The Making of Korean Christianity

STUDIES IN
WORLD CHRISTIANITY

The Nagel Institute for the Study of World Christianity
Calvin College

Joel A. Carpenter
Series Editor

The Making of Korean Christianity

Protestant Encounters with Korean Religions, 1876–1915

Sung-Deuk Oak

BAYLOR UNIVERSITY PRESS

Cover Design by Nita Ybarra
Cover Image: Members of the Session of the Central Presbyterian Church in Pyongyang, Korea in 1909. S. A. Moffett, Kil Sŏnju, and G. Lee are in the center. From George T. B. Davis, *Korea for Christ* (New York: Revell, 1910), 20.
Book Design by Diane Smith

Library of Congress Cataloging-in-Publication Data

Oak, Sung-Deuk.
  The making of Korean Christianity : Protestant encounters with Korean religions, 1876–1915 / Sung-Deuk Oak.
  437 pages cm. -- (Studies in world Christianity)
  Includes bibliographical references (pages 347–396) and index.
  ISBN 978-1-60258-575-1 (hardback : alk. paper)
  1. Christianity and other religions—Korea—History. 2. Christianity—Korea—History. 3. Protestant churches—Korea—History. 4. Korea—Religion. I. Title.
  BR128.A77O25 2013
  275.19'08--dc23
                                                    2012043662

Printed in the United States of America on acid-free paper with a minimum of 30% post-consumer waste recycled content.

For Yoo Hyun, Eun Hyun, and Hyun Bhin

Series Foreword

It used to be that those of us from the global North who study world Christianity had to work hard to make the case for its relevance. Why should thoughtful people learn more about Christianity in places far away from Europe and North America? The Christian religion, many have heard by now, has more than sixty percent of its adherents living outside of Europe and North America. It has become a hugely multicultural faith, expressed in more languages than any other religion. Even so, the implications of this major new reality have not sunk in. Studies of world Christianity might seem to be just another obscure specialty niche for which the academy is infamous, rather like an "ethnic foods" corner in an American grocery store.

Yet the entire social marketplace, both in North America and Europe, is rapidly changing. The world is undergoing the greatest trans-regional migration in its history, as people from Africa, Asia, Latin America, and the Pacific region become the neighbors down the street, across Europe and North America. The majority of these new immigrants are Christians. Within the United States, one now can find virtually every form of Christianity from around the world. Here in Grand Rapids, Michigan, where I live and work, we have Sudanese Anglicans, Adventists from the Dominican Republic, Vietnamese Catholics, Burmese Baptists, Mexican Pentecostals, and Lebanese Orthodox Christians—to name a few of the Christian traditions and movements now present.

Christian leaders and institutions struggle to catch up with these new realities. The selection of a Latin American pope in 2013 was in some respects the culmination of decades of readjustment in the Roman Catholic Church. Here in Grand Rapids, the receptionist for the Catholic bishop answers the telephone first in Spanish. The worldwide Anglican communion is being fractured over controversies concerning sexual morality and biblical authority. Other churches in worldwide fellowships and alliances are treading more carefully as new leaders come forward and challenge northern assumptions, both liberal and conservative.

Until very recently, however, the academic and intellectual world has paid little heed to this seismic shift in Christianity's location, vitality, and expression. Too often, as scholars try to catch up to these changes, says the renowned historian Andrew Walls, they are still operating with "pre-Columbian maps" of these realities.

This series is designed to respond to that problem by making available some of the coordinates needed for a new intellectual cartography. Broad-scope narratives about world Christianity are being published, and they help to revise the more massive misconceptions. Yet much of the most exciting work in this field is going on closer to the action. Dozens of dissertations and journal articles are appearing every year, but their stories are too good and their implications are too important to be reserved for specialists only. So we offer this series to make some of the most interesting and seminal studies more accessible, both to academics and to the thoughtful general reader. World Christianity is fascinating for its own sake, but it also helps to deepen our understanding of how faith and life interact in more familiar settings.

So we are eager for you to read, ponder, and enjoy these Baylor Studies in World Christianity. There are many new things to learn, and many old things to see in a new light.

Joel A. Carpenter
Series Editor

Contents

Illustrations, Tables, Diagrams, and Maps   xi

Preface and Acknowledgments   xv

Abbreviations   xxiii

Introduction   1

1   God   33
        Search for the Korean Name for God, Hanănim

2   Saviors   85
        Images of the Cross and Messianism

3   Spirits   141
        Theories of Shamanism and Practice of Exorcism

4   Ancestors   189
        Confucian and Christian Memorial Services

5   Messages   221
        Chinese Literature and Korean Translations

6   Rituals   271
        Revivals and Prayers

Conclusion   305

Appendix   317

Glossary   337

Bibliography   347

Index   397

Illustrations, Tables, Diagrams, and Maps

ILLUSTRATIONS

Figure 1 Giulio Aleni (1582–1649), *T'ien-chu chiang-sheng ch'u-hsiang ching-chieh* 天主降生出像經解 [Illustrated Expositions of the Incarnation of the Lord of Heaven] (Fukien: Chin-chiang Church, 1637), plate 26. Courtesy of Houghton Library, Harvard University. (**p. 99**)

Figure 2 A. Schall, *Jincheng Shuxiang* [Images Presented to the Chongzhen Emperor], 1640, as shown in Yang Guangxian, *Budeyi* 不得已 (1664). Courtesy of UCLA East Asian Library. (p. 99)

Figure 3 *Bixie jishi* 辟邪紀實 (1861), 13, plate 1. (**p. 106**)

Figure 4 John Bunyan, *The Pilgrim's Progress*, 51st edition (Paisley: A. Weir and A. M'Lean, 1757), 40. (**p. 110**)

Figure 5 John Bunyan, *Tian lu li cheng* 天路歷程 [The Pilgrim's Progress], trans. William Chalmers Burns (N.p., 1852). July 5, 2010. Courtesy of the National Library of Australia. (**p. 111**)

Figure 6 John Bunyan, *Tenro rekitei: iyaku* 天路歷程 意譯 [The Pilgrim's Progress: Free Translation], ed. and trans. Yosimine Satō 佐藤喜峰 (Tokyo: Jūjiyashoho, 1879). Courtesy of UCLA East Asian Library. (**p. 111**)

Figure 7   John Bunyan, *The Pilgrim's Progress*, with notes by the Rev. Robert Maguire, illustrated by H. C. Selous, Esq. and M. Paolo Priolo (London: Cassell, Petter, & Galpin, 1863), 73. (**p. 112**)

Figure 8   John Bunyan, *T'yŏllo yŏkchŏng* 텬로력뎡 [The Pilgrim's Progress], trans. James S. Gale (Seoul: Korean Religious Tract Society, 1895), 38b. (**p. 112**)

Figure 9   Inferred Tonghak *Yŏngbu*. Roderick S. Bucknell and Paul Beirne, "In Search of Yŏngbu: The Lost Talisman of Korea's Tonghak Religion," *Review of Korean Studies* 4, no. 1 (2001): 213. (**p. 116**)

Figure 10   Inferred Tonghak *Yŏngbu*. Drawing by Sung-Deuk Oak. (**p. 116**)

Figure 11   The Designs of the *Pulsap* Used in the Chosŏn Period. Yi Seunghae and Ahn Pohyun, "Chosŏn sidae hoegyŏk hoegwagmyo ch'ult'o sab e taehan koch'al" [A Study of the "Sap" Excavated from the Tombs of Lime-Covered or Lime Coffins], *Munhwajae* 42, no. 2 (2008): 49. (**p. 118**)

Figure 12   The Sorae Church and Its Flag of St. George's Cross, 1898. "Mission Albums of Miss Esther Lucas Shields." Courtesy of the Samuel Hugh Moffett Collections, Princeton Theological Seminary Archives. (**p. 122**)

Figure 13   A Typical Flagpole of a Rural Church, ca. 1902. *Missionary Review of the World* (February 1908): 101. Courtesy of UCLA Library. (**p. 127**)

Figure 14   Japanese Red Cross Society Hospital in Incheon, Korea, 1904. *American Monthly Review of Reviews* (June 1904): 667. Courtesy of UCLA Library. (**p. 132**)

Figure 15   Japanese Military Rule: Execution of Korean Farmers, 1904. Homer B. Hulbert, *The Passing of Korea* (London: Heinemann, 1906), 210. (**p. 134**)

Figure 16   Execution of Korean Patriots, 1907. B. L. Butnam Wheale, *Coming Struggle in East Asia* (London: Macmillan, 1909), 518. (**p. 135**)

Figure 17   A Political Cartoon of *The Sinhan Minbo*, 1909. *The Sinhan Minbo* 신한민보 (September 15, 1909). Courtesy of UCLA Library. (**p. 137**)

Figure 18   Missionary Baptism, 1910. *Yorozu chōhō* 萬朝報 (March 21, 1910). Courtesy of UCLA Library. (**p. 137**)

TABLES (in Appendix)

Table 1   The Names for God Used in the Korean Scriptures, 1882–1905

Table 2   Examples of the Korean Terms Adopted by the Ross Version, 1887

Table 3   Chinese Terms Adopted by Korean Versions from the Delegates' Version, 1887 and 1904

Table 4   The Most Popular Chinese Tracts and Books in 1893

Table 5   Chinese Books and Tracts Used in Korea without Translation, 1880–1900

Table 6   Chinese Tracts Translated and Published in Korean, 1881–1896

Table 7   The Title and the First Stanza of "The Rock of Ages"

Table 8   Various Editions of "Jesus Loves Me, This I Know"

Table 9   Growth of Presbyterian Churches in Korea, 1907–1912

Table 10   General Statistics of the Christian Missions and Churches in East Asia, 1910

Table 11   Educational Statistics of the Korea Mission, PCUSA, 1907–1908

Table 12   Statistics of the Presbyterian Churches in Korea, 1910

DIAGRAMS (in Appendix)

Diagram 1   Religious and Political Factors in the Iconography of the Cross, 1801–1910

Diagram 2   Translation of Christian Texts into Korean, 1876–1915

Maps (in Appendix)

Map 1   Early Protestant Missionary Routes to Korea, 1879–1887

Map 2   Territorial Comity among the Presbyterian and Methodist Missions in Korea, 1912

Preface and Acknowledgments

Korean Protestant Christianity has been known for two things: rapid growth and conservative theological orientation. American evangelicalism has been regarded as a driving force to that effect since the arrival of the first medical missionary to Korea, Horace N. Allen (1858–1932), in 1884, during Japanese colonial rule in 1910–1945, and in the postwar period of the North–South division since 1953. Already by 1900 there were more than twenty-five thousand Protestant Christians, about two hundred thousand in 1910, and then about eight million in 1990. As a result, the monolithic image of rapidly expanding fundamentalistic Korean Protestantism, influenced by American evangelicalism, has dominated its historiography. The missionary literature has lauded the Christian triumph over heathen Korean religions. Conservative Korean theologians and pastors have reproduced similar rhetoric to boost the domestic and foreign missions as well as to buttress their hegemony over any emerging new liberal theology and in their efforts to suppress lenient attitudes toward non-Christian religions. The conservative camp has tried to justify these positions by creating the image of intensely conservative pioneering missionaries. In contrast, the liberal or pluralist camp has criticized the exclusivist missionary theology, its Orientalism, and cultural imperialism that had destroyed traditional Korean religious culture and imposed a Western form of Christianity on Koreans. Most non-Korean scholars have not paid much attention to the history of Protestantism in Korea because it appeared to be a simple story of expansion and thus boring. This book challenges such a lineal historical understanding of

Korean Protestant churches and tries to affirm that the culturally sensitive and biblically sound identity can go hand in hand with a vitally growing constituency and social relevancy. Above all, the contemporary critical situation of declining Protestant churches in Korea calls for a serious reflection on their first decades for their renewal.

This book explores the history of the localization of North American Christianity in Korea through its encounters with Korean religions at the turn of the twentieth century. Using archival materials, this book not only delineates the transpacific transmission of North American Christianity to Korea but also investigates trans–Yellow Sea interactions between naturalized Chinese Protestant mission theories, methods, and literature and emerging Korean Protestantism. The main concern, however, lies in that third integration: the synthesis of Anglo-American–Sino Christianity with congenial elements of Korean religions. This geographical and cultural convergence produced a unique Korean Protestantism in the first generation, and this indigenous identity contributed to the rapid progress of Protestant Christianity as a new national religion in modern Korea. The agency of Korean Christians in this triple integration is particularly emphasized. This is a case study on the interplay between the globalization of Christianity in East Asia and the inculturation of Christianity as a national and local response.

In their encounters with Korean religions—a mixture of shamanism, Confucianism, Buddhism, Daoism, Tonghak, and popular beliefs—young North American missionaries, influenced by the seasoned missionaries in China, dropped their initial goal of radically displacing Korean "heathenism" and otherness with Western Christianity. The heuristic approach that followed was based on what they learned from studying and observing Korean religions and Korean Christians' interpretation of the relationship between Western Christianity and Korean religions. In order to answer to both indifferent and responsive audiences and to become competitive in the rapidly changing religious market, evangelical missionaries, as a utilitarian approach, were open to negotiations and accommodations to the congenial elements of Korean religions. Their evangelical mission theology firmly maintained the finality and superiority of Christ in relation to Korean religions, but they searched for the points of contact within Korean religions that had some foundation for accepting the Christian gospel. The missionaries' combination of confrontational and conciliatory approaches, cross-cultural sensitivity, and moderate fulfillment theory encouraged

Korean Christians to create an indigenous Christianity that grew rapidly in the liminal space of turn-of-the-twentieth-century Korea, where transnationality, translations, traditions, modernity, and coloniality interacted. North American Christianity and its missionary work had a profound impact on early modern Korean religious culture and society; and vice versa, Korean culture and spirituality shaped Protestant missionary endeavors. The other side of the expansion of Western Christianity in Korea was its indigenization as Korean Christianity.

Missionaries and Korean leaders presented Protestantism as a faith to fulfill spiritual aspirations and prophetic longings of the Korean people. They proclaimed that the fulfillment of Korean religions by Christ would be similar to the fulfillment of Judaism by Christ. Without ignoring discontinuities and differences, continuities and means for coexistence were emphasized. The mutual interdependence of Confucianism and Christianity, for instance, was depicted in 1898 through the metaphor of beautiful trees by a sunny spring. Although the pruning of traditional religions' withered branches was needed, the sunlight of Western Christianity would make Korean Confucian trees luxuriant and fruitful, whereas the latter could reflect the brilliance of the spring. Christianity grown in New York, Chicago, Nashville, or Toronto was not brought to Korea in a pot, nor were its seeds scattered on the streets of Seoul and Pyongyang, but a well-naturalized Anglo-American-Sino Christianity was grafted onto Korean religions, so that a new Korean Christianity could flourish. The universal biblical model of the Christian fulfillment of traditional religions took on a local form and facilitated the invention of Korean Christianity, in particular among the plurality of globalized Christianities in non-Christian lands.

This book revises the image of the first-generation North American missionaries and Korean Protestant Christians as the fundamentalist destroyers of Korean religious cultures and instead describes them as moderate evangelicals whose fulfillment theory paved the way for the indigenization of Protestant Christianity in Korea. They searched for the preparations for the gospel in Korean religious culture—such as the monotheistic name for God, Hanănim, from the triune god of the founding shamanistic myth of Tan'gun—and Christianized those points of contact to proselytize in Korea. Though early twentieth-century fulfillment theory was not free from spiritual imperialism, it was the most liberal missionary attitude toward non-Christian religions at that time. The book argues that many representative first-generation North

American missionaries and Korean Protestant Christians were open-minded enough to accept the most advanced contemporary mission theology of religions. This is a specific case study of the cross-cultural theological development by mainline North American missionaries during the period of high imperialism. It challenges the generally accepted interpretation of mainline evangelical (Presbyterian and Methodist) missionaries' role in that period and mitigates the common charges of cultural imperialism, white supremacy, and religious triumphalism.

The book discusses not only various points of conflict between mainline North American Christianity and multiple religions in Korea such as ancestral rite, spirit worship, and idolatry, but also their congenial points of contact in the ideas and practices of monotheism, millenarianism, morality, and vernacularism in the context of nation building, modernization, and anti-Japanese colonialism. The combinations of intolerance and tolerance to the otherness in Korean religions and the ongoing process of negotiations across the boundaries of Western and Eastern religions formulated the indigenous form of Protestant Christianity on Korean soil.

Finally, this book's thesis and findings confirm the general ideas that the globalization of Christianity goes together with the localization and plurality of Christianity; that authentic Christian mission works need networking partnerships among the diverse forms of local Christianity; and that world Christianity, as the totality of such an ongoing mutual friendship and enrichment, encourages open-mindedness to other religious cultures and confidence in the Christian faith as well. The making of Korean Protestant Christianity is a good example of the globalization and localization of Christianity, and the first modernity Korea experienced was such a Christian modernity that facilitated the acceptance of the West from the foundation of the East.

The introduction is a critical and historical reflection of self-imposed interpretations of the first encounters between Protestant Christianity and Korean religions. It challenges the polarized conventional interpretations, which have relied on the prepackaged guidance of others rather than on one's own examination of historical evidence.

Chapters 1, 2, and 3 address the contextualization of the Christian Trinity—God (monotheism, the name for God, the term question), Savior (images of the cross, Christology, and messianic eschatology), and spirits (pneumatology, demon possession, and exorcism). Discussing a genealogy of the term "Hanǎnim," chapter 1 examines a doctrinal side of Christianity in Korea and looks at it as a religion of intellectuals. It emphasizes the historical connections and mutual theological influence among various Chinese, European, North American, and Korean groups, and the complex process of inventing a new Korean Protestant term for God, Hanănim, from the sky god of Korean shamanism to the Christian monotheistic God. Chapter 2 investigates the created images of Christ through the images of the cross and the flag of the cross. It covers the material, symbolic, and social aspects of Korean Protestantism as well the characterization of it as a religion of people in crisis. Chapter 3 deals with the conflicts and negotiations between Korean shamanism and Protestantism, between the shamanic idea of disease and Western germ theory, and between missionaries' Orientalist discourse on demon possession and shamanic healing ceremonies. It explores the spiritual and psychological sides of Korean Christianity, as a religion of women in particular. It stresses missionaries' changing position on shamanism and the continuous practice of Christian exorcising shamanic spirits from Koreans. Chapter 1 deals with the encounters of Protestantism with shamanism and Confucianism, chapter 2 discusses those with Tonghak and folk religion, and chapter 3 focuses on encounters with shamanism, which encompassed popular Buddhism and Daoism in many instances.

The next three chapters (chapters 4, 5, and 6) also recognize the importance of symbols, rituals, and tangible materials as well as printed texts in the understanding of Korean Protestantism, a new modern religion in Korea. Chapter 4 investigates the Chinese background of Korean Protestantism's ongoing prohibitive theology of ancestor worship, North American missionaries' policies and Korean Christians' attitudes, and the formation of Christian theology of filial piety and an indigenous memorial service as alternatives to the traditions. It reveals the encountering of Confucianism and Christianity in the realms of anthropology, soteriology, and morality. Chapter 5 analyzes social classes of the church members and Korean translations of Chinese Christian literature (apologetics, Scriptures, and hymns) in order to identify the vernacularization of the Christian message. Chapter 6 focuses on prayers invented during the revival movement in the first decade of 1900. Chapter 4 emphasizes the confrontational nature and the transformative power of Protestantism when it encountered premodern Korean Neo-Confucianism and its tight family system. The process of the demarcation in the Confucian practice reveals the serious conflicts and compromises between evangelical Protestantism and Chosŏn Neo-Confucianism. Chapter 5 touches on Confucianism and partly deals with Buddhism, and chapter 6 mainly discusses Daoism. I present the indigenized Korean Protestantism more visibly in the final two chapters.

This book is an expansion of the studies published in my dissertation of 2002. I lost an opportunity to publish it as it was, given by the American Society of Missiology in 2002, due to my teaching job at the University of California–Los Angeles (UCLA), other research projects, and above all the change to the target audience. The main audience of my dissertation was seminarians, ministers, and theologians of the Christian churches. My appointment at the Department of Asian Languages and Cultures of UCLA, however, forced me to write for general readers and diverse Koreanists. I do not think that I have completely succeeded in accommodating the changed audience. If you find some biased perspectives and expressions in this book, please let me know so I can avoid them in further research.*

In 2008 I was awarded a generous grant to facilitate the writing of this book by the International Center for Korean Studies (ICKS), affiliated with the Research Institute of Korean Studies, Korea University, Seoul. I was able to revise the manuscript extensively and add several new chapters with their generous support. ICKS was established in 2003 to support scholarship and exploration of Korea in the humanities and social sciences and to promote new research in Korean studies for a wide international audience. I would like to express my profound gratitude to professor Cho Sungtaek, director of ICKS; its editorial board; and reviewers of the Korean studies book series.

In the process of writing, UCLA and my department have provided me with research grants and nonteaching or sabbatical quarters. Special thanks go to the following, who are globally renowned scholars and my respected colleagues—Professors Robert E. Buswell Jr., John B. Duncan, Namhee Lee, Sung-Ock Sohn, Timothy L. Tangherlini,

---

* Korean words in the text are rendered using the McCune-Reischauer system, with the exception of proper names, such as Seoul, Pyongyang, and Incheon, for which alternative names are well established. Korean names follow the standard order—family name first—unless a particular name is traditionally rendered in Western order. In footnotes and bibliography, Korean names in the English source follow the original renderings. Unless a source is specified, all translations of Korean texts are mine.

Christopher P. Hanscom, and David C. Schaberg. I could not have finished this project without their moral support and timely guidance. I owe a great debt of love to Mr. Im Dongsoon and Mrs. Im Mija of the Los Angeles Youngnak Presbyterian Church. Their generous donation created the Im Endowment Chair of Korean Christianity at UCLA in 2007, and my appointment as its first holder provided me the time and space to write this book.

Since I began to study the history of Korean Christianity in 1984, I have had several significant mentors and supporters. Dr. Yi Mahn-yol guided my studies in Korea from 1984 to 1993. My interest in the Koreanization of Western Christianity developed into my doctoral dissertation under the guidance of Professor Dana Lee Robert of Boston University School of Theology. I hope this book can repay my academic debt to my mentors. I also acknowledge those individuals and institutions that have munificently given research grants and project funds over the past eight years. The Henry Luce Foundation provided for my work as Luce Postdoctoral Fellow of Korean Christianity at the UCLA Center for Korean Studies from 2002 to 2003 and from 2005 to 2007. The Reverend Ha Yongjo of the Onnuri Community Church in Seoul gave me a grant to work as a research fellow at the same center from 2003 to 2005. To my great sadness, he passed away in August 2011. From 2003 to 2009, the Korean Bible Society awarded me a grant to put together three volumes of the society's historical documents. In the same period, the Institute of Korean Studies of Yonsei University funded me to make the five-volume series *H. G. Underwood and L. H. Underwood Papers*. The Korean Nurses Association has funded me to research the nursing history of Korea since 2010. These grants have helped me to study diverse aspects of Korean Protestantism and revise this book. I owe a debt of gratitude to Professor Marion Eggert of Ruhr University Bochum in Germany. Her invitation to the Käte Hamburger Kolleg program as a research fellow in 2012 provided me with the time to finalize the manuscript.

Writing a book on the history of early modern Korea requires various kinds of assistance from archives and libraries. I would like to show my appreciation for the generous and professional support I received from the archivists and librarians of the following institutes—the American Bible Society Archives (New York), the British and Foreign Bible Society Archives, Cambridge University (London), the Institute for Korean Church History (Seoul), University of Toronto Library (Toronto), the

Kautz Family YMCA Archives, University of Minnesota (Minneapolis), the Lancaster Historical Society (Lancaster, Pa.), the New York Public Library (New York City), the Presbyterian Historical Society (Philadelphia), the Princeton Theological Seminary Library (Princeton, N.J.), the Rutherford B. Hayes Presidential Center (Fremont, Ohio), the United Methodist Historical Center, Drew University (Madison, N.J.), the Union Theological Seminary Burke Library, Columbia University (New York City), the Yale Divinity School Library (New Haven, Conn.), and the Bodleian Libraries of Oxford University (Oxford, UK). Dr. Samuel Hugh Moffett and Mrs. Eileen Flower Moffett at Princeton provided me with Christian love and valuable primary sources and photos.

Many renowned scholars and friends have offered invaluable comments for the revision of the manuscripts. I would like to express my special thanks to Professor Donald N. Clark of Trinity University, Professor Dana L. Robert of Boston University, Dr. Joel Carpenter of Calvin College, and the Editorial Advisory Board of Baylor University Press Series on World Christianity and its chief editor and director, Dr. Carey C. Newman. Dr. Carpenter read the manuscripts carefully and sent me the most valuable comments. His guidance and encouragement enabled me to finish the final revision. I appreciate Professor Timothy S. Lee of Texas Christian University and Professor Paul S. Cha of Samford University, who read parts of the manuscripts. I am also grateful for the editorial work of David White of Nanzan University (Nagoya, Japan) and my daughter Yoo Hyun. Their comments, suggestions, and copyediting made the book a more readable one. If any errors remain, they belong to me alone.

Above all, my wife, Jin Hye Kyung, has been the rock and foundation in my life of prolonged studentship and job uncertainty. Her anthropological perspective enhanced the quality of this book. I would like to express my deep gratitude for the constant prayer of my mother, Park Seo Hwi, and the ever-loving kindness of my parents-in-law, Jin Young Kun and Oak Hyun Ja. While I was working on this book, my children, Yoo Hyun, Eun Hyun, and Hyun Bhin, entered university, and two of them have already graduated. I hope that they will enrich their lives and others with their cross-cultural experiences, as many figures in this book did in Korea a century ago. Hence, I dedicate this book to them.

Abbreviations

ABS	American Bible Society
AH	*Assembly Herald*
AR	*Annual Report*
BCK	Bible Committee of Korea
BFBS	British and Foreign Bible Society
BFM	Board of Foreign Missions
BFMPCUSA	Board of Foreign Missions of the Presbyterian Church in the USA
BSR	*Bible Society Record*
BW	*Bible in the World*
CA	*Christian Advocate*
CHA	*Church at Home and Abroad*
CMJ	*China Medical Journal*
CR	*Chinese Recorder and Missionary Journal*
CRKM	Correspondence and Reports of the Korea Mission, BFMPCUSA
FM	*Foreign Missionary*
GAL	*Gospel in All Lands*

HKY	*Han'guk Kidoggyo wa yŏksa* [Christianity and History in Korea]
HS	*Hwangsŏng Sinmun* [Imperial Capital Gazette]
HWF	*Heathen Woman's Friend*
IKCH	Institute for Korean Church History
JAMA	Journal of American Medical Association
JRKMC	Journal and Report of the Korea Mission Conference of the MEC, South
KACMEC	Korea Annual Conference of the Methodist Episcopal Church
KF	Korea Field
KH	*Chyosyŏn K'ŭrisŭdoin Hoebo* (1897), *Taehan K'ŭrisŭdoin Hoebo* (1898–1910), *K'ŭrisŭdoin Hoebo* (1911–1914)
KM	*Korea Methodist*
KMF	Korea Mission Field
KMMEC	Korea Mission of the Methodist Episcopal Church
KMMECS	Korea Mission of the Methodist Episcopal Church, South
KMPCUSA	Korea Mission of the Presbyterian Church of the USA
KN	*Kongnip Sinbo* [New Korea]
KR	*Korean Repository*
KRTS	Korean Religious Tract Society
KRv	Korea Review
KS	*Kŭrisŭdo Sinmun* [*Christian News*]
MEC	Methodist Episcopal Church
MECS	Methodist Episcopal Church, South
MFiles	Missionary Files, Correspondence of the Board of Foreign Missions of the MEC, Methodist Historical Center, Madison, N.J.
MR	*Missionary Review*

MRW	*Missionary Review of the World*
MSMEC	Missionary Society of the Methodist Episcopal Church
MSMECS	Missionary Society of the Methodist Episcopal Church, South
PCUS	Presbyterian Church of the United States
PCUSA	Presbyterian Church of the United States of America
RGC	*Records of the General Conference of the Protestant Missionaries in China*
SVM	Student Volunteer Movement for Foreign Missions
SW	*Sinhak Wŏlbo* [Biblical and Church Monthly]
TKB	Transactions of the Korea Branch of the Royal Asiatic Society
TMS	*Taehan Maeil Sinbo* [Korean Daily News]
TS	*Tongnip Sinmun* [Independent]
UMHC	*United Methodist Historical Center*
UPMR	*Missionary Record of the United Presbyterian Church of Scotland*
WFMS	Women's Foreign Missionary Society, the Methodist Episcopal Church
WFMSP	Women's Foreign Missionary Society of the Presbyterian Church, USA
WFMSS	Women's Foreign Missionary Society, the Methodist Episcopal Church, South
WMA	Women's Missionary Advocate
WMC	World Missionary Conference
WMF	*Women's Missionary Friend*
WWFE	*Women's Work in the Far East*
WWM	World Wide Missions
WWW	*Women's Work for Women*

Introduction

Christianity was introduced to the world, as common property of all the world, under Oriental forms and as the blossoming and full perfection of a religion purely Oriental. Japanese, Chinese, and Korean thinkers have assured me that to the Oriental mind there is not only no difficulty whatever in Christianity but that it is all marvelously simple to them, and that obstacles to its reception as elsewhere, are not inherent in the Christian religion but in the materialism which has incrusted it, in the "fact that Westerners have not understood Christianity and prove it by their mutual divergence and animosities; by their insistence on making Christianity a vehicle for the furtherance of their political views and the advancement of their national ambitions," and finally, in the "impertinence of Westerners attempting to explain an Oriental message to Orientals" anyway, even if they had understood it themselves.

—William F. Sands, 1930[1]

On Easter Sunday afternoon, April 5, 1885, Henry Gerhard Appenzeller (1858–1902), the first American Methodist clerical missionary to Korea, arrived at Chemulpo, a small open port to Seoul, with his pregnant wife and the first Presbyterian clerical missionary, Horace Grant Underwood (1859–1917). Appenzeller believed that he had landed "upon

---

[1] William F. Sands, *Undiplomatic Memories: The Far East, 1896–1904* (New York: Whittlesey House, 1930), 83. Mr. Sands (1874–1946), a Roman Catholic, served Emperor Kojong as an advisor of diplomacy from 1899 to 1904, after working in Japan from 1896 to 1898 and in Korea from 1898 to 1899.

terra firma as yet untouched and unimproved by the hand of man," and prayed inside the Japanese Great Buddha Hotel: "We came here on Easter. May He who on that day burst asunder the bars of death, break the bands that bind this people, and bring them the light and liberty of God's children."[2] Appenzeller considered himself to be a chosen vessel, commissioned to bear the Christian light of liberty to the Koreans who lived in that den of slavery: Asian heathenism. His first encounter with the Korean belief in shamanistic spirits demonstrated a pioneer missionary's typical attitude toward Korean religions.[3] When the Korean laborers were digging the foundations for Paejae School at the mission property of Chŏngdong, Seoul, near the palace in 1886, they worked in abject "fear" of the ghosts and spirits that lurked in the soil. No one dared to clear the remains of the large elm tree, planted during the Japanese invasion in 1592. They believed that a strong spirit lived in the tree. But Appenzeller chopped down and burned this sacred tree, and also removed a stone tablet buried under the ground. He remained unscathed, and Appenzeller believed this proved that he was right, and that the God from America was stronger than the spirits of Korea. His first power encounter with shamanism relieved the Korean workers' fear of ghosts. Afterward the missionary compound in Seoul became a "spirit-immunized" area. He intended to "make this end of the city a little bit of America."[4] Chopping down the sacred spirit tree, that is, destroying traditional "superstitions" and replacing them with Christian religion and civilization, was Appenzeller's initial mission method and policy.

POSTCOLONIAL DISCOURSES OF PROTESTANT ENCOUNTER WITH KOREAN RELIGIONS

It is no wonder, then, that most scholarship in recent decades has claimed that fundamentalism or conservative evangelicalism was predominant among pioneer North American Protestant missionaries, and that their belief in white supremacy, religious triumphalism, cultural imperialism, and a mechanical worldview of body–soul dichotomy crusaded against

---

[2] Henry G. Appenzeller, "Our Mission in Korea," *GAL* 10 (1885): 328; *Annual Report of the Missionary Society of the Methodist Episcopal Church* (New York: MSMEC, 1885), 237.

[3] William E. Griffis, *A Modern Pioneer in Korea: Henry G. Appenzeller* (New York: Revell, 1912), 239–40.

[4] Griffis, *Modern Pioneer*, 101.

traditional Korean religious culture. It has been claimed that their premillennial vision of the evangelization of the world in their generation merged with a strategy for propagating "Christian civilization," to eradicate Korean religions. American mission scholars as well as Korean historians and theologians have reinforced this interpretation since the 1950s. In particular, in the aftermath of the civil rights movement and amid ongoing disillusionment with the Vietnam War, American revisionist historians in the 1970s severely criticized American foreign policy and missionaries' collaboration with American expansionism during the heyday of colonialism from 1880 to 1914.[5] In fact, both the liberals and the evangelicals of the late nineteenth century attempted to conquer "heathen religions" in Asia and Africa. A new Anglo-Saxon imperialism armed with the idea of social Darwinism advanced with a sense of the "white man's burden" toward "inferior" races. As Arthur M. Schlesinger Jr. (1917–2007) argued in his provocative article "The Missionary Enterprise and Theories of Imperialism" in 1974, the audacious, ambitious, and arrogant enterprise of Christian foreign missions in East Asia functioned as a part of American cultural imperialism in the name of manifest destiny.[6] Or according to a more nuanced interpretation by William R. Hutchison (1930–2005), the missionary enterprise was a "moral equivalent for imperialism" at best. It transplanted a Western form of Christianity onto Asian fields. The gospel of "Christian civilization" promoted Western education, technology, and secular ideas by means of institutions such as modern hospitals, schools, and printing presses.[7] On the

[5] Until the 1960s, the dominant interpretation of American foreign mission movements was that the religious element reinforced and manifested the "national mission" of the expansion of American civilization—democracy, individual rights, voluntary associations, and social and economic free enterprise. See R. P. Beaver, ed., *To Advance the Gospel: Selections from the Writings of Rufus Anderson* (Grand Rapids: Eerdmans, 1967), "Introduction."

[6] Arthur M. Schlesinger Jr., "The Missionary Enterprise and Theories of Imperialism," in *The Missionary Enterprise in China and America*, ed. John K. Fairbank (Cambridge, Mass.: Harvard University Press, 1974), 360.

[7] William R. Hutchison, *Errand to the World: American Protestant Thought and Foreign Missions* (Chicago: University of Chicago Press, 1987), 124; Hutchison, "Evangelization and Civilization: Protestant Missionary Motivation in the Imperialist Era," in *Missions and Ecumenical Expressions*, ed. Martin E. Marty (Munich: K. G. Saur, 1993), 91–124; David. J. Bosch, *Transforming Mission: Paradigm Shifts in Theology of Mission* (Maryknoll, N.Y.: Orbis, 1992), 298–302; Timothy Yates, *Christian Mission in the Twentieth Century* (Cambridge: Cambridge University Press, 1994), 7–33.

Korean side, especially after the Kwangju Uprising in 1980, critiques of *minjung* theology, parallel with the rise of anti-Americanism, were leveled against traditional hagiographical images of American missionaries as well as conservative pro-American Protestant churches.

A variety of schools of interpretation—nationalist liberal theologians, conservative evangelicals, indigenous theologians, minjung theologians, nationalist church historians, and postcolonialists—have produced the negative images of pioneering missionaries and early Korean Protestant Christians as fundamentalists—puritanical moralists, conservative premillennialists, and rigid exclusivists—in postcolonial and postbellum Korea during the past sixty years.[8]

U.S. forces occupied southern Korea when Korea was liberated from the thirty-six-year rule of Japanese colonialism in 1945. The American military government (1945–1948) employed some American missionaries as interpreters and advisors. During the Korean War (1950–1953) many Korean church leaders were killed, and the Protestant churches split over the "Shinto shrine question." A great number of Christian refugees from communist North Korea formed a constituency in the South. Their conservatism and regionalism complicated the process of church reconstruction, in which some American missionaries were deeply involved, along with an influx of U.S. dollars. Postbellum Korean churches split and deteriorated in the absence of cooperation, leadership, and identity.

Korean nationalism reinforced the negative image of Anglo-American missionaries. In his 1955 dissertation, Chŏn Sŏngch'ŏn (1913–2007) criticized the narrow and limited theology of the early American Presbyterian missionaries as the backdrop for the schisms in Korean churches.[9] Kim Chaejun (1901–1987), a founder of the antimissionary Chosŏn Theological Seminary in Seoul in 1940, separated himself from the majority conservative Presbyterians in 1952 and endorsed Chŏn's assertion in 1956: "The Princetonian missionaries transplanted

[8] Paek Nakchun's doctoral dissertation at Yale University (1927), guided by Kenneth S. Latourette, positively evaluated pioneer missionaries' evangelicalism, ecumenical spirit, social works, and efforts toward indigenization. See George L. Paik, *The History of Protestant Missions in Korea, 1832–1910* (Pyeng Yang: Union Christian College Press, 1929), 149–55. Its Korean edition was published in Seoul in 1973.

[9] Chun Sung Chun, "Schism and Unity in the Protestant Churches of Korea" (Ph.D. diss., Yale University, 1955).

conservative orthodoxy to Korea and established an empire of Korean orthodox Presbyterianism by protecting its conservatism with an iron curtain for five decades."[10] By following Kim's position for the past six decades, liberal theologians have ignored the rich heritage of early Korean Protestantism.

Some progressive theologians began to appreciate Korean religious heritage from the 1960s. However, they assumed that they pioneered the indigenization of Christianity, and criticized the earlier missionaries and Korean Christians as fundamentalists. The Vatican II Council (1962–1965), Paul Tillich's theology of culture, the World Council of Churches' theology of mission, and the emerging Asian theologies all inspired a group of liberal theologians and academic historians to have a positive view of Korean religions as being necessary for the success of Christianity. They attempted to create a Korean theology by reevaluating the continuity between the Christian gospel and certain Korean traditions. They differentiated their theological identity from the conservative majority who held fast to the so-called missionary heritage of fundamentalism. Theologians of indigenization insisted that the legalistic and combative characteristics of Korean Protestant theology originated in American fundamentalism and were passed down by missionaries. Looking for Korean subjectivity in Christian faith through the relationship between the gospel and Korean culture, Ryu Tongsik (1922–) criticized conservative fundamentalism for its exclusive attitude toward Korean religions.[11]

The discourse of the de-Westernization of theology gained currency among the liberals and the pluralists. At the 1984 conference for the centennial of Korean Protestantism, Methodist theologian Pyŏn Sŏnhwan (1927–1995) argued, "not only religious imperialism or exclusivism which demonizes or curses other religions, but also fulfillment theory, which regards them as *preparatio evangelica*, should be discarded."[12]

---

[10] Kim Chaejun, "Taehan Kidoggyo Changnohoe ŭi yŏksa chŏk ŭiŭi" [The Historical Meaning of the Presbyterian Church in the Republic of Korea], *Sipchagun* 25 (1956): 35.

[11] Pyŏn Sŏnhwan, *Han'guk chonggyo wa Kidoggyo* [Korean Religions and Christianity] (Seoul: Christian Literature Society of Korea, 1965); "Han'guk kyohoe ŭi t'och'akhwa yuhyŏng kwa sinhak" [Types and Theology of Indigenization of Korean Church], *Sinhak Nondan* [Theological Forum] 14 (1980): 2–22; and *Han'guk sinhak ŭi kwangmaek* [Veins of Ore in Korean Theology] (Seoul: Chŏngmangsa, 1982).

[12] Pyŏn Sŏnhwan, "T'ajonggyo wa sinhak" [Other Religions and Theology],

His iconoclastic rejection of imported Western theology primarily targeted missionary fundamentalism and exclusive Christology.

From the 1970s minjung theologians, who identified themselves with the suffering people, minjung, and who fought against political and social injustices for the liberation of minjung, retained a strong antimissionary perspective. They declared that the early missionaries introduced a god of Western civilization and killed the god of the Korean people, who had been with them throughout history. Sŏ Namdong (1918–1984) regarded the mission history in Korea as a part of the expansion of Western Christendom and argued that the relationship between Christianity and Korean traditional culture had been mutually exclusive and antagonistic, and thus Christianity remained in the ghetto of Christendom in Korean culture and society.[13] Chu Chaeyong (1933–) contended that the early Korean Protestant church had spent the period of "the Babylonian captivity" under the imperialist theology of the missionaries from 1901 to 1933.[14] The dichotomy between Korean theology and missionary theology continued in the writings of Kim Kyŏngjae (1940–). He stated, "The conservative orthodox mission theologians of the late 19th and early 20th centuries regarded the cultural soil as not only lifeless but also barren and desolate, a wilderness full of poisonous weeds." The early missionaries' theological position, by contrast, was "fundamentalist conservative, combative anti-rationalism, a-historical futurism, and anti-cultural."[15] Kim argued that the mainstream Korean Presbyterian church inherited this kind of fundamentalism.

Theological conservatives, on the other hand, have affirmed the founding missionaries' exclusivism as orthodoxy to buttress their own fundamentalism and to block theological innovations. In 1964 Pak Hyŏngnyong (1897–1978), the godfather of conservative orthodoxy, declared that "his long-cherished desire is to deliver to the new generation the same theology that the Western missionaries brought to Korea

---

Sinhak Sasang 47 (1984): 695; idem, "Other Religions and Theology," *East Asian Journal of Theology* 3 (1985): 327–53.

[13] Sŏ Namdong, *Minjung sinhak ŭi t'amgu* [A Study on Minjung Theology] (Seoul: Han'gilsa, 1984), 73.

[14] Chu Chaeyong, *Han'guk Kŭrisŭdogyo sinhak sa* [A History of Christian Theology in Korea] (Seoul: Christian Literature Society of Korea, 1998), 51–100.

[15] Kim Kyoungjae, *Christianity and the Encounter of Asian Religions* (Zoetermeer, Netherlands: Uitgeverji Boekencentrum, 1995), 121.

eighty years ago."[16] He regarded Commission IV, "The Christian Message in Relation to Non-Christian Religions," of the World Missionary Conference held in Edinburgh in 1910 as the origin of the liberalists' compromise with non-Christians and criticized fulfillment theory of the commission. Pak insisted that the "suitable relationship of Christianity to heathenism is not compromise but conquest."[17] The Presbyterian General Assembly Theological Seminary (Ch'ongshin) and its professors preserved Pak's formula. In 1966 Harvie M. Conn asserted that the history of the Korean church in its early years was the history of conservative, evangelical Christianity and that the early theological leadership was strongly conservative.[18] Since Conn borrowed the term "conservative" from J. Gresham Machen's polarized terms of "Christianity" versus "liberalism," his term "conservatism" implied fundamentalism.[19] Park Yonggyu (1955–) defended the early missionaries' constructive role in the shaping of the conservative biblicism and revivalism of the Korean Presbyterian church.[20]

Nationalist church historians also accepted the stereotypical interpretation of early missionaries' theology as fundamentalism. Min Kyŏngbae (1934–), who initiated the "national church perspective" against Paek Nakchun's (1895–1985) "missionary perspective," popularized the image of the early missionaries as fundamentalists. In 1971 Min defined them as pietistic evangelical Presbyterians and revivalist Methodists and blamed them for the Westernization of Christianity in Korea.[21] Later Min pointed out their negative characteristics of theological

[16] Pak Hyŏngnyong, *Kyoŭi sinhak* [Dogmatic Theology] (Seoul: Ŭnsŏng munhwasa, 1964), "Introduction."

[17] Pak Hyŏngnyong, "Igyo e taehan t'ahyŏp munje" [The Problem of Compromise with Heathenism], *Sinhak Chinam* 134 (1966): 5.

[18] Harvie M. Conn, "Studies in the Theology of the Korean Presbyterian Church: An Historical Outline, Part I & II," *Westminster Theological Journal* 29–30 (1966–1967): 24–25.

[19] See J. Gresham Machen, *Christianity and Liberalism* (Grand Rapids: Eerdmans, 1956).

[20] Park Yong Gyu, "Korean Presbyterianism and Biblical Authority: The Role of Scripture in the Shaping of Korean Presbyterianism 1918–54" (Ph.D. diss., Trinity Evangelical Divinity School, 1991), 248–51.

[21] Min Kyŏngbae, "Han'guk ch'odae kyohoe wa sŏguhwa ŭi munje" [Early Korean Church and the Problem of Westernization], *Kidoggyo Sasang* 14 (1971): 44–50; Min Kyŏngbae, *Han'guk minjok kyohoe hyŏngsŏng saron* [A Study on the Formation of the Korean National Church] (Seoul: Yonsei University Press, 1974), 31–35.

poverty, weak ecclesiology, individualistic soteriology, apolitical quietism, anti-intellectualism, and dualistic faith.[22] Yi Mahnyol (1938–), delving into anti-Christian incidents at the turn of the twentieth century, criticized American missionaries' sociopolitical status as *yangdaein* (great Westerners), their sense of racial superiority, the implantation of Western culture, and their collaboration with Japanese colonialism.[23] Yi Tŏkchu (1952–) identified the evangelical theology of early Presbyterian missionaries with fundamentalism. He stated that early missionaries' closed protectionism curtailed Korean Christians' subjective theological productivity, and the inevitable result was theological dependence on the missionaries.[24] As the pivotal concepts for these church historians were nation and minjung, they were strongly influenced by the sociopolitical discourses of nationalism and minjung theology.[25]

The minjung discourses were combined with antimissionary discourse in the 1980s and leveled at earlier conservative missionaries. Building upon the existing anti-Western critiques of missionary conservatism, anti-American missionary discourses gained currency among students, writers, and scholars with increasing anti-Americanism that followed the Kwangju Uprising in May 1980 and the materialist interpretations of history, influenced by Marxist ideology and *Juche* ideology of North Korea. For instance, Ro Taejun interpreted the Great Revival Movement in 1907 as conservative American missionaries' project to depoliticize the Korean church at the time of Japanese colonization.[26]

---

[22] Min Kyŏngbae, *Han'guk Kidok kyohoe sa* [A History of Korean Christian Church] (Seoul: Yonsei University Press, 1994), 149.

[23] Yi Mahnyol, "Han'guk Kidoggyo wa ch'ogi sŏngyosa" [Korean Christianity and Early Missionaries], *Pit kwa Sogŭm* (December 1987): 112–24; Yi Mahnyol, "Han'guk Kidoggyo wa Miguk ŭi yŏnghyang" [Korean Christianity and American Influence], *Han'guk kwa Miguk* 3 (1988): 65–116; Yi Mahnyol, *Han'guk Kidoggyo wa minjok ŭisik* [Korean Christianity and National Consciousness] (Seoul: Chisiksanŏpsa, 1991), 391–93.

[24] Yi Tŏkchu, "Ch'ogi naehan sŏngyosa dŭrŭi sinang gwa sinhak" [Faith and Theology of the Early Missionaries to Korea], *HKY* 6 (1997): 59; Yi Tŏkchu, "Han'guk Kidoggyo wa kŭnbonjuŭi: Han'guk Kyohoesa jŏk ipchang" [Korean Church and Fundamentalism], in *Han'guk Kidoggyo sasang*, edited by Korea Academy of Church History (Seoul: Yonsei University Press, 1998), 24–29.

[25] See Lee Changsik, "Han'guk kyohoesa ŭi chemunje" [Problems of the Korean Church History], *Han'guk Kidoggyosa yŏngu* 3 (1985): 5–6; Kim Hŭngsu, "Kyohoesa sŏsul panpŏb ŭi saeroun sigak" [A New Perspective for the Writing Method of the Church History], *Han'guk Kidoggyosa yŏngu* 24 (1989): 6–10.

[26] Ro Taejun, "1907nyŏn Kaesingyo taebuhŭng undong ŭi yŏksajŏk sŏnggyŏk"

Since the late 1990s the purveyors of postcolonialism in Korea, studied in the cultural theories of Michel Foucault, Edward Said, John Comaroff, and other scholars, have inundated academic journals with criticism of missionary Orientalism and cultural imperialism for debasing Korean religions as being inferior and primitive. A rising tide of religious pluralism has also meant criticism of Korean Christians' intolerant attitude to other religions. For example, Chung Chinhong (1937–) and Kim Yunseong criticized missionaries' mechanical and dualistic view of the human body, Orientalist episteme, and cultural imperialism.[27] Ryu Daeyoung (1960–) wrote that the American missionaries endeavored to "transplant the evangelical-revivalistic version of American Protestantism" in Korean soil at the dawn of the twentieth century.[28] Ryu, quoting Arthur J. Brown, argued that the early missionaries were "peculiarly conservative" and "Puritan type" and their "religious and ethical rigorism" was imposed on the Korean Christians. Ryu agreed with Brown's assertion that Korean Christians were replicas of conservative American missionaries. In the issue of missionaries' understanding of Korean religions, Ryu argued that they inevitably revealed the Orientalist and Western Christianity–centered perspective.

Most of the aforementioned scholars quoted a comment written in 1919 by Arthur J. Brown (1856–1963), which has been reiterated over and over again in the past two generations. Brown, one of the secretaries of the Board of Foreign Missions of the Presbyterian Church in the USA from 1895 to 1929, initiated the widely accepted stereotype of early American missionaries in Korea. He described "the typical missionary of the first quarter century after the opening of the country" as "a man of the Puritan type" who kept the Sabbath strictly; looked upon

[The Historical Nature of the Protestant Revival Movement in 1907], *Han'guk Kidoggyosa yŏngu* 15–16 (1989): 14–15.

[27] Chung Chinhong, "Early Protestant Medical Missions and the Epitome of Human Body in Late Nineteenth Century Korea: Concerning Problems of Environment," in Korea between Tradition and Modernity: Selected Papers from the Fourth Pacific and Asian Conference on Korean Studies, ed. Chang Yun-Shik et al. (Vancouver: Institute for Asian Research, University of British Columbia, 2000), 308–16; Kim Yunseong, "Protestant Missions as Cultural Imperialism in Early Modern Korea: Hegemony and Its Discontents," *Korea Journal* 39, no. 4 (1999): 205–34.

[28] Ryu Dae Young, "The Origin and Characteristics of Evangelical Protestantism in Korea at the Turn of the Twentieth Century," *Church History* (June 2008): 372.

dancing, smoking, and card playing as sins; rejected biblical higher criticism and liberal theology as heresies; and held the premillenarian view of the second coming of Christ. "In most of the evangelical churches of America and Great Britain, conservative and liberals have learned to live and work together in peace; but in Korea the few men who hold 'the modern view' have a rough road to travel, particularly in the Presbyterian group of missions."[29]

This statement epitomizes the crux of the problem that this study seeks to address. Brown had been in conflict with the majority of the Presbyterian missionaries, especially those in Pyongyang, over deciding the new location of the Union Christian College in Korea and the adjustment of mission schools to the requirements of the Japanese government. He intentionally emphasized an exclusive and uncooperative attitude toward a more liberal and modern view of Christian education, that is, toward his position.[30] Most northern Presbyterian missionaries under his supervision, together with southern, Australian, and Canadian Presbyterians, insisted on educating children of Christians in Pyongyang, the center of the Presbyterian church, rather than implementing a broader secular education in Seoul. After a decade of heated controversy on the "College Question," Brown's evaluation of missionaries in Korea changed from praising their qualifications during

[29] Arthur J. Brown, *The Mastery of the Far East: The Story of Korea's Transformation and Japan's Rise to Supremacy in the Orient* (New York: Scribner, 1919), 540.

[30] Donald N. Clark, *Living Dangerously in Korea: The Western Experience 1900–1950* (Norwalk, Conn.: EastBridge, 2003), 128–33. The board (represented by Brown) supported the minority group of Seoul (represented by H. G. Underwood) against more than two-thirds of the others, including the Pyongyang and Taegu missionaries (represented by William M. Baird, Samuel A. Moffett, and James E. Adams). Methodist missionaries also preferred Seoul as the location of a union college. This heated conflict related to the issue of authority between the New York board and the Korea mission. The issue was whether or not the board could make a decision against the majority opinion of the mission field. Missionaries in Pyongyang opposed establishing a large secular college in Seoul because they feared that it would foster the spirit of institutionalism. See BFMPCUSA, *Presentation of Difficulties Arisen in the Chosen Mission, Presbyterian Church, U.S.A. Because of a Lack of Definition between the Foreign Board and Itself Concerning Their Mutual Responsibilities in the Administration of Field Work* (New York: BFMPCUSA, 1919).

his visits to Korea in 1901 and 1909 to criticizing their exclusivism and conservatism in 1919.[31]

With the simplified portrayal of the founding missionaries as puritanical moralists, conservative premillennialists, and rigid exclusivists, Brown argued that the first generation of Korean Christians naturally reproduced typical missionary characteristics: escapism from a destructive world, manifest evangelistic zeal, strict Sabbath observance, rigid doctrinal conviction, literal acceptance of the Bible from Genesis to Revelation, and inflexible opposition to anything that did not accord with the accepted tenants. If Brown's argument were true, the early Korean church would have been a replica of "strongly conservative" American Protestantism and an enemy of traditional Korean religions—shamanism, Buddhism, Confucianism, and other religions. Both Korean historians and mission historians have recited Brown's caricature uncritically during the past six decades, and they have reproduced these negative images of pioneering missionaries and early Korean Protestant Christians.[32]

Hence these essential questions arise now: "What is Korean Protestant Christianity?" and "Who made it?" Neither the imagined polarization of the conservatives and the liberals nor the reiterated terms "conservative fundamentalism" and "cultural imperialism" by contemporary academic postcolonialists accurately represent the multilayered mission theology of the first-generation missionaries and Korean Christians. Samuel H. Moffett (1916–) stated that the early missionaries belonged to nineteenth-century evangelicalism in the best sense of that word, not to the divisive and polemic fundamentalism of the twentieth century that tore the American church apart into warring segments, with liberals against conservatives and modernists against fundamentalists.[33] Korean religious historiography has been largely a story of the

---

[31] Brown praised Korea missionaries' wise policy and unceasing zeal in utilizing great evangelistic opportunities and defended the positive side of the rapid growth of the Korean church in 1901 and 1909 when he visited Korea. Brown supported a union college in Pyongyang in 1901. See A. J. Brown, *Report of a Visitation of the Korea Mission of the Presbyterian Board of Foreign Missions* (New York: BFMPCUSA, 1902) and *Report on a Second Visit to China, Japan, and Korea* (New York: BFMPCUSA, 1909).

[32] Paek Nakchun's doctoral dissertation at Yale University (1927), guided by Kenneth S. Latourette, positively evaluated pioneer missionaries' evangelicalism, ecumenical spirit, social works, and efforts toward indigenization (Paik, *History of Protestant Missions in Korea*, 149–55).

[33] Samuel H. Moffett, "The Life and Thought of Samuel Austin Moffett, His

politicization projected by historical presentism, whereby "the extraordinary richness of the early 20th century especially is forced into a procrustean bed of predominantly postcolonial category."[34] Against this flattened world of early Protestant Christianity, we need to go beyond the postcolonial path prescribed by various academics. Restoring religious language and metaphors to the study of Korean Christianity in history, while avoiding the nihilistic amnesia of postmodern relativism and academic detachment, is a challenging task for its historians.

Precolonial Missionary Understanding of Korean Religions

In 1668 a Dutch merchant Hendrik Hamel published the first book about Korea in a European language, *Journal van de Ongeluckige Voyage van't Jacht de Sperwer* (The Journal of the Unfortunate Voyage of the Jaght the Sperwer).[35] It was reprinted several times and translated in the beginning of the eighteenth century into English, German, and French. In 1885 William E. Griffis introduced it again in the title of *Narrative of an Unlucky Voyage and Shipwreck on the Coast of Corea, 1653–1667.* Hamel boldly testified, "As for religion, the Coreans have scarcely any. . . . [T]hey know nothing of preaching nor of mysteries, and therefore they have no disputes of religion."[36] Hamel's comment on the lack of religions in Korea became a kind of aphorism in the travelogues written by later European and American visitors.[37]

Children's Memories," in *The Centennial Lecture of Samuel A. Moffett's Arrival in Korea* (Seoul: Presbyterian Theological College and Seminary, 1990), 19.

[34] Kenneth M. Wells, "The Failings of Success: The Problem of Religious Meaning in Modern Korean Historiography," *Korean Histories* 1, no. 1 (2009): 60.

[35] Hamel (1630–1692) was a bookkeeper for the supercargo ship *De Sperwer* of the Dutch East India Company. In 1653, while heading for Japan, he was shipwrecked on Cheju Island along with his thirty-five crewmates. After thirteen years in Korea, Hamel and seven surviving sailors managed to escape to Japan in 1666. Hamel wrote the reports about his experience in Korea in 1668 to get paid his wage. The reports were published in Dutch, and Hamel described the Korean people very negatively. He might have been a Christian trained in the Heidelberg Catechism.

[36] William E. Griffis, *Corea, Without and Within* (Philadelphia: Presbyterian Board of Publication, 1885), 130–31.

[37] Kim Chongsuh, "Early Western Studies of Korean Religions," in *Korean Studies New Pacific Currents*, ed. Suh Dae-Sook (Honolulu: Hawaii University Press, 1994), 141–57.

Did a "religious vacuum" tempt American missionaries to fill the void with spiritual imperialism as a moral equivalent to political imperialism? This question should be investigated precisely because such an aforementioned interpretation has dominated scholarship for the past six decades. An investigation of the North American missionaries' initial and revised responses toward Korean religions reveals their moderate evangelical mission theology of non-Christian religions. Their idea of replacement emphasized the points of conflict with Korean religions, yet their fulfillment theory appreciated the points of contact and the preparation for the gospel found in Korean religions.

Before coming to Korea, North American missionaries collected pieces of information about Korea through several sources. William E. Griffis (1843–1928) became their authority. Griffis began work on his first book on Korea in 1877 during his pastorate at the Dutch Reformed Church in Schenectady, New York, and he published *Corea, the Hermit Nation* in 1882. It was praised as "the best work on Corea which has ever been published in English" and "a work of solid worth and abiding interests."[38] It propelled pioneering missionaries to Korea and remained the reference work on Korea for several decades.[39]

Griffis, however, examined Korean religions through a doubly thick Orientalist lens, shaped both by American Protestantism and by Japanese expansionist pan-Asianism. He supported Japan's colonial mission to civilize stagnant Korea and devalued Korean religions. He considered shamanism the basis of Koreans' faith, especially the Northern Koreans' faith, and "the fibers of Corean superstition" that had not "radically changed during twenty centuries, in spite of Buddhism."[40] He ignored Daoism. He regarded ancestor worship as a link between shamanism and Confucianism and anticipated that ancestor worship would be the

[38] George C. Noyes, "Review of *Corea, the Hermit Nation*," *Dial* 3 (1882): 167; "Corea, the Hermit Nation," *MRW* 6, no. 6 (1883): 409.

[39] Alice R. Appenzeller, "William Elliot Griffis, D.D., L.H.D.: An Appreciation," *KMF* (April 1928): 78; Everett N. Hunt, *Protestant Pioneers in Korea* (Maryknoll, N.Y.: Orbis, 1980), 54.

[40] Griffis, *Corea, the Hermit Nation* (New York: Scribner, 1882), 326. Griffis was an Orientalist scholar, prolific writer, Congregational minister, and supporter of the Christian missions. After graduating from Rutgers University, he went to Japan in 1870 and taught in Feudal Fukui and Tokyo. He graduated from Union Theological Seminary in New York City in 1877 and served for twenty-seven years at three pastorates in New York. His papers are at Rutgers University.

greatest obstacle for the progress of Christianity. He defined Confucianism as a system of morality and philosophy.[41] Griffis dealt with Buddhism more favorably than Confucianism and was inclined to classify Korea as a Buddhist country. He emphasized Korean Buddhism's great influence on Japan, its tendency toward cultural accommodation, and its influence on political and social affairs. He was aware of contemporary Japanese Buddhists' missionary efforts in Chosŏn Korea. He therefore asked a question about the future: "Shall Chosen be Buddhist or Christian?"[42]

Griffis critically reviewed the history of "papal Christianity" in Korea, drawn from Claude Charles Dallet's *Histoire de l'Eglise de Corée* (1874).[43] Griffis criticized "the moral weakness of Roman Catholic methods of evangelization." Because the Korean converts were taught to "believe not only in the ecclesiastical supremacy of the Pope, but also in the righteousness of his claim to temporal power as the Vicar of Heaven," they "played the part of traitors to their country."[44] In addition to his anti–Roman Catholic bias, Griffis was not free from Japanese prejudice toward Korea, since he had no personal experience in Korea, and some of his information depended on Japanese sources.[45] He had no objection to Japanese expansionism. He took it as a matter of course that the Japanese men-of-war opened Korea in 1876 just as the American gunboats opened Japan in 1854.[46] Because his understanding of history was influenced by social Darwinism and American expansionism, he was in favor of a modernized Japan that aspired toward a Westernized identity.[47]

---

[41] Griffis, *Corea*, 328–30.

[42] Griffis, *Corea*, 335.

[43] Griffis regarded the acceptance of Roman Catholicism in 1784 as the beginning of the modern period in Korea. One of the major concerns of his writings was the role of foreigners, especially Protestant missionaries, in the modernization of Japan and Korea.

[44] Griffis, *Corea*, 360.

[45] Griffis visited Korea and Manchuria in 1927 and died in Florida in 1928.

[46] Griffis, *Corea*, vi.

[47] In 1912 he still wrote, "Despite abominable treatment by individual Japanese of the Koreans, or the horrible mess which some of the Mikado's servants made of their business in the peninsula, one must justify the final action of the Tokyo government in 1910, in absorbing the sovereignty of a Court that refused to reform and of abolishing a nation whose rulers had betrayed it." Griffis, *Modern Pioneer in Korea*, 118–19.

Griffis and Hamel created a similar image of Korean religions among the North American missionaries. Both believed that Confucianism was not a religion in a deeply spiritual sense but rather a system of morals, Korean Buddhism was a shadow or a memory, Daoism hardly left a trace, the people were enslaved by superstitious shamanism, and imperialistic Roman Catholicism distorted Christian teachings. In fact, Griffis endorsed Hamel's old claim in 1888: "The Koreans offer the spectacle of a nation without a religion and waiting for one. Hardly else wise, humanly speaking, could the quick success of the American gospelers in Korea be explained. A church reared in four years!"[48] Griffis never saw Korea until 1927. He confessed that if he had had a Korean assistant in 1882, he could have written a much better book on Korea.[49] Griffis' biased perspective was repeated in the literature of early American missionaries to Korea until at least 1907, when the eighth edition of his *Corea, the Hermit Nation* was published.

INITIAL IMAGE: "NO RELIGION"—RELIGIOUS WILDERNESS

When North American missionaries arrived in Korea beginning in 1884, they emphasized the fundamental incompatibility between indigenous religions and intrusive Christianity. Their first impressions used culturally biased vocabularies, saying that the streets were narrow and filthy; the houses were unsanitary and primitive; the people were poor, exceedingly lazy, and dirty; and the political situation was unstable. Their first reports disregarded the existing forms and spirituality of Korean religions.

> The Confucianism of China has been largely adopted by the educated classes, but the real religion of Korea is Shamanism, spirit worship, and low forms of popular superstition. Since Buddhism was put under bans, sevenfold superstitions have entered in to fill the void, yet they are not religions. Wanted, a religion for Korea. What shall it be?[50]

"Wanted, a religion for Korea." This was the slogan of the Korean Protestant missions in their first decade. The Anglo-Saxon missionaries believed that Buddhism was doomed and exerted little if any influence, although priests maintained temples in the mountains. In terms

---

[48] Griffis, "Korea and Its Needs," *GAL* 13 (1888): 371.
[49] Appenzeller, "William Elliot Griffis," 78.
[50] "Foreign Mission Notes by the Secretaries," *CHA* 3 (1889): 117.

of moral code, people followed Confucianism. The remaining void was filled with "superstitions." Dr. Horace N. Allen, who arrived in Seoul in September 1884 as the first resident Protestant missionary and became a diplomat of the American legation in 1890, stated in 1891, "In religious matters the Koreans are peculiar in that they may be said to be without a religion, properly speaking."[51] In 1891 George Heber Jones (1867–1919) reported, "Heathenism in India is vile, in China defiant, in Japan desperate, in Korea indifferent, in Africa triumphant." No better term describes Korea than "indifferent" because the old religious systems had lost their hold on the masses.[52] Jones insisted that a nation without a religion was Christianity's opportunity. This remark revealed the underlying intention of the sweeping statement that "Korea has no religion." It was intended to declare not that Korean people were devoid of all ideas and concepts of religion, but that the old systems had fallen into decay and lost their hold on the people so that for all practical purposes they were nonexistent in the missionaries' eyes.[53]

The example of Henry G. Appenzeller, a pioneer Methodist missionary in Seoul from 1885 to 1902, presents a good illustration of the Protestant missionaries' attitude toward Korean religions at the first stage of their encounter. His mission theory of Christian civilization and its superiority devalued Korean religions. He was convinced that the Koreans' condition was hopeless "without the uplifting, refining, and sanctifying power of the gospel."[54] He insisted that Christianity alone could save individual souls and the nation because Buddhism was derelict, Confucianism brought the country to the verge of ruin, and shamanism failed to elevate its myriads of devotees from the lowest depths of ignorance and superstition. He had a militant antipathy toward heathenism. He compared the Korean people to the Canaanites and himself to Caleb or Joshua, who gave a positive report, unlike the other ten spies of the Israelites. "The five kings of the Amorites (Japan, Korea, China, India, and Islam) will unite against the advancing hosts of Joshua: but

[51] Horace N. Allen, "Korea and Its People," *GAL* 16 (1891): 419.

[52] George H. Jones, "The Religious Development of Korea," *GAL* 16 (1891): 417.

[53] Jones, "The Spirit Worship of the Koreans," *TKB* 2 (1901): 37; Lillias H. Underwood, *Fifteen Years among the Top-Knots, or Life in Korea* (New York: American Tract Society, 1904), 9–10.

[54] H. G. Appenzeller, "#163 Korean Notes," UTS, Appenzeller Papers: Notes, ca. 1890.

'there shall not a man of them stand before thee.' The Church is in this conflict."[55] He viewed ancestral worship as his principal enemy: "Ancestral Worship—around this worship the battle rages. This is the citadel, when it is taken the victory is won."[56] He took the same line as Matthew Yates, a Baptist missionary in China, who claimed that $120 million was expended annually in ancestor worship.[57] Appenzeller's Christ could not be harmonized with Confucius. He agreed with H. G. Underwood, who answered a Korean inquirer that when Christ contradicted Confucius, he must give up the latter.[58] Appenzeller classified Confucianism as a system of ethics, not a religion.[59] He criticized Confucianism's lack of a higher ideal of humanity, degradation of women, and moral legalism. Influenced by Yun Ch'iho's negative understanding of Confucianism, Appenzeller asserted, "Confucianism had for five centuries an undisputed sway in Korea with the result that the country is among the most oppressed and poorly governed in the world."[60]

Another historical example that Appenzeller used to translate a "heathen" society into a Christian one was Kija, who reportedly brought advanced Chinese Confucian civilization to the uncivilized Korean people. Korean scholars believed that Kija, a Shang aristocrat and scholar, arrived in northern Korea in 1122 B.C.E. and founded the Confucian social order and civilization. Missionaries accepted his historicity and emphasized the external influence in the formation of Korean civilization.[61] If Tan'gun, the mythic founder of the ancient Chosŏn nation, was Abraham to the Koreans, Kija was Moses, a virtuous lawgiver and founder of a new civilization. Kija and his "first invasion" established a historical paradigm for Korean cultural renewal and advancement by accepting higher foreign civilization. Appenzeller identified himself as a

---

[55] Appenzeller, "#139 The Report of the Spies," UTS, Appenzeller Papers: Sermons, September 25, 1892.

[56] Appenzeller, "#140 We Preach Christ Crucified," UTS, Appenzeller Papers: Sermons, January 15, 1893.

[57] Matthew T. Yates, "Ancestral Worship," in GCPMC, *RGC* (1878), 385.

[58] Appenzeller, "#152 Native Inquirers," UTS, Appenzeller Papers: Sermons, January 18, 1889.

[59] Appenzeller, "#149 The Faith of Rome," UTS, Appenzeller Papers: Sermons, ca. 1888; "#155 Korea: The Field, Our Work and Our Opportunity," UTS, Appenzeller Papers: Addresses & Essays, 1901.

[60] Appenzeller, "#149" and "#155"; Yun Ch'iho, "Confucianism in Korea," *KR* 2 (1895): 401–4.

[61] Appenzeller, "Ki Tza," *KR* 2 (1895): 83–84.

modern Kija by transferring a higher civilization to Korea and reforming its corrupted traditions.[62]

Appenzeller intended to make a corner of Seoul into a miniature America, with modern schools for boys and girls, clinics and hospitals, and a printing press, as well as churches.[63] He advocated higher education in English for the future leaders of Korea. He edited a religious paper and magazine and managed a printing press and a bookstore. He also supported the progressive political reform movement of the Independence Club. To Appenzeller, "a champion of civilization," Buddhist monks who dwelled in the mountains existed outside the territory of civilization. Appenzeller aimed to challenge what he considered outdated heathenism, change old customs, re-create modern civilization, and finally "create a new nation." He believed that "there would have been no new Japan, no re-civilized Korea, and no modernized China without Protestant missionaries."[64]

American missionaries believed that they had arrived in a religious wilderness thick with the weeds of idolatry. The wilderness was not a virgin soil, but a haunted land where a distorted and tainted imagination had infested the earth, air, sea, trees, and houses with the gods of serpents, tigers, dragons, ancestors, and other supernatural spirits. The spirits' multiplicity made them ubiquitous, and their power for good or evil demanded worship. The pioneering missionaries felt full responsibility for cultivating the evil spirit-infested wasteland into the garden of Christian truth. Hospitals were established to plow up hard hearts, schools to harrow the field of the heathen mind, and churches to plant the seeds of the gospel for a good harvest. One of the first Korean scriptural passages that the missionaries should have memorized was the parable of the sower and the seed (Matt 13:1-23). By their experience, they were convinced of the fact that most seeds fell by the wayside, on stony places, or among thorns in the wilderness.

At the same time, this Orientalist image of the barren wilderness overlapped with that of a religious vacuum waiting to be occupied. The missionaries regarded the religious void, in which a people who

[62] Oak Sung-Deuk, "North American Missionaries' Understanding of the *Tan'gun* and Kija Myths of Korea," *Acta Koreana* 5, no. 1 (2002): 68–70.

[63] Griffis, *Modern Pioneer in Korea*, 239; Daniel M. Davies, *The Life and Thought of Henry Gerhard Appenzeller (1858–1902), Missionary to Korea* (Lewiston, N.Y.: Edwin Mellen, 1988), 119.

[64] Griffis, *Modern Pioneer in Korea*, 101, 160–61, 225–35.

sought religion yet lived without any entrenched religions, as a remarkable opportunity for the progress of Christianity. Their emphasis on the absence of religions in Korea was partly due to the comparison of the religions of China, Japan, and Korea.[65] They imagined that Buddhism had little influence in Korea compared to the strength it held in neighboring countries. Daoism and Shintoism, the alternative systems, were hard to find or unknown in Korea. Therefore missionaries declared, "The Koreans are the least religious of all these Eastern nations."[66]

Not surprisingly, the contemporary Western Christian understanding of the term "religion" defined early Protestant missionaries' understanding of Korean religiosity. They defined religion as "the surrender of the finite will to the infinite, and the absolute identification of one's will with the will of God."[67] Homer B. Hulbert (1863–1949) defined religion as "every relation which men hold, or fancy that they hold, to superhuman, infrahuman or, more broadly or extra-human phenomena."[68] He included in the category of extrahuman the spirits of deceased humans. It was thought that a religion should have visible organizations, ritual systems, disciplined priesthoods, well-built temples, and voluminous scriptures; it should have elaborate doctrines on God, the Holy Spirit, sin, the redeemer, and eschatology. By this standard, shamanism was regarded as mere superstition, and Confucianism as a system of morality. Asian religions were understood as a baneful trap that bound and held ten million souls in the prison of slavery, terror, and ignorance.[69] Even though Anglican bishop Mark N. Trollope, who studied Korean Buddhism academically, acknowledged that Buddhism was a "great religion," he insisted in 1917 that "the one true religion" was Christianity.[70]

On the other hand, Korea was also considered the best example of pagan toleration. People did not believe in any overbearing truth, so as to view other cults as incompatible or intolerable. Through extended association with Koreans for a decade, George W. Gilmore (1857–1933) found that "among the masses the conservatism and intense opposition to a change of religion found among the Chinese has not to be

---

[65] Griffis, *Corea, Without and Within*, 161.

[66] "What Is the Religion of Korea?," *CHA* 6 (1892): 139.

[67] "The Hour for Korea," *FM* 44 (1885): 153.

[68] Homer B. Hulbert, *The Passing of Korea* (London: Heinemann, 1906), 403.

[69] Griffis, *Corea, Without and Within*, 162; Jones, "Spirit Worship," 38.

[70] Mark N. Trollope, "Introduction to the Study of Buddhism in Corea," *TKB* (1917): 1–3.

encountered."[71] The comparatively less religious environment of Korean "heathenism" was interpreted as less adulterated than that of China or Japan.[72] A Methodist missionary wrote,

> This fact has twofold significance in relation to mission work. On one hand, the Korean mind is not one that responds readily to any kind of religious influence. On the other hand, the false religion now in possession does not, for that very reason, place a serious obstacle in the way of the truth. There is not so much weeding to be done as in some other places, but the soil itself is not so fertile.[73]

This hasty and superficial judgment—projecting Korea as a land of religious indifference and barrenness—determined the pioneering missionaries' course of action. Their identity as planters of the true religion was established in a land of false, if any, religions. Their institutional—medical, educational, and literary—mission works were also justified as preparation of this uncultivated soil. At the same time, since they did not fear serious opposition from established religions, launching direct evangelism within the privilege of treaty was plausible as soon as they learned the language.

DIFFERENTIATION FROM ROMAN CATHOLICISM

The Korean government persecuted Roman Catholic Christians from 1791 to 1866 because they disturbed the status quo of the Neo-Confucian political ideology, social morality, and ritual hegemony (ancestral veneration) as well as threatened national security. The authorities stigmatized Roman Catholicism as a religion of foreign invaders and beasts of "no-father-no-king." Over the course of the century, they executed thousands of Christians in the name of orthodox Neo-Confucianism and patriotism.

After the Korea–Japan Treaty in 1876, Huang Zunxian's treatise *Chaoxian Celue* (A Stratagem for Korea, 1880) recommended to Korean intellectuals that the Korean foreign policy should have intimacy with China, association with Japan, and alliance with the United States in order to ward off the imminent threat of Russian expansionism. To

---

[71] George W. Gilmore, *Korea from Its Capital; with Chapter on Mission* (Philadelphia: Presbyterian Board of Publication and Sabbath School Work, 1892), 186.
[72] Samuel F. Moore, "Welcome to Korea," *CHA* 7 (1893): 33.
[73] "Gathering Notes on Korea," *GAL* 16 (1891): 429.

mitigate Korea's fear of the United States, Huang emphasized that America coveted "neither territory nor populations which do not belong to them, nor do they interfere in the domestic affairs of other states."[74] The treatise also stressed that Protestantism, an American religion, held the principle of separation of church and state, unlike Roman Catholicism, a French religion, which had caused a series of domestic and foreign disturbances. Huang's paper encouraged progressive Korean leaders to differentiate Protestantism from Roman Catholicism and to have a positive attitude toward the former.[75] The Korea–America Treaty was instituted in 1882, and it prepared the way for American missionaries to come to Korea.

In this historical background, nineteenth-century American Protestantism's negative view of Roman Catholicism became more extreme in Korea. When Rev. Robert S. Maclay (1824–1907) of the Japan Mission of the Methodist Episcopal Church visited Seoul in June 1884 and sent King Kojong a letter expressing a desire and design to begin mission schools and hospitals, he received royal permission to begin the work "so long as it was Protestant." Maclay found that the "difference between Romish and Protestant missionaries is, happily, quite clear to the mind of this monarch."[76] Dr. Horace Allen's healing of Min Yŏngik, a nephew of Queen Min, who was severely wounded during the coup d'état in December 1884, and the work of other medical and educational missionaries enhanced the usefulness of American missionaries in the national project of civilization and enlightenment. King Kojong believed in opening the country to foreign nations and had great confidence in the United States and American Protestant missionaries.[77]

The primary strategic task of American missionaries was thus to introduce Protestantism as a religion different from Roman Catholicism. They claimed that American Protestantism's principle of political nonintervention would allow them no room to disrespect the Korean

---

[74] William W. Rockhill, *China's Intercourse with Korea from the XVth Century to 1895* (London: Luzac, 1905); Tyler Dennett, "Early American Policy in Korea, 1883–87," *Political Science Quarterly* (March 1923): 82–84.

[75] Lew Young Ick, "Late Nineteenth-Century Korean Reformers' Receptivity to Protestantism: The Case of Six Leaders of the 1880s and 1890s Reform Movements," *Asian Culture* 4 (1988): 159–61.

[76] Robert S. Maclay, "Corea," *Missionary Herald* 80 (1884): 523.

[77] Appenzeller, "The Korean King at Seoul," *GAL* 11 (1886): 7; William B. Scranton, "Letter from Korea," *GAL* 11 (1886): 141.

government's authority. They condemned the Roman Catholic Church's idea of ecclesiastical superiority over civil jurisdiction, and they insisted that Protestantism guaranteed political independence and peace separate from the Pope's ambition.[78]

In 1888, when the Korean government issued a strict order to all missionaries to cease the teaching of Christianity and Appenzeller and Underwood were recalled to the capital from Pyongyang, they blamed the French priests who dared to build a Western-style cathedral on the hill of Myŏngdong overlooking the walls of the palace. Underwood stated that the Romanists had "aroused the ire of the government," yet the American consulate assumed that the trouble was due to the aggressiveness of the missionaries. Indeed, Underwood expressed his burning zeal to preach the Christian gospel in his letter to Dr. Frank F. Ellinwood: "We do not put off the day when there will be full religious liberty." In Underwood's judgment, "the Government is not opposed actively to Christianity, but simply passive on the matter. Protestantism is preferred to Romanism."[79]

American missionaries maintained that Protestant countries such as the United States and the United Kingdom were more civilized and held more national power than Roman Catholic countries such as France and Spain. They consistently asserted that Protestantism, as a religion of "higher civilization," not of idolatry, would help modernize Korea. In 1886, when the king's interpreter questioned Dr. H. N. Allen about

---

[78] John Ross, "Obstacles to the Gospel in China," *MRUPCS* (January 1877): 409; Griffis, *Corea*, 376; Horace Newton Allen, *Horace Newton Allen Diary*, ed. and trans. Kim Won-mo 김원모 (Seoul: Dankook University Press, 1991), May 9, 1886; H. G. Underwood, "Romanism on the Foreign Mission Field," in *Reports of the Fifth General Council of the Alliance of the Reformed Churches Holding the Presbyterian System* (Toronto: Hart & Riddell, 1892), 409–11.

[79] H. G. Underwood, "A Powerful Appeal from Korea," *MRW* (March 1888): 209–11. Allen wrote to Ellinwood from Washington, D.C., that Underwood and Appenzeller were "the principal agitators" who "determined to violate the laws" (H. N. Allen to F. F. Ellinwood, June 11, 1888 and August 20, 1888). In 1889 Underwood baptized thirty-three Koreans on Chinese soil across the Yalu River. When this was reported to Seoul, the government prohibited Christian services. Dr. Heron did not think that the mission should be associated with law breaking. Minster Dinsmore decided that Christian teaching, public or private, was contrary to the law. Underwood, however, stated that the "difficulty is not so much with the government as with our Minister." Underwood thought he had a "higher law than human to go by" (H. G. Underwood to F. F. Ellinwood, May 26, 1889).

the Catholics and their efforts to have a decree of religious liberty, Allen felt it was his duty to deal at length with the subject. After showing the workings of Romanism in China, Japan, Mexico, and Spain, he attacked "Romanism" as a "religion of idolatry" (image worship and worship of the Virgin Mary), immorality (corrupted priests), ignorance of the Bible, and erroneous doctrines (sacerdotalism and papalism).[80] Underwood repeatedly warned that Roman Catholicism could occupy Korea before Protestantism began its work: "The Roman Church is trying to gain Korea, and I fear that if the Protestants do not do their duty we will have a Romish instead of a heathen people to convert."[81] At the annual meeting of the Korea mission in October 1893, Underwood's helper, Sŏ Sangnyun, suggested removing pictures of Bible scenes from the church buildings because nonbelievers "saw them and went out to spread the report that we were Roman Catholics."[82] Appenzeller criticized idolatry of Romanism in his own epilogue to *Dialogues with a Temple Keeper*, published in 1895. "The book clarified . . . that the Jesus doctrine is not like Romanism. The former neither worships the picture of Jesus nor wears a crucifix. The holy Way of God is the Jesus doctrine [Protestantism]. Although Romanism was from one origin, it worships ancestral tablets and images against the commandment of God."[83] He included the icon worship of Roman Catholicism in the category of heathen idol worship. G. Heber Jones thought that Roman Catholicism had been a clog in the regeneration of a nation for a century, and that even "martyrs can accomplish little with a lifeless creed."[84]

Especially Protestant missionaries criticized Roman Catholicism for limiting priests' use of the Bible. By contrast, they pointed out that Protestantism in Korea began with the distribution of the vernacular Scriptures among the people.[85] Because Confucianism, a religion of books,

[80] *Allen Diary*, May 9, 1886; Edward A. Lawrence, "Missions in Korea," *GAL* 12 (1887): 273.

[81] H. G. Underwood, "Romanism Wide Awake," *FM* 45 (1886): 567; Underwood, "A Powerful Appeal from Korea," *MRW* (March 1888): 211.

[82] Samuel F. Moore, "Welcome to Korea," *CHA* 7 (1893): 33.

[83] Appenzeller, "Epilogue," in F. Genähr, *Myoch'yuk mundap* [Temple Keeper], trans. H. G. Appenzeller (Seoul: Paejae Haktang, 1895).

[84] Jones, "Open Korea and Its Methodist Mission," *GAL* 18 (1893): 392.

[85] The Roman Catholics did not translate or publish the whole Korean New Testament until 1971 or the whole Bible until 1977. By contrast, the Protestants produced the first vernacular Korean New Testament in 1887 and the whole Korean

compelled all its followers to study its classics, Jones argued, some Koreans were surprised at the French priests' refusal to give their Scriptures to the seekers and believers. The Koreans believed that it was contrary to the spirit of true teaching and religion and assumed that there must be something wrong with the sacred books of Roman Catholicism.[86]

Some missionaries appreciated the heroic history of Korean Catholicism as the preparation for the entrance of Protestantism. Homer B. Hulbert called the French missionaries "our brothers" and Korean believers "Christ's followers." He praised their great faith under persecution and martyrdom.[87] In 1892 Daniel L. Gifford (1861–1900) stated that one of the grounds for expecting to see great spiritual results within five years was that "Roman Catholicism has in many respects done a preliminary work for us."[88] In addition, the Protestant and Roman Catholic missions cooperated in some areas, such as working to eliminate cholera in 1886, famine relief work in 1888, and sharing information on the Korean nationalists' threat and conspiracy to kill missionaries in 1893 and 1900. Nevertheless, generally speaking, a belligerent competitive spirit existed between the two, which only worsened as the Protestant missions grew rapidly around 1900. The two churches clashed at the Church Abuse Case, *kyoan*, in Hwanghae province in 1902 and engaged in an apologetic literature war in the 1900s.[89]

On the whole, American missionaries, with their biased view on the religions of Korea, initially proclaimed war against Korean heathenism and Romanism. In 1893 Underwood felt that "a kind of mental revolution seems to be in progress throughout the land." Buddhism, Confucianism, and "Demonism" seemed to be losing their power over the people. He believed that it was time to hear the voice of God saying

---

Bible in 1911. From the 1890s, the Catholics used some collections of selected biblical verses during Sunday Latin mass and daily rituals.

[86] Jones, "The Transformation of a Nation," UTS, G. H. Jones Papers, ca. 1900, 18–20.

[87] Hulbert, "A Sketch of the Roman Catholic Movement in Korea," *MRW* 13 (1890): 730–35.

[88] D. L. Gifford to F. F. Ellinwood, November 8, 1892, PHS, CRKM, reel 176.

[89] Yun Kyŏngno, "Ch'ogi Han'guk singugyo kwangye ŭi sajŏk koch'al" [A Historical Study on the Early Relationship between Protestantism and Roman Catholicism in Korea], in *Han'gŭl sŏngsŏwa kyore munwha* (Seoul: Christian Literature Press, 1985), 373–407; Shin Kwangch'ŏl, *Ch'ŏnjugyo wa Kaesingyo* [Encounters and Conflicts between Roman Catholicism and Protestantism in Korea] (Seoul: Institute for Korean Church History, 1998), 78–89.

to his church, "Go work today in my vineyard in Korea."[90] A physical war prepared a path for the spiritual war. The uprising of the Tonghak peasants and the Sino-Japanese War in 1894 changed the entire East Asian political and spiritual situation. China's political suzerainty came to a definite end, and the Chinese gods and spirits proved quite inefficient before Westernized Japan.[91] As Robert E. Speer (1867–1947) said, the Sino-Japanese War disarmed the Korean people's hostility toward and fear of Christianity: "Japan's victory over China made a profound impression to the Koreans, and made Western civilization and religion more highly esteemed. It also demoralized spirit worshippers, killed the worship of Chinese gods, and cut away some of the remaining props of Buddhism."[92] Therefore, beginning in 1895 the Protestant missions were able to accelerate their direct evangelism in the inland areas and their attack on Korean heathenism. After these first impressions and one-way aggression, however, they revised their attitude toward Korean religions during the course of their work.

REVISED RESPONSES
"VERY RELIGIOUS"—RELIGIOUS PLURALISM

Conflicting views of the condition of Korean religions—a religious vacuum, a Buddhist or Confucian land, or a replica of Chinese religions—existed in the early writings of missionaries. Nevertheless, when the missionaries' experience and involvement with the lives of Koreans deepened, they became more sympathetic in their assessment of Korean religions. Although their studies of Korean religions were tainted with late nineteenth-century American Protestant views toward "heathen" religions, they began to take a comparatively academic approach to Korean religions. There were four occasions that advanced missionaries' understanding of Korean religions: the publication of the monthly journal the *Korean Repository* from 1892, the Tonghak Revolution in 1894, the term question from 1893 to 1903, and the Great Revival Movement from 1903 to 1907.

First, Franklin Ohlinger's (1845–1919) founding of the monthly English mission magazine *Korean Repository* in January 1892 was a

---

[90] Underwood, "Religious Changes in Korea," *GAL* (December 1893): 557.
[91] Arthur T. Pierson, "Spiritual Movements of the Half Century," *MRW* 21 (1898): 21.
[92] Robert E. Speer, "Christian Mission in Korea," *MRW* 21 (1898): 681.

significant signal that missionaries were prepared to produce their own research on Korean culture and religions. In 1892 Daniel L. Gifford presented a new insight into the religious pluralism in Korea.

> The religious beliefs of Korea show a blending of Confucianism, Buddhism, and Daoism. . . . The social fabric of the country is largely Confucian. Ancestral worship is Confucian. Again the temples and priests of Buddha are scattered throughout the country—a faith with much of its luster gone, but said to be favored with palace patronage. Daoism has its representatives in the *pansu* or blind sorcerer, the *mudang* of sorceresses, and the *chigwan* or geomancer.[93]

Although Gifford incorrectly classified Korean folk religion and shamanism under the category of Daoism, influenced by Chinese missionary literature on the threefold Chinese religions (Confucianism, Buddhism, and Daoism), he rightly understood the belief system of Korea as a system of hierarchical gods and spirits from the highest Hanănim down to the shamanistic house gods. Gifford illustrated this amalgamated system by analyzing the ancestor worship practiced in Korea. Many Koreans believed that every person had three souls; upon death one went to Hades, one went to the grave, and one took its abode in the ancestral tablet, *wip'ae* or *sinju*. Gifford argued that the origin of ancestor worship was Confucian. But he found that people believed that the Buddhist Ten Judges in Hades decided the fate of the soul of the deceased. And a Daoist geomancer, or *chigwan*, chose the burial site, which they believed influenced the prosperity of the deceased's children. A sacrifice at the grave would be offered to the gods of the ground and mountain for the second soul in the grave. At home, Koreans occasionally offered sacrifices to the third soul in the tablet, which was put into a box and placed in a room or in a little cabinet in the ancestral temple. The regulations for this family worship were mainly Confucian. In conclusion, Gifford asserted that the features of ancestor worship in Korea differed from those in China. As Matthew T. Yates (1819–1888) of China indicated, the Chinese believed that the happiness of the dead and of the living was directly connected to ancestor worship. On the other hand, some Koreans seemed to believe that the condition of the dead was permanently fixed by the sentence of the Ten Judges upon the dead soul's arrival in the other world. They held that whether a man worshipped

[93] Daniel L. Gifford, "Ancestral Worship as Practiced in Korea," *KR* 1 (1892): 169.

his father or not would not affect the happiness of either the father or the son. It affected only the reputation of the son among his acquaintances. Other Koreans believed that if they worshipped their ancestors well, Hanănim, the head deity of Korean mythology, would reward them with happiness; on the other hand, he would punish those who neglected this sacrifice.[94] Gifford verified a distinctive feature of Korean religions—the blending of multiple religions or their harmonious coexistence in a whole system. In the context of this inclusive eclecticism, he may have considered which elements of the system Christianity could choose to adopt. In the analysis of ancestral worship, he found that the idea of Hanănim could be a point of contact for the Christian gospel.

The Tonghak revolutionary movement in 1894 became the second stimulus furthering the missionaries' understanding of Korean religious pluralism. Tonghak (Eastern Learning) was a combination of Confucianism, Buddhism, Daoism, and Roman Catholicism. In 1895 Rev. William M. Junkin (1865–1908) of the Southern Presbyterian Church reviewed its religious aspects. Ch'oe Cheu (1824–1864), the founder of Tonghak in 1859, purportedly had a supernatural experience of Shangdi God. During this encounter with the divine, he asked, "Is Roman Catholicism the true religion?" The answer he received was, "No, the word and the time are the same, but the thought and spirit are different from the true."[95] Ch'oe felt called to found a new religion and proceeded to write the *Tongŏgyŏng taejŏn* (The Great Book of the Tonghak).

> He took from Confucianism the book of the five relations, from Buddhism the law for heart cleansing, from Daoism the law of cleansing the body from moral as well as from natural filth. So one of the names used for this book is made by combining the names of the three religions *You Poul Sun Sam To*. The influence of Romanism may be seen in the term for God in the prayer, *Chun Chu*, being the one chosen. Romanism is also, indirectly at least, responsible for the name they called it, Tong Hak or Eastern Learning in contradistinction to So Hak (Romanism) or Western Learning. This taken in connection with the fact of its being a combination of the true Oriental religions easily accounts for the name.[96]

Junkin believed that Tonghak adopted Confucian morality, Buddhist meditation, Daoist healing and training of the body, and Christian

---

[94] Gifford, "Ancestral Worship," 176.
[95] William M. Junkin, "The Tong Hak," *KR* 2 (1895): 56.
[96] Junkin, "Tong Hak," 57.

monotheism, yet it rejected the Buddhist belief in the transmigration of souls, and used neither images nor sacrifices in worship. The Tonghak people spoke incantations and wore pieces of paper with mystic signs for protection from disease and weapons. Their doctrines contained the "apocryphal gospel" taken from messianism of folk religion. The syncretism of Tonghak, however, was not strange to the Koreans who were familiar with other religions.

In 1895 G. H. Jones asserted that Confucianism and shamanism were entrusted with a different role in the realm of Korean religious life. He found that Confucianism took charge of morality and shamanism of spirituality.[97] Thus when a Korean man turned to Christianity, he had to cope with not only "opprobrium and scorn among friends" and "violent opposition of family and relatives," but also his mental and spiritual shackles.

In 1897 Rev. Robert A. Hardie (1865–1949), a Canadian Methodist doctor, revised an erroneous first impression of Korean religions. He considered spiritism or shamanism the real religion of the Korean people. Isabella Bird Bishop (1831–1904) had the same view.[98] Hardie asserted that ancestor worship was purely shamanistic in its origin, and its practice was a mixture of Confucianism, superstition, and demonolatry. He argued that although the primitive religion of China and Korea was undoubtedly "a vague monotheism," the Chinese and Koreans had always believed in the existence of evil spirits. Thus he devaluated the Korean idea of Hanănim, Lord of Heaven, because they knew him "not as kind and loving Father, whom they may approach in worship, but rather as a being to be feared, one to whom, in the last extremity of despair, we sometimes hear them cry, but hopelessly."[99] Hardie thus concluded that demons alone were the everyday objects of worship. He considered Hanănim as a shamanistic god who was not worshipped in everyday life. Furthermore, Hardie insisted that all forms of worship in Korea—whether bowing before Buddhist images, Confucian tablets, the ancestral grave, or the acknowledged altar of some evil spirit—were basically forms of devil worship (*kwishin yebae*).

As seen above, there was still no consensus on several points. Over a decade the experiences in the field had enabled missionaries to discern

---

[97] Jones, "Obstacles Encountered by Korean Christians," *KR* 2 (1895): 146–47.
[98] Isabella B. Bishop, *Korea and Her Neighbors* (London: John Murray, 1898), 21.
[99] Robert A. Hardie, "Religion in Korea," *MRW* 20 (1897): 927.

the wide influence of popular religions or shamanism among the Koreans, especially among women. The majority of missionaries asserted that almost all Koreans believed in the shamanistic one supreme being, Hanănim, and that all forms of religions in Korea, including Buddhism and Confucianism, were amalgamated with spirit worship.

In 1899 Homer B. Hulbert stated that Korea had not committed itself to either materialistic Confucianism or mystical Buddhism in the realm of religion because the Koreans belonged to a different species than the Chinese and the Japanese, in both intellect and imagination. Hulbert insisted that Korea's real religion was aboriginal shamanism, though it was mixed with Buddhism.[100]

In 1901 Jones argued that the three religions coexisted in ordinary Koreans. They were mutually overlapping and deeply interpenetrating. Buddhism accepted Confucian ethics while absorbing shamanism. In turn, shamanism freely accepted the transcendental objects of Confucianism and Buddhism. Although they theoretically distinguished among them, Koreans in practice believed in all three and that they could attain happiness with their united help. Jones asserted that Koreans were very religious because they had a tendency to spiritualize all natural things, they had a sense of dependence on an existence superior to themselves, and they had established an intercommunicative dimension between humans and spiritual entities.[101]

In 1906 Hulbert made the following remark, which is one of the best summaries of the missionaries' descriptions of the multireligious situation in Korea. The "mosaic of religious beliefs" that was held not only by different individuals but also by any single individual, he argued, demonstrated the antiquity of Korean civilization.

> [The] reader must ever bear in mind that in every Korean mind there is a jumble of the whole; that there is no antagonism between the different cults, however they may logically refute each other, but that they have all been shaken down together through the centuries until they form a sort of religions composite, from which each man selects his favorite ingredients without ever ignoring the rest. Nor need any man hold exclusively to any one phase of this composite religion. In one frame of mind, he may lean toward the Buddhist element and at another time, he may revert to his ancestral fetishism. As a general thing, we may say that the all-round

[100] Hulbert, "Korea and the Koreans," *Forum* 14 (1899): 218–19.
[101] Jones, "Spirit Worship," 37–41.

> Korean will be a Confucianist when in society, a Buddhist when he phi-
> losophizes and a spirit-worshipper when he is in trouble.[102]

Hulbert concluded that "the underlying religion of the Korean, the
foundation upon which all else is mere superstructure, is his original
spirit-worship," for one's practical religion came out when one was
troubled and in need. Hulbert included animism, shamanism, fetishism, and nature worship in the category of spirit worship. Philosophical
Buddhism and political Confucianism, he asserted, "eventually blended
with the original spirit-worship in such a way to form a composite religion." He then added, "Strange to say, the purest religious notion which
the Korean today possesses is the belief in Hananim, a being entirely
unconnected with either of the imported cults and as far removed from
the crude nature-worship."[103] Unlike Gifford's analysis, Hulbert separated Hanănim from the circle of the various other gods and indigenous
spirits, for Hulbert believed that the Koreans were "strictly monotheistic" in their belief in Hanănim. Hulbert supported the Protestant missionaries' identification of Hanănim with Jehovah. The revised view on
Korean religious pluralism led missionaries to consider seriously the
influence of shamanism and the importance of the idea of Hanănim.

Third, the Great Revival Movement of the Korean church from
1903 to 1907 transformed its spiritual life. The revivals stimulated
moribund Korean spirituality, which was rooted in traditional religions. For example, a new form of prayer—audible prayer in unison
(t'ongsŏng kido)—was developed during the revivals. It may have been
influenced by Buddhist or Daoist audible prayer. The dawn prayer meeting (saebyŏk kidohoe), which was initiated in the 1890s, became a regular program of the Bible class in Pyongyang in 1905 and spread to other
regions. Another indigenous form of devotion was "offering of days of
preaching" (nal yŏnbo), which was first presented during the Sŏnch'ŏn
Bible class in November 1904.[104] Korean Christians borrowed this time
offering from the traditional forms of sharing labor in agricultural work
(ture and p'umasi).

The revival movement transformed missionaries' understanding of
Korean spirituality. It was initiated by a missionary's repentance of his

---

[102] Hulbert, *Passing of Korea*, 403.
[103] Hulbert, *Passing of Korea*, 403–4.
[104] Carl E. Kearns, "One Year in Syen Chun Station," *AH* 11 (1905): 602.

lack of spiritual power in 1903, and its final fruit was an awakening of missionaries. They witnessed "the best of the Korean character" and "the inner life" of the Koreans.[105] A missionary confessed that he was liberated from the "contemptible notion that the East is East and the West is West, and that there can be no real affinity or common meeting ground between them."[106] Once they had believed that it was "impossible" to lead Koreans to "higher ground" of Christian life; now they confessed, "we have *seen*, and *know* that we can pray them down to the depths and up to the heights."[107] They found a vision for the Korean church under Japanese colonialism and praised the Korean church as "the Christian lamp that is to lighten the Eastern world."[108] Above all, missionaries appreciated Korean leaders' spirituality. They admired elder Kil Sŏnju's (1869–1935) powerful sermon and deep spiritual experience. When he successfully led the revival meetings in Seoul in March 1907, one missionary was reminded of the powerful preaching of John Wesley (1703–1791) and George Whitefield (1714–1770).[109] James S. Gale (1863–1937) confessed that Kil's spiritual experience seemed more profound than that of missionaries. As Kil entered "the inner chamber of the Divine Presence," his preaching had "a subtle something that has to do with the heart and that God uses to influence men."[110]

The above three occurrences—the publication of the *Korean Repository* in 1892, the Tonghak Revolution in 1894, and the Great Revival Movement from 1903 to 1907—led the missionaries to see not only more diverse and syncretic aspects of Korean religions, but also the aspects of Korean religions congenial with Christianity.

In sum, three decisive discoveries made North American missionaries revise their understanding of Korean religions and spirituality. In the first decade (1884–1893) of their mission work, they discovered the multiple religious identities of the Koreans. This descriptive pluralism led them to study the real condition of Korean religions. In the second decade (1894–1903), they discovered the original Korean monotheism

[105] John Z. Moore, "A Changed Life," *KMF* 3 (1907): 159.

[106] Moore, "Changed Life."

[107] Edith F. MacRae, "For Thine Is the Power," *KMF* 2 (1906): 74; emphasis original.

[108] Moore, "Changed Life."

[109] "Recent Work of the Holy Spirit in Seoul," *KMF* 3 (1907): 41.

[110] James S. Gale, "Elder Kil," *MRW* (July 1907): 495.

in the Tan'gun myth and accepted its Hanănim as the Christian God. Some missionaries engaged in in-depth study of Korean shamanism. In the third decade (1904–1913), they realized the profound spiritual potential of the Korean people through the revival movement. They abandoned their basic assumptions: that the Koreans were different from Westerners, that Koreans could not lead a higher spiritual and ethical life, and that Koreans were incapable of running an independent nation and a democratic society. The emergence of Korean Christian spiritual and political leaders from 1904 to 1907 was proof that such assumptions were invalid and distorted by cultural imperialism.

–1–

God
Search for the Korean Name for God, Hanănim

They [Koreans] have first to learn that in coming to God they must believe that "He is," and that He has sent His only begotten Son into the world to be the Savior of the world. This, therefore, is the first lesson to be learnt by those whose belief in the spiritual world is confined to a belief in ghosts and evil spirits and the efficacy of sacrifices offered at the graves of their ancestors.

—C. John Corfe, 1897[1]

Many of the Christians in Korea first had their interest in the Christian Gospel aroused through their knowledge of Tangoon and his God, and they have recognized that He is one and the same as the God of their Bible.

—C. A. Clark, 1932[2]

The idea of a monotheistic God was one of the most important new elements that Christianity introduced into modern Korean religious culture. It prohibited the worship of all other existing gods and spirits and put the supremacy of God over all other authorities, including political and familial authorities. Thus, it was very difficult for Koreans, who had lived in an agnostic or polytheistic culture, to accept monotheism and practice its demands exclusively. The first controversial issue in the

---

[1] C. John Corfe, "The Bishop's Letter II," *Morning Calm* (May 1897): 37.
[2] Charles A. Clark, *Religions of Old Korea* (New York: Revell, 1932), 143.

encounter of Christian monotheism with local religions was the "term question"—the best vernacular name or term for the Christian God. Just as the Hebrew term "Elohim" became the Greek "Theos," Latin "Deus," and English "God," the term "God" has been translated into different names from one language to another, and this process entailed heated debates among missionaries and produced Christian discourses on the names of local gods, and through these competing narratives the modern idea of monotheism in Korea was formed.

In searching for the proper term for God among the many candidates, missionaries in China and Korea had to investigate the history of traditional religions and their view of gods, the term questions in neighboring countries, the etymologies of the names of local deities, and the contemporary religiosity of the people. In their discursive construction of the best candidate name, some missionaries accepted the idea of primitive monotheism and created new meanings suitable for Protestantism, a modern religion. The debates were entangled with not only theisms of traditional religions, but also contending mission theologies and the politics of various mission societies. Finding a vernacular name for God was the first step in the indigenization of Christianity in a given culture and language group.

The term question was also discussed among the theologians and ethnologists in Europe and America.[3] They asked whether ancient Chinese, Japanese, or Koreans had the idea of God; if they were monotheists, polytheists, or pantheists (which was related to theories on the origin of religions); and what the nature and meaning of the contemporary names of deities was (which was related to the Western understanding of East Asian religions and cultures). The term controversy in China and Korea, therefore, reveals multiple dimensions of the encounters between Western Christianity and Korean religions—the Western-Christian frameworks for the interpretation of the history of East Asian religions, a cross-cultural interaction between West and East, and thus a starting point to decode the cultural and theological genealogy of Protestantism, a new religion in modern Korea.

Two competing options existed among the missionaries and Bible translators. The first was a method of creation—inventing a new term

---

[3] Irene Eber, "Interminable Term Question," in *Bible in Modern China: The Literary and Intellectual Impact*, ed. Irene Eber et al. (Nettetal, Germany: Institut Monumenta Serica, 1999), 135.

or name based on the existing names of gods. The conservative camp preferred this option, for a neologism could block off the danger of syncretism with the names of "heathen" gods. But the shortcoming of a coined name, let alone the phonetization of Deus or Jehovah, lay in its foreignness to the audience and thus its limited circulation. The second option was a method of incarnation—adopting one of the traditional divine names, baptizing it as a Christian name, and, through the use of biblical connotations, educating the people about it. This camp insisted that Christianity could not be understood without this inevitable and pragmatic accommodation. This assimilative method entailed the problems of syncretism with the existing religions, provoking the opposition of those religious groups that claimed that missionaries had stolen their indigenous god and that Christians had no right to call on their god.[4]

This chapter traces the history of the official adoption of Hanănim (하ᄂ님) as the Korean term for the Protestant God and its metamorphosis from 1878 to 1906 from the highest deity of the Korean pantheon into the monotheistic God. It argues that the Korean Hanănim was adopted by the traditional method of choosing an existing name of divinity like the Greek Theos, Latin Deus, English God, and Chinese Shangdi, but that its etymological and theoretical foundation came from an assumed ancient monotheism of indigenous Korean spirituality. The combination of two methods of accommodation and invention was a unique feature of the Korean Protestant God Hanănim. On the other hand, the Korean "shin" (신) was understood as a term for the Greek "daimon," Latin "numen," English "gods" or "spirits," and Chinese "shen" (神), so that it was used in compound words like "Sŏngshin" (the Holy Spirit),

[4] In the early seventeenth century, Chinese anti-Christian scholars accused Ricci and Jesuit missionaries of stealing the Chinese term "Shangdi" from the Confucian classics and of applying a strange Christian color to it. In Korea, Taejonggyo (Religion of the Great Progenitor), founded by Na Ch'ŏl in 1909 and worshipping Hanŏllim, the three-persons-in-one God, insists that Christians stole this name from them and thus had no right to call their God Hanănim. See Kim Sanggeun, *Strange Names of God: The Missionary Translation of the Divine Name and the Chinese Responses to Matteo Ricci's Shangti in Late Ming China, 1583–1644* (New York: Peter Lang, 2004); Donald Baker, "The Korean God Is Not the Christian God: Taejonggyo's Challenge to Foreign Religions," in *Religions of Korea in Practice*, ed. Robert E. Buswell Jr. (Princeton, N.J.: Princeton University Press, 2007), 470–71; Eric Reinders, *Borrowed Gods and Foreign Bodies: Christian Missionaries Imagine Chinese Religion* (Berkeley: University of California Press, 2004).

"kwishin" (evil spirits), and polytheistic "shin" (gods or spirits).[5] This process reveals an aspect of the influence of Chinese Protestant theology on the Korea missions, competing theologies of religions of Protestant missionaries in Korea, and their acceptance of Korean Christians' understanding of Korean religions and their theism. My concern is not with the contemporary debate on the validity of devolution theory that claims that original monotheism degenerated into polytheism, but with turn-of-the-twentieth-century Protestant missionaries' and Korean Christians' discourse on Korean primitive monotheism.[6] This chapter

[5] A controversial issue in the term question in China was the term for the Holy Spirit. The Shengshen/Shangdi camp competed with the Shengling/Shen camp. The Shen camp could not use Shengshen because "Spirit of God" would be translated into "Shen of Shen." In 1904–1907, when the Shen editions of the Scriptures became unpopular among the Chinese, both camps compromised with Shangdi for God and Shengling for the Holy Spirit. But in Korea, as Hanănim was adopted, there was no need for compromise. John Ross' Gospels in 1882 used Syŏngshin (Shengshen), but he changed this to Sŏngnyŏng (Shengling) in 1883. So his New Testament in 1887 and its revised portions published in Seoul in 1892–1893 adopted Sŏngnyŏng. From 1895 to 1936 the Seoul editions exclusively used Sŏngshin because the Shangdi–Shengshen editions of the Chinese Scriptures of the BFBS were used in the Korean–Chinese mixed Testaments from 1906. However, the Revised Version adopted Sŏngnyŏng in 1938–1939, probably because of the influence of the Japanese Kami–Shengling versions.

[6] There have been two conflicting theories in regard to the origin of religion—evolutionism and devolutionism. James G. Frazer's *The Golden Bough* (1890) argued that religions originated from animism and evolved to polytheism, henotheism, and finally monotheism. The devolution theory (or degeneration/nonprogressive theory) of religion with the idea of primitive monotheism was developed by comparative religion scholars like Max Müller (from 1852) and became popular among Christian mission scholars in the 1890s. Andrew Lang's *The Making of Religion* (1909) and Wilhelm Schmidt's *High Gods in North America* (1933) argued that the oldest religion of mankind was monotheistic and that polytheism, magic, and superstitions were later degenerations. The school of Jesuit ethnologists known as the *Kulturkreislehre* (Schmidt, Kluckhohn) and the German Historical School (Jensen, Heine-Geldern) pushed forward the devolutionary idea and argued that God directly revealed himself to early men, communicating fundamental monotheistic theology and natural moral law. So the concept of primitive monotheism played an important role for more than a century (from the 1850s to the 1960s) and was accepted as ethnologically defensible. Devolution theory, defended with an enormous mass of ethnological material by Schmidt and his collaborators, has long since been proven unsound and was abandoned by many scholars. Yet many Christian scholars still hold on to it. So whatever contemporary scholars argue, the historical importance of the concept of primitive monotheism cannot be ignored. In Korea, the debate has not been productive primarily due to the

focuses on the development of a neologism, Hanănim, in relation to the concepts of heavenliness and oneness, and to the Korean founding myth of Tan'gun.

THE TERM QUESTION IN CHINA

The history of the interminable term controversy in China is significant in its influence on the debate in Korea. First, the former became the linguistic and theological background of the latter in Sinocentric East Asian culture. Second, all Chinese terms were imported to Korea and had competed with Korean terms for several decades. The third reason is that theologies and discourses that developed during the controversies in China were studied and used by the missionaries in Korea before reaching a consensus around 1905.

In China, the first camp of the missionaries invented new names for God in order to counteract polytheism. The most widely used method was to combine an adjective prefix with the main word *zhu* (主 lord). The use of the word "lord" came from the traditions of the Jewish Adonai reading of the Tetragrammaton and its Greek translation κύριος (Lord, master of supreme authority) in the Septuagint Old Testament and the New Testament. In China, Nestorians made a new name, Zhenzhu (眞主 True Lord), in the seventh century; Roman Catholics used Tianzhu (天主 Heavenly Lord) from the seventeenth century; and Anglicans used both Tianzhu and Shangzhu (上主 Supreme Lord) in the nineteenth and early twentieth centuries.[7]

ROMAN CATHOLICS
FROM SHANGDI TO TIANZHU

The Jesuit missionary Matteo Ricci (1552–1610), who arrived in China in 1583 and in 1601 was granted permission to reside in Beijing, accommodated Christianity to classical Confucianism. He originally

---

lack of the source materials on ancient Korea and its religions. The oldest existing documents on Korean religions were written in the thirteenth century. See Anthony F. C. Wallace, *Religion: An Anthropological View* (New York: Random House, 1966), 6–13; T. H. Barrett, "Chinese Religion in English Guide: The History of an Illusion," *Modern Asian Studies* 29, no. 3 (2005): 509–33.

[7] See Oak Sung-Deuk, "Competing Chinese Names for God: The Chinese Term Question and Its Influence upon Korea," *Journal of Korean Religions* 3, no. 2 (2012): 89–115.

employed two existing terms for God—Shangdi (上帝 Sovereign on High) and Tian (天 Heaven). Ricci understood original Confucianism as an imperfect ethical theism or a viable natural philosophy that was open to God and compatible with Christianity. He criticized the atheistic elements of Neo-Confucian cosmology. Instead he adopted Shangdi from the Confucian classics, which connoted God as a personal deity who watched over both human affairs and the universe. Ricci's second term was Tian, the transcendental Heaven, which was similar to the Western notion of Providence. Since the term Tian was introduced to Chinese religious culture later than Shangdi—around the beginning of the Zhou dynasty (ca. 1120 B.C.E.)—Tian and Shangdi were used interchangeably in the canonical Confucian classics. However, under the influence of Daoism and Buddhism, by the sixteenth century Tian had long taken on the connotations of an impersonal and natural force.[8] Hence Ricci used the coined term Tianzhu (天主) as well as Shangdi in his *Tianzhu shiyi* (1603). He identified the Christian Tianzhu with the Chinese Shangdi of the Confucian classics and Shen with the Spirit.[9] However, he emphasized that the impersonal *taiji* (supreme ultimate) or *li* (ultimate principle) of Neo-Confucian cosmology could not be the origin of all things, and Tianzhu had nothing to do with the Buddhist *sunyata* (emptiness) or the Daoist *wu* (nothingness).[10] By understanding the character *tian* (heaven) as a compound letter of *yi* (one) and *da* (great), Ricci added a new monotheistic meaning of "Great One" (unicum magnum) to the Heavenly Lord Tianzhu.[11] The Jesuit adoption of

[8] Douglas Lancashire and Peter Kuo-chen Hu, "Introduction. *The True Meaning of the Lord of Heaven (T'ien-chu Shih-I). By Matteo Ricci S.J.*," in *Jesuit Primary Sources in English Translations*, ed. Edward J. Malatesta, S.J. (St. Louis: Institute of Jesuit Sources, 1985), 33–34.

[9] Matteo Ricci, *China in the Sixteenth Century: The Journals of Matteo Ricci, 1583–1610*, trans. Louis J. Gallagher (New York: Random House, 1953), 99–100, 125.

[10] Ricci, *China*, 98–99, 106–7.

[11] Ricci, *China*, 125. According to Xǔ Shèn's *Shuowen Jiezi* (Etymological Dictionary of Chinese Characters) of the Han dynasty in the second century C.E., the etymology of "Tian" was "something most high over a person" (Chu Chaeyong, *Sǒnyu ǔi Ch'ǒnju sasang gwa chesa munje* [Early Confucian Thought of Tianzhu and the Ancestor Worship Question] [Seoul: Kynghyang chapchisa, 1958], 32). The oracle script of the Zhou dynasty depicted a person with a large cranium. Anthropomorphic Heaven was said to see, hear, and watch over all men. Ricci's erroneous understanding of "Tian" as a compound of "one" and "great" was accepted by James Legge in 1880 and G. Heber Jones in Korea in 1892. See James Legge,

the original Confucian terms represented their accommodation to the syncretic spirit of the Ming dynasty (1368–1644), and created a Confucian–Christian synthesis.[12]

When the Manchus established the Qing dynasty in 1644, they became less open to foreign influences, though they hired some Jesuits at the court for their scientific knowledge. Manchu ethnocentrism, chauvinism, and xenophobia, combined with Confucian orthodoxy, made the Jesuit method of blending Christianity with Confucianism less tenable among the Chinese literati. In this milieu, the mendicant orders—Dominicans and Franciscans—adopted a confrontational method and gained their constituency among the lower social classes in rural areas like Shandong, where secret societies like the White Lotus Society were burgeoning. Franciscans prohibited ancestor worship, which they saw as pagan idol worship, promoted the development of confraternities, and organized secret meetings of their followers who were persecuted by the local government.[13] The difference in target audience and constituency led the missionary societies to take different theological approaches to Chinese culture and religions.

During the Rites Controversy over the terms for God and the ancestral rite from the middle of the seventeenth century to the early eighteenth century, Dominicans and Franciscans criticized the Jesuit method of syncretic assimilation to Confucian terms and rituals. When Pope Clement XI banned ancestor worship in 1715, his papal bull *Ex Illa Dei* prohibited the use of Shangdi and Tian, religiously and sociopolitically charged words, replacing them with Tianzhu.[14] The bull prohibited

---

Religions of China: Confucianism and Taoism Described and Compared with Christianity (New York: Fleming H. Revell, 1880), 9; G. H. Jones, "Studies in Korean, Korean Etymology," *KR* 1 (1892): 332–33.

[12] D. E. Mungello, *The Great Encounter of China and the West, 1500–1800* (Lanham, Md.: Rowman & Littlefield, 1999), 22. On the other hand, the Jesuit discourse on the supernatural campaigned against Chinese demonology. Jesuit rationalism, science, and accommodation policy to Confucianism went together with Jesuit discourse on divine miracles and religious iconoclasm. See Qiong Zhang, "About God, Demons, and Miracles: The Jesuit Discourse on the Supernatural in Late Ming China," *Early Science and Medicine* 4, no. 1 (1999): 1–36.

[13] Mungello, *Great Encounter*, 24–26.

[14] The papal bull ordered the designation of the Spirit (*pneuma*) as Shen. See S. W. Williams, "The Controversy among the Protestant Missionaries on the Proper Translation of the Words God and Spirits into Chinese," *Bibliotheca Sacra* 35 (1878): 735.

Shangdi because Vatican theologians thought that the Christian God Deus should not be confused with the Chinese emperor *di*. In response, Emperor Yongzheng proscribed Roman Catholicism as a heterodox cult in his imperial edict of 1724. Pope Benedict VII's bull *Ex Quo Singularii* (1742) more completely denounced the Jesuit accommodation to pagan culture. In reaction the Chinese court banned Christianity. Thus, European cultural and religious pride over East Asian civilization, particularly over Manchu influence, defeated the Riccian method, and the first chapter of European Christianity's encounter with Chinese religions came to a close. The issue of ancestor worship was closely related to that of the term question, and Protestants reopened both issues in the nineteenth century.

PROTESTANTS
DOMINANCE OF SHANGDI OVER SHEN

Many Protestant missionaries belonged to the second camp, which preferred using the existing names of the divine as a medium to convey a new idea of God.[15] Protestantism, as a religion of the Bible, produced vernacular translations of the Scriptures. Different groups in China had varying ideas, linguistically and theologically, on the terms for God. One dominant argument was that Theos (God) should not be translated into Zhu (Lord) because the Lord (kurios) of the Greek New Testament was equivalent to the Tetragrammaton (YHWH).[16] According to this argument, Zhenzhu, Tianzhu, and Shangzhu were Chinese equivalents to Lord, not God. They searched for an alternative, and their solution was adopting the best vernacular name for God—just as the Greeks had done with Theos and the English with God. Another reason for the Protestant missionaries' movement toward assimilation was their need to differentiate Protestantism from Roman Catholicism, a stigmatized foreign religion in China. One of the new developments

[15] For good summaries of the term question in China, see Douglas G. Spelman, "Christianity in Chinese: The Protestant Term Question," *Papers on China* 22A (1969): 25–52; Eber, "Interminable Term Question."

[16] E.g., when one used Tianzhu, the translation of "my Lord and my God" (John 20:28) became "my true Lord and my heavenly Lord" in Chinese. See James Legge, *The Notions of the Chinese Concerning God and Spirits: With an Examination of the Defense of an Essay, on the Proper Rendering of the Words of Elohim and Theos, into the Chinese Language* (Hong Kong: Hong Kong Register Office, 1852), 130.

made by (American) Protestant missionaries was their use of Shen as the term for God, which the Roman Catholics had used universally to designate the Spirit.

Since Robert Morrison (1782–1834) had adopted Shen in his Chinese New Testament in 1813, Protestant missionaries used more than twenty Chinese names for God, some borrowed from the Confucian classics and others coined by combining Shen, Tian, Shangdi, or Zhu with other letters.[17] But it was not just British and American missionaries who disagreed; Baptists, Methodists, Presbyterians, and Anglicans were also unable to find common ground. Protestant missionaries were divided into two major groups—the Shangdi camp (Shangdists) and the Shen camp (Shenites)—at the time the Board of Translators of the Delegates' Version of the New Testament was organized in 1843,[18] and then a third group—the Tianzhu camp—appeared in the 1870s and 1880s.

In 1847 and 1848 many dissertations and tracts on the terms were produced. The Board of Translators could not reach a consensus and consequently published the union version in two different editions in 1850. The liberal camp interpreted Shangdi (Supreme Ruler) of the Confucian classics as a historical and spiritual equivalent to the God Most High of the Bible, and the Chinese Shen as equivalent to the Greek daimon and the Latin numen. Walter H. Medhurst (1796–1857) argued that Shangdi was the substance (*ti*) of Shen, and Shen was the spiritual function (*yong*) of Shangdi.[19]

The Shangdi camp in China signaled a new phase through the notion of "original monotheism." The Jesuits had thought that Christianity

[17] They were (1) the Shen group: 神, 眞神, 眞活神; (2) the Di group: 上帝, 神天上帝, 天上上帝, 眞神上帝, 神天大帝, 天帝, 天皇, 主宰, 眞宰; (3) the Tian group: 天, 上天, 神天, 天父, 老天爺; and (4) the Zhu group: 天主, 神主, 眞主, 上主, 天帝神主. Three favorite names were Shen 神, Shangdi 上帝, and Tian 天. See Walter H. Medhurst, *An Enquiry into the Proper Mode of Rendering the Word God in Translating the Sacred Scriptures into the Chinese Language* (Shanghai: Mission Press, 1848), 157–59; Frank Rawlinson, *Chinese Ideas of the Supreme Being* (Shanghai: Presbyterian Mission Press, 1928), 14.

[18] There were two subgroups in the Shangdists: the first party used Shangdi for God and Shen for Spirit; the second party used Shangdi or Tian for God, *shen* 神 for gods (false gods), and *ling* 靈 for Spirit. The Shenites used Shen for God and *ling* for Spirit. See Williams, "Controversy among the Protestant Missionaries," 738.

[19] W. H. Medhurst, *A Dissertation on the Theology of Chinese with a View to the Elucidation of the Most Appropriate Term for Expressing the Deity, in the Chinese Language* (Shanghai: American Presbyterian Mission Press, 1847), 266, 278; Medhurst, *Enquiry into the Proper Mode*, 15.

and ancient Confucianism were complementary and that the latter was open to theism. Yet the Protestant Shangdists, represented by James Legge (1815–1897), argued that that the Shangdi of the Confucian classics was synonymous with the Greek Theos and the Chinese were originally monotheistic, like the Greeks.[20] The Shangdists believed that Shangdi referred to the monotheistic God, although the ancient Chinese worshipped many lower deities. Their use of Shen for the Spirit had continuity with the use of the Jesuits.

By contrast, the conservative camp insisted that Shen was a much more generic term, meaning gods, God, spirit, or soul, and that they could destroy Chinese gods by using the Christian Shen. Bishop William J. Boone (1811–1874), of the American Protestant Episcopal Church, denied the existence of original monotheism and primitive revelation in ancient China, just as Franciscans and Dominicans had done in the seventeenth century. In 1848 Boone argued that the Chinese were polytheists, and they did not know the true God; therefore the highest being known to them, Shangdi, should be regarded as the chief god of a pantheon. Under these circumstances, he contended that they should choose not the specific proper name Shangdi, but the generic and relative name Shen, just like the Greek New Testament had not adopted the name of the chief god Zeus but the generic and relative term Theos.[21] Like French Jesuit Claude de Visdelou (1656–1737), Boone referred to Zhu Xi's commentaries, which understood creation as an impersonal process beginning with the Great Ultimate (*taiji*), Principle (*li*), and Vital Energy (*qi*). In Korea, H. G. Underwood and his colleagues followed Boone's line and opposed the use of Hanănim in the 1890s because they regarded it as the name of the highest god of the Korean pantheon.

Boone's arguments were so forceful that in January 1850 Medhurst and his five colleagues in Shanghai proposed to temporarily use Aloha (Jehovah) when the opinion of Protestant missionaries was divided between Shangdi and Shen. This compromise, however, met with no

---

[20] Legge, *Notions of the Chinese*, 58–59, 113; Elihu Doty, *Some Thoughts on the Proper Term to Be Employed to Translate Elohim and Theos into Chinese* (Shanghai: Presbyterian Mission Press, 1850), 12–13.

[21] William J. Boone, *An Essay on the Proper Rendering of the Words of Elohim and Theos into the Chinese Language* (Canton: Chinese Repository, 1848), 2–4.

favor from anyone.[22] But the Shenites began to lose their voice under the rising academic influence of James Legge of the London Missionary Society, who began the monumental task of translating volumes of Chinese classics in 1841 (more focused work began in 1857).[23] By 1851 more than one-third of all missionaries in China ceased to use Shen, and gradually one mission after another abandoned the term permanently.[24]

The Victorian missionary James Legge played a pivotal role in the Chinese term question by advocating two new concepts—Shangdi as a relative term and its original monotheism. He used Shen initially, triumphantly believing that the Protestant missionary enterprise was very close to the rapid conversion of darkest Sinim China.[25] However, after studying Chinese classical literature, he accepted Medhurst's scholarship on Confucian classics and in 1848 changed his term form Shen to Shangdi, insisting that God was not a *generic*, but a *relative* term.[26] Legge argued that both God and Shangdi referred not only to the highest God in himself, but to the relationship between himself and all other beings.[27] In 1852 Legge took a step further by insisting that monotheism, though not a pure monotheism, existed in ancient China, stating that the God whom the Chinese worshipped was the same whom Christians adored because God had revealed himself to the Chinese.[28] He discovered documentary evidence for a form of Shangdi monotheism from Ming imperial worship recorded by the restorationists in the *Ta Ming hui-tien* (The Collected Statutes of the Great Ming Dynasty, 1511).[29]

---

[22] Boone, *Defense of an Essay on the Proper Rendering of the Words of Elohim and Theos into the Chinese Language* (Canton: Chinese Repository, 1850), 3, 17; Williams, "Controversy among the Protestant Missionaries," 746–47.

[23] Norman J. Girardot, *The Victorian Translation of China: James Legge's Oriental Pilgrimage* (Berkeley: University of California Press, 2002), 40, 49.

[24] Henry Blodget, *The Use of T'ien Chu for God in Chinese* (Shanghai: American Presbyterian Mission Press, 1893), 3.

[25] Girardot, *Victorian Translation*, 44.

[26] Legge, *An Argument for Shangte as the Proper Rendering of the Words Elohim and Theos in the Chinese Language with Strictures on the Essay of Bishop Boone in Favour of the Term Shin* (Hong Kong: Hong Kong Register Office, 1850), v.

[27] Legge, *Notions of the Chinese*, 2, 86; Keong Tow-yung, "James Legge and the Christian Term Question," *Tsing Hua Journal of Chinese Studies* 37, no. 2 (2007): 472.

[28] Legge, *Notions of the Chinese*, 38.

[29] Legge, *Notions of the Chinese*, 24–31, 40–42; Lauren F. Pfister, "Discovering Monotheistic Metaphysics: The Exegetical Reflections of James Legge

Based on the idea of primitive revelation, Legge believed that monotheism preceded polytheism in China, that Shangdi in the five Confucian classics was a different name from the monotheistic Christian God, and that Chinese had never debased the name in history, though they worshipped many other inferior gods and spirits.[30] Legge, like Matteo Ricci, depended on the metaphysical interpretation of classical Confucianism and the ritual of the imperial court.

In 1859 Legge defended Ricci's liberal method of accommodation.[31] But Legge preferred Shangdi to Tianzhu and rejected the latter as "a Popery invention" from his Protestant freedom. He regarded "Romism" as an exceedingly corrupted form of Christianity, which worshipped both the true God and multiple other beings, and insisted that ancient Chinese monotheism, like Roman Catholicism, had corrupted into polytheism, and that it worshipped both monotheistic Shangdi and other spirits.[32]

In his essay titled *Confucianism in Relation with Christianity* for the General Conference held in Shanghai in 1877, Legge, from Oxford, insisted that Shangdi in the Confucian classics was the true monotheistic God, that Confucius was a man sent of God, and that Confucianism could be used as a schoolmaster to teach the Chinese the knowledge of Christianity.[33] However, Legge acknowledged that the Confucian books did not represent the time when the religion of China was purely monotheistic. Legge reiterated his view on the original monotheism of the ancient Chinese in his book *The Religions of China*, published in 1880. He stated, "Five thousand years ago the Chinese were monotheists—not henotheists, but monotheists"—though he added that even then there was a constant struggle with nature worship and divination.[34] Many Korean Christians and missionaries in Korea accepted Legge's arguments of the

---

(1815–1897) and Lo Chung-fan (d. circa 1850)," in *Imagining Boundaries: Changing Confucian Doctrines, Texts, and Hermeneutics*, ed. Chow Kai-wing et al. (Albany: State University of New York, 1999), 215.

[30] Legge, *Notions of the Chinese*, 58–59, 113.

[31] Legge, *The Land of Sinim: A Sermon Preached in the Tabernacle, Moorfields, at the Sixty-Fifth Anniversary of the London Missionary Society* (London: John Snow, 1859), 58.

[32] Legge, *Notions of the Chinese*, 32.

[33] Legge, *Confucianism in Relation with Christianity* (Shanghai: Kelly & Walsh, 1877), 11.

[34] Legge, *Religions of China*, 16.

primitive monotheistic Shangdi and understood Hanănim as its equivalent. His book *The Religions of China* exerted a great influence among Protestant missionaries in Korea. When H. G. Underwood published his book *The Religions of the Eastern Asia* in 1910, he used Legge's book extensively and advocated the primitive monotheism of Korean Hanănim based on Legge's understanding of Shangdi.

Most British and European missionaries—W. H. Medhurst, W. C. Milne, Karl Gützlaff, John Stronach, George Staunton, and James Legge—supported Shangdi, and most American missionaries—represented by William J. Boone and Elijah C. Bridgman—Shen. Accordingly, the British and Foreign Bible Society (BFBS) and the National Bible Society of Scotland (NBSS) printed the Shangdi editions, and the American Bible Society (ABS) the Shen editions. Although the BFBS had a policy of literal translation, they tolerated the 1854 literary and dynamic translation of the Old Testament by the missionaries of the London Missionary Society. This Delegates' Version (the so-called Wenli Version) of the BFBS became much more popular by 1910 than the Bridgman–Culbertson Version of the ABS, which was faithful to the literal translation. Because American missionaries occupied most of Japan, the Chinese term Shen and its Japanese equivalent Kami were used in Japan. In contrast, since American missionaries worked mainly with the BFBS in Korea, the Shangdi edition of the Chinese Scriptures was distributed in Korea, and Shangdi and its Korean equivalent Hanănim were eventually used in Korean Protestantism.

There was a third camp—the Anglicans—who advocated Tianzhu, which had a strong impact on the missions in Korea in the 1890s. The first bishop of the Church of England in China, George Smith, wrote in 1851 that he preferred Tianzhu because numerous Chinese converts had been made by its century and a half of usage and Protestants had adopted most other religious nomenclature of Roman Catholicism.[35]

---

[35] Blodget, *Use of T'ien Chu*, 6. In 1864 Robert Samuel Maclay (1824–1907) of the Methodist Episcopal Church in Fuzhou proposed to use Tianzhu for God and either Shengshen or Shengling for the Holy Spirit. In 1865 Alexander Williamson (1829–1890), agent of the National Bible Society of Scotland in Chefoo, wrote a paper to urge the missionaries to adopt Tianzhu as the only practicable basis of union for a new Mandarin version. The paper was signed by many veteran missionaries including Joseph Edkins of the London Missionary Society and W. A. P. Martin of the Presbyterian Church, USA. In 1876 Maclay made the same suggestion for the union.

Bishop Samuel I. J. Schereschewsky (1831–1906) was its representative translator. In his 1875 Old Testament translation, he employed Tianzhu for God, Zhu for YHWH, and Shen for (other) gods.[36] Henry Blodget (1825–1903) of the American Board in Beijing convinced Schereschewsky that Tianzhu was the best term. In 1893 Blodget argued that the entire Christian church in China—Protestants, Roman Catholics, and Orthodox—should be united in using the uniform term for God. The experience of eighty-five years proved that Shen could not distinguish between polytheistic gods and the One God. Shangdi had been associated with the national cult, and thus many Catholic and Protestant missionaries regarded Shangdi as just a chief god.[37] He stated that no word in Chinese had more religious reverence attached to it than the word "Tian" (Heaven), and "Zhu" added the personal element.[38] The Anglican proposal for the union was well accepted by younger missionaries in Korea as well as by senior missionaries in China.[39]

Even so, the term question was not resolved in China. The Shanghai Conferences in 1877, 1890, and 1907 could not solve the problem. The three terms, Shen, Tianzhu, and Shangdi, coexisted in the 1890s and 1900s. The Chinese Christians preferred the Shangdi edition published by the BFBS. In the first decade of the twentieth century, nearly all Chinese Protestants used the Shangdi edition, and the Union Bible in 1919 used Shangdi.[40] The Chinese liked the vernacular name and the idea that their ancient ancestors were monotheists, which was strongly defended by James Legge and other liberal evangelical missionaries and translators. The principle of vernacularism and the idea of primitive monotheism of the liberal Protestant missionaries in China influenced the Protestant missions in Korea.

---

[36] Samuel I. J. Schereschewsky, "Terminology in the China Mission," *Churchman* 57, no. 6 (1888): 34–35; Eber, "Translating the Ancestors," 226.

[37] Blodget, *Use of T'ien Chu*, 3–4.

[38] Eber, "Translating the Ancestors," 227.

[39] The board of the translators of the Korean Scriptures decided to use T'yŏnjyu in 1894.

[40] The sales of the Shangdi edition increased rapidly in the 1900s: 38,500 copies (11.6 percent) in 1894, 299,000 copies (78.9 percent) in 1908, and 1,708,000 copies (99.7 percent) in 1913. See Zetzsche, *The Bible in China: History of the Union Version or The Culmination of Protestant Missionary Bible Translation in China* (Nettetal, Germany: Monumenta Serica, 1999), 88.

THE TERM QUESTION IN KOREA

Unlike with the Chinese Protestant missions, the Korean traditional vernacular name Hanănim (하ᄂᆞ님 Heavenly Being) and the Chinese new name T'yŏnjyu (텬쥬 C. Tianzhu) competed in the Korean Protestant missions in the 1890s. The former was an indigenous name of Korean folk religions and was adopted by John Ross, who began to translate the Scriptures into Korean in 1878, whereas the latter was a Chinese term, which had the advantage of ecumenical cooperation between evangelical Protestants (Presbyterians and Methodists) and Anglicans.[41] After debates over several names from 1893 to 1903, the evangelical Protestant missions decided to adopt Hanănim in the vernacular Korean texts and to use Shangdi in the Chinese texts.[42] The Protestant missions in China had engaged in prolonged controversies over the term for God. In contrast, those in Korea came to a consensus for the newly coined Hanănim within two decades of their work. The history of the term question reveals early Protestant missionaries' theology concerning non-Christian religions and their attitudes toward the idea of the primitive monotheism of Korean shamanism, a unique side of Korean spirituality that had affinities with Christianity, and early Korean Christians' agency in the creation of a neologism Hanănim as the Christian God.

ROMAN CATHOLICS' EXCLUSIVE USE OF T'YŏNJYU

Just before the Catholic Church in Korea officially started in 1784, they used Shangdi and Tianzhu interchangeably, influenced by Matteo Ricci. The first Korean vernacular hymns, "Song for Worshipping God" and "Song of the Ten Commandments," composed around 1779, used only T'yŏnjyu (C. Tianzhu). By contrast, Yi Pyŏk (1754–1786) used Shangzhu, Shangdi, and Tian in his Chinese poem "Sŏnggyo yoji"

[41] The following were used as the Korean names for God at this time: 하느님 Hanŭnim, 하ᄂᆞ님 Hanănim, 하나님 Hananim, 텬쥬(天主) T'yŏnjyu, 샹뎨(上帝) Syangdye, 신(神) Shin, 진신(眞神) Chinshin, 춤신(眞神) Ch'amshin, 쥬(主) Chyu, and 샹쥬(上主) Syangjyu.
[42] In the controversy, Syangdye (C. Shangdi) had been dropped earlier, for it was used in the Chinese Scriptures and literature. The coexistence of the Korean Hanănim, which came from Korean shamanism and was favored by American missionaries, and the Chinese Shangdi, which came from Confucianism and was favored by British missionaries, revealed that Korean religions and Christianity had a distinctive identity.

(Essentials of the Holy Teaching), written around 1785. Shangzhu was a combination of the Confucian Shangdi and the Christian Tianzhu.[43]

After the papal bull *Ex Quo Singularii* (1742) prohibited ancestor worship and the use of Shangdi, and a Lazarist (Congregation of the Mission) bishop Alexandre de Gouveia (1751–1808) in Beijing banned ancestor worship in Korea in 1790, T'yŏnjyu was used exclusively in Korean Catholic literature.[44] For example, Chŏng Yakchong's (1760–1801) *Chugyo yoji* (Essentials of the Lord's Teaching, ca. 1800) used T'yŏnjyu, and Chŏng Hasang's (1795–1839) Chinese letter to the prime minister, *Sang chaesang sŏ* (1839), used Tianzhu. Even though French missionaries in Korea knew the name of Hanănim of Korean folk religion, their conservative theology under the papal prohibition of Shangdi and Tian regarded the Korean indigenous Hanănim as a superstitious pagan god. The *Dictionnaire Français-Coréen*, compiled in 1869, therefore used only T'yŏnjyu, and for the entry for "Ciel," the author added that "les payens par respect superstitieux disent 하늘님" (the pagans say 하늘님 with superstitious respect).[45] The *Dictionnaire Français-Coréen* 韓佛字典, published in Yokohama in 1880, did not mention Hanalnim under the entry of 하늘,[46] and only under the entries "Syangdye" and "T'yŏnjyu" was God referred to. Tianzhu (天主, T'yŏnjyu 텬쥬 or Ch'ŏnju 천주) remained the official term for God for Roman Catholicism (天主敎) in Korea throughout the nineteenth and twentieth centuries. Nevertheless, after the Vatican II Council, the Korean Roman Catholic Church moved toward indigenization in the term question. When in 1971 and 1977 they made the Union Version of the Korean Bible in cooperation with Protestants, Anglicans, and Orthodox Christians, they adopted Tianzhu's Korean equivalent, Hanŭnim (하느님).

[43] Kim Okhŭi, *Kwang'am Yi Pyŏk ŭi sŏhak sasang* [Yi Pyŏk's Thought of Roman Catholicism] (Seoul: Kat'olik ch'ulp'ansa, 1979), 95–100.

[44] Some French Vincentians from Paris worked in Beijing after Clement XIV ordered the dissolution of the Society of Jesus in 1773, and a Jesuit bishop, Louis de Grammont (who baptized Yi Sŭnghun in Beijing in 1784), could not work in China any longer.

[45] Stanislas Férron, ed., *Dictionnaire Français-Coréen* (1869; repr., Seoul: Han'guk Kyohoesa Yŏn'guso, 2004), 59. Thus we can say that Koreans were using Hanănim commonly before John Ross' liberal Scottish Presbyterian theology adopted it as the term for God in 1881.

[46] F. C. Ridel, ed., 韓佛字典 *Hanbul chadyŏn: Dictionnaire Coréen-Français* (Yokohama: Levy, 1880), 77.

The Roman Catholic Church continued to use Hanŭnim in its own new version of the Bible, *Sŏnggyong* 성경, published in 2005.

In 1860 Ch'oe Cheu experienced an epiphany of the Shangdi God and founded a new religion, Tonghak (Eastern Learning), as an alternative religion to Roman Catholicism, a Western religion. Yet Tonghak used Tianzhu for the name of God in its Chinese writings until 1880. That was why the Chosŏn government persecuted its members as Roman Catholics. When they published a few vernacular documents in the early 1880s, they began to use Hanullim, which was the vernacular translation of the Chinese Tianzhu.

JOHN ROSS' ADOPTION OF HANANIM

In the interconnection between the Chinese terms and the Korean terms for God, John Ross (1842–1915) and other Scottish missionaries in Shandong and Manchuria provided the missionaries in Seoul with important theological and linguistic discourses. They used Shangdi in Chinese Christian literature and Hanŭnim or Hananim (Heavenly One) in Korean Christian literature that they produced from 1877 to 1893. By using both terms and by referring to the contemporary Manchurian and Korean religiosities, they determined the adoption of Hananim in Korean Scriptures. Here John Ross developed unique discourses on the original monotheism of Confucianism in ancient China, Daoism in Manchuria, and shamanism in northern Korea.

John Ross was sent to Newchwang (Yingkou) in 1872 as the first missionary of the Manchurian Mission of the United Presbyterian Church of Scotland, and he worked among Koreans as well as Chinese in Manchuria until his retirement in 1910.[47] After some contacts with Koreans in Manchuria, he began to translate the Scriptures into Korean *hangŭl* in 1877, and he chose a vernacular name, Hanŭnim (Hananim), as the term for God, from his first Korean gospels of Luke and John in 1882 to his New Testament translation in 1887.[48] The "Ross Version"

[47] The United Presbyterian Church of Scotland was formed in 1847 and in 1900 merged with the Free Church of Scotland to form the United Free Church of Scotland. It was the third largest Presbyterian church in Scotland and stood on its liberal wing.

[48] Oak Sung-Deuk and Yi Mahnyol, *Taehan sŏngsŏ konghoesa* [A History of the Korean Bible Society], vol. 1 (Seoul: Korean Bible Society, 1993), 31–89; vol. 2 (1994), 105–6. In 1883 Ross changed the spelling of Hanŭnim to Hananim. This was the result of his effort to simplify the phonetic value of " · ", which had been

led to the first Korean converts, including Sŏ Sangnyun. They became the first helpers of American missionaries and the seeds of churches in northern Korea (see map 1 in the appendix).

Ross regarded Manchuria and Korea as parts of the larger cultural sphere of Northeast Asia and studied the distinctive Korean language, culture, history, and religions, hoping to evangelize in Korea someday in the future.[49] This vision was transferred from Alexander Williamson, a senior Scottish missionary in China from 1855 and agent of the NBSS in Chefoo, Shandong. Williamson persuaded Robert J. Thomas (1839–1866) to visit Korea in 1865 and board the *General Sherman*, an American vessel, as a colporteur for the fateful voyage of 1866 to Pyongyang. In 1867 Williamson visited the Corean Gate in Manchuria, the gateway village and the official marketplace between Qing China and Chosŏn Korea. He distributed Scriptures and tracts among Korean merchants there and gathered some information about Korea, yet failed to hear about the late Thomas. Williamson yearned for Great Britain and America to open Korea for mission work.[50] Influenced by Thomas and Williamson, Ross visited the Corean Gate in 1874 and 1876 and found a Korean language teacher, Yi Ŭngch'an. After publishing *The Corean Primer* for future missionaries to Korea in 1877, Ross and Yi began to translate the Scriptures into Korean, and the first drafts of three gospels were completed by 1878, before Ross left for England on furlough. John MacIntyre (1837–1905), who joined Ross in 1875 and became his brother-in-law in 1876, continued the translation work with some Koreans in 1879.[51] MacIntyre used Hananim, which Ross and his Korean helpers had adopted. He baptized four Koreans, including Paek

---

pronounced as (a) or (ŭ), into (a). There was no change in his understanding of the meaning of the name.

[49] John Ross, *The Manchus: Or, the Reigning Dynasty of China: Their Rise and Progress* (Paisley, Scotland: J. and R. Parlane, 1880); Ross, *History of Corea: Ancient and Modern* (Paisley, Scotland: J. and R. Parlane, 1881), 7–8; James H. Grayson, "The Manchurian Connection: The Life and Work of the Rev. Dr. John Ross," *Korea Observer* 15, no. 3 (1984): 345–46.

[50] Alexander Williamson, *Journey in North China, Manchuria and Eastern Mongolia with Some Account of Korea*, vol. 2 (London: Smith Elder, 1870), 179–84, 311.

[51] Douglas Christie, "Pioneers: The Rev. John Ross, Manchuria," *Life and Work* 5 (1934): 78; Grayson, "Manchurian Connection," 350–52.

Hongjun and Yi Ŭngch'an, at the Chinese church in Newchwang in 1879.[52] These were the first Protestant baptisms for Koreans.

From 1878 Ross adopted Hanŭnim as an equivalent of Shangdi. Before going to Scotland, he completed the drafts of *History of Corea: Ancient and Modern* and published it in 1881. In the book he argued,

> The Coreans have one native name, and one borrowed from the Chinese, for the Supreme Being. The former is *Hannonim*, from *hanul*, heaven; the latter *Shangde*. The name *Hannonim* is so distinguished and so universally used, that there will be no fear, in future translations and preaching, of the unseemly squabbles which occurred long ago among Chinese missionaries on this subject;—even though the Romanists have introduced the name which they employ in China. The idea conveyed by the term *Hannonim* is much like that of *Tien laoye*, the popular Chinese name for the Almighty, the all-present, but invisible One.[53]

Ross understood that the etymology of Hanŭnim (Hannonim) was *hanŭl* (heaven); Hanŭnim meant the Heavenly Ruler, and thus it was equivalent to the Chinese Shangdi. Ross contended that this term included the meanings of omnipotent, omnipresent, and invisible.

When Ross retuned to Manchuria from Scotland in 1881, he moved to Shenyang, established a press, and began to publish Korean Christian literature. Ross adopted Hanŭnim in his first two Korean tracts, *Yesu sŏnggyo mundap* (Bible Catechism) and *Yesu sŏnggyo yoryŏng* (Introduction to the New Testament), in October 1881,[54] and the first two Korean Gospels of Luke and John in the spring of 1882.[55] From 1883 he then consistently used Hananim in the Korean Scriptures. However, there was no change in the meaning in his shift from Hanŭnim to

---

[52] John MacIntyre, "Baptism at Moukden, Haichang, and Seaport," *UPMR* (January 1, 1880): 14–15; MacIntyre, "Mr. MacIntyre's Report," *UPMR* (July 1, 1880): 278–79; J. Ross, "Manchuria Mission," *MRUPCS* (October 1, 1880): 333–34.

[53] Ross, *History of Corea*, 355.

[54] Ross' *Bible Catechism* was revised by Mrs. Mary F. Scranton and published in Seoul in 1892. It was widely used by Methodists and Presbyterians in Seoul. Rosetta S. Hall, "Women's Medical Missionary Work," *CR* (April 1893): 167.

[55] Ross' first principle of translation was "an absolute literal translation compatible with the meaning of the passages and the idiom of the Corean language." But his actual translation had to accept many Korean idioms (J. Ross to William Wright, January 24, 1883). This moderately dynamic equivalent translation might have been another factor in Ross accepting the indigenous term "Hananim."

Hananim, as it was just a spelling change. Its meaning remained "Heavenly One," the Korean equivalent of the Chinese Shangdi.

Ross adopted Shangdi, like other Scottish missionaries, under the influence of Alexander Williamson of the NBSS and possibly James Legge.[56] In adopting Shangdi, however, Ross had a different approach from that of Legge. Legge depended on documentary evidence, such as Confucian classics and old court records. Although Ross studied Confucian classics, quoted them in his sermons, and included them in the curricula of the mission schools, he had different sources for Shangdi as a term for God—the contemporary Chinese people's understanding of Shangdi. Ross gathered information from his target audience in Manchuria, which consisted of urban merchants and rural farmers, and tried to find the remnants of the monotheistic belief in Shangdi. This fieldwork approach was applied to the search for the Korean term for God. As Ross could not enter Korea, his contact with Koreans was limited to itinerant Korean merchants and the Korean embassies to Beijing via Manchuria. Ross depended on their religiosity and colloquial usage of Hanŭnim, partly because of the scarcity of available documents on Korean religions. On the other hand, his liberal missiology and tolerant attitude toward East Asian religions led him to find and appreciate the Korean people's monotheistic spirituality in practice.

In his anthropological approach, Ross found a third source. This was Manchurian Daoism and a Daoist priest in Shenyang who worshipped Shangdi or the Jade Shangdi. Through written dialogues on chapter 1 of the Gospel of John with Ross, the priest argued that the Christian concepts of Dao, Shangdi, light, darkness, and life were similar to those of Daoism, that Daoist Shangdi was also a creator who had no beginning or end and who was omnipresent, omniscient, and omnipotent; and thus he supported the concepts of Shangdi and heaven of primitive Confucianism, which he thought differed from the li-qi theory of Neo-Confucianism.[57] Ross thought that the Shangdi of contemporary Manchurian Daoism, the Shangdi of original Confucianism, and

[56] See Ahn Sungho, "The Influence of the Term Controversy in the Delegates' Version of the Chinese Bible Translation on the Early Korean Bible Translation (1843–1911)," *HKY* 30 (2009): 230–36. Ahn assumes that Ross was influenced by Legge when they met in London in 1879. But Ross had already adopted Hananim before meeting Legge.

[57] John Ross, "Corean New Testament," *CR* 12 (1883): 494; Ross, "Shang-ti: By the Chief Taoist Priest of Manchuria," *CR* 23 (1894): 123–29.

the Hanŭnim (Hananim) of contemporary Korean shamanism–Daoism were very similar to the Christian God.

Ross was determined to use as many vernacular Korean terms in his translation as possible, so it was natural for him to adopt the Korean Hanŭnim instead of the Chinese Shangdi. Ross obtained information about Hanŭnim from Yi Ŭngch'an and other Korean merchants. He believed that through the employment of Hanŭnim Korea would not have the term controversy that China had, for that term was "so distinguished" from terms for other Korean gods and "so universally used" among contemporary Koreans. He was well aware of the term question in China. Yet his choice of Hanŭnim was based on many interviews and tests with ordinary Koreans. In adopting this term for God, Ross took a different approach from that of James Legge, who had depended on the literary Confucian classics and court records.

When William E. Griffis published *Corea, the Hermit Nation* in New York in 1882, he mentioned the Korean highest God referring to Ross' *History of Corea* (1879) and James Legge's *The Religions of China* (1880). Griffis paraphrased Ross' Hanŭnim as "the King or Emperor of Heaven" and identified him with the Chinese Shangdi, based on Legge's idea of primitive monotheism.[58] Thus it was Griffis who linked Ross' Hanŭnim with Legge's primitive monotheistic Shangdi for the first time.[59] As Griffis' *Corea, the Hermit Nation* became required reading

[58] William Elliot Griffis, *Corea, the Hermit Nation* (New York: Scribner, 1882), 327–28.

[59] Like James Legge in Oxford, Ross regarded Confucianism as a schoolmaster or the handmaid to drive the Chinese to Christ (Ross, "Obstacles to the Gospel in China," *MRUPCS* [January 1877]: 409–11; Ross, *Mission Methods in Manchuria* [New York: Revell, 1903], 250). Like Legge, Ross thought highly of the Jesuits' mission methods and great success in China and their good influence in Korea. Ross evaluated the Jesuits as "in a sense Protestants" because they acted independently of Rome. Yet he criticized French Franciscans in China and Korea who were connected with French military power (Ross, *History of Corea*, 291–94). When Ross' book *History of Corea: Ancient and Modern* was published in 1879, Legge quoted its comment on Daoism—"which divides Chinese attention with Buddhism, is almost unknown in Corea (p. 355)"—in his book *Religions of China* (230). Legge sent Ross a copy of the Oxford edition of Palmer's *The Greek New Testament* (1881) and its English edition (RV) as soon as they were published. Ross used them as the basis of his translation of the Korean New Testament from 1881 to 1887. So the Ross Version became the first translation based upon the critical texts of the Revised Version copies of the Greek and English New Testament (Ross to William Wright, March 24, 1882, and March 28, 1889). Hence Ross omitted the

for missionaries going to Korea and went through nine revised editions in thirty years with the help of missionaries in Korea,[60] early Protestant missionaries in Korea must have been aware of the connections between the Korean Hanănim and the Chinese Shangdi. And through this conjunction, they might have studied the Chinese term question and James Legge's arguments, and Ross' reason for using Hananim.

But Ross did not need to use the idea of primitive monotheism in his adoption of Hanŭnim (Hananim) from 1881 to 1887. He knew that Koreans worshipped multiple gods and spirits of folk religions. But he found the monotheistic Hananim among many gods in Korea. The Shangdists argued that the monotheistic god Shangdi had coexisted with many lower gods in ancient China. By contrast, Ross found that the contemporary Korean monotheistic god Hananim coexisted with many other gods. After the completion of the first Korean NT in 1887, he reaffirmed that the contemporary Korean Hananim was equivalent to the Chinese Shangdi of the classical texts. He wrote, "The Corean for 'heaven' is *hanal*, for 'lord' or 'prince' *nim*, originally Chinese; and *Hananim* is the term by which Coreans everywhere acknowledge the Ruler above and supreme on earth."[61]

> One other remarkable form of worship demands notice. In time of great drought mandarins go, not to the temple of Heaven and Earth, but outside, and standing under the great temple of the blue heaven, they look upwards and pray to *Hananim* for rain. By this term—"Lord of Heaven"—they always translate the Chinese *Shangdi*, the Chinese *shen* being by them always translate *Kueishen* [*sic*], the two being invariably combined. From all I have ever heard of the name *Hananim* I have felt

---

story of the woman caught in adultery of John 8:1-11 in his Korean Gospel of John in 1882 (Ross to William Wright, January 24 and July 22, 1883). But Ross inserted these verses in 1883 by the request of the BFBS, which financially supported Ross' translation and publication. Ross believed that the original religion of the Chinese, though not henotheism, was monotheism, like that of the ancient Jews (Ross, *The Original Religion of China* [New York: Eaton & Mains, 1909], 20–21). Later Ross stated that "there has been no greater Chinese scholar" than Legge (Ross, *The Origin of the Chinese People* [Edinburgh: Oliphant, 1916], 59). Thus we can assume that Ross, influenced by Legge, used Shangdi of the Confucian classics as the Christian monotheistic God (Ross, *Mission Methods in Manchuria*, 247–48; Ross, *Origin of the Chinese People*, 91, 97) and that Ross' adoption of Hananim might have been partly influenced by Legge's idea of primitive monotheism.

[60] E. N. Hunt, *Protestant Pioneers in Korea* (Maryknoll, N.Y.: Orbis, 1980), 54.
[61] Ross, "Corean New Testament," 497.

thankful that the Koreans had a term which should prevent the shade of any difficulty regarding the question which is older times so sadly, and may I add so unseemingly, divided the counsels of good men in China.[62]

Ross tested Hananim in every way with Koreans and became convinced that the introduction of a foreign term was a serious mistake. At the same time, he rejected the Chinese Shen as the term for God, for it was understood as kwishin ("evil spirits") in Korea. He used *shin* for gods in John 10:30 ("You are gods"). And he changed the term for the Holy Spirit from Syŏngshin to Syŏngnyŏng in 1883.[63] His refusal to use T'yŏnjyu served the purpose of differentiating Protestantism from Roman Catholicism, which had been persecuted as a vicious religion by the Korean government.[64]

Ross' adoption of the vernacular name for God, Hanŭnim or Hananim, was closely connected with his translation principle of using the ordinary people's colloquial language, and of his mission policy of indigenization and the Nevius method. His introduction of Hanŭnim (Lord of Heaven), a term that is still in use, was a significant theological foundation for the development of the indigenous Korean Protestant church. He identified the Korean people's contemporary Hanŭnim with the biblical Elohim. He did not introduce a foreign god to the Koreans, but taught them that the Christian God had already been working among them.

HORACE G. UNDERWOOD'S EXPERIMENTS

Horace G. Underwood (1858–1916) raised the term question in Korea. He staunchly opposed the use of the term Hanănim, but finally accepted it as a fully monotheistic term around 1905. From 1887 to 1892, he used Syangdye (C. Shangdi); from 1893 to 1894, he used Jehovah or Ch'amshin (True Shen); from 1894 to 1896, he experimented with several names simultaneously; and from 1897 to 1903, he supported T'yŏnjyu and Syangjyu (C. Shangzhu). After nearly two decades of experimentation and research on the ancient religious history of Korea, as well as contemporary Korean gods, Underwood eventually agreed to

---

[62] Ross, "The Gods of Korea," *GAL* (August 1888): 370.

[63] Thus the Korean Scriptures used Syŏngnyŏng for the Holy Spirit from 1883 to 1893, yet they used Syŏngshin from 1895 to 1936.

[64] Ross, "Gods of Korea," 370.

the adoption of Hanănim as the name for God in the first authorized Korean New Testament in 1906.

When Underwood and H. G. Appenzeller arrived in Chemulpo in April 1885, they brought a bunch of copies of Yi Sujŏng's gospel of Mark, printed in Yokohama. They revised it with Korean helpers, yet found that the term Shin (Shen) in Yi Sujŏng's version was understood as kwishin (evil spirits) in Korea.[65] Thus they changed Shin to Syangdye in its revised edition in 1887, for "Jesus Christ, the son of Shin" gave the impression to the people that he was "the son of a demon."[66] Underwood used Syangdye in his Korean tracts published in 1890 and 1891.

Underwood published a hymnbook at his own expense in 1894. It was the first Korean hymnal with musical notes and contained 117 songs. Because most Protestant missionaries were using Hanănim, Syangdye, or T'yŏnjyu according to their taste, and the Board of Translators of the Permanent Executive Bible Committee (PEBC) had not arrived at a consensus, Underwood decided to use Yŏhowa (Jehovah) with the auxiliary Syangjyu (Supreme Lord) and Chyu (Lord) to address God, instead of using the controversial competing terms. He expected that "no one would oppose Jehovah and everyone will be satisfied with it."[67] But as with Medhurst's proposal for the use of Aloha in 1850 in China, nobody was satisfied with Underwood's use of Yŏhowa, and the term question started in Korea.

---

[65] Yi Sujŏng's Korean edition of the Gospel of Mark, published in Yokohama, Japan, in 1885, used the term "Shen" of the American Bible Society. He sailed to Japan to learn advanced civilization in September 1882. His acquaintances with Japanese Christians and study of the Bible led him to accept Christianity. He was baptized by Rev. George W. Knox in Tokyo on April 29, 1883, as the first Korean Protestant in Japan. His conversion attracted the attention of American missionaries as well as Japanese Christians. Henry Loomis, agent of the ABS, suggested that Yi translate the Scriptures into Korean. With his support, Yi translated the four Gospels and the Acts into Sino-Korean in May 1883, and one thousand copies of each were published in 1884. He also translated the Gospels of Mark, Luke, and John into Korean by the spring of 1885. One thousand copies of the Korean Gospel of Mark were published in February 1885, some of which Horace G. Underwood and Henry G. Appenzeller brought to Korea when they arrived at Chemulpo on April 5, 1885. As Yi's Gospel of Mark was based on Elijah C. Bridgman and M. S. Culbertson's more literal Chinese New Testament (Shanghai: American Bible Society, 1859), which used the term "Shen" of the American camp, Yi's Gospels used "Shin" (C. Shen) as the term for God.

[66] H. G. Appenzeller to E. W. Gilman, August 8, 1887.

[67] L. H. Underwood, *Underwood of Korea* (New York: Revell, 1918), 123.

Like the Shenite Henry Boone in China, Underwood insisted that the Christian God was not a specific name but a generic term. He claimed that because the use of an existing name for the native gods entailed a connection with these gods, a generic term should be selected in order to exclude them; in cases where it was not possible to find such a term, Jehovah should be used.[68] Underwood opposed many missionaries who said, "Koreans understand the word of Hanănim. They have already worshipped Him. What we need is to teach them Hanănim is the only one and the monotheistic God, and to tell them all His nature. Then everything will be easy."[69] Underwood knew that Korean Christians and most missionaries preferred Hanănim, but he considered it a name of the highest god of shamanism. He opposed such an easy and short-term solution as unbiblical syncretism. Because Underwood was trying to create a Seoul version of the New Testament that would replace the Ross Version, he boycotted Ross' Hanănim, just as he rejected Yi Sujŏng's Shin.

Despite Underwood strongly opposing Hanănim, his arguments borrowed from the Shenites were doomed like Boone's term Shen. Underwood's position was being undermined by his Korean tracts translated from the Chinese tracts, mostly authored by Griffith John of the London Missionary Society, who used Shangdi as the term for God. In fact, the first source materials that helped missionaries in Korea and Korean Christians develop a theological idea of primitive monotheism were Chinese evangelistic tracts and books written by Shangdist missionaries in China. Most Chinese tracts translated into Korean around 1891–1895 argued that ancient Chinese sages and Korean people worshipped God, Shangdi in China and Hanănim in Korea. For example, G. John's *Kwŏnjung hoegae* (Exhortation to Repentance), translated and edited by Underwood in 1891, stated, "In the ancient times, all Koreans believed in Syangdye and worshipped only Him. Yet as the world changed and the times passed, they left the truth and followed the false gods. Is it a huge sin of Chosŏn to God?"[70] F. Genähr's *Myoch'uk*

---

[68] Underwood, *Fifteen Years among the Top-Knots, or Life in Korea* (New York: American Tract Society, 1904), 103–4.

[69] Underwood, *Fifteen Years*, 135.

[70] Griffith John, *Kwŏnjung hoegae* [Exhortation to Repentance], trans. and ed. Horace G. Underwood (Seoul: Chŏngdong Church, 1891), 8b. If this passage was composed by Underwood's helper, Song Sunyong, who came from Roman Catholicism, it is probable that Mr. Song was not satisfied with the Franciscan missionaries' conservative theology that prohibited ancestor worship and the terms

mundap (Temple Keeper), translated by H. G. Appenzeller in 1895, emphasized that in the golden period of the ancient sage kings, Yao and Shun, there was no worship of idols at all but the worship of Shangdi.[71]

In 1894, when the term question heated up in Korea, therefore, Underwood stepped aside and experimented with several other terms in his Korean translation of Chinese tracts. He used Jehovah, Ch'amshin (True Shen), and Syangdye in Samyorok (Three Principles), and Jehovah and Ch'amshin in Pogŭm taeji (Great Themes of the Gospel) in 1895. He even published Hanănim and T'yŏnjyu editions of Helen Nevius' Yesugyo mundap (Christian Catechism). In 1895 he used the term Hanănim in Syŏnggyŏng mundap (Bible Catechism), Ch'amshin in Chilli iji (Easy Introduction to Christian Doctrine), and T'yŏnjyu in Kusyegyo mundap (Christian Catechism). This experiment revealed that Underwood was at the formative stage in his mission theology of Korean religions and his mission method.

RIVALRY OF T'YŎNJYU AND HANĂNIM

Other American missionaries were divided into three groups in 1894— the T'yŏnjyu camp, the Hanănim camp, and the compromising camp. Franklin Ohlinger (Methodist Episcopal Church), who was transferred from Fuzhou, China, to Seoul in 1888, supported Syangdye (Shangdi) exclusively. But he left Korea permanently in September 1893. Anglicans were exclusively the T'yŏnjyuists, and Underwood supported the term.

Three junior Presbyterian (PCUSA) missionaries outside of Seoul— James S. Gale in Wŏnsan, Samuel A. Moffett (1864–1939) in Pyongyang, and William M. Baird (1862–1931) in Pusan—belonged to the Hanănim camp.[72] Daniel L. Gifford in Seoul joined them but swung to the T'yŏnjyu camp under the influence of Underwood. Gale and many other Presbyterians opposed T'yŏnjyu because it was a foreign (Chinese) term associated with Roman Catholicism.[73] Their argument for a

---

"Shangdi" and "Hanănim." As Underwood translated many tracts of G. John of the London Missionary Society (who used "Shangdi") in 1889–1895, we can guess that Underwood used "Syangdye" and could consider the validity of John's idea of primitive monotheism.

[71] Ferdiand Genähr, *Myoch'uk mundap* [Temple Keeper], trans. Henry G. Appenzeller (Seoul: Trilingual Press, 1895), 9a–10a.

[72] Gale to F. F. Ellinwood, May 19, 1894; Moffett to Ellinwood, January 12, 1894.

[73] Gale to Ellinwood, May 19, 1894.

unique Protestant and "pure native" term eventually won the controversy in the early 1900s.

The third camp preferred Hanănim to other terms, yet was flexible in using Syangdye and T'yŏnjyu. Two Northern Methodists in Seoul— H. G. Appenzeller and William B. Scranton (1856–1922)—and two junior Southern Presbyterians—William D. Reynolds (1867–1951) and William M. Junkin—voted for this compromising option at the PEBC meeting in May 1894.[74] As Shangdi was universally used in Chinese Christian literature in Korea, they were open to three Korean terms— Hanănim, Syangdye, and T'yŏnjyu. However, Appenzeller moved to Hanănim and Scranton to T'yŏnjyu sooner or later, and Reynolds and Junkin to Hanănim.

A more detailed description of the process of the term controversy will reveal different missiological positions of individual missionaries and denominations, and their relationships. The Board of Translators met in Seoul in April 1894 and adopted T'yŏnjyu over Hanănim by a vote of four to one. H. G. Underwood, William B. Scranton, H. G. Appenzeller, and Mark N. Trollope of the English church mission voted for T'yŏnjyu, and James S. Gale voted for Hanănim. Robert T. Turley, a subagent of the BFBS of China who visited Chemulpo to open a depot, welcomed the adoption of T'yŏnjyu. He understood Hanănim as the Korean equivalent of the Chinese Tianzhu, unlike John Ross, who understood Hanănim as the Korean equivalent of the Chinese Shangdi. The reason Turley emphasized the interchangeability of Hanănim and T'yŏnjyu was that the latter was the Anglican term in East Asia. He criticized the "ultra-Protestant" North American missionaries who opposed T'yŏnjyu because it was a Roman Catholic term.[75] But Scranton, secretary of the PEBC, evaluated T'yŏnjyu as the best choice in terms of church unity between the North American Protestants and the Anglicans. There were three Anglican factors in Korea in the 1890s, which influenced the board's choice of T'yŏnjyu. The BFBS was almost exclusively working in Korea. The Church of England began its Korea mission in 1890. And many veteran missionaries in China had supported the Anglican proposal for uniform terminology since Blodget's dissertation was published in 1893.

---

[74] H. G. Appenzeller to S. A. Moffett, May 18, 1894.
[75] Robert T. Turley to William M. Paul, November 26, 1894.

Nevertheless, the majority of the Presbyterian and Methodist missionaries refuted the decision of the board. James S. Gale in Wŏnsan thought that T'yŏnjyu was a compromise between the terms used by Roman Catholics and Anglicans. As he knew that there were many missionaries in Pyongyang and other cities to whom T'yŏnjyu would not be acceptable, he felt that he should represent their opinion. The other, stronger reason was that "*Tien Chu* is a foreign term introduced with Roman Catholicism and has become so inseparably associated with R. Catholicism that it would take years to dissociate in the minds of the native the name from idolatry of a worse kind, it seems to me, than even ancestral worship."[76] He regarded the whole system of Roman Catholicism as one of political intrigue and disliked its manufactured term for God. Gale thought that most missionaries desired the native word, Hanănim.

The members of the PEBC and its chairman, Samuel A. Moffett, demanded the adoption of Hanănim. In May 1894 W. D. Reynolds and W. M. Junkin of the Southern Presbyterian Mission wrote a circular letter to the missionaries asking them to oppose the exclusive use of T'yŏnjyu and to support the use of Hanănim or Syangdye in the provisional editions of the Scriptures. W. B. Scranton and H. G. Appenzeller now supported this idea. Twenty-five missionaries voted for the Reynolds–Junkin petition and sent it to the Board of Translators. The board refused to reverse its decision and proposed an open debate. In October 1894 a group of missionaries submitted the petition for Hanănim to the PEBC. The number of the signatories increased to thirty-two, which represented more than 80 percent of the Protestant missionaries in Korea.[77]

After the vote of the Board of Translators in May 1894, Mrs. Underwood wrote about Gale, "He is only one in the whole translating Committee unable to accept a compromise term for God. The whole Methodist mission too are willing to give up their pet term and take T'ien Chu, but we Presbyterian are so obstinate and contrary, we never can compromise or yield an inch."[78] Presbyterians did what they thought was right, and H. G. Underwood was one of them. From 1893 to 1895,

---

[76] Gale to Ellinwood, May 19, 1894.
[77] W. B. Scranton to W. Wright, October 24, 1894; S. Dyer to W. Wright, December 21, 1894.
[78] L. H. Underwood to F. F. Ellinwood, May 28, 1894.

therefore, individual translators decided their own terms for God in a dozen Korean evangelistic tracts.

In 1897 Underwood moved toward the use of T'yŏnjyu and Syangjyu, probably influenced by Henry Blodget's 1893 arguments for Tianzhu for uniformity in China. Around 1900 Underwood became the only Presbyterian missionary in Korea opposed to Hanănim. He used T'yŏnjyu in his translation of the Scriptures and tracts, and between 1897 and 1901 he consistently used Syangjyu in his weekly *Kŭrisŭdo Sinmun* (*Christian News*). He remained in the eye of the storm during the term controversy from 1894 to 1903, and then yielded to the Hanănim camp, just as many missionaries in China yielded to the Shangdi camp.

What kind of God did these missionaries and Korean Christians understand? Like the opinion of J. S. Gale, the main idea was exclusive monotheism against idolatry. In 1895 S. A. Moffett and Ch'oe Myŏng'o coauthored *Kusyeron* (Discourse on Salvation), a short evangelistic tract. It stated, "There is only one Hanănim, not two. He is neither heaven, nor Yuhuang, nor Buddha, nor kwishin. He exists by himself, has no beginning and no end, does not change forever, and is the Great Ruler of all things in the world."[79] Appenzeller translated the Chinese tract *Dialogues with a Temple Keeper* into Korean in 1895. It also emphasized exclusive Christian monotheism of Hanănim against all Korean polytheisms of Buddhist bodhisattva, Daoist Yuhuang, Confucian heaven, and shamanistic spirits.[80] In his own epilogue Appenzeller added Roman Catholic saint worship to the list of idolatry.

When the majority of the missionaries and Korean Christians supported Hanănim, the Board of Translators proposed a compromise to the PEBC—one thousand copies of the Gospels and Acts to be printed using Hanănim and five hundred copies using T'yŏnjyu. The PEBC accepted this proposal and published two editions in 1895.[81] The responses to this decision were divided. W. B. Scranton approved of it because the board's preferred term survived. He believed that if Hanănim were adopted, its Chinese equivalents—Shangdi, Tianzhu, and Shen—would be used. But because T'yŏnjyu was adopted, the Chinese Shangdi and Shen were excluded and the way for using Hanănim was opened. Scranton believed

[79] Samuel Moffett and Ch'oe Myŏng'o, *Kusyeron* [Discourse on Salvation] (Seoul: Trilingual Press, 1895), 5.

[80] Genähr, *Myoch'uk mundap*, 13a.

[81] W. B. Scranton to W. Wright, October 24, 1894.

that this solution would satisfy both Catholics and Protestants.[82] He used T'yŏnjyu in his translations until 1900. But Frederick S. Miller (1867–1937), secretary of the PEBC, stated that this evaluation was Scranton's personal opinion and that the publication of the T'yŏnjyu edition was just a temporary solution that considered the demands of the Anglicans. Miller added that the term question was no longer a burning question, since almost all missionaries in Korea preferred Hanănim and rejected T'yŏnjyu to differentiate Protestantism from Roman Catholicism.[83]

The agents of the BFBS in China criticized this majority opinion as ultra-Protestant and wanted the London Committee to sanction the use of both T'yŏnjyu and Hanănim. Of course, Mark N. Trollope (1862–1930) and other Anglican missionaries supported T'yŏnjyu because it was used in the Anglican missions of China and Japan. In this context, the BFBS decided to publish two editions until 1903. But the Korean members of the Church of England were so few in number that the T'yŏnjyu edition remained in stock. The Anglicans composed less than 1 percent of the Korean Protestants, and 99 percent of them preferred Hanănim.

The terms Hanănim and T'yŏnjyu defeated the other existing names and rivaled each other in the Korean Scriptures from 1894 to 1903 (see table 1 in the appendix). Underwood was at the center of the controversy, which heated up beginning in the fall of 1898. Underwood, Daniel L. Gifford, W. B. Scranton, and M. N. Trollope of Seoul used T'yŏnjyu; S. A. Moffett of Pyongyang, J. S. Gale of Wŏnsan, and H. G. Appenzeller of Seoul used Hanănim. It seemed that "the problem was whether to use a Chinese-derived or a Korean-derived word,"[84] but it was a conflict between the ecumenical-minded or more inclusive group in Seoul and the "ultra-Protestant" group centered in Pyongayng. The latter group preferred Hanănim and pronounced it Hananim, a dialect variant.

The most vexing issue was whether Hanănim was a monotheistic god or an ethnic chief god of the polytheistic system. Underwood and Gifford understood Hanănim as the highest god of the syncretistic Korean religions, just as Boone and other Shenites understood Shangdi

---

[82] W. B. Scranton to W. Wright, October 24, 1894.
[83] F. S. Miller to W. Wright, May 5, 1895.
[84] Rutt, *James Scarth Gale and His History of the Korean People* (Seoul: Taewon, 1972), 26.

as the Chinese Zeus. Gifford listed the hierarchy of the gods of the Korean system of belief—Hanănim at the head, just below him Buddha, then *siwang* (the Ten Judges of Hades), then *sanshin* (mountain spirits), and kwishin at the bottom.[85] Although the majority opposed Underwood, whose nickname was the "English bulldog," until he found theological grounds for accepting Hanănim, he did not compromise. After Gifford's death in 1900, Underwood was the only missionary apart from the Roman Catholics and the Anglicans who used T'yŏnjyu until 1903. All of his colleagues used the term Hanănim. He created headaches for the missionaries in Korea, as well as for Alexander Kenmure (1856–1910), who was in charge of the Bible work in Korea as an agent of the BFBS. In 1901 Kenmure noted, "He is the only missionary apart from the Roman Catholics and the English church Mission, who uses the term *Heavenly Lord* as a designation for the Deity. All his colleagues use the term Hananim."[86] Underwood, however, changed his view on Hanănim around 1904, when he found that this term's origins were rooted in a monotheistic religious tradition of Korea.

INVENTING A MONOTHEISTIC GOD HANĂNIM

CONSTRUCTING HANĂNIM AS THE "ONE GREAT LORD"

Both missionaries in China—Griffith John, James Legge, William Martin, and others—and missionaries in Korea—G. H. Jones, H. G. Appenzeller, J. S. Gale, and H. B. Hulbert—provided theological arguments that led Underwood to accept Hanănim. Chinese tracts assumed that the ancient Chinese and Koreans worshipped a monotheistic God. First, Jones connected Hanănim with the highest god of shamanism. Second, Korean editorial staff of the Christian weekly newspapers accepted the arguments of the Shangdists in China and argued for the existence of primitive monotheism in Korea. Third, Gale elaborated the etymology of the term Hanănim as the "One Great One." Finally, Hulbert argued for Tan'gun's worship of the monotheistic god Hanănim with a Trinitarian interpretation. These innovative interpretations combined to create a new monotheistic term, Hanănim, around 1901, and persuaded Underwood to accept it.

---

[85] Daniel L. Gifford, *Everyday Life in Korea: A Collection of Studies and Stories* (New York: Revell, 1898), 88–89.
[86] A. Kenmure to James H. Ritson, June 21, 1901.

Chinese Christian literature used in Korea without translation had a more liberal attitude toward original Confucianism and its primitive monotheism. An educated yangban (governmental official) man, converted to Christianity after reading William M. P. Martin's Christian Evidences, confessed that he had been a nominal Confucianist for fifty years, for he had not worshipped heaven, and that Christians were the true disciples of Confucius because they worshipped heaven.[87] In this milieu, G. Heber Jones opened the way to understanding the etymology of Hanănim as a monotheistic deity in 1892. Like Ricci and Legge in China, Jones argued that just as the Chinese character Tian (heaven) compounded the two letters yi (one or only) and da (great), the Korean Hanănim was composed of two words—hana (one), not hanăl (heaven), and nim (lord).[88]

The second source of apologetic literature that argued for the original monotheism in ancient China and Korea was two Korean Christian weekly newspapers started in 1897—the Methodist *K'ŭrisŭdoin Hoebo* (*Christian Advocate*) and the Presbyterian *Kŭrisŭdo Sinmun* (*Christian News*). Korean leaders, who converted from Confucianism, wrote many articles and editorials in these papers. Although they were screened by the missionary editor, Appenzeller or Underwood, they revealed Korean Christians' own interpretation of Christianity and its relationship with the ancient history of East Asia.

From the beginning, the editorials of *Taehan K'ŭrisŭdoin Hoebo* argued that the Chinese and the Koreans in ancient times worshipped God (Shangdi or Hanănim) like the ancient Jews; as Jehovah was active in ancient Israel, so Shangdi was in ancient China; and just as the ancient Israelites presented offerings of thanks and sacrifices of supplication to Jehovah, so the ancient Chinese sage kings presented theirs to Shangdi.[89]

The worship of Hanănim had been common in all nations. In the East, Shennong founded the sacrificial rite for Heaven and performed it at the end of the year, and Zhuanxu ordered Zhong Nan-zheng offer a sacrifice

---

[87] "Ronsyŏl: Se gaji yoginhan mal" [Editorial: Three Important Words], *KS*, September 9 and 16, 1897.

[88] G. H. Jones, "Studies in Korean, Korean Etymology," *KR* 1 (1892): 332–33; H. G. Underwood, *The Religions of Eastern Asia* (New York: Macmillan, 1910), 5.

[89] Paik Jong-Koe, *Han'guk ch'ogi Kaesingyo sŏngyo undong kwa sŏngyo sinhak* [The Earliest Protestant Mission Movement and Mission Theology in Korea] (Seoul: Han'guk kyohoe sahak yŏn'guwŏn, 2002), 129.

to the Heavenly God. All the services to Heaven and Earth of Xia, Shang, and Zhou Dynasties were offered to God. Emperor Shun offered a sacrifice to Shangdi and Emperor Tang prayed to Supreme Shangdi. So there was no sage emperor who had not worshipped God.[90]

This editorial argued that ancient Chinese and Koreans had not worshipped a mere national god or an ethnic deity, but a God of the universe. Only Korean Methodist leaders like Ch'oe Pyŏnghŏn (1858–1927) and Ro Pyŏngsŏn (1871–1941), who had converted from Confucianism, could write this kind of editorial referring to many passages of Confucian classics and Chinese history books.[91] In other words, Ch'oe and other Korean leaders read the Chinese apologetics and evangelistic books of "liberal" missionaries and extremist Shangdists like J. Legge, W. A. P. Martin, and Ernst Faber. Korean Christians accepted the idea of primitive monotheism of Shangdi and applied it to the Korean term Hanănim around 1897.

Underwood's *Kŭrisŭdo Sinmun* also emphasized in 1897 that there was no idol at all in ancient China and that the sage kings worshipped only the true God Shangdi and offered sacrifices to him for their sins. Yet the customs were gradually degraded into superstitions and idolatry. "The ancient sages revered Syangjyu who created heaven and earth, governs all things, and controls all blessings and punishment." "The ancient sages and saints worshipped Syangjyu sincerely."[92] One editorial, "Confucianism and Christianity: Two Sides of the Same Coin," maintained that Confucianism and Christianity were two sides of the One Way, and that Christianity did not destroy Confucianism but fulfilled it. It depicted their relationship with an analogy of beautiful trees (Confucianism) and the sunny spring (Christianity). "As the beautiful trees become mature, they become more luxuriant and take more sunshine. . . . Who can ignore interdependence of the two religions?"[93] Christianity would let Confucianism grow, blossom, and bear abundant

[90] "Ronsyŏl t'yŏnjyŏron" [Editorial: On the Heavenly Ruler], *KH*, February 10, 1897.

[91] "Kyou No Pyŏngsyŏnssi yŏllamhan il" [No Pyŏngsŏn's Trip to North], *KH*, October 5, 1898; Elmer M. Cable, "Choi Pyung Hun," *KMF* (April 1925): 88–89.

[92] "Hongmunsyŏgol Kyohoe" [Hongmunsu-gol Church], *KS*, July 8, 1897; "Usyang ŭi hŏhan ron" [Emptiness of Idols], *KS*, July 29 and August 6, 1897; "Ronsyŏl" [Editorial], *KS*, October 28, 1897; "Kyohoe t'ongsin" [Church News], *KS*, December 9, 1897.

[93] "Kyohoe t'ongsin" [Church News], *KS*, May 5, 1898.

fruit. The sunny spring needed the beautiful trees of Confucianism to produce flowers and fruits. The same interdependence existed in the grafting of a new branch of Christianity onto the stem of Confucianism. The editorial emphasized the partnership of two religions in religious life in worshipping heaven as well as in the educational and moral life of the nation. The church agenda of evangelization could coexist with the national agenda of state nation building in the discursive public space of the church newspapers.

Besides these two literary sources, a few national political and ritual occasions from 1897 to 1900 stimulated Koreans and Western missionaries to contemplate the meaning of worshipping heaven and Hanănim. At three o'clock in the morning on October 12, 1897, Kojong ascended the three platforms of the Hwan'gudan (the Imperial Altar of Heaven on the Round Mound) in Seoul and bowed reverently before Heaven, while the grand master of ceremonies read a prayer and proclaimed the kingdom and the beginning of the empire, and solemnly assumed the title of the emperor of Korea. Two days later Emperor Kojong declared the kingdom of Chosŏn an independent empire, Taehan Cheguk (the Great Han Empire), and the year 1897 as the first imperial year of Kwangmu. The editorials of the *Christian News* stated that changing the name of the nation meant it had become an independent nation.[94] Actually since the assassination of Queen Min on October 8, 1895, loyalist members of the cabinet had promoted the project of instituting Kojong as emperor. Their motto was "No emperor, no independence."[95] As only Chinese emperors had presided over the ritual of worshipping heaven in Beijing during the Chosŏn dynasty, emperor Kojong's worship of heaven symbolized the independence of Korea from China. Now many people, including members of the Independence Club, began to mention the worship of heaven/Hananim along with referring to Tan'gun as the founder of the independent Korea.[96]

---

[94] "Ronsyŏl: Se gaji yoginhan mal" [Editorial: Three Important Words], *KS*, September 9 and 16, 1897; "Ronsyŏl" [Editorial], *KS*, October 14, 1897; "Tae Chyosyŏn tyeil kyŏngsa" [The Greatest Occasion of the Great Korea], *KS*, October 14, 1897.

[95] Yun Ch'iho, "The Whang-Chei of Dai Han, or the Emperor of Korea," *KR* (October 1897): 387.

[96] "Ronsyŏl" [Editorial], *KS*, October 14, 1897; "Hoejyung sinmun" [Congregational News], *KH*, August 11, 1897; H. B. Hulbert, "Ancient Korea," *KR* (December 1897): 460, 463.

In the spring of 1899, when Korea was afflicted with a serious drought, the central and local governments performed a ritual for rain and prayed to heaven. A vice-minister of the Department of Agriculture, Commerce, and Industry died on the spot during the service. This accident provided an opportunity for Christians to explain who and what God was. The *Christian Advocate* emphasized the importance of sincerity in the worship of God, and the resemblance between the ancient Israelites and the ancient East Asians who prayed to God for rain, whether his name was Jehovah of Elijah or Shangdi of the sage King Tang or Hanănim in Korea. The weekly identified the ancient Chinese Shangdi and the Korean Hanănim with the Christian God.

> Although their pronunciations are different from Confucian Shangdi, the Christian Syangjyu, Syangdye, T'yŏnjyu, Taejujae, or Hanănim are identical in meaning. . . . Examine carefully the Confucian classics. The ancient sage-kings like Yao and Shun, Yu and Tang, Mun and Mu, Zhou, and Confucius and Mencius worshipped Heavenly Shangdi, but neither Yuhuang nor Laozi nor Buddha. . . . Although our Christian Syangdye is in no way different from the Syangdye worshipped by the ancient sages, the ignorant do not worship Hanănim but bow down before idols and evil spirits. As they do not follow the teachings of the ancient sages, they are heretical scholars and rebellious traitors of Confucianism and the very enemies of God.[97]

Korean Christian leaders argued that Confucius and Mencius as well as Yao and Shun worshipped Shangdi or Hanănim. They believed in the continuity between the original Confucian Shangdi and the biblical Jehovah. They accepted the idea of the Confucian primitive monotheism maintained by Legge, Martin, and other progressive missionaries in China, and then applied its concept to the Korean monotheistic god Hanănim.

In 1900 James S. Gale introduced a new etymology for Hanănim. Through discussion with Mr. Chu, a Korean scholar in Seoul, Gale heard a new explanation of Koreans' understanding of Hanănim. Mr. Chu argued that Koreans knew of God before the days of Christianity:

> "Our God," said Chu, "is the Great One, and is called by us Hananim, from the word Hana, meaning one, and nim, meaning lord, master, king.

---

[97] "Incheon Tambangni Kyohoe sŏngt'anil kyŏngch'uk" [Celebration of Christmas at Incheon Tambangni Church], *KH*, January 4, 1899.

> The one great Lord of Creation is Hananim. We associate him with the building of the universe, and also call him Cho-wha-ong, the ancient creator. . . . God is eminently just and wholly impartial, that he is holy; He is the last court of appeal for us mortals.[98]

Gale accepted Mr. Chu's interpretation of the meaning of "hană" of Hanănim as one, and introduced the new etymology of Hanănim as "The Ruling One, The Honorable One, The Great One, The One" and "One Great Lord of Creation" to the Christian church.[99] Gale's transformation and reinterpretation of Hanănim from "Heavenly Lord" to the monotheistic "One Great Lord" was an important turning point in the term question in Korea. Almost all of the Protestant missionaries and Korean Christians had accepted the newly invented monotheistic Hanănim by 1903, and it has been approved as the authorized term for the God of Korean Protestantism ever since.

In contrast, Homer B. Hulbert referred to varied histories and those of minority groups in his writing of ancient Korean history. He used the *Tongsa poyu* (Addendum to Korean History, 1646) and the *Tongsa kangyo* (Outline of Korean History, 1884), which contained the text of the *Samguk yusa* (Memorabilia of the Three Kingdoms, 1281) written by a Buddhist monk, Iryŏn (1206–1289). Moreover, he believed that myths and legends were important in the investigation of the origin of the Korean race. Thus he used them more positively than other missionaries and understood the Tan'gun myth in terms of the origin of the Korean race.[100]

At the first general meeting of the Korea Branch of the Royal Asiatic Society held in November 1900, Gale argued that Korea had been under "a mesmeric spell" at the hands of the great Middle Kingdom since the arrival of Kija in 1122 B.C.E. and that Korean life was an exact replica of Chinese life.[101] Hulbert disproved Gale by arguing that Korea had

---

[98] Gale, "Korean Ideas of God," *MRW* (September 1900): 697.

[99] Gale, "Korean Beliefs," *Folklore* 11, no. 3 (1900): 325–32.

[100] Hulbert, "The Origin of the Korean People," *KR* (June 1895): 220; Hulbert, *The Passing of Korea* (London: Heinemann, 1906), 297–98.

[101] Gale, "Korean Ideas of God," 697. At this time Gale did not accept the historical Tan'gun and his relation to Hanănim. He followed the mainstream historical understanding of the Chosŏn Kingdom and the Taehan Empire (1897–1910), and accepted its emphasis on Kija as the founder of enlightened civilization. Because Gale depended on the *Tongguk t'onggam* (General History of Korea, 1485), the official history of early Chosŏn, which interpreted the founding myths

preserved a "distinct national life" for more than two thousand years. He investigated the archeological remains as "cultural survivals" that were distinctive of Korea and differentiated them from those of China. Moreover, he traced Korean history to Tan'gun.[102] Hulbert emphasized the cultural role of Tan'gun and maintained that the folklores of Tan'gun and other heroes of Korea's origin were strikingly different from those of the Chinese.

Jones mediated the two conflicting opinions. He agreed with Hulbert's contention that there were many customs and institutions that were purely Korean and did not belong to the category of Chinese influence, but agreed with Gale that Chinese influence had gradually spread over Korean society since Kija Chosŏn. Yet Jones pointed out that shamanism was one of the chief Korean aspects that had survived. Jones stated that "Tan-gun, the first worthy mentioned, claimed descent from Ché-sŭk, one of the chief shaman demons. The early kings of *Silla* took the shaman title of seers or exorcists for the royal designation. As far as we know this has always been the Korean's religion."[103] Jones interpreted Chesŏk or Hwan'in as a chief shaman, and Tan'gun as his descendent. Jones did not accept the interpretation of the *Samguk yusa*, which understood Hwan'in or Chesŏk as Sakra-Devanam Indra, a Buddhist god of devas in the Tusita Heaven who governed lightening, thunder, wind, and rain like Zeus, and thus was inferior to Buddha. Instead, Jones emphasized the connection of Tan'gun to shamanism. Since shamanism was the original religion of Korea and Tan'gun was the shaman king, Jones maintained that Hanănim was the highest god of shamanism and the distinctive Korean god who had been worshipped by Tan'gun and the Korean people prior to the Chinese influence on Korea through Kija.

In 1901 Gale and Hulbert exchanged their opinions on Tan'gun. Hulbert began to publish "the History of Korea" in the *Korea Review* beginning in January 1901. In the first introductory note, he presumed that the persistent traditions of Tan'gun and Kija were "founded on facts." The many monuments that corroborated these traditions made

---

from the perspective of Confucian rationalism and morality, his translations largely eschewed the mythical elements of Tan'gun. See Gale, "Korean History," *KR* (September 1895): 321.

[102] Hulbert, "Korean Survivals," *TKB* 1 (1900): 25–26.
[103] "Discussion," *TKB* 1 (1900): 48–49.

him believe in their historical existence. In the first part of chapter 1, Hulbert produced a free translation of the text of the Tan'gun myth of Chang Tong's the *Tongsa kangyo* (Essential History of Korea, 1894), which was based on the *Samguk yusa*.[104]

> In the primeval ages, so the story runs, there was a divine being named Whan-in, or Che-sŏk, "Creator." His son, Whan-ung, being affected by celestial ennui, obtained permission to descend to earth and found a mundane kingdom. . . . A tiger and a bear. . . . They ate and retired into the recesses of a cave, but the tiger . . . could not endure the restraint . . ., but the bear, with geater faith and patience, waited the thrice seven days and then stepped forth, a perfect woman. The first wish of her heart was maternity, and she cried, "Give me a son." Whan-ung, the Spirit King, passing on the wind, beheld her sitting there beside the stream. He circled round her, breathed upon her, and her cry was answered. She cradled her babe in moss beneath that same pak-tal tree. . . . This was the Tan'gun, "The Lord of the Pak-tal Tree." . . . At Mun-wha there is a shrine to the Korean trinity, Whan-in, Whan-ung and Tan-gun.[105]

Hulbert adopted the Christian idea of the Trinity in his translation. He cast Hwan'in as the "Creator," Hwan'ung as "the Spirit," and Tan'gun as the incarnated "Lord." Hulbert described Tan'gun as conceived by the Spirit—the wind—and born of a perfect woman, as in the case of Jesus. He implied that Tan'gun was a god–man as well as a king–teacher–priest like Jesus. Hulbert's acceptance of the motifs of the Korean trinity was another significant turning point in the development of Tan'gun studies among the missionaries and the term question.[106] Yet

---

[104] The *Tongsa kangyo* was a summary of the five great histories of the Chosŏn period—the *Tongguk t'onggam*, the *Tongsa ch'anyo*, the *Wirye ch'amrok*, the *Tongsa poyu*, and the *Tongsa hoegang*. See Benjamin B. Weems, *Reform, Rebellion and the Heavenly Way* (Tucson: University of Arizona Press, 1964), 74–75; Maurice Courant, *Bibliographie coréene: tableau litteraire de la Corée*, vol. 2 (Paris: E. Leroux, 1896), 336–38.

[105] Hulbert, "Part I. Ancient Korea Chapter I," *KRv* (January 1901): 33–35.

[106] In 1963 Yun Sŏngbŏm interpreted the Tan'gun myth in terms of the Christian Trinity, quoting Hulbert's translation. Yun argued that the myth was formed under the influence of Manchurian Nestorianism in the seventh century. Palmer admitted Yun's thesis had some reasonable basis for drawing analogies between old Korean concepts and biblical ideas of God. See Sŏngbŏm Yun, "Hwanin Hwan'ung Wangŏm ŭn kot Hananim ida" [Whanin, Whan'ung, and Wangŏm of the Tan'gun Myth Are God], *Sasanggye* (May 1963): 258–71; Spencer J. Palmer, *Korea and Christianity* (Seoul: Hollym, 1967), 15.

Gale refuted the historical Tan'gun and his divine origin. In his first article on Tan'gun and Kija in the *Kŭrisŭdo Sinmun*, Gale argued that Tan'gun did not come from heaven, but that people had called a man from another country "a spirit being" and made him a king. Gale criticized the mythical elements as false and unreliable.[107]

The controversy between Gale and Hulbert in 1900 and 1901 introduced the topic of Tan'gun to the missionaries in their efforts to understand features distinctive to Korean culture and shamanism. First, Hulbert suggested that the Tan'gun myth could be interpreted using the Christian idea of Trinity, and that Hwan'in of the myth was the Creator, which was the Heavenly Father, Hanănim, to the Koreans.[108] Second, Jones argued that Tan'gun, a shaman king, worshipped Hanănim of shamanism. Many missionaries accepted this opinion. In 1885 Nangok's *Mudang naeryŏk*, the first modern study of Korean shamanism by a Korean scholar, was issued and declared that Korean shamanism originated from Tan'gun.[109] We do not know whether Protestant missionaries read this book or not. But because such a book and such an understanding were circulating when they came to Seoul in the late 1880s, we can surmise that American missionaries (like Jones) connected Tan'gun to the faith in Hanănim and regarded Hanănim as the highest god of Korean shamanism. Third, the new etymology of Hanănim as "One Great One" that Jones initiated and Gale developed was also accepted by the missionaries and Korean Christians. We can thus say that both Hulbert and Gale accepted Hanănim as the monotheistic Creator around 1901, although they did not agree on whether to recognize Tan'gun as a historical figure. The difference was that Hulbert interpreted Hwan'in of the Tan'gun myth as Creator, but Gale interpreted the primary etymology of Hanănim as "one."

[107] Gale, "Tan'gun Chosŏn," *KS*, September 12, 1901; Gale, "Koguryŏ," *KS*, October 17, 1901.

[108] There is no documentary evidence that Hulbert read a traditional Trinitarian understanding of the Tan'gun myth. *Samilshingo* [Divine Words on Triune God], a 366-Chinese-character scripture of Taejonggyo founded in 1906, stated that Hwanin, Hwanung, and Tan'gun were Trinitarian gods. See Ch'a Chuhwan, "Han'guk Tokyo ŭi chonggyo sasang" [Religious Thought of Korean Daoism], in *Togyo wa Han'guk munhwa*, ed. Han'guk Togyo sasang yŏnguhoe (Seoul: Asea munhwasa, 1989), 471.

[109] Sŏ Taesŏk, ed., *Mudang naeryŏk* [A History of Mudang] (Seoul: Kyujanggak of Seoul National University, 1996).

At the nineteenth annual meeting of the Methodist mission held in Seoul in May 1903, D. A. Bunker and Jones proposed that the term T'yŏnjyu be omitted from the Scriptures and changed to Hanănim. This proposal was passed.[110] In 1904 a tentative version of the Korean New Testament was printed using only Hanănim, and its authorized edition was published in 1906.

The adoption of Hanănim in the New Testament partly resulted from the union movement among the missions in Korea. The spirit of unity and federation had been manifested in the mission fields at the turn of the twentieth century. The Presbyterian churches in India met for their first General Assembly in 1904. The General Conference of Protestant Missionaries in Japan, held in Tokyo in 1900, formed a standing committee of cooperating Christian missions in Japan. The Federation of the Protestant Churches in China was formed after the conference at Peitaiho in 1904. Amid a milieu of the ecumenical movement in Asia, the General Council of the Protestant Evangelical Missions in Korea was organized and unanimously decided to establish one Protestant Christian church in Korea in 1905. The adoption of the unified term for God in Korea was desirable for the unity among the Methodists and Presbyterians. Thus Dr. James S. Dennis, author of *Christian Missions and Social Progress*, wrote in 1905,

> The historic controversy about theological terminology in Chinese seems about to disappear through the spirit of compromise and conciliation which this passion for unity developed. Missionaries who had been in the thick of the philological conflicts over the proper terms for deity, seemed amazed at the possibility of harmony on long-disputed points. A union hymnbook, common terms for ecclesiastical functions and places of worship, and general approval of federation as a working plan, were hardly to arouse discussion.[111]

Hulbert's argument on Hanănim was further developed in 1906. He stated that in the days of Abraham, Tan'gun built an altar on the top of Mari Mountain on Kanghwa Island that touched heaven and worshipped God by burning animal offerings. Hulbert asserted that the Koreans who had worshipped Hanănim were strict monotheists. He argued that the Roman Catholic term T'yŏnjyu was used long before

---

[110] "Kim Sangt'aessi ŭi yŏlsim" [Efforts of Mr. Kim Sangt'ae], *SW* 3 (1903): 194.

[111] James S. Dennis, "Union Movement in Mission Fields," *Congregationalist and Christian World* (November 4, 1905): 627–28.

Christianity came and could therefore be considered the name of a heathen god. There were idols bearing the name of Tianzhu in China, Hulbert asserted, yet people had never made any physical representation of Hanănim in Korea.[112]

Gale affirmed his new interpretation of Hanănim in 1909: "He is *Hananim*, the One Great One. His name in Chinese and also in Korean is made up of terms meaning 'one' and 'great.' So he is the Supreme Ruler for whom there is no image or likeness in heaven or earth or under the earth."[113] When Gale's understanding of Hanănim as "the Great One" was conjoined to Hulbert's assertion of Korean monotheistic belief in Hanănim, the result was the transformation of Hanănim as the Lord of Heaven into Hananim as "the Great One," a new God.

Underwood's other source in accepting Hanănim was his study of the ancient myths of Korea. According to his wife, in the course of studying the ancient religions of Korea Underwood realized that the ancient Koreans of the kingdom of Koguryŏ worshipped the "Great One" god, Hanănim. Underwood believed that the contemporary Koreans' idea of Hanănim could be corrected and healed by the use of Hanănim as Hananim, which had a primitive monotheistic meaning. Thus he decided to use the term Hanănim around 1904.[114] The myth that Underwood believed to be the primitive pure monotheism of the ancient Koreans was actually the Tan'gun myth. In lectures on Korean religions at New York University and Princeton Theological Seminary in 1909, he argued,

> In primeval ages there was one divine being named Whanin, who was the "Chai-sok," the Creator. He had with him one other being who came from him, called Whanung, who asked and received permission to come down into this world. Finding difficulty, however, in governing the world as a spirit, he desired incarnation. Seeing a beautiful woman, who, because of self-denial, had been lifted by miraculous power from the condition of an animal to humanity, he breathed upon her, and she conceived and gave birth to Tangun, who became the first king of Korea.[115]

[112] Hulbert, *Passing of Korea*, 288, 404; Underwood, *Religions of Eastern Asia*, 101.

[113] Gale, *Korea in Transition* (New York: Young People's Missionary Movement of the United States and Canada, 1909), 78–79.

[114] Underwood, *Underwood of Korea*, 126.

[115] Underwood, *Religions of Eastern Asia*, 105–6.

Underwood interpreted Hulbert's translation in his own way and stressed Hwan'ung's desire for incarnation, the Bear-Woman's self-denial, and Tan'gun's worship of his Father God, Hwanin. Underwood affirmed that Korea had originally possessed a Trinitarian monotheism. He concluded, "In the Korean concept of *Hananim* there is even less anthropomorphism than is seen in the Jewish ideas of Jehovah." He understood the Christian Hanănim to be adopted from Korean shamanism, yet he believed that this supremacy of Hanănim was acknowledged by Confucianists, Buddhists, and shamanists alike in Korea.[116]

By 1910 North American missionaries believed that the Korean church, whose adherents had grown to over a quarter million in twenty-five years, had solved the term question: "Twenty-five years ago, when missionary work began in Korea, there was no word in the Korean language for the name of God. The missionaries at last agreed upon its nearest equivalent, and added to it a meaning it never had before."[117] This observation showed that the Korean Christians and the missionaries in Korea as well had accepted a new monotheistic Hanănim. The missionaries' theological works had created an indigenous Hanănim, the "Heavenly Lord," to be born again as the monotheistic Hanănim, the "One Great One" in Heaven. Their main historical source for the neologism was the Tan'gun myth. In the 1880s John Ross emphasized the monotheistic vestige of Hanănim, Lord of Heaven, used by the contemporary people. In the 1900s Protestant missionaries in Seoul added the idea of primitive monotheism to Hanănim and created a Korean Protestant name for God, Hanănim, as the "One Great One."

FULFILLMENT THEORY AND HANĂNIM, 1910–1930

Leading Protestant missionaries in Korea accepted fulfillment theory in their approach to Korean religions around 1910. In the case of H. G. Underwood, who initially defended replacement theory and rejected the existence of primitive monotheism in Korea, the term question led him to accept fulfillment theory as well as James Legge's idea of the pure monotheistic Shangdi God. In his book *The Religions of Eastern Asia* (1910), a result of his lectures at Princeton Theological Seminary and New York University in 1909, Underwood supported the devolution

---

[116] Underwood, *Religions of Eastern Asia*, 110; Underwood, *Underwood of Korea*, 216.

[117] "Korea—The Changes of Seven Years," *MRW* (February 1911): 144.

theory—degeneration from monotheism to polytheism or a pantheistic medley—and the fulfillment of corrupt East Asian religions by Christianity.[118] Underwood argued that a pure monotheism, neither a henotheism nor a monolatry, existed in ancient China and Korea, and that it was a common ground on which Christianity and Confucianism or shamanism could meet. As seen above, Underwood agreed with H. B. Hulbert and J. S. Gale, who insisted that the Koreans had held stoutly to the monotheistic Hanănim despite their polytheistic tendencies. Now Underwood maintained that the ancient peoples had the purer and higher ideals of God; that the Chinese Tian or Shangdi, or the Korean Hanănim, was the "One Supreme Ruler"; that the ancient Chinese and Koreans worshipped this God; and that the idea of this God came from the divine revelation. He accepted the theory that when the descendents of Noah's three sons moved to China and Korea, they brought the original monotheism, and the Chinese and Koreans possessed its remnants. Underwood regarded this concept of monotheism as the first point of contact of East Asian religions with Christianity.

In 1910, when the Methodist Episcopal Church celebrated the quarter centennial of the founding of the Korean Mission, G. H. Jones, editorial secretary of the Board of Foreign Missions in New York, related Hanănim to shamanism, and stated that traces of a primitive monotheism could be found in the Korean people's original faith in Hanănim.[119] Jones stated that the shamanistic aspect of Hanănim could explain the religious reasons behind the rapid growth of Christianity in Korea and the mission policy that stressed the evangelization of the ordinary people, especially women, whose main religion was shamanism.

In the book manuscript titled *The Rise of the Church in Korea*, based on his lectures at Boston University School of Theology in 1915, Jones delineated five points of contact between Korean religions and Christianity: the Korean ideas about God, the moral responsibility of man, worship, prayer, and immortality. He wrote that Koreans were not atheists, for over their polytheistic world they believed in a supreme God, Hanănim. Jones insisted that he was a spirit personality unconnected with Confucianism or Buddhism and standing aloof even from the animistic nature worship of the masses. He argued that the literal

[118] Underwood, *Religions of Eastern Asia*, 157.
[119] Jones, *The Korea Mission of the Methodist Episcopal Church* (New York: Board of the Foreign Missions of the Methodist Episcopal Church, 1910), 15–17.

meaning of the term was "Master of Heaven," but its more ancient etymology made the word literally "The One Great One." "This idea of Hananim proved one of the first points of contact between Christianity and native religious conceptions and was early utilized by the missionaries with large practical results."[120] With this ancient term Hanănim as its vehicle, Jones explained, Korean Christianity cured the idolatry of Buddhism, the agnosticism of Confucianism, and the polytheism of shamanism and enriched Koreans' understanding of God. Yet Jones did not elucidate the relationship between Tan'gun and Hanănim.

When the completion of the first Korean Bible was celebrated in 1911, James Gale declared with confidence that Hanănim was Korea's first preparation for the Bible.

> First: The Name of God—*Hananim*, meaning the One Great One, the Supreme and Absolute Being, suggesting the mysterious Hebrew appellation "I am that I am." *Hana* meaning *One* and *Nim*, *Great*. . . . The character *Ch'on* 天, *God* or *Heaven*, being an exact equivalent in Chinese of the Korean name *Hananim*, bring us accord with those who use *Ch'on-ju*, so that today we can claim union in our appreciation of the wonderful appellative by which Korea stood ready to welcome the tributes to the Bible.[121]

Gale accepted fulfillment theory, which acknowledged the preparations of the Christian gospel in indigenous culture and religions. He synthesized the two different meanings of Hanănim: "heaven" and "one." He believed that the transformation of Hanănim from a shamanistic god to a new Christian God would fulfill the original meaning of the term and the aspirations of Koreans. In 1916 Gale reaffirmed his theory of fulfillment and the preexistence of divine revelation in the history of Korean spirituality:

> As God was ever present to the true Hebrew and was spoken of and addressed by a wide variety of names, so it has been with the Korean. For as the Hebrew wrote El, Elohim, Eloah, El-Shadday, Jehovah, etc., expressive of His different attributes and relationships, and yet all pointing to the same God; so the Korean has used many names that point

[120] Jones, *The Rise of the Church in Korea* (Typescript, UTS, G. H. Jones Papers, 1915), chap. 5.

[121] Gale, "Korea's Preparation for the Bible," *KMF* (March 1912): 86. This article was chosen and published again by the same journal as one of the "Past Solutions of Initial Problems" in January 1914.

to the same Spirit, infinite, eternal and unchangeable. Who, though He dwells out of sight of the eye, controls all the doings of the earth. Some of these names are Hananim and Ch'un—the One Great One, Sang-je—the Supreme Ruler, Sin-myung—the All Seeing God, Tai-chu-jai—the Master, Ch'un-koon—Divine King, Ch'u-kong—Celestial Artificer, Ok-whang—the Prince of Perfection, Cho-wha-ong—the Creator, and Sin—the Spirit.[122]

Gale regarded all of the divine names that Korean seekers had used—even Daoist Jade Emperor Okhwang Sangje—as acceptable names for God. Using a list of true seekers after God throughout the history of Korea, Gale concluded that this preparation of the heart and mind was related to "the Korea's ready acceptance of the fuller light of the Gospel."[123] Gale, however, still hesitated to relate Tan'gun to Hanănim. "If we put aside the traditions of Tan-goon, not yet fully investigated, we find that Korea received her first revelation of God about the time of Samuel the prophet. It came from China."[124] Gale reserved his final conclusions on Tan'gun; nevertheless, his attitude toward Tan'gun differed from that of 1901. It was no longer a total negation of Tan'gun's relation to Hanănim, but an ongoing investigation of the issue. In 1916 Gale was considering Tan'gun in the context of Korean monotheism.

In 1917 Gale issued a full account of his research on the texts related to Tan'gun. He presupposed that Tan'gun was "the most mysterious and the most interesting of all religious influences of Korea."[125] He regarded the contemporary attempt to revive the Tan'gun religion as a mere mechanical effort. He translated quotations related to Tan'gun from various Korean and Chinese books. Although Gale did not attempt to draw any conclusions or express any opinion regarding Tan'gun, he arranged various texts under the categories of "the Triune Spirit—God," "the Teaching of Tan-goon," "Miraculous Proofs of Tan-goon's Power," "Places of Worship," and "the Tan Song of T'ai-biak." His first quotation was from *Kogŭmgi* (The Old Record):

Whan-in, Whan-oong, and Whan-gum are the Triune Spirit. Sometimes he is called Tan-in, Tan-oong, and Tan'goon. In the year Kap-ja of Sang-wun (2333 B.C.) and the 10th moon and 3rd day, Whan-gum changed

[122] Gale, "The Korean's View of God," *KMF* (March 1916): 66–67.
[123] Gale, "The Korean's View of God," 70.
[124] Gale, "The Korean's View of God," 66.
[125] Gale, "Tan-goon," *Korea Magazine* (September 1917): 404.

from a Spirit into a man and came with his heavenly scepter and his three seals. He descended to the Tai-baik Mountains and stood beneath the sandalwood trees. There he made known the divine truth and taught the people. . . . Whan-in is God (Ch'un); Whan-oong is the Spirit (Sin); and Tan-goon is the God-man (Sin-in). These three constitute the Triune Spirit (Sam-sin).[126]

Now Gale began to consider Tan'gun in the system of a Korean Trinity. Gale's new understanding of Hanănim and Tan'gun influenced Mrs. Robertson Scott, who visited Korea for three months during the Independence Movement in 1919. She met many Korean Christians and missionaries, including Gale. She praised courageous Koreans in the fight against Japanese colonialism. She found that the foundation of spiritual power of the Koreans against Japanese material power was their belief in Hanănim. "The Japanese have had no understanding of one God in the sense of an unseen central creative power. The Koreans have always worshipped *Hanănim*, a name which covers the idea of one supreme mind, one God. This God of the Koreans is similar to the God of the Jewish Old Testament." Scott attributed the amazing success of Protestantism in Korea to this deep-seated monotheism.[127] If a Korean had faith in such a Hanănim, Scott said, he or she could not be satisfied with Japanese materialism. The Korean wanted to stay Korean, and cling to Korean history, language, and spirituality. The Christian faith in Hanănim was connected with Korean nationalism and spiritualism against Japanese militarism and materialism.

Finally Gale accepted a Trinitarian interpretation of the Tan'gun myth in 1924, when he began to publish his "History of the Korean People" in the *Korea Mission Field*. As the editor, Allen F. Decamp, said, it was "the crowning piece of work by a life-long student of things Korean."[128] On the first page, Gale wrote that ancient Koreans called Tan'gun *shin-in*, divine man, or the third person of a divine trinity. "Tan-goon's teaching was known as the Worship of God, and was observed

---

[126] Gale, "Tan-goon," 404.

[127] William Scott, *Canadians in Korea: Brief Historical Sketch of Canadian Mission Work in Korea* (self-published, 1975), 699. Mrs. Robertson Scott had been residing in Japan for years and was associate editor of the *New East*. Her thesis was that "the Korean problem cannot be solved until the Japanese understand the psychology of the Korean people." She compared the Japanese literal and material mind to the Korean metaphysical and spiritual mind.

[128] Gale, "A History of the Korean People, Chapter I," *KMF* (July 1924): 134.

by bowing before the Almighty and offering sacrifice. Quite apart from Confucius, Buddha, and the old Philosophers in his relation to the Great Unseen, he has been the guiding genius for Korean inspiration through all ages."[129] Although Gale was still not convinced of the historicity of Tan'gun and omitted the role of the Bear-Woman, he acknowledged the Trinity of the Tan'gun myth. With a quotation from *Kogŭmgi*, Gale admitted Tan'gun was the third person of a divine trinity of Korea. This Trinitarian understanding was not limited to Gale.[130] Many Protestant missionaries in the 1920s embraced the Trinitarianism of the Tan'gun myth. The Heavenly Father, the Holy Spirit, and the Son were counterparts of Whan'in, Whan'ung, and Tan'gun. They admired the primitive monotheism of the myth, which explained to them the Korean people's genius for religion. Tan'gun was an incarnated god–man who taught the worship of Hanănim. Gale's understanding of Tan'gun as the third person of the Korean Trinity was the crowning piece of work in his lifelong study of Korean culture. Not only was his understanding of Hanănim as "One Great One" fulfilled by the Korean people's idea of what a divinity should be, but also Gale's Korean scholarship was fulfilled by the acceptance of the Trinitarian structure of the Tan'gun myth.

Various elements had been integrated in the invention of the monotheistic god Hanănim. In this neologism three catalyst theories—degradation theory, primitive monotheism, and fulfillment theory—were used in blending Christian God and Chinese Shangdi (of the editions of the British and Foreign Bible Society) with Korean highest god Hanănim. Shin (Chinese Shen and Japanese Kami of the American Bible Society) was rejected in Korea as early as 1885. And T'yŏnjyu (Tianzhu) was used for ecumenical purposes only for a decade, from 1894 to 1903. When Hanănim became the authorized term for God in the Korean Scriptures in 1906, Shangdi was dominant in China and Kami (Shen) in Japan. As a uniquely Korean Protestant Christianity was emerging in the face of Japanese colonization of Korea, the conflict between Protestant Hanănim nationalism (connected to Korean Tan'gun nationalism) and Japanese Shinto colonialism was inevitably anticipated.

[129] Gale, "History of the Korean People," 134.

[130] The editor stated, "Strangest of all, rumor makes him the third person of a divine trinity. Tangoon not only served men with the truth during his life, but from time to time through the ages, in answer to longing prayers, appeared giving precious gifts to men, such as the power to write and to paint" ("Editorial," *KMF* [July 1924]: 133).

In the space of a generation, the metamorphosis of Tan'gun from the first father and king of the Korean race to cultural hero, to priest of shamanism, to the third person of the Korean Trinity, and finally to the spiritual source of the Christian term Hanănim took place. Although American fundamentalism began to influence the Korean Presbyterian churches from the 1920s onward, fulfillment theory, which had been accepted by some Presbyterian leaders as well as Methodist leaders in the first decade of the twentieth century, formed a strong theological stream in the Korean churches.

Protestant missionaries studiously approached ancient Korean religious history to find vestiges of primitive monotheism or points of contact with Christianity. When they delved into the Tan'gun myth, they thought that they encountered the idea of the primitive monotheistic and the Shamanistic god Hanănim. After a relatively short period of controversy over the terms, missionaries, initiated by Korean Christians, adopted Hanănim as the authorized term for God. They identified Whanin, the Divine One of the Tan'gun myth, with the biblical God, the Creator. They found a parallel between Tan'gun and Abraham, for both worshipped the monotheistic God. The term question in Korea was solved through a series of combined efforts and theological reflection of missionaries and Korean Christians. As seen above, there were nine major factors: (1) Chinese discourses of the term question; (2) John Ross' liberal adoption of Hanŭnim in 1881; (3) William E. Griffis' connection of James Legge's idea of primitive monotheistic Shangdi with Korean Hanănim in 1882; (4) H. G. Underwood's experiments with several terms and his ongoing support for T'yŏnjyu; (5) Korean leaders' acceptance of the imagined primitive monotheism in ancient China and Korea from 1897 to 1899; (6) the invention of Hanănim as the monotheistic God by missionary Koreanist scholars, especially Gale's acceptance of Mr. Chu's understanding of the etymology of Hanănim as "One Great One" in 1900 and Hulbert's Trinitarian interpretation of the Tan'gun myth in 1901; (7) the church union movement among Methodists and Presbyterians around 1905; (8) the confirmation of Hanănim as the biblical God by fulfillment theory; and (9) Hanănim as a symbol of Christian cultural nationalism against Japanese polytheism and colonial modernity.

North American missionaries accepted Hanănim with their own theological reflections. It fitted their evangelical theology of non-Christian religions. The theory of degradation led them to find the vestiges of primitive monotheism and primitive revelation in the Tan'gun myth and its Hanănim. Although the term was contaminated by the Korean pantheistic system, it still had its distinctive original monotheistic nature. Thus, as Underwood expected, the adoption of Hanănim as a Christian God by the Korean church allowed Koreans to recover the original monotheistic and Trinitarian meaning of the term. And fulfillment theory enabled them to find the points of contact in Korean religions and accept them as "preparation for the Gospel." They interpreted the Tan'gun myth in relation to Hanănim, and believed in the fulfillment of fundamental Korean religious longings and aspirations by Christianity.

Four early missionary scholars—J. S. Gale, H. G. Appenzeller, G. H. Jones, and H. B. Hulbert—studiously researched ancient Korean religious history to find vestiges of primitive monotheism or points of contact with Christianity. When they delved into the Tan'gun myth, they created a tradition of monotheism and the shamanistic god Hanănim. After a relatively short period of controversy over divine names, the missionaries, in a movement initiated by Korean Christians, adopted Hanănim as the Christian term for God. They identified Hwanin (Hanănim), the Divine One of the Tan'gun myth, with the biblical God, the Creator. Through the term controversy, H. G. Underwood changed his position from a Korean Henry Boone to a Korean James Legge. He was the only opponent to the term Hanănim around 1900 among the Protestant missionaries in Korea. He argued that as it was a name of the supreme sky god of the Korean pantheon, it was inappropriate for the biblical God. His conservative attitude was totally changed after a decade of debate with other missionaries. He accepted Hanănim as the Christian term for God around 1904.

Other important actors were the Korean editorial staff of the vernacular Christian newspapers. Their editorials from 1897 to 1899 firmly maintained that ancient Chinese sage emperors and Koreans worshipped the primitive monotheistic Shangdi or Hanănim. Korean Christians' active acceptance of the idea of primitive monotheism in ancient China and Korea accelerated the metamorphosis of Hanănim from a chief god of shamanism to the Christian monotheistic God. Many Korean Christians became interested in the Christian gospel through the argument that the traditionally worshipped Hanănim of the Tan'gun myth was the same as the Christian God. They found a new God, Hanănim, in the face of the national crisis between the

Sino-Japanese War and the Russo-Japanese War. The Korean church that believed in Hanănim, as connected to the nationalistic belief in Tan'gun, had a nationalistic identity under the rule of Japanese colonialism. Korean Christians were not satisfied with the material benefits brought by the Japanese imperial government. Because they believed in the one God and the life-loving Spirit, they could resist Japanese materialism, militarism, and Shintoism. The spiritual foundation of the Independence Movement of 1919 and the Shinto Shrine Resistance Movement in the late 1930s was the belief in Hanănim. Early Korean Christianity accepted Tan'gun nationalism and fought against Japanese colonialism to preserve the country's national identity. Therefore, the argument of contemporary conservative Koreans, that they are legitimate heirs of the early Korean church's denunciation of superstitious and idolatrous myths, is historically unsupported.

The process of the adoption of Hanănim of the Tan'gun myth as the Christian God revealed the first-generation North American missionaries' continuous efforts for the indigenization of Korean Christianity, as well as Korean Christians' theological initiative and potentiality. Late nineteenth-century evangelicalism had disregarded Korean religions as superstitious heathenism and attempted to destroy idolatry. The Western evangelical missionaries' final aim was to convert individual Koreans into Christians or to Christianize Korean society entirely. Nevertheless, if we look at the other side of their missiology and Korean studies, we find that the essence of their attitude toward Korean religions was to seek points of contact and to fulfill them with Christianity. They revised their first negative impressions of Korean religions from the middle of the 1890s and began to map the pluralistic situation of Korean religions, and they researched ancient Korean myths, history, and thought to find points of contact with Christianity. The North American missionaries' theology of indigenization and fulfillment theory transformed the shamanistic god Hanănim into the Christian God. This process illustrates that the leading missionaries were not exclusive imperialists but moderate evangelicals and pioneers of Korean theology. Some acknowledged the preexistence of divine revelation in Korean religious history and accepted various divine names as the Christian terms for God. The authorized term for God, "Hanănim," was adopted both on the basis of the triune character of the Tan'gun myth and on the historical basis of its original monotheism. The Korean term Hanănim had a solid theological advantage in its compatibility with a pure monotheistic Trinity, compared with the Chinese terms Shangdi and Shen and the Japanese term Kami. The doctrine of the Trinity also provided the Korean church with more potential for open dialogue with non-Christian religions, which also had their own concept of the trinity.

To be sure, the Christian term Hanănim has some negative connotations rooted in its formational history. Hanănim has not been freed from northwestern provincialism, Confucian naturalism, shamanistic syncretism, and its patriarchal image. Northwestern provincialism resisted the spelling change from Hanănim to Hanŭnim. The adoption of Hanănim relied on numbers rather than theological reflections, to some extent. The Confucian metaphysical idea of the interaction between supernatural principle and the natural process hindered an immanent and personal conception of the Christian God and his revelation in Jesus. Shamanistic syncretism was influential among Christian believers. Their Hananim was no more than a magical machine for material prosperity or a wonder drug for physical health. The patriarchal image of Hanănim came partly from the image of the grandfather Tan'gun, and partly from the Confucian conception of Shangdi. The theological conservatism of the populace, shamanistic syncretism, and Confucian patriarchal structure, exposed in the history of the term Hanănim, are theological challenges for Korean Protestant Christianity. And the contemporary debate on the existence of the primitive monotheism in ancient Korea and the arguments of Taejonggyo, a new indigenous Korean religion, which worships the Korean god Hanŭnim/Hanŭlnim, need to be seriously considered in further study of the Protestant Hanănim.

— 2 —

Saviors
Images of the Cross and Messianism

After the wars [the Sino-Japanese War of 1894–1895 and the Russo-Japanese War of 1904–1905] numerous people discarded lands and houses, left ancestors' tombs, endured endless sufferings in order to find the so-called *sipsŭngjiji* 十勝之地 [ten auspicious places] and finally died in the forest of the strange mountains.

—*Hwangsŏng Sinmun*,
February 9, 1908

Why were numerous people wandering deep into the mountains to find an imagined holy land in turn-of-the-twentieth-century Korea? What was the *sipsŭngjiji*, ten auspicious places, of the *Chŏnggam-nok* (鄭鑑錄 *The Record of Chŏng Kam*)? Was there any relationship between the explosive growth of Protestantism from 1894 to 1910 and the prophecy of the *Chŏnggam-nok*? This chapter aims to connect the apocryphal prophecy of the *Chŏnggam-nok*, especially its most sought-after enigmatic phrase, *sipsŭngjiji* 十勝之地 and *kunggungŭlŭl* 弓弓乙乙, with Protestant churches' use of the image of the cross and the flag of St. George's Cross (the red cross on a white background) in an apocalyptic context. It focuses on the Korean responses to the images of the crucifixion of Jesus and the rhetoric on the symbolism of the cross, for Jesus' cross was one of the most central and powerful symbols of Christianity as well as the most scandalous image for the Chinese, Japanese, and Korean people. Interestingly enough, the cross, especially the empty cross of Protestantism, has acquired a crucial new meaning in East Asia because its shape resembles the Chinese character for the number ten (十). As in the Jewish tradition, East Asian peoples have developed symbolic meanings for numbers.

This chapter traces not only the Koreans' responses to the crucifixion iconography, but also the rhetoric about the cross in their rejection or acceptance of the Christian tenants. It pays special attention to the glyphomancy (*chaizi* 拆字 or *cezi* 測字 in China; *p'acha* 破字 in Korea; the dissection of written Chinese characters) method in the interpretation of the geomantic prophecy, and argues that sociopolitical factors were closely connected to the popular religious factors in the conversion of Koreans to Protestant Christianity from 1894 to 1910, for the glyphomancy factor in Korea was related to the apocryphal prophecy of the dynastic change, and Korea was suffering a catastrophic crisis at that time.[1] This chapter also emphasizes the importance of the role of religious symbols and symbolic languages in ordinary people's lives in the precarious period of transition from premodern Chosŏn to early modern and colonial Korea. In the rapidly changing landscape of the turn-of-the-twentieth-century Korea, the most prominent religious and pseudo-religious symbol was the cross (十字架 *sipchaga*)—the flag of the red cross of the Protestant churches and the red cross of the Japanese military hospitals. This chapter deciphers the social, political, cultural, and religious meanings of these symbols in the context of

[1] In explanations of conversions, many contemporary scholars have used the concepts of relative deprivation and compensation, the strains of modernization, Christian civilization, hegemony, nationalism, and Protestant ethics. David K. Jordan, however, argued that one must not allow these political, economic-sociological, and cultural reasons—however elegant and appealing to social science scholars—to mask the sometimes intellectually implausible worlds of individual believers. Instead he emphasized "the glyphomancy factor" in the conversion of Chinese individuals. By the glyphomancy factor he meant to stress the significance of the logic and experiences that believers themselves find compelling, and to suggest that we should incorporate those experiences into our higher-level "explanations" of changes in religious belief and affiliation. He argued that we need to pay more attention to religious rhetoric and the logic of persuasion invented or imagined by local peoples. I think we need to combine these two approaches—the higher-level grand scheme factors and the lower-level glyphomancy factor—in the conversion of Koreans to Protestantism at the turn of the twentieth century. See David K. Jordan, "The Glyphomancy Factor: Observations on Chinese Conversion," in *Conversion to Christianity: Historical and Anthropological Perspectives on a Great Tradition*, ed. Robert W. Hefner (Berkeley: University of California Press, 1993), 286.

rampant pestilences, severe famines, international wars, and appalling death tolls.

Competing Millennial Visions

North American Evangelical Millennialism

Christian millennialism, the biblical vision of the final messianic kingdom on earth, had exercised dynamic impact on the mainstream movements of North American society and Christianity. Theologically, millennialism was a driving force for the Puritan pilgrims to America with the errand to the wilderness and the establishment of the American colonies as the city on the hill in the seventeenth and eighteenth centuries; the foreign mission movements as the errand to the world in the nineteenth century; and the Civil War (1861–1865), which many Christians in the North believed would bring about the abolishment of slavery and, therefore, the millennial kingdom. However, with mass immigration, rapid urbanization, and industrialization came the systemic ills of capitalism—sharp division of classes, alienation, and violence. Secularism spread through scientific advances and pluralism through the waves of immigrations. Charles Darwin's (1809–1882) theory of evolution, combined with racism, intensified intellectual and social crises. Two different millennial reactions, the postmillennial social reform movement and the premillennial revival movement, competed to redeem sinful society and individuals. However, shaken by the aftermath of the Civil War and disillusioned by the social changes of postbellum America, many Americans and Canadians abandoned postmillennialism and became premillennialists.[2] These premillennialists did not lose the vision for social reform and activism.[3]

In the last decades of the nineteenth century, dispensational premillennialism flourished in many American evangelical groups in contest against liberal theologians and historical-critical scholars. John Nelson Darby (1800–1882) made at least six tours to the United States from

[2] James H. Moorhead, "Searching for the Millennium in America," *Princeton Seminary Bulletin* (1988): 30; George M. Marsden, *Religions and American Culture* (San Diego, Calif.: Harcourt, 1990), 67.

[3] For the social vision of British historic premillennialism and its concept of the covenanted nation, see Martin Spence, "The Renewal of Time and Space: The Missing Element of Discussions about Nineteenth-Century Premillennialism," *Journal of Ecclesiastical History* (January 2012): 81–101.

1859 to 1877, winning prominent ministers and laypersons, especially Baptists and Presbyterians, to dispensationalism, which emphasized the imminent coming of Christ in person.[4] The Niagara Bible Conference, founded in Chicago in 1875, became the most effective meeting to propagate dispensationalism in America. The dispensational schemes reduced the church to a parenthesis within history, and history was rapidly dashing toward its cataclysmic completion.[5]

Most American premillennialists, however, were not true Darbyites, because they rejected the idea of the ruin of the church and had a moderate view on the historical church. At the same time, they were active in the ecumenical movement. For example, William E. Blackstone (1841–1935), a prominent Chicago entrepreneur and Methodist layman, who attracted a wide readership for his book *Jesus Is Coming* (1908), gave heavily to Methodist causes. Rev. Adoniram J. Gordon (1836–1895), as chairman of the American Baptist Missionary Union from 1888 to 1895, supported the interdenominational faith missions and maintained friendships across theological barriers. In addition, many dispensational premillennialists, with their new understanding of the Holy Spirit, emphasized personal holiness. When the premillennialist Keswick teachers repudiated the concept of eradication of inward sin and substituted it for an emphasis on the power of the Holy Spirit to lead away from evil toward righteousness, Dwight Lyman Moody (1837–1899) and American premillennialists felt comfortable with them. Arthur Tappan Pierson (1837–1911) participated in the Keswick movement almost annually after 1897, avoiding radical perfectionism and advocating Christian service as the fruit of holiness.[6] Moody was one of the key figures in the Bible conference movement in the 1880s and

---

[4] Timothy P. Weber, *Living in the Shadow of the Second Coming: American Premillennialism 1875–1925* (New York: Oxford University Press, 1979), 10–11; David W. Bebbington, *Evangelicalism in Modern Britain: A History from the 1730s to the 1980s* (London: Hyman, 1981), 80–85.

[5] The split between those who had a moderate view of the historical church (like A. J. Gordon and W. J. Eerdman) and those who had a sectarian view based on the Plymouth Brethren's pretribulationalism (like C. I. Scofield) ended the Niagara Conference Movement. See C. Norman Kraus, *Dispensationalism in America: Its Rise and Development* (Richmond, Va.: John Knox, 1958), 99–110; David Beale, *In Pursuit of Purity: American Fundamentalism since 1850* (Greenville, S.C.: Unusual Publications, 1986).

[6] Dana L. Robert, *"Occupy Until I Come": A. T. Pierson and the Evangelization of the World* (Grand Rapids: Eerdmans, 2003), 254–61.

1890s. The Gilded Age revivalist preached Christ's imminent second coming throughout the cities. He was pessimistic about the immediate future. Nevertheless, he thought of himself as ultimately an optimist because he believed in the final victory of Christ.

Premillennialism spread wide throughout the Bible schools.[7] Magazines such as *Prophetic Times*, *King's Business*, J. Brookes' *Truth*, A. J. Gordon's *Watchword*, C. Trumbull's *Sunday School Times*, and A. Gaebelein's *Our Hope*, and many popular books, including *Jesus Is Coming* and the *Scofield Reference Bible* (1909 and 1917), were main channels through which many missionaries could find sources and methods of concerning the premillennial interpretation of biblical prophecies. Many Presbyterian and some Methodist missionaries in Korea were under the influence of Moody's revivalism and dispensationalism. Some of them sent their children to Moody's school at Northfield, Massachusetts.

Dispensational premillennialism played a formative role in North American mission theory and the mission movement. The combination of beliefs in the imminence of Christ's second coming and in the hopelessness of those who died without Christ provided a strong drive toward missionary activity.[8] Prominent mission leaders such as A. T. Pierson, A. J. Gordon, and Albert Benjamin Simpson (1843–1919) felt that they were living during a crisis of missions: the Holy Spirit was opening the world to Christianity in preparation for the *parousia*. They believed that engaging in the evangelization of the world would hasten the Lord's return (Matt 24:14). Their premillennial impatience fostered a single-purpose mentality and a quick-result pragmatism that led to the development of independent evangelical missions. Faith missions such as the Christian and Missionary Alliance (1887) and the Evangelical Alliance Mission (1890) were organized and sent Americans to disperse the gospel overseas and to gather individual souls into the lifeboat of Christianity.[9]

[7] See Virginia L. Brereton, *Training God's Army* (Bloomington: Indiana University Press, 1990). Many Presbyterian women missionaries to Korea were trained at the Moody Bible Institute. But the Scarritt Bible and Training School, where a large number of the female Methodist missionaries to Korea were trained, was not a premillennial school.

[8] Weber, *Living in the Shadow*, 67.

[9] Dana L. Robert, *American Women in Mission: A Social History of Their Thought and Practice* (Macon, Ga.: Mercer University Press, 1997), 192–205; Klaus Fielder, *The Story of Faith Mission* (Oxford: Regnum, 1994).

The majority of evangelical American missionaries in Korea, however, served under a denominational mission board, even if they were committed premillennialists.[10] They integrated the premillennial sense of urgency in the saving of individual souls of revivalism with postmillennial social activism of late nineteenth-century dynamic evangelicalism. Horace G. Underwood was a prominent premillennialist.[11] He accepted the support of six missionaries of Lyman Stewart (1840–1923), founder of the Union Oil Company in Los Angeles, who required that the missionaries be fundamentalists and premillennialists.[12] Underwood began to translate the Scofield Reference Bible into Korean with James S. Gale in 1910. Yet Underwood lived the life of an educator of Korean national leaders as well as that of a dedicated itinerant evangelist. Gale, a Canadian Presbyterian and a faithful premillennialist, met Hudson Taylor in Ontario in 1888 and felt encouraged by his prayer. Gale's initial idea of work was like that of the China Inland Mission, and his standard doctrine was the Doctrine of the Evangelical Alliance, formed in London in 1848.[13] Yet he became a missionary scholar and industrious translator in colonial Korea and devoted himself to the lifelong study of traditional Korean literature and contemporary Korean language to connect English readers with the best Korean culture and literature as well as to preserve it for future generations of Koreans.[14] When North American Protestant missionaries' eschatology, a mixture of premillennial dispensationalism and postmillennial conviction in the superiority of Christian civilization, or a critical pessimistic optimism, was introduced to the Koreans, it had the malleability and potential to negotiate with Korean geomantic millennialism of folk religion and new religions that had anticipated the imminent coming of a new messianic kingdom after the destruction of the contemporary dynasty.

[10] D. L. Robert, " 'The Crisis of Missions': Premillennial Mission Theory and the Origins of Independent Evangelical Missions," in *Earthen Vessels*, ed. Joel A. Carpenter and W. R. Shenk (Grand Rapids: Eerdmans, 1990), 30–32.

[11] Moody Bible Institute, *The Coming and Kingdom of Christ: A Stenographic Report of the Prophetic Bible Conference held at the Moody Bible Institute of Chicago, February 24–27, 1914* (Chicago: Bible Institute Colportage Association, 1914), 249.

[12] Lyman Stewart to H. G. Underwood, February 11, 1909, attached to H. G. Underwood to A. J. Brown, February 15, 1909.

[13] Daniel L. Gifford to F. F. Ellinwood, April 25, 1889; Richard Rutt, *James Scarth Gale and His History of the Korean People* (Seoul: Taewon, 1972), 11.

[14] See Rutt, *James Scarth Gale*, 85–87.

APOCRYPHAL PROPHECY OF THE *CHŎNGGAM-NOK*

The traditional Chinese and Korean *chenwei* (讖緯 apocryphal prophecy) on dynastic changes was conveyed through prophetic-apocryphal texts and songs, with phrases and words that had a strong impact on people. The prophecies were often coded and thus subject to alternate readings. The ambiguous meanings were usually decoded by a savant who had studied philosophy and theories of *yinyang*, geomancy (*fengshui*), heaven–human correlation (*ganying*), and talismans. Sometimes a political leader justified his coup d'états or founding of a new dynasty by inventing a chenwei prophecy or a new interpretation of the old prophecy. When the public accepted a new prophecy or interpretation to be valid, it became a true prophecy.[15] Such openness or ambiguity gave longevity to the prophetic texts, but it also meant government repression through strict censorship of fabricated prophecies. Most of the essential coded words were related to the founder of the new dynasty and its capitol, and sometimes to the refuge places for times of tribulation. So the apocryphal prophecies were closely connected to fengshui, a system of geomancy, and the process of searching for the auspicious places where a special life force was formed by topology, the positive energy that aided in the welfare of human beings, dead or alive.

The *Chŏnggam-nok* was a collection of more than thirty prophetic tracts that were compiled in the eighteenth century. The main original tract, the *Kamgyŏl* (The Record of Prophecy), written in symbol-laden Chinese, anticipated the collapse of the Yi dynasty (1392–1910) after the great tribulations of famines, wars, and epidemics, followed by a new Chŏng dynasty, wherein people could live in peace. The main concerns of the *Chŏnggam-nok* were the negation of the contemporary dynasty, preserving lives in the secluded places, a theory of the relocation of the capitol, messianism, and optimistic fatalism. In short, the historical perspective of the book was a kind of secularized eschatological messianism. It was neither afterlife-ism nor escapism from real life, for it anticipated changes and transformations in the near future. However, with little reflection on the past or effort in successfully inheriting

[15] See Lü Zongli, *Power of the Words: Chen Prophecy in Chinese Politics AD 265–618* (Oxford: Peter Lang, 2003); Lü, "Apocrypha in Early Medieval Chinese Literature," *Chinese Literature: Essays, Articles, Reviews* 30 (2008): 93–101.

the blessed future, it fell into magical determinism without the dynamic ethical dimension of eschatology.[16]

The "ten auspicious places" (sipsŭngjiji) were the hidden lands of salvation for the refugees, mentioned in the Chŏnggam-nok. The designated ten best places for the survival, however, were mostly located in the deep valleys of the mountain, making it difficult to pinpoint their locations. This ambiguity led to people wandering around in the search for the exact sites of salvation in anticipation of the coming kingdom. Another hidden keyword of the Chŏnggam-nok was the kunggungŭlŭl, whose cryptic meaning was more mysterious than the sipsŭngjiji. The Kamgyŏl tract said that the most advantageous place to hide one's body during the critical time of the dynastic change was neither in mountains nor in waters, but in kunggung, meaning two bows (as in the archer's bow). Another tract, Yisŏnsaengga changgyŏl (Prophecy Preserved at Mr. Yi's House), confirmed that the advantages were in the kunggungŭlŭl. Later the meaning of the phrase shifted from a location of salvation to a way of salvation through different interpretations.

In the middle of the eighteenth century, the Chŏnggam-nok was mentioned officially for the first time in the Chosŏn wangjo sillok (The Annals of the Chosŏn Kingdom). In 1739, hearing that many people in Hamgyŏng and P'yŏng'an provinces were widely disseminating the chenwei of the Chŏnggam-nok, King Yŏngjo thought that rearing the orthodox Confucianism would naturally eradicate such a heterodox teaching.[17] However, in 1748 several fallen yangban in Ch'ŏngju, Ch'ungch'ŏng province, were arrested for posting what was considered a subversive and dangerous document on the wall, in which they mentioned the kunggung of the Chŏnggam-nok as the refuge place during the coming war. This time King Yŏngjo questioned the leader Yi Chisŏ himself because it was a case of treason related to the issue of national security.[18] The Chŏnggam-nok was listed in the index of books banned by the government. In 1782, the sixth year in the reign of King Chŏngjo, when another plot of treason was discovered, the conspirators confessed

[16] Yun Sŏngbŏm, "Chŏnggam-nok ipchang esŏ pon Han'guk ŭi yŏksagwan" [The Korean Historical Perspective Seen from the Chŏnggam-nok], Kidoggyo sasang (January 1970): 105–19.

[17] Yŏngjo sillok [The Annals of the King Yŏngjo], vol. 42, August 6, 1739.

[18] Yŏngjo sillok, vol. 67, May 23–24, 1748.

that they used a hidden copy of the *Chŏnggam-nok*.[19] The handwritten *Chŏnggam-nok* was widely circulated, especially in northern Korea in the nineteenth century, a century rife with revolts against corrupt local governments.[20] Many participants of the Hong Kyŏngnae Uprising (1811–1812) in P'yŏng'an province believed in the dynastic change based on the *Chŏnggam-nok*. Their conviction in the millennial prophecy, combined with socioeconomic forces, was enough to incite uprisings against the central government.

Some of its believers joined the Roman Catholic Church, for Christian messianic eschatology had somewhat similar elements to the millennial vision of the *Chŏnggam-nok*.[21] They expected that a new Western religion would reveal more about the end time. In their propagation of Roman Catholicism, therefore, these followers used the prophecy of the *Chŏnggam-nok*—the comings of strange foreign ships, people in blue clothes (foreigners), the *chinin* (savior of the world), tribulations of wars and epidemics, and a new dynasty of peace and prosperity under King Chŏng.[22]

Tonghak used the kunggungŭlŭl and the sipsŭngjiji by presenting its own creative interpretations. Ch'oe Cheu, who had been interested in geomantic prophecies and founded Tonghak in 1860, preached about the coming of the Chŏng dynasty prophesized in *Chŏnggam-nok*. He declared, "Yi dynasty will perish and Chŏng dynasty will arise. A great

[19] *Chŏngjo sillok* [The Annals of the King Chŏngjo], vol. 14, November 20, 1782; vol. 14, December 10, 1782.

[20] Paek Sŭngjong, "18 segi chŏnban sŏbuk chibang e ch'ulhyŏnhan Chŏnggam-nok" [The *Book of Chŏng Kam* Appeared in the Northwestern Provinces in the First Part of the Eighteenth Century], *Yŏksahakpo* (September 1999): 99–124.

[21] Chŏng Yakchong's *Chugyo yoji* (Essential Teachings of Roman Catholicism, ca. 1800) had a similar millennial scenario of tribulations in the end of the world.

[22] Cho Kwang, *Chosŏn hugi ch'ŏngjugyosa yŏn'gu* [A Study on the History of Roman Catholicism in the Late Chosŏn Period] (Seoul: Koryŏdaehakkyo minjokmunje yŏn'guso, 1988), 161–62; Nobuaki Suzuki, "Chōsen koki Tenshukyō shisōto Teikanroku" [Roman Catholic Thought and *The Record of Chŏnggam* in the Late Chosŏn], *Chōsenshikenkyūkai ronbunshū* 40 (2002): 60–97; Kim Chinso, "Sinyu pakhae tangsi sŏyang sŏnbak ch'ŏngwŏn ŭi t'ŭksŏng" [Characteristics of the Request of Western Ships at the Time of the 1801 Persecution], in *Sinyu pakhae wa Hwang Sayŏng paeksŏ sagŏn* [The Persecution and the Incident of Hwang's Silk Letter in 1801] (Seoul: Han'guk sungypsa hyŏn'yang wiwonhoe, 2003), 127–36; Paek Sŭngjong, "Chosŏn hugi Ch'ŏnjugyo wa *Chŏnggam-nok*" [Roman Catholicism and *The Record of Chŏnggam-nok* in the Late Chosŏn], *Kyohoesa Yŏn'gu* (June 2008): 5–46.

war will outbreak. Those who do not belong to Tonghak cannot preserve their lives. As our Tonghak people just sit and meditate Tianzhu [the Heavenly Lord] and serve Zhenzhu [the True Lord], they will enjoy the blessing of Taiping [the Great Peace]."[23] Ch'oe identified the kunggungŭlŭl with his own thirteen-letter incantation to Tianzhu God. He made a spiritual talisman of the kunggungŭlŭl for the purpose of healing diseases, and composed songs of "Sipsŭng-ga" and "Kung'ŭl-ga." He was executed in 1864. When the government condemned Ch'oe Sihyŏng (1827–1898), the second patriarch of Tonghak and the leader of its northern branch, to be executed in 1898, he was charged with bewildering people with the talisman of the kunggungŭlŭl.[24] Despite his death, the followers of Tonghak grew in the 1910s and 1920s, especially in northern Korea, and it was reported that their numbers reached around one million.

On the other hand, Pak Chungbin (1891–1943), who founded Wŏn Buddhism in 1916, interpreted the kunggungŭlŭl as the "ilwŏn" (the One Circle) and equalized it with the *taiji* (Supreme Ultimate) of Confucianism. Pak emphasized that the kunggungŭlŭl could be formulated in one's heart, and was not to be found in a certain place.[25]

Some of the believers of Tonghak (Ch'ŏndogyo) and the *Chŏnggam-nok* in northwestern Korea began to migrate to the Kyeryong Mountain, near Kongju and Taejŏn of southern Ch'ungch'ŏng province, in the late 1910s. According to *Chosŏn Ilbo* in 1921, groups of twenty or thirty people, believing in the prophecy of the *Chŏnggam-nok*, moved to the

---

[23] "宣言 李氏將亡 鄭氏將興 大亂將作 非東學者 毋以得生 吾黨但坐念天主 輔佐眞主 將享太平之福." Hwang Hyŏn, "Sup'il Kapsin" [The First Essay in 1884], *Ohagimun* [梧下記聞 Writing down What I Heard under a Paulownia Tree], in Tonghak nongminjŏnjaeng paekchunyŏn kinyŏmsaŏp ch'ujinwiwŏnhoe, *Tonghak nongminjŏnjaeng saryo ch'ongsŏ* I [Collection of Historical Sources of the Tonghak Peasant War] (Seoul: Sayeyŏnguso, 1996), 42–43.

[24] *Kojong sillok* [The Annals of the King Kojong], vol. 37, July 18, 1898.

[25] Paek Sŭngjong, "Chŏnggam-nok sanch'aek (21): Sumŭŏn kiwŏdŭ 'kunggung ŭlŭl' " [Review of the *Book of Chŏng Kam*: A Hidden Keyword "kunggung ŭlŭl"], *Seoul Sinmun*, June 2, 2005. Paekbaek-kyo, a scandalous religion in the 1930s, propagated that their headquarters were located in the *sipsŭngjiji* and sold the paper amulets that had the letters of *kunggungŭlŭl* and the seal of the church for 50 or 100 yen per copy, like an indulgence, for the salvation in the end times. See "Kunggung ŭlŭl hyŏnhokyong koein" [Kunggung ŭlŭl: A Bewildering and Strange Seal], *Maeil Sinbo* [Daily News], April 13, 1937.

town of Sindo in the Kyeryong Mountains, and its population increased to around 2,500. Many of them came from Hwanghae province.[26]

In 1924 there were 1,515 houses and 6,949 people in the town of Sindo. Only 70 households (350 people) migrated before 1918, and most came after the March First Independence Movement.[27] In 1931 it was reported that about 80 percent of the population of Sindo was from the northwestern provinces.[28]

In sum, belief in the prophecies of the *Chŏnggam-nok* had been so strong among some of the people in Hwanghae and P'yŏng'an provinces that they revolted against the government in the nineteenth century or migrated en masse to the town of Sindo in the 1920s with the dream of building a millennial kingdom. This was the fertile spiritual soil in which the encounters between Christian millennialism and the millennial prophecy of the *Chŏnggam-nok* in northwestern part of Korea grew at the turn of the twentieth century. People dreamed that the sipsŭngjiji would be the land of hope and refuge to survive the unprecedented national crisis.[29]

The crisis was closing in on many fronts. The Tonghak Revolution in 1894 triggered the Sino-Japanese War in 1894. The Boxer Movement in China induced some conservatives to plot to kill all Christians in Korea in 1900. The great famine of 1900–1902 hit the middle part of the Korean Peninsula, and the rice crop in 1902 produced one-tenth of the normal annual yield, resulting in the suffering of many, the appearance of roving bandits, and the desire to immigrate to the Hawaiian Islands in 1903. The Russo-Japanese War broke out in 1904, spelling doom for the Chosŏn Kingdom. Cholera epidemics hit Korea in 1886, 1890, 1895, 1902, 1903, and 1905. Smallpox plagues were prevalent from 1899 and reached their zenith in 1903, "a year of epidemics."[30] Thousands of

[26] "Kyeryongsan ŭi Sindo" [Sindo of the Kyeryong Mountain], *Chosŏn Ilbo*, May 6, 1921.

[27] Murayama Chijun, *Chosŏn ŭi chŏmbok kwa yeŏn* [Divination and Prophecy of Chosŏn], trans. Kim Hŭigyŏng (Seoul: Tongmunsŏn, 1990), 571.

[28] "Sagyo ŭi wangguk pokma ŭi chŏndang 'Sindo' Kyeryongsan ŭi pimil" [Kingdom of Cults and Hall of Devils: The Secret of the Town of Sindo in the Kyeryong Mountain], *Chosŏn Ilbo*, January 23, 1931.

[29] The first printed edition of the *Chŏnggam-nok* was Kim Yong-ju, ed., *Chŏnggam-nok* (Seoul: Hansŏng chusikhoesa, 1923). An Ch'un-gŭn, ed., *Chŏnggam-nok chipsŏng* (Seoul: Asea munhwasa, 1981) is a collection of ten different editions.

[30] Oliver R. Avison, "Sickness and Rumor of Sickness: From Annual Report of Dr. O. R. Avison," *KF* (June 1903): 126–27.

Koreans were killed on the battlefields, and tens of thousands were killed by cholera or smallpox or other epidemics.[31] Many people deserted their houses and subsisted on slash-and-burn farming to avoid taxes.[32] Some people wandered deep into the mountains to search for the holy land of salvation, the sipsŭngjiji.

The "four horsemen," described in Revelation 6:1-8, the four beasts that ride on white, red, black, and pale-green horses—symbolizing pestilence, war, famine, and death—seemingly had shown themselves in Korea.[33] During the great famine in northern Korea from 1900 to 1902, "[men], women and children were on the hillsides from early dawn, digging roots and plucking leaves to cook in order to keep body and soul together."[34] On November 22, 1902, Yun Ch'iho wrote in his diary

[31] These statistics are incomplete. The severe cholera epidemics occurred in 1886, 1895, and 1902. The *Journal of American Medical Association* reported in 1890, "More than 80,000 have perished in Japan, Korea and the contiguous Asiatic provinces of Russia. All this loss within a few months" ("Cholera Threatened," *JAMA* [December 20, 1890]: 906). Cholera swept through Korea in August and September 1902, and there were between 50 and 250 deaths daily in Seoul in September ("The Public Service: Cholera," *JAMA* [November 1, 1902]: 1150, 1358; "Editorial Comment," *KRv* [September 1902]: 406–7; "News Calendar," *KRv* [September 1902]: 411). The Wŏnsan police report stated that 61 Koreans died in September 1902 (*Yun Ch'iho Ilgi*, December 4, 1902). Because of a "cattle disease" there was scarcity of bullocks to carry wood and rice in Seoul. Smallpox had been prevalent in Korea for three years, from 1899 to 1902 ("Public Health: Smallpox," *JAMA* [May 1899]: 1012, 1072; [April 14, 1900]: 958; [August 11, 1900]: 395; [February 23, 1901]: 536; [April 1901]: 1082). These epidemics in 1902 and the great famine from 1901 to 1903 created a kind of apocalyptic situation among the people who lived in the middle part of the Korean Peninsula.

[32] E.g., the prefect of Kyodong of Kanghwa Island asked the Finance Department "what should be done about the taxes from 177 houses that were deserted in that district by famine sufferers" ("News Calendar," 413).

[33] Helen F. MacRae, in her biography of her father Duncan M. MacRae, titled the period of 1902–1904 "the Four Horsemen." In Hamhŭng Rev. MacRae got "native fever"; Mrs. MacRae was exposed to smallpox; their daughter was kidnapped by bandits; and they saw the result of famine—numerous deaths by starvation (Helen F. MacRae, *A Tiger on Dragon Mountain: The Life of Rev. Duncan M. MacRae, D.D.* [Charlottetown, Canada: A James Haslam, Q.C., 1993], 99–106).

[34] MacRae, *Tiger on Dragon Mountain*, 105. Mrs. Sarah Nourse Welbon wrote in her diary on July 13, 1902, "First good rain in 3 years" (Priscilla Welbon Ewy, *Arthur Goes to Korea: The Early Life of Arthur Garner Welbon and His First Years as Missionary to Korea, 1900–1902* [Tucson, Ariz.: Self-published, 2008], 265). The editor of the *Korea Field* wrote that no rain for three years was a surprising and unprecedented occurrence in the history of Korea, where there was a rainy season

that "every Korean seems to think these are the last years of the present dynasty."[35] Actually Yun himself was a doomsayer who deplored "the moral degradation of the Boss [Emperor Kojong] and his slaves [in the government]," and criticized Confucian despotism and materialism for leaving Korean officials skillful only at squeezing and swindling the citizenry. In 1904 the crushing hooves of the Rider on the Red Horse (the Japanese Army) passed through Incheon, Seoul, Songdo, Chinnampo, Pyongyang, and Ŭiju. Russian soldiers burned down hundreds of houses in Hamhŭng to punish Koreans for giving false information in the summer of 1904.[36] In this apocalyptic situation, many Protestant churches in the provinces of northern Kyŏnggi, southern Hwanghae, Kangwŏn, and southern Hamgyŏng hoisted the flag of St. George's Cross, a red cross on a white background, as well as the national flag during the decade of 1895–1904.[37] Why did Korean Protestant Christians build these expensive tall wooden flagpoles in their churchyards? What were the symbolic meanings of the red cross flag during the national crisis?

---

in summer. The famine hit the several magistracies fifty miles or so to the northwest of Seoul and in certain others about as far to the south. "Large numbers of people removed to districts better favored. Those who remain have lived on roots and grass and other substances hitherto thought fit only for cattle" ("The Famine Wolf in Korea," *KF* [May 1902]: 33). Underwood, who was on furlough in America, cabled relief funds to mission treasurer, and about 578 yen was used in assisting the worst cases of destitution, if necessary, after investigation of famine tracts by a Korea helper by May 6, 1902 ("Famine Wolf in Korea," 34; Charles E. Sharp, "Famine along the River: From January Report of Rev. C. E. Sharp," *KF* [August 1902]: 59). Arthur Welbon distributed over 300 yen among the famine sufferers in the Paech'ŏn area, Kyŏnggi province. Most received the donation with a thankful heart. Those who had not received enough or had received unequal amounts made trouble (Arthur G. Welbon, "Personal Annual Report for the Year Ending June 30, 1902," in Ewy, *Arthur Goes to Korea*, 259). The Sorae Church and Sŏ Sangnyun were active in helping the churches in the famine area in Hwanghae province (Sharp, "Famine along the River").

[35] *Yun Ch'iho ilgi*, November 22, 1902.

[36] H. F. MacRae, *Tiger on Dragon Mountain*, 112.

[37] One of the initial Christian responses for the famine was the organization of the Society of Christians' Charity at the Sangdong Methodist Church in Seoul. Pae Tonghyŏn donated his house, and the church organized the society to mobilize all the Methodist churches to help the people who were suffering ("Chŏngdong syŏ sinhag ŭl kongbuham" [Theological Class Held at Chŏngdong], *SW* [March 1902]: 116–17).

Roman Catholic Iconography of the Crucifixion

Before discussing Protestant representations of the images of the cross, let us review the Roman Catholic crucifixion iconography and the reactions of the Chinese and the Koreans to this in the eighteenth and nineteenth centuries. From the 1710s to the 1850s, the Korean envoys in Beijing's encounters with the strange images of Jesus on the cross (*shijijia* 十字架, the ten letter frame) generated very negative responses. Jesus, as shown being crucified on the cross, was perceived as being a rebellious criminal and a crazy unfilial son. Unlike the bare cross of Protestantism, the Roman Catholic crucifix had the image of the crucified Jesus on it. Even though the Chosŏn government made it the symbol of anathema and disloyalty, the crucifix also became the symbol of perseverance and spiritual identity for Catholic Christians during the severe persecutions from 1791 to 1866.

Korean Embassies to Beijing in the Eighteenth and Nineteenth Centuries

In the eighteenth century, Chosŏn actively adopted many products of Western civilization, such as astronomical knowledge, the calendar, and clocks, paintings, and organs by way of Qing China. The pipeline of this cultural exchange was the Korean envoy to Beijing. During the 238 years from the beginning of the Qing dynasty in 1644 to the final year of the Tongzhi Emperor in 1874, a total of 870 Korean emissaries visited Beijing, an average of 3.6 envoys per year.[38] These visitors saw Western objects in the four Roman Catholic cathedrals in Beijing. Catholic missionaries welcomed the Korean envoys, and their meetings became an established custom. One of the most shocking things that the Korean envoys encountered was the crucifixion iconography of Jesus. They could not understand why Westerners were worshipping as a god an executed criminal on a cross.

Many Korean travelogues to Beijing, including Hong Taeyong's (1731–1783) *Tamhŏn yŏn'gi* (湛軒燕記, 1765) and Pak Chiwŏn's (1737–1805) *Yŏlha ilgi* (熱河日記, 1780), mentioned the missionary portraits of Jesus.[39] In *Iram yŏn'gi* (一庵燕記 The Records of Travels to Beijing,

---

[38] Jung Jae-Hoon, "Meeting the World through Eighteenth-century *Yŏnhaeng*," *Seoul Journal of Korean Studies* 23, no. 1 (2010): 54.

[39] Hong Taeyong's *Tamhŏn yŏn'gi*, instead of paying attention to nature and

FIGURE 1
Giulio Aleni, *T`ien-chu chiang-sheng ch`u-hsiang ching-chieh*
天主降生出像經解
(Illustrated Expositions of the Incarnation of the Lord of Heaven), 1637

FIGURE 2
Schall, *Jincheng Shuxiang*
(Images Presented to the Chong-zhen Emperor), 1640,
as shown in Yang Guangxian,
Budeyi 不得已, 1664

1720), Yi Kiji wrote that he viewed the portraits of the life of Jesus in Roman Catholic books. He and other Koreans might have read Giulio Aleni's *Tianzhu jiangshen chuxiang jingjie* (天主降生出像經解 Illustrated Expositions of the Incarnation of the Lord of Heaven, 1637) and seen its woodblock print of the crucifixion (figure 1) and similar images in other books. Aleni retained Matteo Ricci's policy of accommodation to Confucianism and used similar supernatural motifs between *Vita Christi* and *Vita Confucii* in explaining their annunciation and birth. However, the visual narratives of the miracles of Jesus, such as casting out demons, walking on the water, and reviving the dead, and, above all, the death of Jesus on the cross and his resurrection, moved beyond the analogy between Jesus and Confucius. Aleni emphasized the supernatural efficacy of Jesus and a Christ-centered spirituality, which ultimately surpassed and complemented Confucianism.[40]

The Chinese Confucian literati perceived the crucifix as a Western tool for sorcery and Jesus as an unfilial son and a rebel executed lawfully by the Roman authorities.[41] When the court eunuch Ma Tang saw the

---

scenery along the route to Beijing, focused more on the culture and institutions of Qing China, like other late eighteenth-century travelogues of the Korean visitors (Jung Jae-Hoon, "Meeting the World," 58). Through their interaction with Qing scholars and advanced culture, Korean visitors, like Hong and Pak Chiwon, had a positive view of the Qing dynasty and abandoned the concept of *Chosŏn chunghwa* ("Korea as the center of Chinese culture"). Moreover, they began to go beyond the boundary of Sinocentrism and tried to learn from Western civilization (Jung Jae-Hoon, "Meeting the World," 61–62).

[40] Gianni Criveller, *Preaching Christ in Late Ming China: The Jesuits' Presentation of Christ from Matteo Ricci to Giulio Aleni* (Taipei: Ricci Institute for Chinese Studies, 1997), 433–39; Junhyoung Michael Shin, "The Supernatural in the Jesuit Adaptation to Confucianism: Giulio Aleni's *Tianzhu Jiangsheng Chuxiang Jingjie* (Fuzhou, 1637)," *History of Religions* 50 (2011): 329–61. G. Aleni's *Tianzhu jiangsheng chuxiang jingjie* (Hangzhou, 1637) was the first illustrated book on the life of Jesus in Chinese. Its fifty illustrations were taken from Geromino Nadal's *Evangelicae Historiae Imagines* (Images of the History of the Gospel, 1593). Missionaries believed that holy pictures conveyed the mysteries of the Christian faith sometimes more effectively than words. Graphic art, a popular medium, was widely used in religious literature in the seventeenth century. A. Schall presented more Chinese-style illustrations (48) on the life of Jesus to Emperor Chongzheng in 1640. See D. E. Mungello, *The Great Encounter of China and the West, 1500–1800* (Lanham, Md.: Rowman & Littlefield, 1999), 40–43.

[41] Anthony E. Clark, "Early Modern Chinese Reactions to Western Missionary Iconography," *Southeast Review of Asian Studies* 30 (2008): 9–14.

crucifix in the bag of Matteo Ricci in 1600, Ma thought that Western missionaries were carrying this charm (the suspended figure of Christ on the cross) to bewitch people with poisonous sorcery.[42] On the other hand, the wild-haired and naked body of Jesus gave the impression of a malicious devil. In this cultural milieu, therefore, Ricci did not mention the crucifixion of Jesus in *Tianzhu shiji* (The True Meaning of the Lord of Heaven, 1603) at all.[43]

In 1665 Yang Guangxian (1597–1669) published *Budeyi* (不得已 I Cannot Do Otherwise, 1664) to attack Christianity using A. Schall's pictures of the Passion of Jesus (figure 2).[44] The style of the painting became Chinese, yet the negative representation did not change. Yang asserted that Jesus was put to death as a convicted criminal.[45] Other Chinese officials condemned Jesus as a subversive rebel leader, as social harmony was their most important political precept.[46]

Koreans' responses to pictures of crucifixion such as the one in Aleni's book or the more indigenous illustration of A. Schall did not differ from those of the Chinese elite. Hong Taeyong visited the south and east churches in Beijing in 1765 and quoted Pan Tingyun's opinion on the crucifix in the section of *Kŏnjŏngdong p'ildam* (Written Dialogues with Chinese Scholars) in his collected writings, the *Tamhŏnsŏ*.

---

[42] Matteo Ricci, *China in the Sixteenth Century: The Journals of Matthew Ricci, 1583–1610*, trans. Louis J. Gallagher (New York: Random House, 1953), 365.

[43] For the christological controversy between Jesuits and mendicants in China, see Criveller, *Preaching Christ*, 76–87.

[44] A. Schall published *Jincheng Shuxiang* (Images Presented to the Chongzhen Emperor). Crown Prince Sohyŏn (1612–1645) was detained in Shenyang on account of a peace treaty after the Korea-Manchu War in 1636. He moved to Beijing in 1644 and communicated with a German Jesuit missionary scholar named Johann Adam Schall von Bell (1591–1666). When Sohyŏn saw the crucifix and Schall's drawings of Jesus, he could not understand why Westerners worshipped a crucified criminal as a god. However, the prince became highly interested in Roman Catholicism as well as Western science through Schall, who looked forward to the spread of Catholicism in Korea. Soon the prince had a positive perception of the suffering of Jesus. When Schall presented the Chinese Scriptures and the crucifix, the prince thanked him for the gifts and wrote that when he looked at the crucifix, it gave him peace of mind and purified his heart. Sohyŏn came back to Korea with some Chinese Catholics, but he was murdered by conservative forces soon after because of his pro-Qing and pro-Western policies.

[45] Criveller, *Preaching Christ*, 393.

[46] Clark, "Early Modern Chinese Reactions," 12.

> When Matteo Ricci entered China at the time of Wanli [Emperor Shen-zong, 1573–1620], Roman Catholicism began to be practiced. There is the cross, the so-called ten-letter-frame. Catholics must worship it, for "the Master of the West was executed on the cross and died." It is ridiculous. The main doctrines of the Western teaching are filled with words of strange, deceiving, and seducing people. And they say, "As the Master of the West was punished to death on the cross in order to found the church, the believers always should shed tears and grieve, yet never forget his death for a moment." How serious their delusion is![47]

Looking at the picture of the crucifixion and the men and women crying over the death of Jesus, Hong felt it was disgusting and could not bear to look at it.[48] When other Confucian scholars in Korea read Hong's travelogue, they shared his negative reaction to the image of the crucified Jesus and the Christian worship of the executed criminal.

When King Chŏngjo died in 1800, his relatively tolerant policies toward Western civilization were terminated. The papal edicts that supported Franciscans' fundamentalist missiology ended the Rites Controversy over ancestor worship and the terms for God in China by 1742, and their dominant influence on Korean Catholic Christians from 1790 aggravated the political situation in Korea. A new Korean government strictly forbade Roman Catholicism, and persecutions followed. The Korean envoys to Beijing, therefore, could no longer visit Catholic cathedrals, and instead the Russian Diplomatic Office in Beijing became the only place where they could see Western instruments such as alarm clocks, organs, mirrors, and cameras.

Some Korean envoys' travelogues depicted their encounters with the crucifix in the church inside the Russian Diplomatic Office. Kim Rosan wrote the following diary entry on June 25, 1828:

> When opening the curtain and entering inside, there is a dead man hanging on the opposite wall. Generally, on the wall, there is a cross-shaped wood panel on which a man is nailed at the head, legs, and arms. It looks like the punishment of tearing a person tied to a cart limb from limb, and the skin of the man is white. His skin, flesh, nails, and hair look alive

---

[47] Hong Taeyong, "Kŏnjŏngdong p'ildam" [Writing Dialogue at Kŏnjŏngdong, Beijing], *Tamhŏnsŏ* [The Writings of Tamhŏn Hong Taeyong, 1765] (Seoul: Korean Classics Research Institute, 1976).

[48] Shin Ik-Cheol, "The Experiences of Visiting Catholic Churches in Beijing and the Recognition of Western Learning Reflected in the Journal of Travel to Beijing," *Review of Korean Studies* (December 2006): 24.

and I cannot tell whether the naked body is real or not. Red blood pours out and drips down from the nailed parts of his body from head to foot, as if he were dead just a few moments ago and did not yet get cold; I felt too dizzy to look straight at it.[49]

Kim thought that the man was executed like a criminal guilty of high treason who was put to death by dismemberment. He wondered why the crucifix was enshrined and the man worshipped as a god. The guide replied that it was Jesus who was punished to death. Kim then understood why Christians in Korea were not afraid of the death sentence and did not renounce their faith at the moment of execution.

The Korean government adopted a policy of the strict prohibition of Roman Catholicism, and major persecutions happened in 1801, 1834–1835, 1839, and 1866–1873. When the police arrested members of the church, they fastened Christians to the flog frame (hyŏngt'ŭl), a cross-shaped wooden frame, and tortured and forced them to renounce faith. Many Christians recited the Christian catechism or sang hymns on the flog frame. The police confiscated the crucifixes, smuggled from China and cherished by the underground church.[50] In 1801 the government found that Catholic Christians made the sign of the cross on their breast before eating, going to bed, or having a secret mass. They reflected on the passion of Jesus in their prayers. Thus the cross became a symbol of suffering and faith for Catholic Christians in Korea.

The Roman Catholic icon of the cross, however, had no meaningful encounters with Korean religious culture. The main concern of the isolated underground churches was the survival of faith communities, whose basic liturgies—prayer, worship service, baptism, and Eucharist—focused on the passion of the crucified Jesus. The Korean Catholic Christians subjectively separated themselves from the world and yearned for the salvation of their souls in heaven after death.[51] The symbolic

---

[49] Shin Ik-Cheol, "The Western Learning Shown in the Records of Envoys Traveling to Beijing in the First Half of the Nineteenth Century—Focusing on Visits to the Russian Diplomatic Office," *Review of Korean Studies* (March 2008): 20.

[50] From 1629 to the 1850s crucifixion became a symbol of the persecution of Christianity or Christian apostasy in Japan. The Tokugawa shogunate required suspected Christians to step on the plate of crucifixion or the image of Mary (*fumie*) to prove that they were not members of that outlawed religion. See C. R. Boxer, *The Christian Century in Japan: 1549–1650* (Berkeley: University of California Press, 1951), 327.

[51] See Deberniere Janet Torrey, "Separating from the Confucian World: The

cross helped to sustain their spiritual identity under severe persecution. However, the cross of Jesus had no hermeneutic point of contact with the Korean prophetic tradition. Likewise, no element of ancestor veneration was added to their liturgy, and a Korean name for God, "Hanănim," was regarded as a sky god of superstitious spirit worship.[52] The crucifix became a symbol of the confrontational policies of French missionaries of la Société des Missions Étrangères de Paris and a cult of martyrdom in the nineteenth century.

Bixie Jishi and the Baby Riot in 1888

The negative image of the cross of Roman Catholicism was imposed upon Protestantism in Korea in the 1880s. The "Baby Riot," the first anti-Protestant disturbance in Seoul in 1888, was caused partly by some anti-Christian Chinese tracts used during the Tianjin Massacre and other anti–Roman Catholic movements in China in the 1870s and 1880s.

Dr. Horace N. Allen's treatment of severely wounded Min Yŏnghwan at the Kapsin coup d'état in December 1884 opened the way to the building of the first modern hospital, Chejungwŏn, and laid the foundation for the beginning of the Protestant mission in Korea. On the other hand, after the Chinese troops suppressed the pro-Japanese coup, General Yuan Shikai was appointed Imperial Resident of Seoul in 1885 and exercised a strong hand as head official from the suzerain until July 1894. Chinese merchants and Chinese literature poured into Chemulpo and Seoul. Yuan and conservative Korean Confucian officials imported Chinese anti-Christian books and tracts to curb the influence of Anglo-American missionaries in Seoul. One of the most notorious anti-Christian books, *Bixie jishi* (辟邪紀實 A Record of Facts to Ward off Heterodoxy, 1861), was circulated in Seoul from 1886.[53] Originally

---

Shift Away from Syncretism in Early Korean Catholic Texts," *Acta Koreana* (June 2012): 127–45.

[52] The *Dictionnaire Français-Coréen*, written in 1869, used only "T'yŏnjyu," and in the entry "Ciel" the author added that "les payens par respect superstitieux disent 하 님" (the pagans say 하 님 with superstitious respect). See Stanislas Férron, ed., *Dictionnaire Français-Coréen* (1869; repr., Seoul: Han'guk Kyohoesa Yŏn'guso, 2004), 54.

[53] John W. Heron to Frank F. Ellinwood, August 27, 1886: "It is stated on good authority that a book [tract] written by a Chinaman entitled, *A Death Blow to Corrupt Doctrines*, now prohibited in China, had been circulating here. I have not

the book targeted Roman Catholicism in China and provoked the Tientsin Massacre in 1870, in which a cathedral and four British and American churches were burned down and two French consular officials, two French Lazarist priests, and approximately forty Chinese Christians were killed.

The anonymous Chinese author of *Bixie jishi* attacked Christian teachings and activities and insisted that the pestilence of Christianity be rooted out of China. Its caricature illustrations were designed to incite a mass audience. They stirred up the Chinese to burn Christian literature and kill Western missionaries and Chinese Christians. The tract depicted Western missionaries as goat-headed men worshipping Jesus, a "grunting heavenly pig," seen removing the fetus from a pregnant woman, gouging out the eyes of a dying convert, and behaving indecorously with Chinese women.[54] The most malicious and sinister woodcut of the pamphlet was the picture captioned "Shooting the Pig and Beheading Goats" (figure 3). The image depicts a stately magistrate ordering two archers to shoot arrows at a crucified pig (Jesus) while another decapitates three goat-headed men with the character *xi* (Westerner) on their chests. This iconographic representation of the crucified pig Jesus on the cross was a culmination of the negative images of the crucifixion of Jesus in China.

This book was circulated in Korea when American missionaries began to work in Seoul, and the book became a literary source of the "Baby Riot" in 1888.[55] Conservative intellectuals imported Chinese books and tracts and used them in their opposition to Western missionaries and Christianity. Although *Bixie jishi* was written in Chinese,

---

seen it, nor anyone who has, but I think it is true. You probably know something of this book, which was said to have caused the Tientsin Massacre, some 17 or 18 years ago. No doubt this inflamed the Koreans and the first measure taken by the government added to it." Its English translation was Gentry and People, *Death Blow to Corrupt Doctrines* (1870).

[54] Paul Cohen, *China and Christianity: The Missionary Movement and the Growth of Chinese Antiforeignism, 1860–1870* (Cambridge, Mass.: Harvard University Press, 1963), 45–60; Roman Catholicism was called "天主教 Tianzhu-jiao" in Chinese. "Zhujiao" sounds similar to the graphs for "pig grunt" (猪叫), pronounced "zhujiao" but with a different inflection. So some Chinese called Catholicism as "天猪叫" and Catholics worshippers of "天猪" (the heavenly grunting pig Jesus). (Clark, "Early Modern Chinese Reactions," 6.)

[55] See n. 53.

FIGURE 3
Bixie jishi 辟邪紀實, 1861

its graphic illustrations "filled with the most loathsome obscenity and the grossest misrepresentations and falsehood" could, to some extent, inflame ordinary Koreans' anti-Christian and antiforeign sentiments.[56]

When some children disappeared from Seoul in 1888 (they had actually been kidnapped and sold to Chinese traders as slaves), a rumor was started among the Koreans that they had been sold to Westerners. The rumor began in the orphanage established by Horace G. Underwood and circulated rapidly throughout all parts of Seoul. Diabolically, it was said that the favorite food of the missionaries was roasted Korean babies, served up whole on tables and eaten; that little children, before being killed, were taken into the cellars underneath foreign houses, their eyes gouged out and their tongues torn out in order to be manufactured into magic drugs with which the missionaries then made photographs, or put into the food they served to Korean guests in order to turn their hearts to God and become Christians. These reports were broadly believed and created an atmosphere of wild excitement. Korean

[56] Henry W. Blodget to N. G. Clark, October 24, 1870, quoted in John King Fairbank, ed., *Chinese Thought and Institutions* (Chicago: University of Chicago Press, 1957), 502.

servants deserted their foreign employers. Plans were laid to attack foreign residences, burn down the houses, and kill all foreigners. Soon several Koreans, however, were arrested and charged with kidnapping children in order to sell them to Chinese merchants. One crazy man claimed that he had sold children to the missionaries. When exposed as a madman by the Korean judge before whom he was tried, he was taken by a mob and stoned to death. The riot was subdued by the immediate actions of the Korean government, which had to respond to the strong appeals of the foreign legations. The ministers intensified their pressure on the Korean government by dispatching their own navy and marine soldiers from Chemulpo to Seoul. After the riot, American missionaries felt that they had passed the period of probation in Korea. Ironically, the Baby Riot provided the missionaries, as American citizens, with an opportunity to be known as "*yangdaein*, Western great men," who were under the protection of American military power as well as the Korean–American Treaty of 1882. The intellectual antagonism of the Korean yangban class toward Western Christianity developed into a popular riot against American missionaries, albeit with less damage and violence than occurred in China. In short, up to the 1880s the iconography of the Christian cross did not have any glyphomantic point of contact with Korean religious culture.

PROTESTANT FLAGS OF THE RED CROSS
AND CODE BREAKING

New iconographic interpretations of the cross by North American missionaries and Korean Christians facilitated the propagation of Protestantism. First, a new image of the cross was provided by a woodblock print in James S. Gale's Korean translation of Bunyan's *The Pilgrim's Progress* in 1895. Second, the Tonghak Uprising, the Sino-Japanese War of 1894–1895, and the Russo-Japanese War of 1904–1905, which created an apocalyptic situation in Korea, opened a fertile religious space for new iconographies and rhetoric of the Christian cross. Korean Christians' glyphomantic interpretation of sipsŭngjiji of the *Chŏnggamnok* invited a millennial meaning of the Christian cross during wartime. Third, in connection with the glyphomantic understanding of the cross and the church as the place for millennial salvation, William MacKenzie's flag of St. George's Cross, hoisted at Sorae, Hwanghae province, in December 1894, symbolized the Western missionaries' political power of extraterritoriality. Many churches began to install flagpoles in the churchyards when the great famine hit Hwanghae, Kyŏnggi, and Kangwŏn provinces, where the village people attempted to protect their property and lives under the red cross flag of St. George's Cross.

There were eighty illustrations in the Korean edition of *Syŏnggyŏng tosŏl* (*The Bible Picture Book*), printed in 1892, whose original Chinese edition was made by Mrs. Sarah M. Sites (1842–1912, wife of Rev. Nathan Sites) in Fuzhou, China. Miss L. C. Rothweiler, a German American Methodist missionary of the Woman's Foreign Missionary Society and a teacher at Ewha Girls' School in Seoul, translated the book into Korean and popularized the Western-style pictures of Bible stories and the lives of Jesus and his apostles. In figure 4, Jesus looks like an Anglo-Saxon man with long hair against the heavy beams of the cross. The Chinese caption emphasizes that Jewish religious leaders—both scribers and priests—persecuted Jesus and made him carry the burden of the cross, but the Korean edition explains simply that Jesus carried the cross. The scene of the crucified Jesus in the book is in the typical Western style, depicting the suffering body of Jesus and the lamenting women under the cross. The Korean caption states, "Jesus was nailed down on the ten-letter frame (*sipchat'ŭl*)." Nonbelievers, upon seeing the picture, might have thought that it was the scene of the execution of a criminal like those depicted in figures 1 and 2.

THE PILGRIM'S PROGRESS AND A NEW IMAGE OF THE CROSS, 1895

New iconographic interpretations of the cross by North American missionaries and Korean Christians facilitated the propagation of Protestantism. James S. Gale's *T'yŏllo yŏkchŏng* (1895) was a Korean translation of John Bunyan's (1628–1688) *The Pilgrim's Progress from This World to That Which Is to Come* (1678). C. C. Vinton's review lauded its Korean illustrations.

> First, no doubt, to attract attention, although we come only now to speak of them, are the illustrations. Artistically they are fairly executed. Anatomically the figures far exceed in merit those of the best Korean drawings. To those for whom they are intended they come with peculiar acceptance because they are meant to represent Koreans and not foreigners.[57]

The book presented not only an evangelical doctrine of the redemptive death of Jesus on the cross, but also a Koreanized image of the cross.

[57] C. C. Vinton, "Literary Department," *KR* 3 (1896): 39.

The Anglo-American style in the *Bible Picture Book* changed into the Korean style of figure 8 in three years (from 1892 to 1895), just as the European style of figure 1 changed into the Chinese style of figure 2 in three years (from 1637 to 1640). It was necessary for the missionaries to make such a rapid indigenization of the Christian images for the propagation of the Christian images and doctrines.

A Korean scholar, Yi Ch'angjik (1866–1936), helped Gale as a language teacher and literary assistant from 1889 to 1927. Gale married Mrs. Heron in April 1892. They began to translate *The Pilgrim's Progress* and its Chinese Mandarin version (1852) by William Burns into Korean with Mr. Yi, whose excellent literary skills made the book one of the best pieces of the early Protestant literature. Mr. Yi deepened his own understanding of evangelical Christianity and tried to strengthen his spiritual resistance to evil desires during the translation of the book.

Gale used the drawings of Korean folk painter Kim Chun'gŭn. Gale had known him since 1889, when he worked in Pusan. Kim's illustrations differed from those of the American, Chinese, and Japanese versions that were available at that time. Kim produced Korean folk paintings for foreign clients who visited the treaty ports of Korea. As a skilled artist, Kim combined the traditional techniques of Korean genre painting with those of Western paintings. His works sold well to foreigners. At the same time his illustrations were well received by Koreans.[58] Therefore, the Korean text was influenced by Burns' Chinese edition, but also included in Gale's edition were forty-two illustrations in the Korean folk style with a slight Western perspective.

Let us compare the illustration of the Christian removing the burden of sin in front of the cross in the first three East Asian editions of *The Pilgrim's Progress*. All three versions use an indigenous style with the main native character—an educated Manchu, a Japanese samurai, or a Korean farmer. William Burns' Chinese edition (1852) adopts a more Western style and perspective (figure 5).[59] Yet it relocates the cross to the left, an unusual position compared to the other versions. Both

---

[58] Shin Seonyoung, "Kisan Kim Chungŭn p'ungsokhwa e kwanhan yŏn'gu" [A Study of Albums of Genre Paintings by Kim Chungŭn], *Misulsahak* 20 (2006): 105–41; Chŏng Hyŏngho, "Kisan Kim Chungŭn ŭi p'ungsokhwa e nat'anan minsok chŏk t'ŭkching" [The Folk Characteristics of Kisan, Kim Junkeun's Genre Painting], *Chung'ang Minsokhak* 13 (2008): 179–223.

[59] John Bunyan, *Tianlu licheng: guanhua* [The Pilgrim's Progress in Mandarin], trans. William Burns (Shanghai: Presbyterian Mission Press, 1852).

FIGURE 4
Bunyan, 1757 F

the Chinese and Japanese editions emphasize the individual Christian's encounter with the cross. In both editions the Christian is looking upward toward the cross in a praying position, representing introspection rather than liberation. Sato Yosimine's Japanese edition (1879) does not emphasize the cross but focuses on the samurai Christian, whose posture on the steep slope represents his inner struggle rather than peace of mind (figure 6).[60]

In contrast, James S. Gale's Korean edition (1895) incorporates the visual of the Christian removing the heavy burden of sin and two female angels putting him in a white robe (figure 8).[61] Its structure is similar

[60] John Bunyan, *Tenro rekitei: iyaku* [The Pilgrim's Progress], trans. Sato Yosimine (Tokyo: Jiujiya, 1879).

[61] John Bunyan, *T'yŏllo yŏkchŏng* [The Pilgrim's Progress], trans. James S. Gale (Seoul: Korean Religious Tract Society, 1895). When *T'yŏllo yŏkchŏng* was published in 1895, the *Korean Repository* praised the book as "the most elegant

圖　任　罪　脫

FIGURE 5
Burns, 1852

FIGURE 6
Yosimine, 1879

CHRISTIAN IN VIEW OF THE CROSS.

FIGURE 7
Maguire, 1863

FIGURE 8
Gale, 1895

가 흰옷을 닙히다
라 죄짐을 버스니련소
괴독도 십즈가에 다다

to that of figure 7, illustrated by Henry Courtney Selous (1803–1890) of the edition noted by Rev. Robert Maguire (1826–1890) in 1863. It is likely that Gale read Maguire's edition as a young man, brought it to Korea, and gave the book to Kim Chun'gŭn, because some of the illustrations in Gale's Korean edition are similar to those in Maguire's English edition. Gale might have chosen Selous' illustration, for the scene emphasizes the triple interaction of the cross, the Christian, and the angels. Kim simplified the background, reduced the angels to two, and removed the old vines from the cross. The illustrations of the Chinese and Japanese versions are individualistic and doctrine oriented, yet Gale's Korean version is relational and narrative oriented. The picture (figure 8) has two female angels who are like Buddhist bodhisattvas or Daoist immortals who touch the Christian, which differs from Bunyan's original illustration, with its three angels who look at the Christian from some distance, giving a sinister atmosphere with its skulls and the dark backside of the cross with a crown (figure 4). Kim's interpretation adopts Selous' illustration but depicts the angels as Korean. In other words, the illustrations of the Gale version reflect both Kim's Korean folk style and Gale's theological selection of the illustrations among the English editions.

At stake here was the image of the cross in figure 8. The bare cross was now represented to Korean readers for the first time as a redemptive place of one's burdensome sin being taken away, and being born again as a righteous person with intimate, heavenly help. The Protestant cross was simple, clean, and empty. There was neither a crucifixion nor a representation of Jesus with a naked and bleeding body, appearing wild and frightening to some. Unlike the samurai Christian of the Japanese edition, Gale's Korean Christian was a commoner, the main target of evangelism in Korea. The cross became available to everyone in Korea. Moreover, the cross was incorporated into Korean religious culture by having angels coexist with the image of a common Korean man, Buddhist bodhisattvas, or Daoist immortals who were equivalent to the Christian angels. Such an interchangeable pantheon can be seen in the final illustration of the book, "Entering the Heaven." The "Christian"

---

specimen of the printer's art thus far placed by foreigners upon the native market, and furthermore the most notable production toward a standard literature as yet made available to the Korean nation" (C. C. Vinton, "Literary Department," *KR* [September 1896]: 377).

heaven looks like a Daoist or Buddhist paradise where immortals are singing and playing the flute. Its structure and motifs came from the Selous' picture and Bunyan's text, yet its imagery was indigenized for Korean readers.[62]

These Koreanized images of the Christian cross and heaven began to circulate among early Korean converts, who later interpreted Christian doctrines with their eyes while staying within the boundaries of North American missionaries' pragmatic and audience-centered evangelical Protestantism. Kil Sŏnju and Ch'oe Pyŏnghŏn wrote stories of the Christian pilgrimage from the earthly world to the heavenly kingdom. Kil's *Haet'aron* (懈惰論 On Sloth, 1905) was a simplified version of *The Pilgrim's Progress*, and Ch'oe's *Sŏngsan Myŏnggyŏng* (聖山明鏡 The Bright Mirror in the Holy Mountain, 1909) was an allegorical novel that dealt with interreligious dialogue in a dream.

CODE BREAKING OF THE PROPHECY OF THE *CHŎNGGAM-NOK*, 1895–1905

For some Korean Christians who had deeply believed in the *Chŏnggam-nok* before joining the church, the key to their decoding of the enigmatic phrases of the book was the cross, 十. The Chinese graphic letter 十 represented not only the shape of the cross but also the number ten. Therefore, the empty cross of Protestantism was easily connected to the number ten of the *Chŏnggam-nok* through the interpretative method of glyphomancy. Before discussing their new interpretation, a short historical review of this method will prove helpful.

The glyphomancy *p'acha* 破字 method in Korea had been used as a traditional decoding method in divination and in deciphering secret geomantic prophecies, especially in times of dynastic change.[63] For example, Yi Chagyŏm (?–1126) began a revolt, believing the prophecy of "十八子爲王" (eighteen sons, meaning Yi 李, will become king), and Cho Kwangjo (1482–1519) was killed based on the fabricated rumor of "走肖爲王" (Cho 趙 will become king).

The *Chŏnggam-nok*, which prophesized the collapse of the Yi dynasty after great tribulations such as famines, wars, and epidemics,

---

[62] The illustration of "Heaven" in Gale's Korean version is more indigenized than those of Burns' Chinese version and Yosimine's Japanese version.

[63] Gale mentioned 破字占 (fortune telling by means of letters) in his diary on June 7, 1915.

and the founding of a new Chŏng dynasty, was widely circulated in the eighteenth and nineteenth centuries. The *Chŏnggam-nok* stated that people would find refuge at sipsŭngjiji and kunggungŭlŭl during the national crisis. As mentioned before, some of its believers joined the Roman Catholic Church, but they had not produced a new interpretation of the enigmatic words sipsŭngjiji and kunggungŭlŭl, which were believed as the most important secret codes that contained the truths and prophecy of the future, and thus the most sought-after lexis to be deciphered to the religious minority groups who were interested in the geomantic prophecy.[64]

However, Tonghak (Eastern Learning), an indigenous and syncretistic Korean religion, actively used these terms in its propagation. Its founder, Ch'oe Cheu, wrote *Sipsŭng-ga* (A Song of Ten Auspicious Places) and made a paper amulet with the four letters of 弓弓乙乙 (kunggungŭlŭl) as a medicine (*yak* 藥) for the sick or weak (*yak* 弱) people. He had them drink water with its ash. People were suffering from epidemics such as cholera and smallpox, famines, and the high taxes of corrupt local officials. Tonghak grew rapidly in poor farming areas in the 1870s and 1880s. In East Asian traditions, in their rebellions political leaders like Kŭngye (857–918) had used the people's belief in Maitreya, a future Buddha in Buddhist eschatology, as a millennial vision for a new dynasty. Ch'oe Cheu's messianism synthesized this Buddhist eschatology and the geomantic prophecy of the dynastic change of the *Chŏnggam-nok* with the Roman Catholic doctrine of millennialism.[65]

---

[64] By combining the four letters *kunggungŭlŭl* 弓弓乙乙, Murayama Chijun (村山智順) interpreted in 1933 that the phrase represented the letter "弱" (weakness), and thus that the weak people would survive the national crisis. He emphasized the prophecy of the fall of the Chosŏn dynasty in the *Chŏnggam-nok* to justify the Japanese colonization of Korea and to criticize the Korean Independence Movement based on the *Chŏnggam-nok*. See Murayama Chijun, *Chosŏn ŭi chŏmbok kwa yeŏn*, 543–44, 558–71.

[65] Tonghak accepted the scenario of the dynastic changes in *Chŏnggam-nok*, which prophesized that the capital of the Wang dynasty (Koryŏ) would be located in Song'ak (Kaesŏng), the Yi dynasty (Chosŏn) in Hanyang (Seoul), the Chŏng dynasty in Kyeryong-san, the Cho dynasty in Kaya-san, and finally the Pŏm dynasty in Ch'ilsan. Tonghak millennialism envisioned "the Great Transformation" (kaebyŏk) of the earth, and Roman Catholic eschatology, based on the Augustinian model of history, anticipated the gradual improvement of the world before the second coming of Jesus Christ, which was similar to postmillennialism of liberal Protestantism in the early twentieth century. Ch'oe's eschatology was

FIGURE 9
Inferred Tonghak *Yŏngbu*
(Bucknell and Beirne)

FIGURE 10
Inferred Tonghak *Yŏngbu*
(Oak)

Bucknell and Beirne insisted that Ch'oe Cheu's talisman resembled half of the Chinese character 弱 yak (weak) (figure 9), for half of the character yak 弱 comes close to being a combination of the mystical *kung* 弓 and *ŭl* 乙.[66] But a more plausible combination might have been the four letters, not two letters—the combination of one half of the letter yak and the other reversed half of the letter yak for a bilateral symmetry, which was a typical design of the talisman. Then Ch'oe's talisman resembles the letter *a* 亞, with two short horizontal lines in each of the lower corners of the letter (figure 10).

The design of this talisman resembled that of *pulsap*, a pair of traditional Confucian funeral fans or the symbol found on coffin cloth or coffins. The fan was originally used to cool the body and to ward off evil spirits. The following *pulsap* were the official designs used by the Chosŏn government.[67] As the letter *pul* 亞 was similar to the letter of "*a* 亞", *pulsap* was called *asap*. The last in the series of figure 11 was used at the funeral of the Empress Min in 1898. As the *pulsap* was widely

similar to that of the Old Testament prophets who insisted that Israel would be destroyed by the enemy, acting as the tool of God, before the renewal of the nation. See Hong Suhn-Kyoung, "Tonghak in the Context of Korean Modernization," *Review of Religious Research* 10, no. 1 (1968): 48–49.

[66] Roderick S. Bucknell and Paul Beirne, "In Search of Yŏngbu: The Lost Talisman of Korea's Tonghak Religion," *Review of Korean Studies* 4, no. 2 (2001): 201–22.

[67] Yi Seunghae and Ahn Pohyun, "Chosŏn sidae hoegyŏk hoegwagmyo ch'ult'o sab e taehan koch'al" [A Study of the "sap" excavated from the tombs of lime-covered or lime coffins], *Munhwajae* 42, no. 2 (2008): 49.

used for the Confucian funerals, I presume that the symbol of the cross-shaped 卍 could be related to the Christian flag of the Red Cross.[68]

From this uniquely Korean tradition of geomantic prophecy, some Koreans devised a Christian interpretation of the *Chŏnggam-nok*. Kim Sangnim (1847–1902) was one of them. He was a traditional Confucian *yangban* scholar at Kyohang, Kanghwa Island. He had failed several times in the government exams but finally passed the first local exam *ch'osi* when he was forty years old. He became a teacher at a private school. He had mastered the *Book of Changes* and the *Chŏnggam-nok*. However, he could not figure out the meaning of sipsŭngjiji of the *Chŏnggam-nok*. After hearing the Christian gospel from a local preacher, Yi Sŭnghwan, in 1893 and studying the Scriptures, Kim decided to become a Christian, believing that the way of sipchaga (the cross) was the sipsŭngjiji. Rev. G. H. Jones baptized Kim in August 1894. The first conversion of a *yangban* scholar became a serious issue for the family clan, yet aroused great interest in Christianity among the islanders. Soon a church was organized at Kyohang under Kim's leadership. After teaching at the East Gate Methodist School in Seoul for a year, Kim worked as a local preacher on the island. By the time he died in 1902, many self-supporting Methodist churches were growing rapidly in Kanghwa. His conversion gave great impetus to the beginnings of the Methodist churches in Kanghwa Island.[69]

Yi Sŭngnyun, a Presbyterian, converted to Christianity in 1894, believing that Jesus Christ was the anticipated Chŏng-doryŏng (Prince Chŏng, the new king of the *Chŏnggam-nok*) and Christianity signaled the fulfillment of the prophecy of the *Chŏnggam-nok*. When the Russo-Japanese War began in 1904, many people called on the *Chŏnggam-nok* and wandered into deep valleys and the mountains of the country in order to find auspicious places, hoping to preserve their lives. Even

---

[68] Kang Hŭinam guessed that the symbol "卍" of *pulsap* originated from the cross of Nestorianism of China in the seventh century (Kang Hŭinam, "Unasab i kajinŭn ŭiŭi" [The Meaning of the Funeral Fans "Unasap"], *Kidoggyo sasang* 12, no. 7 [1968]: 144–46). But no evidence for this argument has been found so far (Yi and An, "Chosŏn sidae hoegyŏk," 51).

[69] "Kim Sangnimssi pyŏlsehasim" [The Death of Mr. Kim Sangnim], *SW* (June 1902): 253–54.; Tŏkchu Yi and Ije Cho, *Kwanghwa kidoggyo 100nyŏn sa* [The Centennial History of Christianity in Kanghwa] (Seoul, 1994), 107; Yi Tŏkchu, *Han'guk t'och'ak kyohoe hyŏngsŏngsa yŏn'gu* [A Study on the Formation of the Indigenous Church in Korea, 1903–1907] (Seoul: IKCH, 2000), 364–65.

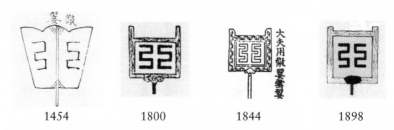

| 1454 | 1800 | 1844 | 1898 |

FIGURE 11
The designs of the *pulsap* used in the Chosŏn period

many Protestant Christians awaited and anticipated the imminent second coming of Christ.[70] In this context, Yi elaborated on his earlier interpretation of the sipsŭngjiji and Chŏng-doryŏng. He criticized the ignorance of those who were still searching for the sipsŭngjiji in Kyeryong Mountain and other places, and presented a spiritual meaning for the ten auspicious places in his interpretation of the first character (亞) of Abraham (亞伯拉罕) in Matthew 1:1 of the Chinese New Testament:

> When we see "A" (亞), the first character of "Abraham" (亞伯拉罕) in Matthew 1:1, it has both "sip" (十) of the *sipsŭngjiji* and *kunggungŭlŭl*. The central white part of the character "A" (亞) is apparently the character "sip" (十). Thus any place where people believe in the Lord's Cross will become the *sipsŭngjiji*. When we see the right and left part of the character "A" (亞), they are obviously *kunggungŭlŭl*. Thus we must study and investigate the Bible. . . . As the three characters of "Chŏng-doryŏng" are "chŏng" (正, right), "do" (道, way), and "ryŏng" (寧, peace), it means that if one follows the right way he or she may live in peace. This is identical to "tohaji 道下旨," which means that God let the *Chŏnggam-nok* foretell the truth of the Lord's Cross to the people. . . . Brothers, do not search for the ten auspicious places any more. If you come before our Lord's Cross, you will find a very auspicious place. Let's discard the imperfect words of the *Chŏnggam-nok*, and propagate the precious character "十" of the "cross 十字架" to wandering compatriots, and let them know the way of eternal life.[71]

[70] Cyril Ross, "Personal Report of Rev. Cyril Ross, September 1903," *KF* (May 1904): 176.

[71] Yi Sŭngnyun, "A pŏgŭm a cha sog i sipchaga ga toem" [The Inside of the Chinese Character "A" Becomes the Cross], *KS*, March 21, 1906.

Using the very method of glyphomancy, Yi Sŭngnyun found Christ's cross (十), the place of salvation (sipsŭngjiji), and the way of salvation (kunggungŭlŭl) inside the first letter (亞) of the name of Abraham. Yi believed that he found the fulfillment of the prophecy of the *Chŏnggam-nok* in Jesus Christ, the son of Abraham. The ten (十) auspicious places (sipsŭngjiji) of the *Chŏnggam-nok* were deciphered as the locations where the cross defeated sin. Now any place where people believed in the ten-letter-frame cross (十) could become one of the ten auspicious places (十勝) of salvation. Yi believed that God gave the *Chŏnggam-nok* to Koreans to foretell the truth of the cross of Jesus Christ. He interpreted a foreign book, the New Testament, from the perspective of a more familiar book, the *Chŏnggam-nok*. The two books were combined in hopes of showing Koreans the way of salvation and providing them hope for the millennial kingdom.

What is significant is that this interpretation was introduced in the official newspaper of the Korean Presbyterian church, *Kŭrisŭdo Sinmun*, edited by H. G. Underwood. It meant that Yi's innovative yet intellectually implausible interpretation was acceptable to some missionaries and Korean Christian groups. It provided some Koreans with a new way of reading the *Chŏnggam-nok* with the New Testament. Beginning in 1894, many churches, Christian schools, and mission hospitals hoisted the flag of the red cross (the Jesus flag). When the glyphomatic interpretation of the cross as a mark of the ten auspicious places of the *Chŏnggam-nok* was projected onto the red cross, those Christian places came to signify protective spaces for life and property of the suffering people. The forces of the missionaries' political and economic power, the Christian message of redemption, and the Christian doctrine of premillennialism with Korean folk beliefs in geomantic prophecy became impelling factors in the conversion of some Koreans to Protestantism. The synthesis of the church as a religious space with the church as a political space was started at the Sorae Presbyterian Church, Hwanghae province, which was established in 1885 by Korean Christians and ministered by William J. McKenzie beginning in 1894. Through this amalgamation of religion and politics, we can determine the early usage and significance of the Jesus flag (the red cross flag or the flag of St. George's Cross) in the early Korean Protestant churches.

FROM THE FLAG OF ST. GEORGE'S CROSS
TO THE JESUS FLAG, 1895–1903

The flag of the red cross had different religious, diplomatic, political, and social meanings at the turn of the twentieth century in Korea. First, William J. McKenzie hoisted the flag at his house and the chapel at Sorae in 1895. It represented his theology of the cross and nonviolence as well as the British legation's protection of the Canadian missionary. Flagpoles were also erected at many churches in Hwanghae, Kyŏnggi, and Kangwŏn provinces. Initially flags with the cross represented the day of Sabbath as well as indicated a place of worship. But gradually the flags symbolized the political power of the Protestant churches against local groups like Roman Catholic Christians and members of the Peddlers, or pro-Japanese societies. Some pseudo-Christians even organized local Protestant churches and hoisted flags with the red cross in order to promote their own private interests.

William J. McKenzie (1861–1895), an independent Canadian Presbyterian missionary, worked at Sorae Church, the first Korean Protestant church, formed in 1884, beginning in February 1894 with the help of Sŏ Kyŏngjo. In November 1894, the second Tonghak Uprising broke out against the Japanese. McKenzie emphasized "the meekness and gentleness of Christ, enduring abuse and hatred without retaliation."[72] All the Tonghak soldiers who sought MacKenzie out were welcomed and counseled. The villagers, who were suffering under the exploitation of the Tonghaks, inquired of Sŏ Kyŏngjo the secret of the Christians' peace. Villagers were trying to "hide under the foreigner's wing when the Japs [sic] come" and "clung the more closely to the preacher as their earthly protector."[73]

On December 12, 1894, McKenzie raised "the flag of Jesus," the flag of the St. George's Cross—which had a centered red cross on a white background—above his dwelling and the chapel, to stand for the dwelling of a British citizen as well as Christianity (figure 12). In his diary he wrote, "We cut the pole some distance off. There were willing workers to have that emblem above them. Tonghaks and all worked, dug the hole and held the ropes, and soon the flag ascended, while we sang 'All hail the power of Jesus' name!'" It was his own idea "to distinguish his

[72] Elizabeth A. McCully, *A Corn of Wheat or the Life of Rev. W. J. McKenzie of Korea* (Toronto: Westminster, 1904), 153.
[73] McCully, *Corn of Wheat*, 154.

little church and the holy Sabbath from the unholy shrines and celebrations of the heathen." The next day he wrote, "The flag is seen from afar, and there is much curiosity as to its meaning. It serves as an object-lesson of the meaning of the cross—purity and suffering for others."[74] A few days later two hundred Tonghak soldiers passed through the village. Their leaders stopped to visit the foreigner because they saw the Jesus flag flying. He received them without fear. Christmas Day passed without celebration. The Japanese were defeating the Tonghaks. On the first Sunday of the New Year, the Sŏ brothers preached to a large crowd at two services. "A fair portion of the congregation were Tonghaks."[75] In February, about fifty men and sixty women began fund-raising for a new church building. Several Tonghaks gave over 600 nyang ($30) in a day. Soon a new church was completed on the former site of the town shrine, and a high pole was erected in front of the gate to designate it as a sacred Christian place.

McKenzie's flag of St. George's Cross and his thoughts inspired the notion that "throughout the land of Korea a white flag with St. George's Cross has become as universal as the church bell of Christian lands."[76] Religiously, the "Jesus flag" symbolized the suffering and redemptive death of Jesus and the Christian principle of nonviolence.

Ecclesiastically, the church flagpole, since its advent at the Sorae Church in 1895, had separated the Christian churches from other secular or religious spaces. The flagpole began to appear in Paech'ŏn and Yŏnan counties of southeastern Hwanghae, where Samuel F. Moore itinerated for pioneer evangelistic works. In 1898 he stated, "The red cross flag in all this area is considered as necessary as the church itself and is a constant reminder to the heathen of the Lord's Day."[77] Every Sunday the Protestant churches hoisted the flag of the red cross in order to inform people of the holy space and time of worship. The flagpole became an essential part of the church building around 1898.

On the other hand, politically, the flagpole was the symbol of the missionary's extraterritoriality, which attracted people who desired to be protected under the "great Westerner."[78] The flag of the red cross,

---

[74] McCully, *Corn of Wheat*, 155.
[75] McCully, *Corn of Wheat*, 158.
[76] McCully, *Corn of Wheat*, 154.
[77] S. F. Moore, "Report of S. F. Moore, 1898," PHS, CRKM, reel 180.
[78] The church flagpole had continuity with the ancient Korean tradition of

FIGURE 12
The Sorae Church and Its Flag of St. George's Cross, 1898

like the Union Jack flying over the British legation and the Stars and Stripes over the American legation and the American missionaries' hospitals in Seoul, represented the political power of the missionaries, who were protected by extraterritorial rights.[79] During the Independence Club Movement from 1897 to 1899, which was the first nationwide civilian political movement for the awakening of the people for nation building, the Protestant churches participated in the public celebration of the national holidays such as Emperor Kojong's birthday and the

---

erecting a *sottae* (a wooden pole for protecting the village or for a good harvest) in a sacred place; *sodo*, which offered protection to refugees; *changsŭng*, village guardians who protected people from epidemics; and *tanggan*, a flagpole of a Buddhist temple. In particular, the flag of the cross had a new meaning to some groups who believed in the prophecy of the *Chŏnggam-nok*.

[79] In the 1890s American missionaries' basic policy in politics was noninterference or passive resistance, whereas that of French missionaries was active resistance. So the political power of French missionaries was so immense that some former officials who lost their lands to Taewŏngun could regain their property by simply joining the Roman Catholic Church in Seoul.

Founding Day of the Chosŏn Kingdom, and hoisted the flag of the red cross along with the Korean national flag. These flags stood for the loyalty and patriotism (*ch'unggun aeguk*) of the Protestant church as well as its political power supported by Western missionaries.

From March 1898 the Independence Club (*Tongnip Hyŏphoe*) Movement developed into the All People's Meeting (*Manmin Kongdonghoe*) in Seoul. Public meetings were held almost daily with more than ten thousand citizens. They criticized the pro-Russian cabinets' concessions and corruption. The students of the Methodist boys' school, Paejae Haktang of H. G. Appenzeller, and many Protestant Christians joined the demonstrations. Yun Ch'iho (Methodist), Hong Chŏnghu (Presbyterian), and Syngman Rhee (Methodist) were leaders of the meetings. On October 29, 1898, a former butcher named Pak Sŏngch'un of the Central Presbyterian Church made a public speech. The meeting adopted the Six Articles that were submitted to the emperor and demanded serious political reforms and the expansion of people's rights. The minister of education asked Appenzeller to disperse the students. On November 15, the election day of the Privy Council (the Lower House), Emperor Kojong ordered the arrest of the leaders of the Independence Club. Many of them, including Yun Ch'iho, found refuge in American missionaries' houses. When Hong Chŏnghu, a deacon of Daniel L. Gifford's Yŏndong Church, was arrested on American property, H. N. Allen of the American legation demanded Hong's release, and it was granted. After attending the prayer meeting and seeing his family, however, Hong "voluntarily gave himself up to the authorities, preferring to share the lot of his compatriots to being free on a technicality."[80] The people and the students did not disperse, and things grew worse.[81] From November 16 to 19, the loyalists of the court reorganized a couple thousand members of the old guild of coolies and merchants known as the Peddlers' Club (*Hwangguk Hyŏphoe*). On November 20 they armed themselves with clubs and attacked the unarmed people, calling them *Manmin Kongdonghoe yŏkjŏknom* (traitors of the populace).[82] About one thousand armed men on each side fought hand to hand until the Peddlers' Club retreated outside the city. The people destroyed the houses of the Peddlers. Dr. Avison's hospital, Chejungwŏn, was filled with wounded

---

[80] O. R. Avison to Robert E. Speer, November 19, 1898.
[81] H. N. Allen to H. G. Appenzeller, November 20, 1898.
[82] H. G. Appenzeller to Robert E. Speer, November 19, 1898.

men with broken bones and bruised flesh. The U.S. minister directed all American citizens to fly their national flag over their houses to protect themselves from the mob. The *Christian News*, edited by H. G. Underwood, criticized the Peddlers' Club and its wicked organizers of the court.[83]

On November 26, Emperor Kojong publicly promised to reform the government and then met the leaders of the Independence Club—Yun Ch'iho, Hong Chŏnghu, and Ko Pyŏngsŏ. But the dispersed people reignited their campaign because the emperor ignored his promises, and the leaders of the Peddlers continued communication with the cabinet members. The Peddlers' Club sent a letter of warning to Paejae Haktang:

> A letter, purporting to come from the Peddlers to the Methodist School reviling the students and all the Christians, caused a good deal of excitement, especially as it threatened the destruction of their school and churches and a few hot-headed ones, taking their cue from the methods followed by the "Independence Club," gathered the Christians from all denominations together, harangued them into a state of fervidity, and, taking several Red Cross banners, marched them in a body to the police court to demand the immediate arrest and punishment of the men whose signatures were on the letter. The frightened Chief of Police promised to have the men arrested within 24 hours and they dispersed with the understanding that they would meet the next day to watch the trial.[84]

Students and so-called Christians marched to the police court with the flag of the red cross. The chief of police resigned and disappeared. Kil Yŏngsu, a leader of the Peddlers, sent a letter to Appenzeller and denied any connection to the abusive letter, "declaring it to be a forgery, and stating that they held the school and the Christians in the highest esteem."[85] When the aforementioned radical Christians planned to meet again, missionaries attempted to persuade Deacon Hong and others not to participate in political demonstrations and had a free discussion with Koreans. However, some of the politically awakened members of the churches, a strong, intelligent body supported the use of force.

The local churches also displayed both the Korean national flag and the flag of the red cross at the ceremony of the emperor's birthday from 1897 to 1907. With the widespread use of the flag of the red cross, its

[83] "Kyohoe t'ongsin" [Church News], *KS*, May 5, 1898.
[84] O. R. Avison to Robert E. Speer, December 16, 1898.
[85] O. R. Avison to Robert E. Speer, December 16, 1898.

meaning shifted from a symbol of peaceful patience to that of masculine power. To some extent, this paralleled the change in the nature of the church from a religious community to a sociopolitical association. Many people joined the church to receive protection and gain power.[86] After the Independence Club was disbanded by the Peddlers' Club in 1899, villagers joined the churches to protect their property from the abuse of the Peddlers. They erected flagpoles in the churchyards to protect against the Peddlers, robbers, and corrupt local officials. Others organized churches by themselves, erected flagpoles, and squeezed money from the villagers by flouting the missionaries' political power and abusing the name of the church. For example, during the Incident of Chŏng Kilddang in 1900–1901, armed Tonghaks, flying the flag of the red cross, beat innocent villagers in Imch'ŏn, Hansan, Sŏch'ŏn, Hongsan, and Namp'o of southern Ch'ungch'ŏng province and insulted local officials under the pretext of the Russian Orthodox Church. This was a typical church abuse case.[87] But when we consider the fact that traditionally there were many peddlers of ramie fabric trade in those towns, it might have been a conflict between peddlers (seemingly sponsored by the Korean government) and villagers (who needed to protect themselves under the flag of the red cross) when the Russian power was at its height on the Korean Peninsula.

The churches that displayed the flag of the red cross became known as places that ensured the protection of lives and property during wars and times of national crisis. After the Sorae Church, the Sap'yŏngdong Presbyterian Church in Munhwa, Hwanghae province, erected a flagpole in 1897.[88] The use of the flag of the red cross began to be popularized in 1898 and greatly proliferated from 1901 to 1903, when a great famine hit central Korea and flagpoles with the red cross flag were erected in the provinces of Hwanghae, Kangwŏn, and Kyŏnggi (figure 13).[89] Crop failure was so severe that it became a major factor in the fall

---

[86] Charles E. Sharp, "Motives for Seeking Christ," *KMF* (August 1906): 182.

[87] Yi Mahnyol, "Hanmal Rŏsia chŏnggyo ŭi chŏnp'a wa kŭ kyop'ye munje" [Propagation of Russian Orthodoxy and Its Abuse Case in the Late Chosŏn Period], in *Kŭrisŭdokyowa kyŏre munhwa* (Seoul: Kidoggyomunsa, 1985), 303–33.

[88] "Kyohoe t'ongsin" [Church News], *KS*, April 8, 1897.

[89] For more pictures, see Frederick A. McKenzie, *The Tragedy of Korea* (London: Soughton, 1908), 114; Jennie F. Willing and Mrs. G. H. Jones, *The Lure of Korea* (Boston: Woman's Foreign Missionary Society, Methodist Episcopal Church, 1913), 33.

of the Chosŏn Kingdom. Many people became beggars, hoodlums, or robbers. They were thirsty, thirsty for everything. Some of them, under the pretext of the powerful foreign missionaries, organized nominal churches to avoid heavy taxes or labor, to protect their lives, to extort money from people, or to win lawsuits for the hill gravesites where they had built fake ancestral tombs to lay claim to the gravesites. Many joined the Roman Catholic churches to be protected under French missionaries. It was in this context that many Protestant churches in the middle part of the peninsula built the flagpoles and hoisted the red cross flag as a banner of political power.

In 1901 James S. Gale, who had emphasized the separation of church and state, became editor of the *Christian News* and treated the erection of flagpoles as a serious issue.[90] In an editorial in May 1901, he equated the worship of the red cross flag, or forsaking Christ on the cross, to the Israelites' idol worship of the bronze serpent that Moses had made in the wilderness.[91] It was in this context that Arthur J. Brown, who visited Korea in the spring of 1901, recommended a nonengagement policy in politics. The missionaries sent a ministerial letter to the Korean congregations that emphasized the strict separation of church and state.[92] Gale continuously criticized flagpole building and insisted that the flagpoles be removed from churches. In early 1902 an idiom—"Pyongyang is famous for faith, Seoul for hymn-singing, and Yŏnbaekch'ŏn for the flagpoles"—was popularized among Protestant Christians. In the counties of Yŏnan and Paekch'ŏn in Hwanghae province, there were "about twenty flagpoles every ten or fifteen *li* and the wooden poles and flags were high and magnificent." Gale warned that if the flagpoles were not prohibited, a bigger problem would arise.[93]

Nevertheless, ecclesiastical authority and missionaries' demarcation could not stop the church abuse cases. Competition between Roman Catholics and Protestants aggravated the situation. The popularization of flagpoles in Hwanghae province was related to the Haesŏ Kyoan (the church abuse case in Hwanghae province) from 1900 to 1903. Two

[90] "Kittae ŭi ŭinon" [Discussion on the Flagpole], *KS*, May 9, 1901.

[91] "Ch'anmi" [Praising], *KS*, May 9, 1901.

[92] "Kyohoe nŭn ch'am ich'i rŭl panp'o hanŭn chŏndosil iji sesamg il ŭnon hanŭn kos i anida" [Church Is Not a Place to Discuss Secular Things but to Preach the True Doctrines], *KS*, August 1, 1901.

[93] "Midŭm gwa ch'anmi wa kitae" [Faith, Hymn Singing, and Flag Poles], *KS*, March 6, 1902.

FIGURE 13
A Typical Flagpole of a Rural Church, ca. 1902

groups competed to occupy the same religious market where a great famine, disorder in the local government's handling of land laws, over-taxation, and Japanese settlers' purchase of farmland had made people desperate. Some joined the Roman Catholic Church and forced villag-ers, including Protestants, to donate money to build churches. They defied the authority of the local government, insisting that they were governed under French law, not Korean law. The case was solved by the active intervention of Anglo-American missionaries and the central Korean government. The Protestant missionaries' victory over French missionaries stimulated the growth of Protestant churches in Hwang-hae, Kyŏnggi, and Kangwŏn provinces. Many Methodist and Presby-terian churches built flagpoles from 1901 to 1903 and hoisted both the red cross flag and the national flag.[94]

The Wŏnsan Revival in 1903 was initiated by Robert A. Hardie, who had repented of his failure in mission work, which was related to

[94] Yi Ŭnsŭng, "Kwangjyu Noromok Kyohoe hyŏngp'yŏn" [Situation of the Kwangju Noromok Church], *SW* (March 1901): 160; "Mutch'inae sae hoedang ŭl hŏngdangham" [Dedication of the New Church Building at Mutch'inae, Suwŏn], *SW* 1 (1901): 351; David H. Moore, "Our Mission in Beautiful, Hospitable Korea," *GAL* (September 1901): 407; Chang Wŏngŭn, "Hwanghaedo kyohoe chinboham" [Progress of the Churches in Hwanghae Province], *SW* (January 1903): 11.

128 — The Making of Korean Christianity

the flagpoles and church abuse cases in his district. Hardie visited Kim-hwa and Ch'ŏlwŏn counties in Kwangwŏn province four times within the year from the summer of 1901 and tried to disband fake churches organized by villagers who needed to protect themselves from the Ped-dlers' Club. Even local government officials could not handle them, fearing their supposed connections with foreign missionaries. Hardie labeled such a fake church "a den of thieves." He informed the local government of the principles of the church, in particular its separation from politics. He ordered the removal of all flagpoles from the churches. He excommunicated a class leader who refused and disbanded his class.[95] When the churches lowered the flags of the red cross, villagers and officials could discern the true churches from the false ones, and the problem of the abuse of the churches began to disappear. The church abuse cases, however, disturbed Hardie, and he could not resolve them until he repented his own lack of spiritual power, repented his superior-ity as a white man, and repented his triumphalism—and had his own awakening in the summer of 1903.

When Korea became a Japanese protectorate in 1905, the flags of the red cross reappeared in churchyards. In March 1906 Miss Catherine Wambold of Seoul reported that people had "a great desire to join some kind of society, and sometimes apply to the missionary to join what they call 'the Christian Society.' Sometimes of their own accord they raise a flag pole and buy a few hymn books and call themselves Christians."[96] Many people cried, "We do not have anywhere to depend on."[97] They joined local or national societies—including the pro-Japanese Ilchinhoe (Progressive Society), pro-French Roman Catholic churches, and pro-American Protestant churches—to protect their property and lives. The last groups used the red cross flag. At this stage some "entered a preach-ing service with political motives" and it was "the most natural thing to become mixed up with politics."[98]

In 1905 many Protestant leaders joined two larger societies. When the Ilchinhoe was organized in 1904, many Christians of Seoul, including

[95] R. A. Hardie, "R. A. Hardie's Report," in *Minutes of the Sixth Annual Meeting of the Korea Mission of the MEC, South* (Seoul: Methodist Publishing House, 1902), 32–33.

[96] Catherine Wambold to A. J. Brown, March 19, 1906.

[97] "A Great Awakening," *KMF* (January 1906): 51.

[98] W. L. Swallen, "Korean Christian Character," *AH* (November 1908): 511.

Sŏ Sangnyun, evangelist of Severance Hospital, actively participated in its meetings. However, secular leadership and political elements got control of the society in 1906. In the country districts, the branch societies used their power to extort money and pay off old grudges. Christian leaders found themselves "being stuck into the old whirlpool of passion, hatred, and violence," so one by one they left the society.[99] Another large society was the YMCA (Kidokkyo Ch'ŏngnyŏnhoe) in Seoul. Mr. Phillip L. Gillett (1872–1938), its first secretary, supported Koreans' anti-Japanese movement. The Methodist churches had their own young people's organization, the Epworth League, which was also called Ch'ŏngnyŏnhoe. Leaders of the Epworth League, especially of the Sangdong Ch'ŏngnyŏnhoe of the Sangdong Methodist Church in Seoul, engaged in the anti-Japanese movement. In this political milieu, "false" churches or societies took some elements of the Protestant church or YMCA and sprung up like bamboo shots after rain.[100] Under these circumstances, people said, "Village changsŭng are falling down, whereas Christian white flags and poles are rising up."[101]

On the other hand, mission schools hoisted the national flag and the red cross flag at graduation ceremonies, sports days, picnic days, and military exercises, sometimes using the American flag. An article of the Korea Daily News expressed that the "Jesus Church" was the hope of the nation, and passionate youth gathered at Protestant churches.[102] Interestingly, the diploma of the Presbyterian Seminary of Pyongyang in 1907 envisioned the evangelism of Korea through the image of the cross lightened by the torch of the gospel and engraved on the Korean Peninsula. Therefore, to some extent, from 1905 to 1910 the flagpoles represented Christians' anti-Japanese imperialist sentiments. This nationalistic nature differed from that of the flagpoles in the early 1900s, which were related to the church abuse cases and group egoism.

Both the flagpoles of the red cross of the local pseudo-religious groups and the nationalistic flags of the red cross of the churches in the 1900s expressed desires for self-defense and self-reliance. Nevertheless,

[99] C. A. Clark to A. J. Brown, December 8, 1906.
[100] C. A. Clark to A. J. Brown, December 8, 1906.
[101] Margaret L. Guthapfel, "Bearing Fruit in Old Age," KMF (January 1906): 41–44.
[102] "Singyojagang" [Self-Strengthening by Protestantism], TMS, December 1, 1905.

it was hard for missionaries to tell them apart, and so they prohibited the flying of any red cross flag in churchyards. The revivalist movement purified the churches and removed all the flagpoles by 1908. This was a result of the application of the American mission policy of the separation of church and state in Korea, a mission field that was becoming a Japanese colony. Now, instead of a red cross flag flying on a pole, a symbol of political power, a simple wooden cross fixed on the roof represented the nature of the churches as religious institutions officially loyal to the colonial government.

JAPANESE COLONIAL IMAGES OF THE RED CROSS, 1904–1910

From 1904 the Christian churches were unable to monopolize the symbol of the cross. The Japanese army's Red Cross hospitals and ambulances symbolized modern Japanese civilization, which was represented by advanced medical science as well as its military power, which was used to occupy Korea. During the war between the Japanese army and the Korean "righteous army" from 1907 to 1910,[103] Japanese soldiers shot many Korean militias to death literally on the cross. The cross was now associated with the powerful and contradictory images of healing and killing, or humanism and colonialism.

JAPANESE RED CROSS HOSPITALS AND NURSES

During the Russo-Japanese War, the Japanese empress presided over the meetings of the council of the Ladies' Branch of the Red Cross Society (hereafter RCS) of Japan to make bandages for the wounded.[104] A red cross was embroidered on the left side of the chest of the Japanese

---

[103] After the enforced abdication of Emperor Kojong and the dissolution of the Korean Army in 1907, voluntary Korean militia soldiers launched a guerrilla resistance movement against the Japanese army. Between 1907 and 1910, more than 25,000 Koreans participated in battles to keep the nation free from Japanese imperialism.

[104] During the Sino-Japanese War, the Japanese Army Medical Service, adapted from the German model, and the Naval Medical Department, originally formed and trained under the British, provided excellent medical services to the Japanese troops. More than 200,000 members of the Red Cross Society were dispatched to three hospitals and supported auxiliary sanatoria. "At these Red Cross Hospitals no fewer than 1,484 Chinese wounded were treated and discharged as cured" (Arthur Diosy, *The New Far East* [London: Cassell, 1904], 133–34).

nurses' uniforms. The international Red Cross Movement originated from European philanthropy and Christian charity. In Japan, however, the RCS was sponsored by the royal family and Shinto priests. The RCS restricted its association with Christianity and reinterpreted the logo of the red cross as the symbol of external neutrality, not a Christian altruism. Although the idea of the red cross was a Western import, the RCS argued, its sacred humanity could be based on traditional Japanese values. Thus the Japanese Army approved its military use as a symbol of universal philanthropy, Japanese civilization, and imperial care of soldiers.[105]

The Japanese army established two RCS hospitals in Incheon and Pyongyang and dispatched an RCS hospital ship to Korea. They hoisted large red cross flags at the hospitals (figure 14). There were thirty-two relief detachments along the battlefronts in Korea, and each detachment consisted of two physicians, one pharmacist, two chief nurses, and twenty nurses or attendants. Japanese nurses, wearing red cross caps, took care of wounded soldiers. The army ambulance parties had medical boxes marked with the red cross. The RCS in Japan was one of the symbols of the "new Japan" from the 1880s onward.[106] A total of 4,700 male and female nurses and attendants were working at the end of 1905.[107]

Korean leaders praised their work with the wounded. "On September 2, Yi Chun, Yi Hyŏnsŏk, and others distributed 10,000 copies of the appeal for the establishment of the society. They organized the Red Cross Society and expressed sympathy to Japan by fundraising for the treatment of the wounded soldiers of the neighboring country."[108] The Japanese nurses' white uniforms with the red cross impressed Koreans, who regarded Japan as the defender of the peace of East Asia against Russian expansionism. Koreans praised the victory of "yellow" Japan over "white" Russia and admired Japan's advanced civilization. The red

---

[105] Aya Takahashi, *The Development of the Japanese Nursing Profession* (London: RoutledgeCurzon, 2004), 50.

[106] George Kennan, "The Japanese Red Cross," *Outlook* (September–December 1904): 27–36.

[107] "The Sanitary Hygiene of the Japanese Army," *JAMA* (March 10, 1906): 747.

[108] Chŏng Sunman, "Kanghwarŭl pangch'ŏnghago tongnibŭl konggokeham" [Observing the Treaty and Strengthening Independence], *TMS*, September 7, 1905. The Korean Red Cross was established by Emperor Kojong's edict on October 27, 1905. The Japanese Red Cross Society annexed it in July 1909.

FIGURE 14
Japanese Red Cross Society Hospital in Incheon, Korea, 1904

cross of the Japanese army was a part of Japanese civilization that Korea sought. In Pyongyang, Korean Christians, American missionaries, and Japanese businessmen organized *Kusegun*, the first RCS, in 1904. Dr. James H. Wells joined this circle of humanitarianism and civilization by organizing the cholera corps, who wore red cross caps and uniforms.

The red cross as a symbol of Japanese medical science during the Russo-Japanese War, however, disguised the actual nature of Japanese civilization—imperialism. Yi Chun (1859–1907) and other Christian leaders, who supported the founding of the RCS in Korea in 1905,[109] did not decipher the hidden meaning of the red cross of the Japanese Army. Dr. James H. Wells (1866–1938) of the Presbyterian Hospital Chejungwŏn in Pyongyang was one of the most enthusiastic supporters of the Japanese rule of Korea in 1905. He stated that the "three most conspicuous features of modern enterprise in northern Korea" were three Ms—Protestant missions, American mines, and Japanese

---

[109] The Korean Red Cross Society Hospital was established behind the Kyŏngbok Palace, Seoul, in 1905. It moved to the south of Wŏnnam-dong in June 1906. The Taehan Hospital, financially supported by the Japanese government, took over its work from March 1907.

merchants.[110] He thought that the increasing Japanese merchants would add energy and activity and "the Japanese whetstone" would give an "edge" to the Koreans as nothing else could. "The Japanese method may not be the gentlest in the world, but it is effective at any rate, and it is the only method in sight."[111] Therefore he exclaimed "Dai Nippon! Banzai!" The editor of the *Korea Review*, Homer B. Hulbert, commented that Wells' opinion was extreme and that Japan's promise of the independence of Korea should be kept after the war.[112] In reply to the criticism of his article, Wells defended his "pro-Japanese proclivities" and praised the gentle and tactful transfer of the administration from Korea to Japan.[113] Wells did not belong to the minority's opinion, but he had many supporters, even among Koreans, in 1905.

EXECUTION OF KOREAN RIGHTEOUS ARMY ON THE CROSS, 1907–1910

When the Japanese police, gendarmes, and army executed Korean militia soldiers and suspicious farmers from 1904 to 1910, some were shot on the simple cross-shaped wooden frame. The first group to be executed was Korean farmers who protested the confiscation of their land, without reasonable compensation, to be used for the Japanese railroads from Pusan to Seoul or Seoul to Ŭiju. Homer B. Hulbert showed the brutality of Japanese military rule in Korea by publicizing the picture (figure 15) of the execution of three Korean farmers who destroyed some rails that bisected their rice field.

The second group to be executed was a bunch of soldiers from the Korean Righteous Army who fought for the independence of Korea from the Japanese protectorate government. From 1907 to 1909, around 120,000 Korean volunteer soldiers engaged in four thousand battles with the Japanese army and police. When the Japanese arrested Korean patriots, they gathered people in the villages and let them watch the Korean guerrilla "gangs" and "spies" being shot to death on the cross (figure 16). Or they executed Korean patriots on the cross without summoning Korean villagers. Japan annexed Korea in 1910 after killing

---

[110] James H. Wells, "Northern Korea," *KRv* (March 1905): 139.

[111] Wells, "Northern Korea," 140–41.

[112] "Editorial Comments," *KRv* (March 1905): 147–48.

[113] J. H. Wells, "An Appreciation," *KRv* (November 1905): 425–26.

FIGURE 15
Japanese Military Rule: Execution of Korean Farmers, 1904

about ten thousand Korean freedom fighters. Many of them were bound to a wooden cross and shot to death.

The cross was saturated with the blood of Korean nationalists. It is hard to find documentary evidence showing the reasons why Japanese killed Korean patriots on the cross.[114] Perhaps the Japanese attempted to make the scene a vivid lesson—the uselessness and inconsequentiality of resisting Japanese rule—for the Korean villagers, who were forced to witness the executions (figure 16). The executed Korean soldiers looked like powerless scarecrows and figureheads (*hōsuabi*). Based on the fact that the Japanese police and army allowed European and American newspaper correspondents to take the photographs of the events, we can presume that the Japanese colonial government intended to justify killing Korean "guerrillas" and "terrorists" by displaying their "civilized" process of execution. These images were widely circulated in newspapers and books. These propagandist pictures justified Japanese colonial rule of Korea by contrasting primitive Korean peasant terrorists

[114] Some readers might have thought that the executed Korean soldiers on the cross were Christians, for the cross was the central symbol of Christianity. Especially as three crosses were often used for the execution, people could regard the executed Korean patriots as Christians.

FIGURE 16
Execution of Korean Patriots, 1907

with well-trained Japanese soldiers. Once again the image of the cross became a fearful symbol of execution to the Koreans, as in the eighteenth and nineteenth centuries when the Chosŏn government had used it as a frame of flogging as well as a symbol of treason.

A new image of crucifixion, however, emerged during the Righteous Army War from 1907 to 1910. Now the cross became a symbol of Korean nationalism against Japanese imperialism, instead of being a symbol of treason against the Chosŏn government in the nineteenth century. The iconography of the Christian crucifixion in East Asia, started by G. Aleni's *Tianzhu jiangsheng chuxiang jingjie* (1637) and followed by the negative reactions of the Chinese, Japanese, and Koreans, came full circle in the form of the execution of Korean militia patriots on the cross by Japanese firing squad. Even though the missionaries and church leaders discouraged Korean Christians (both Catholics and Protestants) from participating in the military resistance, some Korean Christians assassinated pro-Japanese American diplomats like W. D. Stevens, assassinated by Chang Inhwan (1875–1930), a Presbyterian, on March 23, 1908; Japanese high officials like Ito Hirobumi, assassinated by An Chunggŭn (1879–1910), a Roman Catholic, on October 26, 1909; and Korean traitors like Yi Wanyong assassinated by Yi Chaemyŏng (1890–1910), a Presbyterian, on December 22, 1909 (Yi failed to kill him) for the independence of Korea. Others joined the Righteous Army for the same purpose.[115]

Overseas Koreans actively participated in the Independence Movement. In September 1909 *Sinhan Minbo* (New Korea) in San Francisco printed a special cartoon (figure 17) in which a Western-style Korean man is shown holding the cross of judgment in the name of *ch'ŏndo* (Heavenly Way) and *kongpŏp* (international law) and emptying four bullets into the mouth of a Japanese "Rising Sun" man, who wears a necklace (mining), the armband of the Red Cross Society (hospital), and shoes symbolizing the taking of diplomatic power and the railroad, and holds a cane (law) and a hammer (police) in each hand, while trying to consume Korea itself. Here the cross coexists with *kŭmch'ŏk* (the golden measure in the shape of the Korean Peninsula, which was a symbol of the authority and ruling power of the kings of Chosŏn) and a "taiji-shaped emblem" pistol (a symbol of Korean nationalism). Many Korean Americans and Korean Manchurians were Protestant Christians. The cross became a part of the nationalist movements among them. Actually six weeks later, on October 26, 1909, An Chunggŭn, a Roman Catholic soldier of the Korean Righteous Army in Manchuria, with complity of U Tŏkchun, a Presbyterian soldier, shot Itō Hirobumi, Resident-General of Korea, to death at the station of Harbin. Given this context, it is interesting to note this Japanese newspaper cartoon criticizing Protestant missionaries for allegedly administrating a political baptism of anti-Japanese sentiment to Korean Christians in the name of the crucified Jesus (figure 18). The Japanese government and journalists were suspicious of the connection between Protestantism and anti-Japanese nationalism.

In the conversion of Koreans to Protestantism from 1894 to 1910, the glyphomancy factor, which has been mostly neglected by many scholars, played a significant role, and this idiosyncratic glyphomancy factor was closely connected to the sociopolitical and millennial-geomantic prophetic elements in Korea. There are two reasons for the synthesis of these two factors: (1) conventionally, glyphomancy in Korea

---

[115] "Sein ŭi ŭihok: Tongyanggyohoe kamdok Harris kwangye" [Doubt of People: Bishop Harris' Relationship], *KN*, May 6, 1908; Gustave C. M. Mutel, *Mutel Chugyo Ilgi* [Journal of de Mgr. Mutel], vol. 4 (1906–1910) (Seoul: Han'guk Kyohoesa Yŏn'guso, 1998), 413, 433; "Chappo" [Miscellaneous News], *TMS*, December 23, 1909.

FIGURE 17
A Political Cartoon of
The Sinhan Minbo, 1909

FIGURE 18
Missionary Baptism, 1910

had been related to the geomantic prophecy of dynastic change or political revolts; and (2) contemporarily, as the nation building of Korea was rapidly deteriorating and hindered by internal corruption, natural disasters, and external invasions, the religious language and iconography had strong religious-political meanings for local people who needed to protect their lives and property from corrupt local officials and invading Russian and Japanese soldiers. There is no doubt that people joined churches for social, economic, and political reasons. But they did not always convert to Christianity for these reasons. Sometimes they needed a more compelling reason or the logic of persuasion, in which foreign Christianity could be interpreted meaningfully by familiar traditional religions on the one hand and, on the other hand, a Christianity could provide them with significant clues for decoding the unsolved passages of indigenous apocalyptic literature.

The initial encounters between the Roman Catholic crucifix and Korean Confucian scholars in China produced only negative images of the cross in the seventeenth and eighteenth centuries, and the crucifix remained the symbol of the cult of martyrdom of the Roman Catholic Church in the nineteenth century. The in-law politics of the royal familes and antiforeign policies of the Korean government and its Neo-Confucian ideology and ritualism, as well as the conservative theology of French missionaries, thwarted Koreans from finding the glyphomancy factor between Roman Catholicism and Korean religions. Jesus and Korean Catholic Christians were identified as religious and political victims.

Both Protestant missionaries and Koreans tried to change the image of the Protestant cross without using the crucifix of Roman Catholicism and the image of the crucifixion of Jesus. First, the image shifted from "religious martyrdom" to "religious glyphomancy" (the "A" direction in diagram 2 in the appendix). The enigmatic passages of the *Chŏnggamnok* were interpreted in relation to the Christian cross (十字架), and Protestant churches were regarded as sipsŭngjiji ("the place where the cross defeated evil and sin"). Here the image of Jesus was changed from a criminal victim to a cosmic victor who defeated the evil forces. This militant icon had a powerful meaning in the time of international wars and local conflicts. The way for salvation in the time of tribulations, kunggungŭlŭl, was found in Jesus' cross in the first letter 亞 of Abraham (亞伯拉罕), from whom Jesus was begotten. When such a decoding rhetoric was combined with the militant-political symbol of the flag of the red cross of the church and missionaries' extraterritorial status, the people in the famine- and war-afflicted areas of northern Kyŏnggi, southern Hwanghae, Kangwŏn, and southern Hamgyŏng provinces gathered in churches, which were composed of "soldiers of the cross," and sang a hymn of "Stand Up, Stand Up for Jesus." The Protestant churches evolved from religious shelters for the suffering people into semipolitical societies for villagers who attempted to protect their lives and property from the local government and the Peddlers' Club. The "Jesus flag" represented the conditional quality of conversion—political power based on the missionaries' extraterritorial rights and church members' solidarity and active agency for self-defense. The missionaries, therefore, ordered these churches to get rid of flagpoles, launched the revival movement, and strengthened church discipline to eradicate political elements and the rice Christians, who joined the church for material benefits rather than for religious reasons, from the church.

The Japanese images of the cross strengthened the conditional quality of the conversion to Christianity. The flag of the RCS hospitals and the red cross of the military ambulance symbolized modern Japanese civilization. Most medical missionaries welcomed Japanese rule and collaborated with the Japanese colonial government, believing that the Japanese government would be more effective than the Korean government at enhancing the health and hygiene of the people. However, when Japanese soldiers and policemen executed Korean patriots and militias of the Righteous Army on the cross, the meaning of nationalism was added to the image of the cross (the direction "B" in diagram 1 in the appendix). The scandalous iconography of crucifixion in the nineteenth century, a symbol of Christian martyrdom, changed into a political symbol of Korean nationalism (diagram 1, b → b').

Therefore, when the revival movement swept Korean Protestant churches from 1903 to 1908, the cross of the church and the flag of the Christian cross had multiple meanings—a place of redemption, a shelter for refugees, a fortress of the fighters for the interests of the community, political power protected by the missionaries' extraterritoriality, the fulfillment of the traditional prophecy that anticipated the coming of a messiah, Western science and technology, and Korean nationalism. These various meanings coexisted, contesting or complementing each other. One of the missionaries' intentions for the revival movement was to reverse the direction of the political glyphomancy of the cross to religious glyphomancy (diagram 1, a' → a). In other words, the missionaries presented Jesus as "the Lamb of God who bore all the sins of the world" and died for the salvation of the sinful souls, rather than as "the Lion of the tribe of Judah" and the savior (messianic king) of the world.

Four kinds of religious messianism—Tonghak *kaebyŏk* (the great transformation) millennialism, Protestant premillennialism and postmillennialism, and Japanese Shinto colonialism—competed with each other to occupy the Korean Peninsula, where Neo-Confucianism was losing its hegemonic power as the state ideology.[116] Vertically, two religious millennial eschatologies—American dispensationalism and Korean popular millennialism—were amalgamated into the symbol of the red cross flag (Jesus flag) in the church yard from 1894 to 1905. Horizontally, two political-cultural visions—the Christian postmillennial vision and the enlightenment movement—were infused for the nation building in the 1890s and 1900s. But these religious and national visions were distorted by Japanese pan-Asianism of the colonial government from 1905, which sought to civilize and colonize East Asia. Within the competition among various messianic and nationalistic factions, the *Chŏnggam-nok* and the icon of the cross played key roles in the imagination and construction of the heavenly kingdom on earth in the imagination of many.

---

[116] Around 1900 the Christian term "eschatology" was translated into *kaebyŏk-non* (Theory on Transformation) and *kyŏlgukhak* (Study of the Final Events) by Korean Methodists ("Chŏngdong syŏ sinhag ŭl kongbuham" [Theological Class Held at Chŏngdong], *SW* [March 1902]: 117). It seems that the traditional Korean religious understanding of the end of the world, *kaebyŏk*, had some influence on the formation of Protestant eschatology.

— 3 —

Spirits
Theories of Shamanism and Practice of Exorcism

귀신, Koui-sin, 鬼神. Génie: les dieux; les diables; démon; mauvais génies.

—F. C. Ridel, ed., *Dictionnaire Coréen-Français*, 1880

귀신 鬼神. A demon, evil-spirit, a devil.

—H. G. Underwood, *A Korean-English Dictionary*, 1890

귀신 1. 鬼神 (귀신) (귀신). Spirits; demons. See 신.

—J. S. Gale, *A Korean-English Dictionary*, 1897

In his *English-Korean Dictionary* printed in 1890, Horace G. Under-wood, the first American clerical missionary to Korea, defined a "witch" as "무당, 무녀, 마슐ᄒᆞᄂᆞ녀편네, 요슐ᄒᆞᄂᆞ녀편네" (*mudang, sorceress, wretch of magic, and wretch of witchcraft*).[1] Like Korean Confucian yangban elites and French Roman Catholic missionaries, Underwood rejected Korean demon worship, a broad term for folk religions, just as other Christian missionaries rejected magic and wizardry

---

[1] H. G. Underwood, *A Concise Dictionary of the Korean Language in two Parts: Korean-English* (Yokohama: Kelly & Walsh, 1890), 289. A Korean scholar, Song Sunyong, who had participated in compiling 한불ᄌᆞ뎐 *Hanbul chadyŏn: Dictionnaire Coréen-Français* (1880), assisted Underwood's linguistic work. Song transmitted French Catholic missionaries' study of the Korean language to American Protestant missionaries.

in different mission fields. He despised the female *mudang* of Korean shamanism and put their ceremonies on par with Western witchcraft and all of its stigmas. And he defined *kwishin* of Korean shamanism as "a demon, evil-spirit, a devil," which reflected the biblical terms and Christian demonology—the Greek "δαιμόνιον" was translated as "devil" in the King James Version (1611) and "demon" in the English Revised Version (1881), and the Greek "πνεῦμα πονηρὸν" was translated as "the evil spirit" in both versions. By contrast, in 1897 James S. Gale's Korean-English dictionary defined *mudang* as "a witch, a sorcerer, and a female fortune-teller."[2] And it defined *kwishin* primarily as "spirits," using a neutral academic term.

Why did Gale temper Underwood's appallingly negative definitions and use watered-down terms? What happened in the missionaries' study of Korean shamanism in those seven years and beyond? More significantly, did their theoretical and anthropological study influence their practice in the church? With these questions, this chapter examines three topics in the encounter between Christian demonology and Korean shamanism. First, it delineates the initial prohibitive regulations and teachings on demon worship, and the universal practice of decimating fetishes and household gods. Second, it investigates the development of Protestant missionaries' religious and anthropological study of Korea shamanism as "the real religions of Koreans" from 1890 to 1914. Third, it traces theological and ceremonial negotiations resulting from the encounter, especially from the practice of Christian exorcism of demon-possessed women by Korean Bible women.

In the process of iconoclastic encounters with Korean folk religions, Anglo-American missionaries took over a kind of mudang role of casting out "devils and evil spirits." Like French Catholic missionaries, North American Protestant missionaries attacked Korean folk religions on the one hand, and accepted the Korean shamanistic belief in the existence of the spirits, demon possession, and exorcism on the other.[3] The difference

---

[2] J. S. Gale, *A Korean-English Dictionary* (Yokohama: Kelly & Walsh, 1897), 353.

[3] Kim Chongsuh, "Early Western Studies of Korean Religions," in *Korean Studies New Pacific Currents*, ed. Suh Dae-Sook (Honolulu: Hawaii University Press, 1994), 141–57; Boudewijn C. A. Walraven, "Interpretations and Reinterpretations of Popular Religion in the Last Decades of the Chosŏn Dynasty," in *Korean Shamanism: Revivals, Survivals, and Change*, ed. Keith Howard (Seoul: Seoul PressxKorea Branch of the Royal Asiatic Society, 1998), 55–72.

between French missionaries and Anglo-American missionaries was the latter's semiscientific studies of Korean shamanism from the 1890s. The other difference was the hidden process of syncretistic blending of Protestantism with shamanism behind the evident confrontational collision of the two. Koreans' conversion to Protestant Christianity signified more than a one-way push toward enlightenment, modernization, and Christianization of centuries-old beliefs. Even though Protestant missionaries attacked shamanism, burned down fetishes and talismans dedicated to household spirits, and inspired people to abandon "superstitious" beliefs and behavior, many Korean Christians retained their traditional animistic worldviews. In turn, Protestant missionaries' biblical literalism and field experiences led them to accept a Christian version of exorcisms, although their rationalism and the constitutions of the churches denied miraculous healing in modern times. In this sense their field experiences overrode their backgrounds in modern science and theology. In the case of Korean shamanism, an overt Christianity–modernization nexus went hand in hand with a covert Christianity–indigenization nexus.

The syncretistic fusion between shamanism and other world religions was characteristic of Korea's multireligious identity, and Protestantism at the turn of the twentieth century was no exception. A major point of contact between shamanism and Protestantism was a kind of power encounter in healing. Korean people lived in fear of constant afflictions from diseases, disasters, and other imminent misfortunes and believed such phenomena were connected to "evil spirits," over which they had no efficacious means of control. When people saw that the medicines of missionaries could be effective against epidemics like cholera, some joined the church, believing that the missionaries had alternate methods of fighting "evil spirits" unknown to the mudang.

According to the traditional shamanistic worldview, diseases and disasters were caused by a breakdown in the cosmological harmony among spirits, human beings, and nature. A female mediator, mudang, would perform *kut* ceremonies to repel disasters and call for blessings. For example, a healing ritual, *uhwan kut*, attempted to release the anger of household gods or malevolent spirits of ancestors by appeasing them with sacred dancing and singing and offering sacrificial food on behalf of the patients and their family members.[4] The ceremony was intended

---

[4] See Laurel Kendall, *Shamans, Housewives, and Other Restless Spirits: Women in Korean Ritual Life* (Honolulu: University of Hawaii Press, 1985).

to restore the relationship between spirits and human beings, between the dead and the living, and between the body and the cosmic order. Usually mudang and their clients treated the spirits with due respect. Sometimes, however, mudang threatened "evil spirits" in the name of more powerful spirits, using weapons like swords and spears. In contrast, a blind p'ansu, a male practitioner, cast out demons from the afflicted by chanting incantations borrowed from Daoist and esoteric Buddhist sutras.

The coexistence of female shamans and Daoist/Buddhist male exorcists in dealing with diseases and "demon possession" represented the highly negotiated and syncretistic nature of Korean religions.[5] Although the private and public spheres were not completely divided, the roles played by Korean folk religions and Confucianism generally clustered into these two fields. Both domestic ancestral veneration and official governmental ceremonies were under the Confucian liturgical hegemony. However, mudang and p'ansu had spiritual leadership in the private sphere through household kut rituals. The privatization of Buddhism and Daoism by p'ansu reveals that subordinate religions took root in the private realm via syncretistic ceremonies in order to survive under a dominant religion. The encounter of Christianity and shamanism and the survival of the latter in the former followed a similar pattern.

Missionary Iconoclasm against "Demon Worship"

One of the features of nineteenth-century evangelical mission theory was iconoclasm. Missionaries condemned traditional Korean beliefs, including shamanism, as idol or demon worship. The missionary attack on shamanism was rooted in the propounded dichotomies of Christian monotheism against polytheism and Western rationalism against "superstition." Missionaries defined superstition as "an immense body of traditional belief" lying outside the realm of systematized religions like Confucianism and Buddhism and comprising "a vast number of gods, demons, and semi-gods, the legacy of centuries of nature worship."[6] Protestant missionaries and Korean Christian leaders attributed

[5] Lee Jung Young, *Korean Shamanistic Rituals* (New York: Mouton, 1981), 1–10; Walraven, "Religion and the City: Seoul in the Nineteenth Century," *Review of Korean Studies* 3, no. 1 (2000): 178–206.

[6] Jones, "The Religious Development of Korea," *GAL* (September 1891): 415–17.

the prosperity of Anglo-American nations to their belief in one God, and they maintained that the poverty, political weakness, and numerous disasters in Korea were divine punishment for the continued existence of idol worshippers.[7]

Received Tradition: Strict Prohibition of "Demon Worship"

The intolerant stance toward spirit and ancestor worship adopted by the Korea Protestant missions had its roots in existing policies of Chinese missions. Vernacular evangelistic tracts railed against superstitious worship of Buddhist images, Confucian ancestral spirits, Daoist Jade Shangdi, shamanistic spirits, and Roman Catholic icons. This notion of exclusive monotheism, derived from the first and second commandments, was incorporated into the baptismal requirements. In 1895 the Presbyterian missions adopted the seven rules set by John L. Nevius' Catechism for the Candidates for Baptism, as the "Rules for the Native Church in Korea."[8] The first rule was as follows: "Since the Most High God hates the glorifying and worshipping of kwishin, do not follow even the custom of ancestor worship, but worship and obey God alone."[9] Devil worship, ancestor worship, polygamy, and chusaek chapki (drunkenness, sensual pleasures, and gambling) were regarded as "enemies of the cross."[10] The Methodists set similar rules for the probationers in 1895 when they prepared a catechismal system in Korean.

The Sino-Japanese War from 1894 to 1895 sounded the death knell of the traditional worldview of East Asia—Sinocentrism. Religiously, the war served as a great conversion tool for Christian missionaries as doubt grew about the effectiveness of traditional spirits and Chinese gods against Japanese spirits and Western gods. Robert E. Speer, who visited Korea in 1897, stated, "Japan's victory over China made a profound impression in Korea, and made Western civilization and religion

---

[7] "Usyangnon" [Editorial: On Idols], *KH*, April 14, 1897; "Usyang ŭi hŏhan ron" [Emptiness of Idols], *KS*, July 29 and August 6, 1897; "Kyohoe t'ongsin" [Church News], *KS*, May 5, 1898.

[8] John L. Nevius, *Wi wŏnip kyoin kyudyo* [Catechism for the Candidates for Baptism], trans. Samuel A. Moffett (Seoul: Trilingual Press, 1895), 22a–24a.

[9] R. E. Speer, "Christian Mission in Korea," *MRW* 21 (1898): 681.

[10] W. D. Reynolds, "Enemies of the Cross in Korea," *Missionary* 32 (1899): 464–66.

more highly esteemed. It also demoralized spirit worshippers, killed the worship of Chinese gods, and cut away some of the remaining props of Buddhism."[11] Samuel A. Moffett (1864–1939), in Pyongyang, believed that the political and social changes had made it far easier for Koreans "to discard their former superstitions and to neglect the former ceremonies which have now lost much of their importance and significance."[12] Missionaries emphasized faith in Christ, who delivered people from fear of the hostile unseen. The message of the powerful Holy Spirit, who provided guidance and empowered believers to fight against the devil's continuous temptations, appealed to some Koreans who lived in the fear of "evil spirits." In 1897 K'ŭrisŭdoin Hoebo, the Methodist weekly, editorialized that the promise of the fullness of the Holy Spirit at the ascension of Christ was not only for the Jews at the Pentecost, "but also for the Koreans who believe in Jesus."[13] Moffett preached the following simple message to the people who came to the market: "I am not afraid of your evil spirits." Many people at the market who themselves may have been afraid of evil spirits stood around him to listen. "I'm not afraid of the spirits," he went on, "because I know the Great Spirit, Hanănim." The people at the market liked the familiar Korean sound of Hanănim. "I'm not afraid of little evil spirits because Hanănim loves me," he continued, "and if he loves me, no other spirit can hurt me. And the proof of his love is that he sent his only Son, Jesus, to die for me and save me."[14] It was this kind of culturally accommodating message that aided Christian conversion.

During his visit to the Methodist churches in China, Korea, and Japan from 1896 to 1898, Bishop Earl Cranston (1840–1932) preached at Sangdong Church in Seoul in October 1898. His topic was the power of the Holy Spirit. "I heard here that there are many people who are afraid of evil spirits. I have never seen the evil doings of evil spirits, but those of evil persons." He continued, "Why do people do evil things? The devil lets people do those things. What is the Holy Spirit according to

[11] Speer, *Report on the Mission in Korea of the Presbyterian Board of Foreign Missions* (New York: Board of the Foreign Missions, PCUSA, 1897), 7.

[12] S. A. Moffett, "The Transformation of Korea," *CHA* (August 1895): 136–37.

[13] "Yŏnsyŏ" [Editorial: A Speech], *KH*, March 31, 1897.

[14] Samuel H. Moffett, "The Life and Thought of Samuel Austin Moffett, His Children's Memories," in *The Centennial Lecture of Samuel A. Moffett's Arrival in Korea* (Seoul: Presbyterian Theological College and Seminary, 1990), 17.

the Scriptures? He is the Spirit who gives us love and peace and empowers us to do good things."[15] In a pastoral letter, Bishop Cranston and Superintendent William B. Scranton emphasized the importance of the baptism of the Holy Spirit that showed believers the path to heaven and provided them with the power to fight against the devil. Bishop Davis H. Moore (1838–1915), who sailed to China and resided in Shanghai, with jurisdiction over China, Korea, and Japan until 1904, visited Pyongayng in April 1901. He preached that Koreans shared many similarities to the Jewish people: Koreans were the descendents of the Semites according to the books of history, Koreans were of the same race as Jesus, Korean Christians became one body with Jesus, and therefore they should sincerely revere the Heavenly Father.[16] His message was well received by the Korean Christians, who believed that their ancestors in the ancient times had worshipped only one God, not "evil spirits."

PERFORMED CEREMONY: BURNING FETISHES AND DESTROYING DEVIL HOUSES

When Koreans decided to believe in the Jesus doctrine (Protestantism), missionaries instructed them to burn all "fetishes" dedicated to household gods and spirits, for those fetishes were regarded as idols and "fetish worship" as worshipping false gods.[17] Sometimes converts took their fetishes to the edge of the village and cast them as far as they could be thrown. In the eyes of missionaries, new converts needed to cut themselves from the past in a symbolic manner—by destroying the fetishes, which the Christians associated with "evil spirits" and old superstitious beliefs.[18] In 1899, when a mudang gave up her sorcery and decided to become a Christian, she gave the spiritual garment and little brass implements to

[15] "Sŏngt'anil kyŏngch'uk" [Celebration of Christmas], *KH*, December 28, 1898.

[16] "Mungammokk kuisyŏ P'yongyang kyohoe ye osim" [Bishop Moore Came to Pyongyang], *SW* (June 1901): 239–42.

[17] D. L. Gifford, *Everyday Life in Korea: A Collection of Studies and Stories* (New York: Revell, 1898), 115; Martha H. Noble, ed., *Journals of Mattie W. Noble, 1892–1934* (Seoul: Institute for Korean Church History, 1993), 65.

[18] Charles T. Collyer, "A Day on the Songdo Circuit," *KF* 1 (1901): 12–13; C. A. Clark, "The Destroying of a Household God," *KF* 3 (1903): 133; C. G. Hounshell, "The Lord Blessing His People," *KM* (May 10, 1905): 83; Arena Carroll, "Songdo, Korea," *WMA* 26 (1906): 410–11; Georgiana Owen, "Burning of the Fetishes," *Missionary* 41 (1908): 133–34.

Korean evangelists in Pyongyang.[19] Another mudang was required to destroy all her instruments and clothes used for kut ceremony when she was converted to Christianity, just as a number of Ephesians, who practiced sorcery, brought their scrolls together and burned them publicly at the time of the Apostle Paul (Acts 19:19).[20]

Korean evangelists and Christians burned the "devil" (fetishes) during their trips, and the burning performance and ceremony attracted village people. In the spring of 1899, Ch'ŏn Kwangsil, S. F. Moore's helper, burned the "devil" in three houses in Paech'ŏn, Hwanghae province. Moore met three Korean Christian men in another village, who brought a converted mudang and her equipment.

> They had been to four houses that morning to burn the "devil," and had brought along with them a mudang and her outfit, which included drum, gong, cymbals, rattle, necklace of 1,000 beads, garments of all shapes and colors, knives used when impersonating the fighting spirits, and a half dozen large pictures before which she formerly bowed, and sacrificed. She had a small building set apart for the worship of the spirits where all these things were kept. This room she has now set apart as a place of prayer to the true God. This sorceress cannot read, but listened eagerly to the Word and asked me to visit her house and pray. The Koreans here have turned these captured guns upon the enemy. The gong and cymbals make a deafening noise and they use them daily in street chapel meetings, Salvation Army fashion, to draw a crowd.[21]

Korean Christians then "turned these captured guns upon the enemy" by using the mudang's gong and cymbals to draw people to the daily street preaching.

When Charles D. Morris visited Hyech'ŏn, near Pyongyang in 1902, a Christian burned up "all the paraphernalia of his devil worship, and instead of what we destroyed we pasted on the walls of his home the Lord's Prayer, Apostles' Creed, and Ten Commandments in the Korean language."[22] From then on regular Sabbath and midweek services were held in that house. In 1905 Elmer M. Cable with his colleague Charles S. Deming spent a Sunday afternoon "destroying and

---

[19] M. Alice Fish to Franklin F. Ellinwood, April 29, 1899.

[20] W. G. Cram, "Rescued after Years of Bondage," *KM* (September 10, 1905): 149.

[21] S. F. Moore to F. F. Ellinwood, May 27, 1899.

[22] *Annual Report of the Missionary Society of the Methodist Episcopal Church* (New York: MSMEC, 1903), 363.

burning the fetishes in a number of the homes where the families had decided to become Christians" at Kyodong, Kanghwa Island.[23] Korean converts often transferred ideas from old belief systems onto Christianity, including the idea that Christianity simply had more powerful magic, with its own talismans and spirits. Evidence of remnant animistic ideas can be found in the hybrid belief that a piece of a Christian leaflet or a copy of the gospel, which had the smell of Western ink and contained the Jesus doctrine, could be a powerful talisman. Believers in such things put copies of the gospel under their fetishes to cast out their evil influence when they burned the fetishes.

Ella A. Lewis, who came to Korea in 1891, experienced a typical case of the burning ceremony in December 1905. She called it "a holocaust of fetishes."[24] With a Korean Bible woman, Miss Lewis visited many Christian homes in Suwŏn. She listened to stories "well worth hearing of their zeal in the devil's cause, and how he had tortured them when they gave up his service." She witnessed the tearing down and destroying of fetishes, and visited "three people who were said to be possessed with demons." In the village of Changjaenae, she taught women at a Bible class and visited, with them, several neighboring villages, and helped "make way with more fetishes." This time quite a crowd gathered to see the performance. Martha, the wife of Pak the patriarch, took the lead; she called for a gourd, took down a double bag from the wall, emptied the rice into it, and handed it back, saying, "This is enough for your evening meal"; then she went out to a corner of the yard and pulled down a little straw roof which covered a crock half filled with barley chaff (the rats had eaten the grain). She emptied this in the fireplace and burned the whole chaff. The woman of the house called out that there were more fetishes in the closet, being a little afraid to bring them out herself. Pak's wife lost no time in doing so and revealed a basket of summer garments. She tore off the parts that had been nibbled by mice and threw them in the fire. Then the Christian women sang "I Need Thee Every Hour" and another hymn, "My Soul Be on Thy Guard,"[25] believing that these hymns had great power over

[23] *Annual Report of the Missionary Society of the Methodist Episcopal Church* (New York: MSMEC, 1906), 326–27.

[24] Ella A. Lewis, "A Holocaust of Fetishes," *KMF* (May 1906): 134–35.

[25] George Heber Jones and William A. Noble, eds., *Ch'anmiga* [Hymnals] (Seoul: Trilingual Press, 1900), #90. The Korean hymn translated "temptations" of the second verse into "evil spirits."

"evil spirits." After prayer and another hymn, Miss Lewis delivered a short sermon and emphasized that they should have no gods but one. Then she moved on to another house, where they performed the same ceremony. In 1906 a large number of women had been persuaded by Sarah, a Korean Bible woman, "to destroy the various things in their houses connected with devil worship," and now when they were sick it was an established custom to send for a Bible woman to pray with and for them instead of sending for a mudang.[26]

Sometimes Christians destroyed idols, pictures, and fetishes in the shrines. In 1897 a group of Presbyterians of Seoul saw a few blind sorcerers in a shrine revering a statue of Buddha and some pictures of spirits. They exhorted "sorcerers" not to be the servants of the "devil" but to be the worshippers of God. The "sorcerers," fearing of the wrath of the spirits, hesitated to destroy the images. Thus with their consent, Christians broke the statues at one blow and burned all the pictures. They encountered another shrine on their way home. Several women were bowing before the pictures of a Buddha, Buddhist "gods," and spirits when the mudang were dancing. They preached the message of repentance and salvation to the women. The Christians pointed out that the government also prohibited people from performing superstitious ceremonies. The sorceresses were "quite at a loss and begged to be saved." The Christians tore down all the icons and burned them.[27]

A similar incident happened in Seoul on July 18, 1897. Some Christians went to Namsan (South Mount) and entered Kuksadang, a semi-official shrine of shamanism, which housed many pictures of spirits.[28] They called the owner of the shrine and explained to him the evil of spirit worship. As he agreed, Christians took off all the pictures and burned them, except that of T'aejo taewang, the first king of Chosŏn. *Tongnip Sinmun* praised them for doing their civic duty.[29] The year

---

[26] "Annual Report of the Bible Committee of Korea for 1906" (Seoul, 1906), 27.

[27] "Miryŏg ŭi paeham ira" [Destroying Maitreya Statues], *KH*, July 21, 1897.

[28] For the status of Kuksadang in the nineteenth century, see Walraven, "Interpretations and Reinterpretations," 57–58.

[29] "Chappo [Miscellaneous News]," *TS*, July 27, 1897. Walraven interpreted the veneration of the picture of King Taejo, a national symbol, as an "early form of modern national consciousness." See Boudewijn C. A. Walraven, "Religion and the City: Seoul in the Nineteenth Century," *Review of Korean Studies* 3, no. 1 (2000): 199–200.

1897 was the acme of the enlightenment movement, which emboldened some Christians to invade the shrines and destroy the icons of spirits.[30]

Applied Theory: Germ Theory Defeats Evil Spirits

Western medicine and missionary discourse on hygiene crusaded against Korean ideas concerning fate and "superstitions," which held that diseases were caused by the "entering" of kwishin, "evil spirits," into the body, and that their "leaving" or "going out" meant curing and healing.[31] Mrs. Isabella Bird Bishop found that "Koreans attributed every ill by which they are afflicted to demonical influence."[32] Hence medical missionaries understood that Korean doctors frequently used a needle in order that the "evil spirit" might find an exit.[33] People believed that kwishin caused malaria, typhoid, smallpox, cholera, measles, and the like. Smallpox was so common that it was called *mama* (your majesty) or *sonnim* (guest).[34] Both smallpox kwishin and measles kwishin were raised to the status of gods and worshipped in shamanic rites. A principal income source for a mudang was the *mamabaesong kut* (a ceremony for sending off the smallpox spirit). Also, indicating the influence of geomancy, many people believed that some diseases and misfortune were related to the inauspicious site of a house or ancestors' tombs.

Missionary doctors competed with local mudang as well as herbal doctors for the medical market. Many Koreans became interested in Christianity through the treatment of their diseases by Western medicine and surgical skills. Christians advised their neighbors to see the great Western physician rather than a mudang. In 1897 Dr. E. Douglass Follwell, who was sent to Pyongayng in 1895, met a man who was suffering emphysema. He had spent twenty yen for mudang to heal

[30] "Chappo [Miscellaneous News]," *TS*, August 19, 1897.

[31] "Kyohoe t'ongsin" [Church News], *KS*, December 9, 1897; H. N. Allen, *Things Korea: A Collection of Sketches and Anecdotes, Missionary and Diplomatic* (New York: Revell, 1908), 203–4.

[32] Isabella Bird Bishop, *Korea and Her Neighbors* (London: John Murray, 1898), 405.

[33] Lavinia L. Dock, "Foreign Department: Korean News," *American Journal of Nursing* 7 (1907): 34.

[34] Chi Sŏgyŏng (1855–1935) introduced the cowpox vaccination to the Korean public in 1879. In October 1895 the Korean government issued an ordinance on smallpox, Korea's first act of modern vaccination. By 1908 it was reported that nearly all people under the age of thirty were immune to smallpox due to the wide use of the cowpox vaccine.

his disease. Mudang said his trouble had come because his father and mother were buried in bad ground, and not until the remains were removed to a better location would the disease abate. He did as they told him, spending a large sum of money, but the disease grew worse. At last, after all his resources were exhausted, a friar told him if he came to Pyongayng a foreign doctor might heal him. Dr. Follwell performed a surgical operation; the man left in good health and with a public confession of faith in Jesus Christ.[35] In 1901 there was a case concerning a mudang in Suwŏn who had failed to cure her own sick child for three years. She finally brought the child to Severance Hospital in Seoul, where the boy soon recovered. She became not only a believer but also a voluntary evangelist in her village, converting all of her family members and gathering together a Christian congregation of seven women and six men.[36]

Germ theory was an especially effective weapon at destroying people's belief in the dominion of spirits over diseases. The first thing missionary doctors emphasized was boiling water to kill invisible *migyun* (bacteria). They taught that drinking contaminated water caused diarrhea, dysentery, cholera, malaria, indigestion, fever, and so on.[37] There were several cholera epidemics in Korea around the turn of the century. In the summer of 1886, cholera swept through the country. The government did not take proper precautionary measures, and those who fell ill were uncared for. "Booths were erected, at considerable expense, about the city, and the cholera god was prayed to. Battalions of soldiers fired off charge after charge to scare him out of the Palace grounds."[38] Koreans called cholera *chwit'ong* (rat pain), believing that the Rat Spirit brought the disease. Dr. John W. Heron formulated cholera medicine, composed of sulphuric acid, opium, camphor, and capsicum, and the officers of the government hospital (Chejungwŏn) distributed it to the people who came to hospital, as many as a hundred a day.[39] However, in

[35] *Annual Report of the Missionary Society of the Methodist Episcopal Church* (New York: MSMEC, 1897), 244.

[36] "Suwŏn Sanggumyŏn Imuri Kyohoe" [Imuri Church, Sanggu-myŏn, Suwŏn], *KS*, January 2, 1902.

[37] J. Hunter Wells, *Wisaeng* [Introduction to Hygiene] (Seoul: Religious Tract Society, 1907), 5–12, 61–62.

[38] H. N. Allen, "Report of the Health of Seoul for the Year 1886" (Yokohama: University Press, 1886), 5.

[39] John W. Heron to Frank F. Ellinwood, August 27, 1886.

Seoul alone, more than six thousand bodies were carried out for burial in two months in 1886.[40]

When cholera reached Seoul in 1895, the government let Dr. Oliver R. Avison (1860–1956) take responsibility for the government cholera hospital. Many foreign doctors and missionaries volunteered to assist in this work and tried to enforce sanitary regulations and disseminate germ theory to reduce the number of victims. The plague wiped out five thousand people in Seoul and its vicinities in a few months. The missionary staff saw as many as two thousand cases at the hospital and the shelter. Because people believed that cholera was caused by the Rat Spirit's entrance into the body, they posted pictures of cats on the front doors of their houses. Dr. Avison and his staff prepared large posters, which began, "Cholera is *not* caused by an evil spirit. It is caused by a very small particle of living matter called a germ."[41] Proclamations were posted on the city gates, telling people to go to the Christian hospital. When the plague was over, the government sent a letter of gratitude to the missions. The missionaries' hospital work and their extreme emphasis on "the germ" helped both the choleric victims and the publicity campaign against the belief that animistic ideas were tied to disease.[42]

Cholera swept through the country again in August and September 1902. For example, 50 people died among the 92 cases in Chemulpo, and 11 died among the 20 cases in Sŏnch'ŏn, north P'yŏng'an province, on August 17. In September between 50 and 250 deaths happened daily in Seoul.[43] Although some of the most fervent Christians perished, they demonstrated their faith even at death. "The heroism with which the Christian met the disease was in strong contrast with the terror that it inspired among the non-Christian communities. Frequently our people died with a prayer or a word of exhortation on their lips."[44] A Christian woman testified that formerly she believed that "evil spirits were angry with people and sent the scourge of cholera as a punishment; but this

[40] Allen, *Things Korea*, 207.
[41] Allen D. Clark, *Avison of Korea: The Life of Oliver R. Avison, M.D.* (Seoul: Yonsei University Press, 1979), 106; emphasis original.
[42] Graham Lee, "Korean Christians," *MRW* (November 1896): 866; L. H. Underwood, *Fifteen Years among the Top-Knots, or Life in Korea* (New York: American Tract Society, 1904), 136–45.
[43] "The Public Service: Cholera," *JAMA* (November 1, 1902): 1150, 1358.
[44] *Annual Report of the Missionary Society of the Methodist Episcopal Church* (New York: MSMEC, 1903), 361

year the doctor preachers have taught us that it is little insects that get into the water, enter our bodies, and destroy the body; they have no power over the soul." Another confessed, "We know that Satan, going about among us, is more to be dreaded than any cholera germs. I pray God that we may be as diligent in escaping from sin as we tried to be in cholera time."[45] When Western medical science was able to kill the germs of cholera, it eased the minds of Korean converts, who no longer felt they were being punished by spirits or were helpless in the face of disease. The fear of spirits was replaced by the fear of Satan, and germs were painted as physically and spiritually microscopic.

The cholera scourge in 1903 opened up opportunities for the "the Jesus doctrine" and missionary doctors to challenge the Koreans' belief in the power of the shamanistic spirits. As Dr. William B. McGill stated, "The doctors in Korea are holding the tail of the cow while the missionaries are sucking the milk."[46] Medical missions had prepared the soil for more than a decade, and evangelistic missions could now gather converts. They presented Jesus as the Divine Physician who was able to cure the disease of not just the body, but also the soul.[47]

Nevertheless, missionaries were well aware of the prevalence and power of the shamanistic idea of spirituality, even after the destruction of the visible fetishes. The force with which shamanism opposed to the Korean Christian was negative rather than positive. Koreans would quickly cast away the absurd fetishes that adorned their homes and come to regard with intense disgust the superstition they once held; but they found themselves for a time almost unable to comprehend the spiritual conceptions and ideas that are the very essence of Christianity.[48]

Missionaries emphasized the idea that it was not human efforts but the power of the Holy Spirit that could overcome the "evil spirits." The battle between the Holy Spirit and "evil spirits," which will be discussed later, and the defeat of the latter led many Koreans to turn to Christianity. Shamanistic views on spirits and demon possession marked a point of contact with the biblical view of these concepts.

[45] Mattie W. Noble, "After the Cholera—Native Testimonies in a Korean Prayer Meeting," *WMF* (January 1903): 4.

[46] Robert G. Grierson, "The Place of Philanthropic Agencies in the Evangelization of Korea," *KF* (November 1904): 200.

[47] C. C. Vinton, "Literary Department," *KR* (September 1896): 377.

[48] Jones, "Obstacles Encountered by Korean Christians," *KR* 2 (1895): 149.

Protestant Missionary Study of Korean Shamanism

Starting in 1894, G. Heber Jones and other Protestant missionaries began to use "shamanism" as a general term to describe all folk religions in Korea. Recalling that the word "shaman" became a common word at the end of the eighteenth century and that studies on "shamanism" as a scholarly concept and as a heuristic term in the West coving all of the various magico-religious activities date back to the late nineteenth century,[49] it is important to track down the genealogy of this neologism "shamanism" among North American missionaries in Korea. They pioneered the semiscientific study of Korean religions and began to use the single term "shamanism" to refer to the various types of nature and spirit worship in Korea. They also used other popular terms such as superstitious fetishism, sorcery, taboos, devil/demon/spirit worship, and animism in order to replace "backward and primitive" Korean religions with Protestant Christianity. Therefore it is not surprising that in the missionaries' discourse, shamanism emerged as a significant other.

In the Protestant missionary circle, the barely explored terrain of Korean shamanism was mostly mapped by five missionary scholars of Korean studies—George Heber Jones, an American Methodist minister; Eli B. Landis, an American Episcopalian medical doctor; James S. Gale, a Canadian Presbyterian minister; Homer B. Hulbert, an American educator and journalist; and Horace G. Underwood, the first American Presbyterian clerical missionary to Korea. The following comparison of their discourses and definitions of the terms "shamanism," "mudang" (shaman), "kut" (shaman's ritual performance), and various "kwishin" (spirits) demonstrates the missionary origin of Korean shamanism. At the same time, it reveals the development of missionaries' religious understanding of Korean shamanism from a loaded definition of "demon worship" to an academic and neutral one of "spirit worship."[50]

---

[49] Eva Jane N. Fridman and Mariko N. Walter, eds., *Shamanism: An Encyclopedia of World Beliefs, Practices, and Culture* (Santa Barbara, Calif.: ABC-CLIO, 2004), xvii, xxi, 142. French Catholic missionaries in Korea did not use the term "shamanism" in the nineteenth century.

[50] See Bang Won-il, "Ch'ogi Kaesingyo sŏngyosa ŭi Han'guk chonggyo ihae" (The Early Protestant Missionaries' Understanding for Korean Religion) (Ph.D. diss., Seoul National University, 2011).

GEORGE HEBER JONES

Jones was born in Mohawk, New York, and was educated in the public schools of Utica, New York. He began his work in Seoul in 1888 as one of the youngest missionaries.[51] When he was teaching at Paejae School from 1888 to 1893, he studied the Korean language, culture, and history with a Korean teacher, Ch'oe Pyŏnghŏn, who became one of the first yangban Christians in 1893. During these years Jones took college courses through correspondence and received a correspondent bachelor's degree from American University, of Harriman, Tennessee, in 1892.[52] Jones was appointed to Chemulpo as a pioneer missionary to the port city in 1892. He began editing the *Korean Repository* in 1895, and by 1900 he had become one of the foremost scholars on Korea. He was regarded as the authority on Korean shamanism in 1901.[53] He founded *Sinhak Wŏlbo* (Biblical and Church Monthly) for training Korean leaders and theological students in 1900. He also taught church history and other subjects at the Methodist seminary in Seoul. He returned to the Unites States in 1909. As 1910 marked the twenty-fifth anniversary of the Korea mission, he campaigned for the Korea Quarter-Centennial Movement until March 1912 and was appointed a secretary of the Board of Foreign Missions of the Methodist Episcopal Church. He attended the World Missionary Conference, held in Edinburgh in 1910, as a delegate of Korea. He taught mission studies as a visiting professor at Boston University School of Theology and at other universities.[54] One of his academic achievements was a book-length typescript, *The Rise of the Church in Korea*, written from the perspective of fulfillment theory in 1915. It was the first history book of early Korean Protestantism.

His early study of Korean folk religions was influenced by French Catholic missionaries' terminology, such as demonolatry, demon worship, exorcism, and superstition, and American writers' rhetorical

---

[51] He joined the Utica YMCA in 1883 and worked for a telephone company from 1883 to 1886. He worked as assistant secretary of the Rochester YMCA from 1886 to 1888.

[52] James T. White, ed., *The National Cyclopaedia of American Biography*, vol. 18 (New York: James T. White, 1922), 263; W. A. Noble, "George Heber Jones: An Appreciation," *KMF* (June 1919): 146.

[53] Hulbert, "Exorcising Spirits," *KRv* (April 1901): 163.

[54] Noble, "George Heber Jones: An Appreciation," 146; White, *National Cyclopaedia of American Biography*, 263.

notion that there was no religion in Korea.[55] As he did not regard demon worship as a religion, he thought that Korea had no religion. In 1891, therefore, he argued that a country without religion was an opportunity for Christianity.[56] For a female shaman mudang he used the term "witch," which appeared in Underwood's dictionary.[57] Jones emphasized the phenomenon of "pagan toleration" or syncretism in Korean religions. In 1892 he established a new mission station in Chemulpo and worked among the people in the port and on Kanghwa Island. His contact with the seaside people acquainted him with their shamanic practices. He argued that the belief that household gods dwelled in the fetishes was the religion of the Korean homes.[58]

In 1894 Jones began to use the term "shamanism" and focused more on household gods and fetishes. His basic understanding of shamanism was that it was a form of "nature worship" and "demon worship," and his attitude was that of a triumphant power encounter. He viewed the Korean term kwishin (spirit) to be equivalent to the Greek term daimon (demon).[59] And he mentioned that the most conspicuous examples of Koreans' superstitions were the taboo and the common belief in "evil spirits."[60] In 1895 Jones affirmed that Koreans developed "the system of spirit worship which is technically known as shamanism," and that its spirits were identical with the Greek term daimon, in a neutral sense, not a biblically negative sense. Jones' new understanding of Korean shamanism influenced others, including Isabella Bird Bishop, who visited Korea four times from 1894 to 1897 and published a famous travelogue, *Korea and Her Neighbors*, in 1898. According to

[55] Claude Charles Dallét, *Histoire de l'Eglise de Corée* (Paris: Librairie Victor Palmé, 1874), chap. 11, 139–50; W. E. Griffis, "Korea and Its Needs," *GAL* 13 (1888): 371. Dallét acknowledged the existence of Korean Confucianism and Buddhism, yet he accepted other Catholic missionaries' understanding of Korean shamanism as superstitious demon worship, mainly influenced by Marie-Nicholas-Antoine Daveluy and Michel-Alexandre Petinicolas. See Cho Hyŏnbŏm, *Chosŏn ŭi sŏngyosa, Sŏngyosa ŭi Chosŏn* [Missionaries of Chosŏn, Chosŏn of Missionaries] (Seoul: Han'guk kyohoesa yŏnguso, 2010).

[56] Jones, "Religious Development of Korea," 417.

[57] French missionaries translated *malin esprit* as "kwishin," *sorcièr* as "paksu," and *sorcière* as "mudang" (Férron, *Dictionnaire Français-Coréen*, 286).

[58] Jones, "The People of Korea," *GAL* (October 1892): 464–66.

[59] Jones, "The People on the Chemulpo Circuit in Korea," *GAL* (June 1894): 282–84.

[60] Jones to Harry H. Fox, June 11, 1894, in Christopher T. Gardner, *Corea* (Brisbane: Australian Association of the Advancement of Science, 1895), 28–29.

Jones and Bishop, Koreans believed that these spirits were not always evil, but that fortune and misfortune of human life depended upon them. Jones thought that Korean shamanism was an answer to the mystery of human sufferings.[61]

In the article "Obstacles Encountered by Korean Christians," Jones asserted that Confucianism and shamanism were entrusted with different roles in the realm of Korean religious life. Because Confucianism ignored the divine and supernatural side of religion and reduced it to a series of regulations to govern human relationships, Koreans found spiritual fulfillment in "the system of spirit worship." Confucianism took charge of morality and shamanism spirituality. Thus when a Korean man turned to Christianity, he had to cope not only with opprobrium and scorn among friends and violent opposition of family and relatives, but also with mental and spiritual shackles. Jones was concerned with shamanism's negative influence on Korean Christians. A Korean would "throw away the absurd fetishes which adorn his home and come to regard with intense disgust the superstition he once held; but he finds himself for a time almost unable to rise to the spiritual conceptions and ideas which are the very essence of Christianity."[62] Jones believed that only divine help could break Koreans' mental and spiritual shackles of shamanism and would make them the free people of God.

In 1901 Jones published a paper, "The Spirit Worship of the Koreans," which was his full-blown study on the topic. He defined Korean shamanism technically as "spirit worship" and classified the spirits of "the pantheon of shaman." He used an academic term, "spirits," again for kwishin, for their nature was not fixed, but flexible, between benevolent and malicious. He did not pay much attention to the contents (dance, prayers, and songs) of the ceremonies of mudang, nor to female mudang and male p'ansu themselves. He listed seventeen spirits: his eyes moved from the outside shrines dedicated to the spirits (*Obang Changgun, Shinjang, Sanshin, Sŏnghwangdang, T'ojijishin, Ch'ŏnshin, Toggaebi, Sagwi,* and *Yongshin*) to the household gods dwelling in the fetishes in the house (*Sŏngju, T'ŏju, Ŏpju, Kŏllip, Munhojishin, Yŏkshin, Cheung,* and *Samshin*). He contended, "This is the religion of the Korean home and these gods are found in every house." He affirmed, "Their ubiquity

---

[61] Jones, "Obstacles Encountered by Korean Christians," *KR* 2 (1895): 146–47.
[62] Jones, "Obstacles Encountered," 147–48.

is an ugly travesty of the omnipresence of God."[63] He particularly mentioned "the ritual of exorcism" in relation to *toggaebi*, which was "a counterpart of the western ghosts" that haunted "execution grounds, battle-fields, and the scene of murder and fatal disaster." He believed that toggaebi stories and toggaebi folklore were a feature of Korean shamanism. Regarding *ŏpju* (a snake spirit in charge of the fortune of the family), he argued, "This is the symbol of one of the cardinal features of shamanism, namely luck," and compared the Christian idea of blessing with the lower level of luck in shamanism.[64]

Jones' term of "spirit worship" for shamanism might have been influenced by Edward B. Tylor's (1832–1917) theory of animism and his definition of religion as "the belief in spiritual beings."[65] Tylor asserted that the human mind and its capabilities were equitable worldwide and that religions existed universally and evolved from primitive to higher ones. When a society evolved, certain customs were retained that were unnecessary in the new society, like remnant "baggage," which Tylor called "survivals" of primitive culture. He argued that animism as a natural religion was the essence and foundation of all religions, and that the chief feature of animism was a belief in the existence of spirits. Jones identified Korean shamanism with animism in 1907 by saying that "the most universal belief among the Koreans is that of spirit worship, of Animism."[66] His use of animism was shared by other missionaries, including H. G. Underwood.[67]

In 1910 Jones attended the World Missionary Conference, held in Edinburgh. The Report of Commission IV, *The Missionary Message in Relation to Non-Christian Religions*, did not discuss Korean religions. It mentioned that Christian monotheism and the unity and omnipotence of God were the most appealing message to animism in Asia and Africa, including Korea.[68] When Jones attended its discussion session,

---

[63] Jones, "The Spirit Worship of the Koreans," *TKB* 2 (1901): 58.

[64] Jones, "Spirit Worship." Altaic etymology of "kut" is luck, fortune, or fate.

[65] Edward B. Tylor, *Primitive Culture: Researches into the Development of Mythology, Philosophy, Religion, Language, Art, and Custom* (London: John Murray, 1871), 1:377, 384; Bang Won-il, "Ch'ogi Kaesingyo sŏngyosa," 145–46.

[66] Jones, *Korea: The Land, People, and the Customs* (Cincinnati: Jennings & Graham, 1907), 49.

[67] H. G. Underwood, *The Religions of Eastern Asia* (New York: Macmillan, 1910), 113.

[68] WMC, *Report of Commission IV. The Missionary Message in Relation to Non-Christian Religions* (Edinburgh: Oliphant, Anderson & Ferrier, 1910), 218.

he emphasized that if the Christian message were to be appealing to the educated Koreans, Chinese, and Japanese, it should offer the complete and satisfactory answer to "the great conditions and changes in society through modern industrialism, commercialism, and municipalism."[69] As his concern shifted from the animistic religion of older generations in Korea to the rapidly changing culture of younger generations in East Asia, he paid great attention to the social issues and the social responsibility of Christian missions from 1909.

Jones regarded shamanism as the real religion of the Korean people, but he criticized its lack of strict morality. He argued that the three religions coexisted for ordinary Koreans, overlapping and even deeply interpenetrating. Buddhism accepted Confucian ethics while absorbing shamanism. In turn, shamanism freely accepted the transcendental objects of Confucianism and Buddhism. What was lacking in shamanism was the ethical dimension. Although Koreans theoretically distinguished the three, in practice they believed in all of them. A Korean man received a Confucian education but sent his wife to the Buddhist temple to pray for descendants; if he became ill he often sought a shaman or soothsayer. A Korean attained happiness through the united help of these three religions. Shamanism was the oldest and leading religion in Korea, and spirit worship was at its core. Jones asserted that Koreans were very "religious" because they had a tendency to spiritualize all natural things; they had "a sense of dependence" on an existence superior to themselves; they had established "an intercommunicative dimension between humans and spiritual entities"; and they seriously searched for being free from pains and sufferings of souls. He appreciated this spirituality of Korean shamanism, which could pave the way for the Christian idea of divine–human communion.[70]

Jones' assertion of Korean's rich religiosity was based on the contemporary Western theories of religion—Tylor's animism as natural and spiritual worship, Schleiermacher's definition of religion as "the feeling of absolute dependence," and Hegel's "perfect freedom." This shows that Jones was a good student of religious studies as well as of missiological studies of the late nineteenth century. In this sense, we can say that Protestant missionaries were pioneers of the modern scientific

---

[69] WMC, *Report of Commission IV*, 304.
[70] Jones, "Spirit Worship," 37–41; Jones, "The Native Religions," *KMF* 4 (1908): 11–12.

study of Korean religions. And because of their progressive theology of Korean shamanism and the existence of vernacular God Hanănim, the Korea missions had little dilemma integrating "primal" religion into fulfillment theory and utilizing the vitality and immediacy of shamanic faith for church growth.

ELI BARR LANDIS

Dr. Eli Barr Landis (1865–1898), a University of Pennsylvania graduate, joined Bishop Corfe's Korea mission of the Church of England in 1890 and worked in Chemulpo until he died of typhoid in 1898. "From the day of his landing till his death, he gave himself up to his medical work and to studying the Chinese and Korean languages and the people of the country, their history, customs, beliefs, and lines of thought."[71] Through diligent study, he became proficient in Korean history, folklore, and religions as well as Confucian classics like *The Mencius*. The Church of England's exorcism ministry tradition might have propelled his interest in Korean shamanism and its healing ceremonies.[72]

In 1895 Landis claimed that Japanese Shinto was a development of Korean "shamanism."[73] This argument developed from Percival Lowell's comment in 1886 that Korean "demon worship" and Japanese Shinto were related "forms of the common aboriginal superstitions."[74] Landis stated that the major difference was that "whereas in Japan the exorcist is a Shinto priest, in Korea a woman is the chief actor in the scene." Landis' comments implied that Korean shamanism, as the origin of Japanese Shinto, was older and more primitive than the latter, and that Korea was not a country of no religion, but a nation with shamanism as a major religion, as Japan was with Shinto.

In an 1895 article, "Notes on the Exorcism of Spirits in Korea," Landis classified thirty-six spirits of shamanism into three categories.[75]

---

[71] "Obituary Notice: Dr. E. B. Landis," *Journal of the Royal Asiatic Society of Great Britain and Ireland* (1898): 919.

[72] For his researches on Confucian rites, see Landis, "Mourning and Burial Rites of Korea," *Journal of the Anthropological Institute* (May 1896): 340–61; Landis, "A Royal Funeral," *KR* (April 1897): 161; Landis, "The Capping Ceremony of Korea," *Journal of the Anthropological Institute* (May 1898): 525–31.

[73] Landis, "Notes on the Exorcism of Spirits in Korea," *Chinese Review* 21, no. 6 (1895): 399.

[74] Percival Lowell, *Chosen: The Land of the Morning Calm* (London: Trubner, 1886), 207.

[75] Landis, "Notes on the Exorcism of Spirits in Korea," 399–404.

This was the first comprehensive classification of the spirits of Korean shamanism. Of those in the third category, most were wandering spirits of the dead who died of tragic accidents or social injustice. In many cases a mudang was invited to conduct an exorcism ceremony for spirits in turmoil.[76] Landis classified two types of mudang—the possessed (destined) and the hereditary (educated). As he lived in Chemulpo, he could see both types because the possessed mudang were prevalent north of the Han River and the hereditary ones to the river's south. He was also aware of yangban mudang, who practiced only for the higher-class families.[77] Dr. Landis was the first missionary to describe the "sickness" of a mudang during the initiation period. The process of becoming an exorcist was as follows: (1) possession by the spirits and sickness; (2) dreams of peach trees, a rainbow, a dragon, or a man in armor; (3) oracles; (4) an announcement in the name of three messengers from heaven, earth, and lightning; (5) an offering of flowers; (6) getting the clothes of a deceased sorceress; (7) exorcism of the donor's house; (8) obtaining rice at neighboring houses; (9) writing names on a tablet and placing them in a little house to invoke blessings; and (10) going to other houses to exorcise them.

As a medical doctor, Landis paid much attention to the initiation sickness of a mudang and her healing ceremony. He also studied Korean traditional herbal medicine in Hŏ Chun's *Tongŭi pogam* (Precious Mirror of Eastern Medicine, 1610), which combined the Confucian medical system with the Daoist one.[78] Landis consistently used "spirits" instead of "demon," which reflected his academic attitude toward Korean religions. In another paper on Korean funeral, he called the ghost of the dead a "spirit," which was the object of Confucian ancestor worship.[79]

---

[76] Landis mentioned the exorcism of the following twelve spirits: goods and furniture (chief of all exorcism), ridge pole, Yi family, mountain, attendants of Yi family, ancestors, smallpox, one's own self, animal, jugglers, trees and hilltops, and spirits that take possession of young girls and change them into exorcists.

[77] Landis, "Notes on the Exorcism of Spirits in Korea," 404.

[78] Landis, "Notes from the Korean Pharmacopoea," *China Review* 22, no. 3 (1896): 578–88. This was a translation of the section on invertebrates of *Tongŭi pogam*.

[79] Landis, "Mourning and Burial Rites of Korea."

James S. Gale

Gale arrived in Korea in 1888 as a volunteer missionary of the YMCA of the University of Toronto. He joined the Korea mission of the PCUSA in 1891. He married the widowed Mrs. Harriet E. Heron in Seoul in 1892 and adopted her two daughters. The new family then moved to Wŏnsan, an open port on the East Sea. In 1895 two Korean families became Christians because they heard that the name of Jesus was sufficient to save every believer from the attacks of "evil spirits." Gale said, "The idea of possession and demon influence has a great place here in life. The 'Tonghaks' who raised such a commotion in the south last year, professed to have power to cast out devils, and that was one cause of their popularity. We rejoice that the name of Jesus is sufficient."[80] Gale was ordained as a minister at the Presbytery of Albany, New York, during his furlough in 1897.

From 1893 to 1898 Gale used the terms "*kouisin* [*kwishin*] worship," "devil worship," "fetichism" (fetishism), and "spirit worship" interchangeably. He believed that a mudang was a sorcerer, and her ceremony represented a sacrifice to a demon or unclean spirits.[81] In his first book, *Korean Sketches* (1898), he differentiated between p'ansu, a blind fortune-teller, and mudang, a sorceress.[82] In the book, which was written earlier than 1897, he retained his critical understanding of Korean shamanism as fetishism and demon worship.

> Some interested in Korea have thought that there are two religions: one cultured and refined, and understood to be ancestor worship; the other heathenish throughout, the lowest form of fetichism. Koreans themselves how ever make no distinction; they call it all *kwishin* worship, and *kwishin* is a word that is translated "demon" in the Chinese and Korean New Testament. They themselves claim that their worship is all of one origin, which agrees exactly with 1. Cor. x: 20, "But I say that the things which the Gentiles sacrifice they sacrifice to demons and not to God."[83]

When Gale published *An English-Korean Dictionary* in 1897, however, he revised Underwood's definitions of "kwishin" as "a demon, evil-spirit, a devil" to "spirits, a demon." Gale identified its first equivalent

---

[80] Gale, "Letters: Korea," *CHA* (September 1895): 230.
[81] Gale, "Korea—Its Present Condition," *MRW* 16 (1893): 663.
[82] Gale, "Korea—Its Present Condition," 73–81.
[83] Gale, *Korean Sketches* (New York: Revell, 1898), 217–18.

as "spirits" and omitted "evil-spirit, a devil." Gale's acceptance of both "spirits" (a neutral term used by Jones, Landis, and Bird Bishop) and "a demon" (a biblical term used by Underwood, Gifford, Hardie, and other missionaries) represented his in-between position in understanding Korean shamanism. Unlike Jones and Hulbert, he retained a conservative stance toward spirit worship, probably because of his negative experience of shamanism in the costal Korean villages in Wŏnsan. In 1899 Gale reported that when a family in Wŏnsan was converted to Christianity through the work of a Korean Christian, they gathered the "idols of demon worship" and piled them in a heap in the middle of the room. There were "paper gods," rolls of cotton goods, embroidered garments, and trinkets that had been given in sacrifice to "evil spirits." After praying and dedication of the house to God, Gale carried the bundle home with him and kept it "as an evidence of Koreans turning from idols."[84]

In 1900 Gale moved back to Seoul, for the Wŏnsan station was transferred to the Canadian Presbyterian church in 1899. Gale introduced a new monotheistic meaning of Hanănim. Hanănim was a supreme "god of Heaven" in Korean shamanism, but Gale claimed that Hanănim was the "One Great One" whose etymology came from *hana* (one), not from *hanăl* (heaven). He adopted this new meaning from a Korean man named Chu, who argued that the Christian God and the traditional Korean Hanănim were identical.[85] According to Chu, what was added was not the idea of monotheism, but the unconditional and sacrificial love of God. But Gale highlighted the monotheistic etymology of Hanănim, which became the view of the Protestant missionaries.

In his book *Korea in Transition* (1909), Gale accepted the studies of shamanism by Gifford, Jones, Bishop, and Hulbert, yet he continued to use the terms "devils" and "demons" as well as "spirits" for kwishin. He argued that Korea had a syncretistic religion of prevalent superstitions.

> Korea's is a strange religion, a mixing of ancestor worship with Buddhism, Taoism, spirit cults, divination, magic, geomancy, astrology, and fetishism. Dragons play a part; devils (*kwi-shin*) or nature gods are abundant; *tokgabi* (elfs, imps, goblins) are legion and are up to all sorts of pranks and capers; spirits of dead humanity are here and there present; eternal shades walk about; there are personalities in hills, trees, and rivers, in

---

[84] Gale to F. F. Ellinwood, April 21, 1899.
[85] Gale, "Korean Ideas of God," *MRW* (September 1900): 697.

diseases, under the ground and in the upper air, some few ministering to mortal needs, but most of them malignant in their disposition, bearing woe and terror to the sons of men.[86]

After clarifying p'ansu as "blind exorcists" who did "ply their trade of casting out demons,"[87] Gale emphasized that many Korean converts believed in Jesus as the great exorcist and "wonder-worker." Many missionaries also came to believe, after consistently performing exorcisms, that "there are demons indeed in the world; and that Jesus can cast them out; to learn once more that the Bible is true, and that God is back of it; to know that his purpose is to save Asia, and to do an important part of the work."[88] They were on a mission not only to "save" the Koreans, but also to drive out existing "demons" in the form of forcefully dismantling shamanistic practices.

In 1913 Gale translated and published *Korean Folk Tales: Imps, Ghosts, and Fairies*. He mentioned Daoism as a major religious background of the stories, although many others were related to Buddhism, Confucianism, and shamanism. A story of "Ten Thousand Devils" described that the devils were under the control of a poor male hermit. And "The Honest Witch" showed that a true mudang could bring out the spirit of a dead friend of a magistrate.[89] In this book, Gale used both "devils" and "spirits" for kwishin, and "witch" for mudang. Among the missionary scholars of Korean religions, Gale was one of the last ones who used the definitions "devils" and "witches."

HOMER B. HULBERT

A graduate of Dartmouth College in 1884 and New York Union Theological Seminary in 1886, Homer B. Hulbert arrived in Seoul in 1886 with two other Americans, Dalzell A. Bunker and George W. Gilmore. These three served as teachers at Yugyŏng Kongwŏn, the government school. Hulbert was then appointed as a Methodist missionary in 1893. He edited the *Korean Repository* from 1896 to 1898 and the *Korea Review* from 1901 to 1906. He was deeply involved in Korean studies

---

[86] Gale, *Korea in Transition* (New York: Young People's Missionary Movement of the United States and Canada, 1909), 68.

[87] Gale, *Korea in Transition*, 85.

[88] Gale, *Korea in Transition*, 89.

[89] Gale, trans., *Korean Folk Tales: Imps, Ghosts, and Fairies* (New York: E. P. Dutton, 1913), 104–10, 125–29.

and politics. Emperor Kojong appointed Hulbert as a secret envoy to the United States to protest the illegality of the Japanese Protectorate Treaty in 1905. The Japanese government forced Hulbert leave Korea in 1907.

Concerning "shamanistic superstitions," Hulbert wrote in 1895, "The existence and immanence of supernatural beings corresponding to the old Greek idea of the demon is an article of firm belief to the ordinary Korean." He found that "the most prominent idea in connection with these superstitions is the idea of luck. Lucky days, lucky hours and lucky moments; lucky quarters, lucky combinations, lucky omens; luck or ill-luck in everything." Like Jones, Hulbert regarded the ubiquitous idea of luck among the people as a serious obstacle to Christianity.[90]

In 1897 Hulbert began to publicize cases of demon possession and reported cases of exorcism through the prayers of Korean Christians.[91] In 1899 he stated that because Koreans belonged to a different intellectual and imaginative species than the Chinese or Japanese, in the realm of religion Korea had not committed itself to either materialistic Confucianism or mystical Buddhism. He rightly argued, "In other words, when a Korean makes any genuine religious demonstration, he reverts to his aboriginal shamanism, though it be thinly veiled behind a Buddhistic cowl."[92] Hulbert thought that spiritual shamanism helped Koreans maintain a balance between materialistic Confucianism and mystical Buddhism. Thus he insisted that Korea's real religion was shamanism, though it was mixed with Buddhism.

In 1900, as seen in chapter 2, Hulbert debated with Gale regarding the influence of China upon Korea. Gale argued the dominance of Sinocentric culture in Korea from the ancient times and thus that there were no customs and institutions of the Koreans that were not traceable to China. By contrast, Hulbert pointed out archeological "survivals" that had been formed in the Korean Peninsula before Chinese culture came to Korea.[93] Here Hulbert used E. B. Tylor's concept of "survivals" to show the distinctive identity of earlier Korean culture and religions, and argued that "shaman worship" did not come from China.

---

[90] Hulbert, "The Korean Almanac," *KR* (February 1895): 71–72.

[91] Hulbert, "Things in General: Demoniacal Possession," *KR* (January 1897): 24–25; "Part I. Ancient Korea Chapter I," *KRv* (January 1901): 33–35.

[92] Hulbert, "Korea and the Koreans," *Forum* 14 (1899): 218–19.

[93] Hulbert, "Korean Survivals," *TKB* 1 (1900): 25–35.

The native demonology of Korea has united with Buddhism and formed a composite religion that can hardly be called either the one or the other, but running through it all we can see the underlying Buddhistic fabric, with its four fundamentals—mysticism, fatalism, pessimism and quietism. That these are inherent in the Korean temperament I will show by quoting four of their commonest expressions. "Moragĕsso"—I don't know—is their mysticism. "Halsu ŏpso"—It can't be helped—is their fatalism. "Mang hagesso"—going to the dogs—is their pessimism, and "Nopsita"—Let's knock off work—is their quietism.[94]

Hulbert recognized that shamanism and Buddhism formed a composite religion in Korea. However, he perceived four fundamental characteristics of shamanism underlying Buddhism—mysticism, fatalism, pessimism, and quietism—which were inherent in the Korean temperament. As he was a good student of the Korean language, he could detect these four fundamentals in the common expressions.

From November 1902 to February 1903, Hulbert published a series of four papers on Korean divination in the *Korea Review*. He introduced and translated a best-selling vernacular book of fortune-telling, *Manbo Ogilbang* (The Five Rules for Obtaining Ten Thousand Blessings). He deemed that it represented "some of the grossest superstitions of the Korean people" and "a curious mixture of Buddhism and the inborn fetishism of the Korean."[95] But it actually was a mixture of the Daoist astrological divination with Buddhism and shamanism. Chapter 6 of the book dealt with the methods of driving out the imps of sickness from the human body. The natural diseases could be cured by medicine, but the diseases "caused by the presence of an evil spirit" should be cured by exorcising the evil spirit. Different diseases were likely to break out on special days of the months, and the method of curing was writing the name of the disease on yellow or white paper and throwing it in the direction from which the disease came. For example, the first day of the month, "The South-east, 'wood' imp, which was formerly the spirit of a man who died by accident away from home, controls this day. There will be headache, chills, loss of appetite. The cash wrapped in paper must be taken forty paces toward the south-east and thrown."[96]

In 1903 Hulbert published another series of six papers on mudang and p'ansu in the *Korea Review*. He viewed mudang as a sort of medium

[94] Hulbert, "Korean Survivals," 39.
[95] "A Leaf from Korean Astrology," *KRv* (November 1902): 491.
[96] "A Leaf from Korean Astrology," *KRv* (January 1903): 16.

who could move the spirits through her friendship with them, but a p'ansu was an exorcist rather than a medium. Again Hulbert found that the service most in demand was the driving out of spirits of diseases. But why should spirits torment people in this way? Hulbert's answer was that there were "hungry" spirits.[97] He argued that in the exorcism or propitiation of the spirits, "the most malignant spirits of all are the disembodied souls of those who have met a violent death or who have been grievously wronged and have died without obtaining revenge." Before these spirits could "get rest," argued Hulbert, they "must be laid" by the ceremonies of mudang.[98] Hulbert acknowledged the mudang's role in healing diseases though various ceremonies such as a disease kut, a *mamabaesong* kut (a ceremony for sending away the spirit of smallpox), or a kut for sending away the soul of the dead. His idea that the troubled spirits of those who died a sudden death or a death of injustice should be "laid" and "get rest" was an important advance in the missionary study of shamanism and its social role in Korean society.

In his 1906 book, *Passing of Korea*, Hulbert remarked, "As a general thing, we may say that the all-round Korean will be a Confucianist when in society, a Buddhist when he philosophizes and a spirit-worshipper when he is in trouble."[99] This was one of the best summaries by a missionary of the multireligious condition in Korea.[100] The "mosaic of religious beliefs" that was held not only by different individuals but also by any single individual, he argued, demonstrated the antiquity of Korean civilization. Hulbert concluded that "the underlying religion of the Korean, the foundation upon which all else is mere superstructure, is his original spirit-worship," since one's practical religion would come out when an individual was in trouble. Hulbert included animism, shamanism, fetishism, and nature worship in the category of spirit worship. Philosophical Buddhism and political Confucianism, he asserted, "eventually blended with the original spirit-worship in such a way to form a composite religion." He added, "Strange to say, the purest religious notion which the Korean today possesses is the belief in *Hananim*,

---

[97] Hulbert, "Hungry Spirits," *KRv* (March 1903): 111–12.

[98] Hulbert, "The Korean Mudang and P'ansu," *KRv* (April 1903): 145–49.

[99] Hulbert, *The Passing of Korea* (London: Heinemann, 1906), 403.

[100] He defined religion as "every relation which men hold, or fancy that they hold, to superhuman, infrahuman or, more broadly, extra-human phenomena." And he included in the category of extrahuman the spirits of human beings who had died (Hulbert, *Passing of Korea*, 403).

a being entirely unconnected with either of the imported cults and as far removed from the crude nature-worship."[101] Hulbert separated Hanănim from the circle of the other various gods and indigenous spirits because he felt that ancient Koreans were "strictly monotheistic" in their belief in him. Hulbert supported the Protestant missionaries' identification of Hanănim with Jehovah. Like Gale, Hulbert invented Hanănim as a Christian term based on the idea of "primitive monotheism" and fulfillment theory.[102]

HORACE G. UNDERWOOD

Underwood arrived in Seoul in April 1885 as the first Presbyterian clerical missionary to Korea. He did not distinguish shamanism from Daoism and called the former "Demonism" for a decade. He did not use the term "shamanism" until 1905. He repeated that Korea was a land without a religion in the sense that all religions were degraded. Buddhism, Confucianism, and Demonism seemed to be losing their power over people. In 1893 he declared that "a kind of mental revolution seems to be in progress throughout the land," and that the time had come to hear the voice of God saying to his church, "Go work today in my vineyard in Korea."[103] This was a declaration of spiritual war against the Korean religions.

Underwood expounded on Korean shamanism in his seminal work, *The Religions of Eastern Asia* (1910). Like Landis, he compared the historical path of Korean shamanism to that of Japanese Shinto. As Buddhism entered Korea in the fourth century, before shamanism developed into an organized religion, the latter became subordinated to the former, even without temples and an organized priesthood. In contrast, Buddhism entered Japan from Korea in the sixth century, after nature worship had developed into Shinto and both were synchronized.[104]

Underwood argued that Korea had a pure monotheism before the entrance of Buddhism. He found that the religion of the state of Puyŏ in

---

[101] Hulbert, *Passing of Korea*, 403–4.

[102] Oak Sung-Deuk, "Edinburgh 1910, Fulfillment Theory, and Missionaries in China and Korea," *Journal of Asian and Asian American Theology* 9 (2009): 41–50.

[103] H. G. Underwood, "Romanism on the Foreign Mission Field," in *Reports of the Fifth General Council of the Alliance of the Reformed Churches Holding the Presbyterian System* (Toronto: Hart & Riddell, 1892), 409–15.

[104] Underwood, *Religions of Eastern Asia*, 95.

Manchuria and northern Korea was "the worship of the heavens, and *absolutely no mention of any other spirits or lesser deities is made.*" It was Kija who came in the year 1122 B.C. to Korea and introduced "geomancy, sorcery, divination, and spirit worship" to the Korean people. In the Tan'gun legend, he argued, "there is a strong probability of a primitive pure monotheism."[105] He adopted the terms "monotheism" and "henotheism" in his description of the original shamanistic belief of the Korean people.

Underwood, however, was very critical toward the doctrine and pantheon of contemporary shamanism. The shrines were mutually independent, and consequently the doctrines held by one sorceress differed from those of others. The main belief system of Korean shamanism was polytheism that had originated from nature worship: (1) belief in Hanănim and his supremacy and providence, (2) belief in the efficacy of the Samshin (Three Gods) for childbearing, (3) belief in local deities, whose chief was the Obang Changgun (Five-Point General), (4) belief in a host of other deities, and (5) belief in the ghosts or spirits of the dead. Underwood claimed that the gods of shamanism had "wandered from their old monotheism and even to a certain extent from the pure henotheism of later times." He accepted the theory of the degradation of Korean religions and their fulfillment through Christianity.[106]

Underwood was interested in the methods of worship in shamanism. He argued that the worship of the Heavens was "a remnant of an ancient henotheism." Thus in "all the worship of the Heavens, the *mudangs* and *pansus* are not allowed to participate in their official capacities." Underwood accepted Hulbert's definition of mudang as a woman sorcerer or "deceiving crowd," and p'ansu as an exorcist and "destiny decider" or "fortune teller." Yet Underwood still called them "witch" and "wizard" in a broader sense.[107] He noticed that a mudang was always female, generally from the lower classes, and of a bad reputation. She was considered to be a sort of spiritual medium, capable of rapport with the spirits and able to be possessed. However, such possessions were preceded by a series of incantations and rituals and a sort of self-hypnotism in which the mudang, having by her performances thrown herself into a trance (pretended or real), became the mouthpiece

[105] Underwood, *Religions of Eastern Asia*, 104–6; emphasis original.
[106] Underwood, *Religions of Eastern Asia*, 114.
[107] Underwood, *Religions of Eastern Asia*, 140–41.

of the deity. Underwood claimed that the mudang had nothing to do with divination; her chief business was the healing of the sick through the kut ceremony.[108]

The Protestant missionaries in Korea began to use the term "shamanism" in 1894. Most of them, except Underwood and a few others, accepted the term around 1900. Thus we can say that there were individual differences in their understanding and definition of Korean shamanism. Overall, their rationalistic iconoclasm, millennialism, revivalism, and theory of religious degradation consistently projected the negative aspects of Korean shamanism. They paid much attention to the house gods and fetishes. One of their main concerns was the negative influence of shamanism on Korean Christians.

Most missionaries understood the kut as a ritual of inducement offering to the spirits, and some kut, including those of p'ansu, as ceremonies for exorcism of evil spirits, wandering spirits, or disease spirits from the victims. The Korean kwishin was identified with the Greek daimon (devil or evil spirits) used in the New Testament. They were good, bad, or indifferent, but most were unclean, malicious, malign, hungry, and sometimes revengeful. However, some household spirits related to prosperity and fertility were regarded as good and kind.

After a decade of work in Korea, the missionaries were well versed in the religions in Korea and what role they served in the society. The Tonghak Uprising and the Sino-Japanese War provided them with opportunities to experience the multiplicity of religious identities of the Korean people. When the missionaries were allowed to enter the *sarang-bang* (a room for male guests) and *anbang* (an inner room for women), they began to perceive the tenets of shamanism and its importance in everyday live. When D. L. Gifford saw the "superstitions" of Koreans "in a spirit of sympathy" and from "their angle of vision," he confessed that he could understand that "the fear of demons is the cause of frequent and intense mental suffering."[109]

Behind these Protestant missionaries' encounter with a completely different religion, however, was a hidden process of transformation of their theology and worldview. They identified the supreme god of shamanism, Hanănim of primitive monotheism, with the biblical God. They also accepted the Korean shamanistic idea of spirits, demon

[108] Underwood, *Religions of Eastern Asia*, 115–35.
[109] Gifford, *Everyday Life in Korea*, 118.

possession, and exorcism, which was similar to that found in New Testament Palestine. The next section deals with the Christian practice of exorcism in detail. Although the female missionaries did not contribute substantially to the academic study of Korean shamanism, their practice exorcism and burning the fetishes had a great influence on the lives of Korean women who lived with shamanistic spirits every day.

On the other hand, paradoxically, shamanic spirits could find a dwelling place in the Protestant missionaries' discourses on shamanism. In the same way that shamanism and its rituals continued to function during the Chosŏn period by being incorporated into the Confucian scholars' discourses on spirits and liturgical hegemony, so too did shamanism and its spiritism survive at the turn of the twentieth century by being included in the Protestant missionaries' discourses on demonology. During the colonial period, shamanism survived, in a similar manner, in the Japanese scholars' discourse concerning the highly developed nature of Japanese Shinto versus "primitive" Korean shamanism. Japanese ethnologists justified their colonial rule by expounding on the superiority of Japanese Shinto over Korean superstitious shamanism.[110] Further study of the continuity in the logic of assaulting shamanism by Neo-Confucian yangban elites, Protestant missionaries, and Japanese ethnologists will reveal an important aspect of the history of Korean religions.

DEMON POSSESSION AND CHRISTIAN EXORCISM

JOHN NEVIUS AND DEMON POSSESSION IN SHANDONG

John L. Nevius, who worked in China from 1854 to 1892, had experienced cases of "demon possession" from the beginning of his work in Shandong. He asked himself the question, "Is there such a thing as demon possession in the latter part of the nineteenth century?" He had carefully investigated these cases and gathered the facts and testimony of missionaries and Chinese Christians on the incidents in which they expelled spirits and set the victims free. The result was his posthumous book, *Demon Possession and Allied Themes*, published in 1896. Not only was the Nevius method adopted by the Korean missions, but his theory of demon possession and Christian exorcism also influenced the

---

[110] Boudewijn C. A. Walraven, "The Native Next-Door: Ethnology in Colonial Korea," in *Anthropology and Colonialism in Asia and Oceania*, ed. Jan van Bremen and Akitoshi Shimizu (Richmond, UK: Curzon Press, 1999), 224.

missionaries in Korea. The people of Shandong province believed in demon possession. The belief was a part of Chinese animism or spirit worship. Physical suffering and violent paroxysms attended the victims' ordeal. When the narratives of demonic possession given in the New Testament were read, therefore, Chinese Christians recognized the correspondence at once. Nevius and other missionaries proceeded with great caution in this matter. As Frank F. Ellinwood said in the preface to *Demon Possession,*

> They have avoided any measures which might lead the people to suppose that they claim the power to cast out devils even in Jesus' name. Nor does it appear that any native minister has claimed any such power. The most that has been done has been to kneel down and pray to Jesus to relieve the sufferer, at the same time inviting all present to unite in the prayer; and it seems a well established fact that in nearly or quite every instance, the person afflicted, speaking apparently in a different personality and with a different voice had confessed the power of Jesus and has departed.[111]

Nevius argued that cases of demon possession actually existed in China. He described those supposedly cured by Chinese Christians, not by the old methods that exorcists had used, such as burning charms, frightening with magic spells and incantation, or pricking the body with needles, but by hymn singing and praying to God. Some missionaries testified that they felt themselves "transported back to the days of the Apostles" and were "compelled to believe that the dominion of Satan is by no means broken yet."[112] Nevius insisted that the phenomenon of demon possession could be explained not by contemporary evolutionary and psychological theories but only by the Bible.

In 1930 Charles A. Clark mentioned Nevius' book on demon possession in his dissertation: "Exorcism of evil spirits by Christian workers caused much discussion and divided opinion among the missionaries and the church workers. It is mentioned in the 1895 Report about Wŏnsan particularly. Dr. Nevius could have found much more material in Korea for his book on Demon Possession."[113] The aforementioned controversy occurred in the early 1920s when Rev. Kim Iktu healed

[111] John L. Nevius, *Demon Possession and Allied Themes* (New York: Revell, 1896), v.

[112] Nevius, *Demon Possession,* 71.

[113] C. A. Clark, *The Korean Church and the Nevius Methods* (New York: Revell, 1930), 99.

various cases of chronic diseases by prayer at revival meetings.[114] But before the debate in the 1920s, many reports of miraculous healings and exorcism were found around the turn of the century.

CHRISTIAN EXORCISM IN KOREA

As mentioned above by Clark, James S. Gale reported the prevalence of demon possession in Wŏnsan in 1895. His work was disturbed by "special development of spirit worship, or rather of demoniacal possessions." People came to him complaining that "the quiet of their households was disturbed by nocturnal visitations of spirits." Many were possessed by demons. In all such cases exorcists plied their trade. "To the people," said Gale, "these demons are as real as the earth beneath their feet and I am thankful that we have a Gospel that can take away their fears."[115]

In Korea, according to missionary sources and Westerners' travelogues, belief in demon possession or possession by "unclean" spirits was common.[116] It had a peculiar and tenacious grip upon the people; one writer called Korea "the haunted house among the nations, afflicted with the delirium tremens of paganism." A missionary stated that "thousands of people are slaves to evil spirits, in bondage to His Satanic Majesty."[117] Gale wrote that the Tonghaks, who raised a great commotion in 1894, "possessed to power to cast out devils, and that was one cause of their popularity."[118] A spiritual mudang was believed to be possessed by a powerful spirit, and by means of her incantations she could induce this indwelling spirit to evict the one that was causing the sickness by aiding her exorcism. The people in the northern provinces called the possessed mudang *manshin*, a legion of spirits, as her spirit brought with him a legion of other spirits under his control. She performed a kut to drive out "evil spirits" from the afflicted person with music, dance, and incantations.[119] Korean miners also practiced the ceremony of driving out "evil

---

[114] Min Kyŏngbae, *Han'guk kidoggyohoe sa* [A History of the Korean Church] (Seoul: Korean Christian Press, 1984), 411–14.

[115] *Annual Report of the BFMPCUSA* (New York: BFMPCUSA, 1895), 161.

[116] Gilmore, *Korea from Its Capital; With Chapter on Mission* (Philadelphia: Presbyterian Board of Publication and Sabbath School Work, 1892), 194; Bishop, *Korea and Her Neighbors*, 399-408.

[117] David K. Lambuth, "Korean Devils and Christian Missionaries," *Independent* (August 1, 1907): 287–88.

[118] "Letters: Korea," *CHA* (September 1895): 230.

[119] H. N. Allen, "The Mootang," *KR* 3 (1896): 163–64.

spirit." For example, whenever a Korean miner was killed in an accident at the American gold mines at Unsan in north P'yŏngan province, the Koreans supposed that his death was "caused by some spirit of the earth who feels himself aggravated," and that his wife was possessed with those spirits. No sooner did the accident occur than all the miners come flocking from the shaft, offered chickens and pigs to the spirits, and severely beat the wife of the dead miner to exorcise the spirits.[120]

Protestant missionaries testified to numerous cases of demon possession and their exorcism by prayer to Christ. Such "miracles" proved to the missionaries that some Koreans were still possessed by demons in the same way as the people in Palestine in the time of Jesus. Both North American missionaries and the Korean people needed to change their worldview regarding the power of God in exorcism. Missionaries were required to transform their modern, rational, and scientific view of "evil spirits" and miracles into the first-century biblical view. In contrast, Korean people were challenged to accept both the modern medical theories of body and disease and the biblical view of the power of the Holy Spirit over "evil spirits."

In Pyongayng Samuel A. Moffett found that the "real and practical religion of the people, so far as they have any at all, is a species of Animism or spirit-worship."[121] His colleague, Graham Lee, traveled the Sunan circuit and visited five places in 1897. He baptized sixteen adults and one baby and received 109 catechumens. He witnessed a case of healing a demon possession at the Sunan church and observed half of the villagers throwing out their spirits. At Chajak he met a blind man and his father who had given up the demon exorcism business.[122]

The majority of those who believed themselves to be possessed were women, and the Christian claim of expelling evil spirits from their bodies appealed to these women and their families as a last resort. For example, Mrs. Yi Kŭnsŏn Incheon was apparently revived after the prayers of Christians in early 1899. She had been sick and mentally ill for ten years. A great deal of money had been spent on medicine and shamanic ceremonies, yet all efforts toward a cure had failed. When her husband heard that Jesus' church had the power to overcome the devil, he voluntarily came to the chapel to profess his belief in Jesus.

[120] Hulbert, "Part I. Ancient Korea Chapter I," 33–35.
[121] *Annual Report of the BFMPCUSA* (New York: BFMPCUSA, 1895), 121.
[122] G. Lee to Samuel A. Moffett, February 20, 1897.

"Believers visited his house, and found that the insane woman broke the wall frantically and was hiding and shivering in the bed. After they sang a hymn and prayed, they removed the blanket. She drank three bowls of cold water, and prayed together with them. In less than two weeks her insanity disappeared. Now she is a sincere believer."[123] Such stories were propagated and encouraged others to seek the church.

In 1905 a Bible class was held in a village of Pup'yŏng, Kyŏnggi. There was a new believer who had been a sorceress for five years—"an obedient servant of Satan."[124] The Christians prayed for and with her, going to her home every night. The woman said, "I cannot tell how peaceful I felt when those hymns were being sung." On one memorable night, just before being loosed from the power of the "great devil," she rolled on the floor in agony of mind, beat her head with her hands, and pulled out locks of her hair. Repeatedly and in measured tones she said, "Depart from me! Depart from me!" All night long the Christians prayed and sang with her. By dawn she had become a supreme example of missionary exorcism, claiming the devil had left her. Miss Lula A. Miller, who joined the Methodist mission in Korea in 1901, asked her how she knew that it was Satan who had been leading her. She answered, "You know, teacher, when we believe in Jesus, He gives us the Holy Spirit and we know when He is leading us, though we can neither see nor hear Him. So it is when Satan is in our hearts. We know it is he who is leading us. O! I am so happy now, and all my family believes in Jesus, the Savior of the world."[125] In this way, belief in the power of Christian ability to exorcise "evil spirits" shifted slightly in rhetoric to the belief in exorcising Satan and his demons.

At the end of 1905 Dr. William B. Scranton and Rev. George M. Burdick visited a little mountain village, Omoi, on the Suwŏn circuit, where a native doctor was the leader of the Christian group. There was one believer, an intelligent scholar of the upper class of society, whose grandfather, father, and himself had each in turn been the owner and keeper of a mountain spirit house. At about the time of his father's death, the man had become interested in the new faith. His sister went insane or was possessed by the devil. "She grew violent; and the believers in the group met daily to pray for her; but for more than a week there

---

[123] "Hŭihanhan il" [A Rare Thing], *KH*, May 23, 1900.
[124] Lula A. Miller, "The Conversion of a Sorceress," *KMF* 2 (1906): 65.
[125] Miller, "The Conversion of a Sorceress," 65.

was very little improvement. At last she grew better; and thereupon the family gave over to the church, as mementoes of the victory, all the garments and various fantastic decorations connected with this spirit worship."[126] The man also gave the house to the church.

Another case was reported as follows: "During the revival the feeling was so intense that one man fell into raving insanity, his violence and superhuman power breaking to pieces even the iron chains that bound him and snapping an iron bar like glass, evidencing demoniac possession no less real than that of the man in the country of the Gadarenes. The devils were trying to frighten us and our converts into silence." Prayer proved successful. The spirits left the man, and he was renewed. Missionaries continually came into contact with "the most extraordinary cases of apparent demoniacal possession and cure, containing all the phenomena that characterized demonized minds in the days of Christ."[127]

KOREAN BIBLE WOMEN AS EXORCISTS

In a gender-segregated society, the Bible societies or the mission societies employed male colporteurs and helpers in the distribution of Christian literature and biblical instructions among the Korean men and Bible women for the same work among the women. Most Bible women were widows or old women, since younger women were neither respected enough nor allowed the necessary freedom of movement. But a Bible woman was more than just a colporteur. As an itinerant evangelist she taught the vernacular language and the doctrine of the Bible by the example of her own self-sacrificial and happy life. She helped exhausted mothers, cared for sick children, and penetrated the remote country districts where foreign missionaries had never reached. A few Bible women began to be trained at the Bible classes from 1892 and engaged in evangelism as helpers of a female missionary. As the number of the male Korean pastors and helpers was still meager by 1910, a Bible woman could be in charge of an unorganized local church and preach every Sunday. Thus earlier Bible women, who were less educated, had more spiritual authority than those who were trained with the regular

---

[126] George M. Burdick, "Conversion of a Mountain Spirit House Keeper," *KMF* 2 (1906): 88.

[127] Lambuth, "Korean Devils and Christian Missionaries," 288.

curriculum at the women's Bible institutes established in the major cities in the 1920s.[128]

In many cases, a female missionary, her Bible woman, and other female members would together visit the house of a possessed woman and hold a prayer service for her. For example, a possessed woman was healed by a Bible woman in Pyongyang in 1903.

> There is out at the Waysung a young woman who became possessed of devils. Her family called in an exorcist and the most extreme measures were resorted to to rid her of the unwelcome intruders. She was beaten with clubs till she was a mass of bruises from head to foot and a perfectly sickening sight. At this point some Christian neighbors interfered, declaring that they would be witness no longer to such cruelty, and persuaded the husband to take her in to leader Choo's. Here she remained a week or two, being visited daily by Sin Si and others of the believing women. I wish that I might give in detail the conversations as reported by Sin Si, between these Christian women and the devils. They would be interesting to students of demonology. Suffice to say, that after agreeing several times to leave the woman at a certain hour, and begging each time when the moment came for a longer limit, they finally yielded to a loud and stern adjuration from old Sin Si and took their departure, leaving the woman in her right mind.[129]

In March 1907 Miss Mamie D. Myers of Wŏnsan heard from her Bible woman Naomi about a possessed woman. She had learned "witchery" at a "heathen temple" yet had been abused as a "crazy" woman by the crowds in the street all day. They visited her house at South Mount, eight miles from the mission house, with Naomi's sister and other school girls. During their second prayer service, the "crazy" woman fell down on her knees and said, "Your God has driven the marque [devil] out of me, and I want to believe in your God." The news of her restoration spread like wildfire among the people. Christian girls insisted that "the crazy one" should have a name, so Miss Myers gave her a new name, "Poktaigee," meaning "Received Blessings."[130]

---

[128] Margaret Best, "Courses of Study and Rules of Admission of the Pyeng Yang Presbyterian Women's Bible Institute," *KMF* 6 (1910): 152–54.

[129] Annie L. A. Baird, "General Report of Pyeng Yang Station to the Korea Mission, June 1903," in KMPCUSA, *Minutes and Reports*, 1903, PHS, CRKM, reel 232.

[130] Mamie D. Myers, "Poktaigee," *WMA* (December 1909): 269–70.

Many Bible women conducted prayer meetings for exorcism. Some of them were former mudangs who had become Christian "exorcists." Mrs. Sim was one of these crossover mudang in Pyongayng. After some training with Bible study, basic theology, and practical ministry, she was appointed as a Bible woman. Her healing ceremony in 1906 of a young female victim was a typical case of Christian exorcism, composed of the following seven elements. First was a confrontational dialogue with the possessed at her own room: Mrs. Sim asked, "Are you possessed of a demon?" She repeated until the spirit answered. The spirits begged to stay. Second, they prayed for the woman, who hissed at, spat at, and struck the Christian women. Third, congregational hymn singing was repeated until the hatred on the woman's part subsided into a low crying. Fourth, Mrs. Sim ordered the spirits to come out, yet they resisted. Fifth, congregational prayer and hymn singing continued. Sixth, around midnight Mrs. Sim finally ordered the spirits to go away: "Thou foul spirit, I adjure thee in the name of Jesus Nazareth, come out of her!" Finally, the spirits were cast out and the woman was healed.[131] The correspondence between the biblical stories of exorcism and Mrs. Sim's case was the conversation and struggle between "demons" and the "exorcist" while the "demons" were being exorcised from the possessed person. The "demon" first defied the exorcist, but eventually yielded to her. The possessed were healed by the faith of the Christian exorcist and brought back to sanity.

A more peaceful healing process was adopted by another crossover mudang in the Taegu area. Rev. Walter C. Erdman met an old woman in a newly built little country church in January 1908.

> She had walked ten miles to see the missionary. In Africa I suppose she would have been called a witch doctor. She had been a sorceress, and her specialty was exorcising spirits out of the sick. These were not the qualifications usually sought in a candidate for admission to the catechumenate, so we asked her questions, and her statements were corroborated by some who knew her. It was a year since she believed for the first time (these Koreans speak of "believing" as though it were an attack of the measles or something!) and since then she had given up all sorcery. What did she do for a living now? She was still in the doctoring business. How did she go about it since her former equipment was not available, or at

---

[131] Annie L. A. Baird, *Daybreak in Korea: A Tale of Transformation in the Far East* (New York: Revell, 1909), 95–106.

least, inconsistent? Oh, it was simple. She used her herbs and prayed that the Holy Spirit would heal. (Neither had she ever read the last chapter of James.) She was a traveling doctor, with no particular home. How did she spend Sunday? In the nearest church.[132]

A newly converted former mudang used herbs and prayer for healing and prayed that the Holy Spirit would heal the sick. She abandoned old equipment and instruments of the shamanist rituals, yet now she appealed to the Christian Holy Spirit, a stronger spirit, to cast out shamanic unholy spirits. Her understanding of spirits and healing had not changed much. However, the missionary baptized her and gave her a baptismal name. To him, she was evidence of Christian victory over a Korean folk religion and Christian uplifting of Korean womanhood.

On the other hand, Christian exorcism provided the Bible women with opportunities to become new spiritual leaders. Mrs. Mary F. Scranton thus praised them in 1907:

These women are highly respected and are believed to have ability to offer up prevailing prayer. If anyone is in trouble of any sort, in mind, body, or estate, the Bible woman is sent for to pray and sing Psalms. When anyone gets tired of trying to propitiate the evil spirit, it is the Bible women who must come and take down the fetishes and burn them. They are called upon to cast out devils, as well as to offer the fervent effectual prayer for the healing of the sick. Their faith is often greater than that of their teachers, and the all-loving and compassionate Father rewards them accordingly.[133]

A Bible woman's spiritual power was sustained by the Christian ceremony of faith healing and exorcism and through her home visitations with new female members. Her best weapon was the "prevailing" and "fervent effectual" prayer. Protracted prayers of intercession for the possessed were sometimes accompanied by fasting. Mrs. Yi, the first Christian woman in the city of Pyongyang, became president of the missionary society and a Bible woman. She cured a woman of "demon possession through the prayer of a company of women of the Fourth Church."[134] However, negative shamanistic spirituality—fetishism,

[132] Walter C. Erdman, "Korea: 'Unto the Church In,' " *All the World* (April 1908): 45.

[133] Mary F. Scranton, "Day Schools and Bible," *KMF* (April 1907): 53.

[134] C. F. Bernheisel, "The Korean Church a Missionary Church," *Woman's Work* (November 1910), 250.

spirit reductionism, fortune-centered fatalism, and earthly blessing-oriented materialism—also entered the church through these crossover female evangelists, of which some missionaries had warned.

EMBRACING THE PREMODERN VIEW OF DEMON POSSESSION

In 1907 Professor David Lambuth of Vanderbilt University completed a special study on the relationship between Korean spirits and Christian missionaries, based on the letters and reports from American missionaries in Korea. He maintained that "the missionaries in Korea display a sense of the presence of evil spirits markedly in excess of that manifested in other countries where demonology had no such popular hold. The spirit-saturated air has with insidious power waked in the missionaries all the dormant demonology with which the Christian religion was at some time furnished forth."[135] He stated that the point at issue, which was "the unconscious and insidious tendency of the foreigner to accept the native point of view," was prevalent in the writings of the Korea missionaries. North American missionaries not only influenced the individual and social life of Korea but also were influenced by the cultural and religious environment of Korea, especially shamanism. Their testimonies about the phenomenon of demon possession epitomized the interaction of religious conceptions and modes of thought.

The Great Revival of 1907 confirmed both Dr. Lambuth's analysis and the experiences of the missionaries regarding the mutual relationship between Christianity and Korean shamanism. One typical case of such a missionary "conversion" was that of Charles A. Clark of the Central Presbyterian Church in Seoul. Initially Clark was uncomfortable with certain similarities between Korean folk religious practice and what he witnessed at the revival meetings. During his education at McCormick Theological Seminary in Chicago, he had belittled the idea of demon possession, chalking up the symptoms to psychosis or a nervous temperament. In 1906, when he read an account of a missionary casting out demons in China, he regarded it as nonsense, maintaining that there had to be a medical or scientific explanation. But his experience during the 1907 revival changed his view. One man at the meeting disrupted the service with his raving and lashing out at anyone who tried to control him. Clark and Kil Sŏnju left the platform and led the disturbed man to

---

[135] Lambuth, "Korean Devils and Christian Missionaries," 287–88.

an outer room. There he began to rage like a wild beast. He smashed his own hat and ripped off his coat, tore open his leggings, and started to demolish the room. He fell to the floor on his face and prostrated himself before the ancestral box. The veins of his neck swelled until it seemed they would burst.

> Finally I became convinced that it was a devil's manifestation. . . . So I went to him, took firm hold of his shaking hands, and ordered him in Jesus' name to be still. . . . Then I prayed and almost at once he became quiet. . . . The Holy Spirit was doing so great work that I firmly believe the devil entered into that man to make him break up the meeting. . . . As sure as I believe there is a Holy Spirit who can "convince men of sin and righteousness and judgment," I am convinced that the devil can work now in opposition to Him exactly as he did 1900 years ago.[136]

Clark revised his views on the idea of casting out the devil and was convinced that the man was an agent of Satan and possessed by a demon. His colleague James Gale also confessed,

> Into this world comes the missionary with his Book and its stories about demons. The Korean reads and at once is attracted. Plenty of demons in the New Testament, thousands of them, but they are all on the run; down the slopes of Galilee they go; away from Christ's presence they fly. . . . Never before in the history of Korea was the world of demons seen smitten hip and thigh. This Wonder-worker is omnipotent, for verily he has issued a reprieve to all prisoners, all who will accept of him, and has let them out of hell. Throughout the land prayers go up for the demon-possessed in his name, and they are delivered; prayers for healing, and the sick are cured; prayers for the poor, and God send means.[137]

In 1911, after ten years, pastoral experience in Pyongyang, Charles F. Bernheisel confessed that he changed his cessationist view on miraculous healing after witnessing many cases of demon possession being cured by the prayers of Christians. The supernatural gift of miracle was considered to have been bestowed on the early church for providential purposes and to have ceased with the death of the apostles. But experiences in the mission field caused him to reexamine the biblical teachings on the subject and to harmonize what he had been taught at the

---

[136] D. N. Clark, *Living Dangerously in Korea: The Western Experience 1900–1950* (Norwalk, Conn.: EastBridge, 2003), 39–40.

[137] Gale, *Korea in Transition*, 88–89.

seminary with what he saw and heard in Korea. He argued that Koreans distinguished between a *mich'in saram* (insane person) and a *magwi tŭllin saram* (demon-possessed person). He testified that all the characteristics of demon possession as recorded in the Gospels, such as demon speaking through the lips of the possessed one, were present in Korea. He explained the curing procedure:

> The method of cure is unique. The Christians call for volunteers and then they divide themselves into bands which may consist of one or two or more persons and then these bands take turns staying with the patient so that at no time day or night till recovery is complete is the patient left alone. Each band spends its watch in prayer for the afflicted one, in singing Christian songs, in reading the Scriptures and having the patient repeat Scripture verses and in exhorting the demon to leave. Sometimes this is kept up for as long as several days. . . . This continuous cannonade of prayer, Scripture reading, song, testimony and exhortation finally prevails and the demon promises to leave, sometimes giving the very hour on which he will take his departure.[138]

Bernheisel concluded that the gift of miracle was not confined to a few individuals and to a certain time period, but a general power to be exercised, and that demon-possessed people were cured by the prayers of Christians. He became a continuationist.

The first-generation missionaries and Korean Christians accepted Nevius' view on demon possession and Christian exorcism. The Korean belief in shamanistic concepts and a vivid sense of demonical presence provided the missionaries and the Korean people with a point of contact and interaction. North American missionaries accepted the Korean point of view on the possession by "evil spirits," and the Korean people experienced the power of the Holy Spirit. Power encounters provided evidence of Christianity. Christian exorcisms continued after the Korean churches experienced the Great Revival Movement from 1904 to 1908.

Not only did the missionaries introduce and represent Korean shamanism to the English audience, but their own initially rationalistic and modern worldview was transformed by shamanism. First, they accepted the premodern Korean view of spirits, which became a factor of Protestant success in Korea. Second, many missionaries and Korean leaders,

---

[138] C. F. Bernheisel, *The Apostolic Church as Reproduced in Korea* (New York: BFMPCUSA, 1912), 9.

especially Bible women, practiced Christian exorcism of the demon possessed. Third, the missionaries accepted a heavenly god of Korean shamanism, Hanănim, as the term for the Christian God, based on the idea of primitive monotheism. We need to examine their overall meanings in terms of the "conversion" of the missionaries. One missionary confessed that when he read of devil possession in the Bible in the United States, he knew how Christ had dealt with such cases, but he seldom saw a person possessed by demons. But when he came to a mission field, his doubts regarding "devil possession in the latter days" were completely vanquished. That the devil at times made his home in the bodies of men and women, especially in heathen lands, was "a matter of unmistakable evidence."[139]

Three elements—American biblicism, Chinese Protestant exorcism, and Korean shamanistic healing ceremony—were combined in making the Korean Protestant theology of spirits. The result of the power encounter between Protestant Christianity and shamanism in early modern Korea was neither a wholesale destruction of the latter nor a unilateral conversion of Koreans to the former. The first-generation Anglo-Saxon missionaries to Korea condemned shamanism as a "primitive" and "superstitious" form of spirit worship. As most scholars have argued, missionaries attempted to destroy Korean shamanism in the name of Protestant monotheism, iconoclastic rationalism, medical science (germ theory), and Western civilization. On the other hand, their field experience led them to embrace John L. Nevius' theory of demon possession and Christian exorcism as spiritual and supernatural phenomena in modern East Asia, not just in first-century Palestine. Protestant missionaries adopted the premodern Korean view of spirits, and thus they practiced Christian exorcist rituals—burning fetishes and communal prayers for the patients—in contradiction to their home churches' official doctrine on demonic possession and miraculous faith healing.

Culturally, this theological compromise implied that, although it was based on Protestant biblicism and their field experiences, the appreciation of Anglo-Saxon missionaries for the Koreans' premodern worldview revealed their Orientalism, which regarded Korean folk religions and spirituality as primitive and obsolete for modern civilization. The

---

[139] W. G. Cram, "Rescued after Years of Bondage," *KM* (September 10, 1905): 148.

missionaries equated turn-of-the-century Korean society with first-century Palestinian society. One of the similarities to them was the ubiquitous existence of demons and exorcisms. The missionaries' Orientalist ethnography emphasized the vacuum of religions in Korea because it viewed shamanism not as a religion but as a superstition. The missionary iconoclasm misled the Korean Protestant churches to neglect the serious study of Korean folk religions.

Liturgically, shamanic spirits could exist in the Christian fetish burning and exorcism rituals. Both missionaries and Koreans recognized the existence of shamanic spirits. The iconoclastic assault of the spirits paradoxically identified the numerous locations of spirits and their functions in the Korean household and family life. One of the major differences between the Christian exorcist ceremony and the shamanic kut was the church members' protracted communal prayer meetings for the victim.

Ecclesiastically, Korean Bible women, especially those who were former mudang, performed Christian ceremonies of exorcism among female members and nonmembers in a gender-segregated society. Their spiritual leadership complemented the male-dominant Confucian patriarchal structure of the church in its early period, yet it became gradually subordinated to the latter from the 1910s, when seminaries produced many educated male ministers. The emergence of male revivalists, who performed miraculous healings through prayer in the 1910s and early 1920s, paralleled the degradation of the status of Bible women in the Korean Protestant church.

Theoretically, shamanic spirits could exist in the Protestant missionary discourses on Korean shamanism. A semiscientific study on this topic was launched by missionary scholars including E. B. Landis, G. H. Jones, J. S. Gale, H. B. Hulbert, and H. G. Underwood. In the same manner that shamanism and its rituals continued to function, during the Chosŏn period, through being embraced by the Confucian scholars' discourses on spirits and subordinated to Confucian liturgical hegemony, so too did shamanism and its spiritism survive by being incorporated into the Protestant missionaries' discourses on demonology at the turn of the twentieth century. In colonial Japanese scholarly discourse, Korean shamanism was painted as an inferior precursor to Japanese Shinto, as part of the Japanese superiority complex that justified the colonization of Korea. Therefore, the significant lack in study of the encounter between Protestantism and shamanism must be remedied as it bridges the discourses of premodern and colonial periods, with parallels and comparisons to be explored.

Theologically, in the process of the power encounter, Christ was represented to Koreans as the most powerful shaman mudang—both a mediator and a spirit—and the missionaries and Korean Bible women were represented as his agents. The interaction between two world-views—Western Christian rationalism and Korean shamanistic spirit-ism—resulted in mutual religious grafting. At the turn of the twentieth century, Protestant missions integrated the medical mission for the human body with the evangelistic mission for the human soul. The priority of the salvation of the soul included the salvation of the body, though the latter was regarded as a means for the former. Doctors and nurses of mission hospitals and clinics, as agents of Jesus, the "Great Physician," worked for the salvation of the whole being through physical healing. Taking care of lepers was a good example of their holistic approach to human beings. The modern Western dual system of "body to science and soul to religion" was not a dilemma to them.[140] The cases of faith healing of "demon possession" presented both medical missionaries and evangelistic missionaries with a solution for this dichotomy.

The adjunct existence of "premodern" Korean shamanism within the boundary of "modern" Anglo-American Protestantism was one of the most notable features of indigenous Korean Christianity. This symbiosis, however, existed in a precarious state. Above all, like the first-century Jewish people, Koreans sought miraculous signs and healings without faith (Matt 12:39). Missionaries worried about the resilient hidden influences of shamanism on newly converted Korean Christians, especially among women believers.

Around 1910 some Presbyterian missionaries, like Bernheisel, accepted the continuationist view of miracle healing in modern times. Yet when the Korean church went through Kim Iktu's revivalism and faith healing in early 1920s, missionaries rejected the revision of a cessationist article of the Constitution of the Presbyterian Church that stated

---

[140] See Chung Chinhong, "Early Protestant Medical Missions and the Epitome of Human Body in Late Nineteenth Century Korea: Concerning Problems of Environment," in *Korea between Tradition and Modernity: Selected Papers from the Fourth Pacific and Asian Conference on Korean Studies*, edited by Chang Yun-Shik et al. (Vancouver: Institute for Asian Research, University of British Columbia, 2000), 312.

that the supernatural gift of miracle was bestowed on the early church for providential purposes and ceased with the death of the apostles.[141] The missionaries had to face faithless Korean communists' attack on Christianity as a "superstitious" religion, as well as Korean Christians' blind faith in miracle healing. An ongoing problem was Korean Christians' lingering shamanistic ideas on luck and bad luck and *kibok sinang* (prosperity-oriented faith).[142]

[141] Min Kyŏngbae, *Han'guk kidoggyohoe sa*, 354; Oak Sung-Deuk, "Major Protestant Revivals in Korea, 1903–1935," *Studies of World Christianity* 18, no. 3 (2012): 269–90.

[142] The popularity of prosperity theology and the "three-beat salvation" (spiritual salvation, material success, and physical health)—as well as the recurring scandals and persistent materialism of the contemporary Korean churches—reveals that Korean Christians have failed to exorcise kibok sinang and materialistic fetishism from the minds of the leaders and members of the church. The public dimension of Protestantism that fought against "superstitions" and idolatry and promoted national enlightenment and modernization at the turn of the twentieth century deteriorated into the private kibok sinang, which seeks worldly fortune, health, and personal prosperity.

— 4 —

Ancestors
Confucian and Christian Memorial Services

Did all the sages who had died without knowing the Jesus doctrine fall into hell? . . . We believe that if any person in the past had done only good works, he might have gone to heaven by the merits of Jesus.

—Ro Pyŏngsŏn, 1897[1]

In the issue of ancestor veneration, most historiography has depicted Korean Protestantism as having adopted a policy of strict prohibition instead of tolerance and enculturation. Although in the late 1930s, the majority of the Protestant churches accepted Shinto shrine worship not as a religious but as a civic ceremony, under the pressure of the Japanese colonial government, they have stood strong against ancestor worship since 1945, emphasizing the history of the minority groups' anti–Shinto shrine worship movement as well as that of the early Korean Christians' renunciation of ancestor worship. Such a confrontational attitude of Korean Protestantism has been compared to that of Korean Roman Catholicism, which was started by the Jesuit theology of accommodation toward Confucian morality and ancestral rites. The Roman Catholic theology of indigenization and the close diplomatic relationship between the Vatican and the Japanese Empire in the 1930s permitted Shinto shrine worship. Since Vatican II in the 1960s, the Roman Catholic Church has

[1] Ro Pyŏngsŏn, *P'ahok chinsŏn non* [Breaking Off Delusion and Proceeding to the Good: Introduction to Christianity] (Seoul: Korean Religious Tract Society, 1897), 8a.

promoted interreligious dialogue and the Catholic rite of ancestor veneration. Thus a general impression of exclusive Protestants and inclusive Roman Catholics persists among Koreans.

This chapter questions this kind of dualistic trajectory of Protestant confrontational and Roman Catholic conciliatory approaches to ancestor worship. In fact, the Roman Catholic Church in Korea forbade the ancestral rites as idolatry based on the papal conclusion of the Rites Controversy in the 1740s and Beijing Bishop A. Gouveia's decree prohibiting the practice of the ancestral rites in 1790. As a result the Chosŏn government condemned Roman Catholicism as a heterodoxy of "no father and no king" from 1791. The governmental persecutions produced more than two thousand martyrs from 1791 to 1868 in Korea.[2] By contrast, Protestantism developed an indigenous form of the Christian memorial service around 1900. This chapter investigates the Chinese Protestant missionaries' discourses on ancestor worship as a theological and missiological background of the Korean Protestant discourse on the issue, its development in Korea by Anglo-Saxon missionaries, Korean Christians' responses and theological reflections, and Korean Christians' invention of a Christian memorial service, ch'udohoe, and the funeral ceremony as alternatives to Confucian ancestral rites. It discusses the Protestant missionaries' changing views about ancestor worship and its meaning, but the main point is that Korean Christians decided how they would deal with ancestor worship.

THE ANCESTRAL RITUAL IN KOREA

Ancestor worship in Neo-Confucian Korea was not just a part of the cult of the dead but a religious domain in which family and kinship relationships were indispensable. As the care of deceased parents was regarded as an extension of their sons serving them during their lives, the departed parents were not regarded as dead, unlike the Buddhists' belief that the dead would disappear into the air. Thus "the ancestral ritual was a medium through which the living could express filial piety by requiting the ancestors' favor (pobon) and keeping their memories alive (ch'uwŏn)."[3] Through ancestor worship the group's qi (material

---

[2] Claude C. Dallét, *Histoire de l'Eglise de Corée* (Paris: Librairie Victor Palmé, 1874), 588.

[3] Martina Deuchler, *The Confucian Transformation of Korea: A Study of Society and Ideology* (Cambridge, Mass.: Harvard-Yenching Institute, 1992), 175.

force or energy) was activated and descent was thereby ritually reinforced. The descendents were united by the common ancestral substance qi. The ritual heir was to be a thoroughly moral man, a filial and primary son, not a secondary son (sons of concubines). Negligent sons were punished by the law, forbidden to conduct the ritual, or excommunicated from the ancestral shrine worship. The Neo-Confucian ideology implanted the agnatic principle in the matrix of the Chosŏn society and sustained a patrilineal consciousness among the descendents by ancestral veneration.

Koreans believed that the spirits of the dead lived in different forms for at least four generations and that the life of the living was influenced by the welfare of the spirits. There was a dual system in the relationship with the spirits. Bad spirits (*wŏn'gwi*) were the products of abnormal deaths, accidents, or executions; they died outside of their homes with a resentful and bitter feeling, *han*—a wounded heart.[4] Shamanistic or Buddhist requiems and purification ceremonies were performed to console these broken spirits. Good spirits were those who had lived long lives and died normal deaths in their homes; they became ancestral spirits (*chosangshin*) who blessed and protected their families and descendents as their guardians. Neo-Confucian ancestral rituals were offered to the good spirits of these ancestors, including kings of the dynasties and Confucian saints.[5] This chapter explores Christian encounters with the Neo-Confucian ancestral rite.

Protestant missionaries were aware of the moral and religious significance of ancestor veneration. G. H. Jones wrote that ancestor worship was the state creed in Korea and that law and custom united in imposing its obligation upon all people. He observed that the complicated system of ancestor worship was "an ever present factor in Korean life and no Korean can get beyond the sphere of its influence."[6] Ancestor veneration was the basis of the Confucian system, which had its root

---

[4] Korean minjung theologians denote *han* as the inner spirit of minjung who suffered from sociopolitical alienation, economic exploitation, and political oppression (Sŏ Namdong, *Minjung sinhag ŭi t'amgu* [A Study on Minjung Theology] [Seoul: Han'gilsa, 1984], 243). Other sources of *han* were epidemics and natural disasters.

[5] Lee Kwang Kyu, "The Concept of Ancestors and Ancestor Worship in Korea," *Asian Folklore Studies* 43 (1984): 199–214; Choi Kil Sung, "Male and Female in Korean Folk Belief," *Asian Folklore Studies* 43 (1984): 227–33.

[6] Jones, "Obstacles Encountered by Korean Christians," *KR* 2 (1895): 145–46.

in "the most sacred soil of human life—the family." The only unpardonable sin was the lack of filial piety, from which every other virtue flowed. In this system, ancestor worship, *chesa*, was equivalent to filial piety. Not participating in this family function was to subject oneself to the wrath and persecution of the rest of the clan, and the to reviling of outsiders.[7]

The ancestral rite was the occasion for a holy communion among the dead and the living.[8] The ceremonies were celebrated several times a year at the state and local levels and from clans to individual families. The order and frequency of the ritual varied from clan to clan. They were usually performed around midnight. A formal home ritual consisted of the following stages: (1) setting up the table with the tablets, (2) calling the spirits, (3) bowing to the spirits, (4) offering food, (5) offering a cup of wine by the head of the family, (6) praying for the prosperity of the family, (7) offering a second cup of wine by the head of the family's wife and a third by the senior member of the family, (8) offering the incense and having a moment of silence, (9) mixing rice with water or tea in a bowl and meditating for a moment, (10) sending the spirits, and (11) removing the table and sharing the food and wine. In this last stage, the assembled company shared the food offered to the spirits and "drank the blessings." The next morning they shared the food with neighbors.

On the memorial day (*hansik*) in the spring or on the day of the harvest, the full moon day (*Ch'usŏk*) in the fall, most Koreans dressed in their best white clothes, made a long pilgrimage to the family mountain tombs, and performed the annual sacrifice at the graves of ancestors. A grave was a sacred place to the household. It was cleaned, raked, and brushed. Then food and rice wine were arranged in front of the grave, and the people bowed down before it several times. After the veneration, they ate the food that had been offered up to the spirits. Bits of the best food were strewn about the grave, and wine was poured

[7] Gale, "Korea—Its Present Condition," *MRW* 16 (1893): 658–65; William M. Junkin, "The Daily Difficulties That Meet the Missionary in Korea," *Missionary* 30 (1897): 465; W. D. Reynolds, "Enemies of the Cross in Korea," *Missionary* 32 (1899): 464–66; Hulbert, "Kyoyuk" [Education], *KS*, July 12, 1906. Hulbert said that filial piety was the primary virtue in Korea and China, yet in Japan loyalty was the primary virtue.

[8] D. L. Gifford, *Everyday Life in Korea: A Collection of Studies and Stories* (New York: Revell, 1898), 93–97; Gale, *Korean Sketches* (New York: Revell, 1898), 213–14.

on the grave as an offering to the spirits. This act ensured peace and blessings for the year.

Koreans believed that they would achieve immortality by ensuring the continuity of their family bloodline. J. S. Gale stated, "In order to make sure of this eternal life through posterity, the gentleman marries his son off when he is still a mere boy, sometimes but nine or ten years of age."[9] He later wrote, "It is the key-stone of Korea's gateway to the happy lands of prosperity and success. To neglect it blocks the whole highway toward life and hope."[10] The need for the continuation of the priesthood line by a male head of a clan, extended family, or household generated negative by-products, such as a preference for sons, early marriage, concubinage, and degradation of women.[11] Yet the Confucian idea of eternity was guaranteed by this patriarchal succession. Theologically speaking, ancestor worship was the way of Confucian soteriology.[12] By participating in seasonal rituals and sharing holy food, Koreans preserved family identity, sense of community, and mutual interdependence. Ancestor worship was a sacred rite for the prosperity of the living that depended on harmony with ancestors, traditions, and the cosmos.

Therefore, when Koreans were required to abandon ancestor worship to be baptized, many of them left the church. Ancestor worship was a complicated and combustible issue to Korean Christians and to missionaries as well. Nevertheless, their policy regarding ancestor worship was imported from China. The missionaries in China and Chinese Christians had engaged in extensive research and debate on the subject, and their official policy of strict prohibition prevailed in East Asia until the Japanese Shinto shrine issue was raised in the 1930s.

Chinese Protestant Apologetics against Ancestor Worship

The Protestant missions in Korea appropriated the Chinese missions' intolerant policy and apologetics against ancestor worship. Many catechisms and tracts, translated from Chinese into Korean, condemned ancestor worship as idolatry. Walter H. Medhurst's *On Feast of Tombs*

[9] Gale, *Korean Sketches*, 190.
[10] Gale, *Korea in Transition* (New York: Young People's Missionary Movement of the United States and Canada, 1909), 69.
[11] J. Robert Moose, "Sacrifice to the Dead," *KM* 1 (1904): 15.
[12] Jones, "The Native Religions," *KMF* 4 (1908): 11–12.

(1854) and John L. Nevius' *Errors of Ancestor Worship* (1859) provided the Korean churches with an apologetic paradigm against ancestor worship. Especially Nevius' *Errors of Ancestor Worship* was used as a textbook in theological classes for Korean leaders in the 1890s.[13]

Qingming saomu zhilun (On Feast of Tombs, or On the Chinese Custom of Repairing the Graves, 1826, 1854, 1863), by W. H. Medhurst of the London Missionary Society, was one of the most widely read tracts on ancestor worship. It was "a discussion of the practice common among the Chinese, of offering annual sacrifices at the graves of their ancestors, on the *Tsing-ming* (April 6)."[14] It appreciated the Chinese practice of honoring parents—filial piety toward the living parents, taking care of the tomb, and veneration of the ancestors—which is identical to the fifth commandment of the Decalogue. But the tract condemned ancestor worship as idolatry and spirit worship of the dead because it violated the first and second commandments. Even though Confucius had encouraged ancestor worship in the past, the tract argued that it was not necessary for contemporary Chinese people to follow his teachings, for customs and rituals changed from age to age. Behind the idea of the changeability of rituals existed not only the theory of the deterioration of Asian religions from primitive monotheism to polytheism, but also the Western missionaries' conviction of the superiority of modern Christianity in the face of "outdated" Chinese religions.

John L. Nevius' *Sixian bianmiu* (Errors of Ancestor Worship, 1859, 1864) discussed ancestor worship and filial piety in dialogic form.[15] Its main goal was to persuade people to "forsake idolatry, renounce spirit and ancestor worship, and wholly worship the only and one God." It started with the thesis that Christianity, like Confucianism, taught and practiced filial piety. Nevius argued that the original form of ancestor worship in ancient China differed from the post-Confucius practice. Specifically, he contended that the latter had deteriorated into empty formalities and vanity, and thus that the original worship of Heaven practiced by the ancient sages must be recovered. Contemporary ancestor worship had fallen from an earlier pure way, which sought for

---

[13] *Official Minutes of the Annual Meeting of the Korea Mission of the MEC* (Seoul: Trilingual Press, 1893), 11–13.

[14] Alexander Wylie, *Memorials of Protestant Missionaries to the Chinese* (Shanghai: American Presbyterian Mission Press, 1867), 28.

[15] Wylie, *Memorials of Protestant Missionaries*, 224.

forgiveness from sins against heaven. Although Confucius said, "If one sinned against Heaven, there is no place to pray," later customs had devolved to futile spirit or ancestor worship. People forgot that the original root of human beings was not ancestors but God. People had made wooden tablets, yet the spirits did not reside there. More than ten times a year people offered food and wine to the spirits, yet the spirits could not eat or smell. People believed that the spirits of deceased parents would help their descendents, yet they were also in need of divine help. Thus the human principle, filial piety to parents and ancestors, although biblically sound, should be extended to and perfected by the worship of God, the heavenly principle. In conclusion, Nevius' tract recommended the Christian way of filial piety and ancestral veneration—not only being dutiful to living parents and relatives, performing proper funeral services, and taking care of tombs properly, but also having a reverential mind, keeping their good will, and honoring their names through donations, relief work, and good behavior.

Nevius insisted that ancestor worship in the days of Confucius had already deviated from the original sacrifices offered to Shangdi for thanksgiving and atonement, and that the latter anticipated the redemptive sacrifice of Jesus Christ to come. As such, Nevius disapproved the necessity of ancestor worship in connection with Christology. Mrs. Helen Nevius' *Christian Catechism* therefore asked, "Is it proper or not for Christians to worship ancestors?" It answered, "It is not. Because Jesus has already offered a big sacrifice to God with his body and blood, if one offers the second sacrifice, it would make little of Jesus."[16] Nevius acknowledged the historical role of ancestor worship in China yet appraised it as just a needless historical relic after the redemptive sacrifice of Jesus Christ. Medhurst and Nevius argued that ancestor worship was allowed in the past but that now it was superfluous and prohibited.

SHANGHAI MISSIONARY CONFERENCES AND ANCESTOR WORSHIP

A survey on the discussion of ancestor worship at the General Missionary Conferences, held in Shanghai in 1877, 1890, and 1907, gives a broad picture of the missionary ideas regarding Chinese religions,

---

[16] Helen Nevius, *Yesugyo mundap* [Christian Catechism], trans. H. G. Underwood (Seoul: Korean Religious Tract Society, 1893), 16a.

specifically ancestor worship, as the background of mission theology applied to Korean religions. From Liverpool (1860) to Edinburgh (1910), the missionary conferences agreed to the principle that Christianity planted in foreign lands must be adapted to local situations. Their initial attitude toward non-Christian religions, however, was negative. "Heathen" religions were regarded as enemies to the success of Christianity. This tendency began to change at the turn of the century. The Shanghai conferences revealed this missiological trend.

FIRST SHANGHAI MISSIONARY CONFERENCE, 1877

Prominent members of the first General Conference of the Protestant Missionaries of China, held at Shanghai in May 1877, were C. Douglas, John Butler, W. Muirhead, Griffith John, J. Edkins, Alexander Wylie, John L. Nevius, Calvin W. Mateer, J. Hudson Taylor, and M. T. Yates. On the first day, Griffith John, who had arrived in China in 1855 and founded the Hankou mission in 1861, read an opening paper. It represented the motive and the aim of mission of most of the delegates. His missionary aim was simple and clear: "We are here, not to develop the resources of the country, not for the advancement of commerce, not for the mere promotion of civilization; but to do battle with the powers of darkness, to save men from sin, and conquer China for Christ."[17] John's purpose was to save individual souls from sin through the spiritual power of the Christian gospel. He required the converted Chinese to abandon all heathen religions and customs. J. Hudson Taylor of the China Inland Mission agreed with John by saying that "our *great* work is to *preach Christ*."[18]

The conference drew a line against Confucianism and ancestor worship. J. W. Lambuth remarked that the applicants for baptism should renounce their sins and pledge themselves faithfully to forsake idolatry in all its forms, together with ancient customs antagonistic to Christianity;

[17] Griffith John, "The Holy Spirit in Connection with Our Work," in *Records of the General Conference of the Protestant Missionaries in China* (Shanghai: American Presbyterian Mission Press, 1877), 32. On May 16, John confessed that he had no sympathy with the spirit of Dr. Martin's paper that proposed that intellectual culture should be promoted by higher education or secular publications (John, "Holy Spirit," 236–37).

[18] John, "Holy Spirit," 239; emphasis original. Nevertheless, A. Williamson, W. A. P. Martin, Joseph Edkins, and Calvin W. Mateer supported higher education, education for women, and secular publications.

should keep the Sabbath; and should have a born-again experience. "We want a converted membership, not baptized heathen."[19] Joseph Edkins regarded three Chinese religions (Buddhism, Daoism, and Confucianism) as "three mighty fortresses erected by satanic art to impede the progress of Christianity." He proposed that the Christian soldiers first overthrow Buddhism and Daoism, the "strongholds of sin and Satan," and when they were destroyed, "let another earnest effort be made to destroy the last and strongest of the towers of the enemy," Confucianism.[20] Edkins believed that the extension of a system of education would strike at the root of "superstitious" religions.

The topic "Confucianism in Relation to Christianity" had been assigned to Dr. James Legge, but he could not attend the meeting and had no substitute. Therefore, Matthew T. Yates, who had written *Ancestral Worship* in 1867, read an essay. Yates defined ancestral worship as "the direct worship of the dead" and argued that it was "the most formidable obstacle to the introduction of Christianity."[21] After the conference, although some disagreed, Yates' view represented a consensus among the missionary circles until at least the 1920s. Henry Blodget summarized Yates' essay in the second Shanghai Conference in 1890, and *The Encyclopedia of Missions* adopted Yates' opinion in 1904.[22]

James Legge's essay, *Confucianism in Relation with Christianity*, was published in a separate booklet. Legge claimed that the Di and Shangdi of the Chinese classics was the true God. His second argument was that the original Confucian anthropology taught that human beings were the creatures of heaven or God, that the human moral nature endowed by God was good, and that the souls of human beings were immortal. The third was that the teaching of Confucianism on human duty was wonderful and admirable. Legge believed that Christianity was the fulfillment of Confucianism. He concluded that Confucianism was in many important points defective rather than antagonistic, and that missionaries should endeavor not to exhibit themselves as antagonistic

[19] James W. Lambuth, "Standard of Admission to Full Church Membership," in GCPMC, *RGC* (1878), 241–46.

[20] Joseph Edkins, "Buddhism and Tauism in Their Popular Aspects," in *Records of the General Conference of the Protestant Missionaries in China* (Shanghai: American Presbyterian Mission Press, 1877), 71.

[21] Matthew T. Yates, "Ancestral Worship," in GCPMC, *RGC* (1878), 385.

[22] Henry O. Dwight et al., eds., *Encyclopedia of Missions* (London: Funk & Wagnalls, 1904), 40–41.

to Confucianism. He believed that Confucius and Mencius were "raised up by God for the instruction of the Chinese people." Although their system of teaching was not complete, it was in harmony with the divine plan in the communication of truth to mankind. The existence of the errors of religious worship, introduced in the system, did not deny that those men were "specially helped by God," and that "He might keep up some knowledge of Himself, and of the way of duty among the millions of their race."[23] Much of Confucianism, unlike atheistic Buddhism or pantheistic Brahmanism, might be made to serve as a schoolmaster to lead to Christ, like the Old Testament.

These two views of Confucianism—Yates' conservative view and Legge's progressive one—were introduced into Korea from the beginning of its missions. Yates and other conservative missionaries emphasized the points of conflict between Asian religions and Christianity, whereas Legge and some progressive missionaries were concerned with the points of contact between them. These two perspectives coexisted in the Korea missions in creative tension and controversy.

SECOND SHANGHAI MISSIONARY CONFERENCE, 1890

The second Shanghai Conference emphasized social reform and higher education of the native leaders. Franklin Ohlinger, who was transferred from China to Korea in 1887, stressed the need to abandon all native idolatrous and cruel customs such as ancestor worship, opium smoking, drinking, gambling, fighting, polygamy, and foot binding.[24]

One of the most important resolutions adopted by the conference was against W. A. P. Martin's "Ancestral Worship: A Plea for Toleration."[25] Martin suggested that a wise adaptation of means would solve "the most serious impediment to the conversion of the Chinese." Although he admitted that "there is unquestionably a large intermixture of superstition and idolatry" in ancestor worship, he emphasized its threefold good tendencies: (1) to strengthen the bonds of family union and stimulate

[23] Legge, *Confucianism in Relation with Christianity* (Shanghai: Kelly & Walsh, 1877), 10–12.

[24] Franklin Ohlinger, "How Far Should Christians be Required to Abandon Native Customs?" in GCPMC, *RGC* (1890), 603–9.

[25] W. A. P. Martin, "Ancestral Worship: A Plea for Toleration," in GCPMC, *RGC* (1890), 619–31. Martin's basic viewpoint on Asian religions was that they were the preparation for the gospel. See Martin, "Is Buddhism a Preparation for Christianity?" *CR* 20 (1889): 193–203.

active charity, (2) to cherish self-respect and impose moral restraint, and (3) to keep alive a sort of faith in the reality of a spirit world. He insisted that ancestor worship could be modified into harmony with Christianity. He interpreted the word "worship" as a respectful salutation, and after analyzing the essential elements of ancestor worship, such as posture, invocation, and offering, he maintained that these essentials did not necessarily imply idolatry. He evaluated the Catholic custom of praying for the dead as more humane than Protestant extreme sentiment. He suggested that Protestant missionaries in China, who employed a different name for God from the papal term, should reconsider the papal decision that condemned ancestor worship. He believed that a tolerant position might be Protestantism's highway to success in China.

H. Blodget read an essay contrary to Martin's opinion. He stated that Protestantism, Islam, and Roman Catholicism had historically opposed ancestor worship. He insisted that ancestor worship was founded on a distorted view of filial piety, worship of the tablet was idolatrous, and offerings and prayers to the dead were not permissible among Christians.[26] Veteran missionaries opened a heated discussion. Ernst Faber pointed out seventeen evil features of ancestral worship.[27] W. Muirhead said, "I was not aware that there were two opinions on the subject of ancestral worship." Professor Thwing exclaimed, "As Dr. Yates has said, to yield this point is to yield everything. Toleration of idolatry is treason to Christianity!"[28] John Ross, however, suggested a practical way of compromise: not forbidding it absolutely but adapting it without its idolatrous practices or superstitious customs. Timothy Richard and Gilbert Reid attacked the extreme attitude of condemning ancestral ceremony and maintained that native customs should be accepted after excluding idolatrous elements. Suddenly, J. Hudson Taylor suggested, "[A]ll those who wish to raise an indignant protest against the conclusion of Dr. Martin's paper will signify it by rising."[29] Almost the whole audience did so. Reid protested against the action. He

---

[26] Henry Blodget, "The Attitude of Christianity toward Ancestral Worship," in GCPMC, *RGC* (1890), 631–54. Blodget argued that the historical experience of Roman Catholics' Rites Controversies provided Protestant missionaries with the providential and proper direction toward ancestral worship. He accepted the decision forbidding ancestor worship by Pope Clement XI as "not too strict."

[27] Dwight et al., *Encyclopedia of Missions*, 41.

[28] GCPMC, *RGC* (1890), 657.

[29] GCPMC, *RGC* (1890), 659.

defended Martin's orthodox theology and moved to form a committee to consider the issue.

Finally, the conference reached the conclusion that "missionaries should refrain from any interference with the native mode of honoring ancestors, and leave the reformation of the system to the influence of Divine Truth, when it gets a firmer hold on the national mind."[30] Although it anticipated the time when more mature Chinese Christians would reform the system of ancestor worship, the conference did not adopt a wait-and-see policy. It clearly declared that it was against ancestor worship. Members of the conference affirmed their belief that idolatry was an essential constituent of ancestral worship. This antagonistic resolution exerted a crucial influence on the young missionaries in Korea. Just after the conference, Presbyterian missionaries in Seoul invited John Nevius and adopted his method as the guideline for the mission policy. They followed the official conservative approach of the Shanghai Conference to ancestor worship, instead of the tolerant approach of Drs. Ross, Martin, and Richard. The minority opinion, however, did not lose its influence among the missionaries in either China or Korea.

SHANGHAI CENTENARY MISSIONARY CONFERENCE, 1907

The third general conference was originally intended for 1900 but was postponed to 1901 due to the Ecumenical Missionary Conference in New York, and then postponed again due to the Boxer Movement, but it was held in 1907 with many Chinese delegates as a celebration of the close of the first century of Protestant missionary work in China. One of the sessions discussed the issue of ancestor worship, which was still an important, difficult, and delicate subject for the missionaries. Many Chinese people charged that Christians did not revere their ancestors. Therefore, the committee prepared five constructive resolutions, which were presented to the session by James Jackson. They expressed something upon which all could unite, although they might differ in their views on certain aspects. The position taken up was "an ironical position—a mediating position."

> It takes for the truth set forth by the writer of the Epistle of Hebrews, as by other of the New Testament Scriptures, that God has spoken to all

[30] GCPMC, *RGC* (1890), lxiii.

races of men in fragmentary portions and various ways, that He has given to the Chinese people at least some scattered rays of that many colored wisdom of God which emanates from the Eternal Word which has shone and still shines in the hearts of all men. . . . The resolutions . . . acknowledge . . . the true instincts which seek to find expression in the worship of ancestors, while at the same time condemning the distortion of those instincts manifested in some features of that worship.[31]

During the discussion, Dr. J. C. Gibson, chairperson of the session, said that in the worship of ancestors the word "worship" denoted not only proper respect but also religious worship. So he suggested that Christians should adopt the idea of a "memorial service," which might express more closely the Chinese point of view, because there were some good features in ancestor worship. With some discussion the session adopted the following four resolutions one by one:

I. That, while the Worship of Ancestors is incompatible with an enlightened and spiritual conception of the Christian Faith, and so cannot be tolerated as a practice in the Christian Church, yet we should be careful to encourage in our Christian converts, the feeling of reverence for the memory of the departed which this custom seeks to express and to impress upon the Chinese in general, the fact that Christians attach great importance to filial piety. II. That, recognizing the full provision made in Christianity for the highest development and expression of filial piety, this Conference recommends that greater prominence be given in preaching, in teaching and in religious observances, to the practical duty of reverence to parents, and thus make it evident to non-Christians that the Church regards filial piety as one of the highest of Christian duties. III. Recognizing that in replacing the worship of ancestors in China by Christianity, many delicate and difficult questions inevitably arise, we would emphasize the necessity for the continuous education of the conscience of the members of the Christian Church by whom all such questions must ultimately be adjusted, expressing our confidence that through the leading and illumination of the Spirit of God, the Church will be guided into right lines of action. IV. That this Conference recommends our Chinese brethren to encourage an affectionate remembrance of the dead by beautifying graves and erecting useful memorials to parents and asylums, and other charitable institutions as is common in all Christian lands, thus making memorials of the departed a means of helping the living through successive generations.[32]

[31] GCPMC, *RGC* (1907), 606.
[32] GCPMC, *RGC* (1907), 623–24.

The conference continued to prohibit ancestor worship as a religious practice. Yet it encouraged ancestor worship's spirit of reverence for ancestors and practical duties of filial piety to parents. The missionaries thought that their recommendation was just a guideline for the Chinese Christians, who they trusted would decide the subject with mature faith and theology with the help of the Holy Spirit. Compared to the previous conferences, the Centenary Conference, or at least the session on ancestor worship, was dominated by progressive missionaries such as Gibson, Jackson, Martin, and Smith. Although Martin's position, compared to 1890, was moderated in 1907, he still supported the good elements of ancestor worship.

Interestingly, the fourth resolution originally presented by Jackson was not adopted at the session. The resolution, though not strictly connected with ancestor worship, had an important bearing upon it:

> That some effort be made by memorial or otherwise, to induce the Chinese government to follow in the steps of Japan by declaring that the homage paid to the tablets of the Emperor and of Confucius, shall not be regarded as an act of religious worship, but of State ceremony only, so that Christians may perform the required acts of homage without violating Christian principle or Christian conscience, while at the same time escaping the brand of disloyalty.[33]

Jackson explained that the whole subject of ancestor worship, with the collateral subjects of homage paid to the Emperor and to Confucius, had ceased to be a question of conscience in the churches of Japan. The conference, he suggested, might recommend the Chinese government follow in the steps of Japan by declaring that the required acts of homage should be regarded as acts of state ceremony only. Arthur H. Smith seconded the adoption of the resolution and moved that the resolution be referred to the Committee on Memorials. It was defeated by vote. Arnold Foster and D. Z. Sheffield opposed its adoption. They believed that those practices had been regarded as religious worship for a thousand years, and thus the passing of the resolution would entangle the consciences of East Asian Christians. This rejection of emperor worship as state ceremony in China was important for the later Shinto shrine question in Korea in the 1930s.

---

[33] GCPMC, *RGC* (1907), 604.

The conference adopted four memorials: to the Chinese churches, to the home churches, to opium, and to the Chinese government. The last consisted of two parts: "a declaration to the Government respecting the spiritual and philanthropic object of Christian Missions" and "a Petition asking for complete religious liberty for all Chinese Christians." The declaration stated dogmatic similarities and differences between Christianity and Chinese religions in the teachings on God, Christ, human beings, and salvation. It emphasized the gradual reforming and fulfilling power of Christianity for the prosperity of China, the voluntary character of the mission societies, and the nonpolitical character of Christianity. The conference petitioned the Empress Dowager and the emperor, asking for complete religious liberty for all Chinese Christians. The memorial pointed out the trouble arising from the enforced performance of the state religious ceremony in the past in Europe and expressed a desired that China might be saved from "the sorrows that our own countries have suffered through religious intolerance." After mentioning the examples of India and Japan, the document asked that the emperor decree that in the law courts "the question never be asked whether litigants, offenders, or prosecutors are Christians or what religion they follow, but that each case should be considered only on its own merits, and that the same rule should be followed in the appointment of officials and teachers."[34] Religious freedom was one of the most important issues in China, Japan, and Korea. When Ito granted religious liberty to the Korea missions in 1905, missionaries welcomed his administration in Korea. T. Richard and other missionaries in China praised Ito's tolerant policy.

Mission Policy against Ancestor Worship in Korea

The resolutions against ancestor worship at the conferences were introduced to Korea and remained the official guidelines until the middle of the 1930s. The 1877 and 1890 conferences condemned ancestor worship as an idolatrous sacrifice and required all candidates for baptism to abandon it. However, there was a theological tension between the old-generation missionaries and the new-breed college-educated missionaries behind these resolutions. Some liberal conservative or open-minded evangelical missionaries emerged and appreciated the value of

[34] GCPMC, *RGC* (1907), 405.

traditional religious customs. Both the official policy of Chinese Protestantism against ancestor worship and its changing theological openness to Chinese religions were imported to Korea.

In 1891 Henry G. Appenzeller wrote that he was following the decision of the 1890 Shanghai Conference, and as a result he lost a Confucian scholar candidate for baptism, who declared, "If I must give up ancestral worship to be baptized, I will not be baptized."[35] Korean tracts and catechisms condemned ancestor worship. John Ross' *Syŏngyŏng mundap* (Bible Catechism, 1881), reprinted in Seoul in 1895, prohibited "the worship of the dead" in the context of monotheism and idolatry. The fifty-seventh question asked, "Shall we worship the dead people?" The answer was, "Although we revere the life and death of the righteous people, we shall neither worship them nor pray to them."[36]

REASONS FOR THE PROHIBITION OF ANCESTOR WORSHIP

There were five major reasons why Protestant missionaries opposed ancestor worship in East Asia. First, they concluded that ancestor worship was a religious sacrifice to the spirits of the dead and that it was against the first and second commandments. Missionaries insisted that Christian monotheism was antithetical to polytheism and that divine spirituality was incompatible with the idolatry of ancestor worship.[37] Second, although ancestor worship taught the idea of the immortality of the soul, the Confucian belief in a soul that could reside in a handmade tablet, eat sacrificial food, and bless the descendants was unscriptural.[38] The status of the ancestor's soul was too ephemeral. It existed as a kind of material force and gradually vanished with the fading memory of the living. Yet Christianity taught that the invisible and spiritual soul of a person never vanished and that there were two eternal destinations for the soul after death—heaven or hell. The Christian doctrine of

[35] Appenzeller, "Korea—What Is It Worth?" *HWF* 24 (1892): 230–31.

[36] J. Ross, *Syŏngyŏng mundap* [Bible Catechism], trans. and ed. Mary F. Scranton (Seoul: Trilingual Press, 1895), 9a. Although Ross was tolerant of polygamy and other Chinese customs, he followed in his catechism the decision of the 1877 Shanghai Conference against ancestor worship.

[37] W. B. McGill, *Kusye yoŏn* [Essential of the World's Salvation] (Seoul: Trilingual Press, 1895), 2a, 4a; Underwood, "Syŏnggyŏng kangnonhoe" [Bible Study], *KS*, October 6, 1898.

[38] Nevius, *Yesugyo mundap*, 31a; Samuel A. Moffett and Ch'oe Myŏng'o, *Kusyeron* [Discourse on Salvation] (Seoul: Trilingual Press, 1895), 15a; "Ch'ŏsa hoegae" [Repentance of a Scholar], *SW* 1 (1901): 357–58, 435.

the resurrection conflicted with the belief system of ancestor worship.[39] These two arguments emphasized discontinuity between the monotheistic God and the polytheistic gods, and between the living and the dead.[40]

The next two reasons for the Protestant missionaries' denunciation of ancestor worship were related to anti–Roman Catholicism. Evangelical missionaries thought that the Korean idea of mutual influence between the world of the dead and the world of the living was a distorted version of Roman Catholicism's saint worship and its theory of purgatory. Like the sixteenth-century reformers who had rejected the idea of the imputation of the merits of the saints upon believers, Protestant missionaries restricted the meaning of the church as *congregatio sanctorum* (the congregation of the saints) to the communion among *congregatio fidelium* (the congregation of the believers), whether they were dead or alive. Those who died without faith in Christ were excluded from the congregation of the saints. Evangelical missionaries did not pay much attention to the continuation of traditional communities such as clans or families based on Confucianism, but to the formation of a new community of believers in Christ. The evangelical bias against Roman Catholic ritualism worked negatively. It rejected the sacrificial concept of the Roman Catholic mass as unbiblical, criticized its theory of transubstantiation as superstitious, and ridiculed its complicated ritualistic procedures as magical. When they saw similarities between Confucian ancestor worship and the Roman Catholic mass, they could not permit the former. Although Gale admired Ricci's scholarship on Confucianism, Gale criticized Riccian tolerance of ancestor worship as a forbearance of spirit worship.[41]

The fifth reason was practical and ethical. Missionaries believed that ancestor worship was the major source of evil customs, such as early marriage, concubinage, degradation of women, poverty, and national stagnation.[42] Missionaries saw the superstitious, selfish, material, and

---

[39] "Yŏnsyŏ" [Editorial: A Speech], *KH*, March 31, 1897; "Usyangnon" [Editorial: On Idols], *KH*, April 14, 1897; Ro Pyŏngsŏn, *P'ahok chinsŏn non*.

[40] Roman Catholicism used these two arguments—monotheism and dualism between life and death—against ancestor worship and produced thousands of martyrs for a century.

[41] Gale, "Limado ŭi sajŏk" [The Life and Work of Matteo Ricci], *KS*, October 17, 1901.

[42] Jones, *The Korea Mission of the Methodist Episcopal Church* (New York: Board of the Foreign Missions of the Methodist Episcopal Church, 1910), 19.

magical practice of the ancestral cult, not its positive elements. Protestant missionaries countered ancestor worship with theological iconoclasm, sociocultural modernism, economic capitalism, ethical emphasis on family and women's rights (against early marriage, polygamy, and gender discrimination), political progressivism, and social Darwinism. Their worldview, embedded in the rationalism of Western Enlightenment, curbed a more liberal attitude toward such "heathen" ceremonies. Their Puritan tradition and strong opposition to Roman Catholic ritualism, the doctrine of purgatory, and saint worship were imposed through an evangelical bias against ancestor worship.

Burning or Burying the Ancestral Tablets

The ancestor cult was the last thing that many Korean Christians gave up. Abandoning the ancestral rite was not only an iconoclastic behavior, but also a total departure from the traditions of the extended family structure and the local community system. Personal salvation apart from the ancestral line represented an overwhelming existential crisis, and choosing to sever this tie was a difficult choice. Thus some seekers lapsed into the old customs. In September 1895 William L. Swallen of Wŏnsan had to expel two members from communion because they had returned to ancestor worship. After this discipline, he reported, "Now our members all stand firm to a man upon the subject of ancestral worship." He believed that ancestral worship was the greatest idol the Koreans had to give up. "I fear we have been too lenient heretofore on this subject. This will be one of the subjects before us for settlement at the annual meeting this fall."[43] Swallen insisted that a more conservative policy should replace the past lenient attitude because he thought that the greatest idolatry in Korea was ancestor worship.[44]

J. S. Gale of the same church solved the issue in a democratic manner. Before proposing any action upon the subject by the session of the church, he sent out papers to Korean Christians asking them to write down their views of ancestor worship and how it should be dealt with. All replies asserted that ancestor worship was foolish and against the command of God.[45] The subject was settled not by Gale's authority,

[43] William L. Swallen to Frank F. Ellinwood, September 24, 1895.
[44] Swallen to Friends, July 1896.
[45] *Annual Report of the BFMPCUSA* (New York: BFMPCUSA, 1896), 161–62.

but by the Korean believers' participation and determination. Both Gale and his Korean congregation made a wise and discriminating decision. As a result, a year later Swallen baptized fourteen persons who had discarded the old customs of concubinage and ancestral worship and who kept the Sabbath.[46]

New converts gave up ancestor worship and burned or buried the tablets. Some gave the tablets to the missionaries as a token of their conversion.[47] In 1897 new believers in Suwŏn and Yongin burned their ancestral tablets and household fetishes.[48] There was a widow of the eldest son of a clan in Paekch'ŏn, Hwanghae. She lived with her daughter-in-law, who became a widow with a handicapped boy. After hearing the gospel from a Bible woman, the first widow realized that her sin against God had brought disasters to the family. She burned all the tablets and fetishes in the shrine and house. The clan tried to cast out the widows from the house.[49] In 1900 Charles T. Collyer visited the house of Mun Manho, an old gentleman in Songdo. They burned fetishes for six hours. Then Mun gave the ancestral tablet to Collyer, saying, "As they were now treading the heavenly road there was no more use for them." Collyer knew that "the ancestral tablet is always the hardest and the last thing for a Korean to give up, because he believes that if there is no one to pray before the shrine of his spirit after he is gone, then there will be no rest for his soul."[50] Even the high priestess of the royal family in Seoul was converted in 1905, when the upper class at last came freely and worshipped "with those who are of no account socially."[51] In 1907 Cho Sangjŏng, a yangban scholar of Kanghwa, destroyed his ancestral tablets and donated a part of the ancestral burial ground to the church. In addition, he liberated a maidservant.[52] Missionaries also prohibited church members from eating and touching sacrificial food offered to the spirits. They asserted, based on 1 Corinthians 10:21, Acts 15:29, and Revelation 2:14, 20, that eating sacrificial food was a sin identical

---

[46] Swallen to F. F. Ellinwood, September 21, 1896.

[47] "Kim Sangt'aessi ŭi yŏlsim" [Efforts of Mr. Kim Sangt'ae], SW 3 (1903): 194.

[48] "Hoejyung sinmun" [Congregational News], KH, March 3, 1897.

[49] "Kyohoe t'ongsin" [Church News], KS, March 31, 1898.

[50] Charles T. Collyer, "A Day on the Songdo Circuit," KF 1 (1901): 12–13.

[51] Gale, "The Gospel Levels Ranks," KF 5 (1905): 263–64.

[52] Ro Pyŏngsŏn, "Kanghwa sagyŏnghoe chŏnggyŏng" [A Bible Class at Kanghwa], SW 5 (1907): 81. Mr. Cho liberated a maidservant of his house, because he believed in human equality.

to worshipping idols.[53] Ancestor worship, however, stood as a major obstacle to people's conversion to Christianity.

PERSECUTION BY THE COMMUNITY AND FAMILY MEMBERS

In many, if not most, cases, choosing Christ over one's ancestors required not only an iconoclastic conviction but also a severance of all ties with families and friends. Rejecting ancestor worship provoked severe reproach and persecution from family members and neighbors. It incurred physical suffering, financial loss, and social ostracism. Nevertheless, most converts did not turn back to the old customs. In the spring of 1892, S. A. Moffett met a man in Ŭiju who showed him a scar on his forehead that he had received from his aunt. She had knocked him senseless with an ink stone when he refused to sacrifice at his father's tomb.[54] In 1893 Gale reported about Old Kim, his first convert in Wŏnsan. In April Kim was getting weaker, and only after great persuasion could Gale get him to accept some beef occasionally. "I am quite sure that this condition was largely due to starvation, for the village ostracized him after he burned his ancestral tablets, and have also stopped his spring seeding and farm work generally."[55]

At Moffett's house in Pyongayng on January 7, 1894, eight catechumens, having given good evidence of conversion, were publicly baptized as the first Korean Protestant Christians in the city and partook of the Lord's Supper.[56] They were roundly abused as being unfilial, "since it is known that Christians give up ancestral worship, and they were told they would have their heads taken off as were those of the Romanists some 30 years ago."[57] The people of Pyongayng remembered that many Roman Catholics had been killed for their refusal of ancestor worship by the government in 1861 and the General Sherman Incident in 1866. They ridiculed both the Western learning (Roman Catholicism) and the Jesus doctrine (Protestantism) as being "no father and no king" heterodoxy.

In early 1894 H. G. Underwood baptized a young farmer near Seoul. His father had recently died, and the son was to have sacrificed to the

---

[53] "Usang e chyemur ŭl mŏkchi mal kŏt" [Don't Eat Food Offered to Idols], *KS*, September 13, 1906.
[54] Moffett, "Evangelism in Korea," *GAL* 17 (1892): 446.
[55] Gale, "Korea," *CHA* 7 (1893): 211.
[56] Moffett, "Life at a Korean Outpost," *CHA* 8 (1894): 374.
[57] Moffett to F. F. Ellinwood, January 12, 1894.

spirit. But he removed the ancestral tablet and did not bow down before it. His uncle warned him that all interactions with relatives would cease. Soon they said he must surely be crazy. A little child in his family died. "This was believed to have been caused by the father's being a Christian. So his wife left him, saying she could not live with such a man."[58] In Hyech'ŏn county in 1902, a young man was severely tested when his father died. As he was the eldest son, it was his duty to venerate the deceased father. "He was the first Christian in the town to undergo such a test, and although he had been a believer only a few months, he patiently endured the persecution and was true to his faith."[59] In 1904 a new church sprang up at Magungol, Kyŏnggi. Although they had been terribly persecuted by the villagers and the magistrate, they stood firm. "One man was tortured in jail and compelled to pay over 100 dollars Korean. He was the first man in the district who refused to worship his dead mother."[60] Another man was beaten nearly to death, yet he said that he would die in the faith of Jesus rather than offer sacrifice to ancestors.[61] Besides corporal punishment and financial damages, converts were also excommunicated by their clans. Their names were erased from the clan's genealogy. This was the eternal anathema to their apostasy.

THE SEOUL CONFERENCE OF 1904

When the missionaries in Korea had experienced Korean culture for a couple of decades, some senior missionaries began to propose that they should wait until Korean Christians could solve the issue of ancestor worship under the guidance of the Holy Spirit. In September 1904, at a conference marking the twentieth anniversary of the Presbyterian mission in Korea, George O. Engel of the Victorian Presbyterian Mission of Australia read a paper on native customs. After emphasizing the need for adaptation to the Korean context, he suggested that missionaries should take a laissez-faire attitude toward Korean dwellings, food, clothes, and hair. Regarding the customs under which religious ideas

---

[58] William M. Junkin, "Notes from Korea," *Missionary* 27 (1894): 439.

[59] *Annual Report of the Missionary Society of the Methodist Episcopal Church* (New York: MSMEC, 1903), 363; *Annual Report of the Missionary Society of the Methodist Episcopal Church* (New York: MSMEC, 1906), 336.

[60] C. A. Clark, "Stood Firm," *KF* 5 (1905): 266.

[61] Pak Sech'ang, "Innae ro igŭim" [Victory with Patience], *SW* 3 (1904): 341; Yi Sŏkp'ung, "Pukch'yŏng raesin" [News from Pukch'ŏng], *KS*, January 18, 1906; C. A. Clark, "Three Incidents," *KMF* 5 (1909): 18.

lay, such as marriage customs and ancestor worship, he suggested the substitution of the Christian ceremonies, not by missionaries' interference but by Korean Christians' initiative.

> As an illustration of how isolated Korean Christians solve these problems for themselves and change their customs, I beg to mention the following:—One man told me once that on the sacrificial days he assembled his family in the evening, lit candles, but not before the tablets (for they had been destroyed), and prayed that God may have mercy on his departed ancestors who had had no chance to hear the Gospel. While I took occasion to point out to him the danger and heresy of such an action, I could not help thinking that God would accept such a prayer in the spirit in which it was offered. There are many things that will be changed yet by the Korean Christians as they receive more spiritual enlightenment. We can do very little, but *God's Word* and *His Holy Spirit* will bring about the changes in the customs of this nation that will make it a truly Christian nation, as truly Christian as ours in the West, and yet leave it oriental. May God grant that Western civilization, with its baneful influence, will leave the Korean church untouched.[62]

Engel believed that the Holy Word and Spirit would bring about the changes and that spiritually enlightened native Christians would truly become Christians, not Western Christians but Korean Christians. In discussion, J. Robert Moose remarked that "all Korean Christians pray regularly for their departed ancestors, this being the understanding on which they have given up Confucian worship." James S. Gale stated that "the question, what shall be our attitude toward mourning customs, confronts all of us. We must deal gently with the Koreans, who, as they grow in grace, will gradually advance in such matters." Samuel F. Moore felt certain that "such pernicious customs as lotteries, wine drinking, debt, usury, smoking excessively, grave-sorcery, would pass out as the light of God shines in." S. A. Moffett asserted that not all church members were in the habit of praying for their ancestors, and that he had found them willing to abandon it.[63]

In 1909 Gale advised the young and inexperienced missionaries not to touch the issue and to wait until the spiritually mature Korean Christians could solve it.

---

[62] George O. Engel, "Native Customs and How to Deal with Them," *KF* 4 (1904): 205; emphasis original.

[63] Engel, "Native Customs," 205–6.

Confronting the young missionary, in his ignorance, is the stupendous question of the ancestor, rooted deep in the generations that lie buried, and with its tentacles all about the living, associated with the wisest of the Orient, and backed up by the master (Confucius) himself and the sages. What can the young and often callow missionary do to meet this? Can he argue the point? Never. Can he speak of it at all with any effect? No. What can he do? Do as the Negro did when he saw the black dog waiting at the gate, his jaw "big" and his eye "mighty dangersome." What did he do? He let him alone. Let it alone. Know all about it, but don't touch it. There is no need. Ancestor worship is dropped off by the spiritually alive, as the beggar drops off his old garments to become a prince imperial.[64]

Gale believed that Korean Christians would solve the issue of ancestor worship with the guidance of the Holy Spirit.

In sum, the controversies and conflicts surrounding the issue of ancestor worship provided the Korea missions with an opportunity to reflect on the theology of filial piety and to understand the relationship of a Triune God in terms of filial piety—God as Heavenly Father of all beings and community of faith and equality, Jesus as the Filial Son, and the Holy Spirit as the teacher of filial piety. Some senior missionaries with a better understanding of the Korean mind-set hoped that the time would come when Korean Christians would find a modus vivendi in a purified and relevant form of ancestor worship with the inspiration of the Holy Spirit.

Theology of Filial Piety

Confrontational policies neither solved the issue nor satisfied the spiritual need of Koreans.[65] Christian alternatives with a distinct theological identity and cultural relevance were needed to fill the vacuum. A theology of filial piety, a Christian funeral rite, and an indigenous memorial service were introduced out of cultural necessity and the apologetic positions of Korean leaders. Evangelistic tracts stressed the duty of worshipping the Heavenly Father (T'yŏnbu) in addition to that of honoring one's visible parents. It described God as Creator of all things and Father of all people. It used the Confucian argument that children should revere

---

[64] Gale, *Korea in Transition*, 78.

[65] Some believers avoided the occasion when they could not have helped participating in the rite. See Appenzeller, "Woman's Work in Korea," *GAL* 16 (1891): 424; Appenzeller, "Notes from the Stations," *KMF* 6 (1910): 8.

their parents as their foundation. Namely, Christianity required one further step—the filial piety (faith) of all people to the Heavenly Father, the Ultimate Beginning, and the only True Principle.[66] One tract wrote, "Although Jehovah is the Father of all the people in the world, his filial children are few. Only those who believe in Jesus and are transformed by the Holy Spirit are able to have the heart of children and become Jehovah's true children."[67] Thus a series of editorials in the *Christian Advocate* said that, like a king in the palace, a parent in the house, or the soul in a body, God is the Creator and Ruler of the universe:

> The soul is one hundred times more valuable than the body. Yet people revere only the parents who gave the body and do not know how to revere God who endowed the soul. Is it not lack of filial piety? . . . Eastern people say that those who believe in the Western religion do not practice ancestor worship and turn against the foundational root of the family. We do not think so. Ancestor worship does not cover more than four generations. Even if we include the rite for the originator of the clan, it goes back to only forty or fifty generations. It knows neither who the father of the originator was nor how to serve him. It is like loving only flowers without knowing how to cultivate the root of a plant.[68]

The editorial continued, "If we go back from the founding fathers to their fathers, then we finally come to the first ancestor Adam, and then to God. As we serve God first, we Christians truly serve the ancestors. If you want to know the origin of ancestors, please study the Christian Scriptures."[69]

Jesus was presented as the Filial Son to the Father. "Jesus was a filial son to the parents at home for thirty years. . . . He became our elder brother and suffered our punishment instead of the sin of our younger brothers and sisters."[70] When Jesus prayed to God, he called

[66] Martin, *Samyorok* [Three Principles], trans. H. G. Underwood (Seoul: Korean Religious Tract Society, 1894), 11a, 15a–15b; Mrs. J. L. Holmes, *Huna chinŏn* [Peep of Day], trans. Mary F. Scranton (Seoul: Korean Religious Tract Society, 1891), 3a; D. B. McCartee, *Chilli iji* [Easy Introduction to Christian Doctrine], trans. H. G. Underwood (Seoul: Korean Religious Tract Society, 1895), 16b, 22b; M. Jones, *Ch'ohak ŏnmun* [A Korean Primer] (Seoul: Korean Religious Tract Society, 1895), 5b–6a; "Kyohoe t'ongsin" [Church News], *KS*, April 8, 1897.

[67] G. John, *Pogŭm taeji* [Great Themes of the Gospels], trans. H. G. Underwood (Seoul: Korean Religious Tract Society, 1894), 9a.

[68] "Manmul ŭi kŭnbon" [The Origin of All Things], *KH*, March 10, 1897.

[69] "Manmul ŭi kŭnbon" [The Origin of All Things]. *KH*, March 17, 1897.

[70] G. John, *Kusye chinjyu* [The True Savior], trans. W. M. Baird (Seoul: Korean Religious Tract Society, 1895), 7b.

Him "Abba, Father." It expressed a child's trust and affection for his father. Jesus was not only his Father's beloved Son, but also the Filial Son who always made his Father's will the sole purpose of his earthly life. He revered and glorified his Father through radical obedience.[71]

Korean apologetics emphasized filial piety to the living parents, not to the spirits of ancestors. Missionaries thought that such an emphasis on filial piety would mitigate Confucian animosity and appeal to Korean morality. They examined ancestor worship not only in terms of the second commandment but also in terms of the fifth, "Honor your father and mother." In 1901 *Sinhak Wŏlbo*, edited by Jones, covered the issue.

> Question 3. Non-Christians say that Christians do not revere their parents, for they do not offer sacrifice to their ancestors. How can we answer them? Answer: There are three answers. First, answer them with the Bible: The Fifth commandment, Matt. 15:4, Proverbs 2:13, 22, Eph. 6:12, and Col. 3:20. It is not true that Christianity does not teach filial piety. Second, answer them with Christians' behavior. Filial piety to the living parents does not exist in old letters, but in the heart. Making the parents' hearts peaceful lies in love and obedience. In loving and obeying them, Christians should be better than non-believers.[72]

Accordingly, the missionaries praised the examples of Korean Christians' living sacrifice to their living parents. For instance, Yi Hakku of Incheon lived with his old parents. When he became a Christian, he thought that it was right to serve his parents with sincere piety. He not only obeyed the will of his parents, but also gave delicacies and rich viands to them on their birthdays and on holidays. The parents rejoiced in receiving them, and his friends said that Mr. Yi offered a living sacrifice to his parents.[73]

KOREAN CHRISTIANS' INTERPRETATIONS OF ANCESTOR WORSHIP

Korean leaders expressed their opinions on ancestor worship through editorials and articles in the *Christian Advocate* and the *Christian*

---

[71] Jones, *Ch'ohak ŏnmun*, 12a; Yang Chuguk, "Saram i kwihan kŭnbon ŭl algo ŭi rŭl haenghal il" [Men Should Know Their Origin and Practice Righteousness], *SW* 3 (1904): 430–31.

[72] "Sadosingyŏng ronri" [Exposition of the Apostle's Creed], *SW* 1 (1901): 106.

[73] "Hŭihanhan il" [A Rare Thing], *KH*, May 23, 1900.

News, which were founded in 1897. Although most editorials and essays were published anonymously, at least the first drafts, loaded with quotations from the Confucian classics and Chinese history, were written by the Korean assistants of the missionary editors. Thus some part of the above missionaries' arguments on ancestor worship should be attributed to the Korean Christians.

Ch'oe Pyŏnghŏn (1858–1927) was a representative of early Korean leaders and writers. In 1899 he lectured on the relationship between traditional Korean ancestor worship and Christian worship on Korean Thanksgiving Day, Ch'usŏk, which was one of the main holidays for ancestor worship. First, he investigated the history of Ch'usŏk and ancestor worship. When Ch'usŏk originated from the Kabae Festival in the Silla Kingdom in the first century, it was a national holiday for women to dance and play games. Yet it had changed into a national day of sacrificing the first fruits and grains of the harvest to one's ancestors. Likewise, although sacrifices were offered only to God in ancient China, Ch'oe argued, ancestor worship was popularized during the Zhou dynasty; since then, the method of ancestor worship had changed from time to time. He emphasized the changing nature of worship customs, and concluded that it was good to reform the law of the ancestral rite once again. As all grains and fruits as well as ancestors came from God, he said, "I sincerely wish that all believing brothers would offer a living sacrifice with our body to God every Ch'usŏk."[74] His thesis—to offer living worship to a living God, the beginning of all ancestors—was based on three principles: the changeability of the ceremonial laws, the legitimacy behind recovering the original meaning of Shangdi or Hanănim, and thanksgiving for harvest. In 1908 he again argued that ancestor worship could not influence the prosperity of the descendents, but those who walked in the bright way of God would be blessed. Ch'oe emphasized the importance of realizing the signs of the times, namely the dispensational differences. The old customs of ancestor worship that the people had followed were appropriate in the old times, yet contemporary people should worship God in the newly revealed truth. Old customs had died, and new customs and civilization had arisen.[75]

[74] Ch'oe Pyŏnghŏn, "Kojip pult'ong" [A Stubborn Man], *KH*, March 8, 1899.
[75] T'amwŏnja, "Chyesa kŭnbon ŭl ŭinonham" [Discussion of the Foundation of Ancestor Worship], *SW* 4 (1908): 184–91; Elmer M. Cable, "Chesa kŭnwŏnŭl ŭinon ham" [Discussing the Origin of Ancestor Worship], *Yesugyo Sinbo*, November 30 and December 15, 1908.

Other Methodist leaders expressed similar arguments against ancestor worship. One leader said, "The worship of a spirit in the tablet is idolatrous and futile."[76] Another wrote, "Alas! He who worships the idol of the tablet as his ancestor! If he serves God the true Ancestor, he will be blessed eternally after death."[77] In October 1901, when the first Western district conference was held at Asbury Church in Chemulpo, presided over by G. H. Jones, some crucial issues were debated. On ancestor worship, Rev. Kim Kibŏm said that it was very foolish and futile. After the sacrifice, food did not decrease, nor its smell disappear. If the spirit lived on sacrificial food, one meal a year would starve the spirit. Kim Sangnim, a local evangelist, stated that as God should judge one between good and evil after death, he could not receive the sacrifice at his former house. An Chŏngsu asserted that giving food to the dead spirit was as useless as giving straw to a dead calf.[78] Korean Methodist leaders strongly rejected Confucian ancestral veneration as useless idolatry.

The question of the destiny of the ancestors who had died without faith in Christ was not an openly discussed issue. However, it was one of the most troubling questions to Koreans. The normative missionary view explained that human destiny would be decided between heaven and hell immediately after death. The first result of this view was that it was too late to pray for the dead because their eternal destiny had already been determined at death. The second result was that many Christians understood the thousands of years of Korean history as a history of heathenism that had no record of divine revelation. The third was the unbearable estrangement of the heaven-bound Korean Christians from their entire non-Christian family and clan members who were bound for hell. For individualistic North Americans, this was not an issue, but for most Koreans the offer of personal salvation separate from the ancestral line and household represented an overwhelming existential crisis and difficult choice. Thus when a yangban scholar heard the Christian message, he argued that he would be with his parents and friends in hell rather than in heaven alone:

---

[76] Chŏn Yŏkho, "Usang ŭl pyehal kŏt" [Remove Idols], *SW* 3 (1904): 243–45.

[77] Kwŏn Minsin, "Songdo kyo'u ŭi mitŭm" [The Faith of a Christian in Songdo], *SW* 3 (1904): 439.

[78] "Hananim anjŏn e haenghasim" [Behaving before the Face of God], *SW* 1 (1901): 389.

> You said that the way to hell is wide and its gate is large, so there are many who enter there; yet the way to heaven is narrow and its gate is small, so there are few who enter heaven. Thus many a friend of mine must be in hell. And as my parents had not believed in Jesus, they must be destined to hell. Confucius said that he who did not alter the way of his father was a filial son. It is right, therefore, for me to go to where my parents went, and it is joyful to be where my friends stay. How can I go to heaven by myself and become unfilial to my parents and unfaithful to friends?[79]

The evangelical missionary view on the issue was so firm that Korean Christians did not develop a systemized idea on the ancestors who had not heard the gospel of Christ. Nevertheless, Ro Pyŏngsŏn, a graduate of Paejae School and a Methodist local evangelist in Seoul, suggested the possibility of a posthumous salvation of righteous ancestors through Jesus. In 1897 he wrote a small apologetic tract titled *P'ahok chinsŏn non* (Breaking off Delusion and Proceeding to the Good). After presupposing the priority of believing in God and rejecting idolatry, he argued that everyone would be rewarded according to his deeds. Those who did good works would be prized in heaven, yet those who did evil deeds would be punished in hell.

> Then did all the sages who had died without knowing the Jesus doctrine fall into hell? We believe that those who had done only good works must have gone to heaven. The Scriptures say that to those who sinned when there was no law, serious sin will not be imputed, yet those who sin after the law has been established will not be forgiven. We believe that if any person in the past had done only good works, he might have gone to heaven by the merits of Jesus.[80]

Ro understood the issue of those who perished without ever hearing the gospel from the viewpoint of Christ-centered universalism. He combined the redemptive merit of Jesus (grace salvation) with the human merit of good works (merit liberation).[81] Yet other Koreans did not further develop this theological view in the printed documents, which were

---

[79] Ch'oe Pyŏnghŏn, "Chyungch'yu kajŏril" [Korean Thanksgiving Day], *KH*, September 27, 1899.

[80] Ro Pyŏngsŏn, *P'ahok chinsŏn non*. See Acts 14:16 and 17:30, Rom 3:25 and 5:13.

[81] Ryu Tongsik, "Ch'ogi Han'guk chŏndoindŭl ŭi pogŭm ihae" [Early Korean Evangelists' Understanding of the Gospel], *HKY* 1 (1991): 68–83.

controlled and censored by the missionaries. A different innovation, however, appeared in the form of a Christian memorial rite.

THE INDIGENOUS MEMORIAL SERVICE, CH'UDOHOE

Korean Christians gradually assimilated the system of traditional ancestor worship into Christian theology vis-à-vis ch'udohoe, which incorporated filial piety and a Christian memorial service. Memorial services for deceased missionaries had been performed since the death of Dr. John W. Heron in July 1890. When Korean believers saw Christian memorial services, they adapted traditional ancestor worship to a Christian rite, ch'udohoe. It was observed at night. In July 1896 W. L. Swallen of Wŏnsan reported that Mr. Oh decided to follow Jesus and worship the true God only and cease to practice ancestor worship. On the day of the ancestral rite, he invited two Christians and burned up the ancestral tablet and fetishes at the midnight hour, the time when the sacrificing was to be done, instead of offering the sacrifice. Then they worshipped God and sang, read, and prayed.[82] The burning of the tablet meant the end of the Confucian rite several times a year and the beginning of the Christian family service with Scripture reading and prayer every day.

The first formal Christian memorial service by Korean believers was conducted in Seoul in 1897. Yi Muyŏng, a military official and a Methodist, initiated ch'udohoe at his late mother's first anniversary.

> The brother could not restrain the greatest grief and deep emotion. As Christians worship God and believe in the Savior, we ought not to spread out food and offer sacrifice like non-believers. Yet one who has filial piety cannot pass the first anniversary of the late parent for nothing. So he invited brothers and sisters of the church to his house. He hung lanterns and put lighted candles on the floor. They prayed to God for the soul of the late lady, and sang a hymn. Remembering her faith in God, her words of admonition, and her attitude of generosity when she was alive, he wept for a moment. Church members prayed to God for Mr. Yi Muyŏng and spent the night together without sleep. It was a sacrifice to his mother from the heart. How beautiful it was! Other church members may do the same when they observe anniversaries.[83]

The anniversary service was observed at night with candles. The order of the service was a prayer for the departed, a hymn, remembrance of

---

[82] W. L. Swallen to Friends, July 1896.
[83] "Usyangnon" [Editorial: On Idols], *KH*, April 14, 1897.

the departed, and a prayer for the survivors. It retained the cultural and ethical heritage of Confucian ancestor worship, and at the same time it nullified its idolatrous character. This culturally assimilated memorial service became a model for other Christians, and gradually a more fixed ritual was formed. For instance, in May 1903, when Son Ujŏng of Chemulpo observed the first anniversary of his mother's death, he invited dozens of Christians at night. They sang hymns, prayed, read Scripture, and reflected on her faith and deeds. After the service they shared food that she had loved. About this diluted form of the ancestral rite, a member of the church wrote, "This would be better filial piety to the parents than preparing the ancestral table and weeping the whole night with a hoarse voice."[84]

One continuing problem of ch'udohoe was the prayer for the dead parents and grandparents. Missionaries fully discussed this issue at the conference in 1904, for some of the Korean members still were in the practice of praying for deceased ancestors. In addition, the phrase "he went down into hell" of the Apostles' Creed influenced Korean Christians' understanding of the possibility for the salvation of ancestors. Although later Korean translations omitted the phrase from the creed, most early translations in the tracts and hymnals contained it. Its omission in the later translations itself proved that the phrase was understood differently by Korean believers.[85] In 1901 Sinhak Wŏlbo included the phrase of "going down to hell" in the introduction to the Apostles' Creed. Soon it interpreted the phrase of 1 Peter 3:19, "he went and preached unto the spirits in prison," not as Jesus' going down to hell and preaching to the spirits there for three days, but as Noah's preaching to the afflicted people at the time of the flood.[86] Yet, some Koreans continued to believe that Jesus went down to hell and preached to the poor spirits of ancestors for three days.[87]

---

[84] Chang Wŏngŭn, "Noda puin pyŏlsehan narŭl kuiryŏmham" [Memorial Service for Mrs. Noda], *SW* 3 (1903): 296.

[85] It seems that Protestant missionaries omitted the phrase to block the Roman Catholic doctrine of purgatory from the Korean Protestant believers. Another possibility is that pressure from Korean converts caused its omission.

[86] "Sadosingyŏng ronri," 106; "Ch'ŏsa hoegae" [Repentance of a Scholar], *SW* 1 (1901): 357–58.

[87] Kim Hoil, "Ch'am sarang hal kŏt" [Love Truly], *Yesugyo Sinbo*, January 15, 1908.

Christian memorial services were grafted onto the cultural and ethical heritage of Confucian rituals. At the same time, Christian ch'udohoe eliminated elements of ancestor worship such as Confucian *ch'ukmun* (an offering of wine), the Daoist–Confucian practice of geomancy for the tomb site, the shamanistic provocation of departed spirits, the Buddhist ideas of sentencing by the Ten Judges in the afterlife, and the Roman Catholic doctrine of purgatory. By clearly cutting away these polytheistic elements, the Protestant memorial service became a double-edged sword against the traditional Confucian and shamanistic ancestral venerations on one hand, and the incoming Japanese Shinto ceremony for deceased Japanese patriots and royal family on the other hand. Ch'udohoe was a good example of indigenization and Confucian–Christian integration without lose of Christian identity.

The conflict around the issue of ancestor worship provoked severe persecutions and became one of the major obstacles to the proselytization of the Korean people. However, it provided the Korean church with an opportunity to reflect on a theology of filial piety and to rethink the relationship of the Triune God in terms of this issue—the Heavenly Father of all beings, Jesus the Filial Son, and the Holy Spirit, the teacher of filial piety. Some senior missionaries with a better understanding of "the Korean mind" hoped that the time would come when the Korean Christians might find a modus vivendi in a purified form. On the other hand, the Korean church, although it did not develop a theology on ancestors in detail, gradually assimilated the traditional rite of ancestor worship into a Christian memorial rite, which retained the cultural and ethical heritage of the former. This indigenous alternative, initiated by Korean Christians, to some extent satisfied their need for expressing filial piety to their deceased parents. In short, the development of ritual alternatives for ancestral ceremonies was an important element in the ability of Christianity to meet the Korean people's needs.

— 5 —

Messages
Chinese Literature and Korean Translations

As the God-men relationship stands primary, the five relationships come secondary and thus in due order. This is like the foundation of a house, on which all the pillars and rafters should be built, and then the house becomes safe and strong. The five relationships are like precious pearls, which have no flaw. The primary relationship is like a golden string on which the pearls are threaded not to be lost.

—William A. P. Martin, 1854

The advent of the modern Protestant mission era coincided with an explosion in Bible translation and vernacular Christian literature. In the nineteenth century, the Bible was translated into an additional 446 languages, compared to 74 in the previous eighteen centuries. In Asia, the translated vernacular Scriptures appeared in India, Pakistan, China, Burma, Japan, and finally Korea. The first Korean New Testament, translated by John Ross, was published in Shenyang, Manchuria, in 1887, the tentative Committee Version of the Korean New Testament in Seoul in 1900, and the first authorized Committee Version of the Korean Bible in 1911.[1]

---

[1] Joshua Marshman's Chinese Bible was published in India in 1822, Robert Morrison's Chinese Bible in 1823, the Chinese Delegates' Version in 1854, the Japanese New Testament in 1879, and the Japanese Bible in 1888. See William A. Smalley, *Translation as Mission* (Macon, Ga.: Mercer University Press, 1991), 33–40.

Behind the advent of vernacular Protestant literature and Christian printing culture as a modern phenomenon in Korea, however, were strong Chinese–Korean connections in the Christian book publication and translation. The networking between missionaries in China and Chinese books with missionaries in Korea and translated Korean books was formed in the 1880 and 1890s, and many Chinese books were used in Korea with or without translation. Korean Christians used the Chinese New Testament and Bible, hymnals, books, and tracts. Though the authorized Korean New Testament was published in 1906 and the whole Bible in 1911, educated people used the Chinese New Testament and Bible. When the missionaries edited the Korean hymnals, they translated many songs from the Chinese hymnals as well as from the American ones. They also used Chinese commentaries, books, and tracts. From 1882 to 1910, more than sixty Chinese evangelistic tracts and books were used in Korea without translation, and more than sixty Chinese tracts were translated into the vernacular Korean language.

This chapter reviews the influence of Chinese Christian literature in the shaping of early Korean Protestantism. The first topic concerns the aforementioned social and ecclesiastical background of the readership of Chinese Christian literature. The second section discusses the influence of the Chinese Scriptures on the Korean versions, whose impact in the construction of Korean Protestantism cannot be ignored. The third section deals with the influence of Chinese tracts and books on the theological orientation of Korean Protestantism toward non-Christian religions. Through the exclusive use of Chinese Christian apologetics on East Asian religions, mostly produced by European and North American missionaries in China, Korean Protestantism was under the influence of the theological and missiological package of nineteenth-century European–Chinese Protestantism as well as North American–Chinese Protestantism. The last part describes both hymns translated from Chinese and hymns composed by Koreans. The heavy use of Chinese literature by the Korean churches and the Koreans' sifting integration of various elements of the doctrines and practices for its own use was in line with the traditional pattern of other Korean religions—Confucianism and Buddhism—which had practiced a similar pattern of borrowing from China and then inventing an ecumenical or unified form for Korea.

CHRISTIAN PRINTING CULTURES AND MISSIONARY NETWORKS
IN EAST ASIA

Three historical factors facilitated the importing of Chinese Christian literature to Korea. First, Chinese was a universal language in the Sino-centric East Asian culture in the nineteenth century. Moreover, at least up to 1904, Korean intellectuals understood modern Western civilization through Chinese books, as only a few Korean intellectuals could read Japanese or English. As the official written language in Chosŏn Korea was classical Chinese, and a mixed Chinese–Korean script was adopted from 1895, educated Korean Christians preferred Chinese or mixed-script books. Even after the publication of vernacular Korean Christian books, the literary class and church leaders used Chinese or Chinese–Korean editions. Classical Chinese remained the most important written language until the 1910s. For example, the majority of Korean pupils who attended either Christian mission primary schools or *sŏdang*, traditional Korean local primary schools, learned Chinese Confucian classics. The number of sŏdang increased in the 1910s, although the Japanese governor-general government issued regulations for private schools in 1911 and then regulations for sŏdang in 1915. One of the results of the influx of Chinese Christian literature through the Chefoo–Chemulpo or the Shanghai–Nagasaki–Pusan steamship lines and their Korean translations was that missionaries and Korean leaders, who were occupied with proselytizing works, did not feel the need to write new evangelistic and apologetical books in vernacular Korean. Therefore, in using either the Chinese books without translation or the Korean books with translation, early Korean Protestantism was under the strong literary and theological influence of Chinese Protestantism up until at least 1910, when Korea was colonized by Japan and Japanese Christian literature began to be disseminated among Koreans.

Diagram 2 in the appendix shows the linguistic connections in the translation of Protestant literature from English or Chinese into Korean. The Chinese language was the medium between English and Korean. French was a referential and differentiating language between Roman Catholicism and Protestantism. And Japanese began to affect the translations in the mid-1910s.

Second, the American Methodist and Presbyterian missions to Korea were started, guided, and mentored by senior missionaries in China and Manchuria or those who had missionary experience in

China and then were transferred to Japan. The aforementioned context of the East Asian Christian literary market and translational networks facilitated this missionary networking. Robert S. Maclay began working in Fuzhou, China, in 1848, transferred to Tokyo in 1873, visited Seoul for a scouting trip in 1884, and helped found the Korea mission of the Methodist Episcopal Church in 1885. Franklin Ohlinger also began working in Fuzhou in 1870, was transferred to Seoul in 1887, and worked there until 1893. He greatly influenced pioneer junior Methodist missionaries—H. G. Appenzeller, W. B. Scranton, and G. H. Jones. Not only were many Chinese books, tracts, and hymnals made by Maclay and Ohlinger imported to Korea and translated into Korean, but their mission theory of Christian civilization and English education was also adopted by their juniors in Seoul. In the case of Presbyterians, John Ross in Shenyang, Manchuria, John L. Nevius (1829–1893) in Chefoo, Shandong, and James C. Hepburn (1815–1911) in Yokohama were mentors to H. G. Underwood, S. A. Moffett, and the other young missionaries of that time in Korea, who used the vernacular Korean Scriptures translated by Ross and tracts and hymns made by Mr. and Mrs. Nevius as well as adopted their mission policy—the Nevius–Ross method—for the establishment of the indigenous churches and the speedy evangelization of Korea.

The third factor was the existence of many intellectual converts who could read classical Chinese and mixed-script Christian literature. Earlier Christians came from intelligent middle and upper classes as well as from the working classes. There were hundreds of yangban Christians by 1907 in Seoul, and the majority of the church leaders came from the educated yangban and urban "middle classes," including a newly rising merchant class. They used Chinese Christian literature, and through these avenues Protestant mission theories and methods, tested and naturalized in China, were introduced into Korea.

LITERARY CLASSES OF EARLY KOREAN CHRISTIANS

An investigation of social class in the early Protestant church, particularly the existence of Chinese-reading members who became church leaders, will reveal its socioeconomic dimensions as well as its ecclesiastical features. This section challenges a generally accepted image of the constituency of earlier Protestantism—predominantly lower-class and uneducated ordinary people—and emphasizes the role of the literary class in its formation.

Chosŏn society was divided theoretically into two broad classes—
yangmin (freeborn commoner) and *ch'ŏnmin* (lowborn commoner: seven
outcast groups and slaves). Yangmin were again hierarchically divided
into three classes: *yangban* (civilian and military officials and literati),
chungin (middle people: medical officers, translators and interpreters,
technicians in the astronomy and meteorology office, accountants, stat-
ute law clerks, scribes, and government artists), and *sangmin* (farmers, artisans, and merchants). Beginning in the seventeenth century, the
yangban-centered society started to unravel. In the nineteenth century
especially, the number of fallen yangban increased, and the distinction
between legitimate and illegitimate lines of descent became blurred. The
household slaves who occupied at least one-quarter of the population
gradually disappeared after the abolition of slavery in the 1894 Kabo
Reform,[2] and some rich farmers, merchants, and miners employed wage
laborers and accumulated capital. In the eyes of foreigners, in the late
nineteenth century, it seemed that there were generally three classes: the
upper class, consisting of yangban and chungin in Seoul and *hyangni*
(*ajŏn*, petty local officials) in other cities and towns; the "middle class,"
consisting of independent merchants and farmers; and the lower class,
consisting of tenants, shoemakers, hatmakers, coolies, wage laborers,
actors, outcasts, shamans, and slaves.[3]

The early members of the Protestant churches were mostly sangmin commoners (farmers, artisans, and merchants). This was partly due
to the Nevius method, adopted by the Presbyterian church from 1887
to 1891, which targeted the "working class" and women, but not the
higher or lower classes.[4] With more than 90 percent of the population

---

[2] James B. Palais, "A Search for Korean Uniqueness," *Harvard Journal of Asiatic Studies* 55, no. 2 (1995): 414–18.

[3] C. W. Campbell, "Report by Acting Vice-Consul Campbell of a Journey in
North Corea in September and October 1889," in *British Documents on Foreign
Affairs*, I-6 (Washington, D.C.: University Publications of America, 1989), 209–
11. One important class was *hyangni* (*ajŏn*, *hyangban*, or *hyangch'ŏk*: hereditary
country office holders). See H. B. Hulbert, "The Ajun," *KRv* (February 1904): 63
and (June 1904): 255; Hwang Kyung Moon, *Beyond Birth: Social Status in the
Emergence of Modern Korea* (Cambridge, Mass.: Harvard University Press, 2004),
161–207.

[4] The opportunities for evangelism were most easily found among the ordinary people (farmers, artisans, and merchants). The higher classes, including the
gentry and officials, were too satisfied with their own Confucian learning and were
prejudiced against foreign religions; and the lower classes were too busy to attend

illiterate, the Nevius method emphasized the reading skills of the vernacular Scriptures and tracts. However, the "working class" was not wholly made up of illiterate people. They included the "newly rising middle class," such as intelligent urban workers and merchants who engaged in the international trade in the open ports and northern border cities. At the same time, some of the middle (professional) and higher literary classes entered the Protestant church before 1895. Even though the Nevius method adopted a policy of the exclusive use of vernacular Korean literature, Chinese Christian literature was widely used among literate Christians, and the Chinese–Korean mixed-script editions of the Scriptures and books were published for the educated classes.

One of the newly rising classes was the merchants in northern Korea. Missionaries regarded them as part of the "middle class" or the "independent middle class." John Ross of Manchuria divided Koreans into three classes, and the "middle class" consisted of merchants and others able to hire labor.[5] The Korean merchants whom Ross met in the 1870s and 1880s were those who engaged in trade on the Chinese–Korean border. He found that they spoke and wrote Chinese fluently; were open-minded about foreigners, foreign culture, and goods; and even accepted Chinese Christian literature without fear of governmental prohibition.[6]

---

church and too occupied with the effort required for survival in everyday life. Unlike the secluded higher-class women and biased higher-class men, the so-called middle class (land-owning farmers, shop-owning merchants, and artisans) were easily accessible. See O. R. Avison, "Response to the Commission I. Carrying the Gospel to All the World of the World Missionary Conference, 1910," UTS, G. H. Jones Papers.

[5] John Ross, "The Christian Dawn in Korea," MRW (April 1890): 242.

[6] See Lee Chull, "Social Sources of the Rapid Growth of the Christian Church in Northwest Korea: 1895–1910" (Ph.D. diss., Boston University, 1997), 98–181. In the nineteenth century, many merchants in northern Korea accumulated large wealth. They wanted to raise their social status commensurate with their economic power. Some bought yangban status by offering money to the local officials, or by inserting their names in the genealogy of the fallen yangban. Some joined hands with central government officials, and others joined Roman Catholicism or Protestantism to protect their lives and property from the abuse of local officials. As most of Ross' Korean converts came from this newly rising literary merchant class, he was able to hire some of them to assist in translating the Chinese Bible into Korean.

American missionaries affirmed Ross' remarks on the merchant class in northern Korea.[7] When H. G. Appenzeller made his second trip to Pyongyang in the spring of 1887, he commented on the northerners, "The people are more independent than in some parts of Korea. There is a large field here and I believe, should a port be opened, we ought to establish a station at once."[8] In April 1889 H. G. Underwood went to Ŭiju via Pyongyang and baptized thirty-three men, converted by Ross' evangelists and the Ross Version, on the Chinese side of the Yalu River. They were "all men from all classes, from a former deputy magistrate of this city, who now holds the position of governor of about ten miles from here, down to the police and couriers of this place."[9] They were officials, customs officers, doctors, merchants, teachers, and farmers. In 1890, when S. A. Moffett went to Changyŏn, Hwanghae province, he baptized fifteen Christians. Many of these baptized Koreans belonged to the "middle class," "those most free from the moral and political corruption of the country, the class which will certainly become the 'backbone' of a new Korea."[10] In the spring of 1897, William M. Baird, who was transferred from Pusan to Pyongyang, made a trip from Seoul to Ŭiju with Norman C. Whittemore. Baird reported, "I was much pleased with what I saw of the northern work—warmest, aggressive, Scriptural, sensible, seemed to be words applicable to the church work there. The people are mostly able to read, and very eager to read the Bible."[11] He was impressed by the independent, manly spirit of many of the mountain people in the north. He compared the northerners to the southerners:

> A man seems to be more a man in the North than in the South. In looking for the causes of this I find it in the marked absence of the so-called "gentleman" class. In the South the independent middle class is apt to be crushed between the upper and the nether millstones, between the

[7] For a detailed discussion on the social status of the northerners in early modern Korea, see Hwang, *Beyond Birth*, 248–89.

[8] H. G. Appenzeller to E. W. Gilman, August 8, 1887.

[9] L. H. Underwood to F. F. Ellinwood, May 5, 1889.

[10] S. A. Moffett to F. F. Ellinwood, October 20, 1890. Gifford suggested that the mission should go north because "the people in the southern part of the land seem to be an inferior race to that of the northern part" and "the people in the northern part are more the kind of people among whom Presbyterianism is adapted to take hold" (D. L. Gifford to F. F. Ellinwood, October 21, 1890).

[11] W. M. Baird, "Letters from Rev. W. M. Baird, Seoul, Korea, May 14, 1897," *CHA* 11 (1897): 126.

strutting, conceited "yangban" and the obsequious, cringing serf. The North is brighter with hope because of the predominance of an independent middle class, who have to work for their own living, and as a result have more muscle and more brains.[12]

The fewer rice fields, Baird thought, made the northerners more "intelligent, active, energetic kind of human beings" than the southerners. He found that the predominance of an "independent middle class" in the north was a bright hope for mission work.[13] During the early period of the Protestant missions, northerners were the most active in building Christian communities. They gathered for worship, read the Scriptures, built chapels, and organized churches. Their only need was the vernacular Scriptures. Some of them could read the Chinese Scriptures and had to use them because of the scarcity of the Korean Scriptures.

After the Korean–Japanese Treaty in 1876, Christians in China expressed concern for the mission to Korea and attempted to distribute Chinese Scriptures and tracts. Huang Zunxian's *Chaoxian Celue* (A Stratagem for Korea, 1880), mentioned in the introduction, encouraged them to anticipate that the Korean government would have a tolerant policy toward Protestantism. In August 1883 Wang Xichang, who was a close attendant of Li Hongzhang and an officer in the foreign office of the Korean government, tried to offer a copy of the Chinese New Testament and a dozen other Christian books to King Kojong.[14] Arthur W. Douthwaite, an agent of the National Bible Society of Scotland, made a trip from Chefoo to Chemulpo at the end of 1883 and distributed many Chinese Scriptures in the port town and in Seoul for six weeks.[15]

---

[12] Baird, "Notes on a Trip into Northern Korea," *Independent*, May 20, 1897.

[13] W. M. Baird to F. F. Ellinwood, May 22, 1897. In 1912 Greenfield said that one of the causes of the slower development of the church in South Korea was "the psycho-physical racial distinction between the Kyung Sang Man and his brother in Pyeng An." He also said, "Yet in time the slow and timid southern will overtake his strong and independent brother of the north, whose soul is yet untamed by war or famine or persecution." See M. W. Greenfield, "Personal Report to Korea Mission, 1912–13," in *Minutes and Reports of the Twenty-Ninth Annual Meeting of the Korea Mission of the Presbyterian Church in the USA* (Kobe: Fukuin, 1913).

[14] Wang Xichang, "Wang Xichang song yasogyo pŏnsŏ sibibon bunji" [Wang Xichang Sent Various Christian Books], *T'ongsŏ ilgi*, vol. I. (Seoul: Korea University Press, 1972), August 24, 1883.

[15] *Annual Reports of the National Bible Society of Scotland* (Edinburgh: National Bible Society of Scotland, 1884), 795–96; "Corea," *China's Millions* 10 (1884): 25.

He also supplied a Chinese soldier with Chinese Scriptures and tracts. Although their attempts to distribute Chinese literature in Chemulpo and Seoul were prohibited, they stimulated enthusiasm for the Korea mission. In April 1884 Gilbert Reid of Chefoo insisted on "the immediate preoccupation, if not occupation, of Corea" with medical and education missions.[16]

Dr. Horace N. Allen's treatment of Min Yŏngik, a nephew of Queen Min, who was severely wounded during the coup d'état in December 1884, enabled him to win the favor of the court and to begin the Royal Hospital in April 1885. In addition, his treatment of many wounded Chinese soldiers led to a close relationship with Yuan Shikai, director-general resident of diplomatic and commercial relations in Korea, who exercised pervasive power over all political affairs in Korea. Under his protection, Chinese merchants inundated both Seoul and the countryside. After the failure of the Kapsin coup d'état, Chinese power dominated in Korea for a decade. In this milieu, Chinese Christian literature could be imported and distributed through the Korean ports and cities.

Some early believers in Seoul came from the middle and upper classes. In October 1882 Ross sent Sŏ Sangnyun from Shenyang to Ŭiju and Seoul as a colporteur of the British and Foreign Bible Society with five hundred copies of Korean versions of the Gospels and tracts. After working in Ŭiju for three months, he came to Seoul to do evangelistic work. Sŏ received more than one thousand copies of the Chinese and Korean Scriptures and tracts from Ross in 1883 and 1884. By the end of 1883, thirteen of Sŏ's friends "desired to be formed into a congregation." After several written requests, in 1884 Sŏ went to Ross and urged him to visit Seoul to examine more than seventy candidates for baptism.[17] They belonged to the middle and upper classes. Ross reported at the end of 1886,

> I was unable during this year to travel to the remote Corean Valleys to strengthen the baptized and examine the numerous professed believers. I specially regret my inability to go to the Corean capital to examine the professed believers there, now said to number over a hundred, all of the middle and higher classes, to whom the colporteur belongs. As his pastor, he has been anxious for me and no other to go, so that, as he

[16] Gilbert Reid, "The Prospect in Corea," *FM* 43 (1884): 131–32.
[17] John Ross to W. Wright, March 8, 1885; J. Orr, "The Gospel in Corea," *UPMR* (June 2, 1890): 188.

informs me, he has not reported himself to the American missionaries newly settled there.[18]

Although Sŏ did not attempt to contact American missionaries, they could sense the wide-open situation. Underwood could not help testifying to his amazement in June 1887 that instead of waiting and preparing for steady work, "the work has opened up so wonderfully that there is really more to be done than we can undertake."[19] Underwood invited Ross to Seoul in September of 1887, when the first Korean Presbyterian church was organized with the fourteen baptized members, which was the fruit of Sŏ's evangelistic work with Ross' Korean version of the Scriptures. "But what was most interesting to me [Ross] was the assurance that there were over 300 men of that class in the city believers, who were for various reasons not then quite prepared, publicly, to join the Church."[20] Just after the American missionaries settled down in Seoul in 1887, if we accept the above statement, there were several hundred believers or seekers as a result of the work not of American missionaries, but of a Korean colporteur. Moreover, these believers belonged to the middle or upper classes and could read Chinese Scriptures and tracts.

The American missionaries' good relationship with the reform-minded King Kojong and Queen Min motivated some officials to be interested in Christianity. Missionaries handed out Chinese Christian literature to these officials, and some of them began to attend Underwood's Chŏngdong Presbyterian Church. In March 1888 Underwood reported, "A week ago last Sunday I had the privilege of baptizing two more Koreans, one of which was a palace eunuch. . . . There are several other eunuchs that we interested and three or four of them are coming to see me during this week."[21] In August 1888 Underwood met "a couple of Korean officials who have been studying Christianity for some time and now desire to be baptized."[22] In May 1889 Mr. Cho, a student at the government medical school, became a Christian. The president of

---

[18] "Mr. Ross's Report," *UPMR* (June 1, 1887): 226.

[19] H. G. Underwood to F. F. Ellinwood, June 17, 1887.

[20] Ross, "Christian Dawn in Korea," 247.

[21] Underwood to Ellinwood, March 12, 1888.

[22] Underwood to Ellinwood, August 25, 1888. On Sunday, December 23, 1888, eleven young men were baptized by Underwood. The chapel room was filled with about fifty Koreans. In January 1889, the Sunday services were crowded every week, and weekly prayer meetings had a regular attendance of about thirty (H. G. Underwood to F. F. Ellinwood, April 30, 1889).

the hospital did not interfere in his conversion.[23] In 1890 Underwood sent a copy of the Chinese New Testament to every magistrate he had met previously.[24]

The Methodist mission also experienced an influx of "middle-class" converts. When H. G. Appenzeller opened Paejae Haktang in Seoul in June 1886, many young men from the "middle" and upper classes came to the school "to get rank" with a knowledge of English. A majority of the students soon attended the religious services voluntarily, and some converted to Methodism. The majority of the First Methodist Church at Chŏngdong consisted of young students of Paejae Haktang and Ewha Haktang, government officials, and Koreans from the rising urban middle class. In 1891 F. Ohlinger hoped to reach all classes, but he considered getting hold of "the intelligent laboring people" most important at the beginning of the work. "Wherever the literary or gentry class predominates in a church it is hard to win the other, while that class, on the contrary, will always find a comfortable seat among the laboring people should these happen to predominate."[25] Ohlinger welcomed the increase of "the intelligent laboring people"—or the "newly rising urban middle class"—among the probationers of the First Methodist Church. According to Jones, this "urban middle class" consisted of "merchants and real-estate men, farmers, contractors, the lower administrative and executive officers of the government, official secretaries, counselors, writers, clerks, the lower officer at the palace, and the major domos in the residences of the great patricians." And the lower class comprised "the laboring classes and the skilled artisans, carpenters, masons, stone-cutters, paper-hangers, blacksmiths, cabinet makers, upholsterers, printers, store keepers, coolies, servants, soldiers, saloon-keepers, criminals, slaves, butchers, and priests."[26] In 1894 Dr. William B. Scranton reported that the Talsŏng (Sangdong) Church near the South Gate was "composed of the merchant and middle class chiefly, though we have representatives from the low class, and from the officials, in some numbers."[27] In 1898 he reaffirmed, "Although we have ex-governors or

[23] Underwood to Ellinwood, May 26, 1889.

[24] Underwood to Ellinwood, October 21, 1890.

[25] *Annual Report of the Missionary Society of the Methodist Episcopal Church* (New York: MSMEC, 1892), 287.

[26] G. H. Jones, "The People of Korea," *GAL* (October 1892): 465–66.

[27] *Annual Report of the Missionary Society of the Methodist Episcopal Church* (New York: MSMEC, 1895), 244.

ex-magistrates among us, yet our congregation represents the middle class largely and none of the rich are included among us."[28]

The Korean language teachers of American missionaries came from the literary classes, and many of the teachers became Christian converts in due time. Underwood employed Song Sunyong, a Roman Catholic scholar, in 1885. "He has had a good deal of practice in teaching foreigners having taught seven or eight of the Franciscan Fathers and also had something to do in the compiling of the French Dictionary."[29] Mr. Song was an excellent linguist. He introduced the experiences, methods, and principles of the Roman Catholic Church's translation of the Korean tracts and Scriptures to the Protestant missionaries. He worked with Underwood as the authority of the Korean language for many years. Sin Nakkyun, an official at the Royal Hospital, graduated from the government's English school and taught the Korean language to Drs. J. W. Heron and H. N. Allen from 1885. His friend, Ro Ch'ungyŏng, became Allen's language teacher in order to learn about foreigners and Christianity. His reading of the Chinese Gospels led him to meet Underwood, who gave him the Chinese New Testament, commentaries, and tracts such as Genähr's *Dialogues with a Temple Keeper* and McCartee's *Discourse on the Salvation of the Soul* and *Easy Introduction to Christian Doctrine*. Underwood baptized Ro on July 18, 1886, as the first Korean convert in Seoul. Just before his baptism, Underwood wrote, "I find that I shall need some Chinese copies of the scriptures, some Chinese commentaries, some Chinese tracts."[30]

In 1893 two yangban men were baptized in Seoul: G. H. Jones' language teacher, Ch'oe Pyŏnghŏn, and S. F. Moore's teacher, Mr. Han. They had read Chinese Scriptures and tracts before joining the church. Their rejection of ancestor worship scandalized the yangban society in

[28] *Annual Report of the Offical Minutes of the Korea Mission of the MEC* (Seoul: Methodist Printing House, 1898), 45.

[29] H. G. Underwood to F. F. Ellinwood, July 6, 1885. Mr. Sunyong Song—his adult courtesy name was Tŏkcho—was the authority on the Korean and Chinese language for Underwood. In spite of the Franciscan Fathers' persuasion and persecution, Song continued to help Underwood. Song had "intimate acquaintance with the Chinese, combined with his thorough knowledge of the use of the native Eunmun" (H. G. Underwood, *An Introduction to the Korean Spoken Language* [Yokohama: Seishi Bunsha, 1890], Preface). He prepared *An Introduction to the Korean Spoken Language*, published in 1889.

[30] Underwood to Ellinwood, July 9, 1886.

Seoul. Their conversion stories illustrated the ordeals of early yangban Christians. Ch'oe Pyŏnghŏn became Jones' private tutor in the fall of 1888, just when the Baby Riot ended.[31] According to Korean standards, Ch'oe was a well-educated young man.[32] Jones exhorted him to become a Christian and to join him in the effort to give to the Koreans the knowledge of the true God and a better way of life. But Ch'oe was loyal to the faith of his ancestors. Time passed and gradually there grew in Ch'oe's heart the thought that there was no disrespect involved in laying aside the "old book" (Confucianism) and taking the "new book" (Christianity).[33] Ch'oe was deeply moved by Jesus' love for his enemies and the missionaries' kind concern for the poor and sick. One day he said to Jones, "Moksa, I think very differently about it. Now I know that if my ancestors could speak to me from out of the unseen world, their message would be 'Follow Christ, follow Christ. We had no knowledge of him when we were on earth, but if we were living today we would be His followers. So you may follow Him.' "[34] Ch'oe decided to become a Christian after struggling between the old religion practiced by his forefathers and the new religion propagated by the missionaries for the past three years. He buried the tablets of his ancestors as a definite sign of conversion from Confucianism. His determination to enter the Protestant church created a great surprise and disappointment among his aristocratic friends. On the Sunday morning when Ch'oe's baptism was scheduled, several of them went to his house, took his coat, hat, and shoes, and stationed a guard over them all day long. The next day Ch'oe came to Jones and explained his absence. They arranged for a baptismal service, without public announcement, to take place at the midweek prayer meeting. Ch'oe was baptized on Wednesday, February 8, 1893. He spent the next few days visiting his aristocratic friends and

[31] Although Ch'oe came to Jones, he was still suspicious of foreigners. When Jones invited him for tea, Ch'oe suspected that the pastor (missionary) would try to catch him "with his magic drugs and dreadful spell" and managed to get away without touching either the tea or the cake. See Jones, "My Language Teacher," UTS, G. H. Jones Papers, ca. 1902.

[32] Ch'oe was appointed as a local preacher in 1896, ordained as deacon in 1902, and appointed an elder in 1909. He served the First Methodist Church at Chŏngdong as a preacher from 1898 and a pastor from 1903 to 1914.

[33] Jones, "My Language Teacher."

[34] Jones, "My Language Teacher." In 1909 Ch'oe wrote *Syŏngsan myŏnggyŏng*, based on his struggles of conversion.

relatives. When he told them he had become a Christian and wished for them to know the fact, trusting that this would make no difference in their friendship and relationship, in every instance they greeted his confession with ridicule, sneers, and insults. His baptism had placed a gulf between him and his friends that could not be bridged; as he told Jones, he was "a traitor to the ancestors" and he had "no friends left now but Christians and Christ."[35]

Mr. Han was "a man of rank higher up than any other man" in the Presbyterian church in Seoul in 1893. He was thirty-one years old and had been a military official with a sixth rank. Shortly after becoming a believer he began to sell Christian books with Samuel F. Moore and preached the gospel in the streets of Seoul. One day while he was reading a tract and "showing the folly of idol and demon worship," the crowd threw stones at him. Another day, as he was selling books, people thought that he was an ordinary man, a *sangnom*, not a yangban, and beat him. But he endured the abuse, remembering the passion of Jesus.[36] A yangban had the right to arrest and beat any sangnom. All sangnom were supposed to use language indicating the highest respect when addressing a yangban. A *nom* striking a yangban was almost unheard of in Korea. It was also something entirely new and contrary to Korean custom for a yangban to become a preacher and to use respectful talk with sangnom. From 1893 something new began to happen in Korea: yangban began to work as preachers in the streets, using polite words when speaking to ordinary people.[37]

---

[35] Jones, "My Language Teacher." See Mattie W. Noble, comp. and trans., *Victorious Lives of Early Christians in Korea* (Seoul: Christian Literature Society Korea, 1927), 119.

[36] S. F. Moore, "Welcome to Korea," *CHA* 7 (1893): 33.

[37] Moore's converts came from the yangban class as well as from butchers. He opened Sŭngdong Church (Kondanggol Church) near Dr. Avison's Hospital (Chejungwŏn) in November 1893. When Pak Sŏngch'un, a butcher, was baptized in April of 1895, many yangban members left the church, but most of them soon came back. They called each other "brother." A social revolution was taking place. Nevertheless, as the number of butchers in the membership increased, yangban Christians requested segregated seats. Moore stood against it, albeit the mission allowed gender segregated seats. Here we can see that contemporary Protestant ethics placed more emphasis on class equality than on gender equality. The church was finally split in two in 1895: Hongmunsugol Church for the yangban members and the old one for the butchers and ordinary people. See S. F. Moore, "The Butchers of Korea," *KR* 5 (1898): 127–32; Moore, "A Gospel Sermon Preached by a

A good number of the educated yangban class entered the church from 1904 to 1905, when some reform-minded politicians and officials were released from prison and joined the church. After Syngman Rhee was arrested in January 1899, about thirty high officials and enlightened leaders were imprisoned. About fifteen men converted to Christianity in the prison through the efforts of missionaries after reading Chinese Christian literature borrowed from the prison library. When released in 1904, many of them attended Gale's Yŏndong Church and participated in the YMCA movement. Their conversion stimulated other members of the educated classes to join the church. In December 1905 Yŏndong Church had more than six hundred members, and three-fourths of them were from the nobility.[38] They contributed to the Christian patriotic enlightenment and educational movement from 1905 to 1910.

In sum, through various ways and sources, Chinese Christian Scriptures and tracts were widely distributed in Korea from 1882 among the middle and upper classes. In northern Korea, against the backdrop of the scarcity of Korean vernacular Scriptures, the "independent middle class" accepted these Chinese books. In Seoul, the majority of the early believers came from the intelligent "middle" and upper classes. Some governmental officials joined the church, and they demanded Chinese Christian books. The conversion of two yangban men—Mr. Ch'oe Pyŏnghŏn and Mr. Han—in 1893 and their preaching ministry in the streets of Seoul were memorable events in the yangban-centered Confucian society, and a kind of group conversion of the higher class in Seoul happened around the time of the Russo-Japanese War.

CHINESE SCRIPTURES IN KOREA

When the Korean–British Treaty was signed in 1882, it contained a clause insisted on by the Korean authorities that they reserved the right to prohibit the conveyance of books and other printed matter of which they disapproved into the interior of the country. It was directed

---

Korean Butcher," *CHA* 12 (1898): 115–16; C. A. Clark, *First Fruits in Korea* (New York: Revell, 1921), 310–12; A. D. Clark, *Avison of Korea: The Life of Oliver R. Avison, M.D.* (Seoul: Yonsei University Press, 1979), 97–103.

[38] C. A. Clark to A. J. Brown, December 8, 1905; Yi Nŭnghwa, *Chosŏn Kidoggyo kŭp oegyo sa* [History of Christianity and Diplomacy in Modern Korea] (Seoul: Chosŏn Kidoggyo Ch'angmunsa, 1928), 203–4; Yi Kwangnin, "Kuhanmal okchung esŏ ŭi kidoggyo sinang" [Christian Belief in the Prison during the Late Chosŏn], in *Han'guk kaehwasa ŭi chemunje* (Seoul: Iljogak, 1986), 218–22.

chiefly at religious books, namely "obnoxious" Christian Scriptures and tracts.[39] The articles of the treaty, however, did not block the influx or smuggling of the Christian books from China to Korea. For example, in Seoul, a Korean colporteur (Sŏ Sangnyun) employed by the British and Foreign Bible Society distributed 200 Chinese New Testaments and 39 Chinese Bibles, 315 Korean New Testaments, and 1,431 portions of the New Testament in 1889.[40] In addition, Yi Sujŏng's Kunten–Korean version of the four Gospels and the Acts were published by the American Bible Society in Yokohama, Japan, in 1884, and one thousand copies of each were distributed in Seoul by 1892.[41] Henry Loomis wrote about their sale in 1892: "Until translations are made, the Chino-Korean version, made by Rijutei, should have a good sale. We have some stock now in hand and the plates to produce more whenever wanted."[42]

Chinese Testaments were sold in the northern provinces, too. In December 1888 E. Bryant, an agent of the BFBS, wrote that there was no pressing need for the Scriptures in Korean, "as the literary men prefer the Chinese."[43] Such a need began to be heard in 1890 when a visible number of commoners came to the church: "There is crying need for hurrying on the translation as fast as possible, as only a few portions of scriptures are now available, except in the Chinese language."[44] Yet the advent of a Korean Bible was delayed until 1911; meanwhile the Chinese Scriptures, especially the Chinese Old Testament, appeased the Korean Christians' demand for the whole word of God.

The Delegates' Version and the Korean Scriptures

The translation and publication of the Chinese Scriptures was the result of the nineteenth-century Protestant missions. They were translated and printed in three different styles: high *wenli*, easy *wenli*, and Mandarin.[45]

---

[39] *Annual Report of the BFBS* (London: BFBS, 1884), 249.

[40] *Annual Report of the BFBS* (London: BFBS, 1887), 435; *Annual Report of the BFBS* (London: BFBS, 1890), 239, 415. "Portions" refer to separate books like Matthew, Mark, Luke, John, and the book of Acts. In the initial stages of evangelism, cheap "portions" were distributed.

[41] See Oak Sung-Deuk and Yi Mahnyol, *Taehan sŏngsŏ konghoesa* [A History of the Korean Bible Society] (Seoul: Korean Bible Society, 1993), 1:120–76.

[42] H. Loomis to Dr. Gilman, September 6, 1892, ABS Archives.

[43] E. Bryant to W. Wright, December 4, 1888, BFBS Archives.

[44] *Annual Report of the Missionary Society of the Methodist Episcopal Church* (New York: MSMEC, *AR of the MSMEC* (1891), 274.

[45] At the Missionary Conference held in Shanghai, May 1890, three committees

The Delegates' Version (hereafter DV), published in high wenli in 1854, became the most popular Bible in China, for its excellent classical literary style satisfied the taste of the upper class. The DV was not a literal translation, but a liberal one like the Septuagint.[46] The DV paid much more attention to Chinese idiomatic expressions than to the faithfulness to the original text, for the Chinese prioritized flavor over content in literature. Therefore, some words or phrases were paraphrased, changed, or omitted.

The literary DV influenced the translators of the Korean Scriptures. The first Korean version was made in Manchuria by John Ross and his Korean helpers, who translated its first drafts from the DV. Although Ross consulted many versions, including the King James Version, the Byzantine Greek, and the Oxford edition of the Greek New Testament in 1881, his base text was the DV.[47] But his principle of using the vernacular language created many new Korean terms (see table 2 in the appendix).

Ross made continuous efforts to translate the Scriptures into the language of commoners by using as many Korean words as possible. Nevertheless, the final printed text retained many Chinese technical words, Chinese theological terms, and Chinese idioms and expressions. For example, Ross used Chinese terms relating to time, money, and weights. For theological terms, he coined and adopted many Korean–Chinese combined words. Table 3 in the appendix shows the Chinese terms adopted by Ross in the Gospel of John (1887).

Seoul missionaries also adopted a number of Chinese theological terms and expressions from the DV. When we compare the first three chapters of Romans of the DV with the 1904 Korean New Testament, the following Chinese terms were adopted in the latter: apostle (使徒), gospel (福音), prophet (先知者), the Holy Bible (聖經), the Holy Spirit (聖神), the Lord (主), grace (恩惠), peace (平康), righteousness (義), the truth (眞理), sin (罪), repentance (悔改), prayer (祈禱), eternal life (永生),

---

were appointed to select three corps of revisers to make a standard version for China in the three forms: *wenli* (high classical), easy *wenli* (simple classical), and *guanhua* (Mandarin). See Edwin M. Bliss, ed., *Encyclopaedia of Missions* (New York: Funk & Wagnalls, 1891), 277.

[46] The Septuagint translated "יהוה" (YHWH) into "κύριος" (the Lord), and added or omitted some words for the understanding of the readers.

[47] Ross also used the *English Revised New Testament* (1881), the *Oxford Greek New Testament* (1881), and the *Peking Mandarin Version* (1861) (Choi S. 1992, 125–28, 173–85).

judgment (審判), law (律法), idols (偶像), circumcision (割禮), and redemption (贖罪).[48] The Korean version also used the Chinese equivalents by slightly modifying them or adding one character to clarify the meaning. For example, *fusheng* (resurrection) of the DV was changed into *fuhuo* (*puhwal*), *dian* (temple) into *shendian* (*sŏngjŏn*), and *jiushizha* (the Savior of the world) into *jiushizhu* (*kuseju*). Notwithstanding that the Korean New Testament had a totally different structure and terms (Shangdi—Hanănim; *chenyu—myŏlmang*) than the DV and that the translators constantly made efforts to be faithful to the original text and to adopt more vernacular words, they could not help using Chinese terms borrowed from the DV.

Meanwhile, educated Korean Christians and ministers used the DV. When most preachers wrote down their sermons in the mixed Korean–Chinese, they quoted the DV. In this process, they naturally adopted Chinese terminology, which formed their theological thinking. For example, they used Shangdi as the name for God in their sermons and writings. Whatever name the Korean editions adopted for God, Shangdi was another officially authorized name for God in Korea as far as the Chinese versions were concerned. Although Hanănim was fixed in the Korean Scriptures after 1904, it existed side by side with Shangdi of the DV.

Protestant missionary translators in Seoul believed in verbal inspiration, the principle of "whole meaning, no more no less," and the advantages of the literal translation in the first version. However, they yielded to the idiomatic Korean because Koreans and Korean translators, who had a strong taste for literary style and thus liked the DV, desired literary polish as well as faithfulness to the original meaning of the text. As a result, the first Korean Old Testament (1911), completed by William D. Reynolds and his two Korean helpers, became a "very literary and very stilted" version.[49]

---

[48] The Korean version was loaded with other theological and ritual terms from the DV: angels (天使), baptism (洗禮), church (教會), comforter (保慧師), cross (十字架), deacon (執事), devil (魔鬼), elder (長老), the end of the world (終末), fast (禁食), the feast of dedication (修殿節), the feast of tabernacles (帳幕節), gift (恩事), heaven (天堂), hell (地獄), hymns (讚頌), inspiration (默示), kingdom of heaven (天國), laying hands (按手), mediator (中保), New Testament (新約), only begotten Son (獨生子), Passover (踰越節), Pentecost (五旬節), priests (祭祀諸長), Sabbath (安息日), salvation (救援), Son of Man (人子), synagogue (會堂), the Word (道), the world to come (來世), and so on.

[49] "R. Kilgour's Interview with Mr. Hung Miller, January 22, 1917," BFBSA, CBFBS; Oak and Yi, *Taehan sŏngsŏ konghoesa*, 2:131.

The Chinese literary style and terms in the Korean Scriptures, how-ever, unconsciously produced a "clique spirit" among the literary Chris-tians. In the preparation of Christian literature, the Korean helpers from the scholarly and aristocratic classes played an important part. Their inclination to retain the literary style and "the obscure phraseology of a semi-Chinese vocabulary instead of the plainness and simplicity of speech" made the texts somewhat unintelligible to the common people. The intellectualism of the users of Chinese literature created an elite group in the church. Dr. Cadwalladen C. Vinton (1856–1936) argued that it was evidence of a "lack of nationalism" in the face of China or "a modified feudalism" of the aristocracies, who were inclined to retain the privileges of their own caste and the traditional Confucian values.[50] Yet, as is shown in the following section, there were other reasons for the ongoing use of the DV and the publication of the Chinese–Korean ·diglot and mixed versions for the literary classes.

THE CHINESE–KOREAN VERSIONS AND THE MIXED VERSION

While the DV satisfied the demands of the literary class, most Korean Scriptures were printed in vernacular Korean for the ordinary people. Yet in the 1890s, two translated Scriptures were issued in the Chinese–Korean diglot style—Malcolm C. Fenwick's *Yohan pogŭm chyŏn* (Gos-pel of John, 1891) and Mark N. Trollope's *Cho manin gwang* (Lumen ad Revelationem Gentium, 1894). And the Sino-Korean mixed New Testament was published in 1906. These two indigenous mixed-script styles were the result of the translators' efforts to respect the language and literature of the Koreans, especially of the educated classes.

Fenwick's Gospel of John (1891)

With the support of the BFBS, the Trilingual Press in Seoul published the Chinese–Korean diglot edition of the Gospel of John in July 1891. Malcolm C. Fenwick (1863–1935), an independent Baptist missionary, made it with the help of Sŏ Kyŏngjo at Sorae.[51] The gospel was a copy

---

[50] C. C. Vinton, "Obstacles to Missionary Success in Korea," *MRW* 17 (1894): 840–41.

[51] Mr. Fenwick was an independent Canadian missionary who arrived in Seoul in September 1889 and studied the Korean language there for ten months. He went to Sorae with Sŏ to learn the language by living among the Korean people. He studied Ross' version of the Korean New Testament and, with the assistance of Sŏ,

of the text of the DV line by line, with the revised text of the Ross Version beside it. The Chinese–Korean bilingual system was the traditional method used in the Confucian textbooks in Korea. The adoption of the indigenous system was an experiment for members of the educated class. As they used only the Chinese writing system and despised the "vulgar" Korean hangŭl script, the diglot edition aimed to mitigate their criticisms against vernacular editions and to make them more receptive to Christian literature.

This experiment, however, did not succeed.[52] The educated classes stuck to the Chinese Scriptures, and the uneducated people favored the vernacular Korean edition. In 1893 the Bible Committee and the Methodist and Presbyterian missions concluded that they would publish only the vernacular hangŭl edition. Because the needs of the educated class had been satisfied by the DV, the missions felt that they needed to respond to the pressing need for a vernacular version as soon as possible. Fenwick agreed with their opinion. He revised his Gospel of John and published it in hangŭl Korean in 1893.[53]

Trollope's Lumen (1894)

Another diglot edition was published in 1894 by the English church mission, which adopted a policy of detachment or independence from both the French Roman Catholic mission and the American Protestant missions. They applied this policy to Bible translation.[54] The mission of the Church of England to Korea was the outcome of its older missions to China and Japan. The Archbishop of Canterbury consecrated C. John

---

compared it with the DV and the English Bible. The diglot edition of John was prepared as a result of their study. Three thousand copies with 109 leaves were issued.

[52] W. B. Scranton to H. Loomis, February 3, 1892, ABS Archives.

[53] It was called 약한의긔록혼디로복음. It had more Chinese terms than the 1891 edition.

[54] The Church of England Mission in Korea took the via media, or the middle path, between the Roman Catholic and Protestant missions. It cooperated with the Anglican missions in China and Japan with the British spirit of the commonwealth. Bishop Corfe had some experience in China before coming to Korea. He emphasized learning Korean language and culture before direct evangelism. This policy enabled Anglican missionaries, who belonged to the high church tradition, to study Korean culture and to adapt the mission to Korea. It baptized its first Korean convert in November 1897, seven years after the launch of the mission. See "Editorial Notes," *Independent*, August 7, 1897; "Correspondence, M. N. Trollope to the Editor," *Independent*, August 19, 1897.

Corfe (1843–1921) as the first missionary bishop of the Korea mission in 1889. He arrived in Seoul in September 1890 with an American doctor, Eli B. Landis. Soon, Mark N. Trollope of the Society for Propagating the Gospel joined them and engaged in learning Korean and Chinese. As a Greek scholar and a quick learner of Korean, Trollope assumed the chief responsibility of preparing their own Scriptures, and the collation method of translation was adopted among the missionaries and Korean helpers.[55] For a year, they compiled a summary of the gospel, a tract on the fundamental truths of Christianity, as the basis of their teaching and preaching.[56] It was titled *Cho mamin gwang* (Lumen ad Revelationem Gentium), meaning "The Light That Lightens All People." The story was told almost entirely in the words of the Scriptures, translated from a combination of the DV, Bishop Burden's Version, and Griffith John's Easy Wenli Version. "Occasionally all these versions were discarded for a fourth rendering, which would (it was thought) be more intelligible to the Coreans, and would be more readily capable of being rendered into Corean vernacular."[57]

This Anglican tract consisted of thirteen sections: Preface, Annunciation, Nativity, Epiphany, Baptism, Temptation, Ministry, Passion, Resurrection, Ascension, Pentecost, Acts of Apostles, and Conclusion. The Preface began with St. Paul's Areopagus sermon on Mars Hill (Acts 17:24-31), which was "the text for every missionary to the Gentiles."[58] It approached the Athenians with the notion of God and his creation of the world. As the Koreans believed in the spirits and ancestors, Bishop Corfe thought that they must first learn the existence of God the Father before learning his only begotten Son. The first lesson, therefore, covered the doctrine of the creation.[59]

The tract was printed "in two languages, verse by verse, in parallel columns of Chinese and *Eun Moun*, just as Coreans print their editions of the Chinese classical books which are taught in their schools."[60] The diglot style was adopted, for it was the language that the Koreans would understand and respect.[61] The diglot style intended to provide both the

[55] "Lumen ad Revelationem Gentium," MC 46 (1897): 42.
[56] John Corfe, "The Bishop's Letter," MC 42 (1893): 174.
[57] "Lumen ad Revelationem Gentium," 42.
[58] The preface summarized St. Paul's sermon on Mars Hill (Acts 17:24-31).
[59] "The Bishop's Letter," MC 46 (1897): 37.
[60] "The Bishop's Letter," MC 42 (1893): 175.
[61] Yi Tŏkchu, "Sŏnggonghoe palch'we sŏngsŏ Chomanminkwang yŏn'gu" [A

Chinese and Korean Scriptures, and to reach all classes. It was helpful for the Koreans to understand new Christian terms. Another reason the Korea mission of the Church of England adopted the diglot edition was that it had a close relationship with its Chinese mission and accepted its experiences in China. As Manchuria was under Bishop Corfe's episcopacy, he visited there via Shandong or Tianjin, where he met his colleagues and exchanged ideas with them.

Thus the tract borrowed most terms from the Chinese Anglican church and the Chinese Scriptures, especially the DV. For example, *T'yŏnjyu* was adopted as the name for God, and the following Korean terms came from the DV—*Sŏngsin* (the Holy Spirit), *magwi* (Satan), *puhwal* (resurrection), *sŭngch'ŏn* (ascension), *kyohoe* (church), *ansigil* (Sabbath), *mundo* (disciples), and *chongdo* (apostles). On the other hand, most sentence structures and some terms followed those of the Ross Version. The occurrence of a gap in the middle of a column of Chinese or Korean was also adopted from the Ross Version as a sign of respect (equivalent to the use of a capital letter in English) toward the word following terms like God, Jesus, and the Holy Spirit.

Lumen was a compromise between the Chinese and Korean Scriptures in translation, style, and terms. It was used as a tract for evangelism, a lesson for teaching, and a lectionary in the services. Yet its use was restricted to a small number of Anglican Christians. The mission of the Church of England in Korea expressed their regret on "the almost total neglect of 'Chinese' among the French Roman Catholic and the American Protestant Missionaries."[62] They believed that it was necessary for the missions to understand and utilize the spoken language, Korean, as well as the written language, Chinese. Yet the other Protestant missions continued to publish vernacular Korean editions of the Scriptures from 1892 to 1905.[63]

The Chinese–Korean Mixed New Testament (1906)

When the number of educated Korean Christians increased, they demanded a mixed Chinese–Korean version of the NT. They were so

---

Study of the Anglican Church's Scriptural Tract *Lumen ad Revelationem Gentium*], in *Kŭrisŭdogyo wa kyŏre munhwa* (Seoul: Kidoggyomunsa, 1987), 282.

[62] "Lumen ad Revelationem Gentium," 44.

[63] A few tracts were published in the Chinese–Korean diglot style: McCartee, 眞理易知 (1895); Gale and Yi, eds., 訓蒙千字 (1907); and John, 眞理便讀三字經 (1908).

accustomed to Chinese and Chinese–Korean mixed scripts that they could read and understand them more easily than the vernacular Korean edition. In 1898 a number of Christians in Seoul prepared some manuscripts of the mixed New Testament, and visited Underwood to consult on its publication. At the same time, James S. Gale of Wŏnsan had prepared the ninth chapter of the Acts in the mixed script. He had copies printed and sent one to Underwood for his opinion. Although Underwood and Gale agreed on the necessity of a mixed version, a large number of the missionaries expressed great fears that "such a plan would hinder the universal acceptance of the native script by the people of Korea."[64] The mission requested Underwood and Gale to wait three years. In 1903 Korean Christians completed the first draft of the mixed script of the New Testament and raised funds for its publication. Gale and Underwood wanted its publication—"not as a substitute for the native script, not even as a rival to it, but as an alternative vehicle." However, Alexander Kenmure, agent of the BFBS in Korea opposed its publication.[65] In October 1903 the Council of the Presbyterian Missions resolved that "it is not desirable in the present stage of the development of Unmun literature to make use of 'Mixed Script' in the publication of the Scriptures."[66] In December 1903, however, Underwood asked the Bible societies to publish a mixed-script version. The official and middle classes used the mixed script, as did the newspaper with the largest circulation, most government documents, and school textbooks. "Under these circumstances," he insisted, "everyone acknowledges that the scriptures in the mixed script would give us a medium for reaching a large class of people who are untouched by either the Chinese or the native character."[67]

From 1903 to 1906, there were some events that led the missions and the Bible societies to agree on the publication of a mixed-script edition. First, many members of the upper class and scholars converted to Christianity. Gale's Yŏndong Church in Seoul had hundreds of yangban attendants by the end of 1905.[68] Second, in July 1904 the BFBS

[64] H. G. Underwood to J. H. Ritson, December 23, 1903.
[65] A. Kenmure to J. H. Ritson, March 27, 1903.
[66] A. Kenmure to John Sharp, October 16, 1903.
[67] H. G. Underwood to J. H. Ritson, December 23, 1903.
[68] C. A. Clark to A. J. Brown, December 8, 1905; Council of Presbyterian Missions in Korea, "Report of Committee of Mixed Script," in *Minutes of the*

permitted the publication of a mixed edition of the Gospels and Acts as an experiment.[69] The society's decision stemmed from the needs of the educated class. Third, Kenmure resigned as an agent owing to his nervous breakdown and returned to London in the spring of 1905. His successor, Hugh Miller (1872–1957), had a good relationship with Underwood. Finally, Yu Sŏngjun, along with Gale and his helpers, prepared the final draft of the mixed New Testament in November 1905. Some Korean Christians raised funds for its publication and provided one-third of the cost of publication.

In April 1906 twenty thousand copies of the Korean–Chinese mixed New Testament were published by the Fukuin Publishing House, Yokohama. Its basic texts were the DV and the first authorized Korean New Testament printed in 1906. All nouns, verbs, and adjectives were represented by Chinese characters in a setting of Korean syntax. Case renderings, tense and mood signs, conjunctions, prepositions, marks of interrogation, and some pronouns as well as honorific forms were printed in Korean.[70] Thus Chinese characters occupied about 40 percent of the text, which helped the readers to understand the meaning of some ambiguous terms more easily than when they were printed in the Korean script.[71] This mixed-script New Testament was reprinted in 1908, 1909, 1910, and 1911. From 1912 the revised mixed-script Gospels were printed, and finally the revised edition was published in 1916.

The Chinese Scriptures influenced the Korean churches in the following ways. The Chinese version, especially the DV, became one of the bases for the translation of the Korean Bible. While John Ross tried to make a Korean vernacular version for a decade from 1877, his helpers translated the first drafts from the DV. It was inevitable that the Ross Version contained many Chinese idioms and words. The young missionaries in Seoul, although they used various versions in English, Greek, Hebrew, German, and French, produced the Korean Scriptures that had many Chinese terms, as their helpers were chosen from the

Thirteenth Annual Meeting of the Council of Presbyterian Missions in Korea, 1905 (Seoul: YMCA Press, 1905), 38.

[69] Robert R. Kilgour to H. Miller, August 9, 1904; J. Sharp to H. G. Underwood, August 30, 1904; *Annual Report of the BFBS* (London: BFBS, 1905), 381.

[70] A. Kenmure to John Sharp, October 16, 1903.

[71] This mixed-script New Testament, 新約全書 국한문, was offered to Emperor Kojong on April 25, 1906. Underwood, Avison, and Miller presented him with two copies.

literary classes, who preferred Chinese idioms and accepted the DV as their textus receptus.

The Classical Wenli and Easy Wenli Versions were distributed among the educated Korean people. Most early Christian leaders, evangelists, and ministers read the Chinese Scriptures, books, and tracts. They accepted the Chinese theological terms and expressions, which dominated the early Korean church and still coexist today with Korean vernacular terms. Although their policy was to publish Korean editions, the Korean missions and the Bible societies supported the publication of mixed Chinese–Korean scriptures for the educated class. Some were issued in the diglot edition. The educated Korean Christians not only demanded such editions but also supported their translation and publication. The mixed edition contained so many Chinese terms that only a small number of people could understand it. Yet the literary class could read and understand it more easily and more clearly than vernacular Korean editions.

The BFBS and the NBSS worked in Korea from their branches in China until 1895. Their agents occasionally visited Korea to oversee work on the Bible. They exerted influence on the policy and methods of Bible translation, publication, and distribution in Korea. When the Korean agency of the BFBS was established in Seoul in 1895, its first agent, Alexander Kenmure, was transferred from China. His policy was connected with his experiences in China.

Finally, the first Korean vernacular Scriptures were published in Manchuria from 1882 to 1893. The Ross Version, distributed by Korean colporteurs and evangelists, gathered the first Korean seekers and converts for a decade in Seoul, as well as in northern Korea. Before the arrival of the first American missionaries in Korea in 1884, the Scottish missionaries and Chinese Christians in Manchuria helped train Korean converts from 1879 onward and sent them to initiate evangelistic work in the northern part of Korea, Pyongyang, and Seoul. As a result of their work, there were hundreds of Korean Christians in the Korean valleys on the Manchurian side of the Yalu River. Among them, seventy-five men were baptized by Ross in December 1884 and twenty-five more men in the summer of 1885. In Ŭiju, a border city, there were eighteen believers and a preaching hall by the end of 1884. At Sorae, Hwanghae province, a Korean Christian community comprising about twenty candidates for baptism had secret regular services on Sundays as early as from the spring of 1885. Therefore, the Ross Version and its

Korean colporteurs, not the American missionaries, initiated Korean Protestantism.[72]

The adoption of these indigenous styles was the church's effort to show the people how the church respected the languages and literature of the Koreans, especially of the educated classes. Although it fostered the spirit of elitism among the literary class, the existence of Chinese Christian literature helped to contextualize the Christian and biblical message in Korea.

CHINESE TRACTS IN KOREA

In the late nineteenth century, Christian messages adopted two mixed attitudes toward East Asian religions: iconoclasm and accommodation. The former attacked the "superstitious" worship of ancestral spirits and idols and harmful and "cruel" customs such as smoking opium, foot binding, gambling, and polygamy. The latter, more progressive attitude emphasized the congenial points of contact between Christianity and traditional religious heritage and accepted them as preparation for the gospel. However, most studies on the history of Korean Protestantism have described Christian movements in Korea as invariably led by conservative and fundamentalist missionaries armed with biblical literalism seeking to destroy Korean religions.

This section challenges such a monolithic interpretation and depicts dynamic apologetics toward Korean religions. Investigated herein is the influence of Chinese Protestant literature on early Korean Protestantism. The primary goal here is to identify more than forty Chinese books and tracts that were distributed without translation among the educated classes by 1900, as well as more than fifty other Chinese tracts translated into vernacular Korean for ordinary men and women. The almost exclusive use of those Chinese tracts for evangelism was one of the most important factors in shaping the theological orientation of the early Korean Protestant church. A second challenge is to analyze the messages espoused by the tracts, focusing on their apologetics toward East Asian religions. Finally, this section reveals the irenic tradition in early Korean Christianity toward Korean religious heritage. A few studies have researched translated Korean tracts and analyzed their messages, yet they have neglected the Chinese books and tracts that were

---

[72] See Oak and Yi, *Taehan sŏngsŏ konghoesa*, 1:23–119.

distributed and read among the educated classes and Christian leaders.[73] Attention is given herein to the role of Chinese tracts and books in the formation of early Korean Christianity. Analysis of this Chinese literature reveals another major theological stream running beneath the surface of conservative vernacular Korean Christian literature.

The coexistence of these two kinds of approaches, with different apologetics and different target audiences, shaped a dual missiological trend in early Korean Protestantism. Chinese literature promoted more accommodating apologetics toward Korean religions. In contrast, vernacular tracts translated from the Chinese targeted the commoners and had more conservative and iconoclastic messages. The mass production and distribution of the Korean editions contributed to the development of vernacular literature and a democratic orientation in Korean Christianity.

Chinese Tracts Distributed without Being Translated

The pioneer Protestant missionaries in China discovered the power of the press. Tracts and books became one of the most effective means of communication of Christianity and Western civilization, for the Chinese people revered the printed page. Christian books and tracts adopted the styles and forms of the traditional Chinese religious classics, commentaries, and tracts. Modern mission printing houses produced millions of copies, and the itineration and colportage system distributed them widely to every corner of China. In May 1892 Alexander Kenmure, an agent of the BFBS in China, investigated the most popular Christian tracts and books (exclusive of commentaries, hymnbooks, and prayer books) in China. Table 4 in the appendix shows the final result.[74]

These books were introduced into Korea, and most were translated into Korean. When William D. Reynolds traveled to Chŏlla province in the spring of 1894 and 1895, he found the "best books for itinerating trips" were W. A. P. Martin's *Evidences of Christianity*, Griffith John's

---

[73] See Yi Mahnyol, *Han'guk Kidoggyo munhwa undongsa* [A History of the Cultural Movement of Korean Christianity] (Seoul: Taehan Kidoggyo ch'ulp'ansa, 1987), 302–44; Yi, "Hanmal Kidoggyo sajo ŭi yangmyŏnsŏng sigo" [A Review of the Dual Trend of the Christian Thought in Late Chosŏn], in *Han'guk Kidoggyo wa minjok ŭisik* (Seoul: Chisiksanŏpsa, 1991), 221–29.

[74] A. Kenmure, "The Ten Best Christian Books in Chinese," *CR* (July 1893): 340. Kenmure was transferred to Seoul in 1895 and worked until 1905 as agent of the BFBS.

The Gate of Virtue and Wisdom, William Milne's *Two Friends*, Adoniram Judson's *Guide to Heaven*, Griffith John's *Leading the Family in the Right Way*, and Robert S. Maclay's *General Discourse on Faith*.[75]

These printed books, impregnated with the smell of a "foreign devil," as well as Western medicine, were a powerful means of access to the people. The books had two basic purposes: to present the gospel to non-Christians and to aid Christian believers in their faith. As they contained elementary instruction, their doctrinal substance was evangelistic and biblical. They consisted of a set of fundamental doctrines such as the existence of God, creation, the fall, redemption through Jesus Christ, and regeneration through the Holy Spirit. Many simple tracts contained the Ten Commandments, the Lord's Prayer, the Apostles' Creed, and some examples of prayers for the relatively uneducated, but others were more substantial and erudite.[76]

The Korea missions accepted many popular and steady-selling Chinese Christian tracts and books. These tracts were introduced to the Koreans in Manchuria and Japan and then imported to Korea. For example, Martin's *Tiandao suyuan* was read by Ross' Korean converts in Manchuria from 1879 to 1882 and was read by Yi Sujŏng, Son Punggu, Kim Okkyun, and other Korean students and converts in Japan from 1882 to 1884.[77] Confucian intellectuals welcomed the books on Western civilization, which propagated nineteenth-century Protestant natural theology and the scientific worldview framed by the Enlightenment.

More than forty Chinese Christian books and tracts (see table 5 in the appendix) were distributed without translation among the educated Koreans by 1900. They exerted a great influence not only on the conversion of the literary class, but also on the theological orientation of the early Christian leaders. Most were used as required readings at Methodist

[75] W. D. Reynolds, "Diary, 1894–1895," W. D. Reynolds Papers, Presbyterian Historical Center, Montreat, N.C.

[76] See T. W. Pearce, "Christianity in China, Native Heathen Opponents and Native Christian Defenders," *CR* 15 (1884): 457. In 1877 the Shanghai Conference reported that from 1810 through 1875, a total of 1,036 separate Christian works appeared in the Chinese language, only 126 of which were "sacred Scriptures" and 43 of which were "commentaries and notes." See S. L. Baldwin, "Christian Literature—What Has Been Done and What Is Needed," in GCPMC, *RGC* (1878), 206.

[77] "Power of the Word in Corea," *Quarterly Report of the NBSS* (October 1880): 633–34; H. Loomis, "Rijutei, the Corean Convert," *Missionary Herald* (December 1883): 481–83. See Harry A. Rhodes, "Presbyterian Theological Seminary," *KMF* 6 (1910): 149–51.

and Presbyterian theological training classes. From 1903 to 1904, more than a dozen political leaders were converted in Seoul Prison after reading these Chinese books and tracts.[78] After Syngman Rhee was arrested in January 1899, about thirty reform-minded political leaders were imprisoned. In Seoul Prison, about fifteen were converted to Christianity after reading Chinese Christian books borrowed from the prison library that had opened in January 1903. Over a period of twenty months, 229 people borrowed about 2,020 books. They also read books on Western history and civilization. When released in 1904, they attended James Gale's Yŏndong Presbyterian Church and joined the YMCA. Their conversion stimulated other educated people to join the Protestant church. In December 1905 Yŏndong Church had more than six hundred members, and three-quarters of them were from the nobility.[79]

CHINESE TRACTS TRANSLATED INTO KOREAN

More than fifty other Chinese tracts were translated and published in Korea from 1881 to 1896, as shown in table 6 in the appendix. Most were printed in Seoul.[80] These vernacular editions were for ordinary men and women, whereas the Chinese editions were mainly for the educated literary classes. The missionaries in Korea organized the Korean Religious Tract Society in 1889, and the Trilingual Press of the Methodist mission began to publish tracts the same year.

By using the latest technology, from June 1893 to July 1894 the Trilingual Press in Seoul printed 6,000 gospels, 36,700 leaflets, 44,800 tracts (1,355,300 pages), 1,385 English books and pamphlets, and miscellaneous publications totaling 52,185 volumes (1,801,440 pages).[81]

---

[78] Yi Nŭnghwa, *Chosŏn Kidoggyo kŭp oegyo sa*, 203–4; Lee Kwangnin, "Christian Belief in a Prison during the Latter Yi Dynasty in Korea," *Journal of Social Sciences and Humanities* 63 (1986): 1–20.

[79] C. A. Clark to A. J. Brown, December 8, 1905.

[80] The following earlier tracts were published in Manchuria or Japan: Ross' *Yesu sŏnggyo mundap* and MacIntyre's *Yesu sŏnggyo yoryŏng* in Mukden in 1881; Maclay's *Rangja hoegae* and *Miimi kyohoe mundap* in Yokohama in 1885; and Underwood's *Chyesyeron, Sokchoe chido,* and *Sŏnggyo ch'walyo* in Yokohama in 1889.

[81] *Annual Report of the Missionary Society of the Methodist Episcopal Church* (New York: MSMEC, 1894), 249. Thus tracts constituted 75 percent of all printed pages. From June 1897 to July 1898, the same press printed 5,157,195 pages. See George C. Cobb, "Report VII. Trilingual Press," in *Journal of the Fourteenth Annual Meeting of the Korea Mission of the MEC* (Seoul: Trilingual Press,

More copies were printed in the next few years after the Sino-Japanese War. If they had printed 5,000 copies of a tract in each edition and at least two editions had been published, then about 600,000 copies might have been printed and distributed before 1897. If an average of 1,000 copies of a Chinese tract or book had been imported from China, then about 100,000 copies might have been distributed before 1900.

Korean colporteurs and evangelists were the principal distributors of these tracts. Like the early nineteenth-century American Methodist circuit riders, Korean evangelists traveled to all corners of the land. Although missionaries had the authority to translate and write the printed word, it was the Korean itinerant evangelists who did the talking. Those who heard the gospel and purchased the tracts did not separate the texts in their minds from the booksellers. Korean evangelists were religious entrepreneurs in this mass movement. In due time they became leaders of the local churches. As they witnessed the real life of the people and experienced the declining fate of the nation, many of them became devoted to the Independence Movement against Japanese imperialism. This was another aspect of democracy that Christian tracts brought to Korean society.

Korean tracts were distributed for direct evangelism among the ordinary people, whereas Chinese tracts were used as textbooks in seminaries and schools or read by the educated classes. The simple vernacular versions held the conviction of the Enlightenment and the commonsense philosophy that truth was self-evident. Because the people were capable of discerning truth from superstition, they would accept Christianity only if rightly informed.

The Messages of the Chinese Tracts

The impact of the tracts on the early Korean church was decisive in evangelism, apologetics against other religions, doctrinal formation, and cultural views. An analysis of the five most influential and best-selling books or tracts, written by five missionaries in China, will identify the basic messages that the Korea missions preached to the Korean people. It will also show that evangelical apologetics that developed in

---

1898), 41; Yi Mahnyol, *Han'guk Kidoggyo munhwa undongsa*, 309–18. Some Korean tracts were printed in Yokohama, Japan, and at Underwood's private printing press.

China influenced the formation of the early Korean church. The vernacular tracts targeted the ordinary people, whom the missionaries in Korea believed were under the "superstitious" spell of shamanism and idolatrous Buddhism. The last two Chinese tracts—Martin's *Tiandao suyuan* and Faber's *Zixi cudong*—were used without translation among the educated class.

Zhang Yuan liangyou xianglun (The Two Friends, 1819)

William Milne (1775–1822), a Scottish Congregationalist, was sent to South China by the London Missionary Society in 1813. He published *Zhang Yuan liangyou xianglun* in Malacca in 1819. By 1906 there were at least seventeen editions and about two million copies in circulation. His son, W. C. Milne, published revised editions in 1851 and 1857, with more accurate terms. It was the best-selling tract in China for a century. Samuel A. Moffett translated it into Korean in 1892, and at least four editions had been published by 1905.

Daniel Bays attributed its popularity in China to the easy wenli semiclassical style, the extended dialogue between two friends, and the Chinese setting.[82] *The Two Friends* made a clear presentation of Christian doctrines, which was representative of early nineteenth-century mainstream Protestantism. By comparing the differences between Christians and non-Christians, Jesus Christ and the Chinese sages, the mundane life and the eternal blessings, and other themes, Milne gave a clear account of basic Christian doctrines to the Chinese. On the other hand, the tract used standard Chinese religious terms, especially Buddhist terms such as *zui* (sin), *shanren* (good person), *eren* (wicked person), *hougai* (repentance), *xin* (faith), *tiantang* (heaven), *diyu* (hell), *jinsheng* (this world), *laisheng* (the world to come), *yongsheng* (eternal life), *yongfu* (eternal blessing), and *yongfa* (eternal punishment). The tract also partly criticized Confucian ethics and values as imperfect. Yet the tract adopted Confucianism's central principle of filial piety (*xiaodao*) and loyalty (*zhong*), and expanded its object to God. Thus Milne insisted that worshipping God was the real way of filial piety (*zhen xiaodao*). *The Two Friends* exemplified adaptation to the Chinese setting in its dialogic form, use of traditional religious terms, and literary

---

[82] Daniel H. Bays, "Christian Tracts: The Two Friends," in *Christianity in China: Early Protestant Missionary Writings*, ed. Suzanne W. Barnett and John K. Fairbank (Cambridge, Mass.: Harvard University Press, 1974), 19–34.

style. At the same time, it clearly spoke against idol worship, syncretism, and polytheism.

Miaiozhu wenda (Dialogues with a Temple Keeper, 1856)

Ferdinand Genähr of the Rhenish Missionary Society arrived in Hong Kong in 1847. Having been placed under the direction of Mr. Gützlaff in connection with the Chinese Union, he settled in Taiping, Guangdong province. In 1848 he founded a station near Hong Kong and established a school there. His close contact with ordinary people enabled him to understand Chinese popular religions. As a result, he condemned Buddhism and Daoism and most religious practices related to them, such as geomancy, ancestor worship, and spirit worship in general. *Miaozhu wenda* was a straight attack on them. It used "the popular dialogue format to explain Christian doctrine in the context of denouncing the follies of idolatry."[83]

Genähr's tract had the typical iconoclastic attitude of nineteenth-century evangelicalism and intellectualism. It denounced all forms of idolatry—the worship of Buddhist icons, Daoist pictures, Confucian ancestral tablets, and Shamanistic spirits. It condemned them as ignorant and deceitful superstitions and a sign of disloyalty to God. Reason was a powerful weapon by which the missionaries destroyed Asian idols and "false" religions.[84] Although the tract did not mention Roman Catholicism, its severe criticism of any form of idolatry assumed the falsity and erroneousness of Catholicism. In the epilogue of the Korean edition, H. G. Appenzeller stressed the difference between iconoclastic Protestantism and the Roman Catholic custom of wearing a crucifix or worshipping the picture of Jesus.[85] The iconoclasm of

---

[83] Alexander Wylie, *Memorials of Protestant Missionaries to the Chinese* (Shanghai: American Presbyterian Mission Press, 1867), 161–63; Ralph R. Covell, *Confucianism, the Buddha, and Christ: A History of the Gospel in Chinese* (Maryknoll, N.Y.: Orbis, 1986), 95.

[84] The Protestant missions attacked visible religious symbols and idols with the linear symbols of the printed pages. But they used visual media for communication, such as modern machines and inventions (like the magic lantern), chapels and schools, and pictures of Jesus and the cross, for "radical intellectualist anti-idolatry" in the early nineteenth century. See Kenneth Cracknell, *Justice, Courtesy and Love: Theologians and Missionaries Encountering World Religions, 1846– 1914* (London: Epworth Press, 1995), 14–20.

[85] H. G. Appenzeller translated the tract into Korean in 1893. He published

nineteenth-century evangelicalism was a legacy of the European Reformation against Roman Catholicism of the sixteenth century.

The condemnation of most Chinese religious practices as idolatry and superstition was not confined to the realm of morality and religion. It affected the social reform movement of the Christian missions, which believed that religious iconoclasm would transform China into a rich and strong nation. In Korea, the iconoclastic message also attacked the Confucian social and political system, which was based on the ideology of loyalty and filial piety. Protestant iconoclasm ultimately aimed at the reformation of the sociopolitical structure of old Korea as well as its religious and ethical systems.

Tiandao suyuan (Evidences of Christianity, 1854)

William A. P. Martin (1827–1916) worked in China for sixty-six years, first in Ningbo from 1850 to 1860 and then in Beijing until 1916.[86] His lectures to the educated people at Ningbo Presbyterian Church became the basis for *Tiandao suyuan*. It was the most popular evangelistic book in China. Before 1912 it went through thirty or forty editions in Chinese as well as many in Japanese. In 1907 a poll conducted by the Christian Literature Society voted it "the best single book" in Chinese.[87] The book had the same aim as other apologetic tracts: to prove the evidence of Christianity. Yet in order to approach the scholarly Chinese mind, Martin reasoned based on nineteenth-century evangelicalism with the help of Western science, Scottish commonsense philosophy, and William Paley's natural theology. Scottish philosophical realism, which declared the objective reality of the external world and cause and effect, led him to argue for the existence of God. Martin believed in God's personal control over history and the universe. This Calvinistic emphasis strengthened his commitment to philosophical realism.

---

the second edition, which had thirty-five leaves, through the Paejae School Press in 1895. The third one was published in 1899.

[86] For Martin's life and work in China, see Ralph R. Covell, *W. A. P. Martin, Pioneer of Progress in China* (Washington, D.C.: Christian University Press, 1978), 10–19.

[87] A. J. Brown, "The Death of the Rev. W. A. P. Martin," *Minutes of the Board of the Foreign Missions of the PCUSA* (New York: BFMPCUSA, 1916), 321. In 1885 H. G. Underwood began to translate the book into Korean. In 1906 Ch'oe Pyŏnghŏn translated a part of the book. A full Korean edition was not published.

Martin's *Tiandao suyuan* was similar to Matteo Ricci's *Tianzhu shiji* (The True Meaning of the Lord of Heaven, 1603).[88] Chinese officials once regarded Martin as a second Ricci. Both books were published at critical periods in Chinese history: Ricci's book at the end of the Ming dynasty during the Japanese–Korean War (1592–1599) and Martin's between the Taiping Rebellion (1850) and the Second Opium War (1858). Thus *Tiandao suyuan* caught the attention of the reform-minded educated class, especially as the evidential learning of the Chinese classics, which denounced futile doctrinarianism and academicism, was popular among Confucian intellectual circles during the mid-nineteenth century. They welcomed Martin's method and attitude, which were based on scientific facts and tangible evidence.[89] Both books were Christian apologetics and intellectual defenses of the Christian faith in philosophical and theological terms. Ricci and Martin believed that Confucian morality was compatible with Christian ethics. They presented Christianity as a faith that could be adopted by Confucian scholars and asserted that God could be proclaimed in local terms. Yet both were extremely critical of Buddhism. Their message of continuity and methods of accommodation showed that new missionaries had to train their minds to enter into the Confucian intellectual world. Both used the printed word and natural theology to access the educated. Ricci was a product of the Italian Catholic humanism of the sixteenth century, so it was easy for him to relate Catholic humanism to Confucian humanism.[90] In contrast, Martin related eighteenth-century English natural theology and Scottish commonsense philosophy to Confucian natural theology, realism, and morality. With their influence on Korea, both gained an audience among the Confucian classes. Some turn-of-the-nineteenth-century minority Confucians accepted Ricci's

---

[88] Because the Chinese people thought highly of traditions, in the appendices of section 2, Martin introduced the text of the memorial on Roman Catholicism submitted by Xu Guangqi (baptized by Matteo Ricci) to the emperor in 1616 and the Nestorian Monument (established in 781). Martin argued that the Nestorian Monument proved that Christianity was not created by Westerners but was propagated in China by Asians during the Tang dynasty.

[89] Yoshido Tora, *Chūgoku Kirisutokyō dendō bunsho no kenkū: "Tendōkyogen" no kenkū, tsuketari yakuchū* [Studies of Chinese Protestant Missionary Literature: A Study of Tracing the Sources of *The Pilgrim's Progress*: Supplemented with a Japanese Translation and Annotations] (Tokyo: Kyūko Shoin, 1993), 103–4.

[90] Andrew C. Ross, *A Vision Betrayed* (Maryknoll, N.Y.: Orbis, 1994), 142–50.

interpretation of original Confucianism and converted to Catholicism. Likewise, at the turn of the twentieth century some educated Koreans accepted Martin's arguments that Christianity was the fulfillment of Confucianism. However, such an accommodating message was devalued by latecomers—conservative Franciscan missionaries in the case of the Catholic Church, and American fundamentalist missionaries in the 1920s in the Protestant case.

Martin regarded the progress of Western civilization as a means for missions. He identified Christian faith with Western civilization and used the latter as proof of the legitimacy of the former. His missionary work in China closely linked Christianity with civilization, and evangelism with education. There was no doubt that the Enlightenment and Scottish commonsense philosophy had a profound impact on nineteenth-century missions and mission methods, to which Martin's work belonged. He placed a high value on reason. Paley's natural theology had a valuable role in supporting the claims of biblical revelation. The Newtonian worldview declared the universe to be a harmonious system that operated according to the natural laws imposed by God. These laws were moral as well as physical, dictating the course of history as well as shaping the natural world.

Martin's employment of the concept of divine providence was an illustration of the confluence of biblical and Enlightenment influences in fashioning his evangelical worldview. History was an ordered process, under the governance of God and the lordship of Christ, moving toward the fulfillment of the purposes of the divine will. Anglo-Saxon missionaries believed that they had been uniquely commissioned by God to bring the gospel to the world. Accepting this God-given trust, Martin was convinced that he was called by providence to disseminate a package of Christian civilization—Christianity and Anglo-Saxon civilization—to China.[91]

Martin, however, wrote the book in accordance with Chinese modes of thought and Chinese points of reference. He utilized Chinese terminology, illustrations, and concepts to gain points of contact. He expounded Christianity with a dialogic attitude, a classical Chinese style, and an

---

[91] For the relationship between nineteenth-century evangelicalism and the Enlightenment, see Brian Stanley, *The Bible and the Flag* (Leicester: Apollos, 1990), 61–78; Stanley, ed., *Christian Missions and the Enlightenment* (Grand Rapids: Eerdmans, 2001).

accommodating method. He believed that God had already been at work in the Chinese philosophical, ethical, and religious systems, unlike the majority of the missionaries, who assumed that they brought a new God to China. Although he condemned idolatry and ancestor worship, and was partially critical of the theory of *yinyang wuxin*, Martin did not denounce other Chinese beliefs and customs—such as geomancy, opium smoking, and polygamy. The missions were not a question of either Christ or Confucius, but of Christ and Confucius.

In chapter 5 of the second volume, Martin defined the relationship between Confucianism and Christianity with the images of a house and necklace. Christianity was "like the foundation of a house, on which all the pillars and rafters should be built, and then the house becomes safe and strong. The five relationships are like precious pearls, which have no flaw. The primary relationship is like a golden string on which the pearls are threaded not to be lost."[92] The ideal was harmony between the Christian faith and Confucian teachings. Christianity brought Confucianism to perfection; Christianity complemented the latter at critical points. What was important was the order of priority: worshipping God, the heavenly Father and Creator, took precedence over filial piety and other human relationships. In the last chapter Martin answered common objections and doubts about Christianity. To address the most important question facing potential converts, "If I follow this way, must I turn my back on Confucius?" Martin answered,

> Don't you know that Confucianism speaks of human relationships and Christianity also speaks of them, yet adds God to the five relationships as well? After the relationship between God and men is in harmony, the five relationships will naturally get their due order. . . . Confucianism affirms filial piety and brotherly love; Christianity lets men revere the Heavenly Father, respect their parents, make friends with others in brotherly love and with the same love search for the origins of filial piety and brotherly love. If God and men love, filial piety and brotherly love will reach out to the world. Confucianism and Christianity are differentiated in terms of breadth and narrowness, but not in terms of heterodoxy and orthodoxy. Then how can you say about apostasy [if one turns to Christianity]?[93]

[92] W. A. P. Martin, *Tiandao suyuan* [Evidences of Christianity] (Ningbo: Huahua shuju, 1854), 47a. "如屋基有磐石 萬椽裂乎其上 方得安固. 五倫譬如珠寶 不可缺少 首倫譬如金索 貫串無遺."

[93] Martin, *Tiandao suyuan*, II.57a–57b.

Martin's message differed from that of nineteenth-century American evangelicalism in its form but not its content. His Presbyterian faith, as practiced, and commonsense philosophy enabled him to see God as the cause for historical, ethical, social, and religious effects within Chinese society. Martin believed that the deep-seated religious needs of the Chinese people were imperfectly met by Chinese religions. His central message was the restoration of people's right relationship with God through redemption by Christ and regeneration of the Holy Spirit. *Tiandao suyuan* was his masterpiece in presenting the Christian faith and culture to the Chinese.

Dehui rumen (The Gate of Virtue and Wisdom, 1879)

Griffith John (1831–1912) prepared *Dehui rumen* for scholars by compiling some of his own previous tracts and adding new chapters. As soon as it was published, it became a Chinese Christian literature classic. The Chinese liked the book "not only for the good teaching it contains, but also on account of its easy, polished Chinese style. It possesses what the Chinese call 'flavor,' and without that 'flavor' no book may hope to become popular and obtain length of days."[94] It became famous when ten thousand copies were distributed at the state examination in 1879. Tens of thousands of copies of it were distributed afterward to scholars in different provinces and to missionaries of various societies and nationalities.

The book consisted of eighteen chapters. The first five chapters dealt with the origin and source of heaven and earth and natural theology. Chapters 6, 7, and 8 were on God, his nature, names, and the Trinity. Chapters 9 and 10 were on Jesus Christ and his redemption of sin. Chapter 11 was on the Holy Spirit and regeneration. The remaining chapters dealt with salvation by faith, resurrection, great themes of the Bible, Christian life, the eternal blessings, and repentance.[95]

---

[94] Nelson Bitton, *Griffith John: The Apostle of Central China* (London: Sunday School Union, 1912), 126.

[95] At the very least the following nine chapters were compiled from the previous tracts: 6, *Shangdi zhenli* (The Truth Concerning God); 9, *Jiushi zhenzhu* (The True Savior of the World); 10, *Shuzui zhi dao* (On the Atonement); 11, *Zhongsheng zhi dao* (On Regeneration); 12, *Xinzhe dejiu* (Salvation through Faith); 13, *Fusheng zhi dao* (On the Resurrection); 14, *Shengjing dazhi* (Great Themes of the Gospel); 15, *Xinzhe suode zhi zhenfu* (True Way of Seeking Happiness); and 18, *Quanzhong hougai* (On Repentance).

In the preface, John stated that the true way, which covered the entire universe, had no division in the East and the West. He emphasized that Christianity was the true religion for the salvation of the soul and the universal religion for all people, for it originated not from the West, but from God. He stressed the benefits that Christianity would bring to China: the establishment of hospitals and schools, the work among the poor and opium smokers, the awakening of the people, and the development of modern learning and civilization. He warned of the danger of *zhongti xiyong* (Chinese substance and Western function), stating that it put the cart before the horse. The relationship between Christianity and Western technology was like a "root and branch," so that the former was indispensable for the latter.

The first five chapters followed the first part of Martin's *Evidences of Christianity* and adopted a part of Williamson's *Natural Theology*. As their discussions of the origin of the world and natural theology appealed to Chinese scholars, John summarized them and elaborated the topics with more precise and persuasive ideas. In order to explain the deft design and management of the Creator, chapter 1 used various analogies including a watch, a house, and the human soul and its maker. Chapter 2 argued that the relationship between the material universe and God was like a house and a carpenter, or the human body and the soul. John denounced the Confucian theory of *wuji taiji* (the great ultimate) and *li* (principle). These were not God, for they had no sense or spiritual wisdom. As a king governed a state with the law, God governed the world according to his nature, will, and law, which was his li. He concluded that *dao* (way) or wuji taiji was not God, but empty chaos. Chapter 3 criticized the theory of yinyang wuxin (two forces and five agents), based on the Western chemical theory of the elements and compounds. John explained the theory of atoms and molecules by comparing them to the method of making Chinese characters by the combination of strokes of the brush.

About the life and teachings of Jesus, the book tried to show a point of reference in Chinese history, and he stated that Jesus was born in Judea, an Eastern country, in the first year of Emperor Ping of the Han dynasty. In chapter 10, he found such a point in the ancient sacrificial ceremonies performed for the people by the Chinese saint emperors. Unlike the emperors, however, Jesus himself died on the cross as a sacrifice of redemption for the whole world, not just for a country.

As it was hard for the Chinese to understand the doctrine of original sin and the regeneration of sinners by the Holy Spirit, John employed the watch analogy again in chapter 11. If a part of a watch is broken, it does not work properly, even if the other parts are good. Likewise, as good human nature was degraded by the original sin, it easily became wicked, even though it had the five constant virtues. Therefore, human beings do not or cannot do what they think is good. John argued that the Confucian way of *gewu zhizhi* (the investigation of things and the extension of knowledge), which was related to only knowledge, could not change the human heart, but the power of the Holy Spirit could regenerate it.

In the final chapter, John gave apologetic answers to the common objections raised by the people during evangelism. The first objection was that Christianity did not originate in the East. Some claimed that cultivating one's words and behavior is enough and that there is no need to revere and serve God. Others asserted that it was right to revere God, but it was wrong to believe in Jesus. Some maintained that as the soul disperses when a person dies, a religion of the salvation of the soul is useless. Others insisted that as every country had its own religion, it was correct to follow its traditional religion and eschew foreign ones. Most objections were related to Chinese nationalism or humanism. John answered that although missionaries came from Western countries, Christianity came from God. The great way was not limited to a country, and its true principles pass throughout the world, in both the East and the West. If a religion, domestic or foreign, was right and profitable to the individuals and the world, it was acceptable to all, even to the Chinese. John wrote that the relationship between Christianity and Confucianism was like that of the sun and the moon. Although Confucianism was good, it did not have sufficient teachings for the people to know the way of God. Christianity did not destroy Confucianism, but fulfilled it.

Zixi cudong (Civilization, Western and Chinese, 1884)

Ernst Faber (1839–1899), of the Evangelical Missionary Society of Basel, arrived in China in 1865. Among his numerous books, *Zixi cudong* was the most famous.[96] His basic attitude toward Confucianism was that it

---

[96] Ernst Faber, *Zixi cudong: Civilization, Western and Chinese*, 1st ed. (Hong Kong: Religious Tract Society, 1884); *Zixi cudong: Civilization, the Fruit of*

should be "an ally to Christianity." The aim of the book was to awaken the Chinese people by comparing Christian and Chinese civilizations and to introduce the essentialness of the former for the reformation of China in the face of its imminent peril.

Faber's main idea was the "grafting theory"—cutting away the dead and decayed branches of Chinese civilization and grafting the good scion of Christian civilization to the rootstock of the old Chinese tree. He argued that reinvigorating the roots of Chinese culture by grafting Christianity onto it was more important than resorting to the short-lived and ultimately futile efforts of grafting Western technology and secular learning onto Chinese civilization, which he likened to grafting a fresh stem onto a dying branch. He therefore criticized the position of Chinese intellectuals who advocated zhongti xiyong. In another analogy, Faber propounded that Christianity was like the sun or rain, which had the power to grow the trees of China. Therefore, accepting Western technology without accepting Christian religion, Faber insisted, was like Yang Zhu's heterodox materialism and hedonistic egoism or Mozi's utilitarianism during the era of the Warring States. Confucianism taught humans to follow heaven's mandate, while Christianity taught people to follow God's will. These two religions therefore must have something important in common and should make efforts to accommodate each other.

The book consisted of five parts—their titles come from the traditional Confucian *wuchang* (five cardinal virtues). Part 3 discussed ceremonies and rites, which, Faber insisted, should be based on one maintaining sincerity in the auspicious, moderation in the unfortunate, rightness in the court, reverence for guests, and authority in the military. In the section titled "The Errors of the False Rites," he criticized ancestor worship. He advocated the spirit of filial piety to serve one's living parents wholeheartedly, burial of the dead with the proper ceremony, and cherishing the memory of one's ancestors. On the other hand, he criticized the rite for the dead aimed at seeking fortunes, building shrines and worshipping the ancestral tablets, engaging in animal sacrifice, and holding extravagant memorials beyond a family's means. Faber also severely criticized fengshui. Comparing what he regarded as the vanity and falsehood of some Chinese rites with the practicality and

---

Christianity, 4th ed. (Shanghai: Society for the Diffusion of Christian and General Knowledge among the Chinese, 1902). For his understanding of Confucianism, see his paper "Confucianism" (Parliament of Religions, Chicago, 1893), a full-text version of which is in *CR* 33 (1902): 159–75.

truth of Western Christian rituals, he suggested that the former should be reformed and supplemented in the light of the latter.

In the last chapter, "How Can Western Civilization Be Practiced in China?" Faber recommended the reformation of the old laws by appointing those who were awakened and well versed in Western civilization. The contemporary weakness of China, he claimed, resulted from the worship of idols and false spirits and from neglecting the divine commandments. A strong nation, he argued, should heal a weak and sick nation. But if a weaker country does not accept a doctor's prescription, then powerful countries will come and exact fees on it; then without being healed, the weak country will become only poorer. Thus a weak China should seek to become strong by appropriating Western civilization; the Chinese should believe in the possibility of reformation and make strenuous efforts to achieve it. To this end, the Chinese should revere God and seek his help. Good-natured Westerners would then cooperate to reform China.

The message of the Chinese tracts used in Korea can be summarized as follows: First, the Chinese worshipped only God in the ancient golden age. Shangdi, or heaven, whom they worshipped, was not different from the biblical God. There was neither West nor East in the great Heavenly Way of worshipping God. Second, heaven itself was not God, but one of his creations. It was like the relationship between a table and a carpenter. This analogy was borrowed from William Paley's famous analogy of a watch and its maker. Third, the worship of idols, Buddha, ancestors, and evil spirits was a foreign intrusion or degraded form of the original worship of God. They were false and deceitful. Fourth, there were temporary revivals of the tradition of the worship of God through the missions of the Nestorians and Roman Catholics from the seventh century to the seventeenth century. Thus Christianity, which originated from God and began in Judea, was not a modern Western religion. Fifth, missionaries did not bring a Western God, but wanted to teach the Chinese to rediscover more fully the heavenly God who worked in the Chinese philosophical, ethical, and religious systems. Sixth, Christianity does not denounce the traditional sages, but states that Jesus, being both God and man, was superior to all other sages. Jesus' teachings were perfect compared to those of other sages, including Confucius and Buddha, who taught little about the world to come, the afterlife, the way to redemption, the truth of resurrection, the judgment, the eternal blessing, and the eternal condemnation. Confucian ethics were compatible with Christianity. However, although Confucian teachings were good and beautiful, they were imperfect and incomplete, for they vaguely or scarcely sought to establish a relationship with God (*ch'ŏllyun*). Christianity prioritized this primary relationship over the five human relationships (*illyun*). Worshipping God is the real way of filial piety. Seventh, therefore, Christianity did not represent a destruction of Confucianism, but its fulfillment. Finally, Christian civilization would help China become a rich and strong nation. Christianity was the root of Western civilization. Accepting Western civilization without Christian religion (zhongti xiyong) was like a tree without the root, which would not bring the fruits of civilization. Finally, having a new heart through the repentance of sin, belief in the atonement of Christ, and transformation by the Holy Spirit was the most fundamental aspect of a Christian life. Those who have this renewed heart in Christ will love their family and neighbors and work for the order of the nation and peace of the world.

Why was Protestantism readily accepted in Korea at the dawn of the twentieth century? One reason was that the messages of the Chinese tracts, translated or not, were appropriate for late nineteenth-century Korea, whose culture was still under the sway of the Neo-Confucian system, yet sought a modern, enlightened civilization. The Chinese tracts and Scriptures played a decisive role in constructing the Protestant messages in Korea. Missionaries in Korea had not felt the need to write the tracts and books because they could use the existing best-selling Chinese Christian literature. Many important Chinese books and tracts introduced into Korea were written by moderate and progressive missionaries in China, such as Griffith John and William A. P. Martin. They asserted that Confucian moralism was compatible with Christian ethics and that the original worship of Shangdi or Hanănim was monotheistic. Most simple vernacular tracts propagated evangelical messages and criticized Confucian ancestor worship, polygamy, Buddhist idol worship, Shamanistic spirit worship, and Daoist superstition. Nevertheless, Chinese tracts and books took a more tolerant and accommodating attitude toward traditional religions. They claimed that Christianity would not destroy all traditional religious heritages but rather fulfill their aspirations and spiritual longings. Even the later tracts of Griffith John, a conservative veteran, accepted the evolutionary idea of fulfillment. The Koreans could accept these messages indigenized in East Asian culture like a well-prescribed medicine. The Christian apologetics' identification of the fundamental Korean religious elements with their counterparts in Christianity convinced many Koreans to accept the new Western religion.

The Chinese and Korean tracts were accessible not only through their content, style, and language, but also in their quantity and price. Ordinary people could read the Korean translations, whereas the educated classes could use the original Chinese editions. The mass distribution of the tracts was an aspect of nineteenth-century audience-oriented and democratic evangelicalism. The rediscovery and propagation of the vernacular Korean writing system, hangŭl, contributed to the growth of the democratic spirit and the rediscovery of Korean traditional culture as well as the spread of Christianity.

Early Chinese and Korean tracts distributed in Korea had many theological and cultural assumptions: (1) they raised the issues of fulfillment theory and the notion that Korea's traditional religious heritage was monotheistic; (2) they brought up the meaning of the Enlightenment for Protestant missions, through which missionaries believed in the use of reason, the ability of ordinary people to understand logic, and the idea of human progress toward a golden age; and (3) they showed that natural theology and commonsense philosophy were extensively adopted for Christian apologetics, and that the idea of a future heaven and the salvation of the soul were interwoven with progress on Earth. Among these major postulations, all of which presupposed a Christian worldview behind the reasoning in the tracts, as well as rationalistic iconoclasm, the belief in a supernatural phenomenon, the ideology of Christian civilization, the idea of original monotheism, and fulfillment theory were important keywords in understanding the evangelical missionaries' orientation toward East Asian religions and the attitude of early Korean Christians toward Korean religions.

HYMNALS
TRANSLATION AND INDIGENIZATION

The first Korean hymnals were published in the 1890s—a Methodist hymnal, Ch'anmiga, in 1892 by G. H. Jones; the first individual Presbyterian edition, Ch'an'yangga, by Underwood in 1894; and the first official Presbyterian edition, Ch'ansyŏngsi, by missionaries in Pyongyang in 1895. The last one developed into the first authorized Presbyterian hymnal, Ch'ansyŏngsi, edited by the Council of Missions Holding the Presbyterian Form of Government in Korea in 1905. Finally, the General Council of Evangelical Missions in Korea, a united organization of Methodists and Presbyterians, consolidated *Ch'anmiga* and *Ch'ansyŏngsi* into a union hymnal, *Ch'ansyongga*, in 1908. *Ch'ansyŏngsi* (1905) had 151 songs, and 89 came from an American hymnal, *New Laudes Domini* (1892), 24 from *Gospel Hymns Consolidated* (1883), and 8 from *Gospel Hymns No. 5* (1887).[97] *Ch'ansyongga* used similar original English and American hymns.

TRANSLATING CHINESE HYMNS

Therefore, most studies on early Protestant hymns have concluded that missionaries translated them from American hymnals and gospel song books.[98] Those studies, however, ignored the historical fact that those hymns were initially translated from Chinese hymnals. Of course, those Chinese hymnbooks had been edited and translated from the American versions, with some additional hymns composed by Chinese Christians and missionaries in China.[99] The Methodist hymnal *Ch'anmiga* (1892–1905) had many translated hymns from the Chinese hymnals edited by Robert S. Maclay, Franklin Ohlinger, and Bertha S. Ohlinger of the Methodist Mission in Fuzhou. By contrast, Underwood's *Ch'anyangga* (1894) had many translated hymns from *Zanshen shengshi* (Christian Hymns, 1877, 1893), edited by John L. Nevius and Calvin W. Mateer of the Presbyterian Mission in Shandong. Underwood's *Ch'an'yangga* had 117 hymns, and 110 were translated from the Chinese hymnal and thus included the Chinese titles, and the rest (7) were composed by Koreans. And hymn 151, "Paedanssi sipsinga," was a translation of D. Bethune McCartee's "Ten Beliefs." A comparison of the title and the first stanza of "The Rock of Ages" reveals the influence of Chinese hymns on Korean hymnology (see table 7 in the appendix).

[97] Cho Sukja, "Han'guk ch'oech'o ŭi changnogyo ch'ansongga *Ch'asyŏngsi* yŏn'gu" [A Study on the First Presbyterian Hymnal *Ch'ansyŏngsi*], *Kyohoe wa Sinhak* 26 (1994): 498–675.

[98] Cho Sukja, "Han'guk"; Oh Seon-young, "Ch'ansongga ŭi pŏnyŏk kwa kŭndae ch'ogi siga ŭi pyŏnhwa" [The Translation of the Hymns and the Change in the Metrics of Korean Poems in Early Modern Korea], *Han'guk Munhak Iron kwa Pip'yŏng* 13-1 (2009): 143–210. These studies have focused on the musical elements of the hymns, such as metrical forms (a stanza with 8-8-8-8 or 8-6-8-6 syllables), tunes (the Western seven-note scale or the Korean pentatonic scale), and rhythms (a Western iambic long foot or a Korean traditional trochaic eight foot).

[99] For a history of Chinese hymnals, see Fang-Lan Hsieh, *A History of Chinese Christian Hymnody: From Its Missionary Origins to Contemporary Indigenous Productions* (Lewiston, N.Y.: Edwin Mellen, 2009).

The translations of table 7 show the process of negotiation and domestication of American hymns in Korea. Underwood's translation in 1894 reflected both the English text and the Chinese translation. He adopted the Chinese title (基督爲盤石) and a few Chinese nouns for rock (盤石) and side (肋旁). However, he made a new translation of the third line from the English because its Chinese idiomatic translation could not be understood by Koreans. *Ch'ansyŏngsi* of 1895 had better Korean lyrics and appropriate metrics. Jones accepted this new translation in his *Ch'anmiga* and improved it in its seventh and eighth edition, which was adopted by the union version in 1908 with a slight revision. "The Rock of Ages" in Korean, for example, became very different from the Chinese version, and lost some of the original meaning. The second part of the first line simply stated "I enter it" instead of "Let me hide myself in thee," and the second part of the last line pleaded just "cleanse me," not "cleanse me from guilt and power." The Korean churches still sing the hymn with the translation of 1908.

Three different versions of another well-known and widely sung hymn, "Jesus Loves Me, This I Know," also shows that the earlier Korean hymns were translated directly yet freely from the Chinese hymns by Korean assistants (see table 8 in the appendix). It was revised by missionary editors who consulted the original American hymns, and then the committees of the hymnals revised the translations continuously and improved the hymns so that they would suit Korean metrical forms. Many of the hymns adopted in the union edition of 1908 had new Korean titles and Koreanized stanzas, and thus had been sung in the Korean Protestant churches for a century.

It took about thirty years for the Protestant missions in Korea to have a union hymnal, whereas those in China were made in 1905 after a century's work. The Chinese editors had attempted to translate hymns in a style base enough to be readily understood and high enough to command respect among literary classes. They had struggled with many linguistic, poetic, and musical problems in their translation (by editors), transmission (by teachers), and reception (by congregations) of Western liturgical canon. The translation process in Korea was aided by the previous efforts of Chinese hymn translators. Second, Korean vernacular lyrics allowed more liberal translation than Chinese poetics, which required a high style and followed strict rules of tonal rhyme. The first-generation missionaries and Korean Christians completed their translation of Anglo-American-Chinese hymnals into Korean in 1908.

The more important issue was the indigenization of Christian hymnology in Korea, which meant Korean Christians' making of Korean hymnody in both Korean poetical style and Christian tune and melody based on the traditional pentatonic scale. Yun Ch'iho's *Ch'anmiga*, published in 1908, attempted a limited indigenization. It had only fifteen hymns, yet three were patriotic songs. Although he made or edited these new songs through the method of contrafactum (using the tunes of "Auld Lang Syne"), one of them, "Tonghaemul gwa Paektusan i" (The East Sea and the Mt. Paektu), later became the Korean national anthem "Aegug-ga." Yun adopted the reformed spelling system.

> 동해물과 백두산이 말으고 달토록
> 하나님이 보호하사 우리 대한 만세
> 무궁화 삼천리 화려 강산
> 대한사람 대한으로 길이 보전하세.[100]

The culmination of Korean Christians' creation of patriotic songs came in 1897 when the Independence Club was organized and its newspaper, *Tongnip Sinmun* (Independent), began to publish those songs weekly. Korean Protestant Christians' patriotic songs represented Christian nationalism. Yun's other patriotic hymn, "Sŭngja sinson ch'ŏnmannyŏn ŭn" (Excellent and Divine Descendents of the Royal House), emphasized loyalty to the emperor, the emperor's sharing in the joy and sorrow of the people, the peace and independence of the nation, and the responsibility of all people irrespective of rank. Yun reinterpreted the traditional Confucian ideals of king's sovereignty and people's loyalty as mutual and democratic responsibility.

Korean Hymns: Using Buddhist Terminology

On the other hand, Protestant missionaries refuted overall the practical phenomena of Buddhism. They attacked its "idol worship," immoral priesthood, and "superstitious" laity. At the level of theoretical criticism,

---

[100] Yun Ch'iho, *Ch'anmiga* (Seoul: Kwanghak sŏgwan, 1908), 15. My English translation is as follows: "Until the East Sea and Mt. Paektu dries up and wears out, God help our country Korea live long. Our beautiful land of the Roses of Sharon far and wide, We Korean people will keep Korea forever and ever." When 新韓民報 (*New Korea*), the weekly newspaper of the Korean National Association, headquartered in San Francisco, published it in September 1910, they changed its title to "국민가 Kungmin-ga" (Song of the Nation) and noted its author "윤티호" (Yun Ch'iho). Its authorship is still debated.

however, they did not reject all the Buddhist dharma, but offered more nuanced views.[101] As Buddhism furnished Christianity with "fairly adequate terms" for "hell" (*diyu*), "sin" (*zui*), "repentance" (*huigai*), "worship" (*ibai*), and so on, Franklin Ohlinger suggested that these "Koreanized" ideas and terms should be studied "to ascertain whether all those terms that have been thus naturalized in the Empire have also been acclimated in the Kingdom, and vice versa."[102] Although his understanding of Confucianism was biased, among the Protestant missionaries in Korea, Ohlinger evaluated Buddhism most positively and tried to find continuity with Christianity.

Since John Ross adopted "chiok" (diyu) for hell, Korean versions adopted the term.[103] Beside heaven and hell, the Korean Scriptures and tracts accepted the following Buddhist terms, which had been adopted by the Chinese Scriptures:[104] devil (魔鬼), temptation (誘惑), sin (罪), punishment (罰), evil (惡), soul (靈魂), a living soul (生靈), repentance (悔改), to be born again (重生), grace (恩惠), this world (今生), the world to come (來生), the last period of the world (末世), worship (禮拜), chapel (禮拜堂), praise (讚揚), incarnation (降生 or 化身), good person (善人), wicked person (惡人), faith

---

[101] In 1892 Franklin Ohlinger in Seoul argued that Buddhism came nearer to the Christian truths on many points than did Confucianism. He insisted that Buddhism had no form of the atheism found in Confucianism. "Confucianism has (in its ancestral worship) a mere hint at the dogma of immortality, Buddhism promises annihilation. . . . Confucianism proclaims no mediator or savior who could restore original nature . . . , Buddhism does not want to restore it, but seeks to wipe bad nature from the troubled mind. Confucianism never prays, yet Buddhism prays all the time. Confucianism makes slaves of women and children, Buddhism makes all equal. Confucianism leads its adherents to expect all rewards in this life and thus fosters avarice and ambition, Buddhism inculcates self-abnegation and altruism. Confucianism presupposes and tolerates polygamy; Buddhism exalts celibacy. Confucianism countenances deception; the third of eight elementary precepts of Buddhism says: one should not tell lies" (F. Ohlinger, "Buddhism in Korean History and Language," *KR* 1 [1892]: 107–8).

[102] Ohlinger, "Buddhism in Korean History," 108.

[103] Protestantism did not adopt the Buddhist ceremony for the dead, for it was similar to the Roman Catholic mass for the dead. Protestant missionaries also criticized the doctrine of transmigration of souls.

[104] Nestorianism in China accepted terms of Tang Buddhism such as Buddha (阿羅訶) for God, Arhat (羅漢) for saints, Fenshen (分身) for incarnation, the Vessel of Mercy (慈航 Kuanyin, Amitabha, the goddess or "boat" of mercy), Minggong (明宮 Palace of Light) for paradise, Diyu (地獄) for hell, and Meshikha (彌施訶) for Messiah.

(信), eternal life (永生), eternal blessing (永福), eternal punishment (永罰), charity (大慈大悲), law (戒命), angel (天使), merit (功德), patience (忍耐), and believing action (信行).[105]

When some Korean Buddhists were converted to Christianity, they were moved by the Christian themes of the forgiveness of sin through the merit of Christ and liberation from the sinful world.[106] The Christian gospel answered their lifelong search for the pure and sinless heart.[107] The other point of contact was the concept of heaven. Korean Christians often described death as a shift from "this sea of suffering" to "the other hill." In the transition from this world to heaven, the church was understood as a boat of life whose captain was Jesus.[108]

In 1894 Underwood translated the fourth and fifth verses of "Sweet Is the Work, My God, My King" in his Korean hymnal, *Ch'anyangga*. The original fifth stanza was "Then shall I see and hear and know, / All I desire or wished below; / And every power find sweet employ, / In that eternal world of joy." Underwood's free translation in Korean was "Cultivated heart and good work shall help me go to the eternal world; When I depart this world, All things I shall see and hear and know."[109] This translation, based on the Korean helper's draft, hinted that not the heart refined by the Lord's grace but the cultivated heart and the merit of good works should be rewarded with eternal blessings in heaven. The fourth hymn employed a Buddhist term, the great "charity heart," to express the good heart of the Lord. The thirteenth hymn translated "six days' work" into "six days' cultivation and labor" (*kongbu*) and "the holy duties" into "good works." Hence, Buddhist

---

[105] W. A. P. Martin, "Is Buddhism a Preparation for Christianity?," *CR* 20 (1889): 193–203; William E. Soothill and L. Hodous, comps., *A Dictionary of Chinese Buddhist Terms* (London: Oxford, 1934).

[106] Buddhists thought, "[S]in of itself has not a matter but follows the rising of the passions. When passions are destroyed sin itself will cease" ("Buddhist Chants and Processions," *KR* 2 [1895]: 125).

[107] See *SW*, August 1901. A convert from Buddhism selected some passages from the Bible and made them the standards of his faith. They were Rom 3:25, 5:6, 6:6, 8:21; 1 Cor 15:17; 2 Cor 5:21; Gal 1:4, 2:20; Heb 9:28; and 1 Pet 1:21 They testified to the individual and cosmic salvation from the old self and the sinful world through Christ's redemption.

[108] "Ch'anmi" [Praising], *KS*, May 9, 1901.

[109] Underwood, ed., *Ch'anyangga* [Hymns of Praises] (Yokohama: Seishi Bunsha, 1894), 3.

ideas of "compassion" and "good works" found a comfortable location in Christian hymnals.[110]

Furthermore, earlier hymns composed by Koreans contained many Buddhist and Daoist terms and expressions. "The Day of Wrath That Dreadful Day" was one of the seven hymns composed by Korean Christians in Underwood's hymnal of 1894. Its description of the terrible suffering of sinners in hell after death was similar to that of the Buddhist hell.[111] In contrast, "Jesus Thy Name I Heard and Lived," composed by a Korean, contained some Buddhist ideas of heaven and the human body. Its second stanza declared, "As the human body came from the soil, It will return to the soil; Thus, do not think about, Our worthless body."[112] These hymns envisioned the heavenly home where the virtuous and faithful souls would go beyond the worthless body after death. The gospels used "the kingdom of God" frequently, yet the hymns used the terms "the heavenly hall," "the heavenly palace," or "the heavenly temple" (*tiantang*) beyond the sea of troubles and pains of this world (*kuhai*). Although this kind of dualism and otherworldly pessimism was a product of the Sino-Japanese War in 1894, these hymns indoctrinated some popular Buddhist ideas of heaven and hell among Korean believers.

In sum, in the late nineteenth century, Christian messages adopted two mixed attitudes toward East Asian culture and religions: iconoclasm and indigenization. The former attacked the "superstitious" worship of ancestral spirits and idols and harmful customs like opium smoking, foot binding, and polygamy. The latter, progressive attitude emphasized the congenial points of contact between Christianity and traditional religions and accepted them as preparation for the gospel. Chinese Protestant tracts bore abundant fruit as the result of acclimatization and indigenization. Its historical parallel was the acceptance of some Korean Confucian scholars of Riccian Chinese Catholic literature, which had adapted to Confucianism a century before. Chinese mission

---

[110] Later H. G. Underwood argued that the Buddhist dharma gave the Asians "a norm by which to measure conduct, and their treasures of heaven and terrors of hell have added a motive." Besides, Buddhism brought new dimensions of life to Asians and enriched their religious ideals: self-denial, contemplation, introspection, spirituality, holiness, gender equality, merciful goddess, and absolute faith in Amitabha. See H. G. Underwood, *The Religions of Eastern Asia* (New York: Macmillan, 1910), 187–88, 214.

[111] Underwood, *Ch'anyangga*, 124

[112] Underwood, *Ch'anyangga*, 58.

theology and literature worked as a bridge between Western Christianity and Korean religious culture.

To use horticultural imagery, Protestant missionaries did not bring a pot of Christian flowers already grown in North America and plant them in the garden of Korean religions, nor did they sprinkle New England gospel seeds directly onto the rocky paths of Korean religions; rather, they selected only the most promising seeds that had already been naturalized and nursed in the seedbeds of China and sowed them in the fertile soil of Korean spirituality.[113] Or to use a scientific image, in the chemistry of accommodating Anglo-American-Sino Christianity to the Korean context, Chinese tracts worked as a catalyst in blending the wisdom of seasoned Western missionaries in China with the zeal of young North American missionaries in Korea. In the laboratory of modern missions in Korea, the North American missions launched a new project—Christianity made in Korea.

[113] Homer Hulbert used the image of a whole tree (Western Christian civilization) in a different way in 1910. He depicted Japanese civilization as arranged flowers cut off from the flowering trees, for it had adopted Western methods "without Christianity which lies at heart of Western civilization." They were beautiful and fragrant, yet would perish without fruit. Hence he insisted that if Korea should go to the hills and "dig up *the tree by the roots*, and plant it in her social soil, she would secure in time both flowers and fruits" (emphasis original). See H. B. Hulbert, "The Needs of a National Ideal for Korea," *KMF* (January 1910): 24.

— 6 —

Rituals
Revivals and Prayers

Now Koreans say [to the missionaries], "Some of you go back to John Calvin, and some of you to John Wesley, but we can go back no further than 1907 when we first really know the Lord Jesus Christ."

—Willing and Jones, *The Lure of Korea*, 1913[1]

During the Great Revival Movement (hereafter GRM) of 1903–1908, indigenous Christian rituals and spirituality developed within Korean Protestantism, and a group of Korean leaders emerged. Repented, reconciled, spirit-filled, and empowered Korean Christians participated in nationwide evangelistic, educational, and enlightenment movements with the vision of a Christian Korea. The direct effect of the GRM was the emergence of self-supporting, self-propagating, self-governing, and evangelical Korean Protestant churches. In the long run, the revivals provided the young Korean churches with enough spiritual power to endure Japanese colonial rule. From the perspective of the history of Korean religious history, the GRM transformed Protestantism from a foreign religion into a new national religion.

The central figure of the GRM was Kil Sŏnju of Pyongyang, who converted from popular Daoism to Protestantism. The first seismic shift of the revival hit a Methodist church in Wŏnsan, in August 1903, and it reached its peak at the winter Bible class held at the Central Presbyterian

---

[1] Jennie Fowler Willing and Mrs. George Heber Jones, *The Lure of Korea* (Boston: Woman's Foreign Missionary Society, Methodist Episcopal Church, 1913), 21.

Church in Pyongyang, January 1907. Kil made it a nationwide move-ment. As one of the first ministers ordained in 1907 and an assistant pastor at the Central Presbyterian Church in Pyongyang, he initiated the Christianization of several Daoist rituals and relocated them into the church.

This chapter argues that a group of Daoists in Pyongyang had typi-cal born-again experiences of evangelicalism around the Sino-Japanese War in 1894, and that the conversion of Kil Sŏnju became a template for other Christians.[2] It investigates his motives for conversion, which demonstrated a paradigm shift in popular Korean spirituality from its private orientation to the public sphere; it looks at Kil Sŏnju and other Daoist Christians' introduction of the dawn prayer meeting into the program of the Bible training class and regular church liturgy; and it investigates the historical meanings of the revival movement, which antedated the advent of Korean leadership of the church and shifted the center of gravity of the church from Seoul to Pyongyang, which became the "Jerusalem of the East" in the late 1920s and early 1930s. This chapter shows the localized form of Protestantism that was centered in Pyongyang in the 1900s.

DAOIST CHRISTIANS IN PYONGYANG

POPULAR DAOISM IN THE CITIES

Daoism in Korea was a fluid and complex tradition. From its introduc-tion to the land in the fourth century, Daoism mixed with shamanism, Buddhism, and even Confucianism. In Neo-Confucian Chosŏn society, religious Daoism was generally suppressed as a heterodox teaching, though philosophical Daoism was widely and privately accepted by the sociopolitically marginalized educated classes. Daoism was not an orga-nized religion but a submerged folk religion or cult. Popular Daoism in Korea emphasized internal alchemy (*neidan* 內丹) that aimed to culti-vate physical vitality for longevity and immortality.[3] Daoism here does not mean philosophical Daoism, but popular Daoism or religious Dao-ism, which was called *Sŏndo* (仙道 the Way of the Immortals) in Korea.

---

[2] For a definition of "evangelicalism," see A. Scott Moreau, ed., *Evangelical Dictionary of World Mission* (Grand Rapids: Baker Books, 2000), 337–41.

[3] See Yi Nŭnghwa, *Chosŏn togyosa* [History of Daoism in Korea], trans. Yi Chingŭn (Seoul: Posŏng, 1986).

Most Daoists in Korea did not commit themselves to Daoism exclusively, but their predominant religious practices were related to Daoism. Daoism had a great influence on folk religions—morality, the belief in geomancy, stars, exorcism, and incantation for prosperity and healing.[4] Professional geomancers selected auspicious sites for houses and tombs.[5] In addition, people worshipped the Spirit of the Big Dipper (the Seven Stars Spirit), a major household god said to govern the life span of children and the prosperity of family members.[6] People recited a Daoist incantation, *Okch'ugyŏng* (the Thunder Spirit Scriptures) for the sick, believing in the healing powers of incantations and talismans. Many medical books, like Hŏ Chun's (1546–1615) *Tong'ŭi pogam* (Treasury of Eastern Medicine), accepted Daoist health-preserving methods. In addition, Daoist Scriptures—such as *Taishang ganying pian* (Tract of

[4] Byun Kyuyong, "Daoism and Daoists—Its Essence and Development," *Korea Journal* 26 (1986): 1–12; Song Hangnyong, "A Short History of Daoism in Korea," *Korea Journal* 26 (1986): 13–18; Ch'a Chuhwan, "Han'guk Tokyo ŭi chonggyo sasang" [Religious Thought of Korean Daoism], in *Togyo wa Han'guk munhwa*, ed. Han'guk togyo sasang yŏnguhoe (Seoul: Asea munhwasa, 1989), 465–78.

[5] Buddhists and Daoists practiced geomancy extensively in Koryŏ. They continued the practice in Chosŏn, though it was marginalized under the dominance of Confucian geomancy. On the folk religious level, a geomancer in the 1890s might be a Confucian, or Confucian–Daoist, or Buddhist–Daoist practitioner, not always an exclusively Confucian geomancer. Herbal doctors and geomancers combined Confucianism with Daoism in dealing with natural and medical science. Famous prophetic books in the sixteenth century—Chŏng Ryŏm's (1506–1549) *Pukch'ang pigyŏl*, Nam Sago's (1509–1571) *Namsago pigyŏl*, and Yi Chiham's (1517–1578) *T'ojŏng pigyŏl*—were related to Daoist geomancy. See Ch'oe Chunsik, *Han'guk chonggyo iyagi* [Stories of Korean Religions] (Seoul: Hanul, 1995), 437.

[6] Some elite groups practiced inner alchemy in the Chosŏn period, and faith in the Spirits of the Big Dipper was an important part of their religious rituals. Ordinary people in late Chosŏn used *Chilsŏnggyŏng* (Seven Stars Scripture), a Daoist incantation, in their prayer to the Spirits of the Big Dipper. See Kim Nakp'il, "Haedong chndorog e nat'anan Togyo sasang" [Daoist Thought in *The History of Daoism in Korea*], in *Togyo wa Han'guk sasang* [Daoism and Korean Thought] (Seoul: Pŏmyangsa, 1987), 164; Kim Nakp'il, "Chosŏn hugi mingan todyo ŭi yulli sasang" [Ethical Thought of Popular Daoism in the Late Chosŏn], in *Han'guk togyo ŭi hyŏndaejŏk chomyŏng* [Modern Understanding of Korean Daoism], ed. Han'guk togyo sasang yŏnguhoe (Seoul: Asea munhwasa, 1992), 358–60. Chapter 26 of Yi Nŭnghwa's *Chosŏn togyosa* discusses the worship and reverence of the Seven Stars Spirits and their mixture with the Buddhist practice in the Chosŏn period. I think that Korean indigenous faith in the Spirits of the Big Dipper was grafted onto Daoism and Buddhism, and many Korean Buddhist temples built halls for the Spirits of the Big Dipper.

Human Action and Divine Response), extracted from Ge Hong's (283–343) *Baopuzi* (the Master Embracing Simplicity), and *Gongguoge* (Ledgers of Merit and Demerit)—gained currency among ordinary people. These morality books (*sŏnsŏ*) exhorted them to accumulate merit by doing virtuous deeds for divine rewards. A sense of sin developed among the people, and yet most books were Confucianized, and over the course of time the nature of reward shifted from spiritual to material.[7]

With the development of commercial activities and an increase in urban population during the nineteenth century, a kind of religious freedom was given to the denizens outside of the walled cities, and new religious forms emerged as alternatives to the sterility of Neo-Confucianism. In new religions "various heterogeneous elements were welded together and old symbols acquired fresh meaning."[8] One of the seeds of the new syncretistic religions was the cult of Kwan U (Guan Yu), the Chinese Daoist god of war and wealth, which became popular among diverse social classes in Korea.[9] Not only military officers and soldiers but also ordinary people worshipped at the temples and shrines of Kwan U, who was disguised as a symbol of Confucian morality. They venerated the image of Kwan U and paid homage to him at shrines or in their homes. Along the Han River, where there were considerable commercial activities, private, communal, and corporate cult followings of Kwan U flourished through the support and patronage of merchants, soldiers, and other professional groups.[10] In 1904 police raided every house

---

[7] Boudewijn C. A. Walraven, "Religion and the City: Seoul in the Nineteenth Century," *Review of Korean Studies* 3, no. 1 (2000): 192–93.

[8] Walraven, "Religion and the City," 191; Walraven, "Shamans and Popular Religion around 1900," in *Religions in Traditional Korea*, ed. Henrik H. Sorensen (Copenhagen: SBS Monographs, 1995), 127; Ro Kilmyung, "New Religions and Social Change in Modern Korea History," *Review of Korean Studies* 5, no. 1 (2002): 31–62.

[9] Daoists called him Kwansŏngjegun and worshipped him as a god of the world of the dead as well as the god of war and wealth. He was also called Kwan Posal. The worship of Kwan U was a result of mixture of Daoism, Confucian, and shamanism. See Ch'oe Chunsik, *Han'guk chonggyo iyagi*, 59.

[10] Queen Min was a patroness of Buddhism, shamanism, and Daoism. During the Military Mutiny of 1882, she escaped to Changhowŏn and met a widow mudang, Pak Sosa. Her prophecy of the return of the queen to the palace was soon realized. Queen Min let Pak stay at the shrine of Kwan U and consulted with her on every matter. Although King Kojong was not directly connected with this patronage, he vacillated from time to time and consulted with sorcerers on many things.

in Seoul and seized more than three thousand pictures of Kwan U.[11] There were around five hundred shamans and worshippers of Kwan U in Seoul.[12] In 1905 a mudang Yi claimed that she was an incarnation of Emperor Kwan U and induced people to worship at her house shrine.[13] Such claims were repeated from time to time.[14] Even though the government suppressed the cult, beginning in 1904, there were 107 private shrines for Kwan U by 1908.

At the same time, Daoist practitioners left towns and entered into mountainous areas to cultivate their inner vitality by means of physical training, breathing techniques, an herbal diet and fasting, talismanic charms, study of scriptures, meditation, and prayers. There were such religious groups in Hwanghae and P'yŏng'an provinces, which were discriminated against by the Neo-Confucian central government. Some from these religious groups became hermits, and others who dwelt in the cities occasionally retreated from the secular life and practiced forty- or one-hundred-day meditation in the mountains. About one hundred people established a Daoist–Buddhist organization Myoryŏnsa in 1872 in Samgak-san, Seoul. Ch'oe Sŏnghwan, one of its founders, edited *Kagse sinp'yŏn p'algam* (覺世新編八鑑), a selected collection of Daoist Scriptures in 1856. After that, several Daoist moral books and Scriptures were published.[15] Popular Daoist moralism formed an important part of the dominant ethical thought in the late Chosŏn society. These facts show that there were some religious Daoists (Sŏndoists) in late nineteenth-century Korean cities, who cultivated inner alchemy, offered prayers to the spirits, and tried to live ethical lives to be blessed by the spirits. Some of them later accepted Protestantism as an alternative new religion to Confucianism during the Tonghak Uprising and the Sino-Japanese War.

In 1880 he built a new temple to Emperor Kwan U near Ch'angdŏk Palace, and the cult was revived in the court.

[11] "Yosul tunjang" [Witchcraft Fled and Hidden], *HS*, August 17, 1904.

[12] "T'onggŭm chapsul" [Prohibiting Witchcraft], *TMS*, August 23, 1904.

[13] "Kiŏnch'wimul" [Taking Money with Deceiving Word], *TMS*, May 5, 1905.

[14] "Yogoihan inmul" [Weird Woman], *TMS*, July 9, 1910.

[15] See chapter 27 of Yi Nŭnghwa's *Chosŏn togyosa*, written in the 1920s to 1930s (its Korean translation was published in 1977). The Myoryŏn-sa people also believed in Guānyīn Bodhisattva and published *Chejunggamno* 濟衆甘露 (Sutras of Sweet Dew for Saving People) in 1878, believing that it was written by her divine inspiration. They were one of the new indigenous religious groups in the late nineteenth century who blended Buddhism, Daoism, and popular faith.

THE CRISIS OF DAOISTS IN PYONGYANG

During the 1890s, against the backdrop of a crisis in Korean society, a group of Daoist followers in Pyongyang converted to Christianity. The Tonghak Uprising triggered the Sino-Japanese War, which changed the whole political and spiritual picture in East Asia. All of Korea was in anarchy in 1894. Pyongyang was the stormy center of the political disturbance, and many frightened people fled to the mountains and remote villages. The great battle at Pyongyang in September 1894 devastated the city, and more than 20,000 Chinese soldiers occupied the city for some two months and "robbed the people of their homes, their rice and rice kettles, and their wives even, until, when the Japanese army took possession, a city of some 80,000 inhabitants had been diminished to a few hundred."[16] After the war, Japanese merchants invaded with cheap goods made in modern factories and destroyed the traditional economic system.[17] Cholera ravaged the city. People felt that the old religions no longer brought comfort, since they could not function in the face of this national crisis. China's political suzerainty came to a definite end, and the Chinese gods and spirits proved quite inefficient before Westernized Japan. The one strong spell of Sinocentrism was broken, and the war disarmed the Korean people's hostility toward Christianity. A "sort of mental revolution" was in progress throughout the land.[18] In 1897, after his visit to Korea, Robert E. Speer, a secretary of the Board of Foreign Missions of the Presbyterian Church in the USA, reported that Japanese victory over China made a profound impression on the Koreans, and "made Western civilization and religion more highly esteemed. It also demoralized spirit worshippers, killed the worship of Chinese gods, and dismantled some of the remaining props of Buddhism."[19]

Daoists in Pyongyang felt that they could not be religious in the old way. They did not belong to the mainstream Confucian yangban class, but to the newly emerging "independent urban middle class," which included merchants, clerks, innkeepers, and doctors, as seen in the previous chapter. Intellectually and religiously, they were more open

[16] *Annual Report of the Missionary Society of the Methodist Episcopal Church* (New York: MSMEC, 1894), 241; see W. B. Scranton, "Missionary Review of the Year," *KR* 2 (1895): 15; Grahma Lee, "A Visit to the Battle Field of Pyeng Yang," *KR* 2 (1895): 14.

[17] S. A. Moffett, "The Transformation of Korea," *CHA* (August 1895): 136–37.

[18] H. G. Underwood, "The 'Today' from Korea," *MRW* 16 (1893): 817.

[19] Speer, "Christian Mission in Korea," *MRW* 21 (1898): 681.

to Western thought and more tolerant of other religions. However, they did not turn to the religions of Japan (Buddhism and Shintoism), as anti-Japanese sentiment was strong, or to the religion of France (Roman Catholicism), as Roman Catholicism was still stigmatized as a "no-father-no-king religion," but to the religion of America (Protestantism). And they actively engaged in educational, social, and religious enlightenment movements in the 1900s. Many of the "northern enlightenment activists" who "began to coalesce as intellectual, political, and social forces" adopted Protestantism as "a springboard" for their participation in the growing educational nationalistic movement, and Daoist Christians were one group among these religious activists.[20]

The First Christians in Pyongyang

The first groups that converted to Protestantism in Pyongyang, between 1893 and 1894, were merchants and innkeepers. In May 1893 Samuel A. Moffett visited the city to open a station, and stayed at what was formerly an inn inside the East Gate. His helper, Han Sŏkchin (1868–1939), had bought it quietly with mission funding.[21] Moffett held the first Sunday worship service at the house on June 4, 1893, and preached to a company of some twenty persons.[22] He went to Seoul and came back to Pyongyang on September 1. During his absence, Mr. Han led the Sunday services with two or three other Koreans. Han's first convert was Ch'oe Ch'iryang, an innkeeper, who was a respectable man and whose acquaintances were numerous.[23] His conversion experience was

---

[20] Hwang Kyung Moon, *Beyond Birth: Social Status in the Emergence of Modern Korea* (Cambridge, Mass.: Harvard University Press, 2004), 280.

[21] Yi Tŏkchu, "Han'guk Kidoggyo wa kŭnbonjuŭi: Han'guk Kyohoesa jŏk ipchang" [Korean Church and Fundamentalism], in *Han'guk Kidoggyo sasang*, ed. Korea Academy of Church History (Seoul: Yonsei University Press, 1998), 24–29.

[22] S. A. Moffett to F. F. Ellinwood, June 6, 1893.

[23] A portion of rich merchants in northern provinces became powerful in the eighteenth and nineteenth centuries, and some purchased yangban status. Some Korean historians and sociologists—Yi Kwangnin, Yi Mahnyol, Yun Kyongno, Lee Chull, and others—use the term "the rising independent middle class" for the merchant class (including 步行客主, who managed inns for yangban travelers, and 物商客主, who operated a kind of commercial banks) in nineteenth-century northwestern Korea. See Lee Kwangnin, "Kaehwagi Kwansŏ chibang gwa kaesingyo" [Northwestern Provinces and Protestantism in the Open Port Period], in *Han'guk ŭi kŭndaehwa wa Kidoggyo* (Seoul: Han'guk Kidoggyo munhwa yŏnguso, 1974); Hwang Kyung Moon, *Beyond Birth*, 248–49.

difficult and intense due to the ridicule of his friends and his own habit of drinking and gambling.[24] His life was changed by the conversion, and news of Christian teachings spread.[25] Moffett bought a larger tile-roofed house for Mr. Han's family and himself. Moffett commenced the systematic and careful instruction of a class of catechumens as a nucleus around which the number of constant attendants gathered. He traveled to Ŭiju and returned to Seoul to attend the annual meeting of the mission in October. He reported that he had not "opened" Pyongyang but was "occupying" it.[26] He came back to Pyongyang again in November 1893. Moffett opened his *sarang* (a guest room) to anyone and everyone, at all times of the day or night. He believed that "direct contact with the people, living in the midst of them, meeting them every day and all day, entering into their lives, and having them enter into his [house]" was "the true secret of missionary success."[27] He felt that he was rewarded for his discernment of the Korean people's spiritual longing for "the true God" with his first baptisms on January 7, 1894.[28] The Pyongyang Presbyterian Church started with eight baptized members—Ch'oe Ch'iryang, Yi Tongsŭng, Chŏn Chaesuk, Mun Hŭngjun, Cho Sangjŏng, Ŭm Pongt'ae, Han T'aegyo, and Pak Chŏngguk—and two catechumens in January 1894.[29] There were two men around forty years old, and the others were in their twenties. They earnestly studied the Scriptures. Moffett reported that there were fifty-two baptized members in P'yŏng'an province in 1894, and twenty-one more were baptized by October 1895.[30]

The second group that converted to Christianity were former Daoists. The first of these were Song Insŏ (1867–1930) and Kim Chongsŏp (1862–1940). Both studied Confucian classics during their childhoods, but after the death of their fathers, they became wandering loafers, and in their twenties practiced Buddhism and Daoism to try to find the meaning of life. During the Sino-Japanese War, both came in contact

[24] *Annual Report of the BFMPCUSA* (1894), 159.

[25] Moffett to Ellinwood, January 12, 1894.

[26] Moffett, "Report of Work in Pyeng An Province: Pyeng Yang, Eui Ju, Kou Syeng, October 1893," PHS, CRKM, reel 176.

[27] *Annual Report of the BFMPCUSA* (New York: BFMPCUSA, 1894), 158–59.

[28] Moffett to Ellinwood, January 12, 1894.

[29] D. L. Gifford, *A Forward Mission Movement in North Korea* (New York: Foreign Mission Library, 1898), 10.

[30] Moffett, "Evangelistic Work in Pyengyang and Vicinity, Pyengyang Station, October 1895," PHS, CRKM, reel 178.

with Protestantism. After having what they described as special spiritual experiences, they were baptized in 1895. Both were ordained as Presbyterian ministers—Song in 1907 and Kim in 1911.

In 1893 Song Insŏ heard that American missionaries had come to the city and some Koreans had converted. He visited a Christian friend and asked him "what business he had to spoil people with foreign doctrines, and of what use was it to him to throw away Confucianism."[31] In June 1893, he went to a Christian preaching house with the intention of abusing the foreigners, but Mr. Moffett's cordial reception embarrassed him. Song received a Christian tract and Scriptures from Moffett. After reading them, he became interested in Christianity. However, a Daoist teacher of ch'aryŏk (super strength) criticized the Christian doctrine and proposed that he study ch'aryŏk. Song devoted himself to the Daoist practices, yet he felt that his life did not satisfactorily change. When he got drunk, he often resorted to the power of his fists. Han Sŏkchin visited Song over a period of several months and urged him to believe in Jesus. Han elucidated concepts like sin and the judgment, explaining that if he did not repent of his sins, he would undergo an everlasting punishment. In this manner, he was gradually moved to sincere belief. He gave up all the books of Buddhism and Daoism that he had formerly revered.[32]

> He always said that he had studied all things for death in the past. Whenever he met somebody, he preached, "Bear the cross of our Lord Jesus Christ and do not take it off for a moment. His cross saves our body and soul from hell. He will deliver you if you believe in him." When war broke out in 1894, he took refuge in Hanchŏn. He preached the Gospel to the people of the town; a congregation of 100 was formed and they erected a chapel.[33]

As Song was converted from Daoism (and Buddhism) in early 1894, his message focused on the salvation of the body and soul from sin and hell. His concern for immortality was fulfilled by the Christian belief in resurrection and eschatological blessings. Song was persecuted during the "Pyongyang Persecution Incident" of May 1894.[34] When the local

---

[31] R. E. Speer, *Missionary Principles and Practice* (New York: Revell, 1902), 390.

[32] Speer, *Missionary Principles*, 390–92.

[33] Yi Yŏngŭn, "Kyohoe t'ongsin" [Church News], *KS*, December 9, 1897.

[34] See H. N. Allen to F. F. Ellinwood, June 12, 1894; G. Lee, "General Report of the Pyeng Yang Station for 1894," PHS, CRKM, reel 180; R. S. Hall, *The Life*

officers found his name on the church roll, they beat him severely and imprisoned him. Moffett said of him in 1907, "Elder Song had declared himself a Christian after a beating received at the prayer meeting in 1894, when the persecution was inaugurated. He too was tied with the red cord, which meant that his crime was one worthy of death. He has for several years been an itinerating evangelist."[35] Song was baptized in 1895 and worked as one of Moffett's helpers. Song zealously preached the gospel in his hometown and Pyongyang,[36] and his conversion might have influenced Kim Chongsŏp and other Daoist men.

Kim Chongsŏp first heard of Christianity in 1894 through Han Sŏkchin. In 1895 Kim was baptized by Moffett and became a leader (*yŏngsu*) of the church. He preached the gospel to Kil Sŏnju and other friends and led them to the church. The friends included Kim Sŏngt'aek, Ok Kyŏngsuk, Chŏng Ikno, Yi Chaep'ung, Kim Ch'ansŏng, and others. They converted to Christianity around 1895 and became the core group of Presbyterian Christians in Pyongyang.[37] Kim became a helper in 1896 and the first elder of the Central Presbyterian Church in 1899. Kim was ordained as a pastor in 1911 and ministered in a small rural church near Pyongyang until his retirement in 1926.

Kim was a religious man. In childhood, he received a Confucian education, and when he was eighteen his father died. He left home and visited Buddhist monks, Daoist hermits, and Confucian scholars to seek the truth. He studied various classics and practiced Daoist breathing, gymnastics, and abstention from food. For five years he also studied geomancy, medicine, and talismans. People called him a *toin* (a spiritual practitioner). He married in 1884, and got a job at a bookstore. He

---

of Rev. *William James Hall, M.D., Medical Missionary of the Slums of New York; Pioneer Missionary to Pyeng Yang, Korea* (New York: Eaton & Mains, 1897), 272–81; D. L. Gifford, *A Forward Mission Movement in North Korea* (New York: Foreign Mission Library, 1898), 8–16.

[35] S. A. Moffett, "An Educated Ministry in Korea," in *Men and the Modern Missionary Enterprise* (Chicago: Winona Publishing, 1907), 140.

[36] Speer, *Missionary Principles*, 392. Song entered the seminary in 1902 and was ordained in 1907. His first pastoral work was caring for the South Gate Church and nine other groups in the Western Circuit with Pang Kich'ang under the oversight of Swallen. See Swallen, "Narrative Report of Rev. W. L. Swallen for Oct., Nov., Dec. 1907," *KMF* 3 (1908): 43.

[37] Later Kil Sŏnju, Kim Sŏngt'aek, Kim Ch'ansŏng, and Yi Chaep'ung became ministers; Ok Kyŏngsuk, Paek Wŏnguk, and Chŏng Ikno became elders; and Chŏng Yunjo became a deacon.

became a father of twins, and his life seemed to smoothly progress. But his two children, wife, and mother died within a span of three years. His inner spiritual investigation continued through sleepless nights. He created his own incantation formula with eighty-six Chinese letters and chanted it every night.[38] He was a humble seeker who kept silent during the day; he wanted to live the truth. He prayed the incantation to Hanănim for several years. Finally, to some extent, he gained spiritual peace. People came to respect him as a *kiin* (a mysterious man) who could exercise supernatural power, and this rumor attracted a group of young Daoists: Kim Sŏngt'aek, Ok Kyŏngsuk, Chŏng Yunjo, Paek Wŏnguk, Chŏng Ikno, Yi Chaep'ung, and Kil Sŏnju. Kim Chongsŏp remarried, settled down, and had more children. Nevertheless, he was not satisfied with his spiritual life. He retreated into Buddhist temples for several months and prayed to the astronomical stars of the Big Dipper.

In 1891 Moffett came from Seoul to Pyongayng with the Korean evangelist Sŏ Sangnyun. Kim Chongsŏp went to Sŏ to assess his scholarship. Kim found Christians to be intelligent rather than ignorant. In 1893 Moffett came to Pyongayng to open a station with his helper Han Sŏkchin of Ŭiju. As Han had a Confucian family background, Kim was able to make comfortable conversation with him. Han gave him Chinese and Korean Christian tracts. Kim occasionally attended the chapel to learn about Christianity. Yet he could not understand Christian doctrines, such as redemption and revelation. If one washed oneself with the blood of Jesus, might one become polluted with the blood? How could God, a spirit, hand people the Ten Commandments? Han gave him a Chinese New Testament to read. Kim thought that the contents were filled with false and unreliable stories. The Book of Revelation seemed beyond understanding. One day Chŏng Ikno and Kim visited Moffett to check what attitude Moffett had toward Korean religions.

---

[38] Kim Hwasik, "Kim Chongsŏp moksa yakchŏn" [A Short Biography of Rev. Kim Chongsŏp], *Sinang Segye* (June 1940): 22. This is its translation: "In this world of *Sabba*, in the South of Manchuria, in the nation of Chosŏn, in South P'yŏng'an Province, in Pyongyang, a resident, Kim Chongsŏp, born in 1862, dares to pray with sincerity one hundred times bowing, to the gods of heaven and earth. Although having sins of the past, as I am immediately awakened and repenting, and determine to correct evil doings and do good deeds, Oh! Bright heavenly god, please love and pity me, bless me with happiness and prosperity, so that I may accomplish the way of humanity. Although I am not worthy to pray to you, please hear my incantation and remember my humble mind day and night."

He asked Moffett, "You forsook your parents and came to Korea, ten thousand miles away from them. Is this filial piety?" Moffett answered, "Brothers, which is filial piety, obeying the words of parents or disobeying them? My parents told me to go to Korea and preach the Jesus Doctrine."[39] Kim began to let go of his misgivings toward Christianity, and his spiritual journey through Confucianism, Buddhism, and Daoism ended in 1894 with his conversion to Christianity. His conversion did not require a dramatic experience. It was a gradual transformation without intentional effort. In his first prayer to Hanănim at the church, he experienced the Holy Spirit.

> I have known and worshipped the greatest and the holiest *Hanănim* who is the omnipresent and omnipotent god. Therefore, when I first knelt before God, my heart was filled with humility and my body trembled. I prayed with my true heart and with sincerity. I did not know if my body was in heaven or on earth. I was so filled with inspiration that I felt myself under a big mountain. When I finished the prayer, my body was hot and my voice had changed. I experienced the transformation of the Holy Spirit. I was filled with joy.[40]

It was his first mysterious experience of "transformation," which he had expected and desired for a long time. At the Christian chapel, he said that he experienced a mysterious union with God, the supernatural "transformation" that Daoism promised. His old religions seemed to unify with Christianity in a mysterious way with neither an alchemic elixir nor physical practices, but with the Holy Spirit. One day, in 1901, when he was reading and meditating on the passion of Jesus, he fell asleep. In his dream, he fervently preached about the passion to a crowd of hundreds. When he awoke at dawn, his eyes were filled with joyful tears. He went out and could not help dancing in delight. He quit smoking in remembrance of the mystic dream. Everything moved him to tears. He wept for an old beggar in the street, for female missionaries who had left their hometowns, for his late mother who had died without faith, and for the sins of the world. He wept thinking of the passion of Jesus and the devotion of the apostles; he wept at the meal table and on his bed. His tears were said to be the result of his joyful union with Christ.[41]

---

[39] Yi Tŏkchu, *Han'guk kŭrisŭdoin dŭrŭi kaejong iyagi* [Conversion Stories of Korean Christians] (Seoul: Chŏngmangsa, 1990), 55.

[40] Kim Hwasik, "Kim Chongsŏp," 36–37.

[41] Kim Hwasik, "Kim Chongsŏp," 37–38.

THE CONVERSION OF KIL SŎNJU

Kil Sŏnju, one of the first seven Korean Presbyterian ministers ordained in 1907, was once a Daoist. He believed that there must be a great being somewhere, and that a lost line of communication surely existed. He read the books of Confucius, but obtained no answer; then he tried Daoism, which stated, "The name that can be uttered is not the Eternal Name; the way that can be walked is not the Eternal Way."[42]

> Led by such passages he and two of his companions became Daoists. . . . In the performance of their sacred rites, they frequently visited the hills for one hundred days of prayer. In the quiet of the pines and by the side of gurgling water, these three spirits united in an unconquerable effort to find God. It was a long season of fasting these hundred days, with only enough nourishment to keep alive. Thin, wan and gaunt, they prayed on and on if by any means they might find God. The long nights came when sleep must be conquered and prayer kept going if they were to attain to the Eternal One. Out in the piercing wind they prayed still with the shadows all about them, hoping, little by little, to rise into the quiet region where the heart would ache no more. Kil was the leader in this fierce exercise of the soul. Often he poured cold water over his head to expel the insidious onset of sleep. Night after night, with the despair of the drowning, they held on, "O God! O God! O God!" It was a long hopeless struggle. True, there were times of quiet in the soul and intimations of peace, but the finding was still beyond them. So the long vigils were kept up and the praying continued, till in each case the hundred days were over.[43]

Kil practiced Daoism between the ages of twenty-one and twenty-nine. First he learned two short incantations to the Three Spirits of the *Jade Book* from Chang Tŭkhan of Pyongayng. He had recited them ten thousand times in lonely spots on a mountain or in a quiet room for twenty-one, forty-nine, or one hundred days, and he did this for years. He dedicated himself to a life of prayer, meditation, fasting, and vigils. Sometimes he would hear the sound of a jade flute or gunshots during the prayers, and he felt his body, as he sat cross-legged, for a moment jump up into the air several feet. He believed he could communicate with the spirits in heaven. He taught Daoist incantations to his wife, and they prayed together at midnight, trembling. They seemed to become healthier through prayer, and their faith in the power of the

[42] Gale, *Korea in Transition* (New York: Young People's Missionary Movement of the United States and Canada, 1909), 82.
[43] Gale, "Elder Kil," *MRW* (July 1907): 493.

incantations deepened. He mastered several physical practices, such as a method to enhance his physical strength by taking medical tonics and physical exercise, or sexual techniques to produce offspring that would hopefully become future heroic figures. He was known as a spiritual practitioner, a strange person, and a physically strong man. After he had learned prayers and practices from Kim Ch'ansŏng, they worshipped Jade Shangdi every morning at the altar to the Big Dipper. He almost became blind in one eye due to strenuous training.

When the Sino-Japanese War scattered the citizens of Pyongayng into deep corners of the country in 1894, Kil experienced the sad fate of a ruined nation and his inability to help the people in the face of the international war. He began to search for the national dimensions of religion beyond pessimism and the everyday kind of private spirituality. He realized that popular Daoism was not enough. When he returned to Pyongayng in the spring of 1896, he discovered that his friend Kim Chongsŏp had converted to Christianity. "What," said Kil, "do you mean to say that you have forsaken the faith that we have labored for so long?" Kim answered, "But I've found what we sought." Kil said, "No, it is false. I will have none of it." But he stayed on, and Kim was quiet and did not argue. He gave Kil a copy of *The Two Friends* to read. Kim recommended that he pray to God when he read the tract. Kil asked if he needed to pray to a Christian God, Hanănim, for he had worshipped the triune Shangdi whom he thought was similar to the Christian God.[44] Kim advised Kil to pray to the Three Spirits God King that he might know whether Christianity was the true way or a false one. Kil prayed to the Daoist triune god everyday, and his prayers evolved into a struggle to seek out the true way: Christianity or Daoism. Kim gave him *The Pilgrim's Progress* to read. Kil was impressed by the stories. Nevertheless, he could neither know who the Christian God was nor have faith in Jesus. Kim Chongsŏp visited him again and suggested that he pray to the Christian God, the Heavenly Father. Kil responded, "How on earth can I call the holiest Shangdi as Father?" Kim replied, "Well, call him Shangdi and pray to him."[45]

[44] Kil Chingyŏng, *Yŏnggye Kil Sŏnju* (Seoul: Chongno sŏjŏk, 1980), 70; Yi Nŭnghwa, *Chosŏn togyosa* [History of Daoism in Korea], trans. Yi Chingŭn (Seoul: Posŏng, 1986), 266; Kim Insŏ, "Chosŏn ch'odae kyohoe ŭi wigŏl Yŏnggye sŏnsaeng sojŏn sang" [A Short Biography of *Kil Sŏnju*, a Hero of the Early Korean Church], *Sinhak Chinam* (November 1931): 40.

[45] Kil Chingyŏng, *Yŏnggye Kil Sŏnju*, 71. Ritual Daoism (科儀道教) in the

Kil was amazed at the repose of Kim's soul. Kil fixed his gaze upon him. "My eyes burned into his every action, his sitting down and his getting up, his sleeping, his waking. As the days deepened a horror overcame me, for I saw that he had won. What could I do but resort to the old method of prayer, this time in the name of Jesus."[46] Kil prayed to Shangdi at midnight and at dawn that he might find peace of mind through knowledge of the true God.

> By degrees the rope that I had held to so persistently was parting, strand by strand, with my soul dangling over the abyss. Into the region of the lost I entered, where there are no words to depict the agony. It was the seventh night and I fell into a half slumber, worn out and hopeless. How long passed I know not, but in the darkness I was suddenly awakened by a loud call, "Kil Sun-ju!" my name, and the echo was repeated. When I sat up, bewildered, I saw before me a mysterious something—what shall I call it? The room itself became transfigured, and a glorious light shone all about me. Rest and forgiveness settled over my soul, and a tenderness, too. That manifested itself in many tears. Now that I look back I say, "Oh, the joy of it! All my prayers were answered and God, whom I had sought through years of agony, was found at last. I was home in my Father's house, redeemed, forgiven."[47]

Koryŏ dynasty included prayer to many heavenly spirits, including the Jade Emperor and the Spirits of the Big Dipper. Sŏng Hyŏn (1439–1504) wrote about ritual Daoism in Korea. Daoist novels had many cases of prayer to heaven, Shangdi, the Jade Emperor, the Spirit of Heaven and Earth, and the mountain god for bearing a son and family welfare. Daoist chumun is a form of "prayer" or "invocation." The Korean concept of *pildaxpilgi* can be translated into invocation, petition, appeal, and prayer. In this sense, Korean popular religions, including popular Buddhism, popular Daoism, shamanism, and folk religions, had many forms of prayer. Korean inner alchemists, though they aimed to become immortal beings through inner cultivation, did not deny the existence of personal gods. Korean Daoists in the Chosŏn period had personal heavenly spirits to pray to—like Shangdi, the Jade Emperor, the Three Spirits, the Primal Heavenly Being, the Great One Spirit, and the Spirits of the Big Dipper. That is why Kil Sŏnju, as a Daoist, prayed to Shangdi before praying to the Christian God. See Ch'a Chuhwan, "Han'guk Tokyo," 472–74; Yi Chongŭn, "Han'guk sosŏlsang ŭi togyo sasang yŏngu" [A Study of Daoist Thought in the Old Korean Novels], in *Togyo wa Han'guk sasang* [Daoism and Korean Thought] (Seoul; Pŏmyangsa, 1987), 293–95; Kim Nakp'il, *Chosŏn sidae nadan sasang* [Thought of Inner Alchemy in Chosŏn] (Seoul: Hangilsa, 2000), 173.

[46] Gale, "Elder Kil," 494.
[47] Gale, "Elder Kil," 494.

Kil's mouth opened and referred to the Daoist Shangdi as the Christian "Father" for the first time. He wept loudly for his sins. His body seemed to burn like a bundle of fire with the fervent prayer of repentance. Soon, divine peace dominated his mind. His heart was filled with joy.[48] It was a mysterious experience for Kil, meeting the biblical God, the Father, through praying to the Daoist Shangdi. "With nothing but his poor blind Taoist gropings and his hungry heart he came to God, and at once was taken 'far ben,' to the inner chambers of the Divine Presence."[49] It was a similar story to that of St. Paul's encounter with the glorious Christ on his way to Damascus. As the light entered Kil's soul, little by little his eyesight failed him, and he went blind. Like Paul it seemed as though he was shut out for a time and separated from the distractions of vision, so that he might be shut in with God. Kil's external history read, "Once he could see but now is blind." Strange as it may seem, he put it, "Once I was blind but now I see."[50] Kil was baptized by Graham Lee with twenty-eight other Christians on August 15, 1897.[51] Kil was elected as a leader of the church in the spring of 1898. He participated in the Pyongyang branch of the Independence Club with Yang Chŏnbaek and others in 1898.[52] His religious devotion did not lose its national concerns.[53] His Christian faith was an amalgamation of pietism and patriotism. In 1902, at the age of thirty-three, Kil was ordained as an elder by Arthur J. Brown, who visited Korea and Pyongyang, and he entered the theological seminary in that city in 1903.

As seen above, merchants and "the newly rising middle class" in Pyongyang converted to Christianity from 1893 to 1894, and soon

---

[48] Kil's unique conversion experience was introduced to the American Sunday school textbook as a case similar to that of Cornelius in Acts 10.

[49] Gale, "Elder Kil," 494.

[50] Gale, "Elder Kil," 495.

[51] Kil Chingyŏng, Yŏnggye Kil Sŏnju, 87. Speer and W. Grant from New York attended the service.

[52] Kil Chingyŏng, Yŏnggye Kil Sŏnju, 95. Kil Chingyŏng wrote that An Ch'angho (1878–1938) and Kil Sŏnju organized the Pyongyang branch of the Independence Club with fifteen other founders, and Kil Sŏnju was appointed as the head of the department of judicial affairs. The Pyongyang branch actively supported the Club in 1898. About five thousand people gathered at its first mass meeting, where Kil and An Ch'angho delivered speeches.

[53] See Kim In Soo, Protestants and the Formation of Modern Korean Nationalism, 1885–1920: A Study of the Contributions of Horace G. Underwood and Sun Chu Kil (New York: Peter Lang, 1996), 109–23.

a Daoist group—Song Insŏ, Kim Chongsŏp, Kil Sŏnju, and others—joined the church. They became the nucleus of the rapidly growing Presbyterian churches in northern Korea that were centered in Pyongyang. The converted Daoist Christians in particular became key Korean leaders of the early church. At the same time, S. A. Moffett and Graham Lee accepted these Daoists into the Christian church and trained them as its leaders. Although Moffett forbade them from drinking, smoking, polygamy, and ancestor and spirit worship, he was not a missionary scholar or theologian who had drawn a line between Daoism and Christianity, but a missionary minister par excellence who sought to help the spiritual growth of the Korean seekers and converts. Although many historians have regarded Moffett as one of the most conservative missionaries in Korea, he had a tolerant attitude toward Korean religions, at least in his earlier years in Pyongyang. His open-minded pastoral care enabled the Korean Daoists to become interested in Christianity and finally to become the leaders of burgeoning Korean Christianity.

DAWN PRAYER AND KIL SŎNJU
FROM PRIVATE PRAYERS TO COMMUNAL PRAYERS

Kil's life of meditation and prayers—dawn prayers, audible prayers, and mountain-fasting prayers—was molded at the Central Presbyterian Church in Pyongyang and became a paradigm for Korean Protestant Christians. This section traces the origin of the dawn prayer meeting (*saebyŏk kidohoe*), known as one of the most unique rituals of Korean Protestantism, and its transformation into Christian liturgy by Kil. Its concern lies not in the dawn prayer as private practice but as a public or group prayer meeting, in its origin in the 1890s, and in its development in the 1900s. Kil Sŏnju has been regarded as the initiator of the unique Christian dawn prayer meeting during the GRM in 1906–1907. However, a voluntary dawn prayer meeting was initiated at the earlier Bible training classes for helpers and church leaders. Kil combined his personal practice of the dawn prayer with the practice of the Bible classes and developed it into a church program in 1909.

Christians practiced daily early morning prayer from the first century, influenced by the Jewish synagogue tradition and Jesus' example (Mark 1:35). They met at the church for the common morning prayer "people's office" starting in the third century. Monasteries in the Medieval Age preserved this tradition. Benedict of Nursia (ca. 480–ca. 547) made a rule calling for prayers eight times a day and regarded matins/

lauds (the early morning prayer) and vespers (the evening prayer) the most significant divine office of the monks. After the European Reformation, reformers, leaders, and revivalists emphasized the importance of the prayer in the morning, and it became privatized among the Protestants and the Anglicans. Protestant missionaries who worked in China and Korea in the nineteenth century practiced the morning prayers only in their personal devotional lives. Therefore, it would be safe to say that the dawn prayer meeting of the Korean Protestant Church originated not from the Western Protestant tradition but from the Korean religious tradition. What remains to be known is the beginning of the congregational, not personal, dawn prayer meeting of the Koreans at the church.

INITIAL DAWN PRAYER MEETINGS AT THE BIBLE CLASSES

The first group dawn prayer meeting of Korean Christians, recorded in the missionary documents, was held during the winter theological class (Bible class) in Seoul in 1892.[54] Rev. Samuel A. Moffett and Rev. Daniel L. Gifford taught eighteen Koreans from November 28 to December 25. The attendants were male leaders—helpers (Sŏ Sangnyun, Paek Hongjun, and Han Sŏkchin) and invited local leaders and promising Christians (including Yang Chŏnbaek of Ŭiju, Kim Kwangŭn of Snch'ŏn, and Kim Kyusik of Seoul). They learned theological reading of the Bible, the life of Jesus, and the Gospel of John, and they read *The Pilgrim's Progress* at the missionary houses. Gifford reported, "It was a notable feature of the class that the men formed the habit from the outset of meeting not daily only, but many times a day, at dawn and at midnight, for prayer for themselves, their work, their teachers, their homes, and Korea."[55] Korean leaders voluntarily held prayer meetings at dawn and midnight daily for a month. The report does not say where they met for prayer. Probably it was the rooms that they stayed and slept in, for it was too cold to meet every morning at the unheated chapel in December.

---

[54] The first theological class was held at Mr. Underwood's guest room in Seoul from December 1890 to January 1891. Mr. Underwood taught Sŏ Sangnyun, Chŏng Kongbin, and Hong Chŏnghu (Seoul); Paek Hongjun and Kim Kwangŭn (Ŭiju); and Sŏ Kyŏngjo and Ch'oe MyCh'oe Myŏng'o (Sorae). It was the beginning of the training of the Korean leaders, based on the Nevius method, and developed into the theological seminary in 1901.

[55] C. C. Vinton, "Presbyterian Mission Work in Korea," *MRW* (September 1893): 670.

Another earlier case of the dawn prayer meeting was reported at the Bible training class held at the Kangjin Presbyterian Church, Suan, Hwanghae province, in the winter of 1898. The church was built in 1895 when Han Sŏkchin and Ch'oe Ch'iryang of Pyongyang came to the town to escape from the Sino-Japanese War. In 1897 the congregation built a small chapel.[56] The church was under the care of Rev. S. A. Moffett and Mr. Han of Pyongyang. Graham Lee and Norman C. Whittemore visited the church and conducted the winter Bible class in February 1898 with an aggregate enrollment of thirty-one Korean Christians. They reported,

> The zeal of these people is surprising. Long before daylight in the morning they could be heard singing, praying, and studying in the next room. The same songs might be heard through the day until late at night. All expenses were met by the native Christians, including the food of the Korean attendants of the missionaries.[57]

Suan had been a strategic military town between Seoul and Ŭiju. Buddhism had been strong from the Koryŏ dynasty (918–1392), and there was a Buddhist monastery in the mountains nearby. There used to be a Confucian academy enshrining a Koryŏ loyalist, Chŏng Mongju (1337–1392), which was abolished by the order of Taewŏn'gun in 1871. Daoism and shamanism still held power among the town's people. Therefore, when a Christian congregation was formed, they felt needs for strong leadership, good knowledge of the Bible, and firm faith among the multi-religious residents. They invited missionaries and studied the Bible for a week. They woke up long before daylight and voluntarily began their own meeting of singing, praying, and studying. It was one of the first recorded dawn prayer meetings in the history of Korean Christianity.

In February 1901 C. F. Bernheisel reported on his Bible classes in Hwanghae province. Many of the Korean members slept in the public room in the chapel together. "Nearly every morning we were awakened at about four o'clock by the voices of those who commenced their study at that early hour. Again in the evening the same process was kept up till about ten o'clock."[58] Korean Christians initiated the early morning

---

[56] Ch'a Chaemyŏng, *Chosŏn Yesugyo Changnohoe sagi* [A History of the Presbyterian Church in Korea] (Seoul: Ch'angmusa, 1928), 43.

[57] *Annual Report of the BFMPCUSA* (New York: BFMPCUSA, 1899), 168.

[58] C. F. Bernheisel, "Classes in Whang Hai Province," *KF* 1 (1901): 2.

service with prayer, songs, and Bible readings without being directed by the missionaries.

The dawn prayer meeting was included as one of the regular programs at a Bible training class, held for two weeks, from December 31, 1903, to January 13, 1904, at the Pyongyang Presbyterian Church. Nine missionaries taught 610 men, and they had deep spiritual experiences.[59] "A sunrise prayer and song service" was a special program for the Korean Christians who felt the need for prayer. Their hearts were thirsty for spiritual truth and knowledge of the Bible. They prayed for the repentance of sins, for the joy of forgiveness, and for energy for Christian work. At sunrise, they reflected and meditated on the truths that they had learned during the previous day and prepared themselves for the new classes.[60]

The dawn prayer meeting at Pyongyang was molded at a time of national crisis in Korea, and the fire of the revival began to sweep the churches in 1904.[61] The Russo-Japanese War broke out just after class on February 8, 1904. One hundred members—most were former high officials, enlightened educators, and students—joined the YMCA in Seoul from 1903 to 1904. They claimed that a modern religion, Christianity, and its education were the only hope for the country.[62] Kim Ku (1876–1949) attended the above Bible class with O Sunhyŏng, a student of Sungsil Academy in January 1904, and studied the Bible and Christian doctrine. Kim devoted himself to the national and educational movement for the salvation of the nation.[63] He wrote that the new education movement in Hwanghae and P'yŏng'an provinces was developed

[59] *Annual Report of the BFMPCUSA* (New York: BFMPCUSA, 1905), 246–47; Cyril Ross to A. J. Brown, January 9, 1904; Norman C. Whiting to A. J. Brown, January 29, 1904.

[60] "Our Training Class System: From Annual Report of Pyeng Yang Station, September 1904," *KRv* (February 1905): 234.

[61] See J. F. Preston, "The Sah Kyeng Hoi," *Missionary* (November 1904): 546–47; E. Wade Koons to A. J. Brown, February 16, 1904.

[62] For discourse on Protestant national independence, see Chang Kyusik, *Iljeha Han'guk Kidoggyo minjok undong* [Korean Protestant National Movement during the Japanese Colonial Rule] (Seoul: Hyean, 2001), 69–101.

[63] "Country Evangelistic Work: From Annual Report of Pyeng Yang Station, September 1904," *KF* (November 1904): 217; "Progress at the Academy: From Personal Report of Dr. W. M. Baird, September 1904," *KF* (November 1904): 229; "A Reminiscence of a Year: Personal Report of Rev. Sharp, July 1905," *KF* (August 1905): 269.

through Protestantism. "Those who promoted the development of a new civilization devoted themselves to Christianity. . . . Thus it is an undisputable fact that the majority of patriotic people are Christian."[64]

In September 1904, when the political situation was rapidly deteriorating, Methodist missionaries in Seoul held a special revival meeting for the students of Paejae and Ewha for two weeks at the First Methodist Church, right before the start of the new school year. Robert Hardie, who initiated the revival movement in Wŏnsan, preached the message of repentance for the fullness of the Holy Spirit at three services daily. The students of Ewha repented of their sins every evening until midnight. In the early morning, the teachers saw "the girls stealing one by one to the chapel to pray, and many of them, when asked when and where they had felt their sins forgiven, would say when alone on a certain morning in the chapel."[65] This effect of the revival lasted throughout the year.

Another case of the dawn prayer meeting initiated by Koreans happened at the annual Bible class for women at Songdo in April 1905. About forty women came from nearby towns and slept in the church building. Some of them woke up at six o'clock in the morning and prayed after singing hymns for a short time. Korean women received spiritual blessings through this voluntary dawn prayer meeting.[66]

A more protracted dawn prayer meeting, as a church program, was held everyday through the fall and winter of 1906 and 1907 at the Presbyterian Church in Kanggye, a remote border city on the bank of the Yalu River. Presbyterian missionaries invited Rev. Howard A. Johnston to the annual meeting held at the Central Presbyterian Church in Pyongyang in September 1906, and they heard how the Holy Spirit was poured out on the Kassians in India. A Bible colporteur from Kanggye also heard Dr. Johnston. He went home and told the church of 250 believers that the Holy Spirit was promised to them as freely as any other gift of God. They prayed for the gift of the Holy Spirit by meeting

<hr>

[64] Kim Ku, *Paekpŏm ilchi* [Journal of Kim Ku], trans. Yi Mahn-yol (Seoul: Yŏkminsa, 1997), 175. Lee Jongsoo's English translation omitted this part. See Kim Ku, *Paekpŏm ilch: Autobiography of Kim Ku*, trans. Lee Jongsoo (Lanham, Md.: University Press of America, 2000), 140.

[65] Lulu E. Frey, "Ewa Haktang—Seoul," in *Reports Read at the Seventh Annual Session of the Korea Woman's Conference of the Methodist Episcopal Church* (Seoul: Methodist Printing House, 1905), 5.

[66] Arena Carroll, "Songdo Woman's Class," *KM* (June 1905): 103; Yi Tŏkchu, *Han'guk t'och'ak kyohoe hyŏngsŏngsa yŏn'gu* [A Study on the Formation of the Indigenous Church in Korea, 1903–1907] (Seoul: IKCH, 2000), 368.

in the church at five o'clock every morning, through the fall and winter of 1906 and 1907. "They honored God the Holy Spirit by six months of prayer; and then He came as a flood. Since then, their numbers have increased many-fold."[67] This six-month dawn prayer meeting at the Kanggye Church might have been influenced by the practice of the Central Presbyterian Church in Pyongyang.

Kil's Dawn Prayer Meeting and His Method, 1909

In the summer of 1909, the dawn prayer meeting as a church program was held by Rev. Kil Sŏnju at the Central Presbyterian Church in Pyongyang. He had felt for some time that "a kind of coldness had come over the Christians" in the city and resolved with elder Pak Ch'irok to go to the church every morning at dawn to pray. Swallen wrote,

> These two men with humble trustful faith, thus continued in prayer every morning at a little after four for about two months, without having spoken to anyone about it—in fact I think no one knew of it. But somehow when it gradually became known to a few, some score or more united with them in these morning prayers. Then the pastor [Kil] seeing there was a desire on the part of others to join him, announced to the Church on Sunday morning, that any who wished, to pray with them at this time might do so, and that the bell would be rung at 4:30 a.m. The next morning at one a.m. the people began coming, and by two o'clock several hundred had gathered. When the bell was rung there were some four or five hundred Christians present, and after a few days the number who met at this early hour was between six and seven hundred. On the fourth morning while praying, suddenly the whole congregation broke down weeping for their sins of indifference, coldness, and lack of love and energy for work. Then came the joy of forgiveness and a strong desire to be shown ways and means to work for God. Four more mornings were thus spent in prayer, singing praises and asking for God's direction, when the pastor thinking that it was now time to do something, asked how many would give a whole day to go out and preach to the unbelieving souls and lead them to Christ. All hands went up. Then he asked how many will go two days. Again nearly all hands were raised. At the request of three days fewer hands went up but still many, and so on through four, five and six days, the number gradually lessening, but even for seven days there were quite a number.[68]

---

[67] Jonathan Goforth, *When the Spirit's Fire Swept Korea* (Grand Rapids: Zondervan, 1943), 16–17.

[68] William L. Swallen, "A Story of Korean Prayer," *KMF* (November 1909): 182.

This dawn prayer meeting was a program that involved the whole church. From the beginning, about six hundred people gathered at four-thirty in the morning. The characteristic happenings were the repentance of sins, experiencing the joy of forgiveness, and offering days for evangelism. Altogether, they promised to offer over three thousand days of work, adding up to a total of nearly six years of continuous work for one man.

Thus "Mr. Kil's method" seemed to be the right cure for the coldness and carelessness of the church and revitalized the zeal for Christian work during the Million Souls Movement in 1909 and 1910. Many churches adopted the dawn prayer meeting. G. T. B. Davis, an American revivalist, reported that in the fall of 1909, "[a]t Chai Ryung at 5:30 each morning several Koreans came to the home of the missionary with whom I was staying to spend an hour to pray with him."[69] Students also came to the dawn meetings. "In Kunsan, as elsewhere, I found the boys and girls and young men and women in the schools are on fire with evangelistic fervor. I was told that 30 young men in the schools had decided to rise at 5 a.m. each morning for Bible study and prayer; while the girls and women in another school were forming prayer groups to 'pray through' to victory, for the outpouring of God's Spirit, and for souls in that district."[70] In June 1910, when the first YMCA student summer conference was held for a week at Chigwan-sa, a Buddhist temple near Seoul, the participants met for a prayer meeting at six o'clock every morning.[71]

A significant form of prayer was corporate repentance and intercessory prayer for the nation. Korean Christians confessed that the fall and colonization of the nation was the result of the accumulated sins of their ancestors and those now living. They had a keen sense of responsibility for the fate of the nation and repented for the sins of the whole country, as its representatives, before God. They pleaded for national independence to God. The prophetic and collective sense of communal sin was an expression of Christian nationalism during the GRM and the Million Souls Movement. Through these movements, Korean Christians formulated a vision for a Christian Korea, and their prayers had strong national dimensions.

[69] "Korea," *Missionary* (May 1910): 212–13.

[70] George T. B. Davis, "Progress of the Million Movement: A Visitor's Impressions," *Missionary* (August 1910): 398.

[71] W. A. Venable, "Korea's First YMCA Student Conference," *Missionary* (November 1910): 558–59.

In sum, the dawn prayer meetings began in the late 1890s and developed into a Bible training class or church liturgy from 1907 to 1910. The meetings were held for a week, two weeks, or six months. This was a voluntary prayer movement initiated by Korean Christians; it was a special prayer movement practiced during the Bible classes and the revivals; it was a Korean-style prayer movement, indigenized from the popular Daoist forms of prayer and partly from the Buddhist early morning prayer; it was an evangelistic prayer movement adopted along with day offerings and rice offerings during the Million Souls Movement; it was a communal prayer movement that all members of the church attended; it was a patriotic prayer movement for the salvation of the nation from Japanese imperialism. Kil and other leaders transformed a personal Daoist prayer, which was for individuals and family members, to a public and collective Christian form of prayer, which was for the church and the nation. This liturgical innovation—besides the adoption of *t'ongsŏng kido* (audible prayer), *kŭmsik san kido* (mountain fasting prayer), and *ch'ŏrya kido* (all-night prayer) from Daoism and folk religions—was another way in which the GRM further indigenized Christianity in Korea.

KIL SŎNJU'S REVIVALS IN 1907

REVIVAL IN PYONGYANG: EMERGENCE OF KOREAN LEADERSHIP

One of the results of the worldwide revivals in the first decade of the twentieth century—in Australia, New Zealand, Japan, Korea, China, Burma, India, Persia, Uganda, the Philippines, Bulgaria, England, Wales, and different parts of the United States, including Kansas City, Missouri, and Los Angeles, California—was the rising of new leadership from lay people and the empowerment of commoners. The traditional social boundaries were blurred, and even the role of women in leadership was enhanced. The emergence of church leaders among ordinary people contributed to the development of democracy.[72] The Pyongyang GRM was also a revival from the bottom up and from the inside out.[73]

---

[72] Oak Sung-Deuk, "The Azusa Street Revival, 1906–1909: Its Characteristics and Comparison with the 1907 Great Revival in Korea," in *Protestant Revivals in the 20th Century and Pyongyang Great Awakening Movement*, ed. Won-mo Suh (Seoul: Presbyterian College and Theological Seminary, 2005), 353–411.

[73] H. M. Bruen to A. J. Brown, March 1907.

Daoist Christians in Pyongyang became the church leaders (elders and pastors) around the GRM in 1907, and Kil Sŏnju was at the center of its leadership. Methodist missionaries led the revival movement from 1903 to 1906 in Wŏnsan, Songdo, and Seoul, yet the revival at the Central Presbyterian Church in Pyongyang in January 1907 was mainly conducted by Kil. The emergence of such a "Spurgeon of Korea" or "Whitefield of Korea" made the missionaries recognize the depth of spirituality of the Korean Christian leaders, and the ordination of the first seven Korean Presbyterian ministers in September 1907 opened a new chapter for Korean Protestantism.

One of the results of the GRM was the transformation of the missionaries' understanding of Korean spirituality and their repentance of Christian Orientalism. When the revivals swept the churches, foreigners as well as Koreans went through the fire. The revival movement was initiated by a missionary's (Robert Hardie) public repentance of his lack of spiritual power and racism in Wŏnsan in 1903, and a missionary's (Carl E. Kearns) confession of a grave sin in March 1907, at the zenith of the GRM, stunned missionaries and Koreans.[74] Missionaries witnessed "the best of the Korean character" and "the inner life" of the Koreans.[75] A missionary confessed that he was liberated from the "contemptible notion that the East is East and the West is West, and that there can be no real affinity or common meeting ground between them."[76] Missionaries began to overcome their cultural imperialism and religious paternalism through their own spiritual awakening. They not only heard of the terrible moral condition of the Koreans, but also came to see in them in the light of possibilities in the higher spiritual order.[77] They once thought that it was impossible to lead Koreans to the higher ground of

---

[74] Rev. Charles E. Kearns in Sŏnch'ŏn confessed his severe sin (the missionaries' letters did not mention its details, yet it might have been a sexual sin with a Korean woman) before Koreans in March, resigned his missionary position, and returned home. See A. M. Sharrocks to A. J. Brown, March 12, 1907, March 21, 1907; J. Samuels to A. J. Brown, April 8, 1907.

[75] John Z. Moore, "A Changed Life," *KMF* 3 (1907): 159.

[76] Moore, "The Great Revival Year," *KMF* 3 (1907): 118.

[77] William A. Noble and G. Heber Jones, *The Religious Awakening of Korea* (New York: Board of Foreign Missions of the Methodist Episcopal Church, 1908), 28.

Christian life; now they confessed that "we have *seen*, and we *know* that we can pray them down to the depths and up to the heights."[78]

Now missionaries could have more trust in Korean Christian leaders who showed sincerity in repentance and indigenous spirituality in leadership. They admired the elder Kil Sŏnju's powerful sermons and deep spiritual experiences. When he led successfully the revival meetings in Seoul in March 1907, a missionary wrote,

> His preaching is in power and in demonstration of the Spirit. In his mouth the word of God is quick and powerful, sharper than a two edged sword. His prayers are wonderful. People broke down and wept under a burden of sin. . . . Even the leaders in the church confess that they were guilty of horrible sins. . . . I am reminded of the history which records the results that followed the powerful preaching of Wesley and Whitefield.[79]

James S. Gale witnessed,

> So he [Kil] lives on and labors a glad saver of life unto life, with no sight worth speaking of, no money, no social standing, no scientific training, no acquaintance with Greek or Hebrew, no knowledge of the wider world. With nothing but his poor blind Taoist groping and his hungry heart he came to God, and at once was taken "far ben," to the inner chambers of the Divine Presence; while many of us, cultured, refined, rich, wise, entitled to all manner of opinion, sit out on the Palace steps in the chill, where we have only faint glimpses of the glory, and but indistinct murmur of the Voice Eternal.[80]

Missionaries confessed that Kil's spiritual experience was more profound than their own. As he entered "the inner chamber of the Divine Presence," his preaching had "a subtle something that has to do with the heart and that God uses to influence men." There was "no haltering or groping on his tongue, no, not one, but a surprising message of tenderness, confidence, directness, that melts your heart or makes you tremble."[81] In 1909 Gale stated that the outward signs of a lack of religion did not correspond to the inner religiosity of the Korean people.[82]

---

[78] Edith F. MacRae, "For Thine Is the Power," *KMF* 2 (1906): 74; emphasis original.

[79] "Recent Work of the Holy Spirit in Seoul," *KMF* 3 (1907): 41.

[80] Gale, "Elder Kil," 495.

[81] Gale, "The First Presbytery in Korea," *MRW* 31 (1908): 43–44.

[82] Gale, *Korea in Transition*, 67.

Missionaries came to better grasp the inner spiritual world of the Koreans. As Gale respected Kil as a spiritual leader, he asked Kil to baptize his baby son, Georgie, in 1911.[83]

Spoken language played an important role in the emergence of Korean leaders during the GRM. Only a small number of missionaries mastered it, and few could deliver an eloquent and poignant sermon at a revival meeting. Rev. Joseph L. Gerdine, a Methodist missionary in Songdo, was invited to Mokpo, for he was "thoroughly at home in the language, and spoke with directness and simplicity that won all hearts."[84] He was an exception. Most missionaries fumbled their words and so found it difficult to penetrate the souls of the people. As quoted above, the word of God was "quick and powerful, sharper than a two edged sword" in Kil Sŏnju's mouth. His tender, confident, and direct words cut deep down into hearts and laid bare secret sins and hidden cancers of the soul. Where the interpreted words of famous American revivalists or the foreign accent of missionaries could not reach, the mother tongue and local dialects of Korean leaders could evoke subtle feelings and understanding in the Koreans. Most of local revival meetings, Bible study meetings, and Sunday services in small towns and villages were conducted by Korean leaders. Their organization began at the grassroots level and moved upward. These local leaders and elders examined candidates for baptism for the itinerating missionary, who visited a local church to confirm the recommendation and judgment of Korean leaders and conducted the baptismal ceremony for the candidates once or twice a year. The local churches were self-governed.

Furthermore, missionaries found a vision for the Korean church under Japanese colonialism and praised the Korean church as "the Christian lamp that is to lighten the Eastern world."[85] A metamorphosis of the missionary image of Korea followed. Missionaries began to refute the Japanese image of Korea as a hopeless nation and Koreans as lazy people.[86] When they came home on furlough, they found numerous articles declaring that Korea was a decadent nation and that the Koreans were compelled to obey the behest of another.[87] W. A. Noble

---

[83] Gale, "The Baptism of Georgie," *WWW* (November 1911): 243–44.

[84] J. F. Preston, "A Notable Meeting," *KMF* 2 (1906): 228.

[85] John Z. Moore, "The Vision and the Task," *KMF* 2 (1906): 108.

[86] Moore, "A Changed Life," *KMF* 3 (1907): 159.

[87] A war correspondent, George Kennan, wrote numerous pro-Japan articles

compared self-supporting, self-propagating, and philanthropic activities of the Pyongyang district with those of the Wyoming Conference. He concluded, "These several facts prove that in perseverance, self-denial, intelligent activity, and Christian fervor they are second to none."[88] American mission leaders who visited Korea in 1907 praised the spirituality of the Korean church. Dr. John F. Goucher of Baltimore was "impressed with the unity of spirit of the missionaries of Korea and of the surcharged spiritual atmosphere which he met everywhere. He said he had not seen its like before."[89] Gregory Mantle said that the Korean church had "a peculiar mission to the nations to the East."[90] He thought that Korean Christians would explain Christianity to Japan and China and that they would become missionaries to these countries.

North American activist missionaries came to understand the essential characteristics of Korean spirituality—the eternal quest for contemplation or the spirit of meditation.[91] They abandoned their basic assumptions that Koreans were different from Westerners, that Koreans could not lead a higher spiritual and ethical life, and that they were incapable of running an independent nation and a democratic society.

---

from 1904 to 1907, in which he depicted Korea as a "desperate state" and criticized the Korean people as "the product of a decayed civilization." See George Kennan, "Korea: A Desperate State," *Outlook* (October 7, 1905): 307–15; Kennan, "The Korean People: The Product of a Decayed Civilization," *Outlook* (October 7, 1905): 307–15; Kennan, "What Japan Has Done in Korea," *Outlook* (November 18, 1905): 669–73. The other active endorser of Japanese colonization of Korea was Professor George T. Ladd of Yale University. After spending two months in Korea in the spring of 1907 at the special invitation of Resident-Governor Ito, Ladd published articles and a book, *In Korea with Marquis Ito* (New York: Scribner, 1908), which endorsed Japan's protectorate status over Korea, whose people he described as hopelessly corrupt and incompetent.

[88] W. A. Noble, "Korean Decadence," *KMF* 2 (1906): 176.

[89] "What Prominent Men Have Said," *KMF* 3 (1907): 158.

[90] "What Prominent Men Have Said," 159.

[91] Gale wrote in 1913, "Perhaps one of the things that the East finds most wanting in Christian propaganda is the quiet that it has associated with the eternal quest. Recently one of the leaders of the church in Korea said: 'This is not religion, all this noise and confusion of committee and assembly—apparatus and what not. It wearies the soul and dissipates the spirit of meditation. Let's get alone with God'" (Gale, "Convictions of the East," *MRW* 36 [1913]: 689–90). In fact, many Neo-Confucian scholars practiced meditation every morning, and *Simgyŏng puju* (*Xinjing fuzhu*, The Mind-Heart Classic) was important to Confucian scholars' everyday life in Korea. There was also Daoist meditation, which formed an important method of inner alchemy in the Chosŏn period.

The emergence of Korean Christian spiritual and political leaders from 1904 to 1907 proved that such Orientalist assumptions were invalid. The Presbyterian Council ordained the first seven Korean ministers in September 1907, including Kil Sŏnju. The emergence of Korean Christian leadership began to shift the center of gravity of the church from the missionaries to Korean leaders, albeit its process continued up to the March First Movement in 1919.

A visible sign of the establishment of the Korean church and indigenous leadership was the development of the church organization. The Presbyterian Churches in Korea organized its first independent presbytery in September 1907 and the General Assembly in 1912. For the General Assembly 44 missionaries, 52 Korean ministers, and 125 Korean elders were delegated from seven presbyteries. Although missionaries controlled the first assembly, numerically Koreans occupied 80 percent of the delegates, which was another step toward the self-governance. Table 9 in the appendix shows the rapid growth of the Presbyterian churches, which occupied almost two-thirds of the Protestant adherents in Korea from 1907 to 1912 and its trend to the indigenization. Ordained Korean Presbyterian leaders recorded the 446.2 percent growth—from 56 (7 ministers and 49 elders) to 290 (65 ministers and 225 elders) in five years, while the number of total adherents grew 253.3 percent (from 56,943 to 144,260).

Table 10 in the appendix reveals this exponential increase and building up of the indigenous Korean churches in the context of East Asia. The general evangelistic statistics of all the Protestant churches in Japan, Korean, and China in 1910 show that Korea had 307 missionaries and 1,981 native workers for 178,686 adherents and that the Sunday school system was well organized. The Korean churches added 20,053 new communicants in a year. The number consisted of 45.4 percent of new communicants added in the year in three countries. As a result, Korea had more baptized members than Japan. And 178,686 Christian adherents in Korea (about 1.5 percent of the population of 12 million) occupied a fourth of all Christians in the three East Asian countries. An ordained missionary in Korea was responsible for 1,842 native Christians, in Japan 318, and in China 564. This number demonstrates the possibility that missionaries in Korea were overworking, or more probably that native leadership took on a great deal of the ministerial and teaching work.

REVIVAL IN SEOUL: A LEADERSHIP SHIFT
FROM SEOUL TO PYONGYANG

The 1907 GRM fixed the center of gravity of Korean Protestantism in
Pyongyang, and the city, known as the "Jerusalem of the East" beginning in the 1920s, remained as its ecclesiastical capital until 1945. The
majority of Protestant Christians were in Hwanghae and P'yŏng'an
provinces from the beginning. Yet as a result of the GRM, a group
of church leaders from these two provinces formed the mainstream
of Korean Protestantism. Kil's spiritual leadership gave momentum to
the church. Sociologically, the emergence of church leaders in northern
Korea meant the formation of a new social leadership group in Pyongyang aside from the royal family and the yangban class in Seoul who
ruled Chosŏn society.

In 1906 a Christian named Kim Wŏngŭn wrote that Pyongyang,
which had been badly despised and discriminated against by the people
of Seoul for five hundred years under Chosŏn, received the grace of God
the most, and that the churches in Pyongyang rapidly grew and formed
"the first Christian city in East Asia" because of divine providence. He
proudly said, "The non-Christian *yangban* in Seoul cannot get a position in Pyongyang, which is given by God."[92] Such a Christian identity
and self-esteem were formed around 1906–1907 in Pyongyang, when
the churches grew speedily and a group of new leaders formed.

Kil Sŏnju's revival meeting in Seoul represented a typical empower-
ing gathering for the northerners.[93] After conducting revival meetings in
Pyongyang in January 1907, Elder Kil was invited to the united revival
meetings of the Presbyterian churches in Seoul for three weeks from
February 17 to early March. The powerful work of the Holy Spirit was
manifested from the beginning, and many church leaders and yangban
members of the churches confessed their old and hidden sins.[94] One of
the visible changes was the rearrangement of the church seats: "They
sat together with the butchers, the most despised and lowest class, in

[92] Kim Wŏngŭn, "Hanal pyŏsŭr i saram ŭi pyŏsŭl boda naŭm" [Heavenly Positions of the Church Are Better Than Human Positions of the Government], *KS*,
February 8, 1906.
[93] For the rise of the social status of northern Koreans, see Hwang Kyung
Moon, "From the Dirt to Heaven: Northern Koreans in the Chosŏn and Early
Modern Eras," *Harvard Journal of Asiatic Studies* 62, no. 1 (2002): 135–78.
[94] C. A. Clark to A. J. Brown, March 1, 1907.

brotherly love."⁹⁵ The people of Pyongyang had obeyed the rules and orders of the Seoul yangban for a long time, but now Elder Kil, a man from Pyongyang, moved the hearts of the people from Seoul and led them to repent their sins. The yangban Christians in Seoul heard the admonition of a Pyongyang man and accepted his leadership authority.

In 1907 evangelists or church members visited all the houses in Pyongyang at least once or twice. The city began to be called "a Christian city."

> Pyeng Yang is changing and becoming more and more nearly a Christian city. One scarcely ever hears a sorcerer's drum now in going through the city, and it has been a long time since I had heard one in any of the villages out near the compound. Early on the morning of the Korean New Year's Day I heard an exclamation from my Bible woman who had slept in the room next to mine and the words as she put up the window shades "It is a new world." I called out to her asking what she meant. She said "Smoke is rising from the chimneys of all the houses in the neighborhood. Several years ago the people would have passed the night in ancestral worship and later in feasting upon the food offered in sacrifice. In the deep sleep state following such dissipation there was no one to build the fire for the early morning meals. There was no early morning meal." The smoke rising from the chimneys at dawn of New Year's Day spoke eloquently to this woman of homes once heathen, now Christian, and involuntarily the word came to her lips, "Sai saysang io." ("It is a new world!")⁹⁶

Rising smoke from the chimneys of many houses in Pyongyang on New Year's Day symbolized that the city was being transformed into a Christian city, "a new world," in which many people had not offered sacrificial food to the ancestors' spirits on New Year's Eve.

Tables 11 and 12 in the appendix show that the center of the Presbyterian churches in Korea was not in Seoul and the southern provinces but in Pyongyang and the northwestern provinces. The four northern stations of the PCUSA (Chaeryŏng, P'ŏyngyang, Kanggye, and Sŏnch'ŏn; see map 2 in the appendix) had about three times more primary schools

---

⁹⁵ Margaret Best to A. J. Brown, March 12, 1907. The social status of butchers, *paekchŏng*, changed from time to time. They belonged to the seven lowest groups in Chosŏn. In the nineteenth century, many people became butchers because butchers were exempted from taxes. By the Kabo Reform of 1894, they obtained equality before the law, and male butchers could wear hats, a symbol of adult commoners. Yet people still despised them.

⁹⁶ Margaret Best to A. J. Brown, March 12, 1907.

(331 vs. 126) and four times more students (9,650 vs. 1,930) than the four southern stations in 1908. Table 12 shows that in 1910 the northwesterners (of Hwanghae and P'yŏng'an provinces) constituted 67 percent of elders, 60 percent of helpers, and 53 percent of all adherents of the Presbyterian churches. In 1908 they were 71 percent (52/73 elders), 57 percent (91/161 helpers), and 59 percent (55,877/94,981 adherents); in 1909 they were 65 percent (70/108 elders), 61 percent (104/171 helpers), and 58 percent (69,146/119,273 adherents), respectively. These statistics illustrate that northwesterners occupied about two-thirds of the Korean leadership of the Presbyterian churches from 1908 to 1910, and more than half of the total adherents. The number of elders in 1910—68 elders in P'yŏng'an province, yet only 9 in Kyŏnggi (Seoul) and Ch'ungch'ŏng provinces—indicates that the center of the church leadership was not in Seoul, but in Pyongyang and Sŏnch'ŏn in the north.

In sum, a series of spiritual seismic shifts among the Daoist Christians in Pyongyang sent shock waves rippling through Korea at the turn of the twentieth century. These shifts had a far-reaching effect on the transformation of the religious landscape of Korea as well as the formation of the mainstream evangelical spirituality of the Korean church. A group of Daoists in Pyongyang converted to Christianity around the time of the Sino-Japanese War in 1894 and 1895 and became the leaders, elders, and pastors of the Presbyterian church by 1907. They integrated traditional Daoist spirituality with Protestant spirituality during the GRM from 1903 to 1908. Their indigenous Christian forms of prayer and spirituality have been the paradigm of the evangelicalism of the Korean church ever since.

American missionaries in Pyongyang adopted the policy of indigenization as well as that of theological intolerance and iconoclasm that attacked not only the worship of ancestors, idols, and spirits, but also customs such as slavery and polygamy that they considered immoral from the ethical standard of American evangelicalism. By contrast, it was certain that the pragmatic policy of indigenization meant adapting to Korean ways without compromising the integrity of Christianity. The indigenization policy adopted a Korean style for church buildings and the Korean terms for God, trained Korean leaders for self-government of the church, and employed fulfillment theory when approaching traditional Korean religions. Missionaries accepted some congenial Daoist elements as preparations for the Christian gospel. Christianity was presented as a better Daoism, the fulfillment of the aspirations and longings of Daoism. This evolutionary idea was acceptable to the troubled Daoists in Pyongyang in the 1890s and other denizens in the city in the 1900s.

Kil Sŏnju was the pivotal figure in this evolutionary process of the fulfillment of Daoism by Christianity as well as in the GRM. His conversion was a paradigmatic born-again experience of evangelicalism for the Koreans, who confessed their sins and reconciled with God and their neighbors. His case revealed the continuity between Daoism and Christianity. On the other hand, his mode of conversion demonstrated a paradigm shift in popular Korean spirituality from its private orientation to the public sphere. Realizing the shortcomings of privatized Daoist spirituality in the face of the national crisis, he grafted the holistic Christian civilization theory of North American evangelicalism at the turn of the century onto the Korean longing for a modern, independent nation.

Kil Sŏnju and other Daoist Christians introduced dawn prayers, all-night prayers, fasting mountain prayers, and most likely audience prayers into the program of the Bible training class and regular church liturgy. Put differently, these were not imposed by missionaries; they were deeply Korean in spiritual sources and leadership. Daoist Christians played the seminal role in the integration of American, Chinese, and Korean elements in the formation of Korean Protestant prayers and revivalistic spirituality. These Christianized prayers had a stronger public dimension rooted in communities and the nation than their original, more private, Daoist counterparts. Kil's deeper spirituality, powerful preaching style, and native colloquial language, which were more effective in persuading Koreans during the revival meetings, led missionaries to respect him as a Korean Spurgeon, Wesley, or Whitefield. One of the most prominent results of the GRM was the advent of Korean leadership, which began to shift the center of gravity of the spiritual authority of the Korean church from missionaries to Korean leaders like Kil Sŏnju.

Moreover, Kil Sŏnju's revivals and the ordination of the seven Korean pastors in 1907 shifted the center of leadership and spirituality of Korean (Presbyterian) Christianity from Seoul to Pyongyang. Pyongyang remained its main center until the 1940s. At the same time, the predominance of Pyongyang leadership in Protestant Christianity represented a point of significance for Korean society, which had been dominated by the Neo-Confucian yangban class in the area surrounding Seoul. At least in the Protestant communities, from around 1907 northerners (Korean Christians as well as American missionaries in the Pyongyang area) began to form a separate identity from the Seoul–Kyŏnggi; this would have more implications in the 1920s when Christian cultural nationalism and the economic self-reliance movement, like Cho Mansik's (1883–1950) *Chosŏn mulsan changnyŏhoe* (Buy Korean Movement), were launched by the northerners.[97] They were the spiritual descendents of the Daoist Christians in Pyongyang of the 1900s.

[97] See Kenneth M. Wells, "The Rationale of Korean Economic Nationalism under Japanese Colonial Rule, 1922–1932: The Case of Cho Mansik's Products Promotion Society," *Modern Asian Studies* 19, no. 4 (1985): 823–59; Chang Kyusik, *Iljeha Han'guk Kidoggyo minjok undong* [Korean Protestant National Movement during the Japanese Colonial Rule] (Seoul: Hyean, 2001).

Conclusion

Korea has been called the surprise of modern missions. The rapid rise of a church community now approximating 300,000, the early naturalization of Christianity in the Korean environment, and its expression in distinctive and original national forms have challenged the attention of the Christian world.

—G. H. Jones, 1912[1]

World Christianity has migrated across cultural, ethnic, national, and religious boundaries. A study of the nativization of Protestant Christianity in Korea at the turn of the twentieth century must consider not only the transpacific transmission of Anglo-American Christianity, but also the trans–Yellow Sea and trans–Yalu River diffusion of Sinicized Protestantism into the Korean Peninsula. It needs to consider the fact that Chinese Protestantism had acculturated various European and North American elements for two generations before its transfer to Korea. In considering this multifaceted process of inculturation, however, the third synthesis should be scrutinized to identify the agency of Korean Christians. This is the main thesis of this book— that early Korean Protestantism was a particular Korean-created hybrid of indigenous Korean religious cultures, Chinese Protestantism, and Anglo-American Protestantism.

[1] G. H. Jones, "Presbyterian and Methodist Missions in Korea," *International Review of Mission* 1, no. 4 (1912): 412.

This book began by dealing with postcolonial master narratives on the initial encounters between Protestant missionaries and Korean religions, as well as the precolonial discourses on Korean religions produced by missionaries and Korean Christians from 1884 to 1910. Thorough analysis of these two spheres reveals the development of the biased understanding of the first generation of Korean Protestantism in post–Korean War Korea, and the forgotten layers of meaningful encounters between Anglo-American and Chinese Christianity with Korean religions and their role in the indigenization of Christianity in Korea. This hidden legacy challenges the stereotype of the first-generation North American missionaries and Korean Christians as conservative evangelicals and cultural imperialists who crusaded against traditional religions. The previous chapters have emphasized the history of the localization of Anglo-American Christianity in Korea through the medium of Chinese Protestantism. A paradigmatic caricature by Arthur Brown in 1919—describing strongly conservative missionaries and the Korean Christians who mimicked them—has been inexhaustibly quoted by the conservative camp to buttress their fundamentalist position, as well as the liberal camp in order to justify an antimissionary stance. But neither the polarization between conservatives and liberals nor the reiterated term "conservative fundamentalism" correctly represents the theology of the early Korean Protestant church. Its image as a destructive force against Korean religions is incompatible with historical evidence of their diverse efforts to establish indigenous Korean Christianity.

Transpacific Diffusion
North American Evangelicalism to Korea

In the eighteenth century, educated Christians rarely became missionaries. Until 1813 missionaries were chiefly Germans from the peasant and artisan classes, paid with English money. By the end of the nineteenth century, however, the North American Protestant churches sent their best young people to Korea. This new breed of missionaries was made of seminary, college, or Bible school graduates. Socially, they were under the influence of capitalist and moral values of the Anglo-Saxon middle classes. Culturally, they were convinced of the superiority of "Christian civilization"—including Western science and technology. While abroad, they were protected under the flags of extraterritoriality and Western imperialism. The increase in female missionaries was another feature of this new breed of missionaries. At the start of the twentieth century, the number of female missionaries, including single women, surpassed that of male missionaries. Female missionaries were armed with Victorian ideas of home and family. These well-educated young missionaries from mainstream North American denominations—Methodists and Presbyterians—dominated the Protestant missions in Korea. The American and Canadian Presbyterian and Methodist mission boards sent about 540 missionaries, comprising more than 75 percent of all Protestant missionaries to Korea by 1910. They were part of the wave of late nineteenth-century North American evangelicalism, whose diverse yet distinctive features included aggressive activism and ecumenism in the social reform and foreign mission movement, revivalism and the holiness movement, millennialism, and democratic orientation. By 1910, more than 55 percent of Protestant missionaries in Korea were the products of interdenominational student missionary movements—the American Inter-Seminary Mission Alliance and the Student Volunteer Movement for Foreign Missions. Before coming to Korea, they believed that speedy evangelization of the world would "usher" in the premillennial second coming of Christ. Theologically, they had a firm belief in the superiority of Christianity over East Asian religions.

The missionaries' sense of superiority in race, religion, and civilization, however, had to undergo a process of adjustment and adaptation in the new context of the Korea mission field. For example, Yun Ch'iho criticized the condescending paternalism and racism of a newly arrived Methodist missionary, Joseph L. Gerdine, in 1902.[2] But in time Gerdine learned the people's language and became a leader of the revival movement from 1904 to 1908 and a lawyer for Korean Christians who were imprisoned for the fabricated Conspiracy Case in 1913. Missionaries' democratic orientation promoted sensitivity to the needs of the people. Above all, turn-of-the-century evangelical mission theology on non-Christian religions was open to accepting moderate fulfillment theory, which acknowledged the existence of truth and divine revelation in non-Christian faiths. Protestant missionaries in Korea were administered and advised by theologically moderate mission board secretaries and centrist leaders of interdenominational mission organizations like F. F. Ellinwood, A. J. Brown, and A. B. Leonard. The evangelical missionaries to Korea flexibly integrated conservative and progressive approaches to missions. They combined individual salvation with

[2] Yun Ch'iho, *Yun Ch'iho Ilgi* [Diary of Yun Ch'iho], December 4, 1902.

social reform, personal holiness with social sanctification, premillennial urgency with postmillennial holism, and orthodoxy with orthopraxis. Practicality and effectiveness in evangelization were as important as principles and dogmas. The concepts of degradation and fulfillment shaped the perspectives through which they understood "heathenism" in Korean religions. One of the most influential religious comparative books was George M. Grant's *The Religions of the World* (1895), used by the Student Volunteer Movement for Foreign Missions. Some leading missionaries like James S. Gale and G. Heber Jones actively used fulfillment theory in order to make and affirm the Korean god Hanănim as the Christian God. In essence, North American missionaries in Korea belonged neither to strict conservatism nor to militant fundamentalism, but to moderate mainline evangelicalism.

TRANS–YELLOW SEA DIFFUSION
CHINESE PROTESTANTISM TO KOREA

Chapters 1, 4, and 5 emphasized the Chinese influence on the making of Korean Protestantism. The diffusion of Protestantism to Korea through China followed the route of other world religions (Buddhism and Confucianism), the traditional pattern of cultural traffic in the Sinic world of East Asia. Roman Catholicism came to Korea through the Beijing–Seoul road. The transmission of Protestantism from China to Korea was accelerated by the speed of the steamship lines between Chefoo and Chemulpo, and Shanghai and Pusan via Nagasaki. As Roman Catholicism was stigmatized as a French religion and "a religion of no father and no king" and was severely persecuted in the nineteenth century, there was little room for free negotiation with Korean religions, in spite of its acceptance of some Confucian values like loyalty, filial piety, and chastity. In contrast, Protestantism was accepted as an American religion for modernization, nation building, and awakening of the people. Under the Koreans' general anti-Japanese sentiment and Chinese political influence from 1885 to 1894, Chinese Protestantism was imported to Korea by American missionaries. Many Chinese Christian tracts and books were used in Korea, and Chinese mission methods and policies were accepted throughout the coming decades.

Chinese mission literature, policies, and methods traveled to the Korean Peninsula and enriched the North American evangelical missions in Korea. Missionary networks, mission conferences, senior missionaries' mentorship to young missionaries in Korea, and mutual visitations facilitated the migration of Chinese Christian products to Korea. The missionaries in Korea found that qualified Chinese evangelistic books and tracts were ready for immediate use in Korea. As European and American missionaries had accommodated these materials to Chinese culture and religions over the course of two generations, they proved effective for evangelism in the culturally similar Korean context. Therefore, Protestant missionaries in Korea did not feel the need to write their own evangelistic tracts. Chinese Christian tracts and their Korean versions functioned in leading Koreans to Christianity, but also guided the young missionaries to learn about East Asian culture and religions as well as the Korean language. In the process of studying and translating Chinese tracts and books, these young missionaries adopted a progressive view toward Korean religions. This view was championed by liberal evangelical missionary scholars in China such as James Legge, William A. P. Martin, Ernest Faber, and John Ross. Even a conservative missionary writer, Griffith John, employed moderate fulfillment theory in his later books for the educated Confucian Chinese classes, which were widely used by the early Korea missions. William Martin's *Tiandao suyuan* (Evidences of Christianity, 1854) was one of the influential tracts among early educated Korean Christians.

The mission policies and methods developed in China equipped the young missionaries in Korea with working tools for the field. As described in chapters 1 and 4, the Rites Controversy of Roman Catholicism, the term question of Protestantism, and the discussion and decisions of the Shanghai Missionary Conferences held in 1877, 1890, and 1907 exerted great influence in the establishment of mission policies toward Korean religions. Drawing on the theory, advocated by James Legge, John Ross, W. A. P. Martin, and other liberal Protestant missionaries in China, that the Chinese god Shangdi indicated that the original Chinese religion was monotheistic, Anglo-American missionaries in Korea invented the Christian monotheistic God Hanănim (하ᄂ님) from the highest god of Korean folk religion. After a decade of controversy from 1893 to 1903, the evangelical missionaries in Korea reached a unanimous consensus to accept Hanănim as the Christian term for God, which differentiated from the Roman Catholic term Ch'ŏnju (C. Tianzhu). Presbyterians adopted the Nevius–Ross method in establishing an indigenous, self-supporting, self-propagating, and self-governing Korean church, and Methodists espoused the Maclay–Goucher–Ohlinger holistic method of Christian civilization. However, both missions synthesized these two approaches in order to cooperate in evangelistic, educational, medical, literary, and women's works. For example, after a few years' discussion, both missions adopted the policy of total prohibition of polygamy and concubinage for the candidates of baptism. John Nevius was important in contributing not only a mission method, but also mission theory dealing with demon possession, as seen in chapter 3. John Nevius' book on the cases of demon possession and Christian exorcism in Shandong served as a catalyst for the synthesis of North American missionaries' Biblicism with the Korean shamanistic healing ceremony. North American missionaries and Korean Bible women practiced a Protestant-style exorcism—protracted communal prayers and hymn singing by the church members, followed by their leaders' casting out of "evil spirits" in the name of Jesus from the "demon-possessed" victims, just as Nevius and other missionaries did in Shandong, China.

One of the emphases of chapter 5 was the influence of Chinese Scriptures, tracts, and hymnals on their Korean translations. Most Christian terminology created in China was transferred to Korea. Even though the Ross Version (1882–1887) adopted vernacular Korean as the written language of the Christian Scriptures for ordinary people and women, it adopted many terms from the Chinese Delegates' Version (DV) of the New Testament (1854). The Seoul versions used more Chinese terms from the DV. The Chinese–Korean mixed editions for the educated literary people used the DV text, which was popular for its classical idiomatic expressions. Other important Chinese Christian literary sources that influenced the formation of Korean Protestantism, though not discussed in this book, were Chinese commentaries on the Bible, especially *The Centenary Commentary*, Chinese sermon books, and Chinese forms of worship and liturgy. The linguistic-theological continuity between Chinese and Korean Protestant terminology was totally different from the linguistic-theoretical continuity between Japanese and Korean social and natural sciences (especially medical science) and secular literature in early modern Korea. This difference partly contributed to the formation of Korean Christian nationalism against Japanese colonialism.

THE MAKING OF KOREAN PROTESTANTISM

Another significant integration in Korean Protestantism was the fusion of North American evangelicalism and Chinese Protestantism with congenial elements of Korean religions. This dynamic synthesis created a unique Korean Protestant Christianity in a transitory period from 1876 to 1915 when Korea experienced an unprecedented national crisis. In this apocalyptic furnace, Korean spiritual ores were smelted, purified, softened, and tempered to be amalgamated with Anglo-American-Sino Christianity. All previous chapters investigated the cases of this integration, yet chapters 1, 2, 3, and 6 discussed uniquely Korean elements in the formation of Korean Protestantism.

In the genealogy of the terms for God in Korea, investigated in chapter 1, the term Hanănim, adopted in Seoul in 1905, differed from that of John Ross' Korean Scriptures published in Shenyang in the 1880s. The latter, adopted from Korean merchants in Manchuria, was a Korean vernacular equivalent of the Chinese Christian term Shangdi, which was based on the idea of the original Confucian and Manchurian Daoist monotheistic god Shangdi. In contrast, the authorization of Hanănim in Seoul was grounded in the missionaries' study of the Korean founding myth of Tan'gun, whose theism was tinted with Korean shamanism and Daoism (Sŏndo). The missionaries understood Tan'gun as the third person of the Korean trinity and the first shaman–king who worshipped the original monotheistic god Hanănim, who was bestowed by divine revelation, the vestige of which the Korean people still retained. Behind this innovative liberal interpretation, there was the Korean Christians' insistence on the use of Hanănim as the Christian God. The unique elements of the Korean Protestant neologism Hanănim were (1) its primitive monotheism (like Chinese Shangdi of the Confucian classics), (2) its contemporary monotheistic vestige (unlike Chinese Shangdi), and (3) its newly added etymological meaning of Trinitarian oneness to its original heavenliness, based on the newly interpreted theism of the Korean founding myth of Tan'gun. This modern theological novelty, combined with ancient mythology, indigenous spirituality, and the contemporary popular usage of the term, appealed not only to the general Korean audience but also to some nationalists, who adopted the invented monotheistic term Hanănim of the Tan'gun myth as their own god of newly organized nationalistic religions. They borrowed Hanănim from Protestantism, not vice versa.

On the other hand, the coexistence of the Chinese term Shangdi in Chinese literature for the educated classes in Korea and Hanănim in Korean vernacular literature for the ordinary people revealed the continued Chinese cultural and religious influence on Korean Protestantism, just as in the case of Korean Roman Catholicism's acceptance of the

Chinese term Tianzhu. However, the vernacular term Hanănim enabled Korean evangelical Protestantism to have its own identity to differentiate itself not only from Roman Catholicism and Anglicanism (which used Tianzhu/Ch'ŏnju), but also from Chinese Protestantism (which used Shangdi or Shen) and Japanese Protestantism (which used Shen/Kami). In addition, the Protestant theistic paradigm of understanding East Asian religions was applied to Korea: the ancient primitive monotheism was deteriorating under the influence of Buddhism and Daoism, and Christianity came to restore the original monotheism and fulfill its deficiencies. Protestantism proclaimed that it came to Korea to heal and fulfill defects of Korean religions, and the metamorphosis of Hanănim from the highest god of shamanism into the Christian monotheistic God manifested this claim.

In the unparalleled national crisis from 1894 to 1910, some Korean Christians interpreted the Korean popular millennial geomantic prophecy of the *Chŏnggam-nok* by referencing biblical passages and the cross of Jesus, and used glyphomancy to interpret biblical passages. A Christian code-breaking rhetoric for the unsolved passages of indigenous apocalyptic literature appealed to some groups who anticipated dynastic change after great tribulations. The local people did not always join churches for social, economic, and political reasons. Sometimes they needed a more compelling religious factor or a persuasive rhetoric, in which they could find significant clues for decoding the mysterious passages of prophecy regarding the coming of the messianic kingdom. The traditional method of glyphomancy was employed in blending Christian biblical passages and the symbol of the cross with Korean millennialism to envision the transformation of the old world. This intellectually implausible yet powerfully appealing interpretation was a strong hidden motive for conversion for the people in the northern sections of Kyŏnggi, Hwanghae, and Kangwŏn provinces where the four apocalyptic horses—war, famine, plague, and death—passed through constantly from 1894 to 1910. They believed that Jesus as the Savior of the world came to Korea as the fulfillment of the traditional Korean prophecy of the *Chŏnggam-nok*.

As seen in chapter 3, Korean Protestant pneumatology and demonology integrated the exorcist healing stories of Jesus in the New Testament with the spiritual healing ceremony of Korean shamanism. Shamanism, the substratum of all Korean religious experience, has survived in syncretistic relationships with other religions. This pattern continued with

Protestantism in its faith healing and prosperity-oriented spirituality. On the other hand, North American missionaries accepted the premodern Korean shamanic worldview of spiritism against church laws and rational intellectualism. A combination of evangelical Biblicism, missionary Orientalism, and field experience led many evangelistic missionaries to abandon modern rationalism and practice Christian exorcist ceremonies or allow Bible women to perform them. This compromise was challenged on one hand in the 1910s and 1920s by medical missionaries who paid more attention to the psychological aspects of mentally ill patients, and on the other by the increase of the number of ordained Korean male ministers (which decreased the role of Bible women) and the faith-healing revival movement of Rev. Kim Iktu. Socialists and younger generations criticized him as an unscientific and deceiving mudang, and the Japanese government fined him for his illegal and unlicensed practice of healing.

In order to make the messages appealing to the Korean people, the first-generation North American missionaries and Korean leaders presented Christianity not only as a religion of prophetism, which would transform Korean society and religions, but also as a religion for the fulfillment of the Korean people's aspirations. Their primary method was the translation of Chinese Christian literature. However, the Korean churches digested Chinese texts and produced Korean-style spiritual food for the Koreans, which began to be presented in the first Korean Protestant newspapers from 1897. When a group of educated Korean Christian writers was formed in Seoul, they portrayed Christianity as a rejuvenating spring for the old trees of Korean religions. Christianity, they wrote, aimed to revitalize not only the leaves and branches of the tress—instrumental and technological aspects of civilization—but also the root—spiritual and moral grounding. Employing both Western rationalism and evangelical iconoclasm, Christianity pruned the withered branches of spirit worship, ancestor worship, polygamy, and so on. Beneath this external purification, however, there was deep fertilization of the roots—a rediscovery of the original monotheistic idea of Hanǎnim, a reinterpretation of millennial prophecy, an adoption of the Christian form of spiritual healing, an invention of a Christian memorial service, and a Christianization of the indigenous prayers for spiritual communication and awakening. As Jones wrote, they constituted "great gateways through which Christianity may drive its chariot of truth to the very center of life in the great World Field. These things have prepared the people of Korea to recognize the messengers who come to them in that golden chariot."[3] Of course, some Koreans were attracted to values of Western civilization that Christianity provided or to the political and economic power that the missionaries possessed. However, on a deeper level, "the warm reception accorded to the great Western religion grew out of the numerous points of contact between the Korean faith and that of most missionaries."[4] Not just material resources, nor might, but spiritual fulfillment was the fundamental reason for the growth of Korean Protestantism at the turn of the twentieth century. Through this process of localization, Western Christianity was grafted onto Korean religions, and indigenous Korean Christianity blossomed.

One of the flowers of the Koreanized Protestantism was the dawn prayer meeting, invented as a church program by Daoist Christians in Pyongyang during the revival movement in 1900s, as seen in the last chapter. The ship of Korean Christianity had sailed to sea. Strong political and spiritual winds were blowing, and the waves were high. The mainsail of the ship was prayer meetings, and at the helm were the Bible study classes. Korean Christians offered dawn prayers, audible prayers, fasting mountain prayers, Wednesday evening prayers, and all-night prayers for the future of the church and the nation, and heard the voice of the heavens through these prayers.

As W. A. P. Martin's image described, Protestant missionaries gathered isolated pearls of truth from Korean religions and threaded them into a beautiful necklace with the golden string of the monotheistic concept of Hanǎnim.[5] Korean Christians and missionaries adopted many fragments of Korean religions—such as commitment to morality, filial piety, sanctification, longing for salvation and eternal life, messianic hope, and sincere mindfulness in rituals—to create a coherent and adaptable form of indigenous Christianity. To use John Ross' metaphor, the moribund Korean religious heritage was revitalized as well as transformed by Christianity.[6] Another image used was that of a pair of oxen

[3] G. H. Jones, *The Rise of the Church in Korea* (Typescript, UTS, G. H. Jones Papers, 1915), chap. 5.

[4] Louis O. Hartman, *Popular Aspects of Oriental Religions* (New York: Abingdon, 1917), 20.

[5] W. A. P. Martin, *Tiandao suyuan* [Evidences of Christianity] (Ningbo: Huahua shuju, 1854), 46b–47a; see John Ross, *Mission Methods in Manchuria* (New York: Revell 1903), 157.

[6] Ross, *Mission Methods*, 250–51.

plowing the soil together—Christianity became a partner with traditional religions in cultivating Korean spirituality. The grafting, fertilization, integration, and revitalization of Korean religions by Christianity were all diverse expressions of the idea of fulfillment.

Protestant Christianity fulfilled the Trinitarian spirituality of the Korean founding myth of Tan'gun by inventing Hanănim, the Korean name for God; it fulfilled the prophecy of the Chŏnggam-nok by building the churches that became the places of millennial salvation for refugees and the places of the cross, Christus Victor; Protestant literature, especially vernacular hangŭl books and newspapers, fulfilled the intellectual needs of the ordinary Koreans; and various Protestant rituals were invented for ancestors, families, demon-possessed people, and spiritually hungry people.

North American missionaries displayed both openness toward Korean religions and culture and a remarkable ability to Christianize certain elements, while rejecting others. Their evangelical mission theology maintained the finality of Christ in relation to Korean religions. Yet, they searched for points of contact with Korean religions and welcomed the preparation for the gospel in them. The integration of Christian transcendence and inculturation, or the combination of intolerance and adaptability, was one of the major factors for the growth of evangelical Christianity in Korea from 1884 to 1915. In other words, the American missionaries' cross-cultural sensitivity and moderate fulfillment theory helped Korean Christians to stimulate the rapid growth of indigenous Korean Christianity. Therefore North American missionaries' evangelism in Korea moved beyond the level of mere proselytism, proclamation, and cultural imperialism. They were pioneers of a distinctive indigenous Korean Christianity in the specific and particular Korean religious context. They crossed the boundary from one ethnic culture to another, that is, living in openness and harmony in a foreign land. It was a painful process of "conversion," requiring a reevaluation and a relativization of some of their conceptions of what was essential and what was redundant in the Christian message and Christian life. They mastered the language of the Korean people, came to understand their spiritual mind-set, comprehended some of the Confucian classics, honored the ancient history of Korea, and respected its religious heritage. Their contextualized message, evangelical mission policy and method, and fulfillment theory enabled them to find substantial points of contact between Christianity and Korean religious traditions, as well as to identify points of conflict between them. Amalgamating these congenial elements of Korean religions to Anglo-American-Sino Christianity, the missionaries, with the help of Korean Christians, created indigenous Korean Christianity. That Christianity came to Korea not to destroy traditional religions but to fulfill and actualize them was one of the most appealing messages to the Koreans and set the foundation for many accepting Christianity.

Historiography of early encounters between Protestantism and Korean religious culture should be rewritten from the perspective of cultural exchanges beyond cultural imperialism. From the perspective of American religious history, early Korean Christianity was an extension of mainstream American Protestantism (evangelicalism) as well as a transplantation of American capitalism and American middle-class culture. From the perspective of geopolitics, it may be seen as another case of collaboration of Western imperialism and its moral equivalent Western Christianity in the conquest of East Asia at the turn of the century. If we see the history of early Korean Christianity as the combined perspectives of the history of world Christianity and Korean religious history, however, this was the process of the formation of "Korean" Christianity. In the reciprocal process of confluence between Korean religions and Christianity, the latter moved in the direction of indigenization or traditionalization, whereas the former, stimulated by Christianity, moved in the direction of modernization. The heritage of the first generation of the Korean Protestant churches' efforts of indigenization of Christianity and their moderate evangelical mission theory and method provide the contemporary Korean church with a sense of historical continuity and identity and a historical framework from which to engage in active dialogue with non-Christian religions. The creative combination of the principle of Christian universality (vertical transcendence) and that of inculturation (horizontal adaptation) will help Korean Christianity to keep its identity and relevance in the coming decades, in an era of new challenges.

Appendix
Tables, Diagrams, Maps

TABLE 1

THE NAMES FOR GOD USED IN THE KOREAN SCRIPTURES, 1882–1905

Names	'82	'83	'84	'85	'86	'87	'88	'89	'90	'91	'92	'93
Hanŭnim	x											
Hananim		x	x	x	x	x	x	x	x	x	x	x
Hanănim								x	x	x	x	x
Shin		x	x									
Ch'amshin									.	x		
Syangdye				x	x				x			
T'yŏnjyu												x

Names	'94	'95	'96	'97	'98	'99	'00	'01	'02	'03	'04	'05
Hanŭnim												
Hananim												
Hanănim	x	x	x	x	x	x	x	x	x	x	x	x
Shin												
Ch'amshin												
Syangdye												
T'yŏnjyu	x	x	x	x	x	x	x	x	x	x	x	

TABLE 2

EXAMPLES OF THE KOREAN TERMS ADOPTED BY THE ROSS VERSION, 1887

King James Version	Delegates' Version (1852)	Ross Version (1887)	Old Version (Seoul, 1904)
God	上帝	하나님	하ᄂᆞ님
The begotten son	獨生子	외아달	독싱ᄌᆞ [獨生子]
Passover	踰越節	넘넌절	유월절 [踰越節]
The righteous	義人	올운쟈	의인 [義人]
Prophecy	預言	밀이말훔	예언 [預言]
Prayer	祈禱	빌다	기도 [祈禱]

TABLE 3

CHINESE TERMS ADOPTED BY KOREAN VERSIONS FROM THE
DELEGATES' VERSION, 1887 AND 1904

Verse	King James Version	Delegates' Version (1852)	Ross Version (1887)	Old Version (1904)
1	The Word	道	도 [道]	말슴
7	Witness	證	간증 [干證]	증거 [證據]
9	The true Light	眞光	진광 [眞光]	빗
14	Glory	榮	영화 [榮華]	영광 [榮光]
14	Truth	眞理	진니 [眞理]	리치 [理致]
17	The law	律法	늘법 [律法]	률법 [律法]
18	Hath declared	彰明	표명 [表明]	붉히 나타내다
19	Priests	祭司	제사 [祭司]	졔ᄉᆞ쟝 [祭司長]
21	Prophet	先知	션지 [先知]	션지자 [先知者]
32	The Holy Spirit	聖神	성령 [聖靈]	성신 [聖神]
47	Guile	詭譎	궤휼 [詭譎]	간샤 [奸邪]
51	The angels	使者	사쟈 [使者]	ᄉᆞ쟈 [使者]
51	The Son of man	人子	인ᄌᆞ [人子]	인ᄌᆞ [人子]

TABLE 4
THE MOST POPULAR CHINESE TRACTS AND BOOKS IN 1893

Title	Number of Votes
天道溯原 Martin's *Christian Evidences*	32
張袁兩友 W. Milne's *Two Friends*	31
天路歷程 Burns' *Pilgrim's Progress*	24
德惠入門 John's *Gate of Virtue and Knowledge*	18
引家歸道 John's *Leading the Family in the Right Way*	16
正道啓蒙 Burns' *Peep of Day*	12
眞道衡平 Genähr's *Chinese and Christian Doctrines Compared*	11
自西徂東 Faber's *Chinese and Christian Civilization*	11
格物探原 Williamson's *Natural Theology*	8
喩道傳 Martin's *Religious Allegories*	6

TABLE 5

CHINESE BOOKS AND TRACTS USED IN KOREA
WITHOUT TRANSLATION, 1880–1900

I. Christian teaching (theology, natural theology, apologetics, and comparative religions)	Burns, William. 正道啓蒙 *Peep of Day*. Beijing, 1864. Corbett, Hunter. 聖會史記 *Church History*. N.p., n.d. Edkins, Joseph. 釋教正謬 *Correction of Buddhist Errors*. Shanghai, 1857. James, F. H. 兩教合辨 *A Comparison of the Two Religions: Protestantism and Romism*. N.p., n.d. John, Griffith. 天路指明 *Clear Indication of the Heavenly Way*. Hankou: Shengjiao shuju, 1862. ———. 訓子問答 *Child's Catechism*. Shanghai, 1864. Martin, William A. P. 天道溯原 *Evidences of Christianity*. Ningbo, 1854. ———. 喻道傳 *Religious Allegories*. Ningbo, 1858. ———. 救世要論 *Important Discourse on Salvation*. Ningbo, 1860. ———. 格物入門 *Elements of Natural Philosophy and Chemistry*. Beijing, 1868. McCartee, D. Bethune. 耶穌教要訣 *Fundamental Truth of Christianity*. Ningbo, 1849. ———. 救靈魂說 *Discourse on the Salvation of the Soul*. Ningbo, 1852. ———. 西士來意略論 *Western Scholars' Reasons for Coming to China*. Zhengzhou, 1863. Medhurst, William. 清明掃墓之論 *On the Custom of Repairing the Graves*. Batavia, 1826. Muirhead, William. 眞教權衡 *Balance of the True Religion*. Shanghai, 1864. ———. 眞教論衡 *Balance of the True Religion*. Shanghai, 1868. Nevius, John L. 天路指南 *Guide to Heaven*. Ningbo, 1857. ———. 祀先辨謬 *Errors of Ancestral Worship*. Ningbo, 1859. ———. 宣道指歸 *Manual for Evangelists*. Shanghai, 1862. ———. 神道總論 *Compendium of Theology*. Shanghai, 1864. ———. 天牖二光 *The Two Lights*. Shanghai, 1864. ———. 兩教辨正 *The Two Religions Set Right: Romism and Protestantism*. Shanghai, 1890. Nevius, Helen S. 聖徒堅忍 *Christian Perseverance*. Ningbo, ca 1880. Williamson, Alexander. 格物探原 *Natural Theology*. Shanghai, 1876. ———. 基督實錄 *Life of Christ Jesus the Light and Life of the World*. Shanghai, 1879.
II. Civilization (history, international law, politics, and science)	Faber, Ernst. 自西徂東 *Civilization: West and East*. Hong Kong, 1884, 1902. Martin, William A. P. 萬國公法 *International Law* [H. Wheaton's]. Beijing, 1864. ———. 公法會通 *International Law* [J. C. Bluntschli's]. Beijing, 1880. Muirhead, William. 大英國志 *History of England*. Shanghai, 1856. Sheffield, Devello Z. 萬國通鑑 *Universal History*. Shanghai, 1892. Sites, Nathan. 天文學 *Elementary Principles of Astronomy*. Shanghai, ca. 1880. Way, Richard Q. 地球說略 *Compendium of Geography*. Ningbo, 1856.

TABLE 5 (CONT.)

III. Presbyterianism	Synodical Committee. 教會勸懲條例 *Book of Discipline*. Shanghai, ca. 1877. ————. 信道揭要 *Confession of Faith*. Shanghai, ca. 1877. ————. 教會政治 *Form of Church Government*. Shanghai, ca. 1877. ————. 禮拜模範 *Form of Worship*. Shanghai, ca. 1877. ————. 耶穌教要理大問答 *Larger Catechism*. Shanghai, ca. 1877. ————. 婚喪公禮 *Marriage and Burial Forms*. Shanghai, ca. 1877. ————. 耶穌教要理問答 *Shorter Catechism*. Shanghai, ca. 1877.
IV. Methodism	Lambuth, James W. 天道總論 *Compendium of Theology* [Binney's]. Shanghai, 1879. ————. 神之原道 *Elements of Divinity* [T. N. Ralston's]. Shanghai, 1879. Maclay, Robert S. 受洗禮之約 *The Baptismal Covenant*. Fuzhou, 1857. ————. 美以美教會禮文 *Ritual of the Methodist Episcopal Church*. Fuzhou, 1865.
Total	43

TABLE 6
CHINESE TRACTS TRANSLATED AND PUBLISHED IN KOREAN, 1881–1896

Year	Author	Title in Chinese	Title in Korean	Title in English	Translator
1881	J. Ross	[聖經問答]	예슈셩교문답	Bible Catechism	Yi Ŭngch'an, Ross
	J. MacIntyre	[新約要領]	예슈셩교요령	Summary of the New Testament	Yi Ŭngch'an, MacIntyre
1885	J. Legge, R. S. Maclay	浪子悔改	랑즈회기	Prodigal Son	Yi Sujŏng
	R. S. Maclay	美以美敎會問答	미이미교회문답	Methodist Catechism	Yi Sujŏng
1889	R. S. Maclay	美以美敎會問答	미이미교회문답	Methodist Catechism	F. Ohlinger
	G. John	聖敎撮要	셩교촬요	Salient Teachings of the Holy Doctrine	H. G. Appenzeller
	G. John	濟世論	제셰론	Salvation of the World	H. G. Underwood
	G. John	贖罪之道	속죄지도	Redemption	H. G. Underwood
1890	G. John	聖敎撮理	셩교촬리	Salient Doctrine of Christianity	H. G. Underwood
	F. Ohlinger	癩病論	라병론	Sin Like Leprosy	F. Ohlinger
	R. S. Maclay	信德統論	신덕통론	General Discourse on Faith	F. Ohlinger
	R. S. Maclay	美以美敎會綱禮	미이미교회강례	Article of Religion	W. B. Scranton
1891	Mrs. J. L. Holmes	訓兒眞言	훈ᄋ진언	Peep of Day	Mrs. M. F. Scranton
	A. Judson	天路指歸	텬로지귀	Guide to Heaven	W. M. Baird

TABLE 6 (CONT.)

Year	Author				
	G. John	勸衆悔改	권즁회기	Exhortation to Repentance	H. G. Underwood
	G. John	上帝眞理	샹뎨진리	True Doctrine of God	H. G. Underwood
1892	W. H. Medhurst	三字經	삼즛경	Three Character Classic	F. Ohlinger/S. A. Moffett
	W. Milne	張遠兩友相論	쟝원량우샹론	Two Friends	S. A. Moffett
	Mrs. S. M. Sites	聖經圖說	셩경도셜	Bible Picture Book	Miss L. C. Rothweiler
	W. A. P. Martin	救世要言	구셰요언	Essentials of the World's Salvation	W. B. McGill
1893	G. John	德惠入門	덕혜입문	Gate of Virtue and Wisdom	H. G. Underwood
	G. John	重生之道	즁싱지도	Regeneration	H. G. Underwood
	G. John	信者所得之眞福	신즛소득지진복	True Way of Seeking Happiness	H. G. Underwood
	W. C. Milne	眞道入門問答	진도입문문답	Entrance to Truth Doctrine	F. Ohlinger
	F. Ohlinger	依經問答	의경문답	Nast's Larger Catechism	F. Ohlinger
	?	四福音合書	스복음합셔	Harmony of the Gospels	W. B. Scranton
	H. Nevius	耶穌教問答	예슈교문답	Christian Catechism	H. G. Underwood
1894	G. John	引家歸道	인가귀도	Leading the Family in the Right Way	F. Ohlinger
	G. John	福音大旨	복음대지	Great Themes of the Gospels	H. G. Underwood
	Richard Q. Way	地球略論	지구략론	Geography	Mrs. M. F. Scranton
	E. Faber	舊約工夫	구약공부	Study of the Old Testament	G. H. Jones

TABLE 6 (CONT.)
CHINESE TRACTS TRANSLATED AND PUBLISHED IN KOREAN, 1881–1896

Year	Author	Title in Chinese	Title in Korean	Title in English	Translator
	W. A. P. Martin	三要錄	삼요록	Three Principle	H. G. Underwood
	J. K. MacKenzie	救世眞証	구셰진쥬	True Plan of Salvation	S. A. Moffett
	F. H. James	天主耶穌兩教不同問答	텬쥬예수량교부동문답	Romism and Protestantism	S. F. Moore
1895	W. Burns	天路歷程	텬로력뎡	Pilgrim's Progress	J. S. Gale
	D. B. McCartee	眞理易知	진리이지	Easy Introduction to Christian Doctrine	H. G. Underwood
	G. John	大主之命	대쥬지명	Order of the Lord	H. G. Underwood
	?	靈魂問答	령혼문답	Catechism on the Soul	H. G. Underwood
	G. John	救世眞主	구셰진쥬	True Savior of the World	W. M. Baird
	?	救世論	구셰론	Discourse on Salvation	S. A. Moffett
	C. W. Foster	福音要史	복음요스	Story of the Gospel	Mr. and Mrs. D. L. Gifford
	F. Genähr	廟祝問答	묘축문답	Dialogues with a Temple Keeper	H. G. Appenzeller
	R. S. Maclay	洗禮問答	셰례문답	Baptismal Catechism	W. B. Scranton
	?	主日禮拜經	쥬일례비경	Wesleyan Sunday Worship	W. B. Scranton
	W. Muirhead	來求耶穌	릭귀예슈	Come to Jesus	W. L. Swallen

TABLE 6 (CONT.)

Year					
	F. Ohlinger	丁大理傳	틴들더긔	Life of William Tyndale	F. Ohlinger
	J. L. Nevius	爲原入教人規條	위원입교인규됴	Manual for Catechism	S. A. Moffett
1896	?	撤世論	경셰론	Warning to the World	W. L. Swallen
	?	教會史記	교회ᄉ기	Church History	W. L. Swallen
	?	新約問答	신약문답	The New Testament Catechism	W. B. Scranton
	?	舊約問答	구약문답	The Old Testament Catechism	W. B. Scranton
	?	復活主日禮拜	부활쥬일례비	Easter Sunday Worship	H. G. Underwood
	?	敎世敎問答	구세교문답	Christian Catechism	H. G. Underwood
Total	53				

TABLE 7
The TITLE AND THE FIRST STANZA OF "THE ROCK OF AGES"

Title	First Stanza	
Presbyterian Hymnals (Philadelphia: Presbyterian Board of Publication, 1874), ed. Joseph T. Duryea	304 The Rock of Ages Rock of ages, cleft for me! Let the water and the blood Be of sin the double cure;	Let me hide myself in thee; From thy riven side which flowed, Cleanse me from the guilt and power.
Zanshen shengshi 讚神聖詩 (Shanghai: Presbyterian Press, 1878), ed. John L. Nevius and Calvin W. Mateer	28 基督爲盤石 萬古盤石爲我開　讓我藏身在余懷 求用被刺筋肋旁　流的寶血效無彊 消沒罪惡免公刑　洗掉骯髒變爲清	
Ch'anyangga 찬양가 (Yokohama: Seishi Bunsha, 1894), ed. H. G. Underwood	36 基督爲盤石 날위ᄒᆞ야열닌반석　날굼초아줍쇼셔 륵방에셔샹ᄒᆞ야　물과피가나온것 죄의효험겸되게　악과능업시ᄒᆞ게	
Ch'ansyongga 찬숑가 (Yokohama: Fukuin, 1908)	73 만셰반셕 만셰반셕열니니　내가드러감ᄂᆡ다 창에허리샹ᄒᆞ야　물과피를흘닌것 내게효험되여셔　졍결ᄒᆞ게흡쇼셔	

TABLE 8
VARIOUS EDITIONS OF "JESUS LOVES ME, THIS I KNOW"

Edition	Text
The Golden Shower (New York: Ivison, Phinney, 1862), ed. W. B. Bradbury	68 Jesus Loves Me Jesus loves me! This I know, For the Bible tells me so. Little ones to Him belong; They are weak, but He is strong. Yes, Jesus loves me! Yes, Jesus loves me! Yes, Jesus loves me! The Bible tells me so.
Zanshen shengshi (Shanghai: Presbyterian Press, 1878), ed. Nevius and Mateer	34 耶穌愛我 耶穌愛我萬不錯 因有聖書告訴我 小人朋友他肯當 我雖軟弱他強壯 耶穌救主愛我 耶穌救主愛我 耶穌救主愛我 有聖書告訴我
Ch'ansyongga (Yokohama: Fukuin, 1908)	190 날ᄉ랑ᄒ심 예수ᄉ랑ᄒ심은 거륵ᄒ신말일네 우리들은약ᄒ나 예수권셰만토다 날ᄉ랑ᄒ심 날ᄉ랑ᄒ심 날ᄉ랑ᄒ심 셩경에쓰셧네

TABLE 9

GROWTH OF PRESBYTERIAN CHURCHES IN KOREA, 1907–1912

Year	Ministers/Elders	Baptized Members	Catechumens	Total Adherents	Churches/Chapels
1907	7/49	18,081	19,789	56,943	691/1,022
1908	7/63	24,239	24,122	72,968	897/1,130
1909	16/108	30,337	30,065	94,578	1,193/1,580
1910	40/133	39,394	33,790	119,273	1,157/1,632
1911	54/159	46,934	35,508	140,470	1,448/1,635
1912	65/225	53,008	26,400	144,260	1,438/2,054

Source: Charles A. Clark, The Digest of the Korea Mission (Seoul: Religious Book and Tract Society, 1918), 183–99.

TABLE 10
GENERAL STATISTICS OF THE CHRISTIAN MISSIONS AND CHURCHES
IN EAST ASIA, 1910

	Japan	Korea	China	Total
Ordained missionaries	305	97 (7.3)	920	1,322
Physician missionaries (male + female)	10 + 1	24 + 12 (8.4) + (9.4)	251 + 114	285 + 127
Unmarried female missionaries	353	71 (4.7)	1,093	1,517
Total foreign missionaries	1,029 (18.6)	307 (5.5)	4,197 (75.9)	5,533
Ordained natives	474	34 (3.3)	513	1,021
Unordained native workers	1,664	1,887 (12.5)	11,595	15,146
Total native workers	2,138	1,981 (12.2)	12,108	16,227
Church organizations	612	462 (14.9)	2,027	3,101
Communicants added last year	8,639	20,053 (45.4)	15,521	44,213
Total communicants	67,024	57,414 (19.0)	177,774	302,212
Baptized members	82,196	89,609 (23.2)	214,642	386,447
Total adherents all ages	97,117 (13.0)	178,686 (24.0)	470,184 (63.0)	745,987
Sunday schools	1,389	1,291 (28.4)	1,859	4,539
Total Sunday school membership	87,283	110,865 (42.1)	65,482	263,640
Total native contribution ($)	171,694	109,460 (22.1)	213,259	494,413

Source: SVM, World Atlas of Christian Missions (New York: SVM, 1911), 83.
(%): percentage of three nations.

TABLE 11
EDUCATIONAL STATISTICS OF THE KOREA MISSION, PCUSA, 1907–1908

Station	Boarding and High Schools	Students (Boys/Girls)	Primary Schools	Students (Boys/Girls)
Chaeryŏng	0	0/0	83	1,700/323
Pyongyang	3	295/100	110	3,021/ 790
Kanggye	0	0/0	15	191/71
Sŏnch'ŏn	0	0/0	133	2,891/543
Seoul	4	140/65	33	587/265
Ch'ŏngju	0	0/0	6	60/0
Taegu	1	52/0	67	698/144
Pusan	0	16/0	10	167/89
Total for 1908	8	503/165	457	9,315/2,165
Total for 1907	13	603/146	344	5,649/1,093

Source: James S. Gale, Korea in Transition (New York: Young People's Missionary Movement of the United States and Canada, 1909), appendix.

TABLE 12

STATISTICS OF THE PRESBYTERIAN CHURCHES IN KOREA, 1910

Presbytery	Ministers	Elders	Helpers	Baptized Members	Adherents	Churches
South P'yŏng'an	12	55	72	10,842	33,144	241
North P'yŏng'an	10	13	33	7,901	26,968	147
Hwanghae	6	21	30	4,740	13,892	272
Hamgyŏng	8	7	18	1,691	9,889	285
Kyŏnggi-Ch'ungch'ŏng	9	9	12	2,975	8,189	170
Chŏlla	15	16	25	5,509	20,989	201
Kyŏngsang	15	12	34	5,736	27,399	315
Total	75	133	224	39,394	140,472	1,613

Source: The Fourth Minutes of the Presbytery of the Korean Church (Seoul: N.p., 1910), 31.

DIAGRAM 1
RELIGIOUS AND POLITICAL FACTORS IN THE ICONOGRAPHY
OF THE CROSS, 1801–1910

1894–1895
Religious Glyphomancy
(Jesus' fulfillment of the prophecy of the *Chŏnggam-nok* and the Church
as salvation shelter for refugees and sinners)

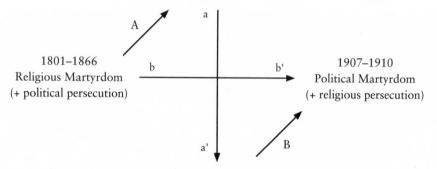

1801–1866
Religious Martyrdom
(+ political persecution)

1907–1910
Political Martyrdom
(+ religious persecution)

Political Glyphomancy
1901–1905
(The missionaries as the "great Westerners" with extraterritorial rights,
and the Church as a semipolitical society for the "rice Christians")

DIAGRAM 2
Translation of Christian Texts into Korean,
1876–1915

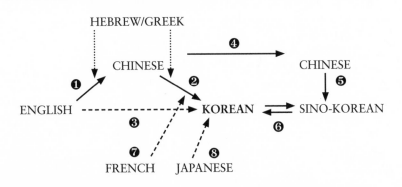

❶ + ❷   Major Process
❸   Major Process
❹   Chinese Christian literature used without translation for the
                 educated people
❺ ❻   Referential factor (mixed script editions for the educated people)
❼   Differential factor (Roman Catholic terms)
❽   Increasing factor (from 1910)

MAP 1
EARLY PROTESTANT MISSIONARY ROUTES TO KOREA, 1879–1887

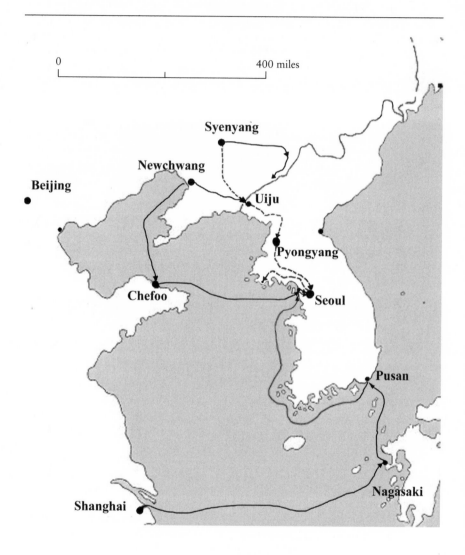

MAP 2
TERRITORIAL COMITY AMONG THE PRESBYTERIAN AND METHODIST MISSIONS IN KOREA, 1912

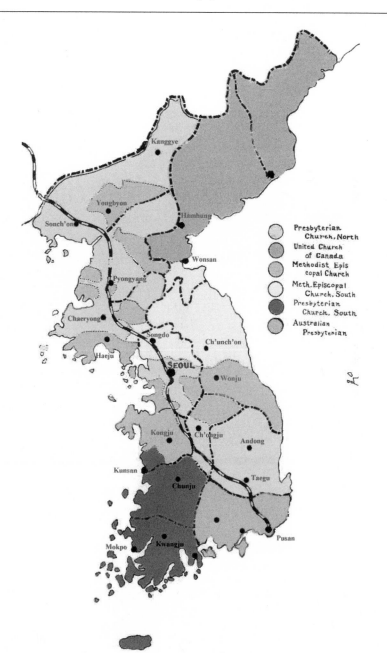

Glossary

A

Aegug-ga	愛國歌	애국가
An Ch'angho	安昌浩	안창호
An Chunggŭn	安重根	안중근
ansigil	安息日	안식일
asap	亞翣	아삽

B

bagua	八卦	팔괘
Baopuzi	抱朴子	포박자
Bixie jishi	辟邪紀實	벽사기실

C

changsŭng		장승
Chaoxian Celue	朝鮮策略	조선책략
Chejungwŏn	濟衆院	제중원
chenwei	讖緯	참위
chesa	祭祀	제사
Chesŏk	帝釋	제석
chigwan	地官	지관
Chilli iji	眞理易知	진리이지
chinin	眞人	진인
Cho mamin gwang	照萬民光	조만민광
Chŏn Sŏngch'ŏn	全聖天	전성천
Chŏng Hasang	丁夏祥	정하상

Chŏng Kam	鄭鑑	정감
Chŏng Yakchong	丁若鍾	정약종
Chŏnggam-nok	鄭鑑錄	정감록
Chŏngjo sillok	正祖實錄	정조실록
chosangshin	祖上神	조상신
Chowhaong	造化翁	조화옹
Chugyo yoji	主敎要旨	주교요지
chungin	中人	중인
chusaek chapki	酒色雜技	주색잡기
chwit'ong	쥐痛	쥐통
Chyangwŏn ryang'u syangron	張袁兩友相論	장원량우샹론
Chyosyŏn syŏnggyo sŏhoe	朝鮮聖敎書會	죠션성교서회
Ch'a Chaemyŏng	車載明	차재명
Ch'amshin	眞神	참신
Ch'anmiga	讚美歌	찬미가
ch'aryŏk	借力	차력
Ch'ilsŏng-gyŏng	七星經	칠성경
Ch'oe Cheu	崔濟愚	최제우
Ch'oe Myŏng'o	崔明悟	최명오
Ch'oe Pyŏnghŏn	崔炳憲	최병헌
ch'ŏllyun	天倫	천륜
ch'ŏndo	天道	천도
Ch'ŏnju	天主	천주
ch'ŏnmin	賤民	천민
ch'ŏrya kido	徹夜祈禱	철야기도
ch'udohoe	追悼會	추도회
ch'ukmun	祝文	축문
ch'unggun	忠君	충군
ch'unghyo	忠孝	충효
Ch'usŏk	秋夕	추석
ch'uwŏn	追遠	추원

D

Dayingguo zhi	大英國志	대영국지
Dehui rumen	德慧入門	덕혜입문
diyu	地獄	지옥

E

Ewha Haktang	梨花學堂	이화학당
ewu zhizhi	格物致知	격물치지

F

fengshui	風水	풍수
fuhuo	復活	부활
Fusheng zhi dao	復生之道	부생지도

G

ganying	感應	감응
Gongguoge	功過格	공과격
Guan Yu	關羽	관우
Guanyin	觀音	관음

H

Haesŏ Kyoan	海西敎案	해서교안
han	恨	한
Han Sŏkchin	韓錫晉	한석진
Hananim		하나님
Hanănim		하ᄂ님
Hanbul chădyŏn	韓佛字典	한불ᄌ뎐
han'gŭl		한글
hansik	寒食	한식
Hanŭlnim		하늘님
Hanŭnim		하느님
Hong Kyŏngnae	洪景來	홍경래
Hong Taeyong	洪大容	홍대용
Huang Zunxian	黃遵憲	황준헌
huigai	悔改	회개
Huna chinŏn	訓兒眞言	훈ᄋ진언
hunpo	魂魄	혼백
Hunsang gongli	婚喪公禮	혼상공례
Hwang Sayŏng	黃嗣永	황사영
Hwangsŏng sinmun	皇城新聞	황성신문
Hwanin	桓因	환인
Hwanung	桓雄	환웅
hyangni	鄕吏	향리
hyo	孝	효

I

ibai	禮拜	예배
Ilchinhoe	一進會	일진회
illyun	人倫	인륜

In'ga gwido	引家歸道	인가귀도
Iryŏn	一然	일연
Itō Hirobumi	伊藤博文	이토 히로부미

J

jinsheng	今生	금생
Jiushi lun	救世論	구세론
Jiushi yaolun	救世要論	구세요론
Jiushi yaoyan	救世要言	구세요언
Jiushi zhenquan	救世眞詮	구세진전
Jiushi zhenzhu	救世眞主	구세진주
Jiushijiao wenda	救世敎問答	구세교문답
Jiushijiao yi	救世敎益	구세교익

K

kaebyŏk	開闢	개벽
kaewha	開化	개화
Kagse sinp'yŏn p'algam	覺世新編八鑑	각세신편팔감
kibok sinang	祈福信仰	기복신앙
Kidok sinbo	基督申報	기독신보
kiin	奇人	기인
Kija	箕子	기자
Kil Sŏnju	吉善宙	길선주
Kil Yŏngsu	吉永洙	길영수
Kim Chaejun	金在俊	김재준
Kim Ch'ŏngsong	金青松	김청송
Kim Iktu	金益斗	김익두
Kim Kibŏm	金箕範	김기범
Kim Ku	金九	김구
Kim Okkyun	金玉均	김옥균
kisu	旗手	기수
Kogŭmgi	古今記	고금기
Kojong	高宗	고종
Kojong sillok	高宗實錄	고종실록
kŏllip		걸립
kongpŏp	公法	공법
Koryŏ	高麗	고려
Kuanyin	觀音	관음
kubon sinch'am	舊本新參	구본신참
kuhai	苦海	고해
Kuksadang	國師堂	국사당

kŭmch'ŏk	金尺	금척
kŭmsik san kido	禁食山祈禱	금식산기도
kunggung ŭlŭl	弓弓乙乙	궁궁을을
Kungmin-ga	國民歌	국민가
Kuseju	救世主	구세주
Kusye ron	救世論	구세론
Kusye yoŏn	救世要言	구세요언
Kusyegyo mundap	救世敎問答	구세교문답
kwagŏ	科擧	과거
Kwan U	關羽	관우
Kwanghyewŏn	廣惠院	광혜원
kwishin	鬼神	귀신
Kwŏnjung hoegae	勸衆悔改	권중회기
kyŏngch'ŏn aein	敬天愛人	경천애인
kyŏngmul	格物	격물

L

laisheng	來生	내생
Laozi	老子	노자
Li Hongzhang	李鴻章	리홍장

M

magwi	魔鬼	마귀
mamabaesong kut	媽媽拜送굿	마마배송굿
Manbo Ogilbang	萬寶五吉方	만보오길방
manshin	萬神	만신
Miaozhu wenda	廟祝問答	묘축문답
migyun	黴菌	미균
Miimi kyohoe mundap	美以美敎會問答	미이미교회문답
Min Yŏngik	閔泳翊	민영익
minjung	民衆	민중
moksa	牧師	목사
Mozi	墨子	묵자
mudang	巫堂	무당
Mudang naeryŏk	巫堂來歷	무당내력
munmyŏng	文明	문명
Myoch'yuk mundap	廟祝問答	묘축문답

N

| nal yŏnbo | 日捐補 | 날 연보 |
| neidan | 內丹 | 내단 |

O

Obang Changgun	五方將軍	오방장군
Okch'u kyŏng	玉樞經	옥추경
Okhwang	玉皇	옥황
ŏnmun	諺文	언문
ŏpju	業主	업주

P

Paehwa Haktang	培花學堂	배화학당
Paejae Haktang	培材學堂	배재학당
Paek Hongjun	白鴻俊	백홍준
Paek Nakchun	白樂濬	백낙준
Pak Hyŏngnyong	朴亨龍	박형룡
Pak Sŏngch'un	朴成春	박성춘
Pang Kich'ang	邦基昌	방기창
Pogŭm taeji	福音大旨	복음대지
puhwal	復活	부활
pulsap	黻翼	불삽
Pyŏn Sŏnhwan	邊鮮煥	변선환
p'acha	破字	파자
P'ahok chinsŏn non	破惑進善論	파혹진선론
p'ansu	判數	판수

Q

Qingming	清明	청명
Qingming saomu zhilun	清明掃墓之論	청명소묘지론

R

Raech'wi Yesyu	來就耶蘇	리취예슈
Rangja hoegae	浪子悔改	랑즈회기
Ro Ch'ungyŏng	盧春京	노춘경
Ro Pyŏngsŏn	盧炳善	노병선

S

saebyŏk kidohoe	晨旦祈禱會	새벽기도회
sagyŏnghoe	查經會	사경회
Samguk yusa	三國遺事	삼국유사
Samshin	三神	삼신
Sang chaesang sŏ	上宰相書	상재상서
sangmin	常民	상민
sangnom		상놈

sanshin	山神	산신
sarangbang		사랑방
Shangdi	上帝	상제
Shangdi zhenli	上帝眞理	상제진리
Shen	神	신
Shin	神	신
shinin	神人	신인
Shinjang	神將	신장
Sin Nakkyun	申洛均	신낙균
Sindŏk t'ongnon	信德統論	신덕통론
Sinhak Wŏlbo	神學月報	신학월보
Sinhan Minbo	新韓民報	신한민보
sipsŭng jiji	十勝之地	십승지지
Sirhak	實學	실학
siwang	十王	시왕
Sixian bianmiu	祀先辨謬	사선변류
Sŏ Kyŏngjo	徐景祚	서경조
Sŏ Namdong	徐南同	서남동
Sŏ Sangnyun	徐相崙	서상륜
sŏhak	西學	서학
Sohyŏn	昭顯	소현
Sŏndo	仙道	선도
Song Sunyong	宋淳容	송순용
Sŏnggyo yoji	聖教要旨	성교요지
Sŏnghwangdang	城隍堂	성황당
sŏngju	成造	성주
Sŏngshin	聖神	성신
sŏngŭi	誠意	성의
Sorae	松川	소래
sottae		솟대
sunyata	空	공
Syangdye	上帝	샹데
Syangdye chilli	上帝眞理	샹데진리
Syangjyu	上主	샹쥬
Syngman Rhee	李承晚	이승만
Syŏnggyo ch'walli	聖教撮理	성교촬리
Syŏnggyo ch'waryo	聖教撮要	성교촬요
Syŏnggyŏng mundap	聖經問答	성경문답
Syŏnggyŏng tosyŏl	聖經圖說	성경도셜
Syŏngsan myŏnggyŏng	聖山明鏡	성산명경

Syŏngsan yuramgi	聖山遊覽記	성산유람기

T

Taehan syŏnggyo syŏhoe	大韓聖教書會	대한성교셔회
Taejonggyo	大倧敎	대종교
Taewŏn'gun	大院君	대원군
taiji	太極	태극
Taishang ganying pian	太上感應篇	태상감응편
Tamhŏn yŏn'gi	湛軒燕記	담헌연기
Tamhŏnsŏ	湛軒書	담헌서
tanggan	幢竿	당간
Tan'gun	檀君	단군
Tiandao suyuan	天道溯原	천도소원
Tianlu licheng	天路歷程	천로역정
Tianlu zhinan	天路指南	천로지남
tiantang	天堂	천당
Tianzhu	天主	천주
Tianzhu shiyi	天主實義	천주실의
tiyong	體用	체용
toggaebi		도깨비
toin	道人	도인
Tŏkhye immun	德惠入門	덕혜입문
tongdo sŏgi	東道西器	동도서기
Tongguk t'onggam	東國通鑑	동국통감
Tonghak	東學	동학
Tongnip hyŏphoe	獨立協會	독립협회
Tongsa ch'anyo	東史纂要	동사찬요
Tongsa kangyo	東史綱要	동사강요
Tongsa poyu	東史補遺	동사보유
Tong'ŭi pogam	東醫寶鑑	동의보감
T'aejo taewang	太祖大王	태조대왕
T'ojijishin	土地之神	토지지신
T'ŏju		터주
t'ongsŏng kido	通聲祈禱	통성기도
T'yŏllo chigwi	天路指歸	텬로지귀
T'yŏllo ryŏktyŏng	天路歷程	텬로력뎡
T'yŏnjyu	天主	텬쥬

U

uhwan kut	憂患굿	우환굿

W

Wang Xichang	王錫鬯	왕석창
wenli	文理	문리
Wi wŏnip kyoin kyudyo	爲願入敎人規條	위원입교인규됴
wŏn'gwi	寃鬼	원귀
wu [mu]	巫	무
wu [mu]	無	무
wuchang	五常	오상
wuji	無極	무극
wuji taiji	無極太極	무극태극
wuwei	無爲	무위

X

Xu Guangqi	徐光啓	주광기

Y

yangban	兩班	양반
yangdaebuin	洋大婦人	양대부인
yangdaein	洋大人	양대인
yangmin	良民	양민
yebae	禮拜	예배
Yesu sŏnggyo mundap	耶蘇聖敎問答	예슈성교문답
Yesu sŏnggyo yoryŏng	耶蘇聖敎要領	예슈성교요령
Yesugyo mundap	耶蘇敎門答	예수교문답
Yi Chaemyŏng	李在明	이재명
Yi Ch'angjik	李昌稙	이창직
Yi Pyŏk	李檗	이벽
Yi Sujŏng (Rijutei)	李樹廷	이수정
Yi Ŭngch'an	李應贊	이응찬
Yinghua Shuyuan	英華書院	영화서원
Yinjia guidao	引家歸道	인가귀도
Yŏngjo sillok	英祖實錄	영조실록
yŏngsu	領首	영수
Yu Sŏngjun	兪星濬	유성준
Yuan Shikai	袁世凱	원세개
Yuanshi Tianzun	元始天尊	원시천존
Yugyŏng Kongwŏn	育英公園	육영공원
Yuhuang Shangdi	玉皇上帝	옥황상제
Yun Ch'iho	尹致昊	윤치호
Yun Sŏngbŏm	尹聖範	윤성범

Z

Zhang Yuan liangyou xianglun	張袁兩友相論	장원량우상론
Zhenshen	眞神	진신
Zhongsheng zhi dao	重生之道	중생지도
zhongti xiyong	中體西用	중체서용
zhongxiao	忠孝	충효
Zixi cudong	自西徂東	자서조동

Bibliography

ARCHIVAL COLLECTIONS

American Bible Society Archives, New York. Correspondence of the Japan Agency, 1882–1910.

British and Foreign Bible Society Archives (BFBSA), Cambridge University Library, London. Correspondence of the British and Foreign Bible Society, Inwards (CBFBS), 1879–1910.

———. Correspondence on Korean Bible Translation, 1895–1955.

New York Public Library, New York. George Clayton Foulk Papers, 1883–1887.

———. Horace Newton Allen Papers, 1883–1909.

Presbyterian Historical Society (PHS), Philadelphia. Adams Family Papers, 1897–1935. Record group 251.

———. Annie Laurie Adams Baird Papers, 1890–1916. Record group 172.

———. Baird Family Papers, 1900–1964. Record group 316.

———. Charles F. Bernheisel Diary, 1900–1907.

———. Correspondence and Reports of the Korea Mission, 1884–1910 (CRKM). Record group 140. The Board of Foreign Mission, PCUSA. Microfilm Series, reels 174–81, 224, 280–85.

———. Korea Mission Records, 1903–1957. Microfilm Series, 31 rolls.

———. William Davis Reynolds Jr. Collection.

———. William Martyn Baird Papers, 1885–1931. Record group 173.

Princeton Theological Seminary Library (PTSL), Princeton, N.J. Robert Elliot Speer Collection, 1896–1910.

———. Samuel Austin Moffett Collection, 1884–1940.

Rutherford B. Hayes Presidential Center, Fremont, Ohio. Reverend Franklin Ohlinger Papers, 1880–1925. GA-36.
Union Theological Seminary Burke Library (UTS), Columbia University, New York. George Heber Jones Papers, 1898–1918.
———. Henry Gerhard Appenzeller Papers, 1883–1902.
———. John Franklin Goucher Papers, 1845–1922.
———. John R. Mott, Addresses and Papers, 1865–1955.
———. John Raleigh Mott Papers, 1865–1955.
———. World Missionary Conference Records, Edinburgh, 1910 (WMCR), 1908–1918.
United Methodist Historical Center (UMHC), Drew University, Madison, N.J. Missionary Files of the Korea Mission, Methodist Episcopal Church Missionary Correspondence, 1884–1912 (MFiles). Microfilm reels 111–15. Wilmington, Del.: Scholarly Resources, 1999.
University of Toronto Library, Toronto, Canada. James Scarth Gale Papers.
Yale Divinity School Library (YDS), New Haven, Conn. Arthur Judson Brown Papers, 1864–1967. Special Collections, record group 2.
———. Franklin and Bertha S. Ohlingerm Papers.
———. John Raleigh Mott Papers, 1865–1955. Special Collections, record group 45.
———. Records of the Foreign Missions Conference of North America, 1913–1950. HR1203.
———. World Missionary Conference Records, Edinburgh, 1910 (WMCR), 1908–1918.

PERIODICALS

All the World. New York, 1905–1919.
Assembly Herald (AH). New York, 1899–1918.
Bible in the World (BW). London, 1905–1920.
Bible Society Record (BSR). New York, 1882–1920.
China Medical Journal (CMJ). Shanghai, 1896–1920.
China's Millions. London, 1882–1910.
Chinese Recorder and Missionary Journal (CR). Shanghai, 1877–1920.
Christian Advocate. New York, 1882–1902.
Christian Work and the Evangelist. New York, 1882–1910.
Church at Home and Abroad (CHA). New York, 1883–1920.
Church Missionary Intelligence and Record. London, 1885–1920.

Chyosyŏn K'ŭrisŭdoin Hoebo (KH) 죠션크리스도인회보 [Korean Christian Advocate]. Seoul, 1897–1899.

Dyeguk Sinmun 데국신문 [Empire News]. Seoul, 1898–1903.

Foreign Missionary (FM). New York, 1884–1900.

Gospel in All Lands (GAL). New York, 1885–1902.

Han'guk Kidoggyowa Yŏksa (HKY) 한국 기독교와 역사 [History and Christianity in Korea]. Seoul, 1991–2012.

Heathen Woman's Friend (HWF). New York, 1885–1895.

Hwangsŏng Sinmun (HS) 皇城新聞 [Imperial Capital Gazette]. Seoul, 1898–1910.

Illustrated Christian Weekly. New York, 1883–1885.

Independent. New York, 1884–1911.

Independent. Seoul, 1896–1899.

International Bulletin of Missionary Research. New Haven, Conn., 1984–2010.

Journal of the American Medical Association (JAMA). Chicago, 1888–1920.

Kidoggyo Sasang 기독교사상 [Christian Thought]. Seoul, 1957–2001.

Korea Field (KF). Seoul, 1902–1905.

Korea Journal. Seoul, 1973–1999.

Korea Magazine. Seoul, 1917–1919.

Korea Methodist (KM). Seoul, 1900–1904.

Korea Mission Field (KMF). Seoul, 1906–1943.

Korean Repository (KR). Seoul, 1892, 1895–1898.

Korea Review (KRv). Seoul, 1901–1906.

Kŭrisŭdo Sinmun (KS) 그리스도신문 [Christian News]. Seoul, 1897–1906.

Missionary. Nashville, Tenn., 1892–1911.

Missionary Herald. New York, 1883–1897.

Missionary Record of the United Presbyterian Church of Scotland (MRUPCS). Edinburgh, 1872–1915.

Missionary Review. Princeton, N.J., 1880–1887.

Missionary Review of the World (MRW). New York, 1888–1911.

Missionary Survey. New York, 1911–1923.

Seoul Press. Seoul, 1907–1910.

Sinhak Wŏlbo (SW) 신학월보 [A Biblical and Church Monthly]. Seoul, 1900–1908.

Student Volunteer. New York, 1893–1898.

Taehan K'ŭrisŭdoin Hoebo (KH) 대한크리스도인회보 [Korean Christian Advocate]. Seoul, 1899–1900.

Taehan Maeil Sinbo (*TMS*) 대한매일신보 [Korean Daily News]. Seoul, 1904–1910.

Toknip Sinmun (*TS*) 독닙신문 [Independent]. Seoul, 1896–1899.

Transactions of the Korea Branch of the Royal Asiatic Society (*TKB*). Seoul, 1901–1930.

Woman's Missionary Advocate (*WMA*). New York, 1896–1910.

Woman's Missionary Friend (*WMF*). New York, 1896–1914.

Woman's Work for Women (*WWW*). New York, 1891–1916.

Woman's Work in the Far East (*WWFE*). Shanghai, 1895–1912.

World Wide Missions (*WWM*). New York, 1889–1912.

World's Work. New York, 1901–1910.

Yesugyo Sinbo 예수교신보 [Christian News]. Seoul, 1907–1910.

LETTERS, REPORTS, ARTICLES, AND BOOKS

Ahn Sungho 안성호. "19세기 전반 중국어 대표자 역본 번역에서 발생한 용어논쟁이 초기 한글 성서번역에 미친 영향 19segi chŏnban chunggugŏ taep'yoja yŏgbon pŏnyŏgesŏ palsaenghan yongŏ nonjaengi ch'ogi han'gŭl sŏngsŏ pŏnyŏge mich'in yŏnghyang" [The Influence of the Term Controversy in the Delegates' Version of the Chinese Bible Translation on the Early Korean Bible Translation (1843–1911)]. *HKY* 30 (2009): 213–50.

Allen, Horace Newton. "Our First Letter from Korea." *FM* 43 (1884): 303.

———. *The First Annual Report of the Korean Government Hospital, Seoul for the Year Ending April 10, 1886*. Yokohama: Yokohama University Press, 1886.

———. "Report of the Health of Seoul for the Year 1886." Yokohama: Yokohama University Press, 1886.

———. Letter to F. F. Ellinwood, June 11, 1888. PHS, CRKM, reel 175.

———. Letter to F. F. Ellinwood, August 20, 1888. PHS, CRKM, reel 175.

———. "Korea and Its People." *GAL* 16 (1891): 419.

———. Letter to F. F. Ellinwood, June 12, 1894. PHS, CRKM, reel 178.

———. "The Mootang." *KR* 3 (1896): 163–64.

———. Letter to H. G. Appenzeller, November 20, 1898. In Yi, *Appenzeller*, 401–2.

———. Letter to H. G. Appenzeller, December 6 and 8, 1898. In Yi, *Appenzeller*, 407–10.

———. *A Chronological Index: Some of the Chief Events in the Foreign*

Intercourse of Korea from the Beginning of Christian Era to the 20th Century. Seoul: Methodist Publishing, 1901.

———. *Korea: Fact and Fancy.* Seoul: Methodist Publishing, 1904.

———. *Things Korea: A Collection of Sketches and Anecdotes, Missionary and Diplomatic.* New York: Revell, 1908.

———. *Horace Newton Allen Diary.* Edited and translated by Kim Won-mo 김원모. Seoul: Dankook University Press, 1991.

American Bible Society (ABS). *The Annual Report.* New York, 1882–1915.

American Tract Society (ATS). *The Annual Report.* New York, 1870–1915.

Appenzeller, Alice Rebecca. "William Elliot Griffis, D.D., L.H.D.: An Appreciation." *KMF* (April 1928): 78–79.

Appenzeller, Henry Gerhard. "Our Mission in Korea." *GAL* 10 (1885): 328.

———. Letter to A. B. Leonard, July 10, 1885. UMHC, MFiles.

———. "The Korean King at Seoul." *GAL* 11 (1886): 7.

———. Letter to E. W. Gilman, August 8, 1887. In Oak, *Sources of Korean Christianity,* 377.

———. "A Trip in Korea by a Missionary." *GAL* 12 (1887): 396.

———. "#149 The Faith of Rome." UTS, Appenzeller Papers: Sermons, ca. 1888.

———. "#152 Native Inquirers." UTS, Appenzeller Papers: Sermons, January 18, 1889.

———. "#163 Korean Notes." UTS, Appenzeller Papers: Notes, ca. 1890.

———. "#134 Memorial Stones." UTS, Appenzeller Papers: Sermons, November 26, 1891.

———. "Woman's Work in Korea." *GAL* 16 (1891): 424.

———. "Korea—What Is It Worth?" *HWF* 24 (1892): 230–31.

———. "#137 Our Father, Matthew 6:9." UTS, Appenzeller Papers: Sermons, May 29, 1892.

———. "#139 The Report of the Spies." UTS, Appenzeller Papers: Sermons, September 25, 1892.

———. "#140 We Preach Christ Crucified." UTS, Appenzeller Papers: Sermons, January 15, 1893.

———. Letter to Samuel A. Moffett, May 18, 1894. In Yi, *Appenzeller,* 359.

———. "Epilogue." In F. Genähr, *Myoch'yuk mundap.* Translated by H. G. Appenzeller. Seoul: Paejae Haktang, 1895.

———. "Ki Tza." *KR* (March 1895): 83–84.

———. Letter to Philip Jaisohn, November 20, 1898. In Yi, *Appenzeller*, 403–407.

———. "#155 Korea: The Field, Our Work and Our Opportunity." UTS, Appenzeller Papers: Addresses & Essays, 1901.

———. "Notes from the Stations." *KMF* 6 (1910): 8.

Australasian Association for the Advancement of Science. *Corea.* Brisbane: N.p., 1895.

Avison, Oliver R. "Cholera in Seoul." *KR* 2 (1895): 339–44.

———. "Disease in Korea." *KR* 4 (March 1897): 90–94 (June 1897): 207–11.

———. Letter to Robert E. Speer, November 19, 1898. PHS, CRKM, reel 178.

———. Letter to Robert E. Speer, December 16, 1898. PHS, CRKM, reel 178.

———. "Severance Memorial Hospital, Seoul, Korea." *Assembly Herald* (1903): 513–16.

———. "Sickness and Rumor of Sickness: From Annual Report of Dr O. R. Avison." *KF* (June 1903): 126–27.

———. "Response to the Commission I. Carrying the Gospel to All the World of the World Missionary Conference, 1910." UTS, G. H. Jones Papers.

Baird, Annie Laura Adams. "General Report of Pyeng Yang Station to the Korea Mission, June 1903." In KMPCUSA, *Minutes and Reports*, 1903. PHS, CRKM, reel 232.

———. *Daybreak in Korea: A Tale of Transformation in the Far East.* New York: Revell, 1909.

———. *Inside View of Mission Life.* Philadelphia: Westminster, 1913.

Baird, William Martyn. "Letters from Rev. W. M. Baird, Seoul, Korea, May 14, 1897." *CHA* 11 (1897): 126.

———. Letter to F. F. Ellinwood, May 22, 1897. PHS, CRKM, reel 178.

———. "Notes on a Trip into Northern Korea." *Independent*, May 20, 1897.

Baker, Donald L. "The Korean God Is Not the Christian God: Taejonggyo's Challenge to Foreign Religions." In Buswell, *Religions of Korea in Practice*, 464–75.

Baldwin, Stephen L. "Christian Literature—What Has Been Done and What Is Needed." In GCPMC, *RGC*, 1878, 206.

Bang Won-il 방원일. "초기 개신교 선교사의 한국 종교 이해 Ch'ogi Kaesingyo sŏngyosa ŭi Han'guk chonggyo ihae" [The Early Protestant

Missionaries' Understanding for Korean Religion]. Ph.D. diss., Seoul National University, 2011.

Barnett, Suzanne Wilson, and John King Fairbank, eds. *Christianity in China: Early Protestant Missionary Writings*. Cambridge, Mass.: Harvard University Press, 1974.

Barrett, T. H. "Chinese Religion in English Guide: The History of an Illusion." *Modern Asian Studies* 29, no. 3 (2005): 509–33.

Bays, Daniel H. "Christian Tracts: The Two Friends." In Barnett and Fairbank, *Christianity in China*, 19–34.

BCK (Bible Committee of Korea). "Annual Report of the Bible Committee of Korea for 1906." Seoul, 1906.

Beale, David. *In Pursuit of Purity: American Fundamentalism Since 1850*. Greenville, S.C.: Unusual Publications, 1986.

Beaver, R. Pierce, ed. *To Advance the Gospel: Selections from the Writings of Rufus Anderson*. Grand Rapids: Eerdmans, 1967.

Bebbington, David W. *Evangelicalism in Modern Britain: A History from the 1730s to the 1980s*. London: Hyman, 1981.

Bernheisel, Charles F. "Classes in Whang Hai Province." *KF* 1 (1901): 2.

———. "The Korean Church a Missionary Church." *Woman's Work* (November 1910): 250–51.

———. *The Apostolic Church as Reproduced in Korea*. New York: BFMPCUSA, 1912.

Best, Margaret. Letter to A. J. Brown, March 12, 1907. PHS, CRKM, reel 281.

———. "Courses of Study and Rules of Admission of the Pyeng Yang Presbyterian Women's Bible Institute." *KMF* 6 (1910): 152–54.

BFBS (British and Foreign Bible Society). *Annual Reports*. London: BFBS, 1876–1911.

———. *Correspondence with the Missions Regarding the Distinct Missionary Responsibility of the Presbyterian Church*. New York: BFMPCUSA, 1907.

BFMPCUSA (Board of Foreign Missions of the Presbyterian Church, USA). *Annual Reports*. New York: BFMPCUSA, 1883–1911.

———. *Presentation of Difficulties Arisen in the Chosen Mission, Presbyterian Church, U. S. A. Because of a Lack of Definition between the Foreign Board and Itself Concerning Their Mutual Responsibilities in the Administration of Field Work*. New York: BFMPCUSA, 1919.

Bishop, Isabella Bird. *Korea and Her Neighbors*. London: John Murray, 1898.

Bitton, Nelson. *Griffith John: The Apostle of Central China.* London: Sunday School Union, 1912.

Blackstone, William R. *Jesus Is Coming.* Chicago: Moody Press, 1908.

Bliss, Edwin M., ed. *Encyclopaedia of Missions.* 2 vols. New York: Funk & Wagnalls, 1891.

Blodget, Henry. "The Attitude of Christianity toward Ancestral Worship." In GCPMC, *RGC,* 1890, 631–54.

———. *The Use of T'ien Chu for God in Chinese.* Shanghai: American Presbyterian Mission Press, 1893.

Boone, William Jones. *An Essay on the Proper Rendering of the Words of Elohim and Theos into the Chinese Language.* Canton: Chinese Repository, 1848.

———. *Defense of an Essay on the Proper Rendering of the Words of Elohim and Theos into the Chinese Language.* Canton: Chinese Repository, 1850.

Bosch, David J. *Transforming Mission: Paradigm Shifts in Theology of Mission.* Maryknoll, N.Y.: Orbis, 1992.

Boxer, C. R. *The Christian Century in Japan: 1549–1650.* Berkeley: University of California Press, 1951.

Brereton, Virginia L. *Training God's Army.* Bloomington: Indiana University Press, 1990.

Brown, Arthur Judson. *Report of a Visitation of the China Missions.* New York: BFMPCUSA, 1902.

———. *Report of a Visitation of the Korea Mission of the Presbyterian Board of Foreign Missions.* New York: BFMPCUSA, 1902.

———. *Report on a Second Visit to China, Japan, and Korea.* New York: BFMPCUSA, 1909.

———. "The Death of the Rev. W. A. P. Martin." In *Minutes of the Board of the Foreign Missions of the PCUSA,* 321–22. New York: BFMPCUSA, 1916.

———. *The Mastery of the Far East: The Story of Korea's Transformation and Japan's Rise to Supremacy in the Orient.* New York: Scribner, 1919; 2nd ed., 1920.

Bryant, Elliot. Letter to William Wright, December 4, 1888. BFBSA, CBFBS.

Bucknell, Roderick S., and Paul Beirne. "In Search of Yŏngbu: The Lost Talisman of Korea's Tonghak Religion." *Review of Korean Studies* 4, no. 2 (2001): 201–22.

Bunker, Dalzell A. "Pai Chai High School." *MSMEC for 1905,* 75–78.

Bunyan, John. *The Pilgrim's Progress: From This World to That Which Is to Come.* London: W. Johnston, 1757.

————. 天路歷程 官話 *Tianlu licheng: guanhua* [The Pilgrim's Progress in Mandarin]. Translated by William Burns. Shanghai: Presbyterian Mission Press, 1852, 1869.

————. *The Pilgrim's Progress: From This World to That Which Is to Come.* London: Cassell, Petter, Galpin, 1863.

————. 天路歷程 意譯 *Tenro rekitei: iyaku* [The Pilgrim's Progress]. Translated by 佐藤喜峰 Sato Yosimine. Tokyo: Jiujiya, 1879.

————. *The Pilgrim's Progress: From This World to That Which Is to Come.* Philadelphia: Henry Altemus, 1890.

————. 텬로력뎡 *T'yŏllo yŏkchŏng* [The Pilgrim's Progress]. Translated by James S. Gale. Seoul: Korean Religious Tract Society, 1895.

Burdick, George M. "Conversion of a Mountain Spirit House Keeper." *KMF* 2 (1906): 88.

Buswell, Robert E., Jr., ed. *Religions of Korea in Practice.* Princeton, N.J.: Princeton University Press, 2007.

Buswell, Robert E., Jr., and Timothy S. Lee, eds. *Christianity in Korea.* Honolulu: University of Hawaii, 2006.

Byun Kyuyong 변규용. "Daoism and Daoists—Its Essence and Development." *Korea Journal* 26 (1986): 1–12

Cable, Elmer M. "제사 근원을 의논홈 Chesa kŭnwŏnŭl ŭinon ham" [Discussing the Origin of Ancestor Worship]. 예수교신보 *Yesugyo Sinbo*, November 30 and December 15, 1908.

————. "宗教上比較學 Chonggyosang pigyohak" [Comparative Religion]. 神學世界 *Sinhak Segye* 1–4 (1916): 51–62.

————. "Choi Pyung Hun." *KMF* (April 1925): 88–89.

Carroll, Arena. "Songdo Woman's Class." *KM* (June 1905): 103.

————. "Songdo, Korea." *WMA* 26 (1906): 410–11.

CHA (*Church at Home and Abroad*). "Foreign Mission Notes by the Secretaries." *CHA* 3 (1889): 117.

————. "What Is the Religion of Korea?" *CHA* 6 (1892): 139.

Ch'a Chaemyŏng 차재명. 朝鮮예수敎長老會史記 *Chosŏn Yesugyo Changnohoe sagi* [A History of the Presbyterian Church in Korea]. Seoul: Ch'angmusa, 1928.

Ch'a Chuhwan 차주환. "韓國道敎의 宗敎思想 Han'guk Tokyo ŭi chonggyo sasang" [Religious Thought of Korean Daoism]. In *Togyo wa Han'guk munhwa*, edited by Han'guk togyo sasang yŏnguhoe, 465–78. Seoul: Asea munhwasa, 1989.

————. "道敎의 永生과 그리스도교의 永生의 問題 Tokyo ŭi yŏngsaeng

gwa Kŭrisŭdogyo ŭi yŏngsaeng ŭi munje" [Daoist Long Life and Christian Immortality]. In *Han'guk chŏnt'ong sansanggwa Ch'ŏnjugyo* [The Korea Traditional Thoughts and Catholic (1)], edited by Catholic Academy for Korean Culture, 301–19. Seoul: T'amgudang, 1995.

Chang Kyusik 장규식. 일제하 한국 기독교 민족운동 *Iljeha Han'guk Kidoggyo minjok undong* [Korean Protestant National Movement during the Japanese Colonial Rule]. Seoul: Hyean, 2001.

Chang Tong 장동. 東史綱要 *Tongsa kangyo* [Essential History of Korea]. 7 vols. Seoul: N.p., 1884.

Chang Wŏngŭn 장원근. "황해도교회진보홈 Hwanghaedo kyohoe chinboham" [Progress of the Churches in Hwanghae Province]. *SW* (January 1903): 11.

————. "노다부인별세흔날을긔렴홈 Noda puin pyŏlsehan narŭl kuiryŏmham" [Memorial Service for Mrs. Noda]. *SW* 3 (1903): 296.

China's Millions. "Corea." *China's Millions* 10 (1884): 25.

Cho Hyeon Beom 조현범. "A Study on the Protestant Discourse of Civilization in Early Modern Korea." *Korea Journal* (Spring 2001): 18–43.

————. 조선의 선교사, 선교사의 조선 *Chosŏn ŭi sŏgyosa, Sŏngyosa ŭi Chosŏn* [Missionaries of Chosŏn, Chosŏn of Missionaries]. Seoul: Han'guk Kyohoesa yŏnguso, 2010.

Cho Kwang 조광. 조선 후기 천주교사 연구 *Chosŏn hugi ch'ŏnjugyosa yŏn'gu* [A Study on the History of Roman Catholicism in the Late Chosŏn Period]. Seoul: Koryŏdaehakkyo minjokmunje yŏn'guso, 1988.

Cho Sukja. "Han'guk ch'oech'o ŭi changnogyo ch'ansongga *Ch'asyŏngsi* yŏn'gu" [A Study on the First Presbyterian Hymnal *Ch'ansyŏngsi*]. *Kyohoe wa Sinhak* 26 (1994): 498–675.

Ch'oe Chunsik 최준식. 한국 종교 이야기 *Han'guk chonggyo iyagi* [Stories of Korean Religions]. Seoul: Hanul, 1995.

Ch'oe Pyŏnghŏn 최병헌. "고집불통 Kojip pult'ong" [A Stubborn Man]. *KH*, March 8, 1899.

————. "즁츄가절일 Chyungch'yu kajŏril" [Korean Thanksgiving Day]. *KH*, September 27, 1899.

————. "성산유람긔 Syŏngsan yuram gŭi" [Traveling to the Holy Mountain]. *SW* (1907): 30–35, 83–88, 126–32, 229–37.

————. 聖山明鏡 *Syŏngsan myŏnggyŏng* [The Bright Mirror in the Holy Mount]. Seoul: Chŏngdong Hwanghwa sŏjae, 1909.

————. "四敎較略 Sagyo gyoryak" [A Short Comparison of Four World

Religions]. *SW* 7, nos. 2–3 (1909): 48–77; 7, nos. 4–5 (1909): 73–93; 7, no. 6 (1909): 31–48.

Choi Hyaeweol 최혜월. *Gender and Mission Encounter in Korea: New Women, Old Ways*. Berkeley: University of California Press, 2009.

Choi Kil Sung 최길성. "Male and Female in Korean Folk Belief." *Asian Folklore Studies* 43 (1984): 227–33.

Choi Sung Il 최성일. "John Ross and the Korean Protestant Church." Ph.D. diss., University of Edinburgh, 1992.

Chŏn Yŏkho 전역호. "우상을폐홀것 Usangŭl pyŏhal kŏt" [Remove Idols]. *SW* 3 (1904): 243–45.

Chŏng Hyŏngho 정형호. "기산 김준근의 풍속화에 나타난 민속적 특징 Kisan Kim Chungŭn ŭi p'ungsokhwa e nat'anan minsok chŏk t'ŭkching" [The Folk Characteristics of Kisan, Kim Junkeun's Genre Painting]. 中央民俗學 *Chung'ang Minsokhak* 13 (2008): 179–223.

Chŏng Sunman 정순만. "講和를 傍聽ᄒ고 獨立을 鞏固케홈 Kanghwarŭl pangch'ŏnghago tongnibŭl konggokeham" [Observing the Treaty and Strengthening Independence]. *TMS*, September 7, 1905.

Chŏng Yakchong 정약종. 主教要旨 *Chugyo yoji* [Essential Teachings of Roman Catholicism]. Manuscripts ca. 1800. Seoul: 1864. Translated by Ha Sŏngrae. Seoul: Sŏnghwangsŏk turugasŏwŏn, 1995.

Chŏngjo sillok 正祖實錄. Vol. 14, November 20, 1782; vol. 14, December 10, 1782; vol. 19, March 15, 1785.

Chosŏn Ilbo 朝鮮日報. "鷄龍山의 新都 Kyeryongsan ŭi Sindo" [Sindo of the Kyeryong Mountain]. May 6, 1921.

———. "邪教의王國 伏魔의殿堂 '新都' 鷄龍山의 秘密 (二) Sagyo ŭi wangguk pokma ŭi chŏndang 'Sindo' Kyeryongsan ŭi pimil" [Kingdom of Cults and Hall of Devils: The Secret of the Town of Sindo in the Kyeryong Mountain]. January 23, 1931.

Christie, Douglas. "Pioneers: The Rev. John Ross, Manchuria." *Life and Work* 5 (1934): 76–78.

Chu Chaeyong 주재용. 先儒의 天主思想과 祭祀問題 *Sŏnyu ŭi Ch'ŏnju sasang gwa chesa munje* [Early Confucian Thought of Tianzhu and the Ancestor Worship Question]. Seoul: Kynghyang chapchisa, 1958.

———. 한국 그리스도교 신학사 *Han'guk Kŭrisŭdogyo sinhak sa* [A History of Christian Theology in Korea]. Seoul: Christian Literature Society of Korea, 1998.

Chun Sung Chun 전성천. "Schism and Unity in the Protestant Churches of Korea." Ph.D. diss., Yale University, 1955.

Chung Chai-sik 정재식. "Confucian-Protestant Encounter in Korea:

Two Cases of Westernization and De-Westernization." *Ching Feng* 34, no. 1 (1991): 51–81.

Chung Chinhong 정진홍. "The Episteme of Body and the Problem of Environment Concerning the Early Protestant Medical Mission in Korea." 종교학연구 *Chonggyohak Yŏngu* 17 (1998): 167–80.

———. "Early Protestant Medical Missions and the Epitome of Human Body in Late Nineteenth Century Korea: Concerning Problems of Environment." In *Korea between Tradition and Modernity: Selected Papers from the Fourth Pacific and Asian Conference on Korean Studies*, edited by Chang Yun-Shik et al., 308–16. Vancouver: Institute for Asian Research, University of British Columbia, 2000.

Chung, David 정대위. "Religious Syncretism in Korean Society." Ph.D. diss., Yale University, 1959.

Clark, Allen D. *Avison of Korea: The Life of Oliver R. Avison, M.D.* Seoul: Yonsei University Press, 1979.

Clark, Anthony E. "Early Modern Chinese Reactions to Western Missionary Iconography." *Southeast Review of Asian Studies* 30 (2008): 5–22.

Clark, Charles Allen. "The Destroying of a Household God." *KF* 3 (1903): 133.

———. "Stood Firm." *KF* 5 (1905): 266.

———. Letter to A. J. Brown, December 8, 1905. PHS, CRKM, reel 281.

———. Letter to A. J. Brown, December 8, 1906. PHS, CRKM, reel 281.

———. Letter to A. J. Brown, March 1, 1907. PHS, CRKM, reel 281.

———. "Three Incidents." *KMF* 5 (1909): 18.

———, comp. *Digest of the Presbyterian Church of Korea.* Seoul: Religious Book and Tract Society, 1918.

———. *First Fruits in Korea.* New York: Revell, 1921.

———. *The Korean Church and the Nevius Methods.* New York: Revell, 1930.

———. *Religions of Old Korea.* New York: Revell, 1932.

———. *The Nevius Plan for Mission Work, Illustrated in Korea.* Seoul: Christian Literature Society Korea, 1937.

Clark, Donald N. *Christianity in Modern Korea.* Lanham, Md.: University Press of America, 1986.

———. *Living Dangerously in Korea: The Western Experience 1900–1950.* Norwalk, Conn.: EastBridge, 2003.

Clark, James Hyde. *Story of China and Japan with a Sketch of Corea and the Coreans, and the Causes Leading to the Conflict of 1894*. Philadelphia: Oriental Publishing, 1894.

Cobb, George C. "Report VII. Trilingual Press." In *Journal of the Fourteenth Annual Meeting of the Korea Mission of the MEC*, 41–42. Seoul: Trilingual Press, 1898.

Cohen, Paul. *China and Christianity: The Missionary Movement and the Growth of Chinese Antiforeignism, 1860–1870*. Cambridge, Mass.: Harvard University Press, 1963.

Collyer, Charles T. "A Day on the Songdo Circuit." *KF* 1 (1901): 12–13.

Conn, Harvie M. "Studies in the Theology of the Korean Presbyterian Church: An Historical Outline, Part I & II." *Westminster Theological Journal* 29–30 (1966–1967): 24–57, 136–84.

Corfe, C. John. "The Bishop's Letter II." *Morning Calm* (May 1897): 37–40.

———. *The Anglican Church in Corea*. London: Livingstones, 1906.

Council of Presbyterian Missions in Korea. "Report of the Pyeng An Committee of Council." In *The Minutes of the Twelfth Annual Meeting of the Council of Presbyterian Missions in Korea, Seoul, Sept. 13–19, 1904*. Seoul: Methodist Publishing House, 1904.

———. "Report of Committee of Mixed Script." In *Minutes of the Thirteenth Annual Meeting of the Council of Presbyterian Missions in Korea, 1905*. Seoul: YMCA Press, 1905.

Courant, Maurice. *Bibliographie coréene: tableau litteraire de la Corée*. 2 vols. Paris: E. Leroux, 1894, 1896.

Covell, Ralph R. *W. A. P. Martin, Pioneer of Progress in China*. Washington, D.C.: Christian University Press, 1978.

———. *Confucianism, the Buddha, and Christ: A History of the Gospel in Chinese*. Maryknoll, N.Y.: Orbis, 1986.

CR (*Chinese Recorder and Missionary Journal*). "A Discourse on Rom. I.18–25." *CR* 11 (1880): 83.

Cracknell, Kenneth. *Justice, Courtesy and Love: Theologians and Missionaries Encountering World Religions, 1846–1914*. London: Epworth Press, 1995.

Cram, William Gliden. "Rescued after Years of Bondage." *KM* (September 10, 1905): 148.

———. *Korea, the Miracle of Modern Missions*. Nashville: Publishing House of Methodist Episcopal Church, South, 1922.

Criveller, Gianni. *Preaching Christ in Late Ming China: The Jesuits' Presentation of Christ from Matteo Ricci to Giulio Aleni*. Taipei: Ricci Institute for Chinese Studies, 1997.

Dallét, Claude Charles. *Histoire de l'Eglise de Corée*. Paris: Librairie Victor Palmé, 1874.

Davies, Daniel M. *The Life and Thought of Henry Gerhard Appenzeller (1858–1902), Missionary to Korea*. Lewiston, N.Y.: Edwin Mellen, 1988.

Davis, George T. B. *Korea for Christ*. New York: Revell, 1910.

———. "Progress of the Million Movement: A Visitor's Impressions." *Missionary* (August 1910): 398.

Dennett, Tyler. "Early American Policy in Korea, 1883–87." *Political Science Quarterly* (March 1923): 82–84.

Dennis, James S. *Christian Missions and Social Progress*. 3 vols. New York: Revell, 1897–1906.

———. "Union Movement in Mission Fields." *Congregationalist and Christian World* (November 4, 1905): 627–28.

Deuchler, Martina. *The Confucian Transformation of Korea: A Study of Society and Ideology*. Cambridge, Mass.: Harvard-Yenching Institute, 1992.

Diosy, Arthur. *The New Far East*. London: Cassell, 1904.

Dock, Lavinia L. "Foreign Department: Korean News." *American Journal of Nursing* 7 (1907): 34–35.

Doty, Elihu. *Some Thoughts on the Proper Term to Be Employed to Translate Elohim and Theos into Chinese*. Shanghai: Presbyterian Mission Press, 1850.

Dwight, Henry Otis, et al., eds. *Encyclopedia of Missions*. London: Funk & Wagnalls, 1904.

Dyer, S. Letter to W. Wright, December 21, 1894. BFBSA, CBFBS. In Oak, *Sources of Korean Christianity*, 275.

Eber, Irene. "Translating the Ancestors: S. I. J. Schereschewsky's 1875 Chinese Version of Genesis." *Bulletin of the School of Oriental and African Studies* (1993): 219–33.

———. "Interminable Term Question." In Eber et al., *Bible in Modern China*, 135–64.

Eber, Irene, et al., eds. *Bible in Modern China: The Literary and Intellectual Impact*. Monumenta Serica Monograph Series 43. Nettetal, Germany: Institut Monumenta Serica, 1999.

Edkins, Joseph. "Buddhism and Tauism in Their Popular Aspects." In *Records of the General Conference of the Protestant Missionaries in China*, 71–72. Shanghai: American Presbyterian Mission Press, 1877.

Engel, George O. "Native Customs and How to Deal with Them." *KF* 4 (1904): 205–6.

Erdman, Walter C. "Korea: 'Unto the Church In.'" *All the World* (April 1908): 43–46.

Ewy, Priscilla Welbon. *Arthur Goes to Korea: The Early Life of Arthur Garner Welbon and His First Years as Missionary to Korea, 1900–1902.* Tucson, Ariz.: Self-published, 2008.

Executive Committee of Foreign Missions of the Presbyterian Church, USA. *Annual Reports.* Nashville: 1892–1920.

Faber, Ernst. "A Critique of the Chinese Notions and Practice of Filial Piety." *Chinese Record* 9 (1878): 94.

———. 自西徂東 *Zixi cudong: Civilization, Western and Chinese.* Hong Kong: Religious Tract Society, 1884.

Fairbank, John King, ed. *Chinese Thought and Institutions.* Chicago: University of Chicago Press, 1957.

———, ed. *The Missionary Enterprise in China and America.* Cambridge, Mass.: Harvard University Press, 1974.

Fang-Lan Hsieh. *A History of Chinese Christian Hymnody: From Its Missionary Origins to Contemporary Indigenous Productions.* Lewiston, N.Y.: Edwin Mellen, 2009.

Federal Council of Protestant Evangelical Missions in Korea. *Minutes of the Annual Meeting.* 1905–1911.

Fenwick, Malcolm C. *The Church of Christ in Corea.* New York: Hodder & Stoughton-Doran, 1911.

Fenwick, Malcolm C., and Sŏ Kyŏngjo tr. 요한복음젼約翰福音傳 *Yohanbogŭmjyŏn* [The Gospel of John]. Seoul: Trilingual Press, 1891.

Férron, Stanislas, ed. *Dictionnaire Français-Coréen.* 1869. Reprint, Seoul: Han'guk Kyohoesa Yŏn'guso, 2004.

Fish, M. Alice. Letter to Franklin F. Ellinwood, April 29, 1899. PHS, CRKM, reel 178.

FM (Foreign Missionary). "The Hour for Korea." *FM* 44 (1885): 153.

Frey, Lulu E. "Ewa Haktang–Seoul." In *Reports Read at the Seventh Annual Session of the Korea Woman's Conference of the Methodist Episcopal Church*, 5. Seoul: Methodist Printing House, 1905.

Fridman, Eva Jane N., and Mariko N. Walter, eds. *Shamanism: An Encyclopedia of World Beliefs, Practices, and Culture.* Santa Barbara, Calif.: ABC-CLIO, 2004.

GAL (Gospel in All Lands). "Customs in Korea." *GAL* 13 (1888): 366.

———. "Gathering Notes on Korea." *GAL* 16 (1891): 429.

Gale, James Scarth. "Korea." *CHA* 7 (1893): 211.

———. "Korea—Its Present Condition." *MRW* 16 (1893): 658–65.

———. *Korean Grammatical Forms.* Seoul: Trilingual Press, 1893.

———. Letter to F. F. Ellinwood, May 19, 1894. PHS, CRKM, reel 178.

———. "Korea—Old Kim with His Savior." *CHA* (July 1894): 33–34.

———. 텬로력뎡 *T'yŏllo ryŏkdyŏng* [The Pilgrim's Progress]. Seoul: Religious Tract Society in Korea, 1895.

———. "Korean History." *KR* (September 1895): 321.

———. "Letters: Korea." *CHA* (September 1895): 230.

———. *A Korean-English Dictionary.* Yokohama: Kelly & Walsh, 1897.

———. *Korean Sketches.* New York: Revell, 1898.

———. Letter to F. F. Ellinwood, April 21, 1899. PHS, CRKM, reel 178.

———. "The Influence of China upon Korea." *TKB* I (1900): 1–24.

———. "Korean Beliefs." *Folklore* 11, no. 3 (1900): 325–32.

———. "Korean Ideas of God." *MRW* (September 1900): 697.

———. "단군 죠션 Tan'gun Chosŏn" [Tan'gun Chosŏn]. *KS*, September 12, 1901.

———. "고구려 Koguryŏ" [Koguryŏ]. *KS*, October 17, 1901.

———. "리마도의 사젹 Limado ŭi sajŏk" [The Life and Work of Matteo Ricci]. *KS*, October 17, 1901.

———. *The Vanguard: A Tale of Korea.* New York: Revell, 1904.

———. "The Gospel Levels Ranks." *KF* 5 (1905): 263–64.

———. "Elder Kil." *MRW* (July 1907): 493–95.

———. "The First Presbytery in Korea." *MRW* 31 (1908): 43–44.

———. *Korea in Transition.* New York: Young People's Missionary Movement of the United States and Canada, 1909.

———. "The Baptism of Georgie." *WWW* (November 1911): 243–44.

———. *A Korean-English Dictionary.* Yokohama: Fukuin, 1911.

———. "Korea's Preparation for the Bible." *KMF* (March 1912): 86.

———. "Convictions of the East." *MRW* 36 (1913): 689–90.

———, trans. *Korean Folk Tales: Imps, Ghosts, and Fairies.* New York: E. P. Dutton, 1913.

———. "The Korean's View of God." *KMF* (March 1916): 66–70.

———. "Tan-goon." *Korea Magazine* (September 1917): 404–5.

———. "A History of the Korean People, Chapter I." *KMF* (July 1924): 134–36.

———. "Address to the Friendly Association, June 1st, 1927, Chosen Hotel Seoul." Gale Papers, University of Toronto Library.

Gale, James Scarth, and Yi Ch'angjik, eds. 훈몽천즈 訓蒙千字 *Hunmong ch'ŏnja* [One Thousand Characters for Children]. Seoul: Korean Religious Tract Society, 1907.

GCPMC (General Conference of the Protestant Missionaries in China).

Records of the General Conference of the Protestant Missionaries in China, Held at Shanghai, May 10–24, 1877, (RGC). Shanghai: American Presbyterian Mission Press, 1878.

———. *Records of the General Conference of the Protestant Missionaries in China, Held at Shanghai, May 7–20, 1890 (RGC).* Shanghai: American Presbyterian Mission Press, 1890.

———. *China Centenary Missionary Conference Records; Report of the Great Conference, Held at Shanghai, April 5th to May 8th, 1907.* Shanghai: American Tract Society, 1907.

Genähr, Ferdiand. 묘축문답 *Myoch'uk mundap* [The Temple Keeper]. Translated by Henry G. Appenzeller. Seoul: Trilingual Press, 1895.

General Conference on the Protestant Missions of the World. *Reports.* New York: Revell, 1888.

Gentry and People. *Death Blow to Corrupt Doctrine.* Translation of *Bixie jishi* 辟邪紀實 [A Record of Facts to Ward Off Heterodoxy]. Shanghai, 1870.

Gifford, Daniel Lyman. Letter to F. F. Ellinwood, April 25, 1889. PHS, CRKM, reel 175.

———. Letter to F. F. Ellinwood, October 21, 1890. PHS, CRKM, reel 175.

———. "Ancestral Worship as Practiced in Korea." *KR* 1 (1892): 169–76.

———. Letter to F. F. Ellinwood, November 8, 1892. PHS, CRKM, reel 176.

———. *Everyday Life in Korea: A Collection of Studies and Stories.* New York: Revell, 1898.

———. *A Forward Mission Movement in North Korea.* New York: Foreign Mission Library, 1898.

Gilmore, George William. *Korea from Its Capital; With Chapter on Mission.* Philadelphia: Presbyterian Board of Publication and Sabbath School Work, 1892.

Girardot, Norman J. *The Victorian Translation of China: James Legge's Oriental Pilgrimage.* Berkeley: University of California Press, 2002.

Goforth, Jonathan. *When the Spirit's Fire Swept Korea.* Grand Rapids: Zondervan, 1943.

Grant, George Monro. *The Religions of the World.* New York: Anson Randolph, 1895.

Grayson, James Huntley. "The Manchurian Connection: The Life and Work of the Rev. Dr. John Ross." *Korea Observer* 15, no. 3 (1984): 345–60.

Greenfield, M. W. "Personal Report to Korea Mission, 1912–13." In *Minutes and Reports of the Twenty-Ninth Annual Meeting of the Korea Mission of the Presbyterian Church in the USA*. Kobe: Fukuin, 1913.

Grierson, Robert G. "The Place of Philanthropic Agencies in the Evangelization of Korea." *KF* (November 1904): 200.

Griffis, William Elliot. *Corea, the Hermit Nation*. New York: Scribner, 1882.

———. *Corea, Without and Within*. Philadelphia: Presbyterian Board of Publication, 1885.

———. "Korea and Its Needs." *GAL* 13 (1888): 371.

———. "Korea and the Koreans: In the Mirror of Their Language and History." *Journal of the American Geographical Society of New York* 27, no. 1 (1895): 1–20.

———. *A Modern Pioneer in Korea: Henry G. Appenzeller*. New York: Revell, 1912.

Guthapfel, Margaret L. "Bearing Fruit in Old Age." *KMF* (January 1906): 41–44.

Hall, Rosetta Sherwood. "Women's Medical Missionary Work." *CR* (April 1893): 167.

———. *The Life of Rev. William James Hall, M.D., Medical Missionary of the Slums of New York; Pioneer Missionary to Pyeng Yang, Korea*. New York: Eaton & Mains, 1897.

Han'guk Kidoggyosa yŏnguhoe 한국기독교역사연구회. 한국 기독교의 역사 *Han'guk Kidoggyo ŭi yŏksa* [A History of Korean Christianity]. 3 vols. Seoul: Christian Literature Press, 1989, 1990, 2009.

Hardie, Robert A. "Religion in Korea." *MRW* 20 (1897): 927.

———. "R. A. Hardie's Report." In *Minutes of the Sixth Annual Meeting of the Korea Mission of the MEC, South*, 32–33. Seoul: Methodist Publishing House, 1902.

Hedges, Paul. *Preparation and Fulfilment: A History and Study of Fulfilment Theology in Modern British Thought in the Indian Context*. Bern: Peter Lang, 2001.

Heron, John W. Letter to Frank F. Ellinwood, August 27, 1886. PHS, CRKM, reel 174.

Holmes, Mrs. J. L. 훈아진언 *Huna chinŏn* [Peep of Day]. Translated by Mary F. Scranton. Seoul: Korean Religious Tract Society, 1891.

Hong Taeyong 홍대용. "乾淨衕筆談 Kŏnjŏngdong p'ildam" [Writing Dialogue at Kŏnjŏngdong, Beijing]. In 湛軒書 *Tamhŏnsŏ* [The

Writings of Tamhŏn Hong Taeyong, 1765]. Seoul: Korean Classics Research Institute, 1976.

Hounshell, C. G. "The Lord Blessing His People." *KM* (May 10, 1905): 83.

HS (皇城新聞 *Hwangsŏng Sinmun*) [Imperial Capital Gazette]. "妖術遁藏 Yosul tunjang" [Witchcraft Fled and Hidden]. *HS*, August 17, 1904.

———. "我同胞〻切勿迷信虛荒 A dongp'o nan chŏlmul misin hŏhwang" [Our People Should Renounce Vain Superstition]. *HS*, February 9, 1908.

———. "韓日赤十字社 合併 Hanil Chŏksipchasa happyŏng" [The Korean and Japanese Red Cross Societies Were Unified]. *HS*, July 25, 1909.

Huang Zunxian. 朝鮮策略 *Chaoxian Celue* [A Stratagem for Korea]. Tokyo: Manuscript, 1880.

Hulbert, Homer Bezaleel. "A Sketch of the Roman Catholic Movement in Korea." *MRW* 13 (1890): 730–35.

———. "The Korean Almanac." *KR* (February 1895): 67–73.

———. "The Origin of the Korean People." *KR* (June 1895): 220.

———. "Things in General: Demoniacal Possession." *KR* (January 1897): 24–25.

———. "Ancient Korea." *KR* (December 1897): 458–63.

———. "Korea and the Koreans." *Forum* 14 (1899): 215–19.

———. "Korean Survivals." *TKB* 1 (1900): 25–50.

———. "Part I. Ancient Korea Chapter I." *KRv* (January 1901): 33–35.

———. "Exorcising Spirits." *KRv* (April 1901): 163.

———. "Hungry Spirits." *KRv* (March 1903): 111–12.

———. "The Korean Mudang and P'ansu." *KRv* (April 1903): 145–49; (May 1903): 203–8; (June 1903): 257–60; (July 1903): 301–5; (August 1903): 342–46; (September 1903): 385–89.

———. "The Ajun." *KRv* (February 1904): 63–70; (June 1904): 249–55.

———. "Editorial Comments." *KRv* (March 1905): 144–48.

———. *History of Korea.* 2 vols. New York: Hillary, 1905.

———. "Kyoyuk" [Education]. *KS*, July 12, 1906.

———. *The Passing of Korea.* London: Heinemann, 1906.

———. "TheNeeds of A National Ideal for Korea." *KMF* (January 1910): 23–24.

Hunt, Everett N. *Protestant Pioneers in Korea.* Maryknoll, N.Y.: Orbis, 1980.

Hutchison, William R. *Errand to the World: American Protestant*

Thought and Foreign Missions. Chicago: University of Chicago Press, 1987.

————. "Evangelization and Civilization: Protestant Missionary Motivation in the Imperialist Era." In *Missions and Ecumenical Expressions*, edited by Martin E. Marty, 91–124. Munich: K.G. Saur, 1993.

Hwang Hyŏn 황현. "Sup'il Kapsin" [The First Essay in 1884], *Ohagimun* [梧下記聞 Writing Down What I Heard under a Paulownia Tree]. In Tonghak nongminjŏnjaeng paekchunyŏn kinyŏmsaŏp ch'ujinwiwŏnhoe, *Tonghak nongminjŏnjaeng saryo ch'ongsŏ* I [Collection of Historical Sources of the Tonghak Peasant War], 42–43. Seoul: Sayeyŏnguso, 1996.

Hwang Kyung Moon 황경문. "From the Dirt to Heaven: Northern Koreans in the Chosŏn and Early Modern Eras." *Harvard Journal of Asiatic Studies* 62, no. 1 (2002): 135–78.

————. *Beyond Birth: Social Status in the Emergence of Modern Korea.* Cambridge, Mass.: Harvard University Press, 2004.

Independent. "Editorial Notes." *Independent*, August 7, 1897.

JAMA (Journal of American Medical Association). "Cholera Threatened." *JAMA* (December 20, 1890): 906.

————. "Public Health: Smallpox." *JAMA* (May 1899): 1012, 1072.

————. "The Public Service: Smallpox—Foreign." *JAMA* (April 14, 1900): 958.

————. "The Public Service: Plague—Foreign and Insular." *JAMA* (August 11, 1900): 395.

————. "The Public Service: Smallpox—Foreign." *JAMA* (February 23, 1901): 536.

————. "The Public Service: Smallpox—Foreign." *JAMA* (April 1901): 1082.

————. "The Public Service: Cholera." *JAMA* (November 1, 1902): 1150, 1358.

————. "The Sanitary Hygiene of the Japanese Army." *JAMA* (March 10, 1906): 746–48.

John, Griffith. 권즁회기 *Kwŏnjung hoegae* [Exhortation to Repentance]. Translated and edited by Horace G. Underwood. Seoul: Chŏngdong Presbyterian Church, 1891.

————. 복음대지 *Pokŭm taeji* [Great Themes of the Gospels]. Translated by Horace G. Underwood. Seoul: Korean Religious Tract Society, 1894.

————. 구셰진쥬 *Kusye jinjyu* [The True Savior]. Translated by William M. Baird. Seoul: Korean Religious Tract Society, 1895.

————. 진리독편삼ᄌᆞ경 *Chilli p'yŏndog samjagŏng* [Easy Three Characters]. Translated and adapted by S. A. Moffett. Seoul: Korean Religious Tract Society, 1908.

Jones, George Heber. "Bishop Fowler in Korea." *GAL* 14 (1889): 32–33.

————. "The Religious Development of Korea." *GAL* (September 1891): 415–17.

————. "The People of Korea." *GAL* (October 1892): 464–66.

————. *The Religious Awakening of Korea*. New York: Board of Foreign Missions of the Methodist Episcopal Church, 1908.

Jones, Margaret J. B. 초학언문 *Ch'ohak ŏnmun* [A Korean Primer]. Seoul: Korean Religious Tract Society, 1895.

————. "The Korean Bride." *KR* 2 (1895): 54.

Jordan, David K. "The Glyphomancy Factor: Observations on Chinese Conversion." In *Conversion to Christianity: Historical and Anthropological Perspectives on a Great Tradition*, edited by Robert W. Hefner, 285–303. Berkeley: University of California Press, 1993.

JRAS (Journal of the Royal Asiatic Society of Great Britain and Ireland). "Obituary Notice: Dr. E. B. Landis." *JRAS* (1898): 919.

Jung Jae-Hoon 정재훈. "Meeting the World through Eighteenth-Century *Yŏnhaeng*." *Seoul Journal of Korean Studies* 23, no. 1 (2010): 51–69.

Junkin, William M. "Notes from Korea." *Missionary* 27 (1894): 439.

————. "The Tong Hak." *KR* 2 (1895): 56–60.

————. "The Daily Difficulties That Meet the Missionary in Korea." *Missionary* 30 (1897): 465.

KACMEC (The Korea Annual Conference of the Methodist Episcopal Church). *Official Minutes*. Seoul: Methodist Publishing House, 1905–1915.

Kang Hŭinam 강희남. "운아삽(雲亞翣)이 가지는 意義 Unasab i kajinŭn ŭiŭi" [The Meaning of the Funeral Fans "Unasap"]. *Kidoggyo sasang* 12, no. 7 (1968): 144–46.

Kaplan, Steven, ed. *Indigenous Responses to Western Christianity*. New York: New York University Press, 1995.

Kearns, Carl E. "One Year in Syen Chun Station." *AH* 11 (1905): 602.

Kendall, Laurel. *Shamans, Housewives, and Other Restless Spirits: Women in Korean Ritual Life*. Honolulu: University of Hawaii Press, 1985.

Kenmure, Alexander. "The Ten Best Christian Books in Chinese." *CR* (July 1893): 340.

————. Letter to James H. Ritson, June 21, 1901. BFBSA, CBFBS.

————. Letter to James H. Ritson, March 27, 1903. BFBSA, CBFBS.

————. Letter to John Sharp, October 16, 1903. BFBSA, CBFBS.

Kennan, George. "The Japanese Red Cross." *Outlook* (September–December 1904): 27–36.

Keong Tow-yung. "理雅各與基督教至高神譯名之爭 James Legge and the Christian Term Question." *Tsing Hua Journal of Chinese Studies* 37, no. 2 (2007): 467–89.

KF (*Korea Field*). "The Famine Wolf in Korea." *KF* (May 1902): 33.

————. "Country Evangelistic Work: From Annual Report of Pyeng Yang Station, September 1904." *KF* (November 1904): 217.

————. "Progress at the Academy: From Personal Report of Dr. W. M. Baird, September 1904." *KF* (November 1904): 229.

————. "A Reminiscence of a Year: Personal Report of Rev. Sharp, July 1905." *KF* (August 1905): 269.

KH (크리스도인회보 *Kǔrisǔdoin Hoebo* [Korean *Christian Advocate*]). "론셜텬졔론 Ronsyŏl t'yŏnjyŏron" [Editorial: On the Heavenly Ruler]. *KH*, February 10, 1897.

————. "회즁신문 Hoejyung sinmun" [Congregational News]. *KH*, March 3, 1897.

————. "만물의근본 Manmul ǔi kǔnbon" [The Origin of All Things]. *KH*, March 3, 10, and 17, 1897.

————. "연셜 Yŏnsyŏ" [Editorial: A Speech]. *KH*, March 31, 1897.

————. "우상론 Usyangnon" [Editorial: On Idols]. *KH*, April 14, 1897.

————. "령혼론 Ryŏnghon ron" [Editorial: On Human Soul]. *KH*, April 21, 1897.

————. "천당지옥론 Ch'yŏndang tiok ron" [On Heaven and Hell]. *KH*, April 28, 1897.

————. "미력의비흠이라 Miryŏg ǔi paeham ira" [Destroying Maitreya Statues]. *KH*, July 21, 1897.

————. "회즁신문 Hoejyung sinmun" [Congregational News]. *KH*, August 11, 1897.

————. "대죠션뎨일경ᄉ Tae Chyosyŏn tyeil kyŏngsa" [The Greatest Occasion of the Great Korea]. *KH*, October 14, 1897.

————. "독립경축회 Tongnip kyŏngch'yukhoe" [The Celebration of Independence of Korea]. *KH*, November 24, 1897.

————. "졍동새회당에셔힝흔일 Chŏngdongsaehoedangesyŏhaenghanil" [Programs of the New Chŏngdong Church]. *KH*, December 29, 1897.

————. "교우노병션씨열람흔일 Kyou No Pyŏngsyŏnssi yŏllamhan il" [No Pyŏngsŏn's Trip to North]. *KH*, October 5, 1898.

————. "통샹교회의게흔편지 T'ongsyang kyohoe ege han p'yŏnji" [A Bishop's General Letter to the Churches]. *KH*, November 2, 1898.

———. "성탄일경축 Sŏngt'anil kyŏngch'uk" [Celebration of Christmas]. *KH*, December 28, 1898.

———. "인천담방리교회성탄일경축 Incheon Tambangni Kyohoe sŏngt'anil kyŏngch'uk" [Celebration of Christmas at Incheon Tambangni Church]. *KH*, January 4, 1899.

———. "강화교항동교회성탄일경축 Knaghwa Kyohangdong Kyohoe sŏngt'anil kyŏngch'uk" [Celebration of Christmas at Kanghwa Kyohangdong Church]. *KH*, January 4, 1899.

———. "부평 굴재회당에서성탄일경축 Pup'yŏng Kuljae Hoedang esŏ sŏngt'anil kyŏngch'uk" [Celebration of Christmas at Pup'yŏng Kulchae Church]. *KH*, January 4, 1899.

———. "희한흔일 Hŭihanhan il" [A Rare Thing]. *KH*, May 23, 1900.

Kil Chingyŏng 길진경. 영계 길선주 *Yŏnggye Kil Sŏnju*. Seoul: Chongno sŏjŏk, 1980.

Kilgour, Robert. Letter to Hugh Miller, August 9, 1904. BFBSA, CBFBS.

———. "R. Kilgour's Interview with Mr. Hugh Miller, January 22, 1917." BFBSA, CBFBS.

Kim Chaejun 김재준. "대한기독교장로회의 역사적 의의 Taehan Kidoggyo Changnohoe ŭi yŏksa chŏk ŭiŭi" [The Historical Meaning of the Presbyterian Church in the Republic of Korea]. *Sipchagun* 25 (1956): 35–37.

Kim Chinso 김진소. "신유박해 당시 서양 선박 청원의 특성 Sinyu pakhae tangsi sŏyang sŏnbak ch'ŏngwŏn ŭi t'ŭksŏng" [Characteristics of the Request of Western Ships at the Time of the 1801 Persecution]. In 신유박해와 황사영 백서 사건 *Sinyu pakhae wa Hwang Sayŏng paeksŏ sagŏn* [The Persecution and the Incident of Hwang's Silk Letter in 1801], 127–36. Seoul: Han'guk sungypsa hyŏn'yang wiwonhoe, 2003.

Kim Chongsuh 김종서. "Early Western Studies of Korean Religions." In *Korean Studies New Pacific Currents*, edited by Suh Dae-Sook, 141–57. Honolulu: Hawaii University Press, 1994.

———. 서양인의 한국 종교 연구 *Sŏyangin ŭi Han'guk chonggyo yŏngu* [Western Studies of Korean Religions]. Seoul: Seoul National University Press, 2006.

Kim Hoil 김호일. "참사랑홀것 Ch'am sarang hal kŏt" [Love Truly]. *Yesugyo sinbo*, January 15, 1908.

Kim Hwasik 김화식. "김종섭 목사 약전 Kim Chongsŏp moksa yakchŏn" [A Short Biography of Rev. Kim Chongsŏp]. *Sinang Segye* (June 1940): 22–37.

Kim Insŏ 김인서. "朝鮮初代教會의 偉傑 靈溪先生 小傳 上 Chosŏn

ch'odae kyohoe ŭi wigŏl Yŏnggye sŏnsaeng sojŏn sang" [A Short Biography of *Kil Sŏnju*, a Hero of the Early Korean Church]. 신학지남 *Sinhak Chinam* (November 1931): 35–40.

Kim In Soo 김인수. *Protestants and the Formation of Modern Korean Nationalism, 1885–1920: A Study of the Contributions of Horace G. Underwood and Sun Chu Kil*. New York: Peter Lang, 1996.

Kim Ku 김구. 백범일지 *Paekpŏm ilchi* [Journal of Kim Ku]. Translated by Yi Mahn-yol. Seoul: Yŏkminsa, 1997.

———. *Paekpŏm ilch: Autobiography of Kim Ku*. Translated by Lee Jongsoo. Lanham, Md.: University Press of America, 2000.

Kim Kyoungjae 김경재. *Christianity and the Encounter of Asian Religions: Method of Correlation, Fusion of Horizons, and Paradigm Shifts in the Korean Grafting Process*. Zoetermeer, Netherlands: Uitgeverji Boekencentrum, 1995.

Kim Nakp'il 김낙필. "해동전도록에 나타난 도교사상 Haedong chndorog e nat'anan Togyo sasang" [Daoist Thought in *The History of Daoism in Korea*]. In *Togyo wa Han'guk sasang* [Daoism and Korean Thought]. Seoul: Pŏmyangsa, 1987.

———. "조선 후기 민간 도교의 윤리 사상 Chosŏn hugi mingan todyo ŭi yulli sasang" [Ethical Thought of Popular Daoism in the Late Chosŏn]. In 한국도교의 현대적 조명 *Han'guk togyo ŭi hyŏndaejŏk chomyŏng* [Modern Understanding of Korean Daoism], edited by Han'guk togyo sasang yŏnguhoe, 355–72. Seoul: Asea munhwasa, 1992.

———. 조선시대 내단 사상 *Chosŏn sidae nadan sasang* [Thought of Inner Alchemy in Chosŏn]. Seoul: Hangilsa, 2000.

Kim Okhŭi 김옥희. 광암 이벽의 서학사상 *Kwang'am Yi Pyŏk ŭi sŏhak sasang* [Yi Pyŏk's Thought of Roman Catholicism]. Seoul: Kat'olik ch'ulp'ansa, 1979.

Kim Wŏngŭn 김원근. "하늘 벼슬이 사람의 벼슬보다 나음 Hanal pyŏsŭr i saram ŭi pyŏsŭl boda naŭm" [Heavenly Positions of the Church Are Better Than Human Positions of the Government]. *KS*, February 8, 1906.

Kim Wonmo 김원모, ed. and trans. 알렌 일기 *Allen ilgi: Horace Newton Allen Diary*. Seoul: Dankook University Press, 1991.

Kim Yunseong 김윤성. "Protestant Missions as Cultural Imperialism in Early Modern Korea: Hegemony and Its Discontents." *Korea Journal* 39, no. 4 (1999): 205–34.

KMF (Korea Mission Field). "A Great Awakening." *KMF* (January 1906): 51.

——. "Revival at Ewa." *KMF* (May 1906): 133.

——. "Recent Work of the Holy Spirit in Seoul." *KMF* 3 (1907): 41.

——. "What Prominent Men Have Said." *KMF* 3 (1907): 158–59.

——. "Notes from the Stations." *KMF* (January 1910): 8.

——. "Kil Moxa." *KMF* (April 1910): 118.

——. "Editorial." *KMF* (July 1924): 133.

KMMEC (Korea Mission of the Methodist Episcopal Church). *Official Minutes of the Annual Meeting.* Seoul, 1893–1910.

KMMECS (Korea Mission of the Methodist Episcopal Church, South). *Minutes of the Annual Meeting.* Seoul, 1899–1910.

KMPCUSA (Korea Mission of the Presbyterian Church of the USA). *Minutes and Reports of the Annual Meeting.* Seoul: KMPCUSA, 1893–1915.

——. *Quarto Centennial Papers.* Pyongyang: KMPCUSA, 1909.

——. *Fiftieth Anniversary Celebration.* Seoul: YMCA Press, 1934.

Kojong Sillok 高宗實錄. Vol. 37, July 18, 1898.

Koons, E. Wade. Letter to A. J. Brown, February 16, 1904. PHS, CRKM, reel 280.

——. "The Power of Christ Demonstrated." *KMF* (July 1910): 181–82.

KR (Korean Repository). "Buddhist Chants and Processions." *KR* 2 (1895): 125.

——. "Christian Missions and Social Progress." *KR* 5 (1898): 68–69.

KRTS (Korean Religious Tract Society). *Annual Reports.* Seoul: KRTS, 1894–1916.

KRv (Korea Review). "Editorial Comment." *KRv* (September 1902): 406–7.

——. "News Calendar." *KRv* (September 1902): 409–15.

——. "A Leaf from Korean Astrology." *KRv* (November 1902): 491.

——. "A Leaf from Korean Astrology." *KRv* (January 1903): 16.

——. "Our Training Class System: From Annual Report of Pyeng Yang Station, September, 1904." *KRv* (February 1905): 234.

KS (그리스도신문 *Kŭrisŭdo Sinmun* [*Christian News*]). "교회통신 Kyohoe t'ongsin" [Church News]. *KS*, April 8, 1897.

——. "충효론 Ch'unghyoron" [Filial Piety and Loyalty]. *KS*, May 27, 1897.

——. "홍문서골교회 Hongmunsyŏgol Kyohoe" [Hongmunsu-gol Church]. *KS*, July 8, 1897.

——. "우샹의허흔론Usyang ŭi hŏhan ron" [Emptiness of Idols]. *KS*, July 29 and August 6, 1897.

———. "론셜: 세가지요긴흔말 Ronsyŏl: Se gaji yoginhan mal" [Editorial: Three Important Words]. *KS*, September 9 and 16, 1897.

———. "론셜 Ronsyŏl" [Editorial]. *KS*, October 14, 1897.

———. "론셜 Ronsyŏl" [Editorial]. *KS*, October 28, 1897.

———. "교회통신 Kyohoe t'ongsin" [Church News]. *KS*, December 9, 1897.

———. "리치의쇼연흔론 Rich'I ŭi syoyŏnhan ron" [The Reason of the Principle]. *KS*, December 16, 1897.

———. "셰시변쳔흐는론 Syesae pyŏnch'ŏnhanan ron" [Change of the Things]. *KS*, December 31, 1897.

———. "셩경강론회 Syŏnggyŏng kangnonhoe" [Bible Study Class]. *KS*, March 10, 1898.

———. "교회통신 Kyohoe t'ongsin" [Church News]. *KS*, March 31, 1898.

———. "교회통신 Kyohoe t'ongsin" [Church News]. *KS*, May 5, 1898.

———. "큰화를자구홈 K'ŭn hwa rŭl chaguham" [Incurring Great Disaster]. *KS*, November 24, 1898.

———. "량교가표리가되는론 Ryanggyo ga p'yori ga toenan ron" [Confucianism and Christianity Are Two Sides of the Coin]. *KS*, December 15, 1898.

———. "찬미 Ch'anmi" [Praising]. *KS*, May 9, 1901.

———. "깃대의의논 Kittae ŭi ŭinon" [Discussion on the Flagpole]. *KS*, May 9, 1901.

———. "교회는참이치를반포흐는전도실이지세상일의논흐는곳이아니다 Kyohoe nŭn ch'am ich'i rŭl panp'o hanŭn chŏndosil iji sesamg il ŭnon hanŭn kos i anida" [Church Is Not a Place to Discuss Secular Things but to Preach the True Doctrines]. *KS*, August 1, 1901.

———. "론셜 Ronsyŏl" [Editorial]. *KS*, August 8, 1901.

———. "장례문답 Changnye mundap" [Questions and Answers on the Funeral]. *KS*, August 15, 1901.

———. "교회와정부사이의교제홀몇가지조건 Kyohoe wa chŏngbu saiŭi kyojyehal myŏk kaji chogŏn" [Several Conditions Regarding the Relationship between Church and State]. *KS*, October 3, 1901.

———. "수원상구면이물이교회 Suwŏn Sanggumyŏn Imuri Kyohoe" [Imuri Church, Sanggu-myŏn, Suwŏn]. *KS*, January 2, 1902.

———. "믿음과찬미와깃대 Midŭm gwa ch'anmi wa kitae" [Faith, Hymn Singing, and Flag Poles]. *KS*, March 6, 1902.

———. "우상에졔물을먹지말것 Usang e chyemur ŭl mŏkchi mal kŏt" [Don't Eat Food Offered to Idols]. *KS*, September 13, 1906.

———. "론셜 Ronsyŏl" [Editorial]. *KS*, September 20, 1906.

Kŭrisŭdokyo wa kyŏre munwha yŏnguhoe 그리스도교와 겨례문화연구회. 그리스도교와 겨례문화 *Kŭrisŭdokyo wa kyŏre munwha* [Christianity and Korean Culture]. Seoul: Kidoggyomunsa, 1987.

Kwŏn Minsin 권민신. "송도교우의밋음 Songdo kyo'u ŭi mitŭm" [The Faith of a Christian in Songdo]. *SW* 3 (1904): 439.

Ladd, George Trumbull. *In Korea with Marquis Ito*. New York: Scribner, 1908.

———. "Economic and Social Change in Korea." *Journal of Race Development* 1 (1910): 248–53.

Lambuth, David K. "Korean Devils and Christian Missionaries." *Independent*, August 1, 1907, 287–88.

Lambuth, James W. "Standard of Admission to Full Church Membership." In GCPMC, *RGC*, 1878, 241–46.

Lancashire, Douglas, and Peter Kuo-chen Hu. "Introduction. *The True Meaning of the Lord of Heaven (T'ien-chu Shih-I)*. By Matteo Ricci S.J." In *Jesuit Primary Sources in English Translations*, no. 6, edited by Edward J. Malatesta, 3–53. St. Louis: Institute of Jesuit Sources, 1985.

Landis, Eli Barr. "Notes on the Exorcism of Spirits in Korea." *Chinese Review* 21, no. 6 (1895): 399–404.

———. "Mourning and Burial Rites of Korea." *Journal of the Anthropological Institute* (May 1896): 340–61.

———. "Notes from the Korean Pharmacopoea." *China Review* 22, no. 3 (1896): 578–88.

———. "A Royal Funeral." *KR* (April 1897): 161.

———. "The Capping Ceremony of Korea." *Journal of the Anthropological Institute* (May 1898): 525–31.

Latourette, Kenneth Scott. *A History of the Expansion of Christianity*. 7 vols. New York: Harper, 1937–1941.

Lawrence, Edward A. "Missions in Korea." *GAL* 12 (1887): 273.

———. *Modern Missions in the East: Their Methods, Successes, and Limitations*. New York: Harper, 1895.

———. *Introduction to the Study of Foreign Missions*. New York: Student Volunteer Movement, 1901.

Lee Chull 이철. "Social Sources of the Rapid Growth of the Christian Church in Northwest Korea: 1895–1910." Ph.D. diss., Boston University, 1997.

Lee, Graham. "General Report of the Pyeng Yang Station for 1894." PHS, CRKM, reel 180.

———. "A Visit to the Battle Field of Pyeng Yang." *KR* 2 (1895): 14.

———. "Korean Christians." *MRW* (November 1896): 866.

———. Letter to Samuel A. Moffett, February 20, 1897. PTSL, Moffett Collection.

Lee Jung Young 이정용. *Korean Shamanistic Rituals*. New York: Mouton, 1981.

Lee Kwang Kyu 이광규. "The Concept of Ancestors and Ancestor Worship in Korea." *Asian Folklore Studies* 43 (1984): 199–214.

Legge, James. *An Argument for Shangte as the Proper Rendering of the Words Elohim and Theos in the Chinese Language with Strictures on the Essay of Bishop Boone in Favour of the Term Shin*. Hong Kong: Hong Kong Register Office, 1850.

———. *The Notions of the Chinese Concerning God and Spirits: With an Examination of the Defense of an Essay, on the Proper Rendering of the Words of Elohim and Theos, into the Chinese Language*. Hong Kong: Hong Kong Register Office, 1852.

———. *The Land of Sinim: A Sermon Preached in the Tabernacle, Moorfields, at the Sixty-Fifth Anniversary of the London Missionary Society*. London: John Snow, 1859.

———. *Confucianism in Relation with Christianity*. Shanghai: Kelly & Walsh, 1877.

———. *Religions of China: Confucianism and Taoism Described and Compared with Christianity*. New York: Revell, 1880.

———. *The Nestorian Monument of Hsi-an Fu in Shen-hsi, China*. London: Trubner, 1888.

Lew Young Ick 류영익. "Late Nineteenth-Century Korean Reformers' Receptivity to Protestantism: The Case of Six Leaders of the 1880s and 1890s Reform Movements." *Asian Culture* 4 (1988): 153–96.

Lewis, Ella A. "A Holocaust of Fetishes." *KMF* (May 1906): 134–35.

Loomis, Henry. "Rijutei, the Corean Convert." *Missionary Herald* (December 1883): 481–83.

———. Letter to Edward W. Gilman, September 6, 1892. ABS Archives, Correspondence of Japan Agency.

Lowell, Percival. *Chosen: The Land of the Morning Calm*. London: Trubner, 1886.

Lü Zongli. *Power of the Words: Chen Prophecy in Chinese Politics AD 265–618*. Oxford: Peter Lang, 2003.

———. "Apocrypha in Early Medieval Chinese Literature." *Chinese Literature: Essays, Articles, Reviews* 30 (2008): 93–101.

Machen, J. Gresham. *Christianity and Liberalism*. Grand Rapids: Eerdmans, 1956.

MacIntyre, John. "Baptism at Moukden, Haichang, and Seaport." *UPMR* (January 1, 1880): 14–15.

———. "Mr. MacIntyre's Report." *UPMR* (July 1, 1880): 278–79.

Maclay, Robert S. *Life among the Chinese.* New York: Carlton & Porter, 1861.

———. "Corea." *Missionary Herald* 80 (1884): 523.

MacRae, Edith F. "For Thine Is the Power." *KMF* 2 (1906): 74.

MacRae, Helen F. *A Tiger on Dragon Mountain: The Life of Rev. Duncan M. MacRae, D. D.* Charlottetown, Canada: A. James Haslam, Q. C., 1993.

Maeil Sinbo 每日申報. "弓弓乙乙 眩惑用怪印 Kunggung ŭlŭl hyŏnhokyong koein" [Kunggung ŭlŭl: A Bewildering and Strange Seal]. *Maeil Sinbo*, April 13, 1937.

Marsden, George M. *Religions and American Culture.* San Diego, Calif.: Harcourt, 1990.

Martin, William Alexander Parsons. 天道溯源 *Tiandao suyuan* [Evidence of Christianity]. Ningbo: Huahua shuju, 1854.

———. "Is Buddhism a Preparation for Christianity?" *CR* 20 (May 1889): 193–203.

———. "Ancestral Worship: A Plea for Toleration." In GCPMC, *RGC*, 1890, 619–31.

———. 삼요록 *Samyorok* [Three Principles]. Translated by H. G. Underwood. Seoul: Korean Religious Tract Society, 1894.

Mateer, Calvin W. *A Review of Methods of Mission Work.* Shanghai: American Presbyterian Mission Press, 1900.

MC (Morning Calm). "The Bishop's Letter." *MC* 42 (1893): 174–75.

———. "The Bishop's Letter." *MC* 46 (1897): 37–38.

———. "Lumen ad Revelationem Gentium." *MC* 46 (1897): 42–44.

McCartee, Divie B. 진리이지 *Chilli iji* [Easy Introduction to Christian Doctrine]. Translated by H. G. Underwood. Seoul: Korean Religious Tract Society, 1895.

McCully, Elizabeth A. *A Corn of Wheat or the Life of Rev. W.J. McKenzie of Korea.* Toronto: Westminster, 1904.

McGill, William B. 구셰론 *Kusye yoŏn* [Essential of the World's Salvation]. Seoul: Trilingual Press, 1895.

McKenzie, Frederick Arthur. *The Unveiled East.* London: Hutchinson, 1907.

———. *The Tragedy of Korea.* London: Soughton, 1908.

Medhurst, Walter Henry. *A Dissertation on the Theology of Chinese with a View to the Elucidation of the Most Appropriate Term for*

Expressing the Deity, in the Chinese Language. Shanghai: American Presbyterian Mission Press, 1847.

———. *An Enquiry into the Proper Mode of Rendering the Word God in Translating the Sacred Scriptures into the Chinese Language.* Shanghai: Mission Press, 1848.

———. 清明掃墓之論 *Qingming saomu zhilun* [On Feast of Tombs]. Xinjiapo: Jian xia shu yuan, 1854.

Miller, Frederick S. Letter to William Wright, May 5, 1895. BFBSA, CBFBS. In Oak, *Sources of Korean Christianity*, 281.

Miller, Hugh. Letter to the Secretaries of the Bible Societies, May 3, 1906. BFBSA, CBFBS.

Miller, Lula A. "The Conversion of a Sorceress." *KMF* 2 (1906): 65.

Min Kyŏngbae 민경배. "韓國 初代教會와 西歐化의 問題 Han'guk ch'odae kyohoe wa sŏguhwa ŭi munje" [Early Korean Church and the Problem of Westernization]. *Kidoggyo Sasang* 14 (1971): 44–50.

———. 韓國 民族教會 形成史 *Han'guk minjok kyohoe hyŏngsŏng saron* [A Study on the Formation of the Korean National Church]. Seoul: Yonsei University Press, 1974.

———. 教會와 民族 *Kyohoe wa minjok* [The Korean Church and the Nation]. Seoul: Christian Literature Society of Korea, 1981.

———. 한국기독교회사 *Han'guk kidoggyohoe sa* [A History of the Korean Church]. Seoul: Korean Christian Press, 1984.

———. 大韓예수教長老會百年史 *Taehan Yesugyo Changnohoe paeknyŏn sa* [Centennial History of the Presbyterian Church of Korea]. Seoul: Assembly of the Presbyterian Church of Korea, 1984.

———. 韓國基督教 社會運動史 *Han'guk Kidoggyo sahoe undongsa* [A History of the Social Movement of Korean Christianity]. Seoul: Christian Literature Society of Korea, 1990.

———. 韓國基督教會史 *Han'guk Kidok kyohoe sa* [A History of Korean Christian Church]. Seoul: Yonsei University Press, 1994.

Missionary. "Korea." *Missionary* (May 1910): 212–13.

Moffett, Samuel Austin. Letter to F. F. Ellinwood, October 20, 1890. PHS, CRKM, reel 175.

———. "Evangelism in Korea." *GAL* 17 (1892): 446.

———. Letter to F. F. Ellinwood, June 6, 1893. PHS, CRKM, reel 176.

———. "Report of Work in Pyeng An Province: Pyeng Yang, Eui Ju, Kou Syeng, Oct. 1893." PHS, CRKM, reel 176.

———. Letter to F. F. Ellinwood, January 12, 1894. PHS, CRKM, reel 178.

———. "Life at a Korean Outpost." *CHA* 8 (1894): 374.

————. "The Transformation of Korea." *CHA* (August 1895): 136–37.

————. "Evangelistic Work in Pyengyang and Vicinity, Pyengyang Station, October 1895." PHS, CRKM, reel 178.

————. "An Educated Ministry in Korea." In *Men and the Modern Missionary Enterprise*, 139–40. Chicago: Winona, 1907.

Moffett, Samuel Austin, and Ch'oe Myŏng'o. 구셰론 *Kusyeron* [Discourse on Salvation]. Seoul: Trilingual Press, 1895.

Moffett, Samuel Hugh. *The Christians of Korea*. New York: Friendship Press, 1957.

————. "The Life and Thought of Samuel Austin Moffett, His Children's Memories." In *The Centennial Lecture of Samuel A. Moffett's Arrival in Korea*, 17–23. Seoul: Presbyterian Theological College and Seminary, 1990.

Moody Bible Institute. *The Coming and Kingdom of Christ: A Stenographic Report of the Prophetic Bible Conference Held at the Moody Bible Institute of Chicago, February 24–27, 1914*. Chicago: Bible Institute Colportage Association, 1914.

Moore, David H. "Our Mission in Beautiful, Hospitable Korea." *GAL* (September 1901): 407.

Moore, John Z. "The Vision and the Task." *KMF* 2 (1906): 108.

————. "The Great Revival Year." *KMF* 3 (1907): 118.

————. "A Changed Life." *KMF* 3 (1907): 159.

————. "The Fullness of the Gospel." *KMF* 3 (1907): 178.

Moore, Samuel F. "Welcome to Korea." *CHA* 7 (1893): 33.

————. Letter to F. F. Ellinwood, March 22, 1893. PHS, CRKM, reel 176.

————. "Report of Session, 1893." PHS, CRKM, reel 176.

————. "Personal Annual Report, 1896." PHS, CRKM, reel 179.

————. "The Butchers of Korea." *KR* 5 (1898): 127–32.

————. "A Gospel Sermon Preached by a Korean Butcher." *CHA* 12 (1898): 115–16.

————. "Report of S. F. Moore, 1898." PHS, CRKM, reel 180.

————. Letter to F. F. Ellinwood, May 27, 1899. PHS, CRKM, reel 179.

Moorhead, James H. "Searching for the Millennium in America." *Princeton Seminary Bulletin* 9 (1988): 17–33.

Moose, J. Robert. "Sacrifice to the Dead." *KM* 1 (1904): 15.

————. *Village Life in Korea*. Nashville, Tenn.: Publishing House of the Methodist Episcopal Church, South, 1911.

Moreau, A. Scott, ed. *Evangelical Dictionary of World Mission*. Grand Rapids: Baker Books, 2000.

MRW (*Missionary Review of the World*). "Corea, the Hermit Nation." *MRW* 6, no. 6 (1883): 409–21.

————. "Korea, the Hermit Nation." *MRW* 12 (1889): 655.

————. "Korea—The Changes of Seven Years." *MRW* (February 1911): 144.

MSMEC (Missionary Society of the Methodist Episcopal Church). *Annual Report of the Missionary Society of the Methodist Episcopal Church.* New York: MSMEC, 1885–1912.

MSMECS (Missionary Society of the Methodist Episcopal Church, South). *Annual Reports of the Missionary Society.* Nashville, Tenn.: MSMECS, 1896–1912.

Mungello, D. E. *Curious Land: Jesuit Accommodation and the Origins of Sinilogy.* Honolulu: University of Hawaii, 1989.

————. *The Great Encounter of China and the West, 1500–1800.* Lanham, Md.: Rowman & Littlefield, 1999.

Murayama Chijun 村山智順. 朝鮮의 占卜과 豫言 *Chosŏn ŭi chŏmbok kwa yeŏn* [Divination and Prophecy of Chosŏn]. Translated by Kim Hŭigyŏng. Seoul: Tongmunsŏn, 1990.

Mutel, Gustave Chares Marie. 뮈텔주교일기 4 (1906–1910) *Mutel Chugyo ilgi* [Journal of de Mgr. Mutel]. Vol. 4. Seoul: Han'guk Kyohoesa Yŏn'guso, 1998.

Myers, Mamie D. "Poktaigee." *WMA* (December 1909): 269–70.

National Bible Society of Scotland. *Annual Reports of the National Bible Society of Scotland.* Edinburgh: National Bible Society of Scotland, 1880–1911.

Nevius, Helen S. Coan. *Our Life in China.* New York: Robert Carter & Brothers, 1876.

————. 예수교문답 *Yesugyo mundap* [Christian Catechism]. Translated by Horace G. Underwood. Seoul: Korean Religious Tract Society, 1893.

————. *The Life of John Livingston Nevius: For Forty Years a Missionary in China.* New York: Revell, 1895.

Nevius, John L. 祀先辨謬 *Sixian bianmiu* [Errors of Ancestor Worship]. Ningbo, 1859.

————. 天路指南 *Tianlu zhinan* [Guide to the Heavenly Way]. Shanghai: Presbyterian Mission Press, 1861.

————. *China and the Chinese.* New York: Harper, 1869.

————. *The Planting and Development of Missionary Churches.* Shanghai: American Presbyterian Printing House, 1889.

————. 위원입교인규됴 *Wi wŏnip kyoin kyudyo* [Catechism for the

Candidates for Baptism]. Translated by Samuel A. Moffett. Seoul: Trilingual Press, 1895.

————. *Demon Possession and Allied Themes.* New York: Revell, 1896.

Noble, Martha H., ed. *Journals of Mattie W. Noble, 1892–1934.* Seoul: Institute for Korean Church History, 1993.

Noble, Mattie Wilcox. "After the Cholera—Native Testimonies in a Korean Prayer Meeting." *WMF* (January 1903): 4.

————, comp. and trans. *Victorious Lives of Early Christians in Korea.* Seoul: Christian Literature Society Korea, 1927.

Noble, William A. *Ewa: A Tale of Korea.* New York: Eaton & Mains, 1906.

————. "Korean Decadence." *KMF* 2 (1906): 176.

————. "George Heber Jones: An Appreciation." *KMF* (June 1919): 146.

Noble, William A., and G. Heber Jones. *The Religious Awakening of Korea.* New York: Board of Foreign Missions of the Methodist Episcopal Church, 1908.

North China Herald, ed. *The Anti-Foreign Riots in China in 1891.* Shanghai: North China Herald Press, 1892.

Noyes, George C. "Review of *Corea, the Hermit Nation.*" *Dial* 3 (1882): 167.

Oak, Sung-Deuk 옥성득. "North American Missionaries' Understanding of the *Tan'gun* and *Kija* Myths of Korea." *Acta Koreana* 5, no. 1 (2002): 51–73.

————. *Sources of Korean Christianity.* Rev. ed. Seoul: Institute for Korean Church History, 2004.

————. "The Azusa Street Revival, 1906–1909: Its Characteristics and Comparison with the 1907 Great Revival in Korea." In *Protestant Revivals in the 20th Century and Pyongyang Great Awakening Movement,* edited by Won-mo Suh, 353–411. Seoul: Presbyterian College and Theological Seminary, 2005.

————. "Edinburgh 1910, Fulfillment Theory, and Missionaries in China and Korea." *Journal of Asian and Asian American Theology* 9 (2009): 29–51.

————. "Competing Chinese Names for God: The Chinese Term Question and Its Influence upon Korea," *Journal of Korean Religions* 3, no. 2 (2012): 89–115.

————. "Major Protestant Revivals in Korea, 1903–1935." *Studies of World Christianity* 18, no. 3 (2012): 269–90.

Oak Sung-Deuk, and Yi Mahnyol. 대한성서공회사 *Taehan sŏngsŏ*

konghoesa [A History of the Korean Bible Society]. 2 vols. Seoul: Korean Bible Society, 1993, 1994.

―――. *Documents of Korean Bible Society. Vol. 1. Correspondence of John Ross and Correspondence of Henry Loomis, 1880–1911.* Seoul: Korean Bible Society, 2004.

―――. *Horace Grant Underwood and Lillias Horton Underwood Papers.* 5 vols. Seoul: Yonsei University Press, 2005–2010.

―――. *Documents of Korean Bible Society. Vol. II. Correspondence of Alexander Kenmure, 1900–1905.* Seoul: Korean Bible Society, 2006.

Oh Seon-young 오선영. "찬송가의 번역과 근대 초기 시가의 변화 Ch'ansongga ŭi pŏnyŏk kwa kŭndae ch'ogi siga ŭi pyŏnhwa" [The Translation of the Hymns and the Change in the Metrics of Korean Poems in Early Modern Korea]. *Han'guk Munhak Iron kwa Pip'yŏng* 13, no. 1 (2009): 143–210.

Ohlinger, Franklin. "How Far Should Christians Be Required to Abandon Native Customs?" In GCPMC, *RGC*, 1890, 603–9.

―――. "Buddhism in Korean History and Language." *KR* 1 (1892): 107–8.

―――. *Thoughts, Words, Deeds and Other Sermons.* Seoul: Trilingual Press, 1893.

―――. "Response to the Commission IV of the World Missionary Conference 1910." Typescript. New London, Conn.: Yale Divinity School Library, 1910.

Orr, James. "The Gospel in Corea." *UPMR* (June 2, 1890): 188.

Owen, Georgiana. "Burning of the Fetishes." *Missionary* 41 (1908): 133–34.

Paek Sŭngjong 백승종. "18 segi chŏnban sŏbuk chibang e ch'ulhyŏnhan Chŏnggam-nok" [The *Book of Chŏng Kam* Appeared in the Northwestern Provinces in the First Part of the Eighteenth Century]. 역사학보 *Yŏksahakpo* (September 1999): 99–124.

Paik, George L. 백낙준. *The History of Protestant Missions in Korea, 1832–1910.* Pyeng Yang: Union Christian College Press, 1929.

Paik Jong-Koe 백종구. *Constructing Christian Faith in Korea: The Earliest Protestant Mission and Ch'oe Pyŏng-hŏn.* Zoetemrmeer: Uitgeverij Boekencentrum, 1998.

―――. *Han'guk ch'ogi Kaesingyo sŏngyo undong kwa sŏngyo sinhak* [The Earliest Protestant Mission Movement and Mission Theology in Korea]. Seoul: Han'guk kyohoe sahak yŏn'guwŏn, 2002.

Pak Hyŏngnyong 박형룡. 교의신학 *Kyoŭi sinhak* [Dogmatic Theology]. Seoul: Ŭnsŏng munhwasa, 1964.

———. "이교에 대한 타협 문제 Igyo e taehan t'ahyŏp munje" [The Problem of Compromise with Heathenism]. *Sinhak Chinam* [Theological Review] 134 (1966): 3–8.

Pak Sech'ang 박세창. "인내로이김 Innae ro igŭim" [Victory with Patience]. *SW* 3 (1904): 341.

Palais, James B. "A Search for Korean Uniqueness." *Harvard Journal of Asiatic Studies* 55, no. 2 (1995): 414–18.

Palmer, Spencer J. *Korea and Christianity*. Seoul: Hollym Corporation, 1967.

Park Yong Gyu 박용규. "Korean Presbyterianism and Biblical Authority: The Role of Scripture in the Shaping of Korean Presbyterianism 1918–54." Ph.D. diss., Trinity Evangelical Divinity School, 1991.

Pearce, T. W. "Christianity in China, Native Heathen Opponents and Native Christian Defenders." *CR* 15 (1884): 457.

Pfister, Lauren F. "Discovering Monotheistic Metaphysics: The Exegetical Reflections of James Legge (1815–1897) and Lo Chung-fan (d. circa 1850)." In *Imagining Boundaries: Changing Confucian Doctrines, Texts, and Hermeneutics*, edited by Chow Kai-wing et al., 213–56. Albany: State University of New York Press, 1999.

———. *Striving for "The Whole Duty of Man": James Legge and the Scottish Protestant Encounter with China*. 2 vols. New York: Peter Lang, 2004.

Pierson, Arthur T. "Spiritual Movements of the Half Century." *MRW* (January 1898): 21.

"Power of the Word in Corea." *Quarterly Report of the NBSS* (October 1880): 633–34.

Preston, J. F. "The Sah Kyeng hoi." *Missionary* (November 1904): 546–47.

———. "A Notable Meeting." *KMF* (October 1906): 228.

Pyŏn Sŏnhwan 변선환. "타종교와 신학 T'ajonggyo wa sinhak" [Other Religions and Theology]. *Sinhak Sasang* 47 (1984): 695.

———. "Other Religions and Theology." *East Asian Journal of Theology* 3 (1985): 327–53.

Rawlinson, Frank. *Naturalization of Christianity in China: A Study of the Relation of Christian and Chinese Idealism and Life*. Shanghai: Presbyterian Mission Press, 1927.

———. *Chinese Ideas of the Supreme Being*. Shanghai: Presbyterian Mission Press, 1928.

Reid, Gilbert. "The Prospect in Corea." *FM* 43 (1884): 131–32.

Reinders, Eric. *Borrowed Gods and Foreign Bodies: Christian Missionaries Imagine Chinese Religion.* Berkeley: University of California Press, 2004.

Religious Tract Society. *The Annual Report.* London: RTS, 1870–1911.

Residency-General. *Recent Progress in Korea.* London: Bradbury, Agnew, 1910.

Reynolds, William D. "Diary, 1894–1895." William D. Reynolds Papers, Presbyterian Historical Center, Montreat, N.C.

———. "Enemies of the Cross in Korea." *Missionary* 32 (1899): 464–66.

Rhee Syngman 이승만. 독립졍신 *Tongnip chŏngsin* [The Spirit of Independence]. Los Angeles: T'aePyongyang chapchisa, 1910.

———. *The Spirit of Independence: A Primer for Democratic Reforms in Korea.* Translated by Han-Kyo Kim. 1904. Honolulu: University of Hawaii Press, 2000.

Rhodes, Harry A. "Presbyterian Theological Seminary." *KMF* 6 (1910): 149–51.

———. *History of the Korea Mission, Presbyterian Church, USA, 1884–1934.* Seoul: Presbyterian Church of Korea, Department of Education, 1934.

Ricci, Matteo. *China in the Sixteenth Century: The Journals of Matthew Ricci, 1583–1610.* Translated by Louis J. Gallagher. New York: Random House, 1953.

Ridel, F. C., ed. 한불ᄌ뎐 韓佛字典 *Hanbul chadyŏn: Dictionnaire Coréen-Français.* Yokohama: Levy, 1880.

Ritson, J. H. "It Is Jesus That We Want." *MRW* 32 (1909): 552–53.

Ro Kilmyung 노길명. "New Religions and Social Change in Modern Korea History." *Review of Korean Studies* 5, no. 1 (2002): 31–62.

Ro Pyŏngsŏn 노병선. 파혹진션론 *P'ahok chinsŏnnon* [Breaking Off Delusion and Proceeding to the Good: Introduction to Christianity]. Seoul: Korean Religious Tract Society, 1897.

———. "다시 사는 리치 Tasi sanan rich'i" [Truth of Resurrection]. *KH*, April 7, 1897.

———. "강화 사경회 졍경 Kanghwa sagyŏnghoe chŏnggyŏng" [A Bible Class at Kanghwa]. *SW* 5 (1907): 81.

Ro Taejun 노대준. "1907년 개신교 대부흥 운동의 역사적 성격 1907nyŏn Kaesingyo taebuhŭng undong ŭi yŏksajŏk sŏnggyŏk" [The Historical Nature of the Protestant Revival Movement in 1907]. *Han'guk Kidoggyosa yŏngu* 15–16 (1989): 14–15.

Robert, Dana L. " 'The Crisis of Missions': Premillennial Mission

Theory and the Origins of Independent Evangelical Missions." In *Earthen Vessels*, edited by Joel A. Carpenter and W. R. Shenk, 30–32. Grand Rapids: Eerdmans, 1990.

———. *American Women in Mission: A Social History of Their Thought and Practice*. Macon, Ga.: Mercer University Press, 1997.

———. *"Occupy Until I Come": A. T. Pierson and the Evangelization of the World*. Grand Rapids: Eerdmans, 2003.

Rockhill, William Woodville. *China's Intercourse with Korea from the XVth Century to 1895*. London: Luzac, 1905.

Ross, Andrew C. *A Vision Betrayed*. Maryknoll, N.Y.: Orbis, 1994.

Ross, Cyril. Letter to A. J. Brown, January 9, 1904. PHS, CRKM, reel 281.

———. "Personal Report of Rev. Cyril Ross, September 1903." *KF* (May 1904): 173–76.

Ross, John. "Visit to the Corean Gate." *CR* (May 1874): 347–54.

———. "Obstacles to the Gospel in China." *MRUPCS* (January 1877): 409–11.

———. *The Corean Primer: Being Lessons in Corean on All Ordinary Subjects, Transliterated on the Principles of the Mandarin Primer*. Shanghai: American Presbyterian Mission Press, 1877, 2nd ed., 1878.

———. "Manchuria Mission." *MRUPCS* (October 1, 1880): 333–34.

———. *The Manchus: Or, the Reigning Dynasty of China: Their Rise and Progress*. Paisley, Scotland: J. & R. Parlane, 1880.

———. *History of Corea: Ancient and Modern*. Paisley, Scotland: J&R Parlane, 1881.

———. 예수셩교문답 *Yesu syŏnggyo mundap* [Bible Catechism]. Shenyang, Manchuria: Mungwang sŏwŏn, 1881.

———. 예수셩교요령 *Yesu syŏnggyo yoryŏng* [Introduction to the New Testament]. Shenyang, Manchuria: Mungwang sŏwŏn, 1881.

———. *Korean Speech, with Grammar and Vocabulary*. Shanghai: Kelly & Walsh, 1882.

———. Letter to William Wright, March 24, 1882. In Oak, *Sources of Korean Christianity*, 35.

———. 예수셩교누가복음젼셔 *Yesu syŏnggyo nuga bogŭm chyŏnsyŏ* [Gospel of Luke]. Shenyang, Manchuria: Mungwang sŏwŏn, 1882.

———. 예수셩교요안늬복음젼셔 *Yesusyŏnggyo yoannae bogŭm chyŏnsyŏ* [Gospel of John]. Shenyang, Manchuria: Mungwang sŏwŏn, 1882.

———. Letter to William Wright, January 24, 1883. In Oak, *Sources of Korean Christianity*, 63–65.

————. Letter to William Wright, July 22, 1883. In Oak, *Sources of Korean Christianity*, 82–83.

————. "Corean New Testament." *CR* (November–December 1883): 491–97.

————. Letter to W. Wright, March 8, 1885. BFBS Archives, Columbia University Library.

————. "Mr. Ross's Report." *UPMR* (June 1, 1887): 226.

————. 예수셩교신약젼셔 *Yesu syŏnggyo sinyak chyŏnsyŏ* [New Testament]. Shenyang, Manchuria: Mungwang sŏwŏn, 1887.

————. "The Gods of Korea." *GAL* (August 1888): 368–70.

————. Letter to William Wright, March 28, 1889. In Oak, *Sources of Korean Christianity*, 133.

————. *Old Wang: The First Chinese Evangelist in Manchuria*. London: Religious Tract Society, 1889.

————. "The Christian Dawn in Korea." *MRW* (April 1890): 241–48.

————. *History of Corea: Ancient and Modern*. London: Elliot Stock, 1891.

————. "Shang-ti: By the Chief Taoist Priest of Manchuria." *CR* 23 (March 1894): 123–24.

————. 셩경문답 Syŏngyŏng mundap [Bible Catechism]. Translated and edited by Mary F. Scranton. Seoul: Trilingual Press, 1895.

————. *Mission Methods in Manchuria*. New York: Revell, 1903.

————. *The Original Religion of China*. New York: Eaton & Mains, 1909.

————. *The Origin of the Chinese People*. Edinburgh: Oliphants, 1916.

Rutt, Richard. *James Scarth Gale and His History of the Korean People*. Seoul: Taewon, 1972.

Ryu Dae Young 류대영. "The Origin and Characteristics of Evangelical Protestantism in Korea at the Turn of the Twentieth Century." *Church History* (June 2008): 371–98.

Ryu Tongsik 류동식. 한국 종교와 기독교 *Han'guk chonggyo wa Kidoggyo* [Korean Religions and Christianity]. Seoul: Christian Literature Society of Korea, 1965.

————. "한국 교회의 토착화 유형과 신학 *Han'guk kyohoe ŭi t'och'akhwa yuhyŏng kwa sinhak*" [Types and Theology of Indigenization of Korean Church]. 신학논단 *Sinhak Nondan* [Theological Forum] 14 (1980): 2–22.

————. 한국 신학의 광맥 *Han'guk Sinhak ŭi kwangmaek* [Veins of Ore in Korean Theology]. Seoul: Chŏngmangsa, 1982.

————. "초기 한국 전도인들의 복음 이해 Ch'ogi Han'guk chŏndoindŭl

ŭi pogŭm ihae" [Early Korean Evangelists' Understanding of the Gospel]. *HKY* 1 (1991): 68–83.

Sands, William Franklin. *Undiplomatic Memories: The Far East, 1896–1904.* New York: Whittlesey House, 1930.

Schereschewsky, Samuel I. J. "Terminology in the China Mission." *Churchman* 57, no. 6 (1888): 34–35.

Schlesinger, Arthur M., Jr. "The Missionary Enterprise and Theories of Imperialism." In *The Missionary Enterprise in China and America*, edited by John K. Fairbank, 336–73. Cambridge, Mass.: Harvard University Press, 1974.

Scott, Mrs. Robertson. "Warring Mentalities in the Far East." *Asia* 20, no. 7 (1920): 693–701.

Scott, William. *Canadians in Korea: Brief Historical Sketch of Canadian Mission Work in Korea.* Self-published, 1975.

Scranton, Mary F. "A Social Advance." *HWF* (September 1895): 65.

———. "Day Schools and Bible." *KMF* (April 1907): 53.

Scranton, William B. "Letter from Korea." *GAL* 11 (1886): 141.

———. Letter to Henry Loomis, February 3, 1892. ABS Archives, New York.

———. Letter to William Wright, October 24, 1894. In Oak, *Sources of Korean Christianity*, 261–65.

———. "Missionary Review of the Year." *KR* (January 1895): 15–16.

Sharp, Charles E. "Famine along the River: From January Report of Rev. C. E. Sharp." *KF* (August 1902): 59–60.

———. "Motives for Seeking Christ." *KMF* 2 (1906): 182–83.

Sharpe, Eric J. *Not to Destroy but to Fulfil.* Uppsala: Swedish Institute of Missionary Research, 1965.

Shin Ik-Cheol 신익철. "The Experiences of Visiting Catholic Churches in Beijing and the Recognition of Western Learning Reflected in the Journal of Travel to Beijing." *Review of Korean Studies* 9, no. 4 (2006): 11–31.

———. "The Western Learning Shown in the Records of Envoys Traveling to Beijing in the First Half of the Nineteenth Century—Focusing on Visits to the Russian Diplomatic Office." *Review of Korean Studies* 11, no. 1 (2008): 11–27.

Shin, Junhyoung Michael. "The Supernatural in the Jesuit Adaptation to Confucianism: Giulio Aleni's *Tianzhu Jiangsheng Chuxiang Jingjie* (Fuzhou, 1637)." *History of Religions* 50 (2011): 329–61.

Shin Kwangch'ŏl 신광철. 천주교와 개신교 *Ch'ŏnjugyo wa Kaesingyo* [Encounters and Conflicts between Roman Catholicism and

Protestantism in Korea]. Seoul: Institute for Korean Church History, 1998.

Shin Seonyoung 신선영. "箕山 金俊根 風俗畵에 관한 硏究 Kisan Kim Chungŭn p'ungsokhwa e kwanhan yŏn'gu" [A Study of Albums of Genre Paintings by Kim Chungŭn]. 美術史學 Misulsahak 20 (2006): 105–41.

Sinhak Chinam 神學指南 [Theological Compass]. "그리스도 종교와 다른 종교에 관계 Kŭrisŭdo chongyo wa tarŭn chonggyo e taehan kwan'gye" [Relationship between Christianity and Other Religions]. Sinhak Chinam 28 (1925): 17–35.

Smalley, William A. Translation as Mission. Macon, Ga.: Mercer University Press, 1991.

Sŏ Namdong 서남동. 민중 신학의 탐구 Minjung sinhag ŭi t'amgu [A Study on Minjung Theology]. Seoul: Han'gilsa, 1984.

Sŏ Taesŏk, ed. 서대석. 무당내력 Mudang naeryŏk [A History of Mudang]. Kyujanggak of Seoul National University, 1996.

Society for the Propagation of the Gospel in Foreign Parts. Annual Reports. London: SPG, 1890–1911.

Song Hangnyong 송항룡. "A Short History of Daoism in Korea." Korea Journal 26 (1986): 13–18.

Soothill, William E., and L. Hodous, comps. A Dictionary of Chinese Buddhist Terms. London: Oxford, 1934.

Speer, Robert Elliot. Report on the Mission in Korea of the Presbyterian Board of Foreign Missions. New York: Board of the Foreign Missions, PCUSA, 1897.

———. "Christian Mission in Korea." MRW 21 (1898): 681.

———. Mission and Politics in Asia. New York: Revell, 1898.

———. Missionary Principles and Practice. New York: Revell, 1902.

———. Christianity and the Nations. New York: Revell, 1910.

Spelman, Douglas G. "Christianity in Chinese: The Protestant Term Question." Papers on China 22A (1969): 25–52.

Spence, Martin. "The Renewal of Time and Space: The Missing Element of Discussions about Nineteenth-Century Premillennialism." Journal of Ecclesiastical History (January 2012): 81–101.

Stanley, Brian. The Bible and the Flag. Leicester: Apollos, 1990.

———, ed. Christian Missions and the Enlightenment. Grand Rapids: Eerdmans, 2001.

———. The World Missionary Conference, Edinburgh 1910. Grand Rapids: Eerdmans, 2009.

Stewart, Lyman. Letter to H. G. Underwood, February 11, 1909. PHS,

CRKM, reel 282. Attached to H. G. Underwood letter to A. J. Brown, February 15, 1909.

Suh Kwangsun 서광선. "American Missionaries and a Hundred Years of Korean Protestantism." *International Review of Mission* 74 (1985): 5–18.

Suzuki Nobuaki 鈴木信昭. "朝鮮後期 天主教思想と 鄭鑑錄 Chōsen koki Tenshukyō shisōto Teikanroku" [Roman Catholic Thought and *The Record of Chŏnggam* in the Late Chosŏn Period]. 朝鮮史研究會論文集 *Chōsenshikenkyūkai ronbunshū* 40 (2002): 60–97.

SW (신학월보 *Sinhak Wŏlbo* [A Biblical and Theological Monthly]). "사도신경 론리 Sadosingyŏng ronri" [Exposition of the Apostle's Creed]. *SW* 1 (1901): 106.

———. "문감목씌셔평양교회예오심 Mungammokk kuisyŏ P'yŏngyang kyohoe ye osim" [Bishop Moore Came to Pyongyang]. *SW* (June 1901): 239–42.

———. "뭇치내새회당을헌당홈 Mutch'inae sae hoedang ŭl hŏngdangham" [Dedication of the New Church Building at Mutch'inae, Suwŏn]. *SW* 1 (1901): 351.

———. "처사회개 Ch'ŏsa hoegae" [Repentance of a Scholar]. *SW* 1 (1901): 357–58.

———. "하ᄂ님안전에행ᄒ심 Hananim anjŏn e haenghasim" [Behaving before the Face of God]. *SW* 1 (1901): 389.

———. "만사문답 Mansa mundap" [Questions and Answers on All Things]. *SW* 1 (1901): 435–36.

———. "셔방데일차디방회 Syŏbang dye ilch'a dibanghoe" [The First Meeting of the Western District]. *SW* 1 (1901): 480–81.

———. "졍동셔신학을공부홈 Chŏngdong syŏ sinhag ŭl kongbuham" [Theological Class Held at Chŏngdong]. *SW* 2 (1902): 116–17.

———. "김상림씨별세ᄒ심 Kim Sangnimssi pyŏlsehasim" [The Death of Mr. Kim Sangnim]. *SW* (June 1902): 253–54.

———. "김상태씨의열심 Kim Sangt'aessi ŭi yŏlsim" [Efforts of Mr. Kim Sangt'ae]. *SW* 3 (1903): 194.

———. "졔물포교우쟝경화씨별세홈 Chyemulp'o kyou Chang Kyŏnghwassi pyŏlsyeham" [Mr. Chang Kyŏnghwa of the Chemulp'o Church Passed Away]. *SW* (November 1904): 376–78.

Swallen, William L. Letter to Frank F. Ellinwood, September 24, 1895. PHS, CRKM, reel 178.

———. Letter to Friends, July 1896. PHS, CRKM, reel 178.

———. Letter to F. F. Ellinwood, September 21, 1896. PHS, CRKM, reel 178.

————. "Narrative Report of Rev. W. L. Swallen for Oct., Nov., Dec., 1907." *KMF* 3 (1908): 43.

————. "Korean Christian Character." *AH* (November 1908): 511.

————. "A Story of Korean Prayer." *KMF* (November 1909): 182.

Takahashi, Aya. *The Development of the Japanese Nursing Profession.* London: RoutledgeCurzon, 2004.

T'amwŏnja 탐원자. "제사근본을의논홈 Chyesa kŭnbon ŭl ŭinonham" [Discussion of the Foundation of Ancestor Worship]. *SW* 4 (1908): 184–91.

TKB (*Transactions of the Korea Branch of the Royal Asiatic Society*). "Discussion." *TKB* (1900): 48–49.

TMS (대한매일신보 *Taehan Maeil Sinbo* [Korea Daily News]). "統禁雜術 T'onggŭm chapsul" [Prohibiting Witchcraft]. *TMS*, August 23, 1904.

————. "欺言取物 Kiŏnch'wimul" [Taking Money with Deceiving Word]. *TMS*, May 5, 1905.

————. "新教自强 Singyojagang" [Self-Strengthening by Protestantism]. *TMS*, December 1, 1905.

————. "雜報 Chappo" [Miscellaneous News]. *TMS*, December 23, 1909.

————. "妖怪한人物 Yogoihan inmul" [Weird Woman]. *TMS*, July 9, 1910.

Tonghak nongminjŏnjaeng paekchunyŏn kinyŏmsaŏp ch'ujinwiwŏnhoe. 동학농민전쟁 사료 총서 I *Tonghak nongminjŏnjaeng saryo ch'ongsŏ* I [Collection of Historical Sources of the Tonghak Peasant War]. Seoul: Sayeyŏnguso, 1996.

Torrey, Deberniere Janet. "Separating from the Confucian World: The Shift Away from Syncretism in Early Korean Catholic Texts." *Acta Koreana* (June 2012): 127–45.

Trollope, Mark N. 照萬民光 *Chomanmingwang* [Lumen ad Revelationem Gentium]. Seoul, 1894.

————. "Correspondence, M. N. Trollope to the Editor." *Independent*, August 19, 1897.

————. "Introduction to the Study of Buddhism in Corea." *TKB* (1917): 1–3.

TS (독립신문 *Tongnip Sinmun* [Independent]). "잡보Chappo [Miscellaneous News]." *TS*, July 27, 1897.

————. "잡보 Chappo [Miscellaneous News]." *TS*, August 19, 1897.

Turley, Robert T. Letter to William M. Paul, November 26, 1894. In Oak, *Sources of Korean Christianity*, 270–73.

Tylor, Edward Burnett. *Primitive Culture: Researches into the Development of Mythology, Philosophy, Religion, Language, Art, and Custom*. 2 vols. London: John Murray, 1871.

Underwood, Elizabeth. *Challenged Identities: North American Missionaries in Korea, 1884–1934*. Seoul: Royal Asiatic Society, Korea Branch, 2003.

Underwood, Horace Grant. Letter to Frank F. Ellinwood, July 6, 1885. PHS, CRKM, reel 174.

———. "Romanism Wide Awake." *FM* 45 (1886): 567.

———. Letter to Frank F. Ellinwood, July 9, 1886. PHS, CRKM, reel 174.

———. Letter to Frank F. Ellinwood, June 17, 1887. PHS, CRKM, reel 174.

———. Letter to Frank F. Ellinwood, March 12, 1888. PHS, CRKM, reel 175.

———. "A Powerful Appeal from Korea." *MRW* (March 1888): 209–11.

———. Letter to F. F. Ellinwood, May 21, 1888. PHS, CRKM, reel 175.

———. Letter to Frank F. Ellinwood, August 25, 1888. PHS, CRKM, reel 175.

———. Letter to Frank F. Ellinwood, December 23, 1888. PHS, CRKM, reel 175.

———. Letter to Frank F. Ellinwood, April 30, 1889. PHS, CRKM, reel 175.

———. Letter to F. F. Ellinwood, May 26, 1889. PHS, CRKM, reel 175.

———. *A Concise Dictionary of the Korean Language in Two Parts: Korean-English & English Korean*. 2 vols. Yokohama: Kelly & Walsh, 1890.

———. *An Introduction to the Korean Spoken Language*. Yokohama: Seishi Bunsha, 1890.

———. Letter to Frank F. Ellinwood, October 21, 1890. PHS, CRKM, reel 175.

———. "Romanism on the Foreign Mission Field." In *Reports of the Fifth General Council of the Alliance of the Reformed Churches Holding the Presbyterian System*, 409–15. Toronto: Hart & Riddell, 1892.

———. Letter to F. F. Ellinwood, November 2, 1893. PHS, CRKM, reel 176.

———. "Religious Changes in Korea." *GAL* (December 1893): 557.

———. "The 'Today' from Korea." *MRW* 16 (1893): 817.

————. "성경강론회 Syŏnggyŏng kangnonhoe" [Bible Study]. *KS*, October 6, 1898.

————. Letter to James H. Ritson, December 23, 1903. BFBSA, CBFBS.

————. *The Call of Korea*. New York: Revell, 1908.

————. "Korea's Crisis Hour." *Korea Mission Field* 4 (1908): 130.

————. *The Religions of Eastern Asia*. New York: Macmillan, 1910.

————, ed. 찬양가 *Ch'anyangga* [Hymns of Praises]. Yokohama: Seishi Bunsha, 1894.

Underwood, Lillias Horton. Letter to F. F. Ellinwood, May 5, 1889. PHS, CRKM, reel 175.

————. Letter to F. F. Ellinwood, May 28, 1894. PHS, CRKM, reel 178.

————. *Fifteen Years among the Top-Knots, or Life in Korea*. New York: American Tract Society, 1904.

————. *With Tommy Tompkins in Korea*. New York: Revell, 1905.

————. "Woman's Work for Women in Korea." *MRW* (July 1905): 491–500.

————. *Underwood of Korea*. New York: Revell, 1918.

Venable, W. A. "Korea's First YMCA Student Conference." *Missionary* (November 1910): 558–59.

Vinton, Cadwallader C. "Presbyterian Mission Work in Korea." *MRW* (September 1893): 670.

————. "Obstacles to Missionary Success in Korea." *MRW* 17 (1894): 837–43.

————. "Literary Department." *KR* 3 (1896): 39.

————. "Literary Department." *KR* (September 1896): 377.

————. 의원의행적 *Ŭiwŏnŭi haengjŏk* [Life of Jesus the Physician]. Seoul: Korean Religious Tract Society, 1896.

Wallace, Anthony F. C. *Religion: An Anthropological View*. New York: Random House, 1966.

Walraven, Boudewijn C. A. "Shamans and Popular Religion around 1900." In *Religions in Traditional Korea*, edited by Henrik H. Sorensen, 107–30. Copenhagen: SBS Monographs, 1995.

————. "Interpretations and Reinterpretations of Popular Religion in the Last Decades of the Chosŏn Dynasty." In *Korean Shamanism: Revivals, Survivals, and Change*, edited by Keith Howard, 55–72. Seoul: Seoul Press/Korea Branch of the Royal Asiatic Society, 1998.

————. "The Native Next-Door: Ethnology in Colonial Korea." In *Anthropology and Colonialism in Asia and Oceania*, edited by Jan van Bremen and Akitoshi Shimizu, 219–44. Richmond, UK: Curzon Press, 1999.

———. "Popular Religion in a Confucianized Society." In *Culture and the State in Chosŏn Korea*, edited by Martina Deuchler and Jahyun Kim Haboush, 160–98. Cambridge, Mass.: Harvard University Asia Center, 1999.

———. "Religion and the City: Seoul in the Nineteenth Century." *Review of Korean Studies* 3, no. 1 (2000): 178–206.

Wambold, Catherine. Letter to A. J. Brown. March 19, 1906. PHS, CRKM, reel 281.

Wang Xichang. "Wang Xichang song yasogyo pŏnsŏ sibibon bunji" [Wang Xichang Sent Various Christian Books]. In *T'ongsŏ ilgi*, vol. 1. Seoul: Korea University Press, 1972.

Weber, Timothy P. *Living in the Shadow of the Second Coming: American Premillennialism 1875–1925*. New York: Oxford University Press, 1979.

Weems, Benjamin B. *Reform, Rebellion and the Heavenly Way*. Tucson: University of Arizona Press, 1964.

Welbon, Arthur Garner. "Personal Annual Report for the Year Ending June 30, 1902." PHS, CRKM, reel 285.

Wells, James Hunter. Letter to F. F. Ellinwood, August 17, 1897. PHS, CRKM, reel 178.

———. "Northern Korea." *KRv* (March 1905): 139–41.

———. "An Appreciation." *KRv* (November 1905): 425–27.

———. 위생 *Wisaeng* [Introduction to Hygiene]. Seoul: Religious Tract Society, 1907.

Wells, Kenneth M. "The Rationale of Korean Economic Nationalism under Japanese Colonial Rule, 1922–1932: The Case of Cho Mansik's Products Promotion Society." *Modern Asian Studies* 19, no. 4 (1985): 823–59.

———. *New God, New Nation: Protestant and Self-Reconstruction Nationalism in Korea, 1896–1937*. Honolulu: University of Hawaii Press, 1990.

———. "The Failings of Success: The Problem of Religious Meaning in Modern Korean Historiography." *Korean Histories* 1, no. 1 (2009): 60–80.

WFMS (Woman's Foreign Missionary Society of the Methodist Episcopal Church). *Annual Reports*. Boston, 1885–1887; New York, 1888–1920.

———. *Fifty Years of Light*. Seoul: Woman's Foreign Missionary Society, Methodist Episcopal Church, 1938.

WFMSP (Woman's Foreign Missionary Society of the Presbyterian Church, USA). *Annual Reports*. New York, 1885–1920.

———. *Historical Sketches of the Missions under the Care of the Board of Foreign Missions of the Presbyterian Church*. Philadelphia, 1886, 1891.

WFMSS (Woman's Missionary Society of the Methodist Episcopal Church, South). *Annual Reports*. Nashville, 1897–1920.

White, James T., ed. *The National Cyclopaedia of American Biography*. Vol. 18. New York: James T. White, 1922.

Whiting, Norman C. Letter to A. J. Brown, January 29, 1904. PHS, CRKM, reel 280.

Williams, S. W. "The Controversy among the Protestant Missionaries on the Proper Translation of the Words God and Spirits into Chinese." *Bibliotheca Sacra* 35 (1878): 732–78.

Williamson, Alexander. *Journey in North China, Manchuria and Eastern Mongolia with Some Account of Korea*. Vol. 2. London: Smith Elder, 1870.

Willing, Jennie Fowler, and Mrs. George Heber Jones. *The Lure of Korea*. Boston: Woman's Foreign Missionary Society, Methodist Episcopal Church, 1913.

WMC (World Missionary Conference). *Report of Commission I. Carrying the Gospel to All the Non-Christian World*. Edinburgh: Oliphant, Anderson & Ferrier, 1910.

———. *Report of Commission IV. The Missionary Message in Relation to Non-Christian Religions*. Edinburgh: Oliphant, Anderson & Ferrier, 1910.

Wylie, Alexander. *Memorials of Protestant Missionaries to the Chinese*. Shanghai: American Presbyterian Mission Press, 1867.

Yang Chuguk 양주국. "사람이 귀한 근본을 알고 의를 행홀 일 Saram i kwihan kŭnbon ŭl algo ŭi rŭl haenghal il" [Men Should Know Their Origin and Practice Righteousness]. *SW* 3 (1904): 430–31.

Yang Guangxian 楊光先. *Budeyi* 不得已. Vol. 1. 1664. Reprint, China: Zhong She, 1929.

Yates, Matthew Tyson. "Ancestral Worship." In GCPMC, *RGC*, 1878, 367–87.

Yates, Timothy. *Christian Mission in the Twentieth Century*. Cambridge: Cambridge University Press, 1994.

Yi Chongŭn 이종은. "한국 소설상의 도교사상 연구 Han'guk sosŏlsang ŭi togyo sasang yŏngu" [A Study of Daoist Thought in the Old

Korean Novels]. In *Togyo wa Han'guk sasang* [Daoism and Korean Thought]. Seoul: Pŏmyangsa, 1987.

Yi Kiji. 이기지. 一庵燕記 *Iram yŏn'gi* [The Records of Travels to Beijing]. 1720.

Yi Kwangnin. 이광린. "개화기 관서 지방과 개신교 Kaehwagi Kwans chibang gwa kaesingyo" [Northwestern Provinces and Protestantism in the Open Port Period], in Han'guk i k ndaehwa wa Kidoggyo, 239-54. Seoul: Han'guk Kidoggyo munhwa y nguso, 1974.

———. "구한말 옥중에서의 기독교 신앙 Kuhanmal okchung esŏ ŭi kidoggyo sinang" [Christian Belief in the Prison during the Late Chosŏn]. In *Han'guk kaehwasa ŭi chemunje*, 218–22. Seoul: Iljogak, 1986.

Yi Mahnyol 이만열. 한국 기독교와 역사의식 *Han'guk Kidoggyo wa yoksa ŭisik* [Korean Christianity and Consciousness of History]. Seoul: Chisiksanŏpsa, 1982.

———. 아펜젤러 *Appenzeller* [H. G. Appenzeller: The First Missionary to Korea]. Seoul: Yonsei University Press, 1985.

———. "한말 러시아 정교의 전파와 그 교폐 문제 Hanmal Rŏsia chŏnggyo ŭi chŏnp'a wa kŭ kyop'ye munje" [Propagation of Russian Orthodoxy and Its Abuse Case in the Late Chosŏn Period]. In *Kŭrisŭdokyowa kyŏre munhwa*, 303–33. Seoul: Kidoggyomunsa, 1985.

———. 한국 기독교 문화 운동사 *Han'guk Kidoggyo munhwa undongsa* [A History of the Cultural Movement of Korean Christianity]. Seoul: Taehan Kidoggyo ch'ulp'ansa, 1987.

———. "한국 기독교와 초기 선교사 Han'guk Kidoggyo wa ch'ogi sŏngyosa" [Korean Christianity and Early Missionaries]. *Pit kwa Sogŭm* (December 1987): 112–24.

———. "한국 기독교와 미국의 영향 Han'guk Kidoggyo wa Migug ŭi yŏnghyang" [Korean Christianity and American Influence]. 한국과 미국 *Han'guk kwa Miguk* 3 (1988): 65–116.

———. 한국 기독교와 민족의식 *Han'guk Kidoggyo wa minjok ŭisik* [Korean Christianity and National Consciousness]. Seoul: Chisiksanŏpsa, 1991.

———. "한말 기독교 사조의 양면성 시고 Hanmal Kidoggyo sajo ŭi yangmyŏnsŏng sigo" [A Review of the Dual Trend of the Christian Thought in Late Chosŏn]. In *Han'guk Kidoggyo wa minjok ŭisik*, 221–29. Seoul: Chisiksanŏpsa, 1991.

———. 한국 기독교와 민족통일운동 *Han'guk Kidoggyo wa minjok*

t'ongil undong [Korean Christianity and the National Reunification Movement]. Seoul: IKCH, 2001.

Yi Nŭnghwa. 이능화. 朝鮮基督敎及外交史 *Chosŏn Kidoggyo kŭp oegyo sa* [History of Christianity and Diplomacy in Modern Korea]. Seoul: Chosŏn Kidoggyo Ch'angmunsa, 1928.

———. 朝鮮道敎史 *Chosŏn togyosa* [History of Daoism in Korea]. Translated by Yi Chingŭn. Seoul: Posŏng, 1986.

Yi Seunghae and Ahn Pohyun 이승해 안보연. "조선시대 회격·회곽묘 출토 삽에 대한 고찰 Chosŏn sidae hoegyŏk hoegwagmyo ch'ult'o sab e taehan koch'al" [A Study of the "Sap" Excavated from the Tombs of Lime-Covered or Lime Coffins]. 문화재 *Munhwajae* 42, no. 2 (2008): 43–59.

Yi Sŏkp'ung. "이석풍. 북청래신 Pukch'yŏng raesin" [News from Pukch'ŏng]. *KS*, January 18, 1906.

Yi Sŭngnyun 이승륜. "亞 버금 아자 속이 십자가가 됨 A pŏgŭm a cha sog i sipchaga ga toem" [The Inside of the Chinese Character "A" Becomes the Cross]. *KS*, March 21, 1906.

Yi Tŏkchu 이덕주. "성공회 발췌 성서 '조만민광' 연구 Sŏnggonghoe palch'we sŏngsŏ Chomanminkwang yŏn'gu" [A Study of the Anglican Church's Scriptural Tract *Lumen ad Revelationem Gentium*]. In 그리스도와 겨례문화 *Kŭrisŭdogyo wa kyŏre munhwa*, 263–301. Seoul: Kidoggyomunsa, 1987.

———. 한국 그리스도인들의 개종 이야기 *Han'guk kŭrisŭdoin dŭrŭi kaejong iyagi* [Conversion Stories of Korean Christians]. Seoul: Chŏngmangsa, 1990.

———. "초기 내한 선교사들의 신앙과 신학 Ch'ogi naehan sŏngyosa dŭrŭi sinang gwa sinhak" [Faith and Theology of the Early Missionaries to Korea]. *HKY* 6 (1997): 30–64.

———. "한국 기독교와 근본주의: 한국 교회사적 입장 Han'guk Kidoggyo wa kŭnbonjuŭi: Han'guk Kyohoesa jŏk ipchang" [Korean Church and Fundamentalism]. In 한국기독교 사상 *Han'guk Kidoggyo sasang*, edited by Korea Academy of Church History, 24–29. Seoul: Yonsei University Press, 1998.

———. 한국 토착 교회 형성사 연구 *Han'guk t'och'ak kyohoe hyŏngsŏngsa yŏn'gu* [A Study on the Formation of the Indigenous Church in Korea, 1903–1907]. Seoul: IKCH, 2000.

Yi Tŏkchu and Cho Ije 조이제. 강화 기독교 100 년사 *Kwanghwa kidoggyo 100 nyŏn sa* [The Centennial History of Christianity in Kanghwa]. Seoul, Miral Kihoek, 1994.

Yi Ŭnsŭng 이은승. "광쥬 노로목교회 형편 Kwangjyu Noromok Kyohoe hyŏngp'yŏn" [Situation of the Kwangju Noromok Church]. *SW* (March 1901): 160.

Yi Yŏngŭn 이영은. "교회 통신 Kyohoe t'ongsin" [Church News]. *KS*, December 9, 1897.

Yŏngjo sillok. 英祖實錄. Vol. 67, May 23–24, 1748.

Yoshido Tora. 吉田寅. 中國 キリスト敎 傳道文書の 硏究: 「天道溯源の 硏究」, 附譯註 *Chūgoku Kirisutokyō dendō bunsho no kenkū: "Tendōkyogen" no kenkū, tsuketari yakuchū* [Studies of Chinese Protestant Missionary Literature: A Study of Tracing the Sources of *The Pilgrim's Progress*: Supplemented with a Japanese Translation and Annotations]. Tokyo: Kyūko Shoin 汲古書院, 1993.

Yun Ch'iho 윤치호. "Confucianism in Korea." *KR* 2 (1895): 401–4.

———. "The Whang-Chei of Dai Han, or the Emperor of Korea." *KR* (October 1897): 385–90.

———. *Yun Ch'iho Ilgi* [Diary of Yun Ch'iho]. December 4, 1902.

———. *Ch'anmiga*. Seoul: Kwanghak sŏgwan, 1908.

———. *Yun Ch'iho Ilgi*. 8 vols. Seoul: National Institute of Korean History, 1973–1986.

Yun Kyŏngno 윤경로. "초기 한국 신구교 관계의 사적 고찰 Ch'ogi Han'guk singugyo kwangye ŭi sajŏk koch'al" [A Historical Study on the Early Relationship between Protestantism and Roman Catholicism in Korea]. In 한국 성서와 겨레문화 *Han'gŭl sŏngsŏwa kyore munwha*, 373–407. Seoul: Christian Literature Press, 1985.

Yun Sŏngbŏm 윤성범. "환인 환웅 왕검은 곧 하나님이다 Hwanin Hwan'ung Wangŏm ŭn kot Hananim ida" [Whanin, Whan'ung, and Wangŏm of the Tan'gun Myth Are God]. *Sasanggye* (May 1963): 258–71.

———. "단군신화는 *Vestigium Trinitas* 이다 Tan'gun sinhwa nŭn *Vestigium Trinitas* ida" [The Tan'gun Myth Is a Vestige of the Christian Trinity]. *Kidookyi sasang* (October 1963): 14–18.

———. "정감록 입장에서 본 한국의 역사관 *Chŏnggam-nok* ipchang esŏ pon Han'guk ŭi yŏksagwan" [The Korean Historical Perspective Seen from the *Chŏnggam-nok*]. 기독교사상 *Kidoggyo sasang* (January 1970): 105–19.

Zetzsche, Jost Oliver. *The Bible in China: History of the Union Version or the Culmination of Protestant Missionary Bible Translation in China*. Monumenta Serica Monograph Series 45. Nettetal, Germany: Monumenta Serica, 1999.

———. "The Work of Lifetime: Why the *Union Version* Took Nearly

Three Decades to Complete." In Eber et al., *Bible in Modern China*, 77–100.

———. "The Missionary and the Chinese 'Helper': A Re-appraisal of the Chinese Role in the Case of Bible Translation in China." *Journal of the History of Christianity in Modern China* 3 (2000): 5–20.

Zhang Qiong. "About God, Demons, and Miracles: The Jesuit Discourse on the Supernatural in Late Ming China." *Early Science and Medicine* 4, no. 1 (1999): 1–36.

Index

Abraham, 17, 72, 80, 118–19, 138
Acts, Book of, 148, 207, 216, 241, 286
Adams, James E., 10
Aegug-ga, 266
Ahn Pohyun, 116
Ahn Sungho, 52
ajŏn, 225
Allen, Horace N., 16, 21–23, 78, 104, 123, 151–53, 174, 229, 232, 279
American Bible Society, 45, 56, 79, 236, 240
American Tract Society, 16, 57, 153
American University, 156
An Chunggŭn, 135–36
An Ch'angho, 286, 337
anbang, 71
ancestor worship, 13, 17, 26, 28, 39–40, 48, 57, 102, 145, 162–64, 189–219, 232, 252, 256, 260, 262, 313
ancestral spirits, 145, 191, 246, 269
ancestral tablet, 26, 162, 199, 204, 207, 209, 215, 217
Anderson, Rufus, 3, 15, 108, 184, 190, 255, 306
Anglo-American, 4, 104, 109, 127, 142–43, 145, 266, 270, 305–6, 309, 311, 316
Anglo-Saxon, 3, 15, 108, 184, 190, 255, 306

anti-: Americanism, 4, 8; Christian, 8, 35, 104, 106; Japanese, 129, 136, 277, 308; intellectualism, 8; missionary, 8; rationalism, 6; Roman Catholic, 14, 104, 205; Shinto shrine worship, 189
apocryphal, 28, 85–86, 91
apologetics, 24, 64, 194, 211, 216, 253, 259
Apostles' Creed, 148, 218, 248
Appenzeller, Alice R., 13, 15
Appenzeller, Henry G., 1–2, 16–18, 21–23, 56, 58–64, 81, 123–24, 204, 211, 224, 227, 231, 252, 322, 324
asap, 116–17
astronomy, 225, 320
atonement, 195, 262
Australia, 209, 294
Avison, Oliver R., 5, 13

Baby Riot, 104–5, 107, 233
Baird, Annie L. A., 178–79
Baird, William M., 10, 58, 212, 227–28, 290, 322, 324
Baker, Donald L., 35
Baldwin, Stephen L., 248
Bang Won-il, 155, 159
Baopuzi, 274
baptism, 103, 136, 147, 180, 196,

203–4, 229, 232–34, 297, 238, 245, 297, 310; requirements, 145
Baptist, 17, 88, 239
Barnett, Suzanne W., 251
Barrett, T. H., 37
Bays, Daniel H., 251
Beal, David, 88
bear, 70
Beaver, R. Pierce, 3
Bebbington, David W., 88
Beijing, 37, 46, 48, 52, 66, 98, 100–103, 190, 253, 308, 320
Beirne, Paul, 116
Bernheisel, Charles F., 180, 182–83, 185, 289
Best, Margaret, 178, 301
Bible: class, 30, 149, 176, 271, 288–91; Committee, 150; translation, 23–24, 45, 221, 240, 245; women in the, 142, 149–50, 177–80, 184–86, 207, 301, 310, 313
biblicism, 3, 11, 184, 310, 313
Big Dipper, 273, 281, 284–85
bishop, 19, 23, 42–43, 45–46, 48–49, 57, 62, 81, 127, 146, 147, 241
Bishop, Isabella Bird, 28, 151, 157–58, 164, 174
Bitton, Nelson, 257
Bixie jishi, 104–6
Blackstone, William E., 88
Bliss, Edwin M., 237
Blodget, Henry , 43, 45–46, 106, 197, 199
Boone, William J., 42–43, 45, 57, 62, 81
Bosch, David J., 3
Boston University, 75, 156, 226
Boxer, C. R., 103
Boxer Movement, 95, 200
Brereton, Virginia L., 89
Bridgman, Elijah C., 45, 56
British and Foreign Bible Society, 36, 45–46, 54, 59, 62–63, 79, 229, 236, 239, 243–45, 247
British legation, 120
Brown, Arthur J., 9–11, 90, 126, 128–29, 235, 243, 249, 253, 286, 290, 294–95, 300–301, 306–7

Bruen, Henry M., 294
Bryant, Elliot, 236
Bucknell, Rodercik S., 116
Buddha, 2, 26, 61, 63, 67, 69, 79, 115, 150, 252, 261, 267
Buddhism, 11, 13–19, 24–30, 38, 53, 61, 68–69, 75–76, 94, 113–15, 122, 144–46, 150, 157, 160, 164–69, 191, 197–98, 219, 222, 251–52, 254, 262, 266–69, 272–82, 285, 289, 293–94, 308, 312, 329
Bunker, Dalzell A., 72, 165
Bunyan, John, 109–10
Burdick, George M., 176–77
Burns, William, 109, 111, 319–20, 324
Buswell, Robert E., Jr., 10, 35
butcher, 123, 234
Byun Kyuyong, 273

Cable, Elmer M., 65, 148, 214
Calvin, John, 271
Campbell, C. W., 225
Canadian, 10, 28, 78, 90, 120, 155, 164, 239, 307
Carpenter, Joel A., 90
Carroll, Arena, 147, 291
catechism, 12, 51, 58, 103, 145, 195, 204; *Bible,* 51, 58, 204, 322; *Child's,* 320; *Christian,* 58, 195, 323, 325; *Larger,* 321; Methodist, 322; *Shorter,* 321
cessationist, 182, 186
Chang Inhwan, 135
Chang Kyusik, 290, 304
Chang Tong, 70
Chang Tŭkhan, 283
Chang Wŏngŭn, 127, 218
Chang Yun-Shik, 9, 186
changsŭng, 122, 129
Chaoxian Celue, 20, 228
chapel, 120, 148, 175, 228, 230, 252, 267, 279, 281–82, 288–89, 291
Chejungwŏn, 104, 123, 132, 152, 234
chemistry, 270, 320
Chemulpo, 1, 56, 59, 104, 107, 153, 156–57, 161–62, 215, 218, 223, 228–29, 308; *see also* Incheon
chenwei, 91–92

Chesŏk, 69
Cheung, 158
chigwan, 26
Chilli iji, 58, 212
China's Millions, 228
Chinese Recorder and Missionary Journal, 51–52, 198, 247–48, 260, 268
chinin, 93
Cho Hyeon–Beom, 157
Cho Ije, 117
Cho Kwang, 93
Cho Kwangjo, 114
Cho manmin gwang, 239, 241
Cho Mansik, 304
Cho Sangjŏng, 207, 278
Cho Sukja, 264
Choi Kil Sung, 191
Choi Sung Il, 237
cholera, 24, 96, 115, 132, 143, 151–54
Chŏn Chaesuk, 278
Chŏn Sŏngch'ŏn, 4
Chŏn Yŏkho, 215
Chŏng-doryŏng, 117–18
Chŏng Hasang, 48
Chŏng Hyŏngho, 109
Chŏng Ikno, 280–81
Chŏng Kam, 85, 93–94
Chŏng Kidang, 125
Chŏng Kongbin, 288
Chŏng Mongju, 289
Chŏng Ryŏm, 273
Chŏng Sunman, 131
Chŏng Yakchong, 48, 93
Chŏng Yunjo, 280–81
Chŏngdong, 2, 57, 97, 140, 230–31, 233
Chŏnggam-nok, 85, 93–95, 107, 114–15, 117, 119, 138
Chŏngjo sillok, 93
chosangshin, 191
Chosŏn, 4, 14, 17, 49–50, 57, 66, 68–71, 86, 92–95, 98, 100, 115–18, 123, 125–26, 135–36, 142, 150, 157, 172, 185, 190–91, 225, 235, 247, 272–73, 275, 281, 284–85, 298, 300–301
Chosŏn Ilbo, 94–95
Chosŏn mulsan changnyŏhoe, 304

Chosŏn wangjo sillok, 92
Chow Kai-wing, 44
Chowhaong, 68, 77
Christian: civilization, 3, 16, 86, 90, 224, 255, 260, 262–63, 270, 303, 306, 309, 319; exorcism, 313; memorial service 313; nation, 210; nationalism, 266, 293, 310; universality, 316
Christian Evidence, 319
Christie, Douglas, 50
Christmas, 67, 121, 147
Christus Victor, 315
Chu Chaeyong, 6, 38
Chugyo yoji, 48, 91
Chung Chinhong, 9, 186
Chungin, 225
Church: Central Presbyterian (Pyongyang), 272, 280, 287, 291–92, 295; Central Presbyterian (Seoul), 123, 181; Chŏngdong Presbyterian (Seoul), 57; East Gate Methodist (Seoul), 117; First Methodist (Seoul), 231, 233, 291; Kanggye (Presbyterian), 292; Kangjin Presbyterian, 289; Kwangju Noromok Church (Kyŏnggi), 125; Sangdon Church (Seoul), 231; Sap'yŏngdong Presbyterian (Hwanghae), 125; Sorae (Presbyterian), 97, 119–22, 125; South Gate (Pyongyang), 280; Tambangni (Incheon), 67
church bell, 121, 292
chusaek chapki, 145
chwit'ong, 152
Ch'a Chaemyŏng, 289
Ch'a Chuhwan, 71, 273, 285
Ch'amshin, 47, 55, 58, 317
Ch'anmiga, 149, 263–66
Ch'an'yangga, 264
ch'aryŏk, 279
Ch'oe Cheu, 27, 49, 93, 115–16
Ch'oe Ch'iryang, 277–78
Ch'oe Chunsik, 273–74
Ch'oe Myŏng'o, 61, 204, 288
Ch'oe Pyŏnghŏn, 65, 114 156, 214, 216, 232–35, 253
ch'ŏllyun, 262
Ch'ŏn Kwangsil, 148

ch'ŏndo, 136
Ch'ŏndogyo, 94
Ch'ŏnju, 24, 38, 48, 93, 309, 312
ch'ŏnmin, 225
ch'ŏrya kido, 294
ch'udohoe, 190, 217–18
ch'ukmun, 219
Ch'usŏk, 192, 214
ch'uwŏn, 129
civilization, 2–3, 17–18, 21–22, 29, 40,
   56, 68, 86, 90, 130–32, 139, 168,
   196, 214, 223–24, 247–49, 258,
   260–63, 291, 298, 303, 306–7, 309,
   313–14; Confucian, 17; higher, 18,
   22, 56; Japanese, 130–32, 139, 270;
   Korean, 17, 29, 168; Western, 6, 25,
   98, 100, 102, 145, 184, 210, 223,
   247–48, 255, 261–62, 270, 276, 314
Clark, Allen D., 153
Clark, Anthony E., 100–101, 105
Clark, Charles A., 33, 129, 147,
   173–74, 181–82, 209, 235, 243, 249,
   300, 328
Clark, Donald N., 10, 182, 235
Cobb, George C., 249
Cohen, Paul, 105
Collyer, Charles T., 147, 207
Colporteur, 50, 177, 229–30, 236,
   245–46, 250, 291
commonsense philosophy, 253–55,
communion, 160, 192, 205–6
concubinage, 193, 205, 207, 310,
Conference: Bible (Chicago), 88, 90;
   Ecumenical Missionary (New York),
   224; General Missionary (Shanghai),
   44, 72, 196–98, 200–2, 204, 236,
   248; Quarter Centennial (Seoul),
   209; World Missionary (Edinburgh),
   7, 156, 159, 226; YMCA Student
   (Seoul), 293
confession, 152, 234, 295
Confucianism, 11, 13–17, 19–20,
   23–30, 37–39, 42, 44, 47, 49, 52–53,
   64–67, 75–76, 92, 94, 100, 140,
   144, 157–58, 160, 165–66, 168–69,
   194, 196–98, 205, 222, 233, 251–52,
   255–56, 259–62, 267, 269, 272–75,
   279, 282, 308

Confucius, 17, 44, 64, 67, 79, 100,
   194–95, 198, 202, 211, 216, 256,
   261, 283
Conn, Harvie M., 7
Conspiracy Case, 307
continuationist, 183, 186
conversion, 43, 56, 86, 117, 119, 136,
   139, 143, 145–46, 181, 184, 198,
   207–8, 231, 233, 235, 248–49, 272,
   277–78, 280, 282, 286, 303, 312,
   315
Corbett, Hunter, 320
Corean Gate, 50
Corean Primer, 50
Corfe, C. John, 33, 240–41
Council of Presbyterian Missions in
   Korea, 243–44
Courant, Maurice, 70
Covell, Ralph R., 252–53
Cracknell, Kenneth, 252
Cram, William G., 148, 184
Cranston, Earl, 146–47
creed, 23, 191, 218
Criveller, Gianni, 100–101
cross, 85–86, 97, 98, 100–14, 117–40,
   145, 179, 238, 252, 258, 279, 283,
   305, 312, 315
Culbertson, M. S., 56

daimon, 35, 41, 157, 171
Dallet, C. Charles, 157, 190
Daoism, 13, 15, 19, 26–27, 38, 49,
   52–53, 71, 144, 165, 169, 197, 252,
   271–75, 278–79, 282–85, 287, 289,
   294, 303, 311–12
Davies, Daniel M., 18
Davis, George T. B., 293
dawn prayer meeting, 30, 273, 287–94,
   314
Decalogue, 194
Delegates' Version (DV), 237–45, 310
Deming, Charles S., 148
demon, 56, 141–42, 155, 157, 162–64,
   166, 171, 175, 179, 183; possession,
   142, 144, 154, 166, 172–75, 180–84,
   186, 310, 315; worship, 141–42, 144,
   154–57, 161–64, 234
Dennett, Tyler, 21

Dennis, James S., 72
Deuchler, Martina, 190
devil, 101, 141–2, 146–48, 150, 155, 163–64, 171, 175–76, 178, 182, 184, 238, 248, 267; worship, 28, 148, 150, 163; *see also* daimon
devolution theory, 36, 74–75
Dialogues with a Temple Keeper, 23, 58, 61, 232, 252, 324
diglot style, 241
Dinsmore, Hugh A., 22
Diosy, Arthur, 130
discipline, 139, 206
dispensationalism, 87–90, 140, 214
diyu, 251, 267
Dock, Lavinia L., 151
Dominican, 39, 42
Doty, Elihu, 42
Douthwaite, Arthur W., 228
dragon, 162
dream, 95, 114, 282
Dwight, Henry O., 197, 199
Dyer, Samuel, 60

Easter, 1–2, 325
Eber, Irene, 34, 40, 46
ecumenical, 4, 11, 47, 62, 72, 79, 88, 222, 307
Edkins, Joseph, 45, 196–97, 320
education, 3, 19, 18, 20–21, 66, 123, 160, 181, 196–98, 201, 224, 229, 235, 271, 277, 280, 290, 310,
elder, 31, 212, 233, 238, 280, 286, 292, 296
Ellinwood, Frank K., 22, 24, 58, 60, 90, 104, 148, 152, 164, 173, 206–8, 227–28, 230–32, 277–79, 307
elm tree, 2
emperoe, 40, 53, 65–66, 97–102, 122–24, 130–31, 166, 202–3, 244, 254, 258, 266, 275
Engel, George O., 209–10
Erdman, Walter C., 179–80
eschatology, 19, 90, 92–3, 115, 140,
eternal: blessing, 251, 262, 268; life, 118, 193, 237, 251, 268, 314; punishment, 251, 268

ethics, 17, 29, 86, 160, 234, 251, 254, 262
evangelical, 7–10, 13, 46–47, 80, 87, 89–90, 108–9, 114, 144, 203, 205–6, 216, 250, 255, 262–63, 271, 302, 307–9, 312–13, 315–16
evangelicalism, 2, 4, 11, 82, 90, 252–53, 255, 257, 263, 272, 302–3, 307–8, 310, 316
evangelism, 20, 25, 113, 129, 177, 225, 236, 240, 242, 246, 250, 255, 259, 293, 309, 315
evangelistic, 11, 57, 61, 65, 121, 145, 154, 186, 222–23, 229–30, 245, 148, 253, 271, 293–94, 299, 309–10, 313
Evidences of Christianity, 253–58, 309, 314, 320
evil spirits, 18, 28, 33, 36, 55–56, 67, 116, 141–47, 149, 150–51, 153–54, 157, 163–64, 167, 171, 173–76, 180–81, 183, 261, 310
evolutionary, 27, 36, 173, 262, 303
Ewha Haktang, 108, 231, 291
Ewy, Priscilla W., 96–97
exorcism, 142, 156, 159, 161–62, 166, 168, 171–72, 174–76, 179–80, 183–85, 273, 310

Faber, Ernst, 65, 199, 259–61, 309, 320, 323
Fairbank, John K., 3, 106, 251
famine, 24, 95–97, 108, 125, 127, 139, 228, 312
Fang-Lan Hsieh, 264
fans, 116–17
fasting, 180, 275, 283, 287, 294, 303, 314
fengshui, 91, 260
Fenwick, Malcolm C., 239–40
Ferron, Stanislas, 48, 108, 157
fetishes, 142–43, 147–50, 154, 157–58, 171–72, 180, 184–85, 207, 217
filial piety, 190–95, 199, 201–2, 211–13, 217–19, 251, 253, 256, 260, 262, 282, 308, 314
Fish, M. Alice, 148
flag: American, 129; Jesus, 120–21,

139–40; Korean national, 97, 123–24, 127, 129; red cross/St. George's, 85–86, 97, 107–8, 117, 119–30, 138–40; Red Cross Society, 139
flagpole, 121–22, 125–28
Follwell, E. Douglass, 151–52
forgiveness, 195, 268, 285, 290, 292–93
Foster, Arnold, 202
Fowler, Charles H., 23
Fox, Harry H., 157
France, 22, 277
Franciscan, 39, 42, 53, 57, 102, 232, 255
Frazer, James G., 36
French, 12, 21–22, 24, 42, 48, 53, 104–5, 122, 126–28, 138, 141–43, 155–57, 223, 232, 240, 242, 244, 308
Frey, Lulu E., 291
Fridman, Eva J. N., 155
fulfillment theory, 5, 7, 13, 74, 76, 79–82, 156, 161, 169, 263, 302, 307–9, 315
fundamentalism, 2, 5–8, 11, 80, 88, 277, 306, 308
funeral, 161–62, 190, 195, 211
Fusheng zhi dao, 268

Gale, James S., 31, 58–63, 67–79, 81, 90, 109–10, 112–14, 126, 141–42, 155, 163–66, 169, 174, 182, 185, 192–93, 205, 207–8, 210–11, 242–44, 283, 285–86, 295–98, 308, 324, 330
Gate of Virtue and Wisdom, 248, 257–59
Genähr, Ferdiand, 23, 58, 61, 252, 324
General Council: Protestant Evangelical Missions in Korea, 72; Evangelical Missions in Korea, 263–64
Genesis, 11
geography, 320, 323
Gerdine, Joseph L., 297, 307
German, 12, 34, 36, 101, 108, 130, 244
gewu zhizhi, 259
Gifford, Daniel L., 24, 26–27, 58, 62–63, 90, 147, 164, 171, 192, 227, 278, 280, 288, 324

Gilman, E. W., 56, 227, 236
Gilmore, George W., 19–20, 165, 174
Girardot, Norman J., 43
Goforth, Jonathan, 292
gold mine, 175
Gongguoge, 274
Gordon, Adoniram J., 88–89
Gospel Hymns Consolidated, 264
Gospel Hymns No. 5, 264
Goucher, John F., 298, 309
Gouveia, Alexandre de, 48, 190
grace, 210, 216, 237, 267–68, 300
Grammont, Louis de, 48
Grant, George M., 308
Grayson, James H., 50
Greek, 34–5, 37, 40–2, 53, 142, 157, 166, 171, 237, 241, 244, 296
Greenfield, M. W., 228
Grierson, Robert G., 154
Griffis, William E., 2, 12–15, 18–19, 22, 53, 80, 157
Guan Yu, 274–75
Guanyin, 275
Guthapfel, Margaret L., 129
Gützlaff, Karl, 45, 252

Haesŏ Kyoan, 126
Hall, Rosetta S., 51, 279
Hall, William J., 280
Hamel, Hendrik, 12, 15
han, 191
Han Sŏkchin, 277, 279–81, 288–89
Han T'aegyo, 278
Hananim, 30, 47, 49–55
Hanănim, 26–83, 104, 146, 161, 164, 168–69, 170–71, 184, 214–15, 238, 262, 281–82, 284, 308–9, 311–17
Hanbul chădyŏn, 48, 141
hangŭl, 49, 240, 263, 315
hansik, 192
Harbin, 136
Hardie, Robert A., 28, 127–28, 164, 291, 295
Harris, Merriman C., 136
healing, 21, 27, 94, 130, 143, 151, 161–62, 168, 171, 175, 179–80, 182, 184, 186–87, 273, 310, 312–13

heathen, 3, 17–8, 23, 25, 35, 73, 121, 178, 184, 196–97, 206, 301
heathenism, 2, 7, 16, 18, 20, 24–25, 82, 215, 308
Hebrew, 34, 76, 244, 296
Heidelberg Catechism, 12
helper, 23, 57, 97, 148, 277, 280–81,
heresy, 210
Hermit Nation, 13, 15, 53
Heron, John W., 22, 104, 152, 163, 217, 232
holiness, 88, 269, 307–8
Holmes, Mrs. J. L., 212, 322
Holy Spirit, 19, 31, 35–36, 45, 55, 79, 88–89, 146–47, 154, 175–76, 180, 182–83, 196, 202, 209–12, 219, 237, 242, 248, 257, 259, 262, 282, 291–92, 296, 300, 318
Hong Kyŏngnae, 93
Hong Taeyong, 98, 101–2
hospital, 104, 123, 129, 131–32, 136, 152–53, 229, 231–34
Hounshell, C. G., 147
Hu, Peter Kuo-chen, 38
Huang Zunxian, 20, 228
Hulbert, Homer B., 19, 24, 29–30, 63, 66–75, 81, 133, 155–56, 164–69, 175, 185, 192, 225, 270
Huna chinŏn, 212
Hunt, Everett N., 13, 54
Hutchison, William R., 3
Hwang Hyŏn, 94
Hwang Kyung Moon, 225, 227, 300
Hwang Sayŏng, 93
Hwanin, 70–71, 74, 81
Hwanung, 71
hyangni, 225
hygiene, 139, 151
hymnals, 263–69

idol(s), 58, 65, 67, 73, 147, 150, 164, 206, 215, 238, 246, 252, 261, 269, 302
idol worship, 23, 126, 144, 208, 234, 252, 262, 266
idolatry, 18, 22–23, 60–61, 65, 76, 82, 187, 190, 193–96, 198–200, 204, 206, 215–16, 252–53, 256

Ilchinhoe, 128
immorality, 23
immortality, 75, 193, 204, 267, 272, 279
Incheon, 67, 97, 131–32, 175, 213; see Chemulpo
Independence Club, 18, 66, 122–25, 266, 286
Independent, 228, 240, 266
India, 16, 72, 203, 221, 291, 294
innkeeper, 277
International Law, 320
Iryŏn, 68
Itō Hirobumi, 135–36

James, F. H., 320
Japanese, 1, 2, 13–14, 29, 34, 78, 85; Buddhist, 14; Christians, 56; colonialism, 4, 8, 14, 31, 78–79, 82; government, 10; Great Buddha Hotel, 2; Kami, 36, 45, 79, 83; materialism, 78, 82; militarism, 78; military hospital, 86; polytheism, 80; samurai, 109; Shinto, 79
Jerusalem, 272, 300
Jesuit, 35–40, 42, 48, 100, 101, 189
Jesus Is Coming, 89
Jewish, 37, 74, 78, 86, 108, 147, 186, 287,
Jiushi zhenzhu, 257
John, Gospel of, 52, 54, 237, 239–40, 288
John, Griffith, 57–58, 63, 196, 212, 241, 247–48, 257, 262, 309, 320, 322–24
Johnston, Howard A., 291
Jones, G. Heber, 16, 19, 23–24, 28–29, 38–39, 63–64, 69, 71–72, 75–76, 81, 117, 125, 144, 149, 154–60, 164, 166, 185, 191, 193, 205, 213, 215, 224, 226, 231–34, 263, 265, 271, 295, 305, 308, 313–14, 323
Jones, Margaret, 212–13
Jordan, David K., 86
Journal of American Medical Association, 96, 131, 153
Jung Jae-Hoon, 98, 100
Junkin, William M., 27, 59–60, 192, 209

Kagse sinp'yŏn p'algam, 275
Kang Hŭinam, 117
Kanghwa, 72, 96, 117, 149, 157, 207
Kearns, Carl E., 30, 295
Kendall, Laurel, 143
Kenmure, Alexander, 63, 243–45, 247,
Kennan, George, 131, 297–98,
Keong Tow-yung, 43
Kija, 17–18, 68–69, 71, 170
Kil Chingyŏng, 284, 286
Kil Sŏnju, 31, 114, 181, 271–72,
   280–87, 292, 294–97, 299–300, 303
Kil Yŏngsu, 124
Kilgour, Robert, 244
Kim Chaejun, 4
Kim Chinso, 93
Kim Chongsuh, 12, 142
Kim Chungŭn, 109
Kim Ch'ansŏng, 280
Kim Hoil, 218
Kim Hwasik, 281–82
Kim Iktu, 173, 186, 313
Kim Insŏ, 284
Kim In Soo, 286
Kim Kibŏm, 215
Kim Ku, 290–91
Kim Kyoungjae, 6
Kim Nakp'il, 273, 285
Kim Okhŭi, 48
Kim Okkyun, 248
Kim Rosan, 102
Kim Sanggeun, 35
Kim Sŏngt'aek, 280
Kim Wŏngŭn, 300
Kim Wonmo, 22
Kim Yunseong, 9
King James Version, 142, 237, 318
King's Business, 89
Knox, George W., 56, 88
Kojong, 1, 21, 66, 94, 97, 122–24,
   130–31, 166, 228, 230, 244, 274
Kojong sillok, 94
Kŏnjŏngdong p'ildam, 101
Koons, E. Wade, 290
Korean Religious Tract Society, 110,
   189, 195, 212, 249
Korean Repository, 17, 25–28, 31, 39,

66, 68–69, 108, 113, 154, 156, 158,
   161, 165–66, 174, 191, 234, 267–68,
   276
Korea Review, 69–70, 96, 133, 156,
   165–68, 225, 290
Koryŏ, 115, 273, 285, 289
Kuksadang, 150
Kulturkreislehre, 36
kŭmch'ŏk, 136
kunggungŭlŭl, 85, 92–94, 115, 118–19,
   138
Kungmin-ga, 342
Kung'ŭl-ga, 94
Kŭrisŭdo Sinmun, 61, 64–65, 119
K'ŭrisŭdoin Hoebo, 64
Kwan U, 274–75
Kwangju Uprising, 8
kwishin, 28, 36, 55–56, 61, 63, 142,
   145, 151, 155, 157–58, 163–65, 171
Kwŏn Minsin, 215
Kwŏnjung hoegae, 57

Ladd, George T., 298
Lambuth, David K., 174, 177, 181
Lambuth, James W., 196–97, 321
Lancashire, Douglas, 38
Landis, Eli B., 155, 161–62, 164, 169,
   185, 241
Lang, Andrew, 36
Laozi, 67
Latin, 24, 34–35, 41
Latourette, Kenneth S., 4, 11
Lawrence, Edward A., 23
Lazarist, 105
leader, 92, 94, 178, 215, 289
Lee Chull, 226, 277
Lee, Graham, 153, 159, 175, 279,
   286–87, 289
Lee Jung Young, 144
Lee Kwang Kyu, 191
Legation: American, 16, 122–23; Brit-
   ish, 122
Legge, James, 38, 40, 42–46, 52–54, 63–
   65, 67, 74, 80–81, 197–98, 309, 322
Leonard, Adna B., 307
Lew Young Ick, 21
Lewis, Ella A., 149–50

Li Hongzhang, 228
Life of Christ, 320
Lo Chung-fan, 44
local preacher, 117, 233
London, 43, 52, 62, 90, 244
London Missionary Society, 43–45,
  57–58, 194, 251
Loomis, Henry, 56, 236, 240, 248
Lord's Prayer, 148, 248
Lowell, Percival, 161
Lu Zongli, 91
Luke, Gospel of, 49, 51, 56, 236
Lumen ad Revelationem Gentium,
  239–42

Machen, J. Gresham, 7
MacIntyre, John, 50–51, 249, 322
Maclay, Robert S., 21, 45, 224, 248–49,
  264, 309, 321–22, 324
MacRae, Edith F., 31, 296
MacRae, Helen F., 96–97
magwi, 183, 242
malaria, 151–52
mama, 151, 168
Manbo Ogilbang, 167
Manchuria, 14, 49–54, 70, 136, 170,
  221, 223–24, 226, 237, 242, 245,
  248, 249, 281, 311, 314
manshin, 174
Mantle, Gregory, 298
Mari Mountain, 72
Mark, Gospel of, 56, 236, 287
market, 146
marriage, 193, 205–6, 210
Mars Hill, 241
Marsden, George M., 87
Martin, William A. P., 45, 63, 65, 67,
  196, 198, 200, 202, 212, 221, 253–
  57, 262, 268, 309, 314, 320, 324
Marty, Martin E., 3
martyrdom, 24, 104, 138–39
Mateer, Calvin W., 196, 264, 326–27
Matthew, Gospel of, 118, 236
McCartee, Divie B., 212, 242, 320, 324
McCully, Elizabeth A., 120–21
McGill, William B., 154, 204, 323
McKenzie, Frederick A., 125

McKenzie, William J., 119–20
measles, 151, 179
Medhurst, Walter H., 41–42, 45,
  194–95, 320, 323
medical, 9, 20–21, 51, 96, 130–32, 139,
  151, 154–55, 161–62, 175, 181, 184,
  186, 225, 229–30, 273, 280, 284,
  310, 313
merchant, 12, 224, 226–27, 231, 277
messianism, 28, 85, 87, 90–91, 93, 115,
  140, 312, 314
Methodist, 64, 97, 129, 231, 233, 291;
  Episcopal Church, 2, 21, 45, 58, 75,
  125, 148–49, 152–53, 156, 194,
  205, 209, 224, 231–32, 236, 249,
  271, 276, 291, 295, 321; Episcopal
  Church, South, 128; missionary, 1,
  10, 16, 20, 60, 89, 108, 165, 224,
  291, 295, 297, 307; theologian, 5
Miaozhu wenda, 23, 58, 61, 232,
  252–53, 324
middle class, 225–28, 231–32, 235,
  276–77, 286, 316
Miller, Frederick S., 62
Miller, Hugh, 238, 244
Miller, Lula A., 176
Million Souls Movement, 293–94
Milne, William, 45, 248, 251
Min Kyŏngbae, 7–8, 174, 187
Min Yŏngik, 21, 229
Ming dynasty, 35, 39, 43
Moffett, Samuel A., 10–11, 58–62,
  145–46, 175, 204, 208, 210, 224,
  227, 251, 276–82, 287–89, 323–25
Moffett, Samuel H., 11, 146
Mokpo, 297
Moody, Dwight L., 88–90
Moody Bible Institute, 89–90
Moore, Davis H., 127, 147
Moore, John Z., 31
Moore, Samuel F., 20, 23, 121, 148
Moorhead, James H., 87
Moose, J. Robert, 193, 210
Moreau, A. Scott, 272
Morning Calm, 33, 161
Morris, Charles D., 148
Moses, 17, 126

Mozi, 260
mudang, 26, 71, 141–44, 147–52, 155, 157–58, 162–63, 165, 167–68, 170–71, 174, 179–80, 185–86, 274–75, 313
Mudang naeryŏk, 71
Muirhead, William, 196, 199, 320, 324
Muller, Max, 36
Mun Hŭngjun, 278
Mungello, D. E., 39, 100
Murayama Chijun, 95, 115
Mutel, Gustave C. M., 136
Myers, Mamie D., 178

Na Ch'ŏl, 35
nal yŏnbo, 30, 294; see also offerings
National Bible Society of Scotland (NBSS), 45, 50, 52, 245, 248
natural philosophy, 38, 320
neidan, 272
Nestorian Monument, 254
Nestorianism, 70, 117, 267,
Nevius, Helen S., 58, 195, 204, 224, 320, 323
Nevius, John L., 145, 172–73, 183–84, 194–96, 200, 224–26, 264, 288, 309–10, 320, 325–27
Nevius method, 55, 172, 225–26, 288
New Laudes Domini, 264
New York University, 74
Newtonian, 255
No Pyŏngsŏn, 65
Noble, Martha H., 147
Noble, Mattie W., 154, 234
Noble, William A., 147, 149, 156, 295, 297–98
Noyes, George C., 13
numen, 35
nurses, 18, 131

O Sunhyŏng, 290
Oak Sung-Deuk, 18, 37, 49, 116, 169, 187, 236, 238, 246, 294
Obang Changgun, 158, 170
offerings, 64, 199; animal, 72; day, 30, 294; rice, 294
Oh Seon-young, 264

Ohlinger, Bertha S., 264
Ohlinger, Franklin, 25, 58, 198, 224, 231, 264, 267, 309, 322–23, 325
Ok Kyŏngsuk, 280–81
Okch'ugyŏng, 273
Okhwang Sangje, 77
ŏpju, 159
Oriental, 1, 27, 43, 314
Orientalism, 9, 184, 295, 313
original monotheism, 36, 41–44, 49, 64, 75, 82, 263, 312; see also primitive monotheism
Orr, James, 229
Our Hope, 89
Outlook, 131, 298,
Owen, Georgiana, 147

Paejae Haktang, 2, 23, 123–24, 156, 216, 231, 253, 291
Paek Hongjun, 50–51, 288
Paek Nakchun, 4, 7, 11
Paek Sŭngjong, 93–94
Paek Wŏnguk, 280
pagan, 19, 39–40, 48, 157
paganism, 174
Paik, George L.: see Paek Nakchun
Paik Jong–Koe, 64
Pak Ch'irok, 292
Pak Chiwŏn, 98, 100
Pak Chŏngguk, 278
Pak Chungbin, 94
Pak Hyŏngnyong, 6–7
Pak Sech'ang, 209
Pak Sŏngch'un, 123, 234
Pak Sosa, 274
pak-tal tree, 70
Palais, James B., 225
Palestine, 172, 175, 184
Paley, William, 253, 255, 261
Palmer, Spencer J., 70
Pang Kich'ang, 280
Park Yong Gyu, 7
patriotism, 20, 123, 286
Paul (Apostle), 148, 286
Paul, William M., 59
P'ahok chinsŏn non, 189, 205, 216
p'ansu, 144, 158, 165, 167–68, 170

Pearce, T. W., 248
Peddlers' Club, 123–25, 128, 139
Peep of Day, 212, 319–20, 322
Pentecost, 146, 238, 241
Pfister, Lauren F., 43
Pierson, Arthur T., 25, 88–89
Pilgrim's Progress, 107–10, 114, 254, 284, 288, 319, 324
Plymouth Brethren, 88
Pogŭm taeji, 58, 212
polygamy, 145, 198, 204, 206, 246, 256, 262, 267, 269, 287, 302, 310, 313
Pope Benedict VII, 40
Pope Clement XI, 39, 199
postmillennialism, 87, 115, 140
prayer, 30, 66, 75, 90, 103, 123, 148, 150, 153, 173–75, 178; all-night, 294, 303, 314; audible, 30, 287, 294, 314; dawn: *see* dawn prayer meeting; fasting mountain, 287, 303, 314; meeting, 123, 233, 280, 293, 314
preaching, 12, 30–31, 51, 128, 148, 201, 218, 235, 241, 245, 279, 296, 303
premillennial, 3, 87, 89–90, 307–8; Premillennialism, 87, 89, 119, 140
Presbyterian, 1, 6–12, 20, 22, 27, 41–43, 45, 48–49, 58, 61, 64, 72, 80, 89–90, 109, 117, 119–20, 123, 125, 127, 129, 132, 135–36, 145–46, 155, 164, 169, 174, 178, 181, 194, 196–97, 223, 255, 228, 230, 234, 240, 243–44, 248–49, 252–53, 257, 263–64, 271–72, 276, 278–80, 283, 287–92, 294–95, 299, 300–303, 305, 307, 326–27, 328, 331, 335; Church, 4; Church, USA, 7, 45, 58, 146, 163, 228, 253, 276, 301, 330; Mission, 60, 209; Mission Press (Shanghai), 41–43, 109, 194, 196–7, 252; missionary, 4, 8, 10, 61, 120, 186, 200, 291
Preston, J. F., 290, 297
primitive monotheism, 34, 36, 45–47, 53–54, 57–58, 63–67, 74–75, 79–83, 169, 171, 184, 194, 311–12
Princeton Theological Seminary, 73–74, 87
printing press, 18, 250

prison, 218, 235, 249
Privy Council, 123
pro-: American, 4, 128; French, 128; Japanese, 104, 120, 128, 133, 135, 297; Qing, 101; Russian, 123; Western, 101
prophecy, 85–86, 91, 93–95, 114–15, 117, 119, 122, 138–39, 274, 312–13, 315, 332
prophet, 77, 237
Prophetic Times, 89
Psalms, 180
p'umasi, 30
Puritan, 9, 87, 206
Pyŏn Sŏnhwan, 5–6
Pyongyang, 10–11, 22, 30, 50, 58, 60, 62, 97, 126, 129, 131–32, 146–48, 178, 180, 182, 227, 245, 263, 271–72, 276–81, 286–87, 289–92, 294–95, 298, 300–304, 314, 330

Queen Min, 21, 66, 229–30, 274
Quingming, 194

Rawlinson, Frank, 41
red cross, 85–86, 97, 108, 119–32, 139–40
Red Cross, 68, 124, 130–32; hospital, 130; International, 131; Japanese, 130–32, 136; Korean, 131
Reid, Gilbert, 199, 229
Reinders, Eric, 35
Revelation, 11, 96, 207, 281
revival, 30–2, 87, 139, 174, 177, 181, 271–72, 290–91, 294–97, 300, 313–14; Great Revival Movement, 30, 139, 271, 287, 293–95, 297, 300–303, 307
Reynolds, William D., 59–60, 145, 192, 238, 247–48
Rhodes, Harry A., 248
Ricci, Matteo, 35, 37–38, 44, 47, 64, 100–102, 205, 254
Ridel, F. C., 48, 141
Righteous Army, 133, 135–36, 139
Rites Controversy, 39, 102, 190, 199, 309
Ritson, J. H., 63, 243

Ro Kilmyung, 274
Ro Pyŏngsŏn, 65, 189, 205, 207, 216,
Ro Taejun, 8
Robert, Dana L., 88–89
Rockhill, William W., 21
Roman Catholic/Catholicism, 1, 14–15,
    20–24, 27, 37, 40–41, 44–49, 55,
    57–63, 72, 93, 98, 100–105, 115,
    120, 122, 126–28, 135–36, 138, 141,
    145, 189–90, 199, 205–6, 208, 218–
    19, 223, 226, 232, 240, 242, 252–54,
    261, 267, 277, 308–9, 311–12, 333
Romans, 237
Ross, Andrew C., 254
Ross, Cyril, 118, 290
Ross, John, 22, 36, 47–55, 57, 59, 74,
    80, 199–200, 204, 221, 224, 226–27,
    229–30, 237, 239–40, 242, 244–45,
    248–49, 267, 309–11, 314, 318, 322
Rothweiler, Louisa C., 108, 323
Russia, 96, 131
Russian Diplomatic Office, 102
Russo-Japanese War, 82, 85, 95, 107,
    117, 130, 132, 235, 290
Rutgers University, 13
Rutt, Richard, 62, 90
Ryu Dae Young, 9
Ryu Tongsik, 5, 216

Sabbath, 9, 11, 120–21, 148, 197, 207,
    238, 242
sagyŏnghoe, 207
Salvation Army, 148
Samgak-san, 275
Samguk yusa, 68–70
Samshin, 158, 170
Sands, William F., 1
Sang chaesang sŏ, 48
Sangdong Methodist Church, 97, 129
sangmin, 225
sangnom, 234,
sanshin, 63, 158
sarang, 171, 278
Sato Yosimine, 110–11
Schall von Bell, Adam, 101
Schereschewsky, Samuel, 46
Schlesinger, Arthur M., 3

Schmidt, Wilhelm, 36
Scofield, C. I., 88
Scofield Reference Bible, 89
Scott, Mrs. Robertson, 78
Scott, William, 78
Scottish, 48–50, 52, 245, 251, 253–55
Scranton, Mary F., 51, 180, 204, 212,
    322–23
Scranton, William B., 21, 59–62,
    147, 176, 180, 224, 231, 240, 276,
    322–25
self-governing/propagating/supporting,
    117, 271, 297–300, 302, 309
Selous, Henry C., 113–14
Seoul, 1–2, 4–8, 10, 12, 16, 18, 21–24,
    31, 36, 49, 51, 57–59, 62, 66–67,
    71–72, 74, 96–97, 104–8, 115, 117,
    122–23, 126, 128–29, 132–33, 146,
    150, 152–53, 156, 163–65, 169,
    181, 200, 204, 207–9, 216–17,
    221, 224–25, 227–39, 241, 243–45,
    247, 249, 267, 272, 275, 277, 281,
    288–91, 293, 295–96, 300–4, 308,
    310–11; Prison, 249; YMCA, 129,
    244, 249, 290, 293
Septuagint, 237
Seven Stars, 273
Severance Hospital, 129, 152
shaman, 69, 71, 155, 157–58, 160, 166,
    186, 311
shamanism, 2, 11, 13, 15–16, 19, 26,
    28–30, 32, 47, 49, 53, 57, 63, 69, 71,
    74–76, 80–81, 141–44, 150, 154–72,
    181, 183–86, 251, 272, 274, 285,
    289, 311–12
Shangdi, 27, 35–59, 61–62, 64–65, 67,
    74–75, 79–81, 83, 145, 195, 197,
    214, 238, 257, 261–62, 284–81, 309,
    311–12
Shangdists, 36, 41–42, 54, 57, 61, 63, 65
Sharp, Charles E., 97, 125, 290
Sharp, John, 243–44
Sharrocks, Alfred M., 295
Sheffield, Devello Z., 202, 320
Shen, 36–46, 55–58, 61, 79, 83, 312
Shenk, W. R., 90
Shin, 56–57, 79, 102–3

Shin Ik-Cheol, 102–3
Shin Junhyoung M., 100
Shin Kwangch'ŏl, 24
Shin Seonyoung, 109
Shinjang, 158
Shinto, 4, 19, 79, 82, 131, 140, 161, 169, 172, 185, 189, 193, 202, 219, 277
Shuowen Jiezi, 38
Sin Nakkyun, 232
Sinhak Wŏlbo, 156, 213, 218, 346
Sino-Japanese War, 25, 82, 85, 95, 107, 130, 145, 171, 250, 269, 272, 275–76, 278, 284, 289, 302
Sino-Korean, 56, 239
sipsŭngjiji, 85, 92–96, 107, 115, 117–19, 138
Sites, Nathan, 320
Smalley, William A., 221
smallpox, 96, 115, 151, 162, 168
Smith, Arthur H., 202
Smith, George, 45
Sŏ Kyŏngjo, 120, 239, 288
Sŏ Namdong, 6, 191
Sŏ Sangnyun, 23, 50, 97, 129, 229, 236, 281, 288
Sŏ Taesŏk, 71
Society for Propagating the Gospel, 241
Society of Christians' Charity, 97
Sohyŏn, 101
Son Punggu, 248
Sŏnch'ŏn, 30, 295, 302, 330
Sŏng Hyŏn, 285
Song Insŏ, 278–80, 287
Song Sunyong, 57, 141, 232
Songdo, 97, 147, 207, 215, 291, 295, 297
Sŏnggyo yoji, 48
Sŏnghwangdang, 158
sŏngju, 158
Soothill, William E., 268
Sorae, 107, 120, 239, 245, 288
sottae, 122
Speer, Robert E., 25, 123–24, 145–46, 276, 279–80, 286
Spelman, Douglas G., 40
Spence, Martin, 87

spirit worship, 15, 25, 29–30, 104, 150, 155, 157–60, 163–64, 168, 170, 173–75, 177, 184, 194–95, 205, 252, 262, 287, 313
spiritism, 28, 172, 185–86, 313
spirits, 2, 18–19, 25–26, 28, 30, 33, 35–36, 44, 54–56, 61, 63, 67, 116, 142–85, 191–95, 204, 207, 213, 218–19, 241, 246, 252, 261, 269, 275–76, 283, 285, 301–2, 310
spiritual: function, 41; imperialism, 13; medium, 170
spiritualism, 78
spirituality, 15, 28, 30–31, 35, 47, 52, 76, 78, 100, 154, 158, 160, 180, 184, 204, 269, 270–72, 284, 295–96, 298, 302–3, 311, 313; Daoist, 302–3; shamanistic, 180; Trinitarian, 315
Stanley, Brian, 255
Staunton, George, 45
steamship, 223, 308
Stewart, Lyman, 90
Stronach, John, 45
Student Volunteer Movement, 307–8
Suan, 289
suffering, 6, 85–86, 95, 97, 101, 103, 108, 115, 119–21, 139, 158, 160, 171, 173, 208, 268–9,
Sunday, 1, 24, 121, 148, 177, 180, 230, 233, 277, 292, 297, 299, 324, 325, 329; school textbook, 286; School Times, 89; School Union, 257
Sungsil Academy, 290
sunyata, 38
superstition, 13, 15–16, 19, 28, 144, 154, 156, 158, 185, 198, 250, 253, 262
Suwŏn, 127, 149, 152, 176, 207
Suzuki Nobuaki, 93
Swallen, William L., 128, 206–7, 217, 280, 292, 324–25
Syangdye, 47–48, 55–60, 67, 317
Syngman Rhee, 123, 235, 249
Syŏngsan myŏnggyŏng, 233

Ta Ming hui-tien, 43
Taehan Cheguk, 66, 68

Taehan Hospital, 132
Taegu, 10, 179, 330
T'aejo taewang, 150
Taejonggyo, 35, 71, 83
Taewŏn'gun, 289
Taiping, 94, 252, 254
Taishang ganying pian, 273
Takahashi Aya, 131
Tamhŏn yŏn'gi, 98
Tamhŏnsŏ, 101
Tan'gun, 18, 32, 66, 68–82, 170, 311, 315
Taylor, J. Hudson, 90, 196, 199
Ten Commandments, 148
term question, 25, 31, 34–80, 309
Thanksgiving Day, 214, 216
Tiandao suyuan, 248, 251, 253–57, 309, 314
Tianzhu, 37–41, 44–49, 59, 61, 73, 79, 94, 100–101, 105, 135, 254, 309, 312
Tianzhu shiyi, 38
Tillich, Paul, 5
toggaebi, 158–59
T'ojijishin, 158
T'ŏju, 158
Tokyo, 13–14, 56, 72, 224
Tonghak, 25, 27–28, 31, 49, 93–95, 107, 115–16, 120–21, 140, 171, 275–76, 348; Uprising, 107, 120, 171, 275–76
Tongsa ch'anyo, 70
Tongsa hoegang, 70
Tongsa kangyo, 68, 70
Tongsa poyu, 68, 70
t'ongsŏng kido, 30, 294
Tong'ŭi pogam, 273
Toronto, 163
Torrey, Deberniere J., 103
translation methods, 45
trinity, 70, 78–79, 83, 311
Trollope, Mark N., 19, 59, 62, 239–41
Truth, 89
ture, 30
Turley, Robert T., 59
Two Friends, 248, 251, 284, 319, 323
Tylor, Edward B., 159–60, 166

T'yŏnjyu, 46–48, 55–56, 58–63, 72, 79, 242, 317
typhoid, 151, 161

uhwan kut, 143
Ŭiju, 97, 133, 208, 227, 229, 245, 278, 281, 288–89
Ŭm Pongt'ae, 278
Underwood, Horace G., 10, 17, 22–23, 42, 45, 55–57, 59–60, 64, 74, 80–81, 90, 106, 119, 124, 141, 155, 159, 169, 185, 195, 208, 212, 224, 227, 230, 232, 243–44, 253, 269, 276, 286, 322–25
Underwood, Lillias H., 16, 56, 60, 153, 227
Union Theological Seminary, 13, 165
United Free Church of Scotland, 49

Vanderbilt University, 181
Vatical II, 5, 48
Venable, W. A., 293
Victorian Presbyterian Mission of Australia, 209
Vinton, Cadwallader C., 108, 113, 154, 239, 288
Virgin Mary, 23

Wallace, Anthony, 37
Walraven, Boudewijn, 142, 144, 150, 172, 274
Wambold, Catherine, 128
Wang Xichang, 228
Watchword, 89,
Way, Richard Q., 320
Weber, Timothy P., 88–89
Weems, Benjamin B., 70
Welbon, Arthur G., 96–97
Welbon, Sarah N., 96
Wells, James Hunter, 12, 132–33, 152
Wells, Kenneth M., 304
Wesley, John, 271
White, James T., 156
White Lotus Society, 39
Whitefield, George, 31, 295
Whiting, Norman C., 290
Whittemore, Norman C., 227, 289

Williams, S. W., 39, 41, 43
Williamson, Alexander , 45, 50, 52, 196, 258, 319–20
Willing, Jennie F., 125, 271
wine, 192, 195, 210, 219
Wŏnsan, 58, 60, 62, 96, 127, 163–64, 173–74, 178, 206, 208, 217, 243, 271, 291, 295
World Council of Churches, 5
World Missionary Conference, 7, 156, 159, 226
wuchang, 260
wuji taiji, 258
Wylie, Alexander, 194, 196, 252

Xu Guangqi, 254

Yang Chuguk, 213
Yang Guangxian, 99, 101
yangban, 64, 92, 107, 117, 141, 156, 162, 172, 207, 215, 224–26, 228, 232–35, 243, 276–77, 303; Christians, 156, 224, 234–35, 300–301
yangdaein, 8, 107
Yates, Matthew T., 196
Yates, Timothy, 3, 17, 26, 196–99
YHWH, 40, 46, 237
Yi Chaemyŏng, 135
Yi Chaep'ung, 280
Yi Ch'angjik, 109
Yi Chongŭn, 285
Yi Kiji, 100
Yi Kwangnin, 249, 277
Yi Mahnyol, 8, 49, 125, 236, 247, 250, 277
Yi Nŭnghwa, 235, 249, 272–73, 275, 284

Yi Pyŏk, 47–48
Yi Seunghae, 116
Yi Sŏkp'ung, 209
Yi Sujŏng, 248, 322
Yi Sŭnghun, 48
Yi Sŭngnyun, 117–9
Yi Tŏkchu, 8, 117, 241, 277, 282, 291
Yi Tongsŭng, 278
Yi Ŭngch'an, 53
Yi Ŭnsŭng, 127
Yi Yŏngŭn, 279
YMCA, 129, 156, 163, 235, 244, 249, 290, 293
Yokohama, 48, 56, 141–42, 152, 224, 232, 236, 244, 249–50, 268, 326–27
Yŏnan, 121, 126
yŏngbu, 116
Yŏngjo sillok, 92
Yongshin, 158
Yoshido Tora, 254
Yu Sŏngjun, 244
Yuan Shikai, 104, 229
Yugyŏng Kongwŏn, 165
Yuhuang, 61, 67
Yun Ch'iho, 96–97, 123, 307
Yun Kyŏngno, 24, 277
Yun Sŏngbŏm, 70, 92

Zanshen shengshi, 264
Zetzsche, Jost O., 46
Zhang Qiong, 39
Zhang Yuan liangyou xianglun, 251
Zhenzhu, 37, 40, 94,
Zhongsheng zhi dao, 257
zhongti xiyong, 258, 260, 262
Zixi cudong, 259–61